PSYCHOLOGY
AND
EFFECTIVE BEHAVIOR

PSYCHOLOGY AND EFFECTIVE BEHAVIOR

A revision and amplification of *Personality Dynamics and Effective Behavior*

by JAMES C. COLEMAN

Professor of Psychology / The University of California at Los Angeles

SCOTT, FORESMAN AND COMPANY

PREFACE

It has been almost a decade since the first edition of this book was published. During this period the world has undergone major crises and changes. We have seen wars, violence, and tragic events, but at the same time we have seen man's rapidly increasing capabilities of controlling himself and his environment and the emergence of new hope that he can build a "good" future for himself.

During these years, marked advances have been made in psychology. Although we still have much to learn about the complexities of man's nature and behavior, we have seen major contributions to the better understanding of personality development and adjustment; we have seen important steps toward the better understanding of group behavior; and we have seen the focus of scientific endeavor enlarge to include both the individual and his social habitat. In this new edition, we have attempted to incorporate these new findings and trends, to indicate where they seem to be leading us, and to show their implications for the achievement of more adequate personal adjustment and growth.

In noting these advances in psychology, it is gratifying to find that the concept of man as an "open system" capable of a high degree of self-regulation and self-direction has received increasing emphasis and acceptance. In 1960 this concept was just beginning to emerge from experimentation and theory in the biological and social sciences. Now this model seems capable of capturing the uniqueness and "humanness" of the individual and of encompassing the complex transactions between the individual and the physical and sociocultural field in which he lives and functions.

The scientific and eclectic orientation of the present text—taking full cognizance of the humanistic, behavioristic, psychoanalytic, and existential models of man—is set forth in the Prologue and Chapter 1 and need not be elaborated here. To provide a comprehensive picture of man and the problems of human existence and personal adjustment, this book has been organized into four parts:

Part One considers the basic nature of man, the determinants and patterning of personality development, and the factors in healthy and faulty development. Part Two focuses on man's basic strivings as well as on the unique motive patterns of individuals, on problems of adjustment and our reactions to them, and on the nature of effective and faulty patterns of adjustment. Part Three deals with the group setting of behavior, the interaction and mutual influence of individual and group, relevant findings and concepts concerning marital and occupational adjustment, and resources for personal growth and change. Part Four attempts to show the application of contemporary psychological concepts and principles to the achievement of more effective behavior through increased intellectual, emotional, and social competence and concludes with the crucial significance of our quest for values. Finally, there are 11 selected readings to extend and enrich the concepts developed in the text.

The author is indebted to the many scientists and writers whose work he has drawn upon in preparing this text. His theoretical position has been greatly influenced by such men as Gordon Allport, Hadley Cantril, Arthur Combs, Sigmund Freud, Erich Fromm, Harold Kelley, A. H. Maslow, James G. Miller, O. H. Mowrer, Gardner Murphy, and Carl Rogers, and has been sharpened by the writings of many with other orientations, such as B. F. Skinner and H. J. Eysenck. He is grateful for the generous permission given by some of these and many others, and by their publishers, to reprint brief selections throughout the chapters and complete articles in the Readings section at the end of the book.

On a more personal level, the author is indebted to Professor Eugene Raxten for critical evaluation and suggestions over the whole manuscript, as well as for his care and resourcefulness in preparing the accompanying *Instructor's Manual;* to Dr. Malathi Sandhu for her assistance with several chapters including those on personality development; to Dr. Andrew Comrey for assistance with material on psychological assessment, counseling, and psychotherapy; to Mrs. Rita Knipe for encouragement, critical evaluation, and creative ideas; and to Dr. Howard Adelman, John Harris, and Janice Stone for helpful suggestions. He would like to express his most sincere and profound appreciation to Mrs. Marguerite Clark, College Editor of Scott, Foresman and Company, without whose capable and dedicated assistance this book could not have become a reality. To his wife, Betty, he expresses gratitude for patience and understanding over the long hours of sustained pressure required to bring the manuscript to its present form.

JAMES C. COLEMAN

Malibu, California
Spring 1969

CONTENTS

Prologue
___

SCIENCE AND HUMAN ADJUSTMENT

Progress and Anxiety
Man's Unique Problem of Self-Direction
Three Key Questions
Man's Quest for Answers

The tremendous and accelerating advances of modern science and technology have led to unprecedented progress and unprecedented problems. On the one hand, we can point to man's increasing mastery of the secrets of nature, to an economy of abundance, to the conquest of disease, and to spectacular cultural advances; on the other, we see the dangers of a divided world, of thermonuclear warfare, of a population explosion, of grinding poverty side by side with abundance, and of other complex problems which man has never before faced. These problems press for solution if man is to survive and move forward. And the solution to these problems appears to depend less upon increased technological know-how and more upon a better understanding of man and his social systems.

PROGRESS AND ANXIETY

We are living in an affluent society. The average person in the United States today is better fed, housed, clothed, and medicated than any man in all history. He is served by myriad slaves—powered by electricity instead of human labor—which remove much of the drudgery from his everyday living and give him more time for creative pursuits. He can enjoy the finest literature, music, and art; he can experience the stimulating rewards of travel; he can participate in sports and other leisure-time activities that formerly were available only to the very rich. Through motion pictures and television, he is entertained by spectacles that would have taxed the imagination of ancient kings. His achievements in medicine have made him the healthiest man of all time and have greatly increased his life span. He has almost unlimited opportunities for educational and creative pursuits and freedom for self-development. He lives in an exciting age of scientific wonders that have placed man on the threshold of conquering space. In fact, man has never before possessed such opportunity for self-determination and for enjoying life to its fullest. It would seem indeed that he is entering upon a Golden Age.

Yet it is apparent that all is not going exactly as we might hope and expect. Paradoxically, the same scientific and technological advances that have made this a Golden Age pose many problems and threats which also make it an Age of Anxiety. We have squandered the earth's resources, polluted our air and water, and made parts of our planet uninhabitable. A seething nationalism embraces half the earth; new weapons for mastery and destruction are being placed in uncertain hands; a population explosion is outstripping the world's food and other resources; there are almost universal problems of illiteracy, poverty, and disease; and there is an inevitable awareness of the "have-nots" that their lives could be improved by social change. The impact of our scientific age upon the hopes and fears of man has been well described by the psychologist Hadley Cantril (1958).

"As more and more people throughout the world become more and more enmeshed in a scientific age, its psychological consequences on their thought and behavior become increasingly complicated. The impact comes in a variety of ways: people begin to feel the potentialities for a more abundant life that modern technology can provide; they become aware of the inadequacies of many present political, social, and religious institutions and practices; they discern the threat which existing power and status relationships may hold to their own development; they vaguely sense the inadequacy of many of the beliefs and codes accepted by their forefathers and perhaps by themselves at an earlier age.

"The upshot is that more and more people are acquiring both a hope for a 'better life' and a feeling of frustration and anxiety that they themselves may not experience the potentially better life they feel should be available to them. They search for new anchorages, for new guidelines, for plans of action which hold a promise of making some of the dreams come true, some of their aspirations become experientially real." (pp. vii-viii)

Wherever we look, we see the world changing with incredible rapidity —and established customs, traditions, and values changing with it. Few are the places in the world today where the children follow, as a matter of course, the patterns of their fathers. Communication problems stemming from a "generation gap" have become a matter of real concern. Indeed, one of the major problems today is the constant adjustment individuals and complex social organizations must keep making to rapidly changing conditions and to change itself. To complicate matters further, advances in communication and transportation have reduced the "size" of the world. Whether we like it or not, we have become members of an interdependent society of the world. This means learning to understand and deal with over three billion people, most of whom have different languages, different beliefs, and different-colored skins from ours. In this world context, two major ideologies— democracy and communism—are fighting a "cold war" for men's minds and the shaping of our world. And there is always the possibility that this cold war may erupt into global conflict—into chemical, biological, and thermo-nuclear warfare that would doom modern civilization and perhaps even mankind. Thus global unrest, conflict, and change form the background against which we function as we try to deal with the problems that confront our nation and to find our own personal way in an increasingly complex, bureaucratic, and impersonal mass society.

The strain of modern life in our own society is revealed in the incredible amounts of tranquilizing drugs, the tons of sleeping pills, and the billions of dollars worth of alcoholic beverages which Americans consume each year. It is revealed in preoccupation with LSD, marihuana, and other "consciousness-expanding" drugs. It is reflected in the vast literature on the "lost selves," the "lonely crowd," and the "dehumanization" and "alienation" of modern man. It is revealed in the large numbers of young people today who have lost faith in and are actively rebelling against many accepted standards of society, and in the many others who lack involvement and commitment and "drop out" of the mainstream of society. In an equally dramatic way, it is revealed in the high incidence of personality maladjustment and mental disorder; in the alarming rise in juvenile delinquency and adult crime; and in racial tension, riots, and epidemics of violence. This is, indeed, an Age of Anxiety as well as a Golden Age.

In pointing to the problems of modern man in our "Golden Age of Anxiety" we are not advocating a return to the "good old days." We have come far toward realizing man's dream of a great and creative society, and few would care to exchange the benefits of modern civilization for the allegedly greater stability of an earlier age. In any case, we have set out upon a path of change and there is no road back. We recognize both the necessity and the utility of change. Our hope lies not in reversing change or in trying to hold the line but in guiding change and developing new values and modes of adaptation which are appropriate to the problems and challenges of our contemporary world. In this process we must constantly guard against the danger of discarding the essential for that which is new but trivial or unsound. For change in and of itself is no guarantee of progress. As Haskins (1968) has pointed out, we must be continually aware of the danger that "in embracing new and experimental courses on myriad fronts of movement with the ardor that we must, we do not at the same time discard long-tested values and long-tried adaptive courses which, if they are lost, will only have, one day, to be rewon—and probably at enormous cost."

MAN'S UNIQUE PROBLEM OF SELF-DIRECTION

Throughout his long history, man has pitted his abilities against the world in his struggle to survive. In this he is not unique, for all living things strive to maintain themselves, to resist destruction, and to grow and function in accordance with their inner natures. The process by which an organism attempts to meet the demands placed upon it by its own nature and by its environment is called *adjustment*. Living things never cease to adjust. Adjustive behavior may be more or less *successful*, in terms of how well it meets external demands and satisfies the needs of the organism, but it goes on continuously. It is as basic to life as breathing—itself a form of adjustive functioning.

In the universal struggle for survival, many different adjustive patterns have emerged in the animal world. Some species manage to survive by sheer number of offspring; others rely heavily upon defensive armaments such as poisons, camouflage, or speed. Though widely different, these various patterns have one thing in common: they rely largely upon "wired-in" adjustive know-how. While most animals are capable of some learning, their behavior is determined primarily by adjustive patterns that are instinctive. We might say that they come factory equipped with adjustive know-how. As Branden (1965) has put it:

"Given the appropriate conditions, the appropriate physical environment, all living organisms—with one exception—are set by their nature to originate automatically the actions required to sustain their survival. The exception is man." (p. 2)

With man, nature has tried out a dramatically different solution to the problem of survival. Endowed with superior mental capacities, man has few, if any, instinctive behavior patterns beyond the level of the simplest reflex. He must rely instead on his ability to learn and reason in working out the most satisfactory mode of adjustment, continually modifying his behavior to meet the demands of new situations. His superior mental gifts—and consequently, his superior adaptability—have enabled man to become the unchallenged master of the animal kingdom and to go far toward conquering his physical environment. But man's unique gifts have also created unique problems, for man alone is faced with the responsibility of deciding what behavior is appropriate and developing whatever competencies it entails. This, in turn, means that he must determine the kind of creature he is and the basic role he should play as a human being. As the Overstreets (1956) put it:

"Although he has a role to play—a form to grow into, a function to carry out—he is unlike every other creature in the fact that he does not grow into this role naturally, by just staying alive long enough. He has to decide for himself what his own basic role is. . . .

"Here is where our chief troubles have arisen. We have been as confused about ourselves, often—as uncertain about what our human nature is and what it requires of us—as an acorn would be if it were not sure whether its proper destiny was to be an oak or a cabbage. . . ." (pp. 240-241)

In directing the "human enterprise" then, man must not only acquire information about himself and his world and develop the competencies for dealing with his problems, but he must also come to grips with the problem of values—of what is good for him and what is not—and ultimately with the meaning of his existence—of what his role is in the universe. For our purposes, we may think of these problems in terms of two categories: "know-how" and "know-why."

The Problem of "Know-How"

To direct his behavior effectively, man must first of all acquire *information* about himself and his world. He must learn about his needs, his potentialities, his rational and irrational tendencies, and the many other facets of his nature so as to fill in a realistic self-picture. Man must also learn about the world in which he lives—not only the inanimate world, but the world of plants and animals and human groups. He must learn about its dangers, its potentialities for meeting his needs, and the principles inherent in its operation—

information that will enable him to understand his world and to some extent control it.

Man's views of himself and his world, whether accurate or inaccurate, are primary determiners of his behavior. For the goals he strives after and the means he selects for trying to achieve them are largely determined by what he conceives himself to be, by what he conceives himself able to become, and by the way he pictures the opportunities and limitations of the world around him. Thus the opportunity for self-direction places a heavy demand upon man to acquire accurate information so as to be able to predict the consequences of different courses of action and choose the ones best suited to his ends.

In addition to information, man must also acquire the competencies requisite for carrying out his purposes and for getting along in human society. Each of us must spend a major portion of his life acquiring the information and competencies required for effective behavior—in acquiring the know-how for living. And as scientific and technological progress continues, the amount of information and the complexity of the skills we need continue to increase. Thus the problem of acquiring know-how for living becomes increasingly difficult and time consuming and continues all our lives.

The Problem of "Know-Why"

Coping with social and personal problems and achieving a "good future" is not simply a matter of acquiring information and developing competencies. Man must also solve the problem of "know-why"—he must find a comprehensive value system to guide his choices and adjustive behavior. From among the many goals and ways of living that are available to him, he must identify and choose those he thinks will best meet his needs and assure his greatest well-being and progress. As Kluckhohn (1954, p. 403) has pointed out: "Surely one of the broadest generalizations to be made by a natural historian observing the human species is that man is an evaluating animal. Always and everywhere men are saying, 'This is good'; 'that is bad'; 'this is better than that'; 'these are higher and those lower aspirations.'" Thus while information helps man to see what *is* or *could* be, values are concerned with the *desirable*—with what *ought* to be.

The problem of values inevitably involves man with a consideration of *meaning*—of what human existence is all about. This concern with meaning, so basic to human thought and action, is unique to man. Other animals are not concerned with their "proper" roles or with the meaning of their existence. Nor are they concerned—or probably even aware—of their finite existence here on earth, an awareness which adds a crucial note of urgency to the human situation. As the psychoanalyst Erich Fromm (1955, pp. 23-24) has pointed out: "Man is the only animal who finds his own existence a problem which he has to solve and from which he cannot escape." Thus for the first time in the history of the animal kingdom, psychological problems centering around values and meaning enter into and complicate the adjustive process.

Eloquent testimony to man's need for know-why and to the difficulty of finding it in modern society is the widely noted sense of alienation and disillusionment—especially among young people—and the often feverish search for "authenticity" and "commitment." Many are questioning the wisdom of a world that can split the atom but cannot unite humanity, or that can put men into space but cannot ensure peace on earth. Often they are repulsed by what they perceive as the superficiality, hypocrisy, materialism, and over-concern with images in the adult world or "establishment." Yet replacement values are not always easy to find or agree upon—particularly with the be-wildering choice available among the many conflicting and changing values of our contemporary world.

Surprisingly, it is only recently that man has come to realize that his so-cial structures are man-made and subject to change. As McCall and Simmons (1966, p. 254) have pointed out: "Most people, throughout most of history, have reflected the cultures they grew up in in the important sense that they have taken the culturally defined patterns and meanings of life for granted, even though they may have balked and quibbled about specifics." However, the systematic study of different cultures, carried out mainly in the last hundred years, has made us aware of how many different answers human be-ings have worked out to the problems of existence. Today we are much more critically evaluative of our existing value patterns and social structures and also much more aware of possibilities for planned change.

The question of value judgments is crucial to man's well-being for if he chooses values which are not consonant with either the needs of his own nature or the realities of the world, they will work toward his destruction. Although he is free to act against the requirements of his nature, he is not free to escape the consequences—anxiety, misery, and destruction.

THREE KEY QUESTIONS

We have spoken of man's problem of self-direction—of his need to solve the uniquely human problems of acquiring both "know-how" and "know-why." For the individual, this means trying to find the answers to three key questions: *Who am I? Where am I going? Why?* These questions deal with one's self-concept, one's life plans, and one's value patterns—in essence with the self-knowledge, goals and competencies, and value judgments involved in self-direction.

The meaningfulness of these questions varies, of course, depending upon the person's opportunities. In many parts of the world the individual's freedom for self-direction is severely curtailed by the sheer struggle for physical survival or by authoritarian forms of social organization which answer these questions for him. Even in the United States, personal limita-tions or stresses in a person's life situation may shift the emphasis from these questions to simply "How can I cope?" Nevertheless, most of our young people have a life situation which provides unprecedented opportunities for shaping their own lives.

Who Am I?

By delineating the characteristics common to all men, we can understand much about ourselves, for we are all members of the human species. We can fill in more details by studying the patterns and values of the culture and family setting in which we have grown up. But each individual is unique and therefore has the problem of getting to know and understand *himself*.

It is an interesting facet of our educational system that we study almost everything else before getting around to studying ourselves. Yet we must live with ourselves and work with our resources to make our lives productive and satisfying. By understanding our physical functioning, we can avoid needless damage to our bodies and ensure greater energy and vigor. On a psychological level, there are equally good reasons for adequate self-knowledge. Failure to understand the irrational forces in our make-up may play havoc with our lives, as when we blame others for our mistakes at the high price of being unable to analyze and profit from them. An inaccurate picture of our own capabilities may lead to unrealistic goals and hurtful failures. A blurred sense of self-identity may make it difficult for us to plan courses of action and make decisions that are right for us. Or we may simply be bewildered by some of the apparently irrational things we do. The latter point is made humorously by Rebecca McCann in a little poem called "Inconsistency":

> *"I'm sure I have a noble mind*
> *And honesty and tact*
> *And no one's more surprised than I*
> *To see the way I act!"*

The need for a clear-cut and realistic sense of "who we are" has become particularly crucial in modern society, where the individual often feels himself a puppet in the hands of a vast impersonal bureaucracy and may lose faith in his own identity or in his ability to find a place for himself.

Where Am I Going?

As we acquire knowledge about ourselves and our world, we are in a better position to delineate our goals and how we can hope to implement them. For the question "Where am I going" centers around our *life plans*—our goals, the means for achieving them, and the hazards we are likely to encounter along the way. Goals focus our energy and effort, help to determine what competencies we need to develop, and provide a basis for deciding between alternative courses of action.

The choice of long-range goals is particularly important to the individual since they dictate the subgoals that are appropriate as well as the means for achieving them. It is the long-range goals that give coherence and continuity to one's life. Some goals, of course, are more appropriate than others in relation to the individual's personal resources and opportunities, and some goals are better than others in the satisfactions which they afford. The pursuit of unrealistically high goals leads to failure and frustration; the pursuit of goals that are too low leads to wasted opportunities and lost satisfactions; the pursuit of "false" goals leads to disillusionment and discouragement.

Inability to formulate meaningful life plans also leads to serious difficulties. Here one is reminded of the poignant lines of Biff in Arthur Miller's *Death of a Salesman* when he says "I just can't take hold, Mom. I can't take hold of some kind of a life." Such individuals appear to drift through life with little or no sense of direction and usually experience a sense of dissatisfaction, aimlessness, and being "lost."

Although the specific skills required will vary with the circumstances, certain general competencies appear basic for reaching one's goals.

1. *Physical competencies*—the practice of good physical hygiene measures and the use of medical resources to keep one's body functioning efficiently.

2. *Intellectual competencies*—the acquisition of essential information about oneself and one's world and the achievement of efficiency in learning, problem solving, and decision making.

3. *Emotional competencies*—the ability to love and be loved and to deal with fears, anxieties, anger, and other problem emotions that we all experience.

4. *Social competencies*—the ability to deal effectively with other people and to build satisfying interpersonal relationships in marriage and other life areas.

Failure to develop these competencies can prevent us from "getting where we want to go," even when our goals are potentially within our reach. Despite our superior power to reason, many of us are crippled by emotional prejudices and lack of training in problem solving and decision making. Often we fail to achieve satisfying relationships with those close to us. Many marriages, for example, drag along or break up for want of the know-how that might have made them rich and satisfying experiences.

Besides such general competencies, we also need to equip ourselves to meet specific hazards and responsibilities that we can anticipate along the way. Although we cannot foresee all the problems we will have to face during our lifetime, there are certain adjustments—such as obtaining an education, preparing for satisfactory life work, building a satisfying marriage, bringing up children, finding a satisfying philosophy of life, and growing old gracefully—which most of us will want to make. We can increase the probability of success if we know what difficulties may be involved and what information and competencies we will need in dealing with them. Such knowledge also helps us to avoid inappropriate means, which can readily defeat our plans.

Why?

"Why this life plan rather than another?" What kind of life is good or bad for human beings in general and for me as an individual? What makes this goal good and that one bad? From among whatever alternatives we see open to us, we all make choices in terms of what we see as most desirable and most likely to be satisfying to us. As Cantril (1950, p. 37) has put it, values "are the compass which give man his direction both as to how he should act and what his action is for." Whether or not the individual has thought through his values or is even clearly aware of them, his life plans reflect his value patterns. Even if he forfeits his chance to plan for himself and blindly follows the dictates of others, he is making a choice and in this sense is living out a value decision.

Since self-direction requires decision making and action, it is important that the individual develop an adequate system of values for guiding his behavior. Lacking such values, he may find himself confused and unable to find meaning in his life, or he may pursue goals based on false values whose achievement is frustrating rather than satisfying. As Turner (1965, pp. 307-308) has put it: "How can we order our own lives and maintain health and stability if we have no overriding purposes or values, if we are busy treading the activity cage to nowhere."

The degree to which the individual trusts the soundness of his values will determine how much he actually relies on them in making choices; how free he is from inner conflict; how successfully he can withstand setbacks and frustrations; and how much effort he will put forth in working toward his goals and living up to his commitments.

The quest for values is not an easy one. We live in a rapidly changing world in which many old values are giving way to new ones and in which value conflicts seem to be the order of the day. And the values that prove satisfying and fulfilling for one person may not appeal to another. Yet science, religion, and the experience of the human race all offer evidence that certain values are likely to prove more realistic and satisfying than others. And as modern science provides us with increasing information about man's nature, about man in relation to man, and about man in relation to his environment, we increase our base for making valid value decisions.

Whether or not he finds adequate answers, modern man is searching—sometimes desperately—for values he can depend on and for a sense of purpose and meaning. We do not easily accept the doctrine of despair so dramatically portrayed in the lines of Shakespeare that life "is a tale/ Told by an idiot, full of sound and fury/ Signifying nothing."

MAN'S QUEST FOR ANSWERS

Most people would consider it sheer folly to attempt to climb a high mountain peak without procuring the necessary equipment, studying the possible routes that might be taken, and obtaining a clear understanding of the hazards to be faced. Yet many of these same people expect that inadequate knowledge, competencies, and values will carry them successfully through the journey of life—a far more difficult undertaking than the conquest of a mountain peak.

The High Cost of "Muddling Through"

For many of us, living is a matter of muddling through. Instead of using the knowledge and resources which human history and modern science have put at our disposal, we go through life making many costly and needless mistakes and wasting much of our potential for self-fulfillment. Even today, literally millions of people guide their lives by superstitions, assumptions, and "common-sense" notions of human nature which science has proved to be false. They prepare for the wrong occupations, choose incompatible mates, and bring up their children with a naïve hope that good intentions will be sufficient. But behind the brave front of confidence that they present to the world are apt to lie deep-seated feelings of bewilderment, inadequacy, and unhappiness. The price of muddling through is ordinarily a high one. At best, it is likely to lead to a serious waste of opportunities and human resources. More commonly, it takes a high toll in unnecessary failures, missed satisfactions, and emotional wear and tear.

As the biologist Herrick (1956) has pointed out, the mistakes we make because of ignorance and immaturity have a way of catching up with us in the long run. Violation of the laws of man's nature are inevitably punished.

"Transgression of these laws brings its own penalty. No prosecutor is required. If you drink whisky to excess, your health is impaired. If you drink wood alcohol, you die. . . . The wages of sin is death, if not of the person, certainly of his richest values and satisfactions. And ignorance of the law excuses no man." (p. 148)

It is a curious facet of man's nature that one of the most frustrating of all experiences is awareness of lost satisfactions—of "what might have been."

Science As a Source of Dependable Knowledge

Today the findings of modern science are reducing man's "ignorance of the law." As people become aware of the fallibility of custom and common sense in guiding their lives, they look increasingly to modern science—particularly to psychology—for dependable sources of information. This is not to say that psychology can fully answer the questions of Who, Where, or Why or provide infallible guides. Nevertheless, contemporary psychology can give us some partial answers, and it can reduce the probability of our getting inaccurate answers.

Although still a young science, psychology has made itself felt in diverse areas of human endeavor. In the study of human development and functioning—on both individual and group levels—psychology has acquired a substantial body of information concerning human learning, motivation, problem solving, reactions to stress, and many other aspects of behavior. This information has provided new and generally effective guides for child rearing, education, marriage, and vocational planning and adjustment; it has been useful in selecting and training personnel in business, industry, and the military services; it has contributed to a better understanding of how groups function and to methods for improving group efficiency; and it has contributed to promising gains in the assessment, treatment, and prevention of personality maladjustment and mental disorders.

Psychologists have been reluctant to apply research findings to specific human problems for fear of going beyond what is actually known and falling into the same trap as the popular literature on "personality" and "adjustment," which often has only the sketchiest of scientific underpinning. Many psychologists, too, are reluctant to come to grips with values, seeing them as inherently a philosophical rather than a scientific concern. Yet we cannot wait until all of the scientific answers are in; we must operate on the basis of the information that we do have. Nor can we avoid the problem of values. The counselor who tries to help a couple with their marital problems must inevitably make assumptions about what is "good" and "bad." In fact, our faith in science itself as a means of helping man is a value assumption. But while we cannot entirely avoid such problems, we can proceed with caution and make clear the difference between scientific findings and value judgments.

The Orientation of This Book

It is our conviction that a sound and comprehensive study of personality dynamics and effective behavior should be based on the following:

1. *A scientific approach to human behavior.* In our discussion, we shall emphasize man's need for ever increasing knowledge about himself and his world. Any comprehensive view of human behavior must be based on information from a variety of scientific fields, including genetics, neurophysiology, psychology, sociology, and anthropology. In our attempt to integrate this information into a coherent view of man and his behavior, we shall strive to be as objective and eclectic as possible. We shall also emphasize the need for more research in the behavioral sciences, for these fields have lagged dangerously behind the progress made in the physical and biological sciences.

In taking this approach we do not assume that science is infallible, although it does have built-in correctional tendencies. Nor do we assume that science can solve all of man's problems. While science can supply the means for coping with the world population explosion, for example, the decision to use these means is a matter of values. Science can predict the outcome of using or not using birth control measures but it cannot say which outcome is desirable and which undesirable. This is a value judgment. So we will use science as far as we can but not expect the impossible of it. And while we will view science as the most dependable source of information about man and his world, we will remain free to utilize information from other specified sources.

2. *Awareness of man's existential problems.* There are many experiences common to human existence about which science has as yet little to say. Included here are such vital experiences as courage, hope, faith, concern, love, alienation, despair, and death. Man is the only animal who can recount his experiences, describe his feelings, and compare them with those of others. Often in literature and autobiographical accounts we find poignant and authentic renditions of experiences which are meaningful to all of us. To ignore man's existential problems would be to run the risk of dehumanizing man; no description and explanation of human behavior will be complete that does not encompass the intimate experiences which characterize human existence. So in subsequent pages we shall not hesitate to draw upon the humanities—literature, art, history, religion, and related fields—for insights into human behavior. However, we shall distinguish such information from that obtained by scientific endeavor.

3. *Belief in the growth potential of the individual.* The statement of the Ethical Standards of Psychologists, as formulated by the American Psychological Association (1963), begins as follows:
"The psychologist believes in the dignity and worth of the individual human being. He is committed to increasing man's understanding of himself and others." (p. 56)
Implicit in this statement is a belief in the growth potential of the individual and in his ability to direct his own life. Man is seen not as the helpless battle-

ground on which heredity and environment vie for control of his behavior but as an active agent who can develop and use his abilities, his knowledge, and his environmental resources to build the kind of life he chooses.

It is not proposed, of course, that great personal growth and effectiveness can be achieved by simply reading a book. Nor does the presentation of research findings about ourselves and others ensure that we can or will utilize such findings in our own behavior. Despite medical research showing the harmful effects of smoking cigarettes, the incidence of their use has not been greatly affected in the United States. Modern psychology can help by providing dependable information about man and his world, but the mastery and effective use of this knowledge is up to the individual. A key finding of modern psychology, however, is that most individuals, given the opportunity, do show good potentiality for continued intellectual, emotional, and social growth and for responsible self-direction—and hence for achieving more satisfying and fulfilling lives.

The purpose of the present book, then, is to show how the core findings of contemporary psychology (and of allied biological and social sciences) can give us a better understanding of ourselves and others and help us to develop our resources for effective living in today's world. This effort will lead us to an inquiry into man's basic nature and potentialities; his intellectual, emotional, and social development; how he perceives himself in relation to his environment and is motivated to act; the kinds of problems he faces and how he goes about trying to solve them; and the nature of interpersonal and individual-group relationships. Although the emphasis will be on identifying underlying principles of human development and adjustment, we will also be concerned with their implications for effective personal behavior.

In his book, *Man's Emerging Mind,* John Berrill (1955) has discussed man in the perspective of evolutionary time. His beautifully expressed statement of purpose encompasses our present intent as well.

"I am a human being, whatever that may be. I speak for all of us who move and think and feel and whom time consumes. I speak as an individual unique in a universe beyond my understanding, and I speak for man. I am hemmed in by limitations of sense and mind and body, of place and time and circumstances, some of which I know but most of which I do not. I am like a man journeying through a forest, aware of occasional glints of light overhead with recollections of the long trail I have already traveled, and conscious of wider spaces ahead. I want to see more clearly where I have been and where I am going, and above all I want to know why I am where I am and why I am traveling at all." (p. 1)

Part One

HUMAN NATURE
AND DEVELOPMENT

In order to understand the dynamics of human behavior and the factors that lead to effective or ineffective adjustment, we must first try to get an overall picture of the human system. Thus Part One begins with a consideration of man's basic nature and the influences of inner and outer determinants in shaping human development.

As a first step toward defining the fundamental characteristics of man, Chapter 1 examines some of the conflicting evidence about "human nature." Is man basically cooperative and loving or selfish and aggressive? Is his behavior primarily rational or irrational? Is he capable of intelligent self-direction or is he the helpless pawn of influences beyond his control? These age-old questions are seen from a new perspective when we look at man as a living "energy system" in continuing transactions with an environmental field—transactions that result in changes in both system and field.

Chapter 2 goes further toward explaining the seeming diversity in human nature by showing how development and behavior (structure and functioning) are shaped by the combined influences of heredity, environment, and the unique self-structure which each individual gradually develops. These determinants operate to make each individual both similar to and different from all other human beings.

Chapter 3 continues the story of human development by outlining the characteristic patterns of growth toward physical and psychological maturity. Despite individual and cultural variations in definitions of *maturity*, there are several general trends in growth toward maturity that seem universally characteristic of personality development. There also are predictable sequences in sensory-motor, intellectual, emotional, and social development.

Chapter 4 comes to grips with the problem of identifying healthy and unhealthy personality development. It then summarizes the common causes of faulty development and the key conditions that foster healthy development.

With this perspective on the structure and development of the human system, we shall then be ready to take a closer look at the dynamics of adjustive behavior—at the functioning of the human system.

Chapter 1

WAYS OF VIEWING MAN

The Problem of Man's Basic Nature
Psychological "Models" of Man
Man As a Living System

If the crew of a spacecraft were to report finding intelligent beings on another planet, our first question would probably be "What sort of creatures are they?" Through the centuries man has asked the same question about himself without getting a satisfactory answer.

One reason for the difficulty in getting a clear answer is that there are so many differences to be accounted for. Man comes in many "shapes and sizes" and behaves in many diverse ways. Of the more than three billion people who inhabit the earth, no two are exactly alike. The vast differences among them have made it hard to identify what they share in common as human beings. Contrast, for example, the embezzler, the civic-minded businessman, the mother who beats her infant son to death, the brutal dictator, the skid-row derelict, the sex deviate, the kindly priest. It is difficult to see what "human nature" these fellow human beings have in common, and when we expand our horizons to include the people of other cultures, we find even greater differences—in values, goals, and ways of life.

Is there a hidden order beneath this diversity, comparable to the order that scientists have found in the rest of nature? Just

what sort of creature is man "down underneath"? This question is not an idle one, for on its answer hinges the type of life man should lead, the form of government that is best suited to him, and the kind of world he should try to construct for himself.

In the present chapter we will examine some of the conflicting historical views of man, survey the major psychological "models" of man, and try to get a new perspective on "human nature" by noting what man shares in common with—and how he differs from—other living things.

THE PROBLEM
OF MAN'S BASIC NATURE

The psychologist Floyd Allport (1967) has described the human situation by an analogy:

"Suppose the ill-fated occurrence of an atomic holocaust had come to pass on earth, and after the debris had cleared the only two remaining objects to be seen were an ultra-primitive man and a watch, still going, which he had picked up in the desert. Since the man might be presumed to be in a state of

almost complete ignorance, all realization of the purpose of the watch had now been obliterated from the earth. That this structure would present the primitive man with a puzzle if he were to try accurately to describe it, to say nothing of explaining its origin, seems evident. We, too, are like watches— lost in the desert of time. And similarly, we are at a loss to understand either our origin or our essential nature." (p. 1)

But we have certainly tried to understand both. Long before modern science entered the arena, philosophers, theologians, and politicians had argued over the problem of man's basic nature. From a welter of conflicting views, three questions have kept recurring: whether man is basically *good or evil;* whether he is basically *rational or irrational;* and whether his behavior is the result of *determinism or free will.*

Good or Evil

Some people have asserted that man is basically selfish and self-seeking. Others have denied it. Some have seen him as competitive by nature, others as cooperative. Some have maintained that his "real" nature is hostile and cruel, others that it is friendly and kind. All these issues become involved in the larger one of whether man's nature is basically good or evil.

Human nature as evil. The view that man is a basically "sinful" creature has received substantial support from both religion and science—as well as from the experience of the human race. The Christian doctrine of original sin has taught that man, once capable of living a good and perfect life, was corrupted by the Fall. Without divine help, he now is unable to resist the temptations of evil. *Genesis* (8:21) tells us, "The imagination of man's heart is evil from his youth." In short, the Christian view of man's nature is not a very charitable one.

While contradicting the traditional Christian explanation of the origin of man,

Charles Darwin's theory of evolution seemed to lend scientific support to a view of man as basically selfish and cruel. In his monumental work *On the Origin of Species by Means of Natural Selection,* published in 1859, Darwin pictured the natural world as the battleground for a ruthless struggle for survival in which man as well as the lower animals participated. In this universal struggle, the fittest would always win out at the expense of their weaker rivals. Actually, Darwin himself viewed man as a basically friendly creature who tended to follow the Golden Rule, but the general impact of the theory of evolution was to strengthen belief in the essential competitiveness, agressiveness, and cruelty of man.

The theories and writings of Sigmund Freud, which have had such a pervasive impact on psychological thought, have also presented a negative view of man's basic nature. In his *Civilization and Its Discontents,* Freud depicted man as essentially a predatory animal:

". . . men are not gentle, friendly creatures wishing for love, who simply defend themselves if they are attacked, but . . . a powerful measure of desire for aggressiveness has to be reckoned as part of their instinctual endowment. The result is that their neighbor is to them not only a possible helper or sexual object, but also a temptation to them to gratify their aggressiveness . . . to seize his possessions, to humiliate him, to cause him pain, to torture and to kill him. . . .

". . . Anyone who calls to mind the atrocities of the early migrations, of the invasion of the Huns or by the so-called Mongols under Jenghiz Kahn and Tamurlane, of the sack of Jerusalem by the pious crusaders, even indeed the horrors of the last world-war, will have to bow his head humbly before the truth of this view of man." (1930, pp. 85-86)

The chain of violence and cruelty evidenced by man reaches from the most ancient times to today's headlines, and it is not surprising that the view of human nature as basically evil has dominated much of Western thought. As Montagu (1955) has summed it up:

"The secular experience of humanity during the last 2000 years, the internecine wars, the bloodshed, plunder and treachery, the general inhumanity of man to man has in almost every way served to confirm the . . . view of the natural depravity of man." (pp. 402-403)

Human nature as neutral. Despite man's deplorable record of pillage, rape, betrayal, torture, and destruction of his fellow human beings—often on a grandiose scale—there is another side to the picture.

Studies of different cultures have shown that there are many peoples in the world who as a group are friendly and kind. The Arapesh, a primitive tribe living in the mountains of New Guinea, were found by the anthropologist Margaret Mead (1939, p. xix) to be a peaceful people who thought that "all human beings . . . are naturally unaggressive, self-denying . . . concerned with growing food to feed growing children." Even though life was difficult in the rocky terrain which they inhabited, the Arapesh were a gentle and cooperative people who seldom showed hostile aggressive behavior. Curiously enough, a neighboring tribe, the Mundungumor, were highly aggressive, warlike, and cruel.

Maslow (1954) has described a similar lack of hostile aggressiveness among the Northern Blackfoot Indians. Among this group, which had a constant population of about 800, he found a record of only five fist fights in fifteen years and no other signs of overt hostility.

"These are not a weak people by any means. The Northern Blackfoot Indians are a prideful, strong, understanding, self-valuing group. They are simply apt to regard aggression as wrong or pitiful or crazy." (p. 175)

Similarly, the pygmies of the Ituri rain forests of Africa do not hurt or kill each other even though they have blow guns and other weapons (Poppy, 1967); and in a recent study it was found that only three murders were committed in Iceland during a period of fifty years (Winchester, 1966) as compared with the 14,000 or more homicides in the United States each year.

Such contrasts have led many social scientists to the conclusion that man is a highly educable animal who is neither good nor bad by nature but has potentialities to develop in either direction. Whether he becomes selfish, cruel, and warlike or self-sacrificing, kindly, and peaceful will depend largely upon the culture in which he grows up. Similarly, differences within a given culture are to be explained by differences in family background and in other specific circumstances and experiences. When circumstances are normal or favorable, the individual is likely to learn to behave in "good" ways; when circumstances are undesirable he may learn to behave in "bad" ways. While he admittedly has the inherent capacity for selfish and cruel behavior, he clearly also has the capacity for love and goodness.

Human nature as good. Swinging still further from the view of man as essentially evil is the conception of man as basically good. The Judaic-Christian tradition, while emphasizing man's tendencies to "innate depravity" if left to his own resources, has also taught that man was created in the likeness of God; that there is a divine spark in each of us. Jesus said, "The kingdom of heaven is within you."

Belief in man's essential goodness was particularly strong in the late eighteenth and early nineteenth centuries and was forcefully expressed in the writings of many Romantic poets and philosophers, who believed that if men were allowed to live "naturally" much of the evil in the world would disappear. For example, in *Émile*, a treatise on education published in 1762, the philosopher Jean Jacques Rousseau maintained that the aim of education should be self-expression rather than the suppression of natural tendencies—that the chief function of the school should be to provide the child with opportunities to develop his natural gifts, unhampered by the corrupting influence of society.

Although they approach the problem of

human development more realistically, a growing number of psychologists are coming to accept a positive view of man's essential nature. They believe that under favorable conditions man develops his basic propensities toward friendly, cooperative, constructive behavior. Aggression and cruelty are viewed as pathological behavior resulting from the denial, frustration, or distortion of man's essential nature. On the basis of extensive clinical studies of clients in psychotherapy, the clinical psychologist Carl Rogers (1961) found:

". . . the basic nature of the human being, when functioning freely, is constructive and trustworthy. . . . When we are able to

"HUMAN NATURE" UNDER STRESS

"In the history of American arms, the most revealing chapter as to the nature of the human animal does not come from any story of the battlefield but from the record of 23 white men and two Eskimos who, on August 26, 1881, set up in isolation a camp on the edge of Lady Franklin Bay to attempt a Farthest North record for the United States."

"The Expedition under command of First Lt. A. W. Greeley, USA, expected to be picked up by a relief ship after 1 year, or 2 years at most. Its supply could be stretched to cover the maximum period. . . .

". . . June of the second year came and passed, and no relief ship arrived. In August, Greeley decided on a retreat, intending to fall back on bases which were supposed to hold food stores. Thereafter disaster was piled upon disaster. . . . When the Greeley Expedition was at last rescued at Cape Sabine on June 22, 1884 . . . seven men remained alive. Even in these, the spark of life was so feeble that their tent was down over them and they had resigned themselves to death. . . .

". . . That any survived was due to the personal force and example of Sgt. (later Brig. Gen.) David L. Brainard, who believed in discipline as did Greeley, and supported his chief steadfastly, but also supplied the human warmth and helping hand which rallied other men, where Greeley's strictures only made them want to fight back. Brainard was not physically the strongest man in the Expedition, nor necessarily the most self-sacrificing and courageous. But he had what counted most—mental and moral balance.

"Among the most fractious and self-centered of the individuals was the camp surgeon, highly trained and educated, and chosen because he seemed to have a way among men. Greeley was several times

Department of Defense, 1950, pp. 99-102.

at the point of having him shot; the surgeon's death by starvation saved Greeley that necessity.

"Among the most decent, trustworthy, and helpful was Jens, the simple Eskimo, who died trying to carry out a rescue mission. He had never been to school a day in his life.

"There were soldiers in the party whom no threat of punishment, or sense of pity, could deter from taking advantage of their comrades, rifling stores, cheating on duty and even stealing arms in the hope of doing away with other survivors. . . .

"But in the greater number, the sense of pride and of honor was stronger even than the instinct for self-preservation. . . .

"Private Schneider, a youngster who loved dogs and played the violin, succumbed to starvation after penning one of the most revealing deathbed statements ever written: 'Although I stand accused of doing dishonest things here lately, I herewith, as a dying man, can say that the only dishonest thing I ever did was to eat my own sealskin boots and the part of my pants.'

"Private Fredericks, accused in the early and less-trying period of meanness and injustice to his comrades, became a rock of strength in the weeks when all of the others were in physical collapse or coma. . . .

"There is still an official report on file in the Department of the Army which describes Sergeant Rice as the 'bravest and noblest' of the Expedition. He is identified with most of its greatest heroisms. The man was apparently absolutely indomitable and incorruptible. He died from freezing on a last forlorn mission into the Arctic storm to retrieve a cache of seal meat for his friends. . . .

"Such briefly were the extremes and the middle ground in this body of human material. . . ."

free the individual from defensiveness, so that he is open to the wide range of his own needs, as well as the wide range of environmental and social demands, his reactions may be trusted to be positive, forward-moving, constructive. We do not need to ask who will socialize him, for one of his own deepest needs is for affiliation and communication with others. As he becomes more fully himself, he will become more realistically socialized. We do not need to ask who will control his aggressive impulses, for as he becomes more open to all of his impulses, his need to be liked by others and his tendency to give affection will be as strong as his impulses to strike out or seize for himself. He will be aggressive in situations in which aggression is realistically appropriate, but there will be no runaway need for aggression. His total behavior, in these and other areas, as he moves toward being open to all his experience, will be more balanced and realistic, behavior which is appropriate to the survival and enhancement of a highly social animal." (p. 194)

The concept of man's essential goodness is supported by two other lines of evidence. Bodily functions are most efficient when emotions are pleasant. Visceral activities accompanying unpleasant emotions such as anger—although useful in coping with many emergencies—disrupt the normal functioning of the body. Over a period of time such negative emotions can actually damage bodily tissue. On a psychological level a parallel can be drawn with our common experience of well-being and happiness when we are loving and "good" and of unhappiness and discontent when we are dominated by selfishness and hate.

On the basis of his work in the area of international tensions, the psychologist Gordon Allport (1954) concluded:

"Normal men everywhere reject, in principle and by preference, the path of war and destruction. They like to live in peace and friendship with their neighbors; they prefer to love and be loved rather than to hate and be hated. . . . While wars rage, yet our desire is for peace, and while ani-

mosity prevails, the weight of mankind's approval is on the side of affiliation." (p. xiv)
It is a curious reminder of history that the most "inhuman" aggressions and cruelties have been inflicted in the name of justice and moral righteousness. Men do not normally follow leaders they perceive as evil and destructive.

These diverse views of human nature as evil, neutral, or good have important social implications. All agree that man is a highly educable creature and that his development for good or evil can be markedly influenced or even controlled by cultural conditions. But here the agreement ends. If man is by nature selfish, predatory, and evil, society must shape him into a social creature by stringent discipline and social control. If, on the other hand, his natural tendencies are toward friendly, cooperative, and constructive behavior, then society can best achieve its purposes by encouraging spontaneity, naturalness, and self-direction. Techniques of restriction and control give way to techniques designed to encourage the fulfillment of inner potentialities.

Rational or Irrational

The indictment of man over the ages has not been confined to pointing out evidences of his selfishness, cruelty, and aggression. He has also been characterized as irrational and irresponsible. Political dictators from the time of the Romans to our own day have belittled the ability of the masses and have given them great public spectacles to divert their attention from complex political and social problems which were allegedly beyond their comprehension. In every age there have been those who scoffed at man's much-touted gift of reason. The seventeenth-century satirist John Wilmot, Earl of Rochester, in "A Satire Against Mankind" spoke of,
"Reason, which fifty times to one does err, Reason, an ignis fatuus of the mind."
Even our own Alexander Hamilton spoke with contempt of "the imprudence of democracy, where the people seldom judge or de-

termine right." The ordinary person, he insisted, is governed by emotion and is changeable and unpredictable.

Early faith in man's rationality. But from earliest times reason has also had its champions. The ancient Greeks considered man to be a highly rational animal and exalted reason as the epitome of man's virtues. The Roman aristocrats emphasized man's rational nature and prided themselves on their pragmatic approach to social problems. Although belief in reason had its setbacks during medieval times, it emerged again as the basic fabric on which the democratic social organization of Western man is based—the belief that man, given sufficient information and opportunity, can direct his own affairs and those of his society with wisdom and responsibility.

In the eighteenth century, reason was elevated almost to the level of a cult, as poets, philosophers, and statesmen expressed their faith in man's capacity to achieve perfection by exercising his own superior reason. The American and French revolutions reflected and enhanced a widespread spirit of optimism about the ability of the common man to guide his own destiny. Thomas Jefferson, an aristocrat by birth, maintained that the average person could reason and judge rightly if given access to the facts: "Enlighten the people generally, and tyranny and oppressions of body and mind will vanish like spirits at the dawn of day." In his first inaugural address Abraham Lincoln expressed a similar faith when he asked: "Why should there not be a patient confidence in the ultimate justice of the people? Is there any better or equal hope in the world?"

Deprecation of rationality in modern times. Our own age has seen this faith in man's innate rationality questioned and deprecated. Research in psychology and the social sciences has delineated many cultural, emotional, and motivational conditions that can distort man's thinking and lead him to irrational solutions to his problems.

Despite our great scientific advances,

we seem to have no end of difficulties in "reasoning together" and developing a more orderly, equitable, and harmonious world. Even such a seemingly straightforward problem as the population explosion continues without serious attempt at solution despite dire predictions that hundreds of millions of people will starve to death if present population trends continue.

Two of the major schools of psychological thought—psychoanalysis and behaviorism—have contributed to the downgrading of man's rationality. In his *Psychopathology and Everyday Life,* Freud emphasized the unconscious and irrational influences that are evident in much of our thinking and behavior. Reading of "repressed sex drives," of "unconscious hostility," and of "rationalization" and "projection," many come to the seemingly obvious conclusion that man's behavior is inherently and inevitably self-deceptive and irrational. In fact, according to Freud's view, even man's "finer" sentiments and aspirations are only sublimations of animal instincts which lurk just beneath the surface of his civilized veneer. Man is seen as the victim of instinctual drives and unconscious processes which distort his reason. Only as he masters the unconscious and irrational side of his make-up can he hope to behave in rational ways.

Behaviorists have denied the overwhelming influence of unconscious forces in man's thinking, but have undermined our faith in our essential rationality by picturing man as a passive, malleable creature whose thinking and behavior are shaped by his culture through the mechanism of conditioning. Man may think rationally if his conditioning has been in that direction, but the existence of any inherently rational force in man's make-up is denied. Man is essentially a puppet manipulated by the strings of his sociocultural environment.

Unquestionably, too, rapid social change, with the uprooting of many cherished beliefs and values, has led man both to confusion and to a questioning of his own vaunted rationality. If he could have believed so firmly in things which he now considers false, how much faith can he place in the rationality of his newer ideas and convictions? Viewing the inequities, confusions, and conflicts which permeate our world, we can well wonder whether we have any basic propensity to be rational.

Continuing evidence of man's rationality. Although faith in man's rationality has been substantially weakened in recent times, it has by no means been destroyed. Many modern statesmen, philosophers, and scientists believe that man's natural tendencies are toward common sense and reason. Again we may refer to the conclusions which Rogers (1961) has drawn from his extensive study of clients in psychotherapy:

"One of the most revolutionary concepts to grow out of our clinical experience is the growing recognition that the innermost core of man's nature, the deepest layers of his personality, the base of his 'animal nature,' is positive in nature—is basically socialized, forward moving, rational and realistic." (pp. 90-91)

Here one might wonder whether rationality is not a logistic built into all animals and essential for their survival. In any event, rationality is built into computers that simulate organisms.

No one denies that man's tendencies toward rationality can readily be distorted by environmental influences. Man can be misled by false information, all but stupefied by repetitive and blatant stimuli from mass communication media, restricted by cultural deprivation, handicapped by lack of training in learning and problem solving, and overwhelmed by the number and complexity of issues he is expected to act upon. Even man's vaunted science, with its worship of scientific objectivity, can mislead him if it causes him to regard as nonexistent or meaningless aspects of his experience which have not yet been studied scientifically—or if it makes him forget his own limitations as an observer in a universe of incredible complexity and vastness.

The achievements of modern science, nevertheless, indicate man's capacity and in-clination for dealing with his problems in rational ways. His unremitting efforts to probe the secrets of the universe and to make sense of his world, to obtain accurate information and sound values for dealing with his problems, and to establish order in both his physical surroundings and his social relationships all seem to indicate not only a potentiality for rational behavior but a basic propensity for it.

Free or Determined

In his everyday life man operates on the assumption that he is free to make decisions and choose his course of action, at least within certain limits. He sees himself as continually weighing alternatives and deciding among them. Yet many philosophers, theologians, and scientists have raised the question of whether his freedom of action is real or *illusory*—whether man is an active and responsible agent with some measure of "free will" or a puppet whose behavior is actually determined by forces beyond his control.

The assumption of determinism. Various kinds and degrees of determinism have been argued since ancient times. The great dramatic tragedies of Aeschylus and Sophocles, for example, are pervaded by the ancient Greek belief that man, for all his nobility, is in the last analysis a pawn of fate. There is an inevitability to his actions, an end from which he cannot escape. This fatalism is clearly illustrated in the well-known legend of Oedipus, who in trying to avoid fulfilling the oracle's prophecy that he would kill his father and marry his mother turned headlong into fate's trap and unwittingly did as prophesied. The Calvinist doctrine of predestination, which holds that at the time of his birth every individual has already been elected to salvation or condemned to damnation, is a later example of philosophic or religious determinism.

Another kind of determinism is the cornerstone of modern science. This is the assumption that the universe is an orderly place where all events occur in keeping with natural laws. Everything follows cause-and-effect relationships. In essence, the universe is a sort of giant machine which functions according to certain built-in principles. If we had complete information about the machine, we could understand and predict its functioning in every detail.

Applied to human behavior, the doctrine of determinism holds that human behavior is lawful. Psychologists have taken it as axiomatic that a cause must precede its effect and thus have usually looked for the causes of behavior in the past history of the individual. Given a complete knowledge of the past experiences of the individual, we would be able to predict how he will—indeed must—act. This assumption has led many psychologists to view man as a "reactive" organism and the concepts of freedom and self-determination as illusory. As B. F. Skinner (1953) has put it: "The hypothesis that man is not free is essential to the application of scientific method to the study of human behavior." Thus man becomes a helpless pawn of whatever influences happen to shape him.

For evidence, psychologists adhering to this "strict" determinism have pointed to the diverse customs and beliefs of people throughout the world, all shaped by cultural conditioning. They have emphasized the experimental finding that peoples' beliefs and values can be manipulated through punishment and reward, and that suggestion and imitation are important forces shaping a person's assumptions and behavior. Despite his "illusion" of freedom, the individual is regarded as completely at the mercy of his past conditioning.

Carried to its logical extreme, strict determinism is essentially predeterminism—since all events are determined by what has happened before. "What will be will be," and we are only puppets who play our part as it is written with no chance of altering the script.

The assumption of freedom. In our own personal lives, probably none of us believes in a strict determinism. As Shibutani (1964) has expressed it:

"Each person believes that he is able to exercise some measure of control over his own destiny. He is capable of making decisions and of selecting among alternative lines of action. It is this widespread belief that provides the basis for the doctrine of 'free will' and for the concept of moral responsibility. Since men are assumed to be capable of making choices, they are held accountable for their deeds." (p. 233)

We all distinguish between behavior for which we feel responsible and behavior that occurs when we are "not ourselves"—for example, when we are under the influence of drugs, in a condition of severe shock, or mentally disordered. Our courts, too, distinguish between degrees of accountability for one's actions. Our whole way of life, with its freedom of discussion, ballot boxes, democratic institutions, and assumptions of personal responsibility, is based on the concept of man's freedom for self-determination. And curiously enough, many of the most ardent advocates of strict determinism are among the most zealous fighters for democracy. As Gordon Allport (1955) has pointed out:

"No paradox is more striking than that of the scientist who as citizen makes one set of psychological assumptions and in his laboratory and writings makes opposite assumptions respecting the nature of man." (p. 100)

The apparently irreconcilable paradox of determinism vs. freedom has been well pointed up by Carl Rogers (1961) in relation to the therapeutic situation.

"In the therapeutic relationship some of the most compelling subjective experiences are those in which the client feels within himself the power of naked choice. He is free—to become himself or to hide behind a façade; to move forward or to retrogress; to behave in ways which are destructive of self and others, or in ways which are enhancing; quite literally free to live or die, in both the physiological and psychological meaning of those terms. Yet as we enter this field of psychotherapy with objective research methods, we are, like any other scientist, committed to a complete determinism. From this

point of view every thought, feeling, and action of the client is determined by what preceded it. There can be no such thing as freedom. The dilemma I am trying to describe is no different than that found in other fields— it is simply brought to sharper focus, and appears more insoluble." (p. 192)

Although the paradox of freedom vs. determinism has by no means been resolved in modern psychology, a number of psychologists have adopted a "soft" determinism. This view accepts the law of causation in human behavior but sees this law operating through the "self-determining" powers of the human mind. While acknowledging that human behavior is heavily influenced by the individual's background of experience, scientists adhering to this viewpoint are impressed with man's self-awareness, with his ability to reflect and to reinterpret and reorganize his past experience, to be critical and evaluative of his own behavior, and to formulate and weigh alternatives on the basis of both past satisfactions and probable outcomes. They are impressed by his ability to imagine new possibilities different from anything he has experienced and to change his plans in the light of new information or new dreams of the future.

Here "freedom" is seen as essentially an *emergent* quality in the evolutionary process (Muller, 1961; Collier, 1964). While physical and biological events follow the principle of determinism—except perhaps for some measure of indeterminism in subatomic physics—the development of self-awareness, reasoning, and other higher thought processes provides the individual with a range of possible actions in many situations. In high-level choice situations, man's transcendent ability to reflect, to imagine, to reorganize the past in relation to the present and the future makes it impossible to predict the outcome or to know what considerations will be the determining ones until after the event has occurred. Rather than a passive automaton, man is viewed as an active determinant in shaping his own destiny.

If we view man as having some degree of freedom and the potential for choice based on reason and anticipation rather than merely past reinforcements, then he should profit from living in a free society. In fact, an authoritarian society, which seeks to indoctrinate and rigidly prescribe the behavior of its members and hence to reduce man to an automaton, would be considered pathological. The fact that such efforts have never been wholly or lastingly successful seems to indicate man's basic tendency to be evaluative and active rather than simply passive and reactive.

What conclusions can we draw from our examination of these conflicting views of human nature? It seems evident that man is capable of both good and evil, of both rationality and irrationality, of being both active and reactive. These are not mutually exclusive types of behavior but poles on a continuum. Though we may operate closer to one pole at a given time, we retain the potentiality for both. None of us is always rational or irrational, selfish or altruistic, active or reactive. However, the patterns of a given society or the life style of a given individual may tend toward one extreme or the other.

In the section which follows, we shall attempt to broaden our perspective of man's nature by reviewing the psychoanalytic and other major "models" of man.

PSYCHOLOGICAL "MODELS" OF MAN

A model is essentially an analogy which can help a scientist to see important relationships. For example, the use of the computer model of the human mind has made it commonplace in psychology to talk about input, information processing, output, and feedback. The use of models follows a strategy of successive approximations—with each refinement making it a more adequate and accurate representation. In psychology, as in other sciences, models serve to keep investigators from being overwhelmed by masses of unwieldy factual information while at the same time avoiding the necessity of premature all-embracing theories.

SOME SALIENT CHARACTERISTICS OF PSYCHOLOGY AS A SCIENCE

GOALS

Explanation of the underlying order in the confusions and complexities of man's nature and behavior. Accomplished by gathering data, interpreting them, and integrating them into a theoretical framework that will explain all the known facts.

Prediction of an event in order to prepare for and perhaps prevent or facilitate it. Dependent upon identification of consistent relationships between events, situations, and conditions.

Control of an event—influencing or changing the "natural" course of events, as in teaching and therapy. Facilitated by increases in both the extent of factual information and the accuracy of prediction.

LEVELS OF INVESTIGATION

Biological level, concerned with the bodily bases of behavior. Biological variables relevant for study include genetic processes, age, brain pathology, drugs, hormones, nutrition, illness, fatigue, and bodily injury.

Psychological level, concerned with understanding the nature and role of psychological variables in human behavior. Relevant are such general categories of behavior as striving, thinking, feeling, and acting, and more specific manifestations such as values, beliefs, attitudes, emotions, dreams, habits, learning, problem solving, decision making, conflicts, and frustrations.

Sociological level, concerned with the effects of sociocultural conditions upon the behavior of individuals and groups. Relevant sociological variables include social roles, status, leadership, patterns of communication, propaganda, social pressures, and interpersonal relationships.

Interdisciplinary approach is often profitable. By working cooperatively, scientists from different disciplines often arrive at a more comprehensive understanding of behavior.

METHODS OF GATHERING DATA

Survey method obtains data by means of written questionnaires or oral interviews from a selected group of individuals, usually a representative sample of some larger group or universe of people.

Field study method, the oldest research technique, involves making direct observations of natural events. The investigator goes into the field and makes observations without manipulating or trying to hold constant the conditions under which his subjects are operating.

Clinical case study method explores the life history and present life situation of a person with a view to uncovering the causes of, and arriving at a solution to, some adjustment problem.

Experimental method tests hypotheses by the manipulation and control of the relevant variables. The experimenter studies the effects of systematic variations of certain conditions (independent variables), on specified aspects of behavior (dependent variables).

Comparative method involves the study of non-human species, especially where complexity or humanitarian considerations prevent use of human subjects.

Statistical method involves the use of mathematical techniques to simulate experimental manipulation or control of variables. Statistical analysis may be used to identify or assess the action of individual variables as well as the interaction of two or more variables.

OUTCOMES

Factual information—either quantitative or qualitative data from observation; data can then be organized into a coherent, orderly, logical framework (model or theory).

Models—analogies which enable the scientist to see relationships among his data. Models keep psychology from being overwhelmed by a mass of unwieldy facts, while at the same time avoiding the necessity of formulating premature, all-embracing theories.

Theories—organizations of a large body of empirically validated facts, inferences, and generalizations. Theories provide a framework within which all the known facts can be explained and, in turn, suggest hypotheses which may be tested experimentally.

Since facts owe no prior allegiance to any scientist, they can often be interpreted in several ways. This is especially true in a relatively new science such as psychology where data are far from complete. Thus we find considerable difference in the psychological models of man which have been formulated.

Psychoanalytic Man

The psychoanalytic model of man is based on the pioneering work of Sigmund Freud (1856-1939) which extended over a period of fifty years of observing and writing. The major principles of his model are based on the clinical study of individual patients undergoing psychoanalysis. Basic to this approach is the method of free association in which the patient is asked to provide an unrestricted running verbal account of whatever comes into his mind, leaving nothing out.

The concepts formulated by Freud and elaborated by his followers have been woven into the fabric of our thinking about man and have profoundly influenced our view of ourselves. The psychoanalytic model of man is a complex one, but its general outlines can be sketched in terms of three sets of concepts and their interrelationships.

Id, ego, and superego. Fundamental to the psychoanalytic model is the concept that behavior results from the interaction of three key subsystems within the personality: the id, the ego, and the superego.

The *id* contains the innate, primitive, biological drives of man, such as hunger, thirst, and aggression. These primitive drives are seen as being of two types: (1) constructive drives, primarily of a sexual nature, which provide the basic energy of life, or *libido;* and (2) destructive and aggressive urges, which are more obscure but tend toward self-destruction and death. In essence, *life* instincts are opposed by *death* instincts. It may be pointed out that Freud used the term "sex" in a broad way to refer to practi-cally anything of a pleasurable nature—from eating to bathing.

The id, according to Freud, operates in terms of the *pleasure principle* and is concerned only with immediate gratification. It is completely selfish and unconcerned with reality or moral considerations. Although the id can generate images and wishes related to need gratification (primary process), it cannot undertake direct action toward meeting its needs. Thus a second key subsystem—the *ego*—develops to mediate between the demands of the id and the realities of the external world. Although the primary purpose of the ego is that of meeting id demands, it must do so in such a way as to ensure the individual's survival. This requires the use of reason and other intellectual resources (secondary process) in dealing with the realities of the external world as well as the exercise of control over id demands. Hence the ego is the central control or decider system of the personality and is said to operate in terms of the *reality principle.*

However, the id-ego relationship is merely one of expediency that does not make allowance for moral values. Hence Freud introduces a third key system—the *superego*—which is the outgrowth of learning the taboos and moral values of society. The superego is essentially what we refer to as *conscience* and is concerned with the good and the bad, the right and the wrong. With the development of the superego, we find an additional inner control coming into operation to cope with the uninhibited desires of the id. However, the superego, as well as the id, operates through the ego system. Thus the superego strives to compel the ego to inhibit desires which are considered immoral.

The interplay of these intrapsychic forces of id, ego, and superego is of crucial significance. Often the instinctual desires and demands of the id are in conflict with superego demands or with the demands of the external world. The adequate resolution of such conflicts by the ego is considered essential to personality adjustment. Neurotics are viewed as persons unable to resolve such inner conflicts.

Anxiety, defense mechanisms, and the unconscious. Freud distinguished three types of anxiety or "psychic pain." *Reality* anxiety stems from dangers or threats in the external world; *neurotic* anxiety arises when id impulses threaten to break through ego controls and cause behavior which will lead to punishment. *Moral* anxiety arises when the individual does something or even contemplates doing something that conflicts with his superego values and arouses feelings of guilt.

Anxiety is both a painful experience and a warning of impending danger and hence forces the individual to do something about the situation. Often the ego can cope with anxiety by rational measures; but when these do not suffice, the ego resorts to irrational protective measures—such as rationalization and repression—which are referred to as *ego-defense mechanisms*. These mechanisms will be discussed in Chapter 7.

Of key importance here is the concept of unconscious processes. Freud thought that the conscious represents a relatively small area of the mind; while the unconscious, like the submerged part of an iceberg, is much the larger portion. In the vast domain of the unconscious are the images, desires, and wishes that have been either forgotten or repressed because they arouse anxiety. The individual is unaware of many of these unconscious desires, but they actively seek expression and may be reflected in dreams and fantasies, when ego controls are temporarily lowered.

In a broad context, Freud viewed man's unconscious strivings—especially sexual and aggressive strivings—as reflecting an inherent conflict between the individual's instinctive animal strivings and the inhibitions and regulations imposed by society.

Psychosexual development. A third fundamental psychoanalytic formulation is that of the critical importance of infancy and childhood for adult personality.

Freud saw psychosexual development as a succession of stages, each characterized by a dominant mode of achieving libidinal pleasure. According to his formulation, the *oral stage* occurs during the first year of life when libidinal pleasure is achieved primarily through stimulation of the lips and mouth in sucking, nursing, and related activities. The *anal* stage involves the second and third years of life, in which libidinal pleasure is associated with defecation. The *phallic* stage occurs from about 3 to 5 years when self-manipulation of the genitals becomes the chief source of libidinal pleasure. This is followed by the *latency* stage from the sixth to twelfth year, when sexual stimulation presumably recedes in importance and the child is preoccupied with developmental skills. Finally, if all goes well, the *genital* stage makes its appearance at puberty with the deepest feelings of pleasure usually coming from heterosexual relations. This stage ideally culminates in marriage, sexual relations with a loved mate, and childrearing.

Libidinal gratification during each stage is important if the individual is not to be *fixated* on a given level. For example, an individual who did not receive adequate oral gratification during infancy may be prone to excessive eating or drinking in adult life. In addition, each stage of development poses demands and conflicts which must be dealt with for normal progress toward maturity. One of the important problems during the phallic stage, for example, is the Oedipal conflict, in which the son has incestuous desires toward his mother. If this conflict is not adequately resolved, he is not likely to achieve satisfactory relationships with members of the opposite sex later, as a young adult.

Essentially, then, this is psychoanalytic man. He is a man dominated by instinctual biological drives and by unconscious desires and motives. While there is the constructive libidinal side to his nature, there are also the darker forces pushing him toward destruction and death. Although the ego tends toward rationality, intrapsychic conflict, defense mechanisms, and the unconscious all tend toward a high degree of irrationality. And although man is driven by his inner desires and impulses, he is essentially a reactive organism, conditioned by his early experiences.

Behavioristic Man

The behavioristic model of man is far from complete but is sufficiently distinctive to warrant a brief sketch. The general format of modern behaviorism stems from the early work of John Watson (1919). Watson concluded that if psychology were ever to become a science of behavior, it must limit itself to the study of events that could be observed objectively. Thus he rejected the introspective study of conscious states or processes as being essentially mentalistic and prescientific—because such observations were not open to verification by other investigators.

Starting with this basic assumption, Watson changed the focus of psychology from inner psychic processes to outer behavior which is objectively observable. Only through the objective observation of such behavior and the stimulus conditions which brought it about could psychologists learn to predict and control man's behavior. Many of the principles underlying the behavioristic model have been formulated on the basis of research conducted with animal subjects, but it is assumed that the same general principles apply to human behavior as well. Largely as a consequence of its scientific flavor and its success in formulating and applying principles of learning, behaviorism has become a dominant theme in modern American psychology and has greatly influenced our view of man.

Respondent and operant conditioning. Since most observable behavior is learned, behaviorists have addressed themselves primarily to the question of how learning comes about. In trying to answer this question, they have focused on conditions in the environment—stimulus conditions that could be related to the acquisition, modification, and weakening of behavior patterns.

As a starting point, behaviorists commonly make a distinction between *respondent* and *operant* behavior. Respondent responses include relatively simple reflexes and emotional responses which are elicited by appropriate stimuli even prior to learning. For example, a bright light leads to the constriction of the pupil of the eye; a sudden loud noise leads to a fear response. Through conditioning, such responses may come to be elicited by a wide range of other stimuli—essentially in the manner first demonstrated by the Russian physiologist Pavlov. Thus an animal, after hearing a bell consistently when food is presented, will start salivating to the sound of the bell alone. On the human level, the well-known experiment of Watson and Rayner (1920) demonstrated the conditioning of fear in a human infant. A sudden loud noise—the unconditioned or natural stimulus for fear—was paired with the sight of a white rat, and after several such presentations the sight of the rat alone or any other furry object elicited a fear response (crying). The conditioning of respondent behavior is often referred to as *classical conditioning.*

Of greater practical significance is the conditioning of operant responses. The term *operant* is used because in such responses the individual "operates" upon or modifies the environment. Instead of presenting a stimulus which elicits a known response, the psychologist places an animal in a situation in which it learns to make a response that brings about the attainment of a goal or the satisfaction of a need. For example, a hungry rat is placed in a cage which has a lever; in the course of exploring the cage, the rat eventually presses the lever and is immediately given a bit of food. Before long, he presses it again and the same thing happens. The rate of lever pressing increases, until it becomes an established response that occurs as soon as he is put into the cage and continues at a high rate as long as he is hungry. In learning to press the bar to obtain food, the rat has undergone *operant conditioning.*

Reinforcement. Crucial to both respondent and operant conditioning is *reinforcement*—which refers to the strengthening of the new response by the presentation of an appropriate stimulus. In the experiment of Watson and Rayner, for example, successive repetitions of the loud noise with the white rat strengthened or reinforced the conditioned fear response to the rat. In the operant conditioning example, the food received by the rat after he presses the lever is the reinforcer—it makes the lever-pressing response more probable on subsequent occasions.

Reinforcement may be negative as well as positive. In respondent conditioning the eliciting stimulus may be pleasant, as in the case of food, or unpleasant, as in the case of the loud noise. And in operant conditioning a rat may learn to press a lever if in so doing he escapes from or avoids an electric shock or other noxious stimulus. Here the escape or avoidance behavior is strengthened by the removal of the aversive stimulus.

In both classical and operant conditioning, when reinforcement is later withheld, the conditioned response eventually becomes *extinguished*. It is assumed that any response of which the subject is capable can be produced, maintained, or eliminated by the appropriate scheduling of reinforcement or lack of it, if one has complete control of the subject's environment.

Reinforcement is effective because it reduces the level of the tension created by the operation of *primary* and *secondary drives*. The former are innate, biological drives like hunger, that are directly related to the meeting of physiological needs; the latter are psychological or social drives like self-esteem and social approval, assumed to be learned through conditioning.

Generalization and discrimination. To fill in our basic sketch of the behavioristic model of man, we need to add the concepts of *generalization* and *discrimination*. Generalization is the tendency for a response which has been conditioned to one stimulus to become associated with other similar stimuli. For example, we noted in the experiment of Watson and Rayner that the infant's fear generalized from white rats to other furry animals. The greater the similarity of stimuli,

---

CONTRASTING EXPLANATIONS OF A PHOBIA

The differences in viewpoints of the psychoanalytic and behavioristic models of man are vividly underscored in the following illustration:

In 1909 Freud reported the case of little Hans to exemplify the role of sexual urges in the development of phobic reactions (irrational fears). Hans was terrified that he might be bitten by a horse. According to Freud, the basis for this phobic reaction lay in the Oedipus complex. Little Hans felt both love and hatred for his father, who represented an obstacle in the expression of his sexual feelings toward his mother. He was also afraid that his father would punish him for having incestuous impulses—a fear experienced as castration anxiety. Freud believed that this conflict had been resolved by Hans' ego through repression of his ambivalent and incestuous desires and displacement of his fear to a symbolic representation—the fear of being bitten by a horse.

The phobia dated from the time of a bus ride that Hans had taken with his mother. Hans had become very frightened when the horse which pulled the bus fell down and was hurt. Freud regarded this incident as the precipitating cause of the phobia, with Hans' unconscious intrapsychic conflict as the real basis of the disorder.

Behaviorists, however, using the same descriptive data, would explain Hans' phobia as a simple conditioned fear response. In that day of horses and buggies, Hans had likely been sensitized to horses by earlier unpleasant experiences involving seeing horses beaten, being hurt while playing "horses," and being warned to avoid horses because they might bite. Thus a fear response might partially have been conditioned already, and the incident on the bus might have been the final learning trial which established it. In any case, the phobic reaction, once established by classical conditioning, was maintained by operant conditioning, because each time Hans successfully avoided a horse his anxiety was reduced; thus his avoidance behavior was strengthened and reinforced (DeNike & Tiber, 1968; Wolpe & Rachman, 1960).

the greater the generalization. Discrimination occurs when the individual learns to distinguish between similar stimuli and respond to one but not another as a consequence of differential reinforcement. According to the behavioristic model, complex processes such as perceiving, forming concepts, solving problems, and making decisions are based on an elaboration of the basic discrimination operation.

Although we could enlarge our picture with additional concepts—such as secondary reinforcers, higher-order conditioning, and response generalization—the preceding concepts represent the core of the behavioristic model of man. By means of these relatively few concepts, behaviorism attempts to depict the acquisition, modification, and extinguishing of all types of behavior, whether adjustive or maladjustive. Its techniques have been applied with increasing sophistication to complex problems in education and psychopathology as well as to basic research.

The behavioristic model makes allowance for man to behave in ways which are good or evil, rational or irrational, depending upon his conditioning. But rather than attribute the causes of behavior to inferred constructs, such as an ego and a superego —which cannot be objectively observed— the behaviorists look for the causes in the reinforcement history of the individual. Behavioristic man is thus completely at the mercy of his previous conditioning and present environment; his alleged freedom of choice is an illusion. Yet such convictions have not kept behaviorists—such as Watson and Skinner—from repeatedly emphasizing the potential use of modern science, with its methods of behavior modification and control, for planning a better future world for man—almost as if they could *choose* to use it in one way rather than another.

Humanistic (Self) Man

The humanistic model of man is far from complete but consists of a number of under-lying themes and principles which can be fitted together into a more or less coherent picture. This picture is based on the contributions of many distinguished psychologists, among whom are Allport, Maslow, Murray, and Rogers.

Although their thinking is influenced by both the psychoanalytic and the behavioristic models, the humanistic psychologists are in disagreement with both. They view the behavioristic model, with its emphasis upon the stimulus situation, as an oversimplification: they feel that it needs to be balanced by a consideration of the internal psychological make-up of the individual. At the same time, they do not concur with the negative and pessimistic psychological dynamics of the psychoanalytic model. Rather they emphasize the essentially positive and rational propensities of man and view him as having some measure of freedom for self-direction.

Sources of data for the humanistic model include both clinical studies of individual cases and findings from the experimental laboratory; they include studies of normal and exceptional people as well as of the maladjusted. They make only limited use of animal studies.

A positive view of man. Humanistic psychologists think the psychoanalytic and behavioristic models are unduly negative and deterministic in their view of man. As Allport (1955) once succinctly stated the matter:

"Up to now the 'behavioral sciences,' including psychology, have not provided us with a picture of man capable of creating or living in a democracy. . . . They have delivered into our hands a psychology of an 'empty organism,' pushed by drives and molded by environmental circumstances. . . . But the theory of democracy requires also that man possess a measure of rationality, a portion of freedom, a generic conscience, [personal] ideals, and unique value. We cannot defend the ballot box or liberal education, nor advocate free discussion and democratic institutions unless man has the potential capacity to profit therefrom." (p. 100)

Allport was not advocating, of course, that our democratic ideals should dictate our scientific findings. Rather he was concerned with what he considered the imbalance of existing models which view man as essentially a conditioned robot. The humanistic model emerged as an attempt—based on scientific evidence—to remedy this imbalance by focusing on the positive aspects of man. Thus the humanistic model attributes great importance to human learning—but emphasizes reflection, reasoning, and creative imagination rather than conditioning. Although unconscious and irrational motives occur, man also has strong propensities for overcoming irrationality—for conscious planning and rational choosing. Sex, aggression, and other biological drives are recognized, but man is seen as just as basically concerned with values, meaning, and personal growth. And although much of human behavior is influenced by past conditioning and experience, the view of man as simply a reactive organism or robot does not seem to tell the whole story. Man is also self-aware, evaluative, future-oriented, and capable of resisting environmental influences.

"Self" as a unifying theme. The humanistic model assumes that man cannot be understood in terms of external stimulus conditions alone; internal psychological structures and processes also have a causal influence on his thinking, feeling, and action.

Although William James in 1890 made extensive use of the self-concept in his *Principles of Psychology,* the concept of self was later dropped by behaviorists and other psychologists because of its "internal" and hence unobservable nature. Eventually, however, the need for some kind of unifying principle of personality—as well as for some way of taking cognizance of the subjective experience of each individual—led to its reintroduction in the humanistic model. Although the concept of self is used as somewhat synonymous with the psychoanalytic concept of "ego"—in that it represents an inferred subsystem concerned with decision making, planning, and coping—the human-

istic approach also extends the concept to include tendencies toward growth and actualization.

Foremost among contemporary self theorists is Carl Rogers. His particular model of personality has been stated in a series of propositions (1951) which are summarized in shortened form below:

1. Each individual exists in a private world of experience—the phenomenal field—of which he is the center.

2. A portion of this total field becomes differentiated as the conscious self—as the I, me, or myself—and is the individual's most valued possession.

3. The most basic striving of the individual is toward the maintenance, enhancement, and actualization of the self.

4. The individual's perceptions and interpretations determine his behavior. He reacts to "reality" as it is perceived by him.

5. The individual behaves in ways that are consistent with his concept of himself and tends to reject or distort incoming information that is inconsistent with or threatening to the self.

6. Perceived threat to the self is followed by defense—including the narrowing and rigidification of perception and coping behavior.

7. Maladjustive behavior results when the individual feels too threatened to acknowledge his own experiences and to be himself.

8. The individual's tendencies are toward growth and wholeness, and when his experiences and alternatives are clarified, he chooses the path of personal growth.

Rogers and other humanistic psychologists also place great emphasis on values and the process of evaluation. It is of crucial importance that the individual's values be based on his own thought and choice rather than on a blind acceptance of the values fostered by his social environment.

Uniqueness of the individual. Not only is man unique as a species, but each individual, by virtue of his great potentiality for learning and his own particular background of experience, is unique. In studying man, psychologists are thus faced with the dual task of describing the development and behavior both of individuals and of man as a species. This problem has led to a strategy conflict between psychologists who adhere to the *nomothetic* approach of seeking laws that apply to man in general and psychologists who adhere to the *ideographic* approach, which seeks to describe and understand individuals. Although these approaches are often used to complement each other, humanistic psychologists feel that psychology generally has stressed the nomothetic approach at the expense of an adequate understanding of the true uniqueness of each individual human being. They point out that there are usually a sizable portion of cases to whom nomothetic laws do not seem to apply. For example, the nomothetic approach can delineate the conditions which typically result in high achievement motivation; such a statement, however, does not explain why a particular child exposed to these conditions failed to acquire such motivation. Only an intensive study of a given child, his life situation, and his own interpretations of events can be expected to reveal the answer.

The humanistic model—with its positive view of man, its utilization of the concept of self, its emphasis on the uniqueness of the individual, and its recognition of man's concern with values and self-actualization—has had an important and increasing influence upon our contemporary view of man.

Existential Man

Although similar in many respects to the humanistic model, the existential model of man had its origins in philosophy and literature rather than science. Again we do not find a close-knit school of thought but rather certain common themes and concepts stemming from the writings of such European philosophers as Heidegger, Jaspers, Kierkegaard, and Sartre. Especially influential in existential thought in the United States has been the American psychologist Rollo May.

Existentialists are very much concerned about the social predicament of modern man. They emphasize the breakdown of traditional faith, the depersonalization of man in a standardized mass culture, and the loss of meaning in human existence. In such a situation it becomes the task of the individual to stand on his own, to shape his own identity, and to make his existence meaningful—to make his life count for something—not on the basis of philosophical or scientific abstractions but through his own experience of being.

Like the humanistic model of man, the existential model emphasizes the uniqueness of the individual, his quest for values and meaning, and his freedom for self-direction and self-fulfillment. However, the existential model represents a somewhat less optimistic view of man, with more emphasis on the irrational trends in man's nature and the difficulties inherent in self-fulfillment. And the existentialists place considerably less faith in modern science for dealing with man's deepest problems and more faith in the inner experiencing of the individual.

Existence and essence. A basic theme in existentialism is that the individual's existence is given, but that what he makes of it—his essence—is up to him. The child who defiantly blurts out "Well, I didn't ask to be born" is stating a profound truth. But it is irrelevant. For whether he asked to be born or not, here he is in the world and answerable for himself—for one human life. What he makes of his existence is up to him. It is his responsibility to shape the kind of person he is to become and to live a meaningful life.

Finding a meaningful and fulfilling way of life, however, is not an easy task. In an age of profound cultural change and conflict, traditional beliefs and values no longer provide adequate guides for the good life or meaning for human existence. And in our bureaucratic mass society the individual tends to be depersonalized and submerged in the group. Thus modern man has become alienated and estranged—a stranger to God, to himself, and to other men. In the social context of contemporary life he is confused and fearful that he will fail in his quest for a fulfilling life.

Yet his predicament can be viewed as a challenge to make something worth while of his life. In his striving for increased self-definition in *his own experience of being* lies the perilous path to self-fulfillment. "Being" is seen as a matter of commitment to increased self-awareness and self-definition, to true communication with others, to concern with values and evaluation, and to acceptance of the responsibility for making choices and directing his own destiny.

Freedom, choice, and courage. The individual's essence is created by his *choices.* For his choices reflect the values on which he bases and orders his life. As Sartre put it: "I am my choices."

In choosing what he is to become, the individual is seen as having absolute freedom; even refusing to choose represents a choice. Thus the locus of valuing is within the individual. He is inescapably the architect of his own life. Morris (1966, p. 135) has stated the situation in the form of three propositions:

1. *I am a* choosing *agent, unable to avoid choosing my way through life.*

2. *I am a* free *agent, absolutely free to set the goals of my own life.*

3. *I am a* responsible *agent, personally accountable for my free choices as they are revealed in how I live my life.*

Although man values his freedom, the problems of choice and responsibility often become an agonizing burden. For finding satisfying values is a lonely and highly individual matter. He must have the courage to break away from old patterns, to stand on his own, and to seek new and more fulfilling pathways. In a sense, his freedom to shape his own essence is "both his agony and his glory."

Often the individual lacks "the courage to be"—to follow the path to greater self-definition and actualization—and so cuts himself off from new possibilities for being. Many individuals do not want their essence to be left up to them; they want some outside au-

thority like religion or society to advise them on how to act and what to believe. But if blind conformity and immersion in the group leads to a wasted life, the individual cannot blame anyone else or evade the consequences. To the extent that he fails to realize his potentialities for being, he is a failure and feels guilty. To flee from one's freedom and obligation to life is to *be unauthentic,* to *show bad faith,* and to *live in despair.*

Meaning, value, obligation. A central human characteristic is a will-to-meaning. This is primarily a matter of finding satisfying values and is a highly individual matter. For the values that give one life meaning may be quite different from those which provide meaning for another. Each person must find his own pattern of values.

This emphasis upon individual value patterns is not to be construed as moral nihilism, however. For there is a basic unity to mankind, and all people are faced with the task of learning to live constructively with themselves and others. Hence, there will be an underlying continuity in the value patterns chosen by different individuals who are trying to live authentically.

Existentialism also places strong emphasis upon the individual's *obligation* to his fellow man. The most important consideration is not what one can get out of life but what one can contribute to it. One's life can be fulfilling only if it involves socially constructive values and choices.

The encounter with nothingness. A final existential theme which adds an urgent and painful note to the human situation is that of *nonbeing* or *nothingness.* In ultimate form it is death, which is the inescapable fate of all human beings.

This encounter with nothingness is unique to man; he is the only creature who must live with the constant awareness of the possibility of nonbeing. And this awareness adds a new and crucial dimension to his existence. Thus the encounter with nothingness becomes an overpowering theme of existentialism. We can deny victory to nothingness by living a life that deserves a better fate, that counts for something, that should not be lost. If man is perishable, we can at least perish resisting—living in such a way that nothingness will be an unjust fate.

Although there are many variations on the four major models of man which we have reviewed, the basic models remain relatively distinct and to some extent contradictory ways of viewing man. Although each has some "evidence" to support it, all four depend ultimately on generalizations from particular kinds of events and experiences. Like the blind men feeling different parts of the elephant and describing it as a different animal, each model makes a contribution to the part of the puzzle of human experience and behavior that it has tackled but does not seem to be adequate for some of the parts it has not tackled.

In this book we shall not limit ourselves to any one model, but shall maintain an eclectic approach, utilizing concepts from differing theoretical orientations, including that of a fifth model—behavior systems theory. This fifth model takes cognizance in a systematic way of both man's inner experiencing and his outer behaving, both his propensities for action and his transactions with his environment. It is a model that recognizes both his continuity with other living things and his uniqueness. We will explore this model in the next section.

MAN AS A LIVING SYSTEM

Physical and biological scientists have long been accustomed to thinking in terms of *energy systems,* and recently a number of behavioral scientists have found it helpful to approach their study of man in much the same way—viewing man as a living energy system, comparable to other living systems in many basic ways.[1]

An energy system is an assemblage of parts held together by some form of interaction or interdependence. There are non-

living systems, such as our solar system, and living systems, such as plants and animals. Living systems, in turn, can be arranged in a hierarchy extending from cells to organs, organisms, groups, organizations, societies, and supranational bodies such as the United Nations. Each higher-level system is composed of lower-level systems.

General Properties of Living Systems

All living systems have certain characteristics in common. For example, living systems contain genetic material (DNA)—indicating the common origin of all living things. Similarly, living systems contain a "decider" and other subsystems, integrated in such a way as to make the total system capable of self-regulation, development, and reproduction. But the particular mechanisms at different levels of the evolutionary scale vary greatly.

Living systems, whether simple or complex, can be seen as having three kinds of properties: *structural, integrative,* and *field* properties.

Structural properties. Each living system contains parts or subsystems which are highly independent, whose combined action enables the system to function as an integrated unit. The human organism, for example, has respiratory, circulatory, nervous, and other observable and distinguishable subsystems. Still other subsystems, such as an ego subsystem, we do not observe but infer on the basis of the functioning of the system. Thus the human system has both observed biological and inferred psychological structures.

Structural properties—and hence potentialities for behavior—vary greatly from one type of living system to another. The behavior potentialities of a virus or a fish are obviously quite different from those of a man. This is why it is important to understand the structure of a system if we are to understand its behavior.

---

[1]For the discussion of behavior systems theory, the author is indebted particularly to J. G. Miller, 1965a, 1965b; and to Buckley, 1968.

LIVING SYSTEMS RESIST DISINTEGRATION

Living systems tend to develop according to a pattern that is characteristic for their species and to resist disintegration or distortion. This tendency has been shown dramatically in studies with pine trees and sponges. When the vertical leader (terminal shoot) at the top of a pine tree is cut off, one of the lateral branches turns up to form a new leader (figure a). Sometimes two or more branches compete briefly, but when one takes over as the vertical leader, the others drop back and grow again at the normal angle for side shoots. If a branch is tied up or down, the free end tends to resume the normal direction (figures b and c). In such studies it has been found that a reddish substance called *reaction wood* forms on the side of the branch away from the direction in which it needs to bend in order to restore the characteristic growth pattern of the tree. The branch curves away from the reaction wood, because its cells have greater lengthwise extension than other wood cells. The formation of reaction wood is controlled by a hormone, *auxin,* but the regulatory mechanism which, in turn, controls the secretion of auxin is still unknown (Sinnott, 1952).

Wilson's classic study of sponges provides an even more remarkable demonstration of self-regulatory mechanisms. A sponge was cut up finely and forced through fine bolting cloth into a container of sea water. The minute particles sank to the bottom and promptly began to form small conglomerations and then larger ones. After eight days the new mass had formed the characteristic internal structure of the original sponge (Wilson, 1910).

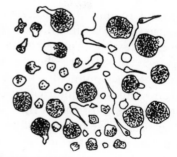

Cells just pressed out

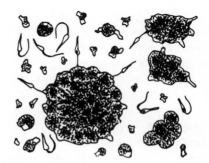

After ten minutes

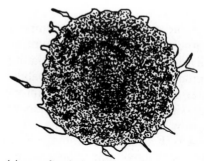

1 hour after being pressed out

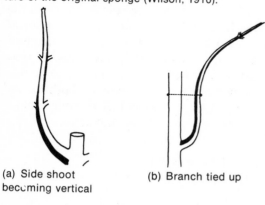

(a) Side shoot
becoming vertical

(b) Branch tied up

(c) Branch tied down

Eight days later

Living systems are "open systems"—they are not self-sufficient but can continue to exist only if they can maintain certain kinds of transactions with their surroundings. These transactions require the processing of *matter-energy,* as in the assimilation of nutrients, and the processing of *information,* as in the recognition of danger. The human brain, for example, is continually processing information concerning internal bodily functioning as well as information from the environment via our sense organs and using this information as a basis for adjustive action. An organism's structure determines the refinement and level of sophistication with which it will be able to process both matter-energy and information. An amoeba obviously has fewer options and less flexibility in both respects than a human being; on the other hand, it has fewer requirements for healthy and adjustive functioning.

Integrative properties. Living systems have built-in tendencies to maintain their organization and functional integrity. If a system's equilibrium is disturbed, it tends automatically to take the action necessary to restore itself.

Although the mechanisms they employ vary considerably, depending on the type of system, all living systems are self-regulating and self-maintaining insofar as their capabilities for matter-energy processing and information processing permit. A hungry person will take action to obtain food. The body tries to defend itself against an invading virus. A nation will resist subversion. The amazing ability of a mutilated sponge to restore itself was demonstrated many years ago by the biologist H. V. Wilson, whose remarkable experiment with sponges is described on page 35.

Another integrative characteristic of living systems is their tendency to develop in accordance with their inherited potentialities throughout a life cycle characteristic for each species. An acorn may develop into a stunted, gnarled tree or into a magnificent specimen of "oakhood" depending upon its environment; but it will always become an oak, never

a birch. Similarly, polliwogs grow into frogs and behave like frogs. Although man shares this developmental tendency, his infinitely greater potential for variations in development and his capacity for helping guide his own development pose unique problems.

Field properties. Each lower-level system is part of a higher-level system or field—usually one among several such parts. For example, an organ is a subsystem of an individual; an individual, a subsystem of a group; and a group, a subsystem of society. The total field for a human being, of course, includes the physical environment as well as the social environment. The important point here, however, is that the energy system model does not view people as completely separate and distinct from their environment but as integral parts of it—both physically and socially.

Each living system is in continual transaction with its field, and this constant interchange modifies both system and field. Even in such a simple matter as eating a steak, the individual both alters and is altered by his environment. On a more complex level we can see that a child both influences and is influenced by his family; a leader both influences and is influenced by his group members. Individuals take an active role in trying to modify their environment by working for political, economic, and social change; at the same time, the school and other agencies of society are trying in many ways to shape or modify the behavior of individuals. It thus becomes apparent that to understand human behavior, we will have to study both the inner and outer factors that together determine an individual's condition and actions.[1]

Special Characteristics of the Human System

Although all energy systems share the basic structural, integrative, and field properties outlined above, different levels of systems reveal many unique characteristics. Living

---

[1]The article by Buckley on society as an adaptive system on page 495 is relevant both here and in connection with Chapter 9.

systems are different in many ways from non-living systems, and as we go up the scale from simple to complex living systems we find that new structural and functional properties begin to appear. On the other hand, it often happens that properties present in rudimentary form at lower levels of life become further refined and more influential at higher levels. The evolvement of the nervous system, for example, can be traced from a very simple segmental apparatus in a worm to the highly complex brain of man.[1]

While sharing many general characteristics with lower-level systems, man reveals many characteristics that are different and some that are unique. Among the most significant characteristics of man as a species are his self-awareness and self-direction; his ability to modify his behavior to meet varied situations; his use of symbols; the richness of his transactions with his environment; and his concern with information, values, and meaning.

Self-awareness and self-direction. Responsiveness to stimulation—sometimes called irritability—is a property of all living things. Though it is not known at what point in the scale of life this irritability becomes associated with consciousness, there is no doubt that man's consciousness reaches a depth and precision far beyond the types of awareness that exist in lower animals. As Collier (1964) has pointed out, man alone seems to have evolved to the level of *reflective consciousness*—to be not only aware of his world but also able to reflect upon, review, and criticize aspects of his own experiences.[2]

It is this unique type of self-awareness, coupled with the ability to delay action over sustained periods of time, that provides man with his unusual potentialities for thought, evaluation, and self-direction. To a far greater extent than any other species, he has the ability to transcend the stimulation of the moment and thus to shape his own future and control his own destiny.

Modifiability of action. Reflective consciousness would be of little use to man if he were limited to reflex or instinctive behavior. Of all creatures, man is the least bound by "built-in" patterns and the most capable of changing his behavior. His resources for learning, reasoning, and imagining give him almost unlimited flexibility for coping with new and changing situations in appropriate and often original ways. And these same resources enable him to evaluate the effects of his actions and to keep making indicated corrections.

One of the lessons that may be learned from evolution is that those organisms unable to adapt to changing environmental demands have perished from the earth. In our modern world, with its complex and shifting demands, man's ability to adapt himself to rapidly changing environmental conditions is thus a critical advantage. Man has a further advantage in that he can not only adapt to change but can also control and direct many of the changes themselves, preventing or reversing changes that threaten his welfare.

Use of symbols. While other creatures show flexibility and resourcefulness in coping with problems, they are unable to deal in any complex way with absent situations by thinking about them. Man's thought processes, on the other hand, may be concerned largely with ideas—symbols of absent or even imaginary objects, events, and concepts. This makes possible man's superior ability to understand the order inherent in his world, to anticipate the probable outcome of a given course of action, and to make plans in the light of past, present, and future conditions.

Man's ability to use symbols has also made it possible for him to communicate more precisely with others as well as to communicate with individuals or groups far removed in space or time. Without language symbols, it would be difficult to exchange

---

[1]For delineation of the relationships between nonliving and living systems and between subsystems, systems, and suprasystems, see Feibleman's article on page 456.
[2]For a fuller statement of Collier's position, see his article on consciousness as a regulatory mechanism, starting on page 459.

MAN AS AN ENERGY SYSTEM

COMMON CHARACTERISTICS OF ENERGY SYSTEMS		EXAMPLES IN MAN
STRUCTURAL	Internal structure, subsystems	Bodily equipment, constitution, personality structure
	Changes in structure with time	Maturation, learning, aging
INTEGRATIVE	Energy sources	Motives, drives, emotions
	Stabilizing resources	Homeostatic mechanisms, healing and restoration after damage
	Adjustive resources	
	a) Information handling	Perception, evaluation, decision
	b) Information storing	Memory
	c) Modification of behavior	Learning, reasoning
	d) Emergency resources	Emotions, compensation
	e) Communication devices	Neural and chemical (within system); language, other symbols (with field)
	Reproduction	Reproductive system
FIELD	Relations with lower-order systems	Relations with animals and inanimate objects
	Relations with same-order systems	Relations with other individuals
	Relations with higher-order systems	Individual-group and group-group relations

Adapted by permission from Grinker, 1956, p. 303.

ideas or to share feelings with others. Nor could Greek writers dead over two thousand years still challenge our thinking. Our written languages have made it possible for each new generation to build on the findings of previous generations, thus enabling man to avoid many actions that have already been shown to lead to undesirable or disastrous consequences.

Complexity of transactions with field. Whereas lower animals must usually eat what they can find or starve, rely on instinctual responses for coping with bodily disease or damage, and live where the climatic changes are not extreme, man is not so limited. In fact, there seems to be almost no end to the ways in which man can change and control his surroundings for his own convenience. As a consequence, his relationships and transactions with his environment have become far more complex than those of other species. Increasingly, in fact, man lives in a world of his own making, and the demands he must meet are demands made by the complex physical and social environment that he himself has created.

Man's transactions with his social and interpersonal environment are equally complex. Cultural standards and values, the complicated sentiments we share as members of a group, and the varying role requirements that different societies develop have no real counterpart in animal groups. Although some animals have rather complicated social organizations, these are based primarily on built-in instinctual patterns and are similar for all groups of a given species. They are far removed from the complex cultural and interpersonal patterns evolved by man.

Concern with information, values, and meaning.
Since man's behavior is not limited to instinctual patterns of adjustment, he must decide for himself what goals to pursue and what means are appropriate for trying to achieve them. In selecting goals and means, man must not only obtain information about himself and his world—about what is and what could be—he must also make judgments of what is desirable and undesirable, good and bad for him. In short, he must come to grips with the problem of values.

As we have noted in the Prologue, the problem of values inevitably becomes coupled with that of meaning—of trying to ascertain the meaning of one's existence. These concerns are uniquely human. They can arise only in an energy system which has a high degree of self-awareness, flexibility in behavior, and opportunity for choice among alternatives.

Changes in the System with Time

All living systems are subject to continual change. Changes within either the system or its field bring corresponding changes in the other and in system-field transactions. Such changes may be minor or drastic, slow or fast, reversible or irreversible.

In man, as in other living organisms, the basic pattern of change comes as part of a genetically determined and predictable life cycle extending from conception to old age and death. In the early phases of the life cycle, the changes are toward increased size, complexity, and competence. In the later phases they are toward entropy—in the direction of decreasing ability, deterioration, and eventual disintegration of the system.

Not all change is genetically determined. Often change is caused by accidents, deficiencies, or disease. And in man, especially on the psychological level, a tremendous amount of continuing change results from experience and learning. As the individual develops, we find the emergence of a fairly consistent structure of beliefs, attitudes, and habits which guide his behavior and lead to a life style which is characteristic for him. As we shall see, psychological structure itself becomes an increasingly important influence on further learning and change. For he tends to learn what is consistent with his past learning and to ignore or deny new experiences which do not fit.

Thus the human system can be viewed as a "time gestalt" with an increasing "closure" of the system as the psychological configuration is filled in. For this reason, environmental conditions tend to exercise their greatest influence during early development. By adulthood, the personality structure is relatively well defined and stable. Although it may continue to change in minor ways, a radical change in a person's environment is usually required for a major change in his outlook and life style.

SUMMARY AND A LOOK AHEAD

In viewing man as a living system, we have by no means resolved the issues concerning his basic nature. However, we have tried to clarify these issues and to show the ways in which he is both like and unlike other living creatures. Man has emerged as neither a mechanistic, stimulus-response automaton nor a mystical being with qualities not amenable to scientific investigation. Rather we see him as a highly educable creature, shaped in different ways as the result of his complex transactions with his environment. Lacking built-in mechanisms to guide most aspects of his behavior, he may become many things. But he has integrative tendencies which guide his growth and behavior in certain directions when environmental conditions permit. These tendencies seem to be in the direction of love and cooperation, rationality, and the active and purposive direction of his own behavior. Finally, in viewing man as a living system, we have found a framework that encompasses both his uniqueness and his continuity with the universe of living things.

To understand why people behave as they do—and the likenesses and differences among them—we must examine the structural, integrative, and field properties of the human system in more detail—the physical and psychological make-up and strivings of the individual and the physical and social world of which he is a part. This examination will take us, in the next three chapters, into a study of how personality develops: what conditions influence it, what changes can be expected during the life cycle, and what conditions are associated with healthy or unhealthy development.·

Key terms used in this chapter include:

determinism, free will (pp. 22-24)
pleasure principle, reality principle (p. 26)
id, ego, superego (p. 26)
oral, anal, phallic, latency, genital stages (p. 27)
psychoanalytic, behavioristic, humanistic, existential models of man (pp. 26-34)
respondent vs. operant behavior (p. 28)
reinforcement, generalization, discrimination (p. 29)
being and nonbeing (p. 33)
structural, integrative, and field properties (pp. 34-36)
energy system (p. 34)

Chapter 2

DETERMINANTS
OF DEVELOPMENT

Heredity
Environment
Self As a Third Determinant

Development is a process of becoming. Personality development—the becoming of a person—starts at conception and continues until death. Each day of his life the individual is a little different from what he was the day before. Nothing that is alive can long remain exactly the same, though the rate and degree of change are far from constant. In Chapters 3 and 4 we shall study what changes can be expected and when—and the degree of variation that is within the range of "normal" development. But first we need to understand the how and why of development—what forces interact to produce development.

In this chapter, then, we shall first examine man's genetic endowment, which provides his potentialities for growth and behavior. Next, we shall note the role of the physical and social environment in determining the way and extent to which his inherited potentialities are realized. Finally, we shall see how the individual's self-structure, including his sense of personal identity, comes to act as a third important influence on his ongoing development. The continuous interweaving of hereditary, environmental, and self influences shapes us all into the recognizable mold of human beings and, paradoxically, makes each of us a little different from everyone else.

HEREDITY

On our earth there are about a million different kinds of animals and some half million different kinds of plants. Despite the tremendous variety of life, each kind of living thing breeds true. Zinnia seeds produce zinnias; deer give birth to fawns and never to lambs.

It thus becomes apparent that each type of living thing accurately transmits specific hereditary information from one generation to the next. But what is the nature of this information, how is it transmitted, and how does it operate in guiding development?

Although we cannot even begin to encompass the findings of modern genetics, let us briefly sketch a few highlights concerning the nature and influence of our genetic inheritance.

The Nature of Our Genetic Inheritance

A human life really begins at conception when the egg cell of the female is fertilized by the sperm cell of the male. At this time the new human being receives a genetic inheritance which provides the basic potentialities for his development and behavior.[1] This endowment includes potentialities not only for his physical structure but also for striving, thinking, feeling, and acting, and for patterns of growth and change throughout a predictable life cycle.

Reproduction and growth. The process by which an individual develops from a single-celled *zygote*—as the fertilized egg cell is called at the moment of conception—into an adult human being with his trillions of cells has been called "the climax of all wonders." And indeed, it would appear to be.

When the male sperm enter the cervix of the female, they make their way—at about the rate of 3 inches per hour—through the cervix and uterus to the Fallopian tubes, in one of which they meet the egg cell. Although more than 200 million sperm are engaged in this race, only one wins and fertilizes the egg.

After fertilization has occurred, the complex process of growth begins. The new cell divides into two cells; and these in turn divide into four cells, and the process continues. Soon specialized cells and systems make their appearance. By the eighteenth day, a primitive heart has begun beating, and a week later the beginnings of eyes, spinal cord, nervous system, lungs, and other organs have developed. By the eleventh week all the bodily systems have formed and are functioning. After a period of some 9 months the baby is born, but the orderly sequence of development and change—as provided for by our genetic instructions—continues throughout a predictable life cycle.

Chromosomes, DNA, and genes. One of nature's best kept secrets has been how our genetic inheritance can possibly specify the great wealth and complexity of details required for manufacturing a new human being. Not only must the new individual develop into a member of the human species, but characteristics such as eye color, blood type, and sex must somehow be specified. In addition, our genetic instructions must regulate development in a typical and orderly sequence all the way from fertilized ovum to adult human being.

Most cells consist of two parts: a centrally located nucleus and a surrounding fluid called the *cytoplasm*. Inside the nucleus of the cell are tiny rod-like structures called chromosomes. These chromosomes come in matched pairs. For example, the fruit fly Drosophila has 8 chromosomes (two each of 4 different kinds) in each cell nucleus, while normal cells in man contain 46 chromosomes (23 pairs).

Each chromosome, in turn, is made up of long molecules of deoxyribonucleic acid (DNA for short) which are arranged in two strands twisted together to form a double spiral or helix that looks like a coiled ladder. In a series of epic research studies, scientists have shown that our genetic instructions are stored in this DNA helix or "book." Since there are 23 pairs of chromosomes in man—one of each pair coming from the mother and one from the father—there are in essence 23 DNA books that make up the instructions for manufacturing a new human being.

The "sentences" in the DNA book of instructions are the genes, following one another much as beads are strung together to form a necklace. Each gene carries the instructions, either singly or in combination with other genes, for specific body traits. For example, there are genes which control eye color, hair curl, and blood type. Genes are thus the discrete units or bearers of heredity.

With the breaking of the genetic code, man can now read the DNA books. Interestingly enough the genetic code appears to be

---

[1]Technically, of course, what is provided is a genetic blueprint, a set of instructions which will make possible the development of certain structures and behaviors under particular environmental conditions. The term *potentiality* is a "shorthand" term for ease of discussion.

THE GENETIC CODE

The instructions carried in the DNA make provision for two main functions. The first is reproduction of cells by the making of exact copies. Were it not for this power of the DNA to duplicate itself, cells could not split in two—each with a complete set of genetic instructions. Replacement of worn-out cells and further growth or reproduction of the organism would be impossible. The second key function provided by the DNA instructions is direction of the activities in each cell, including the making of proteins. Proteins are the "building blocks" of life: structural proteins play a crucial role in the development of body tissues and organs, and protein enzymes regulate bodily processes. In fact, it is by means of proteins that the genetic instructions are carried out—that a living organism is created and its growth and functioning are implemented.

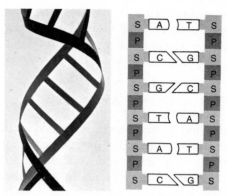

The double spiral of the DNA molecule resembles a ladder. A DNA molecule replicates itself by separating down the middle, or "unzipping." Then each half of the separated DNA molecule picks up the appropriate new base units from the surrounding area and the duplication is complete. In this way, for example, a new liver cell or red blood cell is formed which, in turn, is capable of replicating itself.

The sides of the DNA ladder are made up of sugar and phosphate (S and P); the rungs of the ladder are made up of pairs of four chemical bases—adenine and thymine (A and T) or cytosine and guanine (C and G). A single DNA molecule may have many thousands of these pairs. It is in the specific sequencing of these rungs on the ladder that the genetic information for making proteins is encoded.

In breaking the genetic code, it was found that each base represented a letter in the genetic alphabet. Just as the uniqueness of each word in the dictionary depends upon a specific arrangement of the 26 letters of the alphabet, the uniqueness of each word in the DNA ladder depends upon the sequencing of these chemical letters or bases. All DNA words are short, however—never more than 3 letters long.

Each 3-letter word stands for one of the 20 different varieties of amino acids which are used in the production of proteins. Each of the proteins, or "building blocks" of life, is made up of a different sequencing of these amino acids, a given protein typically requiring a linear sequence of some 300 to 500 amino acids. The DNA *sentence* or *gene* specifies the sequence of amino acids for manufacturing one type of protein. Since there are only 20 different amino acids a question might be raised about the other 44 possible words in the DNA code. It turns out that more than one base triplet, or word, can be used to signify the same amino acid and that some words are used as "start" and "stop" instructions.

The proteins are actually assembled in the cytoplasm of the cell by means of an ingenious arrangement. Too precious to leave the fortress-like security of the cell nucleus, the DNA makes an intermediary chemical called *RNA (ribonucleic acid)*, which is similar but not identical to DNA. The molecules of RNA serve as genetic messengers, journeying from the nucleus of the cell to sites in the cell protoplasm where proteins are to be manufactured. One type of RNA, *messenger RNA*, serves as a template in regulating the sequence of amino acids in protein manufacture. Another type, *transfer RNA*, scavenges in the surrounding area to pick up the amino acids needed for protein manufacture and transports these to the sites where the protein molecules are being assembled. The prodigious feat of the DNA in producing precise instructions for manufacturing the proteins required for the developmental and functional needs of the organism has been compared to the operation of a fantastically complex electronic computer.

Interestingly enough, each cell in the human body contains all the DNA information needed for producing a new human being; somehow "turn-off" mechanisms manage to delete all the DNA information except what is needed for the cell to duplicate itself or to produce a particular protein.

Some idea of the difficulties inherent in breaking the genetic code can be gleaned from noting that the vast information stored in the DNA is written in such a tiny script that all the DNA in all the fertilized egg cells that have given rise to the approximately three billion people on earth would fit into a 1/8-inch cube (Beadle, 1964).

Based in part on Beadle, 1964; McClearn, 1968; Pfeiffer, 1964; Watson, 1965; and Wooldridge, 1968.

the same for all living things—each virus, plant, or animal resembling the stock from which it was descended because of the specific DNA instructions which it inherits. Thus we see the oneness of the living world.

Variations in Genetic Endowment

Although the entire human race receives a characteristic genetic inheritance that is identifiably human and different from that of any other species, there are many noticeable differences among both groups and individuals.

Individual and family differences. Except for *identical twins* (monozygotic), who develop from a single fertilized egg and are assumed to have identical heredity, each individual has a somewhat different genetic inheritance. *Fraternal twins* (dizygotic), since they develop from two separate fertilized eggs, do not resemble each other any more closely in their genetic make-up than ordinary siblings. To understand the genetic differences among family members, let us note certain additional details of the working of our genetic inheritance.

1. *Reduction division.* If, in the process of procreation, a male cell bearing 46 chromosomes were to be fused with a female cell bearing the same number, the offspring would have twice the normal number of chromosomes in their cells. Nature solved this problem by devising the process of *reduction division,* whereby each mature egg or sperm cell receives only one of each pair of chromosomes from the parent cell. Thus unlike other body cells, sperm and ova contain only 23 chromosomes. And since a process of chance selection determines whether the germ cell receives one or the other from each pair of chromosomes, the germ cells from the same individual may have very different selections of chromosomes—much like different hands that can be dealt from a deck. So in the mating of any two parents, there are over 8 million possible combinations of chromosomes—and the likelihood that any one of these combinations would occur more

than once in the offspring of a given family is so small as to be virtually nonexistent.

Thus a tremendous range of individual differences is possible among children of the same parents. And as we go from the immediate family to cousins and more distant relatives, we find that differences in genetic make-up increase—for, by the laws of chance, the average number of shared chromosomes becomes smaller.

2. *Dominance and recessiveness.* The operation of dominant and recessive genes accounts for still further differences within families. After fertilization, the chromosomes carrying genes affecting the same general traits line up in pairs. Thus the genes which determine eye color from the paternal side become paired with genes for eye color from the maternal side. But suppose genes for brown eye color from the father are paired with genes for blue eye color from the mother. In this case, because the brown-eye genes are *dominant*, the offspring's eyes will be brown. The *recessive* blue-eye genes still remain as part of the new individual's chromosomal structure, however, and may show up in later generations. For example, if he marries a person who also carries genes for blue eye color, any of their offspring who receive only genes for blue eye color will be blue eyed. By this mechanism, recessive traits which are not visibly evident in either parent may show up in their children.

Several traits are known to be determined by dominant genes or recessive genes. Some of the traits of both kinds are normal while others are pathological. Blood type and dwarfism, for example, are determined by dominant genes; while blue eyes and albinism ("dead white" skin with pink eyes and white hair) are determined by recessive genes. However, much remains to be learned about the actual number of dominant and recessive genes in human beings and about the function of genes in determining intermediate traits—for example, in determining hazel or gray eye color rather than simply brown eyes or blue eyes.

3. *Sex determination.* The pair of chromosomes that determine sex are alike in the female and are called *X chromosomes;* in the male, sex is determined by one X chromosome and one of a different kind called a *Y chromosome.* Reduction division leaves all the female egg cells with X chromosomes, but half of the male sperm will carry an X chromosome and the other half a Y chromosome. If a sperm carrying an X chromosome fertilizes the egg, the child will have two X chromosomes, and be a female; if a sperm carrying a Y chromosome fertilizes the egg, the child will have an X and a Y chromosome and be a male. Thus the father who is disappointed when a daughter is born can only blame himself since the characteristic of sex is decided by the sperm cell. Curiously enough, for reasons not yet known, the odds for a boy baby are slightly greater than those for a girl baby—106 boys being born for every 100 girls.

Other genes in addition to the sex-determining ones are located on the X and Y chromosomes. Traits which are determined by those genes are said to be *sex-linked.* Females are less susceptible to aberrations involving sex-linked traits because they have two X chromosomes; if either one contains faulty genes, the other will ordinarily be normal and do the work of development. But since the male has only one X and one Y chromosome, he is in for trouble if either is faulty. Red-green color blindness is an example of a sex-linked trait determined by faulty genes on an X chromosome. Unless both of a female's X chromosomes are defective, she will not show the trait. But if the defect occurs in the single X chromosome of the male, he will be color blind. Consequently color blindness is much more common among men than among women.

The fact of being male or female—while making little if any difference in our inherited capacity for most types of achievement—contributes significantly to our development because of differing cultural expectations for men and women and the role of women in child bearing.

4. *Mutations.* When changes occur in a gene, the gene is said to have undergone a mutation. Mutations consist of changes in the rungs of the DNA ladder—involving deletions, additions, or modifications of the base chemicals.

Mutations are usually for the worse, for if any detail of our genetic instructions is missing or garbled—as we might misspell *cat* as *cut*—normal development may be impaired. In sickle-cell anemia, for example—a debilitating and often fatal blood disease of hereditary origin—one amino acid in a sequence of 574 making up the hemoglobin molecule has been put in the wrong place because of altered genetic instructions. The result is a distorted hemoglobin cell with impaired capacity for carrying oxygen through the blood stream. Various other diseases and congenital malformations, possibly including cancer, are associated with faulty DNA instructions due to gene mutations.

Most mutant genes are recessive. For this reason the hazards of various mutagens—agents which cause gene mutations, such as ionizing radiations from the testing of nuclear weapons—often are not immediately apparent but may show up in future generations. In Chapter 4 we shall examine some of the causes of gene mutations and the growth abnormalities that are most typically associated with them.

Population (group) differences. The peoples of the world have customarily been classified into three racial strains or population groups: the Mongoloid or yellow, the Negroid or black, and the Caucasian or white. This classification has been based primarily upon observed differences in physical traits like skin color, eye shape, and the distribution of blood types—all of which seem to be genetically determined.

Many of the *physical* differences observed between peoples living in different geographical regions appear to represent long-range changes in genetic make-up which are particularly adaptive to a given environment. For example, dark-skinned peoples are generally found in tropical regions, and it has been argued that this is the result of natural selection since heavily pigmented skin is a protection against strong sunlight, whereas a lighter skin is more adaptive in regions where less vitamin D from sunlight is available.

The extent to which *psychological* differences among racial groups are genetically determined is obscured by two key factors. First, our criteria for defining *race* are relatively crude and in everyday usage we confuse racial groups with ethnic ones. For example, to speak of Negroes as a racial group in America leads to a host of scientific errors, whereas we may speak of American Negroes as an ethnic group with some measure of assurance. Second, observed differences among population groups in such traits as aggression, competitiveness, and introversion may be the result of cultural rather than genetic influences. Even if there were a genetic basis for such psychological differences, it could be the result of the selective survival of those members of the original group who were best adapted to a given environment or of long-term selective mating or inbreeding in accordance with local social dictates.

In general, it would appear that the essential characteristics of man's genetic endowment are basically the same for all racial and ethnic groups. All populations are highly variable, and the differences *between* groups with respect to any trait are less than the range of differences *within* groups. Even a characteristic like skin color, which can be measured on a continuous scale, varies greatly in a given population, and there is much overlapping between different populations. Because identification as a member of a particular racial group may lead to differences in role, status, and opportunity, however, there are often wider differences in development than genetic differences alone would seem to explain.

Investigation of the frequencies of various genetic patterns in given population groups and the manner in which such frequencies may be affected by assortive mating, inbreeding, mutations, and natural selection is the primary purpose of the scientific field known as *population genetics*. As this field progresses, we shall eventually be able to answer questions for which we can now only make tentative assumptions.

The Role of Heredity in Development

We have noted the role of our genetic inheritance in providing for individual differences as well as in establishing the overall pattern of growth and change that is typical of the human life cycle. Now let us consider the potentials for behavior that our genetic endowment provides, the reaction tendencies that seem to be present at birth, the continuing influence of genetic instructions through maturation, and the continuous interweaving of genetic and environmental "input" that takes place during growth.

Behavior potentials. In Chapter 1 we summarized some of the salient characteristics of the human system—self-awareness and self-direction, modifiability of action, use of symbols, richness of transactions with the environment, and concern with information, values, and meaning. We also noted that human beings, like all living systems, tend to maintain themselves and to grow and function in accordance with their inherent potentialities. These characteristics are made possible by our genetic inheritance, although the exact form they take depends upon the particular physical and sociocultural environment in which our development takes place.

More specifically, we may think in terms of five categories which are of particular interest to psychologists:

1. *Perceiving, learning, and thinking*—receiving, integrating, and storing information and using it creatively in symbolizing, reasoning, problem solving, and decision making.

2. *Feeling*—experiencing fear, anger, love, joy, humor, and other emotions that contribute to the meaning of experience and often help to motivate action.

3. *Striving*—making plans, setting goals, and initiating purposeful behavior as the

individual strives to meet his maintenance and actualization needs.

4. *Acting*—executing adjustive responses. This includes automatic responses, such as habits, which leave conscious processes free for more difficult problems and for mobilization of resources for dealing with emergencies.

5. *Defending and repairing*—including the development of rationalization and other defense mechanisms for maintaining our psychological integration and damage-repair mechanisms such as crying and "talking it out."

To some extent these are behavior potentials of all higher animals, but they are considerably greater in scope for man than for any other species. Man has almost limitless capacity for learning, reasoning, and imagining; his emotional range and depth is far greater than that of other species and makes possible a great richness of conscious experience. Only man among all living creatures laughs at jokes, worries about dying, and anxiously tries to make the most of his existence.

However, the characteristic that appears to set man most clearly apart from other species is his great potential for flexibility in behavior—for responding appropriately to new situations. Man is far less restricted than other species by built-in adjustive patterns. In this connection it is interesting to compare man with another remarkable species, the ant.

Ants can lift more than twenty times their own weight and perform numerous other remarkable feats. The famed leaf-cutting parasol ants of Latin America have mastered a simple type of gardening; they gather leaves, chew them to a pulp, and make an underground compost heap in which they grow mushroom spores. Even the social structure of ants may be well organized and complex. The carnivorous driver ants of Africa, for example, march in orderly formation flanked by larger "officer" ants who organize, discipline, and direct the troops. Scouts bring back reports on the territory to be invaded and then act as an advance guard

for the expedition. The ants move rapidly through the jungle devouring every edible thing in their path (Crompton, 1954).

Given a favorable environment, ants function effectively, but they have relatively little capacity for changing their behavior in the light of experience or adapting to new conditions for which they are not "programed." Man, on the other hand, has tremendous flexibility in his adjustive behavior and has worked out many patterns of social organization. But as we have seen, man's great capacity for learning and modifying his behavior also complicates his existence, for it confronts him with the problem of values and meaning and the need for choosing what he will do and be.

Constitutional reaction tendencies. The term *constitution* refers to the relatively unique and enduring biological make-up of the individual that results from the interaction of genetic and (largely prenatal) environmental influences. Included here are such traits as physique, sex, energy level, and temperament. Some constitutional traits influence development primarily by providing a particular level and quality of potential. Others, such as physical appearance, exert their influence largely through the reactions of other people. Still others, such as temperament, appear to influence basic patterns of reactivity which appear early and are relatively consistent throughout the individual's life span. It is with the latter that we are primarily concerned here.

One of the most striking things about these constitutional reaction tendencies is their unique patterning for each individual from very early in life. On the basis of their pioneering studies of early development Gesell and Amatruda (1945) concluded that:

"Every embryo is unique. The uniqueness is so fundamental that it pervades the whole life cycle. It expresses itself in psychic constitution, temperament, motor demeanors, and distinctive modes of growth." (p. 248)

This uniqueness means that each child's reaction to the conditions of his environment will be a little different from that of every other child; what he learns from his successive, unique confrontations will contribute cumulatively to the unique personality that he develops. Some of the constitutional reaction tendencies that are apparent soon after birth are described on page 49.

Although much remains to be discovered about the role of various constitutional tendencies in human development, it is clear that their special significance lies in their influence on the way the individual characteristically reacts to his environment and is influenced by it. Very early, children begin to develop a *coping style*—a set of strategies for dealing with problems. Although subject to change, such coping styles often appear to characterize their long-term adjustive behavior.

Maturation. By *maturation* we mean development which occurs after birth in which hereditary instructions play a major role. Thus maturation reflects the continuing action of heredity long past the prenatal period. This delayed carrying out of hereditary instructions is evident in all the changes of body structure, physiological functioning, and behavioral patterns that are characteristic of the human life cycle regardless of the social setting. Examples are the hardening of the bone matrix, the loss of childhood fat, the toning up of the muscles, and the appearance of primary and secondary sex characteristics. Throughout the life span we see similarities among people of the same age that reflect the genetically guided growth and change of physical and mental potentials. Though their exact form and timing vary, such changes are predictable in the life cycle of a human being. The interplay between maturation and learning, especially in the early years, will be discussed in Chapter 3.

Interaction of genetic and other influences. The question often arises as to the relative contribution of genetic and environmental influences. For example, eye color seems to be determined primarily by genetic influences, while political attitudes are determined pri-

marily by environmental influences. Intelligence, long considered to be determined primarily by genetic factors, is now considered to be the end product of both genetic and environmental influences, with both playing highly significant roles.

Strictly speaking, only genes are inherited. Any *trait* has both genetic and environmental components because it is forged from countless and cumulative interactions between hereditary endowment and environmental conditions. As Eiduson and Geller (1962) have described it:

". . . *development is a long process of continuous changes, starting with a given genetic array acting in a given environment. The first interaction product then constitutes the background . . . for the next step of interaction with the environment. . . . Thus, at whatever point one arrests the sequential reactions for study, one can no longer— except arbitrarily—point to certain factors as genetic and others as environmental."* (pp. 344-345)

Since different individuals react differently to similar environmental conditions as a result of both unique genetic endowments and unique sequences of past experience, it cannot be expected that the same environmental conditions will be optimal for every child. No longer can we hope to delineate *the* most favorable environmental conditions for all. The implications of this fact have been well elaborated by Caspari (1968):

". . . *The challenge of education appears to me to reside in the problem of how to create educational methods and environments which will be optimally adjusted to the needs of unique individuals. The main contribution which a geneticist can make to educational research is to stress the fundamental biological fact that every human being is a unique individual and that his genetic individuality will be expressed in the way in which he reacts to environmental and educational experiences."*

Although complicating the problems of parents and teachers, this viewpoint gives us more realistic expectations in dealing with children.

PRIMARY REACTION TENDENCIES

Several studies have shown that even very young babies have distinctive ways of behaving and that these patterns continue into the childhood years. Among these constitutional reaction tendencies are:

1. *Activity level (vigor)*. Both the vigor and the persistence of activity appear from the beginning to be consistently higher among some infants than others. Passive babies are not likely to be demanding and their behavior does not have the forceful, energetic, staccato quality typical of active babies. These characteristics influence the infants' exploratory actions and inevitably color their reactions to situations and people around them. In general, active babies appear more capable of protesting (as when offered disliked foods), of persisting in given behavior patterns, and of fending off environmental pressures.

2. *Sensitivity*. Even during the first few weeks of life, babies differ greatly in their sensitivity to stimulation. Some are startled by even slight sounds and cry or whimper if sunlight hits their faces. Others are seemingly insensitive to such stimulation. Thus the same environment may have different effects on different infants; conditions that one can tolerate may be quite upsetting or even overwhelming to another. Such sensitivity can be aggravated or minimized by parental handling—or possibly induced in the first place by a tense, anxious, unstable mother. In general, however, it would appear to be strongly influenced by genetic factors and, in turn, to continue to influence development and behavior throughout the individual's lifetime.

3. *Emotional disposition*. Often the term "quality of mood" is used to refer to the amount of pleasant, joyful, and friendly behavior characteristically displayed by a child, as contrasted with anxiety, crying, sullenness, and similar patterns. The degree of emotional reactivity also appears to differ among children and to be relatively consistent for a given individual. Some children, for example, tend to be relatively stable emotionally and not easily aroused to intense fear, anger, joy, or anxiety. Others tend to overreact to even minor setbacks or successes. Emotional reactivity is likely to color the individual's experiences and have a cumulative effect on his development. Typically, of course, high sensitivity and emotional reactivity go hand in hand in the production of a "nervous child."

4. *Adaptability (vulnerability)*. Infants and children show marked differences in their ability to cope with new or changed situations and to recuperate from physical and psychological upsets. Situations like changes in diet, temporary separation from the mother, and minor accidents are taken in stride by some children but prove highly upsetting to others. Within an overall level of adaptability, there may be areas of special vulnerability—either physical or psychological. A particular subsystem of the body may be especially vulnerable to stress and more likely to show a reaction to any disturbance in the overall functioning of the organism. Thus in response to minor stress one baby may develop a digestive disturbance and another a sleep disturbance. Although mental disorders are not inherited, it would appear that genetic factors may play a role in our vulnerability to the development of depressive, schizophrenic, or other mental disorders under stressful conditions.

5. *Other constitutional tendencies*. Various other primary reaction tendencies have been delineated in longitudinal studies of infants and children. Among these are rate of processing stimulation, approach or withdrawal as a characteristic response to new situations, regularity of bodily functions such as hunger and sleep, distractability, length of attention span, and intensity of response. Although these reaction tendencies probably also contribute to the development of the "coping style" of the child, there is less evidence as to their long-range stability.

The effect of a particular reaction tendency depends on the context in which it occurs. In general, for example, under favorable environmental conditions, children of low sensitivity, low emotional reactivity, and good general adaptability will function smoothly, with moderate encounters with the environment, and will tend to obtain and be satisfied with mild satisfactions. Children of high sensitivity, high drive level, high emotional reactivity, and good adaptability will tend to participate actively in environmental interactions, show a wide range of coping strategies, and have a high level of gratification and success. However, their behavior will lead to more conflictual encounters with the environment which, in general, they will be able to resolve satisfactorily. By contrast, children with the same high sensitivity and high drive level but low adaptability will likely experience great coping difficulties and a disproportionate number of unpleasant encounters with the environment (Murphy, 1962).

ENVIRONMENT

No trait is so dependent on heredity as not to require certain minimal environmental conditions for its development. Huxley (1965) has pointed up dramatically the importance of environmental influences:

"*Anatomically and physiologically, man has changed very little during the last twenty or thirty thousand years. The native or genetic capacities of today's bright city child are no better than the native capacities of a bright child born into a family of Upper Paleolithic cave-dwellers. But whereas the contemporary bright baby may grow up to become almost anything—a Presbyterian engineer, for example, a piano-playing Marxist, a professor of biochemistry who is a mystical agnostic and likes to paint in water-colours—the paleolithic baby could not possibly have grown into anything except a hunter or food-gatherer, using the crudest of stone tools and thinking about his narrow world of trees and swamps in terms of some hazy system of magic. Ancient and modern, the two babies are indistinguishable. Each of them contains all the potentialities of the particular breed of human being to which he or she happens to belong. But the adults into whom the babies will grow are profoundly dissimilar; and they are dissimilar because in one of them very few, and in the other a good many, of the baby's inborn potentialities have been actualized.*" (p. 69)

At any given moment an individual is the product of countless interactions between his genetic endowment and his physical and sociocultural environment. His physical environment includes climate, terrain, food supplies, disease germs, and other aspects of the natural world surrounding him. His sociocultural environment includes not only other individuals and groups but also customs, values, and man-made objects.

Physical Environment

The peoples of the earth live under widely diverse conditions of climate, terrain, and natural resources. Some live in dense jungles, others on barren deserts; some live on high mountains, others on flat prairie lands. Some live where it is extremely cold, others where it is oppressively hot; some live where it rains most of the time, others where there is chronic drought. In some places, food and other resources are plentiful; in others, they are so scarce that most of the individual's life is spent in eking out a bare subsistence. In some areas, people are surrounded by disease and other hazards to physical safety; in others, there is relatively little disease and danger.

Climate and terrain. Man as a species is adaptable to a wide range of environmental conditions. At an altitude of 15,000 feet, for example, acclimatization takes place in some ten days, and similar adaptations can be made to moderate extremes of heat and cold.

Peoples inhabiting areas where conditions of climate and terrain are extreme and unfavorable typically undergo adaptive physiological changes. The circulatory system of the Eskimo lies deep within a protective fatty layer which conserves his body heat. The native Indians who work the tin mines in the mountains of Bolivia at altitudes as high as 19,000 feet have more red corpuscles than we do and a lung capacity demonstrably larger and more efficient than ours (Newman, 1961). The extent—and limits—of man's adaptability to diverse environmental conditions has become an important consideration in his conquest of space.

The effects of climate and terrain on psychological development are less well understood. We have no definitive answers to such questions as whether growing up in tropical jungles leads to different personality traits from growing up on open plains, or whether people who live in cold climates differ in consistent ways from those who live in hot ones.

In one of the few pertinent studies, McClelland (1961) reported that he found achievement motivation greatest in societies living where there were average temperature variations of between 40 and 60 degrees. It has also been suggested that the cold and the long winter darkness may have a depressing effect on people who live near the Arctic Circle. Where children grow up under extreme environmental conditions, there undoubtedly are biological and psychological adaptations as well as other effects on development. But systematic studies of such conditions have yet to be made.

Resources and limitations. Both natural and man-made resources vary greatly for the peoples of the world. According to a United Nations estimate, two thirds of the world's population lives in "less developed areas," suffering from a lack of adequate food, housing, and medical attention. Adverse physical conditions not only take a tremendous toll in reduced physical vigor, bodily damage, and lowered life expectancy but also influence the satisfactions, frustrations, and way of life of the group and hence exert a direct influence on the development of individual members. Again however, it is difficult to arrive at definitive conclusions. Some groups appear to bring up psychologically well-adjusted children even under severe conditions of environmental deprivation and hardship, while in other groups living under comparable conditions there is a high incidence of what might be called individual and social pathology.

An example of the combined influence of adverse physical conditions and non-adaptive cultural patterns on personality development was provided by the Sirono Indians of eastern Bolivia, as observed some years ago (*Science News Letter*, 1950):

The Sirono Indians live in thick, tropical rain forests where food is very scarce. This nomadic group lives in an almost perpetual state of semistarvation. Food and the quest for food—game, fish, nuts, berries, fruit—have assumed prime significance in their lives. The effects of this centering of their existence around food are reflected in their customs, values, and general personality makeup. Women do not marry for love but are wooed by promises of fat meat or wild-bee honey. Wives do not resent their husbands making love to another woman unless he gives her food. To avoid sharing food with others, they lie about how much they have and eat mainly at night so that they can consume more without others knowing about it. Their goal in eating seems to be to swallow the most food in the least time. The thoughts, chants, and dreams of these primitive Indians are mainly of hunting and food. Although the Sironos reveal stable personality development in terms of stress tolerance, they are selfish and completely unconcerned with others—usually refusing even to help anyone in trouble. When a Sirono grows too old or sick to hunt or obtain food, he is abandoned to die.

Although the unfavorable physical environment undoubtedly influenced the development of these cultural and personality patterns, it is difficult to assess its influence accurately or to explain Sirono practices which seem inconsistent with their dominating concern for food. For example, these Indians have failed to develop methods of storing food, and they hunt only when their immediate food supply is exhausted. In addition, regardless of how hungry they are, they refuse to eat snakes—which are edible and plentiful in Bolivia. Nor can we overlook the fact that other peoples who live in areas where food is scarce—such as Eskimos—have become highly cooperative and concerned about others.

Population density. At the time of the early Roman Empire, there were an estimated 200 million people on the earth. By 1600 A.D. the population had increased to some 500 million. Today the world's population is over six times as great—exceeding 3 billion—and this figure is expected to be doubled by the year 2000. It is likely, therefore, that the sheer number of people around us will be an important factor in the physical environment and will determine many of the adjustive demands made on us.

The effects of population density on human development and behavior have not been systematically studied. One might expect that children growing up in sparsely settled areas would be exposed to somewhat

PSYCHOLOGICAL AND SOCIAL EFFECTS OF POPULATION DENSITY

In an interesting experiment, Calhoun (1962) allowed a population of laboratory rats to increase in a confined space. Although adequate food and nesting materials were available, he found that a high incidence of behavior pathology developed in both males and females.

"The first sign of disruption was a failure to build the nest to normal specifications. These females simply piled the strips of paper in a heap, sometimes trampling them into a pad that showed little sign of cup formation. Later in the experiment they would bring fewer and fewer strips to the nesting site. In the midst of transporting a bit of material they would drop it to engage in some other activity occasioned by contact and interaction with other individuals met on the way. In the extreme disruption of their behavior during the later months of the population's history they would build no nests at all but would bear their litters on the sawdust in the burrow box." (p. 91)

Infant mortality ran as high as 96 per cent. Pregnancies decreased, disorders of pregnancy in-creased, and by the sixteenth month a quarter of the females had died.

Many of the males developed equally pathological behavior: some made sexual advances indiscriminately to males, juveniles, and females not in estrus; others showed extreme passivity, ignoring all rats of both sexes, and moved through the colony "like somnambulists"; and still others were both hypersexual and homosexual and at times cannibalistic. Even the aggressive, dominant males, who were the most normal animals of the group, exhibited occasional signs of pathology, such as going berserk, attacking females and juveniles, and showing a peculiar predilection—which rats do not normally display—for biting other animals on the tail.

It was evident that in time the colony would have died out. Even when the four healthiest pairs were taken out of the overcrowded situation after 18 months and restored to a normal environment, they produced fewer litters than normal during the next six months and none of the young survived.

different patterns of sharing, cooperation, affiliation, schooling, health care, and related conditions than children growing up in areas of moderate or high population density.

Even where physical resources are adequate for all, the crowding itself may possibly have important effects. The illustration above describes the effects of high population density on a group of laboratory rats. Such findings with rats do not, of course, answer the question of what effects population density may have on man. Man, with fewer built-in patterns and a much greater capacity for change and learning has far better resources for coping with overcrowding as with other unusual conditions. But Spitz (1963) has pointed out several parallels between the abnormal patterns developed by these rats and forms of abnormal behavior observed in the crowded cities in our society —in particular, the frenetic overactivity of some individuals and the pathological withdrawal and alienation of others.

The growing scientific field of *ecology*, which studies man in relation to his total surroundings, will undoubtedly help to answer many of our questions concerning the effects of our physical environment. However, aside from extremely stressful physical environments—as where food is so scarce that the growing child suffers serious physical impairment—it would appear that the sociocultural environment plays the key role in the shaping of psychological development and behavior.

Sociocultural Environment

In much the same sense that man receives a genetic heritage which is the end product of millions of years of biological evolution, he receives a sociocultural heritage which is the end product of many thousands of years of social evolution. This heritage varies dramatically from one cultural group to another, but the various societies of the world have enough in common to enable us to speak meaningfully of "human culture." Every group, for example, has language, customs, values, family and social structure, music and art. These elements of culture have developed out of the cooperative process of satisfying human needs in a particular setting.

The crucial importance of culture in shaping development has been well summarized by anthropologist Margaret Mead (1953):

"... the functioning of every part of the human body is moulded by the culture within which the individual has been reared—not only in terms of diet, sunlight, exposure to contagious and infectious diseases, overstrain, occupational ... hazards, catastrophes, and traumatic experiences, but also by the way he, born into society with a definite culture, has been fed and disciplined, fondled and put to sleep, punished and rewarded ...

Culture is seen ... as a principal element in the development of the individual, which will result in his having a structure, a type of functioning, and a pattern of irritability different in kind from that of individuals who have been socialized within another culture. ..." (pp. 377-378)

In this section we shall deal with the features of a culture which have a direct bearing upon development in general, and on the process of socialization in particular.

Culture and subculture. A complex society such as ours has both an overall culture—a way of life shared by most members—and many subcultures. Americans as a group share the same language, live under the same political system, follow many of the same customs, use the same system of money, are exposed to television and other technological innovations, and have a mass of accumulated knowledge available to them. These are facets of our general American culture. At the same time various subcultures exist in the United States defined by ethnic, religious, social class, and regional boundaries. While sharing the same general culture of our society, these subgroups may vary markedly in

their specific beliefs, customs, values, and ways of life.

Each society systematically teaches its concepts, values, and desired behaviors to its children in order to develop group members who can maintain and perpetuate the society. This instruction is largely accomplished by social institutions such as the home, school, and church—and in more highly developed countries by the mass media of newspapers, movies, and television. Such systematic instruction makes for a considerable degree of uniformity and tends to establish a basic personality type for that particular society—a *modal personality.*

Despite uniformities, however, the process of socialization permits a considerable measure of individual variation. For the individual's basic personality structure is affected not only by the larger social group but also by the various *subgroups* to which he belongs—groups based upon his family membership, religion, age, sex, and social class. Each subgroup tends to foster certain values, beliefs, and approved behavior patterns which may in turn be subject to restrictions imposed by society as a whole. The fact that each individual belongs to a somewhat different pattern of subgroups tends to produce individual differences, just as common membership in the larger cultural group makes everyone somewhat alike.

The groups with which an individual identifies, or with which he would like to be identified, are called his *reference groups*— for it is in reference to their norms and values that he sets his goals, models his behavior, and evaluates his worth. Sometimes reference groups from which the individual is excluded have greater influence on him than groups in which he actually has membership. For example, a youth from a lower socioeconomic family of immigrants may adopt the values, attitudes, and behavior patterns of a more privileged group, divorcing himself insofar as possible from his own family and social class.

The individual's value system is grounded in the core values of his culture, and there is usually considerable uniformity of value

Each of us usually occupies a number of different positions and hence must play a variety of roles. A young person may play the roles of son, student, Boy Scout, and team captain; an adult may play the roles of lawyer, father, husband, scoutmaster, and civic leader. Usually the individual thinks of his various roles within the context of some broad role that he considers more important than others—typically the one that is associated with the highest status or that he most closely identifies with his "real self."

patterns among the members of a given society. A major problem in our contemporary world is to discover ways in which groups and nations with divergent value orientations can cooperate for the welfare and progress of mankind.

Position and role. In every society there are a variety of distinguishable positions—doctor, teacher, nurse, parent, student, child, and so on—each of which contributes in some way to the total functioning of the group and is accorded a certain social rank or status. Position carries with it both privileges and responsibilities and gives the holder a status in the group. The medical doctor, for example, has the privilege of practicing medicine and is also held in high regard by other members of the society. In return, he is expected to follow the ethical code of his profession and to maintain competence as a physician.

To clarify what is expected of a person with a given position, society establishes social roles. Thus the role of army general

calls for loyalty, decisiveness, courage, and resourcefulness; the physician is expected not only to be competent and ethical but also to be sympathetic, wise, and dedicated to the welfare of his patients. Each person, young or old, tends to develop the skills, behavior, and values that a given role seems to demand. If he deviates too far from what is expected, he is likely to encounter difficulties in his social relationships. And if he violates role expectations in ways that are perceived as detrimental to the welfare of the group, society may even revoke his status.

The extent to which status and role expectations can influence development is well illustrated by Margaret Mead's study (1949) of the Tchambuli, a New Guinea tribe in which the sex roles are practically the reverse of ours. Women are supposed to earn the living, handle business transactions, take the initiative in courtship, and in general head the family. Men, on the other hand, are expected to be coquettish, graceful, prone to gossip, good homemakers, and interested in dancing and theatricals. The established roles for men and women among the Tchambuli obviously tend to channel personality development along lines very different from those in our own culture.

The individual's positions and roles may change considerably as he moves from childhood through adolescence and adulthood, and later we shall examine other aspects of social roles, such as role conflicts and differences between the way the individual perceives his role and the way others may see it. But throughout his life the specific demands made by each of the roles he plays will be influential in shaping his development and behavior.

Interpersonal environment. Much of an individual's personality development reflects his specific experiences with other people. In many societies a certain pattern of interpersonal relationships predominates over others—for example, the norm may be for competition or cooperation, hostility or friendliness. In such societies the individual learns to label and relate to people in accordance with the predominant social pattern, whatever it is. In a complex society such as ours, however, interpersonal relationships contribute to individuality. The experiences of competition and cooperation, love and hate, acceptance and rejection, understanding and misunderstanding, which mark our interactions with other people are in each case relatively unique.

Although we have many kinds of interpersonal relationships in the course of our lives, it is our relationships with our parents and with members of our peer groups that have the greatest influence in shaping our early development. Parents may be warm and accepting or cold and rejecting; they may be rigid disciplinarians or given to overindulgence. Each particular patterning of parent-child relationships tends to shape personality development in a somewhat different way. A child whose parents make him feel loved and wanted and who allow him freedom to be "himself" will develop a picture of himself and his world—and patterns of behavior—very different from those of a child who feels rejected, misunderstood, and unreasonably restrained.

As a child grows older and participates increasingly in activities outside the family, his relationships with other people, including "peers"—others of his own age—assume greater importance in shaping his development. The child who is intimidated and bullied by other children, for example, may lose his self-confidence and come to feel that his only safe role is a submissive one. As the child reaches adolescence, his peer group becomes increasingly important to him. The adolescent's success or failure in winning social acceptance from both boys and girls is a major influence on his later development. Later, the type of relationship the individual establishes in his marriage becomes crucial to both his immediate happiness and his continued growth.

Although we have singled out parent-child and peer-group relations as perhaps the most important, it is apparent that many other types of interpersonal relationships—those with brothers and sisters, grandparents, teachers, neighbors, for example—may play a significant part in shaping personality development. Even a chance meeting with some unusual person may change the direction of our lives.

Socialization and Development

Each society provides institutional arrangements and approved ways for accomplishing the socialization of its young—ways of shaping their psychological and social development in accordance with the purposes and patterns of the group. These arrangements vary considerably from one society to another, but each group has its explicit goals for development, the designation of agents for achieving these goals, favored methods and techniques for motivating and instructing the child, and rough timetables for achieving given stages of the process.

Agencies of socialization. In our society, the agencies responsible for socialization of the child include the family, the school, the peer group, the church, youth organizations such as the Boy Scouts, and the mass media of radio, motion pictures, and television. These agencies carry out their socialization functions both formally and informally. For example, besides the explicit lessons that parents teach deliberately are the lessons implicit in their everyday actions and attitudes; the school teaches not only through its formal curriculum but also through many informal learning situations, including exposure to patterns of interaction with other children with differing backgrounds and attitudes.

Let us briefly summarize the influence of four of these major agencies of socialization: the family, the school, peer groups, and the mass media.

1. *The family.* During infancy and early childhood, the social heritage is transmitted to the child almost exclusively through the family. Each family is an ongoing social system with its own unique pattern of organization and functioning. In this social system, each family member occupies a position with defined responsibilities, privileges, and expected behavior. Each family has its own goals, communication patterns, value orientations, procedures for solving problems and making decisions, and methods for maintaining equilibrium and achieving family purposes.

From the moment of his entry into the family the child is an active participant in this social system, and it is through his interactions in this group that he learns his first lessons in social living. As Havighurst and Neugarten (1962) described it:

"It is within the family that the child learns his first set of social roles, and in doing so, takes a major step in the process of socialization. He learns what is expected of him as a child; how he should relate to other people, older and younger than himself. He learns how to be a son and how to be a brother. He learns, also, what behavior is appropriate to a male in our society and what behavior is inappropriate. It is within the social setting of the family, furthermore, that the child forms his self-concept; what kind of person he perceives himself to be,

what assets and what liabilities he sees himself possessing, and what he expects of himself in the present and in the future.

"In still more general terms the child learns within the family how to live within a social system; how to organize his behavior in consistent ways and to adapt his behavior to that of others; and how to relate himself to others within a complicated network of social relationships. He learns, in short, how to fit into a social organization."(p. 101)

Thus in the family system the child develops a self-concept, certain role behaviors, and a set of assumptions about his world in relation to himself. These patterns may be modified or reinforced by his school experiences, but they constitute the foundation upon which his further social learning is based. Whatever the nature of the particular family setting, it largely determines the boundaries of the child's early experiences and thus channels his development in certain directions rather than others.

2. *The school.* At about the age of 6 in our society—or earlier if the child enters nursery school or kindergarten—the child begins a long period of formal education directed toward shaping him into a mature, competent member of our society.

Besides providing the child with important intellectual tools—reading, writing, reasoning, problem solving, and so on—the school teaches the child the values, goals, aspirations, and approved ways of behavior of the particular society to which he belongs. It also provides a social setting in which the child has an opportunity to learn new social rules—how to behave toward peers and adults other than family members—and a new set of adult models. The "feedback" he gets from classmates and teachers, as well as the exposure to new models and standards, may have a moderating effect on characteristics shaped earlier by idiosyncrasies of his parents.

The school serves still another important function—that of sorting and selection. Education has become the principal avenue of opportunity for achieving social status, and during the school years it is the educational system that identifies the most capable young people and prepares them for the advanced training that will lead to high-status positions in our society.

Our schools differ greatly in their physical plants and settings, in the personnel making up the school staffs, in their types of curriculum, in their facilities and materials for instruction, and in the social class and other subgroups from which their children come. Each school has its own "mix" of all these elements and hence its own unique sub-

SOCIAL CLASS AND SOCIALIZATION

A good deal of research has been directed toward examining the effects of social class membership on the development of values and attitudes. The following are generalizations from many studies:

ATTITUDES TOWARD:	UPPER	MIDDLE	LOWER
FAMILY	Family tightly knit; concern for maintaining family name and prestige. Great importance placed on genealogy and family history.	Emphasis on independence of nuclear family; married children tend to drift away from parents.	Families tend to break up one or more times through desertion, divorce, or separation. Family ties tend to be weak.
EDUCATION	Emphasis on quality of education and prestige of schools; training for high-level administration rather than financial gain. Otherwise, similar to middle-class attitudes.	Education seen as important to eventual success; children expected to excel and encouraged to seek achievement and success.	Family needs take priority over child's education. Frustration and failure at school expected; child's effort determined largely by personal relationship with teacher.
AGGRESSIVENESS	Guilt and anxiety about overt expression of anger developed early. Rigid controls—learn to inhibit these impulses.	Similar to that of upper class.	Children often permitted or even encouraged to settle differences by fighting. Destructive acts common.
PROPERTY	Property and ownership highly valued.	Similar to upper class.	Property and ownership less valued, seen as exploitative. Resentments often expressed in destruction to others' property.
TIME	See own generation as part of historic sequence.	Preponderance of effort toward investing in and building for future.	Live in present: do and get what you can today.
RESPONSIBILITY	"Noblesse oblige."	Strong feeling of responsibility for own behavior. Obligation to own family and social group.	"Victim" image common: feeling of helplessness, of control by other persons and external conditions.

Differences in development that arise from different social class membership reflect both contrasting values and differing opportunities. For example, the apparently lower valuing of college among lower socioeconomic parents is partly a matter of different values and partly a realistic assessment of the possibilities.

culture. The result is that schools foster differences as well as likenesses in development.

3. *Peer groups.* In a sense, a child grows up in two worlds—the world of his parents and other adults and the world of others his own age. Peer groups range from informal play groups and neighborhood gangs to organized community groups such as the Boy Scouts. In the course of growing up, children interact with a succession of such peer groups, each of which has its own group structure and expectations for its members.

As a socializing agency, the peer world performs three key functions. *First,* like the home and the school, most peer groups transmit the wider culture. Although some peer groups—such as delinquent gangs—are in conflict with the adult world, most peer groups reflect the adult society and reinforce most of its beliefs, values, and patterns of behavior. *Second,* the peer world serves as a "reality check." If the family has overindulged and spoiled a child, he may be in for a rude awakening at the hands of his age-mates. Although often harsh, peers are frank and relatively impartial judges in criticizing inaccurate beliefs and undesirable behavior. Thus the peer world tends to have a "normalizing" influence. *Third,* the peer world helps children and youth to achieve emotional independence. Particularly during adolescence, identification with a peer group tends to provide support for a young person's gradual emancipation from his family's dictates and for his growth toward adult independence.

4. *The mass media.* The mass media function both incidentally and by design in the socialization process. Inevitably they transmit the culture of the broader society in terms of beliefs, values, ideology, approved and disapproved behavior patterns, and models for behavior. Through watching the heroes and villains on television and in movies, young people learn what goals are valued in our society and what means are rewarded or punished.

Although television and other mass media have great potential for arousing interest, imparting information, stimulating ideas, and widening horizons, this potential has not been fully utilized, and the effects are not well understood. As we shall see, conflicting findings and interpretations of various research studies have led to considerable confusion concerning the effects of the violence depicted in movies and television as well as of the increasing frankness in dealing with aberrant sexual behavior and other "adult" themes.

Two generalizations can be made, however, concerning the effect of the mass media on development and behavior. Since the same content is imparted to vast numbers of people—particularly by television—the mass media tend to make people alike in information, beliefs, values, manners, and esthetic tastes. On the other hand, as we have seen in so many other situations, people do not simply receive passively what is presented to them. To television and the other mass media, as to other experiences, they bring their own needs, interests, assumptions, and attitudes. And of course, the individual can either select or tune out given programs and materials. So it can be expected that exposure to the mass media will lead to differences as well as uniformities in development.

Methods of influence. Learning is taking place constantly during the individual's encounters with the environment. Some learning is incidental and unplanned by either the individual or those around him; some is sought by the individual; and some is planned for systematically by the various agencies of socialization.

Some of the ways in which the planned learning involved in socialization is accomplished are summarized briefly below. Although listed as separate methods, they usually supplement each other in a given case of learning.

1. *Formal and informal instruction (teaching).* Instruction or teaching includes showing how, guiding discovery by supplying the right props and questions, and explaining through the use of symbols. In the family and the school, as well as in less formal settings, the child is taught the beliefs and values of his culture, is helped to develop

Different physical and social environments provide different lessons to be learned. Some of these lessons are unintentional and unplanned by anyone—simply adjustive responses children make in trying to understand and cope with their surroundings. Some are lessons someone thinks they should learn. Ways in which others—especially adults—may try to guide and help children's learning include explaining, providing a model, showing, rewarding or punishing, and setting standards and expectations.

needed competencies—physical, intellectual, emotional, and social—and is guided toward adult status in the society.

The more complex a culture, the more formal instruction young people will need in order to master the information and skills requisite for effective adult participation in the society. In our own society, this is reflected in increasingly long and intensified formal education.

2. *Reinforcement.* A large body of research as well as everyday observation supports the generalization that behavior can be manipulated and "shaped" through direct reinforcement.

If a child is praised for helping his little brother (positive reinforcement), he is more likely to do it again; conversely, if he hits his little brother and is punished, he is less likely to engage in such behavior in the future. Ignoring or not rewarding certain undesirable forms of behavior, such as showing off, may also lead to its extinction.

In socializing the young, parents and other agents of society may utilize a variety of rewards and punishments. Some of these are tangible reinforcers, such as gifts or physical punishment (or the threat of it); others are nontangible reinforcers, such as approval or disapproval and the display or withdrawal of affection. The latter are often referred to as "love-oriented" techniques. Both tangible and nontangible reinforcers are of key importance in shaping development.

3. *Models.* In many cultures children learn more from observing and imitating the behavior of parents and other adult models than from formal instruction or reinforcement of overt responses already made. Such models provide examples which demonstrate to the child what is appropriate and expected of him by his social group. Thus much learning represents a patterning of our own behavior after what we see others do.

In our own society, the child learns not only from observing his parents, teachers, and other models with whom he has face-to-face contact but also by watching what have been called "symbolic" models—such as the characters in movies and television programs.

Many symbolic models are also presented in our folklore via historical national heroes such as George Washington and Abraham Lincoln. And finally, the individual's reference groups provide important models for the shaping of his development and behavior.

4. *Standards and role expectations.* Much of what we do and become is shaped by the standards, norms, roles, and other "rules of conduct" which have evolved to guide the individual's behavior and to maintain the society.

These standards and rules are enforced not only by social controls—such as rewards and punishments—but also by the expectations of "significant others." Much of what we do is shaped by the expectations of those around us, and much of our sense of success or failure and even of personal worth derives from the degree to which we see ourselves as meeting or failing to meet these expectations. Our unique position in society, as we have seen, is of key importance in determining what social expectations we are expected to meet.

5. *Identification and inner controls.* Although society relies heavily on reinforcement, models, and other external controls in a child's early years for shaping his patterns of behavior, the ultimate aim is to develop inner guides and controls. Thus the child is pressured not only to behave in socially approved ways and to emulate approved models, but also to *identify* with them and adopt their beliefs, standards, and values as his own. This process eventuates in the development of conscience, which supplements the external controls and operates even when they are not present.

Individual likenesses and differences. In the preceding discussion we pointed up some of the ways in which the sociocultural environment tends to make us alike as human beings and as members of a particular cultural group and ways in which it also can foster individual differences. What generalizations can be made about these influences?

1. *Information and competencies fostered by the environment.* The sociocultural environment largely determines the type and amount of information available to the individual. In some societies, for example, the individual has unusual opportunities for acquiring information (knowledge) about his world and himself and for general intellectual development. Other societies mistrust freedom of inquiry and believe that children should be indoctrinated to accept particular beliefs. Still others are so saturated with superstition and taboos that the individual's intellectual horizons are greatly restricted.

The sociocultural environment also determines both the competencies that are needed and the competencies that individuals can develop. Whether they learn wilderness tracking or computer programing depends quite as much on when and where they live as on their genetic potentialities. The many differences between societies and between subgroups within them thus assure wide differences in the competencies developed by human beings despite the similarity that their genetic potentials would make possible.

2. *Uniformity and continuity of the environment.* In general, the more uniform and less changeable the sociocultural environment, the more alike the members of the group will be—the more nearly they will approximate the modal personality fostered by the culture. Dictatorships take advantage of this principle by systematically indoctrinating their young people with rigid political and economic beliefs and values and preventing them from having exposure to other ideas. Isolated and self-contained cultures, such as those of many so-called primitive groups, also tend to produce considerable uniformity. In such groups, the values of society as a whole and of the various subgroups within it tend to be consistent, and the basic personality type emerges as clearcut and standardized.

SELF AS A THIRD DETERMINANT

In the preceding discussion, we examined the roles of genetic and environmental influences in shaping the development of personality. We discussed constitutional differences that foster variations in development and noted the effects of uniform and heterogeneous sociocultural conditions on individuality. Now as we proceed to a discussion of *self* as the third determinant of personality development, we shall concern ourselves with yet another factor that contributes to the uniqueness of every human being. For as the individual achieves a sense of his own identity, he tends to view each situation in the light of his own motives, assumptions, and feelings. Thus, the effects of a particular environment become increasingly dependent upon the way it is *experienced* by the individual.

In introducing the concept of self as the third determinant of man's development, we must be careful to avoid the idea of some "little man" sitting up in the brain deciding how we should behave. When psychologists refer to "self" they are thinking in terms of a conceptual structure rather than a physical one. Like gravity, the self cannot be observed directly but is inferred from various phenomena which *can* be observed and which seem to operate according to some unifying principle. The self, in other words, is not a mystical entity but a useful and seemingly necessary construct for explaining many aspects of individual behavior. Hall and Lindzey (1957) stated it thus:

"The self, whether it be conceived as object or as process or both, is not an homunculus or 'man within the breast' or soul; rather it refers to the object of psychological processes or to those processes themselves, and these processes are assumed to be governed by the principle of causality. In other words, the self is not a metaphysical or religious concept; it is a concept that falls within the domain of a scientific psychology. Self theory represents a serious attempt to account for certain phenomena and to conceptualize one's observations of certain aspects of behavior." (p. 468)

We shall view the self as a complex psychological process which has a developmental course, is influenced by learning, is subject to change, and can be studied by means of scientific procedures. In this context, we are particularly interested in two aspects of self: (1) the self-concept—the individual's perception of himself as distinct from other persons and things, and (2) the self as a centralized decider system—as a central reference point for evaluating new experience and guiding behavior. We shall see that both of these views of self provide us with important conceptual tools for understanding human development and behavior.

The Self-Concept

The individual's self-concept is his picture or image of himself—his view of himself as distinct from other persons and things. This self-image incorporates his perception of what he is really like (self-identity) and of his worth as a person (self-evaluation), as well as his aspirations for growth and accomplishment (self-ideal).

Self-identity. We are not born with a sense of self. In fact, the newborn infant apparently does not know where his own body leaves off and his environment begins. Only gradually does he discover the boundary lines of his own body and learn to distinguish between the *me* and the *not-me*. This early perception of the physical self is called the *body image* and appears to form the primitive core of his self-concept. Since others perceive and react to the individual—at least partially—in terms of his physical appearance, it is not surprising that the individual's body-image may continue to be an important component of his identity and self-concept throughout his life.

Many other inner and outer forces help to shape the child's growing sense of self-identity. As he acquires language and learns labels for his mommy, his daddy, his toys, and other objects, he also acquires a tool for forming a progressively clear-cut picture of himself. An important aid here is the child's own name. He continually hears such phrases as "Where is Johnny's nose?" "Johnny is a good boy." "Johnny, please do what I tell

you." By hearing his name repeatedly in different contexts, he is helped to see himself as a person separate from other people and things.

Although initially the self-concept is heavily weighted with "me" elements in which the child is an object referred to by others, parents soon place demands upon him to control himself and take responsibility for various aspects of his behavior. These demands force him to equate himself to some extent with his feelings and actions—"I want to do this" or "I must not do that" or "I have done that." This, in turn, fosters his emerging self-awareness as well as a sense of autonomy in the direction of his own behavior. Now "I" elements become increasingly incorporated in the self-concept—experiences in which the individual perceives himself as the agent or source of action. "I can dress myself." "I can throw a ball." "I am a boy."

As the individual's experience broadens, his self-identity comes to include things outside of himself with which he feels strong personal involvement. When we think of *me* or *my,* we may include possessions such as our home, the people we love, the groups we are loyal to, and the values we believe in. Of key importance here is the individual's position and role. The individual is treated in consistent ways by others in accordance with his position in the group; and role behavior considered appropriate to his status is demanded and reinforced by those around him. Thus his self-identity is confirmed by recurrent and relatively consistent social interactions.

We have noted earlier that we all play a variety of social roles—and sometimes we feel as though we have several different "selves." Thus a young mother who teaches school may play the role of wife, parent, and teacher—each with its different role expectations and demands. When such roles are in conflict or cannot be integrated into a coherent "master role" of some sort, the individual may have difficulty in establishing a stable sense of identity. This is often a problem during adolescence in our society, when social roles are often unclear and conflicting. A young wife may assume an adult role in her marriage but revert to the role of a child when she is with her parents. In more extreme form, such "identity diffusion" may lead to a chameleon-like pattern in which the individual adopts whatever role he thinks is suited to the particular setting in which he finds himself.

With time, however, such role problems are usually resolved into a reasonably coherent self-identity in which the *I* aspect of personality evidences considerable consistency across a wide range of situations and behaviors. It is in terms of his awareness of himself as a unique person that he sets goals, hopes, prays, fears, and makes decisions. He exists as the center of a changing world of experience, and most events in his world are perceived and dealt with in relation to the *me* and *I*.

Self-evaluation. As a child achieves a sense of self-identity, he begins to make value judgments about himself. Thus he may evaluate himself as superior or inferior, worthy or unworthy, adequate or inadequate.

During early life, the child's self-evaluation is heavily dependent upon the way in which others view him—particularly his parents and other important people in his life. For during these early years, he has no other standards for measuring his adequacy and worth than those supplied by the people around him. If their words and behavior label him as inadequate and unworthy of love and respect, he has little choice but to accept their negative evaluation. If, on the other hand, he is warmly accepted, respected as a person, and viewed as adequate and capable, his self-evaluation will probably be positive. He will show a high level of *self-esteem.*

These early evaluations of his capability and worth have a continuing effect on his personality development. Later experiences can sometimes change them but never quickly or easily. The child who grows up thinking of himself as inferior to other children or as unworthy of his family because he cannot live up to their high expectations will need many experiences of success and acceptance before he will begin to evaluate himself in generally positive terms. He is likely to interpret even the small failures that are inevitable in anyone's life as adding to the already overwhelming proof of his inadequacy. On the other hand, the child who grows up feeling adequate and secure can take considerable failure in stride and realistically accept many personal shortcomings without altering his basic self-picture.

As we grow older, culturally defined standards of social desirability—particularly peer group standards—increasingly provide the yardstick against which the individual now compares himself with respect to physical appearance, intellectual ability, athletic prowess, social status, and other characteristics, depending upon his particular peer-group identifications. Such standards vary considerably, of course, from one peer group to another, although the standards of the larger society tend to form a background context. Thus the individual's particular reference groups may have a great deal to do with his level of self-esteem. For example, a middle-class adolescent may feel inferior and devaluated if he receives failing grades in his high-school or college work, while a lower-class adolescent whose peer group disapproves of academic achievement may feel inferior and devaluated if he gets good grades.

Obviously there is no one-to-one relationship between a person's actual assets and liabilities and the way he evaluates himself. A highly talented person may have deep feelings of inferiority and unworthiness, while a person with mediocre or even inferior ability may be convinced of his superior capacity and skill. Fortunately, however, there are corrective tendencies in our social interactions which tend to make for some consistency between our self-evaluation and the way others evaluate us. For example, the lionized high-school athlete who begins to believe his own "press notices" may be forced to an agonizing reappraisal after graduation into a world where his previous exploits no longer enable him to maintain his accustomed status. Whether fanciful or realistic, negative or positive, the individual's self-evaluation plays an important role in his subsequent development and behavior.

Self-ideal. The individual's self-concept includes not only a sense of personal identity and of worth but also aspirations for accomplishment and growth. An individual's image of the person he would like to be and thinks he should be is called his *self-ideal.*

Depending upon whether a person's aspirations are difficult or easy to achieve in relation to his abilities and environmental opportunities, we say that he has a high or low *level of aspiration.* It is important that one's level of aspiration be realistic. If it is too high, he will suffer inevitable failure and self-devaluation no matter how well he actually performs; if it is too low, he will waste his personal resources and opportunities. Sometimes family expectations induce unrealistic aspirations. For example, a youth's parents may have their hearts set on his becoming a physician even though this goal is not in accord with his own interests and abilities. The expectations and reinforcements of the family and other social groups can work constructively as incentives for the individual to achieve his potentialities, or, by allowing too little room for individuality, can force him to accept goals that are not compatible with his own make-up. When a person accepts too easily the goals and expectations others set for him, it usually indicates that he lacks adequate self-knowledge and a clear sense of his own identity.

Typically our self-ideals are closely related to the identifications we make with various models—parents, friends, prominent personalities, national heroes, and other persons we admire. The identifications we make in childhood, especially with the parent of our own sex, are the source of many of our most basic goals for self-growth and are important in providing the early direction for our development. These early identifications tend to be modified by later peer-group and cultural models and still later by composite models. Although the mechanism of identification can continue to work constructively

in adulthood, the mature person is more likely to set his aspirations for self-growth in terms of thought-out values based upon a realistic assessment of his prior accomplishments and failures, his present assets and liabilities, and the opportunities and limitations of his environment.

In general, members of a given culture share many common standards about what is socially desirable and hence have similar conceptions of the ideal self. In a heterogeneous culture such as our own, however, conceptions of the ideal self may vary markedly with subculture as well as among the individuals in a given group.

It seems likely that some discrepancy between a person's existing self-image and self-ideal is necessary for the fostering of personal growth, but we do not know how wide a discrepancy is desirable. We do know, however, that a marked discrepancy between one's "real" and "ideal" self can lead to serious inner conflict and self-devaluation.

Self As a "Decider" Subsystem

The behavior systems theorist James G. Miller (1965a) has pointed out that each living system contains an executive or administrative subsystem which controls the entire system. He describes it as:
"a decider subsystem which receives information from all parts of the system, and from the environment, makes decisions, and transmits command information which controls a significant part of the process of the units of the system." (p. 214)

An example of such a decider subsystem on a group level would be the leader, who functions as a director of planning, coordinating, and decision making. On an individual level, we infer self processes which function as a decider subsystem. And as we have seen, our self or decider subsystem has the unique property of self-awareness.

Once the self-concept develops, the individual comes to perceive himself as an active agent in determining his own behavior—as indicated in such statements as "I know," "I want," and "I will." In essence, our experience of self-direction involves the self as knower, striver, and doer.

Self as knower. In his encounters with the environment, the individual gradually builds up an inner *cognitive map* or *frame of reference* which provides him with a meaningful picture of himself and his world. Key elements in the individual's frame of reference are the assumptions he makes concerning *reality, value,* and *possibility:*

1. *Assumptions concerning reality*—of how things *really are.* Included here are the individual's assumptions about himself as a person, about other people, and about the world in which he lives. Thus he may assume that he is a capable and worthy person or inadequate and worthless; that other people are for the most part honest and concerned or deceitful and selfish; that the world is a place of opportunity or a concrete jungle of dead-end streets.

2. *Assumptions concerning value*—of how things *should be*—incorporating his judgments of what is good and bad, desirable and undesirable, right and wrong. Thus he may come to assume that aggression and violence are acceptable means of achieving important goals or that even a good end does not justify violence as a means; that persons as young as 18 should be permitted to vote or that such a change in voting age would be bad for the country; that interpersonal relationships are more important than material success or perhaps that status and prestige are all-important.

3. *Assumptions concerning possibility* —of how things *could be,* of possibilities for change and improvement. The student may assume that a college degree will enable him to get the kind of job that would not otherwise be open to him; the people of an underdeveloped country may assume that once they become industrialized and technologically proficient, they will no longer have problems; the slum child may assume that nothing he might do could ever break the pattern of poverty his family has always known.

The goals men strive for, the things they value, their views of work and play, and the relationships they try to establish with others are determined largely by the pattern of assumptions they acquire. Without a coherent frame of reference an individual would be incapable of consistent and purposeful action. In evaluating new situations and choosing appropriate modes of response, he must rely upon the cognitive map which he has constructed as a basic guide. In a general sense, a person's frame of reference—together with the various competencies he develops—represents his learned know-how and know-why for coping with the world.

If his cognitive map were a simple mirror which accurately reflected the individual and the outer world, it would greatly simplify matters. But it is not. Rather his picture of reality, value, and possibility is built upon his own experiences—and these experiences are not only limited but often are biased by need, desire, emotion, propaganda, and other factors. Thus the individual's assumptions may be relatively accurate or inaccurate depending upon how well they correspond to "objective reality." To the extent that an individual's assumptions about either himself or his environment are inaccurate, his development and behavior are likely to be adversely affected.

Fortunately, our assumptions are subject to modification with experience—although some are much more resistant to change than others. Thus again we see a "wired-in" corrective factor in the human computer. There is no guarantee, of course, that the individual will undergo new experiences that will enable him to correct his faulty assumptions.

Self as striver. Each of us is motivated to seek or avoid things in terms of their meaning for us—whether they promise to benefit us in some way or seem to threaten our physical or psychological well-being. And regardless of the many external influences that press in on us, each perceives *himself* as the active force in initiating his strivings. It is *I* who want or need this and who try to avoid that.

SELF-FULFILLING PROPHECIES BASED ON THE SELF-IMAGE

A plastic surgeon, Maxwell Maltz (1960), found that in some but not all of his patients there was dramatic personality and behavior change following successful surgery. Investigation showed that the presence or absence of change depended on whether or not the patient had developed a new self-image. Maltz went on to study the role of the self-image in the adjustment of people generally. He concluded that, "The self-image is a 'premise,' a base, or a foundation upon which your entire personality, your behavior, and even your circumstances are built. Because of this our experiences seem to verify, and thereby strengthen our self-images, and a vicious or a beneficent cycle, as the case may be, is set up." (p. 2)

"Harry N . . . had won none of the external symbols of success. Yet he had had many opportunities, all of which he muffed. Three times he had been on the verge of landing the job he wanted and each time 'something happened'—something was always defeating him just when success seemed within his grasp. Twice he had been disappointed in love affairs.

"His self-image was that of an unworthy, incompetent, inferior person who had no right to succeed, or to enjoy the better things in life, and unwittingly he tried to be true to that role. He felt he was not the sort of person to be successful, and always managed to do something to make this self-fulfilling prophecy come true." (p. 121)

Maltz hypothesizes that the goals we knowingly or unknowingly pursue are goals in keeping with our self-image and that subconscious or unconscious mechanisms automatically subserve these underlying goals and keep us "on target" much as a servomechanism keeps a missile on course.

Miller, Galanter, and Pribram (1960) have conceptualized behavior as the formulating and carrying out of plans—somewhat analogous to the program of a computer. Like computer programs, such plans are arranged in hierarchies, with some taking precedence over others. There are long-range plans, such as a plan to complete one's education or become an astronaut; there are short-range plans, such as a plan to attend a football game or concert. Some plans are executed; some are modified or held in abeyance; some are abandoned.

Because the self is experienced as the very core of our existence, its maintenance and enhancement become matters of very special concern. Thus we strive to maintain our existing frame of reference and to protect our self-concept from devaluation. For without our assumptions concerning reality, value, and possibility, in relation to both ourselves and our world, we would have no reference points for guiding our behavior and would be lost indeed. So we tend to resist dissonant information and to relinquish an assumption only in favor of one that has equal or greater appeal—for example, one

that raises our feelings of personal worth or adequacy. In many direct and indirect ways we try to maintain a favorable picture of ourselves and to enhance it whenever possible. In the face of failure or other sources of self-devaluation, we are quick to call on rationalization and other defensive mechanisms to protect ourselves from hurt and maintain our feelings of adequacy and worth. In a later chapter we shall examine these mechanisms.

Self as doer. The vast quantity of information we receive from our internal and external environment is evaluated, integrated, and stored with reference to its perceived significance to the self and its usefulness to us in the pursuit of our goals. When a new demand is made on us, the typical adjustive sequence appears to involve: (1) perceiving and defining the situation by comparing it with information already on file in our "memory banks," noting how similar situations have been dealt with in the past and formulating alternative possibilities for dealing with this situation, (2) making a decision—choosing the alternative which appears most suitable, and (3) putting it into action and utilizing "feedback"—noting how well the solution is working out and making corrections if they are necessary and possible. In all these steps the individual sees himself as an active and responsible agent with conscious intent—as a doer with the capacity for self-direction and full responsibility for his acts.

In viewing the self as a knower, striver, and doer, we are focusing on the key processes involved in self-direction. We shall elaborate on these processes throughout the remainder of this book.

Self-Direction and Development

The emergence of the self adds a new dimension to human development. For as the self system emerges, other psychological processes—such as memory, thinking, feeling—are organized around it; thus the self-system becomes a highly selective factor in shaping the subsequent course of development and behavior. In this context, three aspects of the self merit further mention.

Interpreting new experiences. As we have noted, the self becomes a central and constant reference point in a world of changing experience, and each new experience is interpreted in terms of its meaning and significance to this self. Rogers (1951) has described it this way:

"As experiences occur in the life of the individual, they are either (a) symbolized, perceived and organized into some relationship to the self, (b) ignored because there is no perceived relationship to the self-structure, (c) denied symbolization or given a distorted symbolization because the experience is inconsistent with the structure of the self." (p. 503)

As a consequence of this screening process, by which incoming information is selected, organized, and possibly distorted, each individual experiences events and environmental conditions in a somewhat personal way. And if we are to understand an individual's reaction, we must examine the way he has perceived the situation. Often

a problem which seems insignificant to us is highly stressful to another person. Failure to be invited to a big dance may constitute a major crisis for one girl but be brushed aside as inconsequential by another with more self-confidence or different values. Although another person's response to a particular situation may seem irrational to us, we can assume that it is relevant to the situation as he perceives it. As Combs and Snygg (1959) have pointed out:

"People do not behave according to the facts as others see them. They behave according to the facts as they see them. . . ."

"When we look at other people from an external, objective point of view, their behavior may seem irrational because we do not experience things as they do. Even our own behavior may, in retrospect, seem to have been silly or ineffective. But at the instant of behaving, each person's actions seem to him to be the best and most effective acts he can perform under the circumstances." (p. 17)

In general, the activities, objects, and events that we see as potentially enhancing or threatening the self are what command our attention and exert the most significant influence on our development. And since the aspects of the environment with which one person is self-involved may be quite different from those which seem important to another, we can see how the development of the self-concept contributes to differences in development.

Self-consistency and continuity. Because the ongoing activities of the human system are organized in relation to self, each individual tends to establish a relatively consistent life style. He develops a characteristic way of doing, thinking, reacting, and growing that tends to distinguish him from everyone else. He puts his personal stamp on every role he plays and every situation he encounters. These patterns of behavior are consistent with his assumptions concerning himself and his world.

Of key importance here is the individual's self-concept. For whether it is accurate

DETERMINANTS OF DEVELOPMENT

	HEREDITY	ENVIRONMENT	SELF-STRUCTURE
UNIVERSAL LEVEL	Potentials for physical characteristics of human species Potentials for growth, aging (life cycle) Potentials for behavior (self-awareness, self-direction, modifiability by learning, concern with values and meaning, use of symbols, rich transactions with field) Resources for routine and emergency responses	Physical setting, requiring adaptation Cultural setting, with prescribed roles, mores, values, language, family and social structure, ideology Social setting (relationships with family members and others)	Awareness and evaluation of self Development of basic assumptions and attitudes about (1) what is real or true, (2) what is valuable, important, good, and (3) what is possible Tendency to screen, evaluate, and distort perceptions in ways consistent with own attitudes and needs
COMMUNAL (COMMUNITY) LEVEL	Racial characteristics (e.g., skin color, endemic diseases) Family characteristics; genes for particular recessive and dominant traits	Resources or limitations of the particular setting (e.g., climate, food supply) Demand for particular competencies Sociocultural structure and social climate of particular group (e.g., values stressed, opportunities and limitations)	Assumptions and values held in common with other members of group—"basic personality type" Motives and goals typical of group Characteristic degree of self-differentiation and sense of responsibility
INDIVIDUAL LEVEL	Unique physical characteristics Unique pattern of psychological capacities Constitutional reaction tendencies (e.g., temperament, sensitivity, energy level, resistance, resilience) Male or female	Membership in unique pattern of subgroups Unique role demands Unique relationships with other individuals Unique satisfactions and frustrations from interaction with physical and sociocultural environment	Unique frame of reference (assumptions and attitudes about self and the world in relation to self) Unique pattern of abilities, habits, interests Unique "life style" (generally consistent way of behaving)

or not, he assumes it is and acts accordingly. Thus the girl whose parents continually criticize her for being stupid and clumsy is likely to develop an unflattering picture of herself and to behave in ways consistent with this picture, which is then further reinforced. And it is apparent that her experiences and learning will be different from those of a child who is constantly praised for cleverness and adeptness. Each day's learning necessarily builds upon what has gone before, and day after day growth is further slanted in the direction of the existing self-concept. In this way the self-concept tends to foster consistency not only in day-to-day behavior but also in long-term development.

Consistency and continuity do not, however, necessarily imply rigidity. Indeed it is considered a sign of healthy development when new experiences and new information —about one's self and one's world—can be assimilated into the self-system without unduly disturbing its integration. In general it would appear that the more realistic an individual's views of himself and his world, the more readily he will be able to modify his assumptions and self-concept to incorporate larger segments of "reality." In fact, Rogers (1961) has described this "openness to experience" as one of the outcomes of successful psychotherapy.

An interesting aspect of the continuity of self over time is the subjective experience of this continuity. Despite changes in our body and physical appearance, in status and role behavior, and in our knowledge and assumptions, we maintain continuity in our basic feelings of self-identity. We think of ourselves as pretty much the same *I* today that we were yesterday and that we will be tomorrow. Our sense of continuity between past, present, and future contributes to our awareness of self and to the continuity of our development and behavior.

Degree of self-differentiation. In some societies the individual is so much a part of his group—so "immersed in the herd"—that he develops very little sense of individuality or self. His self-identity appears to be collective rather than individual in nature. In such instances the individual does not perceive himself as having a high degree of volition and choice, nor does he feel responsible for directing the course of his own development.

In a study of the natives of Kenya, Africa, for example, Carothers (1947) found that social roles were rigidly prescribed and that most behavior was group determined, with individual achievement strongly discouraged. Lacking the opportunity for self-direction, there was little reason for these individuals to feel personally responsible for or self-critical at failure. In fact, Carothers found the Kenyans virtually free from the use of self-defense mechanisms, such as rationalization, as well as from feelings of anxiety, depression, and guilt. Self-blame and the use of self-defense mechanisms are common in our society; they are possible only in persons with a clear-cut sense of identity, who are also capable of evaluating themselves in reference to certain self-defined ideals.

In our society, each individual is held responsible for his own acts from an early age and is encouraged to develop and use his own unique capacities. Though there are many pressures toward conformity, we tend to value the individual as a unique person—in principle at least—with the right to a high degree of individuality and self-determination. This deep-rooted emphasis on individuality, responsibility, and self-direction inevitably sharpens our sense of self and makes for greater self-differentiation.

SUMMARY AND A LOOK AHEAD

In this chapter we have seen that our genetic endowment sets the limits for our development by providing our potentials for growth and behavior; it also influences certain constitutional or primary reaction tendencies which channel our modes of interaction with our environment. Environment, the second major determinant of human development helps to determine how the hereditary potentials are built upon and used. While both physical and psychological development require a minimally favorable physical environment, it is the sociocultural environment that plays the significant role in shaping the development of our distinctly human characteristics. Through our experiences, the self emerges to become a third major influence on our ongoing development. As the individual begins to experience himself as a unique person capable of self-direction, the self becomes the key reference point around which his experiences and actions are integrated—the reference point for evaluating new experiences, making plans and decisions, and undertaking adjustive action.

In examining heredity, environment, and self as the forces which shape human development, we have seen that they operate to produce both likenesses and differences in development. Conditions that obtain for all human beings are said to operate on the *universal* level. Examples are the common genetic inheritance that distinguishes mankind from all other species and the creation of language, social roles, and other aspects of culture. Conditions that influence the members of one society or group but are not characteristic of other groups are said to operate on the *communal* (community) level. Examples are genetic characteristics for a particular skin color, special climatic conditions, and particular group customs. Conditions which influence one member of the group but not others are said to operate at the *individual* level. Examples are genetic variations among members of a family, the individual's unique pattern of group memberships and roles, and the somewhat unique experiences through which each individual develops his own frame of reference. The end result is that "every man is like all other men, is like some other men, is like no other man." (Allport, 1961)

Against this background of the determinants of development, we are ready now to look at the sequences and patterns characteristic of human development.

Key terms used in this chapter include:

chromosomes, DNA, genes, genetic code (pp. 42-43)
monozygotic twins, dizygotic twins (p. 44)
cytoplasm, reduction division, dominance, recessiveness (p. 44)
X chromosome, Y chromosome (p. 44)
mutation (p. 45)
populations genetics (p. 46)
behavior potentials, maturation (pp. 46-47, 48)
constitutional reaction tendencies (pp. 47-49)
coping style (p. 48)
sociocultural environment, culture, subculture (pp. 52-53)
modal personality, reference group, peer group (pp. 53, 58)
position, role, interpersonal environment (pp. 54-55)
socialization (p. 55)
instruction, reinforcement, models, role expectations, identification (pp. 58-60)
self-concept, self-identity, self-evaluation, self-ideal (pp. 62-64)
frame of reference, cognitive map (p. 65)
assumptions of reality, value, and possibility (p. 65)
self-differentiation (p. 69)

Chapter 3

THE PATTERNING
OF DEVELOPMENT

The Direction of Human Development
The Sequencing of Development
Highlights in Key Areas of Development

In the preceding chapter we examined the forces that shape our development—our genetic endowment, our physical and sociocultural environment, and our self-structure. And we have seen that one characteristic of the human species is a predictable life cycle with an unusually long period of immaturity during which to make maximum use of our remarkable ability for change through experience. In the present chapter we shall focus on this life cycle—especially the formative period—to see how growth is patterned under the combined influence of inner and outer determinants. We shall see that within limits human development proceeds in a characteristic direction and follows an inner timetable, but that the maintenance of this developmental schedule depends on a favorable environment and on the learning of essential knowledge and competencies along the way.

Since the specific outcomes of development vary greatly from one cultural group to another as well as among individuals within a given group, we shall be concerned here primarily with identifying underlying trends in development which appear to be characteristic of the human species. This will lead us to a consideration of the direction of development, the sequencing and scheduling of development, and highlights of development in physical, intellectual, and other key areas.

THE DIRECTION
OF HUMAN DEVELOPMENT

With the advent of a new baby in the family, the focus is on the future. How far will his subsequent development and abilities simply follow a pattern already present in his genes? How important will his early experiences be in shaping his adult personality? What would he become if he were never exposed to human society? How much control do his parents have for fostering the kind of young man or woman they want their child to become? These are some of the questions that enliven the study of human development. They are questions about the goals toward which a child's development will lead, and about the extent to which the setting and achievement of these goals is within the control of the parents or, in time, the child himself.

Some Guiding Principles

There are certain basic principles of development which apply both to its direction and to its patterning. A brief review of these principles should help to provide us with some guideposts for understanding human development.

1. The general direction of development is toward the actualization of growth poten-

tials. The members of each species tend to grow and function in accordance with their inherited potentialities. Different environmental conditions can lead to variations in the final outcome, but each species has somewhat distinctive inherent potentialities; development, for its members, is an actualization of these potentialities.

2. Development normally proceeds in an orderly fashion although the rate of development is not constant but shows spurts and periods of slow growth. In addition, each part and subsystem has its own pattern and sequence of development. The patterning of neural development differs from that of the glandular system, and the patterning of intellectual development from that of emotional development. But because they are parts of a larger whole, the development of one subsystem influences and is influenced by the quality and rate of development of other subsystems.

3. Development can be viewed in terms of stages, each stage having its own characteristic features. Although there is an underlying continuity to the human life cycle, we can point to differing characteristics of infancy, childhood, adolescence, adulthood, and old age. For example, walking and talking are key concerns of infancy and early childhood, while achieving a clear-cut sense of personal identity and learning about members of the other sex are key concerns of adolescence.

4. Each new stage of development builds on and is limited by previous development and, in turn, provides the foundation for the stages which follow. What happens in childhood is influenced by the events of infancy, and in turn influences adolescence. Each stage of development leads into and remains a part of successive stages. Thus again we perceive both the directionality and continuity of development over the life cycle.

5. There are both similarities and differences in the development of different people. All of us go through the same stages, and for each of us development is largely a process of gaining identity as an individual and as a member of society. But there are many dif-ferences in individual patterns and outcomes of development, leading to wide differences among the members of any age group. In fact, each person is a unique event in the universe never to be replicated.

6. An overall view of growth from birth to maturity reveals a general sequence *toward increasing differentiation, integration, and complexity*. This sequence can be readily seen in physical development (Smith, 1966):

"First, there is a staggering proliferation of the number of parts—from a single cell at conception to roughly one million-million cells in the adult. Second, there is progressive differentiation of structure and function. For a short period after conception all cells in the embryo have equal potentiality to become any part of the body. Soon, however, the cells respond to regional changes and various organs and functions become differentiated. Some of these changes take many years. Sexual maturity, for example, does not occur until puberty. Third, there is increasing integration among the parts of the body. As they become differentiated and capable of independent action, the separate systems remain in communication and function in coordination with each other. In short, the change from simple to complex involves an increase in number, differentiation, and integration of the constituent parts of the system." (pp. 1-2)

A comparable pattern of increasing differentiation and integration is apparent in emotional, intellectual, and other aspects of psychological development—with concomitant changes in the nature and amount of information that can be processed by the system.

The period of growth and maturity is followed by a period of old age or "entropy" in which growth processes are reversed, leading to the deterioration and death of the system. In a very broad sense, the fulfillment of the potential of any living system is thus represented by the characteristic changes of its life cycle—including both the increasing differentiation and complexity of the early years and the later deterioration and eventual death.

Trends Toward Maturity

As we have seen, each social group tries to guide the development of its children in accordance with its ideas about desirable adult behavior. Although children's growth is shaped in different ways in different socio-cultural contexts, there are certain general trends that characterize development toward maturity in any society—whether primitive or advanced. These trends center around an increasing awareness of one's identity, an increasing concern with values and self-direction, and an increasing participation in and contribution to one's social setting. Seven such trends will be briefly examined here. Although we shall take each trend up separately, we shall see that they are closely interrelated.

Dependence to self-direction. One of the most basic pathways to maturity is from the nearly total dependency of infancy to the independence and self-direction of adulthood. The infant's inner growth tendencies together with guidance and pressure of his sociocultural environment lead to ever greater ability and willingness to take responsibility for his own actions and accept their consequences.

The transition from dependence in childhood to the self-direction of adulthood is often a difficult one to make. For to become self-directing, an individual must gain a clear-cut sense of his own identity and acquire the information, competencies, and

values essential for adult living. And even under the best of conditions, the assumption of adult responsibilities may be a stressful task. The inconsistency of adolescent behavior often reflects a very real ambivalence: the adolescent wants to have freedom for self-direction but is not yet ready to give up the security of dependence or to assume the responsibilities that go with independence. Nor is self-direction simply the attainment of freedom from outside authority. The adult who remains the victim of his own impulses and immaturities is really no more free to direct his life than the child whose behavior is restricted by the prohibitions of his parents. Learning responsible self-direction is also complicated by the fact that close adult relationships require both independence and interdependence.

Probably few of us ever completely outgrow our dependency needs. We continue to lean upon family and friends for help and approval. And occasionally we may dream of a carefree life on some South Sea island, or in the face of special stress we may regress to childish patterns of dependent behavior. But despite conflict and occasional backsliding, the trend of development is toward increased self-direction with all that this implies in terms of the assumption of adult responsibilities.

Pleasure to reality. As we saw in Chapter 1, Freud believed that human beings universally tend to seek pleasure and avoid pain

NEGATIVISM OF TWO-YEAR-OLDS

An important early milestone on the journey from dependence to self-direction is the child's discovery, at about the age of 2, that he can say, "No." This discovery begins a period of strongly self-assertive activity usually involving negativism: the child may refuse to obey, protest loudly even at activities he might enjoy if self-initiated, insist on doing things without help, resort to passive resistance, and generally refuse to meet any demands imposed on him

from without. After several months of testing and establishing his potentiality for some degree of autonomy, he becomes more accommodating and cooperative.

This behavior is viewed not as some mysterious "negativistic phase" but as an important developmental period when the child is learning to define himself as an active agent and is testing the limits of his potential autonomy and capabilities.

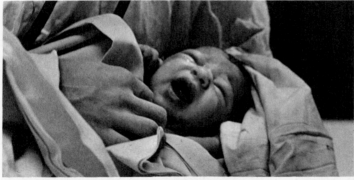

but that the development of the ego enables them to operate according to a *reality principle,* meeting their needs by accommodating to social requirements.

Whether or not we accept psychoanalytic theory, we can readily see that the pathway to maturity does indeed involve a growing ability to perceive and cope with the demands and limitations of the "real world." Among other things, this means that the individual must learn to delay immediate pleasures and gratifications—even to forego certain ones altogether—in order to achieve goals that are more important to him. For example, the medical student must put in long hours of study which preclude many of the social activities he would like to enjoy; and it is by no means always easy to develop and maintain the self-discipline that is required. Each individual learns that the realities of adulthood require that he sacrifice many of his own desires—that he learn to share, to cooperate, and even sometimes to put the needs of others before his own.

Facing the realities of life also implies the development of stress tolerance. The maturing individual learns to take in stride the many inevitable delays, frustrations, failures, hurts, and disappointments of living. The young child may be completely distraught by minor frustrations, as when another child takes a toy away from him, but he gradually learns to control his emotions, to remain coherent when excited or upset, and to look for ways of coping with a frustrating situation. By the time he has reached adulthood, an individual has usually learned to "roll with the punches." This does not mean, of course, that adults are so emotionally insulated from life that they do not suffer hurt. Rather it means that they have learned to take most of the inevitable frustrations of life in stride and to show good resiliency when stress situations do hurt and disturb them.

Ignorance to knowledge. The human infant is born with certain simple reflexes related to survival, such as the sucking motions that enable him to take food, but his ignorance of

himself and the world is total. In the classic statement of William James (1890, p. 488) "The baby, assailed by eyes, ears, nose, skin, and entrails at once, feels it all as one great blooming, buzzing confusion."

As he starts to achieve his enormous knowledge potential, the infant rapidly acquires a great deal of information, but the process of organizing it all into a meaningful whole—into a meaningful picture of himself and his world—is a much slower one. Gradually, however, the child develops an integrated picture of his immediate world—typically beginning with his home and extending to his community and his state, and eventually including the complexities of a global view.

Without going into critical issues—such as the "information explosion," which has created serious problems in the storage, retrieval, and communication of information—it is apparent that one major pathway toward maturity is that of increasing knowledge. As the person extends his knowledge of himself and his world, he also extends the range of situations that he can evaluate and react to in meaningful ways.

Incompetence to competence. To a great extent the process of achieving maturity is one of developing the various competencies necessary for effective adult living in one's particular culture. Teaching these competencies is the task of the home, the school, and other social institutions; learning them requires a major portion of a young person's time, particularly in a technological society. As we have seen, the competencies that will be required are determined by one's particular role in one's particular society, but physical, intellectual, emotional, and social competencies in some form are needed by adults in any society. In Part Four we will examine the basic competencies required in our society.

Diffuse sexuality to heterosexuality. We now know that sexuality is not some mysterious force that suddenly appears at puberty but is present from early infancy. Its initial expressions are relatively diffuse and generalized, but even infants have been observed to experience pleasure from genital stimulation; and in childhood "crushes" that have a high degree of sexual involvement are common. During later childhood, the child may go through a period that has been called "normal homosexuality," in which his interests are directed toward another member of the same sex. This does not ordinarily involve overt sexual behavior. However, it is not until puberty that heterosexuality becomes clearly differentiated.

Sexual behavior thus normally passes through progressive stages of development —varying with the social roles expected and the training administered by the particular social group—and normally ends in heterosexuality in adulthood. The development of heterosexuality can, of course, be retarded or blocked by various types of training; or distortions in development may occur, as in the case of homosexuality and other sexual deviations. For most people, however, sexual development follows a predictable course from the diffuse sexuality of infancy to the differentiated heterosexuality of adolescence and adulthood.

Maturity in sexual behavior eventually involves far more than a physical relationship with some member or members of the opposite sex. In marriage, for example, mature sexual behavior includes the establishment of an intimate and satisfying personal relationship. The individual's sexual maturity is thus influenced by his maturity in other life areas.

Amorality to morality. The newborn infant is amoral—in the sense that he has no concept of "right" or "wrong." Very early, however, he learns that he is loved and rewarded for "good" behavior and punished for "bad" behavior. This early awareness of good and bad eventually develops into a cluster of ethical or value assumptions and attitudes which we have referred to as the *conscience* or *superego*. With the development of conscience, the individual acquires "inner controls" which foster "good" behavior and tend to prevent "bad" behavior, thus elim-

 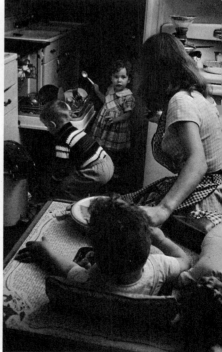

inating much of the need for outer controls. One key aspect of socialization, as we have seen, is learning to guide one's behavior in keeping with the standards and value assumptions of one's society.

Many adults fail to develop a mature conscience. In some instances, the individual fails to learn or internalize social values and lacks effective inner controls of his behavior. In other cases, the individual may blindly accept the values of his group without thought or question. Although such "borrowed values" may serve as effective inner controls of behavior, they do not reflect a mature degree of morality since the individual is more a robot than an evaluating and self-directing human being.

Later in this chapter we shall examine the sequence of events in the progression from immature to mature conscience and morality.

Self- to self-other-centered. One of the most important goals of development—important to both the individual and group—is learning to care and be concerned about the well-being of others. The infant is almost exclusively concerned with his own needs and wants, but with time there is normally an expanding understanding and concern with the needs of others as well as his own. Thus the mature adult is concerned about family and friends and participates in worth-while social causes.

The experience of man provides eloquent testimony that the ability to care deeply about something outside oneself—whether it be family, community, country, value patterns, or social ideologies—helps to give life meaning and to promote self-fulfillment. It is this other-centeredness that keeps a Florence Nightingale ministering to the needs of wounded and dying soldiers and an Albert Schweitzer serving in his jungle hospital— or a mother giving loving care to her children. Thus the choice is not between self-fulfillment and fulfillment for others, but a broadening of concern and involvement so that promoting others' welfare becomes one source of self-fulfillment.

The investment of self in others and in worth-while causes often involves considerable sacrifice of what, in a narrower context, seems best for the I or me. Yet it is only through what might be called an extension of self to concern for others that the individual achieves a feeling of belonging to the "human enterprise."

In a general sense, all these pathways to maturity involve actualization of the individual's growth potentials and development into a productive and effective member of society.

THE SEQUENCING OF DEVELOPMENT

All living creatures develop in terms of a "ground plan" based on their genetic make-up. It is this ground plan that provides for the orderly sequencing of development through the characteristic life cycle.

We know more about the nature of this ground plan for lower animals than we do for human beings; but research studies are gradually filling in the picture on the human level as well. A knowledge of the early sequencing of development is important for several reasons: (1) it provides information essential to an understanding of basic psychological processes such as learning, thinking, and feeling; (2) it provides a framework and norms for appraising a particular child's developmental status and for helping children who are having problems; and (3) it provides a general basis for assessing new concepts and "fads" in child rearing.

Developmental Sequences and Norms

Looking through the family album and seeing our pictures as babies and later as children and adolescents, most of us have been intrigued by the way we have changed in size and appearance. We have probably noted, too, that our bodily development followed a rather definite pattern and that our motor skills, such as walking and talking, fitted into this developmental sequence. We are less likely to realize that our psychological development has also followed a definite sequence. Yet intensive studies of infants and children have shown the sequencing of intellectual, emotional, and social as well as physical development.

Much of the pioneer work in describing the sequencing of early physical and psychological growth of the child was done by Arnold Gesell and his associates (Gesell, 1940; Gesell & Ilg, 1946; Ilg & Ames, 1955). These investigators observed the behavior of infants and children at regular intervals in standardized situations in an attempt to establish norms for early development. They found that the average infant in their samples could sit up without support by about 7 months and walk alone by about 15 months; similarly, on the average, infants spoke their first words at about 12 months and used their first phrases or sentences by about 2 years. These norms involve behavior to be expected "on the average" at a given age—with about 50 per cent of the children manifesting the behavior, 25 per cent not yet reaching the stage, and 25 per cent having gone beyond it in their development.

Unfortunately, Gesell's findings were too often viewed as prescriptive instead of simply descriptive, and some parents worried unnecessarily about their child's normalcy when a given behavior did not appear at the typical age. Although marked retardation in developmental sequencing is often a cause for concern, babies who are slow in the acquisition of motor skills may develop normally in intelligence, and even some intellectually gifted children do not speak until they are 2 or 3 years old. Even the "typical ages" for given behaviors may vary in different cultures and may be affected by social advantages and disadvantages or by innovations like television and teaching machines. Thus emphasis has shifted from the concept of *norms* to that of *stages*. Three ways in which such sequencing has been viewed are summarized on page 79.

Since Gesell's pioneering work, many other investigators have helped to put his findings into perspective as well as to fill in more details concerning the determinants and typical sequencing of development in given areas. In a later section of this chapter, we shall examine the sequencing of physical, intellectual, emotional, and social development.

Developmental Tasks

At each stage of development there are fairly specific tasks—skills, attitudes, understandings—which are appropriate to that level of maturity and which society expects the individual to master at that time. A major task of infancy, for example, is walking; during adolescence the tasks of establishing a mature sense of identity and of preparing for work and marriage come to the fore. Some of the major developmental tasks for each life period in our society are listed in the summary chart on page 80.

If these tasks are not mastered at the appropriate stage of development, the individual will be at a serious disadvantage in making subsequent adjustments. A young child who has not learned to talk is at a serious disadvantage in entering nursery school; the adolescent who does not date misses a key opportunity for acquiring information about himself and members of the opposite sex that he will need later for selecting a satisfactory mate. The demands of a given developmental period may be relatively easy or difficult to meet, depending on how well the tasks on prior developmental levels have been mastered.

In a broader perspective, of course, developmental tasks vary not only with stage of development but also with group membership. Although children in all societies learn to walk and talk, they do not all have to master reading or the skills involved in hunting and fishing. Even among subgroups within the same society, developmental tasks vary considerably. In our own society, psychologists tend to list developmental tasks in terms

MODELS OF PSYCHOLOGICAL SEQUENCING

1. *The growth-readiness model*—associated with the pioneering work of Arnold Gesell. Development is viewed in terms of a schedule determined by age: a certain level of physiological maturation is necessary before given type of learning can take place. For example, it was formerly assumed that a child must reach the age of about 6 before his nervous system and sense organs would be ready for learning to read; this assumption was based on the fact that most of the children observed seemed to reach readiness at about that time. Now it is realized that with provision of particular learning tasks and experiences children as young as 3 can be taught to read. Emphasis has shifted, accordingly, from maturation to the sequencing of experiences in early learning.

2. *The cognitive adaptation model*—developed by Jean Piaget. Stages and sequences of physical and psychological development are viewed as innately determined but modifiable by experience within certain limits. Interaction of the child with his environment is seen as essential for intellectual de-

velopment. New experiences are assimilated into his already existing cognitive structures, which then permit increased accommodation to environmental demands. This model is popular today and has stimulated extensive research.

3. *The cumulative-learning model*—proposed by Robert Gagné. Learning is emphasized as the major causal factor in development. The child develops from one point to the next by building on previous learning in progressively complex fashion through the processes of differentiation, generalization, recall, and transfer. Stages are not age-bound or even maturation-bound except in the sense that learning takes time and is a product of the planned and unplanned events which have filled the individual's life up to present. Intellectual development "may be conceived as the building of increasingly complex and interacting structures of learned capabilities." (Gagné, 1968, p. 190) The degree of similarity in different children's development is determined by the extent to which their sociocultural environment and learning experiences are similar.

Based in part on Gagné, 1968; and Bijou, 1968.

DEVELOPMENTAL TASKS

EARLY CHILDHOOD 0-6 YEARS	Acquiring a sense of trust in self and others. Developing healthy concept of self. Learning to give and receive affection. Identifying with own sex. Achieving skills in motor coordination. Learning to be member of family group. Beginning to learn physical and social realities. Beginning to distinguish right and wrong and to respect rules and authority. Learning to understand and use language. Learning personal care.
MIDDLE CHILDHOOD 6-12 YEARS	Gaining wider knowledge and understanding of physical and social world. Building wholesome attitudes toward self. Learning appropriate masculine or feminine social role. Developing conscience, morality, a scale of values. Learning to read, write, calculate, other intellectual skills. Learning physical skills. Learning to win and maintain place among age-mates. Learning to give and take, and to share responsibility.
ADOLESCENCE 12-18 YEARS	Developing clear sense of identity and self-confidence. Adjusting to body changes. Developing new, more mature relations with age-mates. Achieving emotional independence from parents. Selecting and preparing for an occupation. Achieving mature values and social responsibility. Preparing for marriage and family life. Developing concern beyond self.
EARLY ADULTHOOD 18-35 YEARS	Seeing meaning in one's life. Getting started in an occupation. Selecting and learning to live with a mate. Starting a family and supplying children's material and psychological needs. Managing a home. Finding a congenial social group. Taking on civic responsibility.
MIDDLE AGE 35-60 YEARS	Achieving full civic and social responsibility. Relating oneself to one's spouse as a person. Establishing adequate financial security for remaining years. Developing adult leisure-time activities, extending interests. Helping teen-age children become responsible and happy adults. Adjusting to aging parents. Adjusting to physiological changes of middle age.
LATER LIFE	Adjusting to decreasing physical strength. Adjusting to retirement and reduced income. Adjusting to death of spouse and friends. Meeting social and civic obligations within one's ability. Establishing an explicit affiliation with age group. Maintaining interests, concern beyond self.
TASKS AT ALL PERIODS	Developing and using one's capacities. Accepting oneself and developing basic self-confidence. Accepting reality and building valid attitudes and values. Participating creatively and responsibly in family and other groups. Building rich linkages with one's world.

Based in part on Erikson, 1963, 1966; and Havighurst, 1952.

of middle-class expectations rather than in terms of the expectations of lower socio-economic groups. Thus an adolescent who lacks motivation for continuing his education and drops out of school is a failure with respect to middle-class expectations but not necessarily with respect to the standards held by his own socioeconomic group. The members of each society and major subgroup face somewhat unique patterns of developmental tasks. And, of course, with social change, new developmental tasks may arise for those at all life stages.

Underlying the many particular developmental tasks for each life stage are certain continuing *general tasks* that must be met by members of all social groups. These general tasks focus on: (1) achieving a realistic frame of reference about oneself and one's world; (2) developing the physical, intellectual, emotional, and social competencies needed in one's culture; and (3) learning about and preparing for the problems likely to be encountered in living.

These general tasks are met in different ways at different ages. A 4-year-old and a college student are both achieving understandings and competencies though at quite different levels of complexity. But each, at his own level, should be broadening his present horizons and extending his current competencies so that he can not only deal effectively with present problems but be ready for the problems he will encounter as he progresses to the next stage of his life cycle.

Maturation and Learning

In the last chapter we saw that the influence of genetic factors is a continuing one, through the process we referred to as *maturation*. We also noted the high degree of modifiability in the human infant, resulting in a key role for learning in socialization and psychological growth. In this section we are concerned with the interaction of maturation and learning in the sequencing of human development. It is only comparatively recently that we have begun to realize the range in potential that a particular genetic input supplies and the importance of the particular sequence of environmental conditions in determining the rate and quality of the development that actually takes place.

Maturation and readiness. In an interesting early study, Dennis (1940) demonstrated the effects of maturation on walking. Using Hopi Indians as subjects, he was able to find 63 mothers who had kept their children on a cradle board from birth until the infants were 9 months old. The cradle board is a plank about a foot wide to which the baby is firmly bound; it greatly restricts his movements. Dennis then compared this group with another group of 42 Hopi children whose mothers had not used the cradle board and had allowed their infants freedom of movement. Curiously enough, the mean age of walking was about 15 months for both groups, indicating that the restricting experience of the cradle board during the first 9 months of development had had no retarding effect upon learning to walk.

Although the onset of walking seems to be guided chiefly by maturation, the same is not true of talking: a child cannot learn to speak till nerves, muscles, vocal cords, and general intelligence have developed to

Children are taught whatever skills are needed for participation in their society. What they can learn is usually limited by what competencies others in their society have already developed.

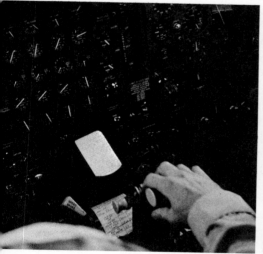

a stage of readiness. But once that point is reached, he will learn speech only if he hears it, and the particular speech patterns he learns will depend on what ones he hears. For most kinds of human behavior, maturation establishes the necessary preconditions but learning determines the direction that development takes. Increasingly, too, even the preconditions necessary for particular new learning require both maturation and previous learning. Thus the first-grader cannot learn to read unless he has learned to understand and use language and to differentiate between similar sounds. When he gets to the middle grades, in turn, he can learn academic subjects adequately only if he has learned to read.

After minimal readiness is achieved, specific training can be helpful. Training started too soon, however, is wasted and may be frustrating to the child; training at the most minimal stage of readiness may be much less efficient than training started a little later when the individual is more fully ready to profit from it.

Several early experiments brought out these relationships. In one, 10-month-old twins were the subjects. At the start of the experiment, neither could climb stairs. Over a period of six weeks, one twin was given a 10-minute practice session each day. By the end of this period, she could climb stairs while her twin still could not. At this point the same training schedule was started with the other twin, who then caught up in only two weeks with the level of skill shown by her sister (Gesell & Thompson, 1941). But although carefully sequenced, enriched experiences can accelerate readiness up to a point, maturational processes still establish a ceiling.

Early and later learning. With good reason babies have been called "information-digesting machines." Almost from the day they are born they seem to thrive on stimulation from and interaction with their environment. Even during the first few weeks of life, experiments have shown that babies are able to use past experience; for example,

they can follow and anticipate a pattern of blinking lights which they have seen before and memorized. Rheingold, Gewirtz, & Ross (1959) found 3-month-old infants making increasingly frequent vocalizations to an adult when such vocalizations were immediately followed by the adult's smiling, making "tsk, tsk" sounds, and touching the infant lightly on the abdomen. When such reinforcement was discontinued, the infants' vocalizations decreased greatly in frequency. The conditioning and generalization of fear responses during the latter part of the first year have also been demonstrated.

Despite several decades of intensive research in human learning, there is a good deal of controversy concerning the ways in which we learn and what actually takes place in learning. Often a distinction is made between simple or associative learning, in which particular responses are learned, and complex or cognitive learning, in which concepts, generalizations, principles, or rules are learned which the individual can then apply selectively and appropriately in new situations. Simple learning takes place through conditioning, observation and imitation, and blind trial and error. Complex learning can take place through observation, discovery, abstraction, inference, or other thought processes in which data from past or present experience are restructured or transformed. Actually, there is no clear dividing point between these two kinds of learning, and both simple and complex learning may result from the same experience.

Although both simple and complex learning are important in shaping the course of human growth, it would appear that simple associative learning plays a particularly significant role during the early years of life. For example, simple conditioning is common in early childhood and provides many new response patterns—often without the individual's awareness of such learning. As the child's perceptual, retentive, and rational capabilities develop, however, he becomes an increasingly active agent in selecting and shaping his own learning. By the age of 4, he has a fairly clear picture of himself and his world, and his ability to discriminate, interpret, and evaluate experience makes him less susceptible to simple conditioning (Gagné, 1968).

In later childhood and adolescence, learning usually focuses on the problems of school achievement as well as those of everyday living. Although the individual is by no means immune to conditioning, his new learning typically depends to a large extent on what he already knows, on what his present motives and purposes are, and on how he views the situation at hand. Now he is able to evaluate, to organize and reorganize his concepts, and to use creative imagination. The result of such learning is a new understanding of himself and his environment —new ways of perceiving, wanting, evaluating, and feeling—which lead to changes in his frame of reference. These tendencies may reinforce or modify his existing tendencies to solve problems and respond to his environ-

ment in particular ways, but they go far beyond acquiring simple conditioned responses.

Although human beings are highly modifiable, even at later ages, the importance of early learning—leading to our habitual ways of thinking, feeling, and acting—has been emphasized by most psychologists. The plasticity and enduring imprint of these early years was claimed dramatically by the pioneer behaviorist J. B. Watson (1930):

"Give me a dozen healthy infants, well-formed, and my own specific world to bring them up in and I'll guarantee to take any one at random and train him to become any type of specialist I might select—doctor, lawyer, artist, merchant-chief, and yes, even beggarman and thief. . . ." (p. 104)

Such control does not exist, of course, in real life. Nor do most modern psychologists accept such strict behaviorism, for hereditary and constitutional factors have been shown to have a far greater influence on development than Watson realized. Neverthe-

BEHAVIORAL CONTROL: AN EXAMPLE FROM LITERATURE

For behaviorists, the causes of behavior lie in the environment: behavior is controlled by reinforcement. In theory, at least, society could use reinforcement to produce people with whatever traits it considered desirable—docility or initiative, competitiveness or cooperativeness, and so on. The possible misuse of conditioning in a totalitarian society is portrayed in Aldous Huxley's *Brave New World:*

Eight-month-old infants of a group destined to be menial workers were brought into a large, bright room where big bowls of flowers and brightly colored picture books had been set out. ". . . the babies . . . began to crawl towards those clusters of sleek colours, those shapes so gay and brilliant on the white pages. . . . From the ranks of the crawling babies came little squeals of excitement, gurgles and twitterings of pleasure. . . . Small hands reached out uncertainly, touched, grasped, unpetaling the transfigured roses, crumpling the illuminated pages of the books. The Director waited until all were happily busy. Then, 'Watch carefully,' he said. And, lifting his hand, he gave the signal.

"The Head Nurse, who was standing by a switch-

board at the other end of the room, pressed down a little lever.

"There was a violent explosion. Shriller and ever shriller, a siren shrieked. Alarm bells maddeningly sounded.

"The children started, screamed; their faces were distorted with terror.

"'And now,' the Director shouted (for the noise was deafening), 'now we proceed to rub in the lesson with a mild electric shock.'

"He waved his hand again, and the Head Nurse pressed a second lever. The screaming of the babies suddenly changed its tone. There was something desperate, almost insane, about the sharp spasmodic yelps to which they now gave utterance. Their little bodies twitched and stiffened; their limbs moved jerkily as if to the tug of unseen wires. . . .

"Books and loud noises, flowers and electric shocks—already in the infant mind these couples were compromisingly linked; and after two hundred repetitions of the same or a similar lesson would be wedded indissolubly. What man has joined, nature is powerless to put asunder." (1932, pp. 13-14)

less, it is generally agreed by psychologists of both the "active" and "reactive" viewpoints that the early years of life are of crucial importance in shaping the individual's basic ways of viewing and coping with his world.

Critical Periods and Stimulation

Recent research has made it quite apparent that there are periods, especially during the early years, when certain types of stimulation and activity are essential for normal physiological and psychological development. If the needed stimulation or opportunity for activity is lacking at the *critical period,* then given functions: (1) may not appear, (2) may be slower in making their appearance, or (3) may be only partially adequate. Research concerning critical periods has focused on sensory-motor, social, and intellectual development.[1]

Critical periods in sensory-motor development. A number of experiments have shown the effects of deprivation of stimulation and activity on sensory-motor development— particularly in lower animals. For example, Riesen (1947) reared chimpanzees in total darkness for the first year of life and found that their vision was permanently impaired. In another early study Dennis (1941) found that if the wings of buzzards were tied down for a period of 10 weeks or longer after hatching, the birds never learned to fly as well as other members of their species. Similarly, tadpoles immobilized for 13 days or longer showed permanently impaired swimming patterns; chicks kept in darkness for up to 5 days showed no apparent defects in their pecking responses, but if kept in darkness for 8 or more days were unable to learn to peck (Hunt, 1961). On the basis of such studies, Scott (1962, 1963, 1967) has concluded that an organism denied early sensory and motor experiences customary to its species, including a chance to experience and adapt to unfamiliar situations, will show impairment in adulthood, even in much behavior formerly regarded as genetically determined.

On the human level, we have little definite information about critical periods in sensory-motor development—and apparently there is a much longer period of grace before permanent damage occurs. However, children with severe and uncorrected strabismus (cross-eyedness) end up with one eye which is blind even though it started out as a structurally sound eye. The explanation for the loss of vision is that since two discrete visual images are confusing, the brain neglects the messages from one eye, with the result that the unused eye eventually becomes unable to function (Lemkau, 1961). This condition can be prevented if the vision of each eye is obstructed alternately so that each one gets some use until a corrective operation is possible.

Conversely, the enrichment of early stimulation has been found to accelerate the development of certain motor skills in human infants. In the celebrated studies of the twins, Johnny and Jimmy, McGraw (1935) gave one of the twins special training in various motor skills and found that the results varied with the skill involved. For example, the time of onset of walking was not affected by help and practice, but development of other skills could be greatly speeded up. Thus the twin receiving special training could roller-skate almost as soon as he could walk. In certain activities, however, early practice led to inferior final performance because of the formation of faulty habits. McGraw (1946) concluded from her studies that there are "critical periods" for motor learning which vary with the type of activity—that for each type there is an optimum period during which guidance and practice lead to the most rapid and effective learning.

Critical periods for social attachment. Studies of *imprinting*—the tendency of the young of certain species to become attached to and remain near adults of their own kind—have

---

[1]The brain structures whose maturation may both underlie these critical periods and make possible different kinds of learning are discussed in the article by Bronson beginning on page 464.

proven helpful in understanding the formation of social bonds in animals. For example, it had long been known that ducklings will follow the first moving object they see and thereafter show a preference for this object and others like it. Usually the first object they see is the mother and this process of imprinting ensures that they will thereafter seek out and remain close to members of their own species. But ducklings can be imprinted to other animals, including human beings.

In an attempt to identify the critical period for imprinting, Hess (1959) exposed mallard ducklings of different ages to a model of an adult mallard and then tested them for strength of imprinting (social attachment) by measuring their tendency to follow and remain near the model. It was found that maximum imprinting took place when the ducklings were between 13 and 16 hours old. Prior to 9 hours and after 20 hours after hatching, exposure to the model was ineffective—imprinting did not take place. Other studies have delineated the critical period for social attachment with other species. For example, the critical period for puppies to form social attachments is between 3 and 12 weeks of age with the peak at about 6 to 8 weeks (Scott, 1958; Freedman, King, & Elliot, 1961). This bears out the common observation that dogs raised too long in a kennel do not make good pets—they have formed social attachments to dogs rather than to human beings.

Harlow and Harlow (1966; 1967) have identified normal sequences in the development of both infant-mother and infant-infant relationships in rhesus monkeys. Both kinds of interaction during the early months seem essential for normal social and sexual relationships in adulthood. If infant monkeys have no chance to interact with or even see another animal for three months after birth and then are permitted contact with age-mates, they show emotional shock at first, with self-clutching and crouching, but soon are able to establish social relationships and show essentially normal social and sexual adjustment in adolescence. If deprivation is continued as long as six months, however,

even with only partial deprivation in which they can see but not interact with other infant monkeys, there are permanent inadequacies in social and sexual development. Similarly, infants either raised by their mothers but with no peer contact or raised with peer interaction but no mothers show deviations in normal social development—the deviations being greater for those infants deprived of peer-group contact. The recent finding that chimpanzees do not show permanent impairment from the same conditions shows again the importance of genetic input and the need for caution in generalizing from one species to another (*Science News,* 1968a).

In human infants, the relevant variables in the learning of social attachments are more complex and less well understood, and it is evident that there are wide individual differences in the effects of early social deprivation—some infants apparently being more severely affected than others. However, there is a growing body of evidence—derived mainly from studies in institutions where large numbers of infants have been cared for by a small staff—that the critical period for the formation of social attachments in humans is from about 6 weeks to 6 or 7 months (Gray, 1958; Schaeffer & Emerson, 1964; Scott, 1967). Social deprivation during this period typically results in later inability to form deep emotional attachments or to be concerned about the feelings or well-being of others. Often antisocial behavior is also associated with such early deprivation. On the other hand, infants who form stable social attachments during this critical period tend later to identify with, emulate, and seek the approval of adult models, and are able to form warm and loving relationships with others.

The timing mechanisms which open and close the critical period for the formation of social bonds appear to be found in the processes of growth and differentiation. Scott (1962) has pointed to various *positive mechanisms,* varying from species to species, which usually bring infant animals close to other members of their kind at the critical time. Examples are the clinging response of young rhesus monkeys, the following response of ducklings, lambs, and other herd animals, the tail wagging and playful fighting of puppies, and the smiling and exploratory investigation of the human infant. All these approach patterns, by leading the infant to contact with and emotional stimulation by adult members of their kind (usually the mother initially) facilitate the formation of social bonds.

The critical period appears to be terminated by *negative mechanisms* which thereafter prevent such attachments from being formed. Perhaps the most common of these negative mechanisms is the development of a fear response in which the young animal withdraws and avoids contact with strangers. In ducklings, this fear is at its height after 20 hours; in dogs, after 14 weeks. In human infants, there is a period between 5 and 12 months when there is a mounting fear of strangers. Such fear occurs at a particular stage of development for each species— whether or not imprinting has taken place— and thereafter prevents its normal occurrence.

Critical periods in the development of intelligence. Several animal studies have highlighted the importance of particular kinds of experience during a given developmental period in determining later levels of ability. A number of investigators have compared the later performance of rats raised in a barren environment with that of rats raised in a "rich" environment, including many objects and playthings that provided opportunities for exploration, lively activity, and spontaneous learning. A consistent and dramatic advantage in intellectual development has been found for those given the enriched environment (Cooper & Zubek, 1958; King, 1958; Thompson, 1960; Bennett *et al.,* 1964; Schultz, 1965; Rosenzweig, 1966). In an attempt to pinpoint the period when such enrichment is most effective, Forgays (1962) found that the major effect of such an enriched environment was limited to the period from 20 to 30 days after birth. Similar experience before or after this period produced

little effect on later skill in learning and problem solving.

Comparable findings have been reported for children:

Skeels (1966) reported on the adult status of two groups of individuals who had been placed in an orphanage as infants. One group of 13 children, ranging between 7 months and 3 years of age, had been transferred to another institution in which more stimulation was provided, as well as an opportunity for closer relationships with adults. A follow-up study 21 years later showed an average gain of 31.6 IQ points for this group, as compared with an average loss of 20.6 IQ points for a matched (control) group of 12 children who had stayed in the original institution. All of the experimental group were self-supporting; of the control group, 6 were unskilled laborers, four were in institutions, and one had died. Interestingly enough, the twelfth member of the control group turned out to have had an enriched environment for a year at age 5, as part of another special study; at the time of the follow-up study he was married, with four children of normal IQ, and working as a compositor and typesetter with an income higher than that of all the other control subjects combined.

The same process is probably at work in children from disadvantaged slum areas, who usually show normal development for the first year or so and thereafter show such slow mental development that there is a progressive loss in IQ. In recent years experimental programs to give them the extra stimulation and the broader experience of nursery-school activities have produced most encouraging results: there is increasing evidence that such experiences can prevent or reverse the usual loss of IQ. For example, Gray and Klaus (1965) found that disadvantaged children who had been given nursery-school experience for even as little as one or two summers started the first grade at a higher level of ability than a matched group of children who had not had this experience. Although the first grade brought a spurt in mental growth for both groups, the children who had had the nursery-school experience maintained their lead. Such findings provide the basis for extensive early enrichment programs such as Head Start, though the Head Start programs usually go far beyond the usual nursery-school curriculum in providing compensatory experiences for deprived children.

Demonstration of the dramatic and lasting effects of both deprivation and stimulation during early development have led to a marked change in our view of intelligence. Formerly it was assumed that intelligence was "fixed" by genetic factors. If a baby could be tested accurately at birth, we would obtain an IQ that would stay with him for life —unless he suffered brain damage. If he had a high IQ, well and good; if not, nothing could be done about it.

Although the genetic potential undoubtedly sets upper limits to the level of intelligence that can be developed, even in an ideal environment, it now appears clear that the actual intelligence a child shows is also heavily dependent upon his cumulative interactions with the environment—especially during his first five or six years. With an early enriched environment, his potential will be more fully developed; with early deprivation of stimulation, less fully so. By the age of 6, the child's intelligence level is usually fairly predictive of what it will be in adulthood; before the age of 6, it is predictive only within very broad limits and only if his environment does not undergo drastic change.

A number of investigators contend that the growth and maintenance of the neural structures themselves are dependent upon the functional demands made upon them during the developmental period (Krech, 1967; Hunt, 1961, 1964; Bronson, 1965). For example, working with rats, Rosenzweig (1966) has found evidence that enriched stimulation, with opportunity for interaction with a complex environment, leads to a thicker and heavier cerebral cortex. In fact, he has been able to modify brain areas selectively by early programs of particular kinds of deprivation or enrichment. As yet, we can only conjecture about the implications of such studies for the effects of enrichment or dep-

rivation on the human brain, but the level of intellectual *functioning* is certainly changed by early deprivation of stimulation and activity.

Thus it becomes apparent that if our basic "ground plan" is to be implemented in development—in terms of the actualization of inherent growth potentials—certain inputs from the environment as well as opportunities to perform certain functions are essential. And it is also apparent that in many cases these inputs and opportunities must come during critical periods of development. Critical periods seem to be periods of especially rapid growth or availability of new capacities, periods when basic structuring is taking place. Once structuring has occurred, restructuring in a different way is difficult and may be impossible.

HIGHLIGHTS IN KEY AREAS OF DEVELOPMENT

"As a growing child gains experience in coping with environment, many changes occur in the patterns of his behavior. The vague, general tensions of infancy become transformed into motives, concerns, wants, and aspirations. General emotional feelings become refined into delicate shades of sentiment, love, and affection, or into awesome states of fear, fright, or anger. Early massive efforts to cope with environment have given way to specific patterns of behavior varying in terms of the possibilities for action in any given situation. Uncertainties regarding himself and the world of which he is a part become replaced by systems of value and belief. . . ." (Knutson, 1965, pp. 369-370)

In the main, psychologists have focused their research efforts on the early years of the human life cycle, possibly because these years appear so important in shaping personality development. As yet, however, the vast array of findings with respect to physical and psychological development have not been organized into a coherent view of early development; nor have these findings been systematically related to adulthood and later maturity. As we have seen, for example, we are just beginning to understand the far-reaching effects of early deprivation or enrichment of stimulation on long-range intellectual development and functioning.

Nevertheless, it will help us to fill in our present picture of development to trace briefly the patterning of development in four key areas—physical, intellectual, emotional, and social—with special attention to the early years.[1]

Physical Development

One major goal in the study of human development is to chart the course of bodily growth and its relation to psychological growth. This includes the establishment of norms for physical development, as well as acceptable variations from such norms, and the effects of body changes and of one's body image upon behavior.

Bodily structure. Any review of the patterning of physical development should, of course, include the approximately nine-month period of prenatal life. In Chapter 2 we briefly traced the course of prenatal development, noting that during the third week after conception the primitive heart begins beating, and that by the eleventh week all of the body subsystems are formed and functioning. The subsequent fetal period is largely one of further growth, differentiation, and integration of biological subsystems—and the preparation of the organism to sustain itself in the new environment it will encounter after birth.

At birth the typical infant weighs about seven and a half pounds and measures approximately twenty inches in length. At this time his body proportions are by no means identical to those of an adult—for example, his head is about a fourth of his body height, whereas it will be only about a tenth of his height in adulthood. Overall physical growth is very rapid during the first year of life, then slows somewhat, averaging about three inches in height and six to seven

pounds in weight yearly until shortly before puberty. At this time, changes in the activity of the pituitary and the sex glands lead to the development of the secondary sex characteristics and to differences in male and female body proportions. For the boys, there is a broadening of the shoulders, and the appearance of facial and body hair; for the girls there is breast development and a widening of the hips. Both also show a growth spurt followed by a gain in weight and, finally, the maturing of the reproductive organs. Although there are wide individual differences, these changes, on the average, come about two years earlier for girls than for boys. Thus there is a period of a few years when girls tend to be somewhat taller and heavier than boys.

Although some changes in body proportions continue throughout one's lifetime—particularly in weight distribution and physical appearance—the individual's adult bodily structure is attained by about the age of 21. This is followed by a so-called "prime of life" period extending into the early 40's and then by a period of physical decline—usually mild until about the age of 70 and more rapid thereafter. These changes may vary considerably, depending upon differences in biological make-up, physical health measures, and the environmental conditions under which the individual lives. Under adverse conditions, for example, as in some underdeveloped countries, the average person is physiologically old by 35 and looks it. But although the life span may be lengthened or foreshortened, we all follow the same characteristic life cycle.

Sensory-motor development. The sense organs of the newborn infant are relatively well developed, and most kinds of sensitivity have been demonstrated within a few hours or days after birth. And in the weeks and months that follow he makes rapid progress in his

---

[1]An excellent discussion of the available research findings, issues, and horizons in infant development is found in articles by Ricciuti, Horowitz, and other investigators in the *Merrill Palmer Quarterly,* January 1968, Vol 14.

ability to discriminate, interpret, and integrate incoming sensory data. For example, the week-old infant may pay more attention to other sounds than to the human voice, but by the time he is a month old, he is more responsive to human voices, which presumably have been more related to the meeting of his needs.

Similarly, the newborn infant is capable of a surprising variety of motor responses including primitive adaptive responses to stimulation—such as making mouth rejection movements to sour or bitter-tasting substances, which are likely to be harmful. During infancy, motor development continues rapidly. By the tenth day he can follow slowly moving objects with his eyes. In succeeding months he develops control over large-muscle groups and learns to sit up, crawl, pull himself to a standing position, and walk (at about 15 months). Although he will continue to be dependent on others for many years, his ability to explore and manipulate his environment, his rapidly acquired ability to understand and use language (his first words occurring typically at about 12 months), and his remarkable capacity for cumulative learning provide new potentialities for further development.

We shall not attempt a review of the progression of sensory-motor development from infancy to adulthood. However, the growing individual makes continuing strides in perceptual development and in the coordination and precision required for motor skills. Like general body growth, sensory-motor development continues up to a given age—depending on the skill involved—after which precision begins to decline. For example, the age of maximum proficiency in professional football, ice hockey, and other strenuous sports appears to fall in the middle to late 20's or early 30's for most athletes (Lehman, 1951). Of course, there are marked individual differences, and certain types of sensory-motor skills may be acquired or improved at almost any age. In general, however, visual and auditory acuity and muscle strength and coordination tend to decrease during the later period of life.

Intermeshing of physical and psychological development. We often tend to take the course of physical development pretty much for granted and not fully realize its importance for psychological development. Yet many facets of physical development have direct and indirect consequences for psychological development.

During early growth, the child's level of maturation sets limits upon the learning that is possible at a given point. Variations from the average in rate of physical development, body build, or other physical characteristics may also influence psychological development. Late-maturing adolescents of both sexes tend to have less adequate self-concepts; sheer bigness may be an avenue to prestige for the male—as in team athletics—while extreme tallness in a girl may be a handicap. Viewing one's body as being too different from the standards valued by the group can be disruptive for a member of either sex (Jones & Mussen, 1958; Garn, 1966). As Hurlock (1968) has pointed out, "It is difficult for a pubescent to be self-

One's reflection in the mirror is a big part of one's body image and hence of one's self-concept. Judged against the prevailing standards of attractiveness, it can go far to bolster or undermine one's self-confidence.

FUNCTIONS OF LANGUAGE IN HUMAN DEVELOPMENT

COMMUNICATION	Language is a key means of transmitting and receiving information. Through language, a child is able to express his needs, feelings, and views to others and receive comparable information from them.
THOUGHT	Language facilitates thinking in many ways. Naming objects and events makes them easier to remember and helps a child to make differentiations. Language is the primary device for translating raw experience into meaningful symbols and concepts and for representing and thinking about objects and events not physically present.
INNER REGULATION OF BEHAVIOR	Having learned to speak, the child can talk to himself and give himself the orders he has heard often from his parents—thus internalizing parental control. Later the use of language makes possible complex dialogues with himself involving value judgments that guide his behavior.

acceptant when he is anxious and concerned about his changing body and when he is dissatisfied with the image of himself he sees reflected in the mirror." (p. 376) In our youth-oriented society, it is also difficult to accept the physical deterioration of aging. And, of course, physical disease or damage at any time during the life span, as well as the deterioration that comes with aging, may not only lessen the individual's functional capacity but also lead to self-devaluation and impaired adjustment.

In Chapter 2 we have also noted ways in which constitutional factors, such as primary reaction tendencies, may influence our environmental interactions. Our physical development and status have far-reaching implications for our coping styles and for our self-concept—in short, for our overall pattern of psychological development and functioning.

Intellectual Development

Intellectual or cognitive development is growth and change in such processes as learning, language use, concept formation, reasoning, and imagining. As we have already seen, the course of such development is dependent both on inner maturational processes and on opportunities provided by our environment—especially opportunities

for acquiring language, knowledge, and competencies. As Bruner (1964) has pointed out:

"... the development of human intellectual functioning from infancy to such perfection as it may reach is shaped by a series of technological advances in the use of mind. Growth depends upon the mastery of techniques and cannot be understood without reference to such mastery. These techniques are not, in the main, the invention of the individuals who are 'growing up'; they are, rather, skills transmitted with varying efficiency and success by the culture—language being a prime example. Cognitive growth, then, is in a major way from the outside in as well as from the inside out." (p. 1)

From the standpoint of inner maturational processes, Bloom (1964) has estimated that 50 per cent of adult intelligence is developed by age 4 and 80 per cent by age 8. However, as we have noted, the degree to which the individual's inherent potentialities are realized—aside from the general timing of maturation processes—depends heavily upon the quality of his sociocultural environment.

Language development. The development of language as a means for thinking and communication is a remarkable human achievement. Man has developed words and other abstract symbols for everything visible or invisible that he wishes to think about and communicate about with others. Since words can be written as well as spoken, they enable us to record and communicate events of the past as well as the present and to contemplate the ideas of people remote from us in time and place. And since language symbols are basic tools for thinking, acquiring them is a key step in the individual's intellectual growth that vastly increases his potential for further growth.

Although man matures slowly in comparison with other species, he starts the process of language acquisition very early. By the age of 3 to 5 months the infant begins to babble and to experiment and play with sounds; and a few months later he can make most of the sounds that appear in all the world's languages. Interestingly enough, these prelinguistic utterances are the same for infants the world over and even for those who are deaf—thus indicating the importance of maturational processes in guiding language development (Smith, 1966; Chomsky, 1968). In succeeding months, the sounds which are not used in the language of those around him gradually disappear, while the infant learns to put the remaining ones into the form that will become his native language.

As we have noted, the average infant uses his first words by about 12 months; from this point on, his vocabulary development is quite rapid. By the age of 6, the child has a passive vocabulary (words he can understand) of about 5000 words and an active vocabulary (words he can use correctly in speaking) of about half that number. During the early school years, the child extends his vocabulary, achieves an explicit understanding of the rules of grammar, and acquires written language. By the time he finishes high school, the average young adult understands about 50,000 words, can use about 10,000 words, and has achieved a relatively high level of proficiency in reading, writing, and speaking.

Interestingly enough, man is apparently the only animal who uses language symbols. The use of words by parrots and other birds is simply the imitation of sounds; their words are not used for conceptualizing their environment. Chimpanzees can learn an extensive sign language but can learn to speak only a few words—and then only with difficulty and only as labels.

The importance of language in the intellectual development of children is dramatically illustrated by the classic study of Kellogg and Kellogg (1933):

In this study a 7-1/2-month-old chimpanzee named Gua was brought into the psychologist's home and raised along with their 9-month-old son Donald. For the following eight months Gua and Donald were given equal care—in terms of affection and training. Interestingly enough, Gua soon began to surpass Donald in many "civilized" tasks—such as using a spoon, drinking out of a cup, exercising bowel and bladder control, and responding to spoken instructions. By the age of 18 months, however, Donald had begun to use language; from this point on, his ability to learn and solve problems rapidly and permanently outpaced that of the chimp.

Thus even in early development, language gives man a tremendous advantage in giving him a tool for representing and thinking about objects, events, and relationships.

Concept formation. Closely related to language development is development of the ability to form and use concepts like "roundness" or "larger than." A concept is derived from the identification of common properties or relationships in many different situations. Thus it is a generalization that is exemplified in many objects or situations but exists apart from its manifestations in any particular one.

The general sequence of concept development is believed to move from the concrete and specific toward the more general and abstract. Initially the words which the child learns are labels for specific objects. For example: the child may learn that the family pet is a "dog," and at first he may overgeneralize, calling all furry animals "dogs." However, he soon learns to discriminate between animals that fall into this category and those that do not. Later he learns to group dogs, cats, elephants, and other creatures into the more abstract and unifying concept of "animal" and eventually can use concepts like "mammal" which are based on similarities other than visually apparent ones. As his intellectual growth progresses, his concepts become highly abstract, as illustrated by such terms as "evolution" and "death." Much of the questioning that is so characteristic of children—typically beginning with "What?" and progressing to "Why?" and "How?"—helps them to form and sharpen concepts pertaining to their world and the demands it is making on them. Much of our education consists in acquiring and learning to use complex abstractions in our thinking.

With the development of concepts, the individual acquires powerful intellectual tools. For his concepts represent the categories into which he sorts incoming experience so that he can deal with it. For example, by placing an unfamiliar object in the category of "human female," he can make an important preliminary step in identifying it. Usually, of course, an unknown human female is categorized in more than one way, so that his preliminary identification might be elaborated by use of such categories as age, appearance, and marital status—she might be judged young, pretty, and unmarried. Such categorizations, in turn, would suggest certain general guidelines for an appropriate response. If it were not for our ability to categorize new objects and events and deal with them in terms of categories developed through past experience, we would be overwhelmed by the complexity of the environment and every new situation would present a potential crisis.

Curiously enough, many complex concepts have been personalized in concrete form. In Christian cultures, for example, evil has been personalized as a devil called Satan, complete with tail and pitchfork.

Development of thinking. In psychology a rough distinction is usually made between perceiving, learning, and thinking—the latter referring primarily to such processes as remembering, reasoning, imagining, and evaluating. Often a further distinction is made between *autistic* thinking and *realistic* thinking. Fantasy, daydreams, and wishful thinking which are not directed toward the meeting of current demands are examples of autistic thinking, while reasoning and evaluation are examples of realistic thinking. Thus thinking may simply involve daydreaming about popularity with the opposite sex, or it may take the form of trying to find a solution to the problem of economic inflation, or of imagining and planning a "dream city" of the future.

As background for reviewing the development of thinking, it is helpful to note three kinds of tools which we use in thinking: (1) images, which are memory "pictures" of an object or event not now present to the senses; (2) symbols, like words or mathematical notations which represent an object but do not look like it; and (3) concepts, which, as we have seen, are abstractions or generalizations. Language symbols and concepts are particularly important in reasoning, evaluative thinking, and imagining since they greatly extend the individual's ability to explore and understand situations or problems and to formulate new ideas and possibilities.

Present views of the development of thinking have been greatly influenced by the pioneering work of the Swiss psychologist Jean Piaget, who has devoted most of his life to the study of thinking in children (Piaget, 1926, 1936, 1964).[1] Piaget views mental growth as an extension of biological growth, governed by the same general principles. Piaget recognizes, of course, that the *content* of thought is determined primarily by the environment—that the particular language, concepts, and values that the child acquires depend on his particular environmental input. But the sequence and general timing in the development of ability to form

[1]The author is indebted to following sources also for the discussion of Piaget: Bronfenbrenner, 1963; Flavell, 1963; Furth, 1968; Tuddenham, 1966; Wolwill, 1967.

and use images, symbols, and concepts are guided genetically if the necessary environmental inputs are provided.

According to Piaget, the development of thinking is based on development of an innate tendency toward organization of and adaptation to incoming information. The newborn infant starts with no specific knowledge but with this tendency to organize and adapt to sensory information he receives. The tendency involves two basic mental operations: assimilation and accommodation. *Assimilation* is the process whereby incoming information is perceived and interpreted in relation to existing schema that he has already established through previous experience. *Accommodation* is the changing of his inner schema or frame of reference as a result of new information—the structuring or restructuring of his mental organization.

As a consequence of assimilation and accommodation—together with the increasing maturation of the nervous system—the development of thinking involves progressive changes in thought patterns. In a broad sense this development progresses from the very limited processes of infancy through the stages summarized on page 94. Piaget's emphasis is on the sequence of these stages rather than on exact age periods. His findings clearly have many implications for education and child rearing. They suggest the importance of providing opportunity and help to facilitate the child's progression from one stage to the next, as well as the possibility of accelerating the pace of development by such assistance.

A slightly different formulation has been worked out by Bruner (1964), with emphasis upon three stages by which a child learns to

---

PIAGET'S STAGES IN COGNITIVE DEVELOPMENT

According to Piaget, the development of thinking progresses in an orderly fashion through the following periods or stages:

1. *Sensorimotor period*—from birth to about 2 years. In this early stage the infant learns to coordinate simple perceptual and motor responses and bring them under control. Incoming visual, auditory, and other sensory data are organized into a meaningful picture. The child's perceptions of external objects at first focus on his functional relations to them; their "existence" is dependent on his activities relative to them. He begins to see his role as an agent capable of modifying them before he seems able to conceive of them as having a continuing, independent existence. Toward the end of the period he also begins to show foresight or contemplation prior to action.

2. *Preoperational stage*—2 to about 7 years. In this period the acquisition of language enables the child to deal with his world symbolically instead of only directly through motor activity. By a process of "decentering" he gradually learns to conceive of a world of space and time that exists independently of himself and his actions. In dealing with physical objects and quantities, he seems able to consider only one dimension at a time during this period; for example, he may conclude that there is more water in a

taller glass than a shorter one without noting that the taller glass is also smaller in diameter.

3. *Concrete operations*—6 to 7 to about 11 years. During this period the child shows an increasing capacity to reason though still at a relatively concrete level. Among his logical acquisitions are numbering, classifying, and ordering in series. Now he can handle variations in more than one dimension at a time. For example, he may realize there is as much water in the short glass as in the tall one because he notes the difference in their diameters. But the child does not go beyond the situation as it is: his symbols and concepts are literal representations of what he has experienced. He is not ready for abstraction or imagination of relationships not already experienced. To solve inferential problems, he needs concrete objects to manipulate.

4. *Formal operations*—from about the age of 11. Now the child can deal readily with words and abstract relationships and can examine the form of an argument as well as its content. He is also increasingly capable of solving problems involving the simultaneous manipulation of several variables and for the first time can intellectually examine and manipulate the merely hypothetical and systematically evaluate several alternatives.

deal with information and form internal representations of his world: (1) motor representations from past actions—corresponding roughly to Piaget's sensory-motor period, (2) images—that stand for events in much the same way that pictures do, and (3) symbols—such as words and numbers—which provide a means not only for representing experience but also for transforming it. The translation of experience into symbolic form—which becomes increasingly important between 4 and 12 years of age—not only augments but even supersedes the child's earlier modes of processing information and "opens up realms of intellectual possibility that are orders of magnitude beyond the most powerful image-forming system." (pp. 13, 14) The extent to which such possibilities are fulfilled depends upon the nature of the culture to which the growing individual is exposed and the degree to which it fosters a higher level of intellectual development. In some primitive cultures, even adults do not learn to use abstractions to any great extent. In our society, extensive use of abstractions is necessary for adaptation.

Emotional Development

Although we are vividly aware of our own experience of emotions—such as fear, anger, and love—the term *emotion* is a very difficult one to define. Perhaps the simplest approach is to describe an emotion as a complex state involving: (1) conscious feeling, (2) physiological changes, and (3) an evaluation of a given situation as having significance of some kind for the individual. Many emotions also are accompanied by action tendencies toward approach or withdrawal. For example, if we evaluate a situation as dangerous, various emergency physiological changes take place in the organism, accompanied by a conscious feeling of fear and, typically, a tendency to withdraw or flee.

It would appear that we have certain "wired in" resources for emotional behavior that tend to develop in a pattern characteristic of the human species. In an early study,

Goodenough (1932) found that the emotional responses of a 10-year-old girl born deaf and blind were similar to those of normal 10-year-old children. The general patterning of emotional development appears to be universal for the human species and to be heavily dependent upon maturation. Nevertheless, learning plays a key role in determining which situations elicit emotion, the type and intensity of emotional arousal, and the ways we control and express our emotions.

Early differentiation of emotions. Immediately after birth the infant can register distress, which is characterized by crying and general muscular tension; by the second week after birth a variety of strong stimuli—such as direct sunlight shining in his eyes, restraint of his arms, and pressing the bottle nipple into his mouth—can elicit this distress reaction. However, it is not until the end of the second month that clear "pleasurable" responses make their appearance, characterized chiefly by smiling and increased vocalizations in response to a human face. Thereafter these two primitive emotions—pleasure and distress or "unpleasure"—differentiate into more specific positive and negative emotional patterns.

By the fifth month the infant shows unmistakable anger responses when some interesting activity is interfered with; and about this time the fear response to strange persons and situations begins to appear. By the seventh month elation makes its appearance in response to some activity initiated by the infant which has a successful outcome—such as making an interesting noise by banging a spoon. By 10 to 11 months most infants show signs of affection and love for certain adults, and by 15 months the infant shows affectional interactions with other infants. About the middle of the second year jealousy makes its appearance; during the second and third year humor appears and the infant "plays tricks"; and during the fourth year shame and guilt are shown, as well as grief and anxiety. By about the fifth year, all the basic emotions have been differentiated (Bridges, 1932).

During infancy and early childhood, emotional arousal is relatively intense and of short duration. As a consequence, emotional behavior may change dramatically in a very short time: one minute the infant is crying and the next he is smiling. With time, there is more continuity in emotional behavior and the child moves more slowly from one emotional state to another. In addition, he soon learns that the uncontrolled expression of emotion is not acceptable, and he gradually learns to control his overt emotional responses as well as to express his emotions in socially approved ways.

Long-range changes in emotional patterns. During childhood and adolescence there is a further differentiation of emotions, characterized in large part by changes in the stimuli which evoke emotions and in increasing subtlety and richness of emotional experience.

As a consequence of learning and experience the situations which elicit emotions undergo marked changes. In part, this involves learning to bear frustration and hurt, so that the older child and adolescent are not upset by many minor frustrations that would earlier have elicited intense emotional responses. In part, too, the change reflects an extension of the individual's cognitive development and greater concern with symbolic situations. Thus fears which initially focus around strange persons and situations may extend to imaginary creatures—such as monsters, ghosts, and bogeymen—and eventually to dangers relating to one's hopes and plans. As the individual's intellectual horizons expand and an increasing number of objects, events, and situations become of significance to him—whether dangerous, exciting, promising, disappointing, threatening, or otherwise meaningful—they take on the ability to arouse his emotions. Thus emotional and cognitive growth go hand in hand.

With growth toward maturity, the differentiation of emotions also involves many refinements and nuances of feeling, including the development of emotionally toned attitudes and sentiments. Thus we find the emergence of worry, crushes, loyalty, and patriotism. Moods are rare in childhood, but become common during adolescence and young adulthood—particularly moods of depression, which may last for hours or even days. During adolescence and adulthood, emotions are usually richly varied and characterized by increasingly complex patterns of anxiety, humor, love, joy, wistfulness, and many other emotions.

With the advent of old age, there often appears to be a constriction in the range and depth of emotion, perhaps due in large measure to the usual restriction of social and other aspects of the older person's life situation (Banham, 1951). The older person also becomes more upset by certain situations, such as those which necessitate adapting to

---

THE DEVELOPMENT OF FEAR

1. The fear response typically makes its first appearance at about 5 months in response to strange persons, objects, and events. As the child learns more about his world, many of his early fears disappear. Even in adulthood, however, we often tend to fear the strange and unfamiliar.

2. An unfeared object or idea may come to be feared through being experienced as associated with a feared one (conditioning). Fears may generalize from an original fear-eliciting situation to situations perceived as similar.

3. A person's particular fears depend upon his experiences and on the generalizations—or failures of discrimination—he has made.

4. Stimuli eliciting fear show a progression from the tangible and concrete to the less tangible—for example, from fear of strangers to fears of ghosts and bogeymen and, later, to fears relating to personal inadequacy.

5. The sources of fear tend to differ from one society to another, as well as in different subgroups within the same society.

change; in general, he tends to show less resilience than younger persons with the result
that his emotional responses may be unduly
prolonged and overly exhausting—particularly negative responses, such as fear and
depression.

Variations in emotional development. There
are marked cultural as well as individual differences in emotional differentiation and expression. For example, fear is a much more
dominant emotion in some societies than in
ours, is elicited by different stimuli (such as
fear of bewitchment), and is expressed in
ways characteristic for the particular group.
Some groups foster expressiveness, others
a concealment of feelings. In our society men
are generally not expected to be as emotionally expressive as women.

Similarly, marked individual differences
in emotional patterns often exist among the
members of a given group. We are all used to
differences in emotionality among the people we know. Thus we may refer to someone
as having a violent temper, or having a good
sense of humor, or being essentially negative in his feelings, or being unable to give
or experience love. Such differences appear
to be based upon varying admixtures of constitutional and experiential factors, reflecting both the genetic make-up and the life
experiences of the individual. The important
point is that each of us develops a relatively
consistent and enduring pattern of emotional
behavior which is an important characteristic
of our "life style."

Emotions play a pervasive role in our
lives, and in later chapters we shall deal with
fear, anxiety, and other key emotions in more
detail. We shall see that our emotions not
only add zest to living but are an invaluable
adaptive resource; we shall also see, however, that under certain conditions emotions
can seriously impair our mental health and
adjustive efforts.

Social Development

In a broad sense, social development includes the entire gamut of behavior involved
in learning to be a participating member of a
social group. We shall restrict our discussion here, however, to three key facets of
social development: (1) the development of
social interactions, (2) sex-role development,
and (3) the development of moral values and
conscience.

Development of social interactions. During the
first weeks of life the infant is said to be
"nongregarious" in that he shows a complete
lack of interest in people. By the second to
third month, however, he expresses pleasure
in the presence of others by smiling, kicking,
and waving his arms. As the fear response to
strangers makes its appearance, around the
middle of the first year, he begins to limit his
positive reactions to the adults with whom he
has had relationships—and particularly to his
mother. Then during the latter part of the
second year, as he becomes more proficient
in dealing with his environment, his fear of
strangers gradually diminishes, although
some measure of timidity and shyness in the
presence of strangers may continue into
childhood.

Although the infant's early social interactions typically involve his parents and siblings, early social development can also be
viewed in relation to his interactions with
other infants. Maudry and Nekula (1939)
utilized a "baby party" technique to study
changes in social interaction from 6 months
to 25 months of age:

*This technique involves putting two babies in
a playpen and providing them with a new toy
every few minutes. It was found that infants
between 6 and 8 months of age were not interested in either the toy or the other infant;
from 9 to 13 months, the infants responded
first to the toy and second to the partner.
Fighting during this period was maximum,
apparently stemming from a tendency to perceive the other infant as an obstacle to obtaining the toy. From 14 to 18 months the
behavior of the infants was predominantly
friendly, with the partner receiving more attention than the toy. It was also found that
cooperative play began during this period.
From 19 to 25 months, play materials were*

used as a means of establishing social contacts, and the frequency and length of positive social interaction increased.

Thus we see the trend toward more complex and sophisticated social behavior even during the first two years.

In the early years, a child's relations with other children can be better characterized as companionable than as friendly. In essence, the young child just wants someone to play with. When other children are not available, he may even invent imaginary

TWO KEY DIMENSIONS OF SOCIAL INTERACTIONS

Several dimensions of social interaction have been studied in an effort to identify the extent to which the patterns that children develop are learned and hence subject to control by parents and teachers. One such dimension is cooperation versus competition; another is aggressiveness versus friendliness.

1. *Cooperation vs. competition.* Before about the age of 4, there appears to be little rivalry or competitive behavior among children in the sense of trying to excel or outdo others on a task. (Competitive striving for parental attention among young siblings is common.) The degree of subsequent competitiveness which does develop appears to be heavily dependent upon learning. For example, Greenberg (1932) found that most 4- and 5-year-olds evidenced competitive behavior when told to perform better than their partners. Competitive behavior also appears to be more common when the child is in a situation where he sees that competition rather than cooperation is more likely to lead to reward or goal attainment—when available rewards cannot be shared by everyone but must fall to some at the expense of others. On the other hand, when children are encouraged to cooperate in the achievement of group goals and are in a situation in which cooperation brings greater rewards, social interaction tends to be predominantly cooperative and integrative rather than competitive (Azrin & Lindsley, 1956).

Some societies have been described as highly cooperative and others as highly competitive. For example, when basketball was introduced to Hopi children—an Indian tribe noted for its cooperative behavior—they took it up with enthusiasm but refused to keep score (Benedict, 1953). In our own highly competitive society, most children by the age of 5 or 6 show competitive behavior in some situations and cooperative behavior in others.

2. *Aggressiveness vs. friendliness.* Studies of aggressiveness and friendliness in children have shown that although friendly approaches are more common in childhood than aggressive ones, aggression does appear to be a common phenomenon—taking either a direct form, as in physical or verbal attack upon another person, or an indirect form, as in teasing. In a study of children's aggression, as reported by 379 mothers, Sears, Maccoby, and Levin (1957) found that every mother had been forced sometime to cope with angry outbursts or quarreling on the part of her children; and 95 per cent of the mothers reported instances of strong aggression directed against the parents. The latter might be expected, since parents must frequently thwart or frustrate the child and aggression is a common response to frustration.

By means of example and expectation, as well as through rewards and punishment, parents and other social agencies teach their children to what degree, in what manner, toward whom, and when aggression can be expressed. As we shall see, studies indicate that children readily imitate aggressive models—both parental models (particularly the father for boys) and movie and television models (Bandura & Walters, 1963; Bandura, Ross, & Ross, 1963b).

The young child usually expresses his aggression directly in physical attacks, but he soon learns that verbal attacks are safer and more socially approved. However, a double standard is often utilized in our society, with aggressive behavior being condemned for girls but often condoned and sometimes even encouraged for boys. Thus it is not surprising that aggression is more common among boys in our society—especially direct physical attack (Bandura & Walters, 1963).

In societies and subgroups where aggressive behavior is praised or rewarded, there is likely to be a high incidence of aggression; if overt aggression is disapproved, it is much less likely to occur. In Chapter 1, we noted that aggression is practically unknown after childhood among the Blackfoot Indians of Montana, where friendliness is encouraged and admired and aggression is deprecated and regarded as abnormal.

A CRITICAL PERIOD IN SEX-ROLE LEARNING?

The existence of a critical period for the learning of one's sex role has been suggested by a study of the development of hermaphroditic children (children with sex organs of both sexes) who had been reared as members of one sex for a time and then treated as members of the other. Very little emotional disturbance was evident when the change had occurred before the middle of the third year. After that period, however, the change had been very difficult to make and had led to serious emotional problems (Money *et al,* 1957). Thus there may be different critical periods for specific aspects of social development. Most of the research so far has focused on the formation of the original social attachment to one's species.

companions and derive pleasure from playing with them. Later he begins to want "friends" —people with whom he can talk and exchange ideas as well as play. Initially friendships are usually based upon fortuitous circumstances such as simply being in the same place and willing to do things together. Throughout the primary grades (approximately 6 to 12 years of age) friendships may change considerably over short periods of time; usually quarrels and changes in interests and values account for the dissolving of friendships.

With the advent of adolescence, friendship patterns increasingly become based on common interests and mutual satisfaction and are more constant and enduring. During middle and late adolescence, the focus of social interaction is on dating and related heterosexual relationships; during young adulthood it shifts to choosing a mate and making the various adjustments involved in marrying and starting a new family.

Sex-role development. In Chapter 2 we discussed the effects of others' expectations on the development of one's behavior. Nowhere is this influence more clearly seen than in the development of male and female sex roles. From the time of birth, the infant's sex elicits certain behavioral expectations from his parents, and he tends to be approved and rewarded when his behavior conforms to these expectations and to suffer disapproval and punishment when he falls short of them or shows behavior regarded as appropriate for the other sex. Ordinarily children's parents

serve as key role models for the development of their sex-role behavior (Josselyn, 1967).

Lynn (1959) has distinguished three stages in sex-role development: (1) *Sex-role preference,* in which the individual learns to prefer the sex role he is assigned. For example, some small boys would prefer to be girls and some small girls would prefer to be boys. Presumably, establishing the appropriate sex-role preference is an important first step if the process of sex-role development is to proceed normally. (2) *Sex-role adoption,* involving attempts to act out the appropriate sex-role behavior. Now the child strives to conform to the sex-role which he has adopted. (3) *Sex-role identification,* in which the child's self-concept includes that of being a boy or girl—in which he identifies himself clearly as male or female.

The timetable for sex-role development varies for both individuals and groups. However, available studies indicate that by the age of 4, most children have progressed to the adoption of their appropriate sex role. This is reflected in the play activities they choose as well as in the fantasy roles they take in their play. For example, girls tend to prefer dolls and playing house over wheeled toys, guns, and the cowboy games played by boys. Similarly, the girl is likely to enact a female role, such as that of the mother, in her play activities; while the boy is likely to enact a male role, such as that of a soldier or a cowboy. Once the sex-role identification is complete, it serves as an important "governor" in shaping many aspects of psychological development (Kagan & Moss, 1962).

For the individual strives to develop and behave in ways compatible with his concept of what is appropriate for members of his sex.

Cultural standards in regard to masculinity and femininity have a far-reaching influence on the development of the sex role. Such standards differ greatly in different societies, but in any society the following are included:

1. *Physical attributes.* For example, characteristics we consider desirable in women include medium height, a slender, hairless body, and moderately sized breasts. In some societies such characteristics as fatness or a muscular physique are greatly admired. In recent years, many young people in our own society—particularly males— have come to prize long hair and beards. A young person who accepts peer-group standards may feel sure of his masculinity only by following current norms; however, he may find himself in conflict with parents and other authority figures if they consider such peer-group norms undesirable.

2. *Feelings, attitudes, motives, and wishes.* For example, we regard as desirable for females the ability to elicit sexual arousal in a male, the desire to be a wife and mother, and the capacity to give love and nurturance to one's husband and children. In males we tend to admire a pragmatic attitude, the ability to make a living, and the ability to play the roles of husband and father, as defined in our own society. Again, however, there may be some measure of conflict between established norms and changing peer-group standards.

3. *Overt behaviors.* For example, as already noted, inhibition of physical aggression is considered appropriate for girls, whereas boys are given considerably more leeway and often even encouraged to be aggressive. Similarly, females are often supposed to inhibit the display of their sexual urges while men are expected to take the initiative in sexual behavior. These traditional standards are changing, with girls being expected to take more initiative.

CULTURAL DIFFERENCES IN SEX ROLES

The strikingly different sex roles that develop in different societies were mentioned in Chapter 2, where the Tchambuli, one of the New Guinea tribes studied by Margaret Mead (1939), were described. The contrasts she found among the three tribes she studied highlight the extremes that are possible—and the extent to which the "human nature" a child will develop is dependent on his experiences as he grows up.

1. *The Arapesh.* In this tribe both sexes showed characteristics and behavior that would be considered feminine in our own society. Both men and women were encouraged to be unaggressive, mild, cooperative, and responsive to the needs of others. Neither sex took an aggressive role in courtship. The ideal marriage was a mild, responsive man married to a mild, responsive woman.

2. *The Mundungumor.* In this tribe both sexes would be characterized as masculine by our standards. Both men and women were encouraged to be aggressive, violent, and ruthless; gentleness and tender behavior were at a minimum. The ideal marriage was that of a violent, aggressive male married to a violent, aggressive female.

3. *The Tchambuli.* While neither the Arapesh nor the Mundungumor had clearly defined roles which distinguished the behavior of the sexes, the Tchambuli did have such roles, but, as we saw in Chapter 2, they were reversed by our standards. The women were characteristically dominant, impersonal, and businesslike and took the initiative in courtship and sexual behavior. By contrast, the men were irresponsible, emotionally dependent on the women, relatively passive, concerned about their physical appearance, and interested in arts and home activities.

In this study, then, we see three societies in which sex roles differ considerably from our own. In two, the roles are social rather than specifically sexual; there is very little distinction between the norms for the two sexes but a striking difference between the norms of the two societies. In the third, there is a reversal of sex roles as compared with ours.

PIAGET'S STAGES OF CONSCIENCE DEVELOPMENT

Piaget (1932) asked children of different ages to make moral judgments about hypothetical situations, and concluded that moral development—like intellectual development in general—followed a genetically directed sequence in which two main stages could be distinguished:

Stage 1. The morality of constraint—lasting until about 7 to 9 years of age—in which the child regards adults as dominant and omnipotent and accepts without question the moral rules handed down by them. Three specific characteristics of stage 1 are especially noteworthy:

a) Moral realism—the belief that acts should be judged on the basis of consequences and not intent. If Johnny inadvertently knocks over a cup and breaks it, he should be punished.

b) Immanent justice—the belief in inevitable punishment for misdeeds, emanating from things themselves. If Johnny disobeys orders and cuts himself while playing with a knife, the cut is viewed as punishment arising from the knife itself.

c) Punishment as learning and expiation—the view that the evil doer must be punished to realize the seriousness of his wicked action and as a means of expiation. Within reason, the more severe the pun-

ishment, the better it is regarded as being.

Stage 2. The morality of cooperation—at about the age of 9—involving the emergence of a more mature morality of cooperation, reciprocity, and mutual respect. Rules are no longer regarded as fixed and absolute but as based on mutual give-and-take and capable of being altered. Now the child thinks in terms of:

a) Subjective responsibility for respecting the rights of others.

b) Equity in fitting the magnitude of the punishment to the magnitude of the misdeed and consideration of possible mitigating circumstances.

c) Restitution—the view that the wrongdoer should put things right rather than just suffer for his misdeed.

d) The intent behind the act, as well as its consequences. Now child can understand and forgive.

Again, it is the sequence rather than the exact timing that is predictable. And with moral values as with the development of thinking, Piaget recognized that the actual *content* is supplied by the life experiences of the individual in his particular society. Later studies of conscience development have yielded somewhat uneven support for Piaget's findings.

These of course are only samples of the many differences in sex-role standards for males and females in our society. Since the broad dimensions of sex-role standards are relatively stable from childhood through adulthood, the long-range influence of sex-role identification is apparent in many important domains of individual development and behavior and in the establishment of family roles.

The individual's self-concept, in turn, may be heavily influenced by the degree to which he sees himself as measuring up to the sex-role standards. Here it is of interest to note that despite increasing permissiveness in the role behavior accorded to both males and females in our society, sex-role stereotypes continue to be clearly defined and generally agreed upon by college men and women (Rosenkrantz *et al.*, 1968).

Moral values and conscience development. Conscience has been somewhat facetiously defined as "that which keeps us from doing what is wrong even when no one is looking" and as "that part of personality which is dissolved in alcohol." In a more scientific sense, conscience is the learned system of moral values by which the person judges his own acts or proposed acts.

Research studies of conscience development have been limited in scope and often somewhat contradictory in their findings. Piaget's early studies of mental development included an investigation of moral development; the two stages he delineated are described above. Most of the studies since Piaget have put their emphasis on social learning factors rather than factors related to increased age and maturation. This work has led to the delineation of three important aspects of conscience development:

1. *An inner control or behavioral component,* which reflects the internalization of cultural standards and enables the individual to resist the temptation to break a rule even when he is not likely to be detected or punished.

2. *A self-critical component,* involving shame, guilt, self-recrimination, and anxiety when the individual does deviate from internalized cultural standards.

3. *An evaluative or judgmental component,* which implies the capacity to make moral judgments in terms of internalized standards and to justify maintaining these standards to oneself and others. Development of these three aspects may be quite discrepant: an individual may verbalize high moral standards but have little ability or inclination to follow them in his behavior.

Research findings indicate that conscience development is a gradual process in which the child first learns which acts will bring reward and approval and which acts will result in punishment and disapproval. Eventually such standards are internalized

TYPES OF MORAL JUDGMENTS

Kohlberg (1963, 1964), studying boys aged 7 to 16, found three general levels of moral judgment which he further subdivided into six types, or stages. These six levels were related to characteristic stances with respect to 32 aspects of morality. The levels, and an example of their stances on one aspect of morality, "motivation for rule following or moral action," are summarized below:

	TYPES	MOTIVATION FOR MORAL ACTION
PREMORAL	**1.** Punishment and obedience orientation	Obey rules to avoid punishment
	2. Naïve instrumental hedonism	Conform to obtain rewards, have favors returned
MORALITY OF CONVENTIONAL ROLE-CONFORMITY	**3.** Good-boy morality of maintaining good relations and approval	Conform to avoid disapproval or dislike by others
	4. Authority maintaining morality	Conform to avoid censure by legitimate authorities and resultant guilt
MORALITY OF SELF-ACCEPTED MORAL PRINCIPLES	**5.** Morality of contract, of individual rights, and of democratically accepted law	Conform to maintain respect of impartial spectator judging in terms of community welfare
	6. Morality of individual principles and conscience	Conform to avoid self-condemnation

At age 7, Types 1 and 2 were most prevalent, with Types 4, 5, and 6 virtually nonexistent. By age 16, Types 4, 3, and 5 were most prevalent, in that order, with Type 1 and 2 still dropping off and Type 6 rising.

Kohlberg argued for an explanation of these types not in terms of increased learning of the culture's verbal morality but as successive products of the child's attempt to make sense out of his social experiences. He found evidence that they do not seem to show a steady accretion in a given direction, but to be a series of organizations and reorganizations in which earlier types are replaced by later ones. Evidence for the same sequence of stages has been found in middle- and working-class children, in Protestants and Catholics, in boys and girls, in popular and socially isolated children, and in several different cultures. Interestingly, though all children seem to move through the same sequence of stages—as far as they go—middle-class children progress more rapidly than lower-class children and popular children more rapidly than socially isolated ones. But all children experience conflicts between individual and group needs, which contribute to the development of moral values.

by the child; now he assumes the role of the parents in delivering rewards and punishments to himself. For example, the two-year-old may slap his own wrist and say, "No, no; bad boy" when he is tempted to misbehave or after he has misbehaved. These moral values or standards have been accepted uncritically, but they come to act as inner controls of behavior. When the child fails to measure up to his standards, he may experience shame and guilt. Shame appears to arise earlier than guilt and to hinge on anticipated punishment and disapproval from others, while guilt involves self-criticism and lowered self-esteem rather than the expectation of reprisal from others (Kagan, 1968). In a general sense, conscience development on this early level seems to be a conditioned anxiety response built up by pairing "wrongdoing" with punishment and "right-doing" with reward or approval.

Later, with more advanced intellectual development, the adolescent gradually frees himself from blind acceptance of the moral dictates he has accepted and becomes able to examine them critically—rejecting some, modifying others, and accepting still others (Kohlberg, 1964). The ethically mature person is thus considered an evaluating individual who is capable of making moral decisions on the basis of value assumptions he has thought through and consciously accepted as valid. However, such mature conscience development is a long and difficult process which is fully accomplished only under highly favorable circumstances. In fact, Rogers (1964) concluded from his study of patients in psychotherapy that the usual adult retains many values which he has uncritically accepted from others as "right." Only as he learns to rely on his own valuing processes in constructing his value patterns does he achieve mature conscience development.

SUMMARY AND A LOOK AHEAD

In this chapter we have looked at *what* comes *when* in the development of a human being after birth. We have seen that the general direction of development is toward the actualization of potentialities, that development normally proceeds in an orderly fashion through predictable stages (though not at an even rate), and that the quality of development at each stage is limited by what has gone before. Growth from birth to maturity is in the direction of increasing differentiation, integration, and complexity and includes development from dependence to self-direction, from impulsiveness to self-discipline, from ignorance to knowledge, from incompetence to competence, from diffuse sexuality to heterosexuality, from amorality to morality, and from self-centeredness to a concern for both self and others. The rate and quality of development depend both on the genetic timetable and on facilitating and inhibiting environmental conditions; the developmental tasks of each life period also are set both by genetic programing, through maturation, and by the sociocultural environment. There seem to be critical periods, especially in the early years, when appropriate stimulation and practice are required if genetic potentials for sensory-motor abilities, social attachment, and intelligence are to develop normally; even neurological development seems to require both genetic instructions and certain types of experience.

Intellectual development is especially dependent on the quality and timing of experience; the particular sociocultural environment sets limits on the cognitive skills that the child can develop, even with maximum genetic potential. Our human capabilities for language and abstraction make it possible for us to transform and re-create the environment in which we live and thus to be far less limited by the natural environment than are other species; as a child acquires language, a store of concepts, and the ability to manipulate symbols, he becomes increasingly able to delay and control his responses to environmental demands and to use the environment for his own purposes instead of simply reacting to or being controlled by it.

Emotional development follows a characteristic sequence of increasing differentiation and complexity and increasing ability to control overt expressions of emotion. The presence of typical emotional responses in blind and deaf children attests to the strong genetic component in emotional development; as with other aspects of development, however, it is the sociocultural environment, through reward and approval of some forms of expression and not others, that determines the patterns of emotional expression that become typical of members of the society.

Social development shows perhaps the widest range of variety of all. The presence of aggressive and nonaggressive groups, of cooperative and competitive groups, and of widely differing sex-role standards in different societies indicates how heavily such traits depend on learning and how little their form is limited by genetic "human nature."

Studies of conscience development show that there is a typical sequence in the child's capacity for making moral judgments and controlling his own moral behavior. Here, too, the precise timing and the concepts and responses actually learned depend on what the environment provides.

In our study of human development, we have now looked at the determinants of development—heredity, environment, and self—and at the typical patterns and sequences in development. In the final chapter in this group we shall try to distinguish between healthy and unhealthy development and delineate conditions that influence development in one direction or the other.

Key terms used in this chapter include:

differentiation, integration, complexity (p. 72)
developmental sequences (p. 78)
developmental tasks (pp. 79-80)
maturation, readiness (p. 81)
simple, associative learning (p. 82)
complex, cognitive learning (p. 82)
critical periods (p. 84)
imprinting, positive and negative mechanisms (pp. 84-85)
sensory-motor development (pp. 88-89)
intermeshing of physical and psychological development (p. 89)
intellectual development (pp. 90-93)
emotional development, differentiation of emotions (pp. 94-96)
social development (pp. 96-102)
sex-role development, sex-role preference, sex-role adoption, sex-role identification
    (pp. 98-100)
conscience development (pp. 100-102)

Chapter 4

HEALTHY AND FAULTY DEVELOPMENT

Variations in Development
Early Conditions Conducive to Faulty Development
Early Conditions Fostering Healthy Development

Up to this point we have examined development in terms of relatively objective data—the key determinants and the general patterning of development. Now as we turn to an examination of healthy and faulty development, we are inevitably faced with the problem of making value judgments—of deciding what is desirable and what is undesirable.

On a biological level, we have relatively well-defined norms for height, weight, blood pressure, glandular balance, and other aspects of bodily development and functioning. On a psychological level, too, we have norms for infancy and early childhood which provide us with guidelines for assessing development. Beyond this point, however, we lack adequate criteria for evaluating the enormous variations we find in psychological development. In essence, we have no "ideal model" by which we can gauge whether the personality development of a given individual is faulty or healthy. For example, if an 18-year-old youth is fascinated by mathematics but shows no interest in girls, should we consider his development faulty? If he sees no value in competitive achievement and does not care to strive for status, is he showing faulty development? Answers to such questions require value judgments—

there are no scientific data on which we can base an adequate answer.

In this chapter we shall first deal with the nature of developmental variations and the problem of defining "healthy development"; then we shall note some of the forms which faulty development may take; and finally we shall examine some of the specific conditions that commonly lead to healthy or faulty development.

VARIATIONS IN DEVELOPMENT

It is apparent that people differ from each other in physical appearance, rate of growth, intelligence, temperament, interests, attitudes, and almost any characteristic that could be named. Some of these differences, such as sex differences, are qualitative—differences in kind. But in most ways people differ quantitatively, or in degree. Everybody has *some* intelligence, *some* height, and *some* musical ability, for example, but certain individuals have more than others.

As psychologists use the term, a *trait* is any distinguishable and relatively enduring characteristic of the individual. A given trait may be inclusive or general (such as intelligence) or highly specific (such as an interest in tennis); it may refer to biological or psychological structure or functioning; and it may be determined primarily by heredity or environment. Going a step further, we may define *personality* as the individual's unique pattern of traits—the pattern that distinguishes him as an individual and accounts for his unique and relatively consistent ways of interacting with his environment.[1]

Nature of Developmental Variations

Variations may occur from one individual to another in (1) the *nature* of a given trait, such as blood type or skin color, (2) the *differentiation* or extent to which a given trait is developed, as in ability to do abstract thinking, (3) the *integration* of traits or harmony among them, as between self-image and self-ideal, and (4) the overall *pattern* of traits, which we have referred to as personality.

Two additional aspects of trait variability are of immediate interest as background information for evaluating development—the patterning of trait variability among groups of people and the significance of trait variations.

Patterning of trait variability. In measuring individual differences, psychologists find that traits typically are distributed among the population along a continuum, with most measures clustering around a midpoint and the number of cases rapidly falling off toward either extreme of the range.

This pattern can be seen pictorially in the graph at the bottom of this page; psychologists refer to it as a *normal distribution*. In any large group selected at random, most traits—intelligence, artistic ability, height, sociability, introversion, and so on—would be distributed according to this pattern.

Of course, if we measure personality traits in a selected sample of the population rather than a random one, we may obtain a *skewed* distribution. For example, intelligence scores of a group of third-year graduate students in physics would be expected to cluster toward the high end of the intelligence scale. On the other hand, the intelligence scores of school dropouts might cluster in the lower half of the intelligence scale. Thus we can compare group variations in given traits as well as trait variations among individuals; similarly, we can compare the score of a given individual with the scores of a particular group in which we may be interested. The concept of the patterning of trait variability is thus a highly useful one in understanding variations in development.

[1]This does not mean that the individual's behavior is determined solely by his personality make-up. Given behavior is always the result of the situation and other "outer" determinants as well as of "inner" determinants.

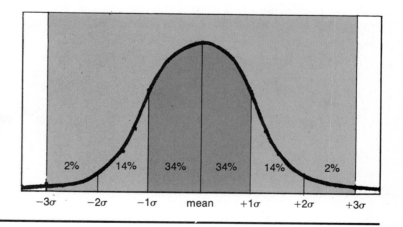

THE NORMAL CURVE OF DISTRIBUTION

In any normal distribution, no matter how widely or narrowly the scores are scattered, about 68 per cent of the cases fall within the middle third of the range—statistically within one standard deviation (σ) on either side of the mean. Virtually all the cases fall within three standard deviations either side of the mean.

2%   14%   34%   34%   14%   2%

-3σ -2σ -1σ mean $+1\sigma$ $+2\sigma$ $+3\sigma$

Significance of trait differences. The significance of developmental variations depends upon the particular trait in question, the degree of possession of the trait, and its relation to the total trait pattern.

It is apparent that some traits have far more significance for human behavior than others. For example, intelligence is far more important than an interest in art when it comes to determining a person's behavior and role in the group. General traits are usually more important than specific ones, since they influence behavior in a far wider range of situations. For example, specific traits such as fear of heights are likely to operate only in a relatively small range of situations; while general traits such as self-control and intelligence are significant in almost every situation a person encounters. If the individual's trait position is very much above or below the average, the trait in question is likely to play a more important role in his behavior than if his trait position is near the norm. Extreme variations in intelligence, for example, whether above or below the average, have implications that extend into most areas of the individual's life. The same thing is true of upper and lower extremes of honesty, self-confidence, and other inclusive traits.

The extent to which a given trait influences behavior also depends upon the way it is related to the individual's overall trait pattern. For example, a high degree of aggressiveness means something quite different in the context of a personality with strongly developed ethical values from what it does when it occurs with poorly developed ethical values and a high level of hostility toward society. Similarly, low intelligence in a girl of outstanding physical beauty may have a quite different effect on her life than low intelligence coupled with unattractive physical attributes.

When we consider the almost limitless variety of traits and trait patterns, we gain some perspective on the vast range of individual variations in personality development. Now the problem arises of assessing such variations in terms of their desirability —in terms of what we mean by "healthy" and "faulty" development.

The Problem of Defining "Healthy" Development

Various views of healthy development have been advanced. *One* popular view considers development as healthy when there is no apparent physical or psychological pathology and no marked deviation from the average of the group. A *second* view considers development as healthy to the extent that there is an optimal realization of the individual's potentialities; lack of pathology or deviation is not sufficient. A *third* approach to healthy development is to set up criteria—such as autonomy or a realistic frame of reference—which are commonly agreed upon as essential for psychological health.

"Normal" vs. "optimal" as healthy. Viewing healthy development as absence of disease or pathology is a projection of the medical view that physical health is a lack of disease. Since the human system tends toward normality and health—on both biological and psychological levels—health is viewed as an almost universal phenomenon under favorable conditions, and development is considered "normal" or "healthy" when it does not deviate markedly from the norm.

Such a negative approach, however, is not very satisfactory when dealing with personality development. Take the case of an adolescent, for example, who is making passing grades in his schoolwork, getting along well with his classmates and teachers, and showing no indications of delinquency or serious maladjustment, but drifting along and using only a fraction of his superior intellectual ability. Such an adolescent is not sick but is he healthy?

Considerations such as this have led to a more positive view of healthy development. As defined by the World Health Organization, health is "a state of complete physical, mental, and social well-being and not merely the absence of disease or infirmity." Here healthy development, by implication, would go beyond the average or norm in the direction of optimal development —toward the "fulfillment of potential" and "self-actualization."

The concept of optimal development is a meaningful one, but we are a long way from agreeing on just what pattern of traits or behaviors constitutes optimal development. What people regard as desirable and optimal inevitably reflects both the customs, demands, beliefs, and values of the larger society and the personal beliefs and values of the person making the judgment. Thus optimal development is a general principle and not something we are yet in a position to define and measure precisely. But as a principle, it appears to be gaining adherents as modern science enables man to eliminate many conditions long assumed to be an inevitable part of the human condition and to specify and create conditions conducive to fuller development of physical and psychological potentialities.

Multiple criteria approach. Neither a view of health as freedom from pathology nor a definition in terms of optimal development solves the problem of actually specifying what development is healthy. For neither approach supplies us with criteria for evaluating development in given cases.

In an attempt to supply such criteria, two major approaches have been utilized. The first derives such criteria from the conceptual framework of a particular model of man. For example, psychoanalysis provides a general conceptual framework for evaluating development in terms of progression through psychosexual (libidinal) stages and the development of ego and superego.

The second approach consists of arbitrarily listing qualities—for example, self-confidence and a realistic frame of reference —which appear to be components of healthy development. Such lists, of course, vary considerably depending upon the theoretical and value orientation of the investigator constructing the list. Yet there are a number of characteristics which are common to most

lists and on which most investigators would agree. One comprehensive approach of this type by Jahoda (1958) is summarized in the chart on p. 108.

Although these criteria provide useful guides for assessing development, they are limited both qualitatively and quantitatively. By *qualitative* limitations, we refer to the somewhat arbitrary nature of any list not based upon "hard" scientific data. Why these criteria rather than others? The emphasis on autonomy and self-actualization in Jahoda's list, for example, clearly reflects values of our particular culture. By *quantitative* limitations we refer to the lack of specification. Again referring to the Jahoda list, what perception is "objective"? How much self-direction is "adequate"? How much stress tolerance is "good"? Who is to say, and on what basis? And how wide a variation is "normal"? The problem of the overall patterning of such criteria in a healthy personality is also left unspecified. And finally, in applying such criteria to a given case, it is apparent that allowances would have to be made for age, sex, social class, and other sources of variation.

The whole problem is further complicated by the fact that as we learn more about human development, we keep changing the criteria by which we make judgments. The quiet, polite little boy who never expressed anger was admired in the Victorian era but today is usually regarded as inhibited and out of touch with his real feelings. Similarly, with improved educational procedures, the intellectual development that is average or normal for a six-year-old today may be considered indicative of mental retardation in the world of the year 2000.

Although we need much more knowledge about man's potentialities and needs before we can establish adequate standards for evaluating an individual's psychological development, the basic dimensions and the criteria which we have examined appear to point to the variables with which we are going to have to deal. Now let us turn briefly to an examination of some forms of faulty development, about which there is more

CRITERIA OFTEN USED IN ASSESSING "MENTAL HEALTH"

ATTITUDES TOWARD THE SELF	Realistic self-concept, objectivity about self, clear sense of identity, self-acceptance.
GROWTH, DEVELOPMENT, ACTUALIZATION	Motivation toward growth and involvement, actualization of potentialities.
INTEGRATION	Harmony among parts of personality, a unifying philosophy of life, good stress tolerance.
AUTONOMY	Self-direction, with perception of self as an organic part of larger whole.
PERCEPTION OF REALITY	Objective perception, free from need distortion, combined with social sensitivity.
ENVIRONMENTAL MASTERY	Adequacy in love, work, and play, with ability to solve new problems.

Adapted from Jahoda, 1958.

agreement. Many of our ideas about healthy development, in fact, have been derived by inference from what we know about faulty development.

Forms of Faulty Development

Although the basic tendency of the human system is toward health and normality, it is all too evident that this tendency does not automatically assure healthy development. Three common types of unhealthy psychological development—more than one of which may occur in a given individual—have been delineated: (1) arrested development, (2) special vulnerability, and (3) distorted development. In one way or another, all of these impair the individual's coping ability and adaptation.

Arrested development. As the individual develops his potentialities—intellectual, emotional, and social—he achieves increasingly diversified and flexible resources for coping with inner and outer demands. Thus the mature and more highly differentiated person is far more capable of dealing with new and complex problems than is a less well differentiated adult or a child.

It is doubtful, of course, that any human being has ever achieved full differentiation of his potentialities in all areas of development. In speaking of arrested development, however, we are concerned with immaturities and fixations that seriously impair the individual's adjustive resources. For example, the adolescent who remains emotionally dependent on his mother and avoids interaction with anyone his own age shows arrested development that is likely to impair his ability to cope with the demands of choosing a satisfactory mate and establishing a happy marriage. The person who never learns to delay gratification of his impulses lacks a necessary prerequisite for mature planning and choice.

Immaturities may be pervasive or limited to certain facets of one's development. For example, an individual may show a high degree of differentiation and effectiveness in intellectual development but be immature in emotional and social development—as reflected in impulsivity, inability to feel deeply about others, and arrested conscience development. On a more restricted level we might cite the case of the young adult who throws temper tantrums and sulks when he does not get his way, or the middle-aged Don Juan who is unable to form a stable or meaningful heterosexual relationship. Sometimes development appears to be totally arrested in a given area at an immature level of functioning; more commonly, we move ahead but carry a residue of immature attitudes and behavior patterns into later developmental stages.

Sometimes, as a consequence of brain damage or excessive stress, development undergoes *dedifferentiation.* Brain damage, for example, may result in the loss of previously differentiated intellectual abilities; or a young child may regress to baby talk and bed-wetting when a new baby enters the family picture. In the latter case, such regression or dedifferentiation is usually temporary. Under certain conditions, however—as in senile brain deterioration associated with old age—regressive trends may become more pronounced with time.

Special vulnerabilities ("weak spots"). Life experiences, especially during early stages of development, sometimes leave a lowered resistance to certain types of stress. On a biological level, a severe case of influenza may lead to increased vulnerability to later respiratory disorders; or injury to the kidneys may leave the individual vulnerable to later stresses that happen to involve these organs.

On a psychological level, early traumatic experiences may leave "psychic wounds" which never completely heal, thus leaving the individual unusually vulnerable to certain types of stressful situations. For example, a child who has been deserted by his parents may have unusual difficulty in coping with rejection by others in later life. Or a daughter who has shared her mother's intense feelings of devaluation and hurt during a traumatic divorce may suffer a "nervous breakdown" later when her own marriage does not appear to be working out. Although there is no way to predict the lasting effects of trauma in a given case—in fact, trauma that the individual can handle adequately may lead to increased resistance to stress—it would appear that traumas occurring during any life period may leave a residue of increased vulnerability if experienced as acutely threatening and self-devaluating. Probably most of us have a more or less vulnerable "Achilles' heel" as a result of earlier life trauma.

Distorted development. Sometimes development proceeds in grossly undesirable forms or directions. Such distortions in development are readily apparent on biological as well as psychological levels. Children born without lower limbs, with a cleft palate, or with other physical anomalies are examples of such distortions on a biological level.

On a psychological level distorted development is somewhat more difficult to pinpoint since, as we have noted, we have no model of the ideal man to use as a base of reference. Although allowance must be made for a range of normal variation, society is eventually forced to draw the line—usually in terms of the consequences of such behavior in relation to the purposes and goals of the group. Thus most societies consider professional criminals, ruthless demagogues, chronic juvenile delinquents, homosexuals, and individuals suffering from certain chronic mental disorders as representing distortions in development. Grossly inaccurate assumptions or unreasonable attitudes would also be regarded as reflecting distorted psychological development. The extreme racist, the youth who commits a murder for "kicks," the adolescent girl who turns to prostitution to support her drug habit, and the confidence man who preys on the elderly—all these show distorted development.

In the preceding discussion we have noted the nature of developmental variations, have pointed up the problem of defining "healthy development," and have categorized the ways in which development can get off the track. In the two sections which follow we shall summarize first several conditions known to be conducive to faulty development, and then several conditions whose influence is in the direction of healthy development. In both instances our focus will be on early development rather than on adulthood or later maturity.

EARLY CONDITIONS CONDUCIVE TO FAULTY DEVELOPMENT

As an introduction to their *Rousseau and Revolution* Will and Ariel Durant (1967) ask this dramatic question:

"How did it come about that a man born poor, losing his mother at birth and soon deserted by his father, afflicted with a painful and humiliating disease, left to wander for twelve years among alien cities and conflicting faiths, repudiated by society and civilization, repudiating Voltaire, Diderot, the Encyclopedie and the Age of Reason, driven from place to place as a dangerous rebel, suspected of crime and insanity, and seeing, in his last months, the apotheosis of his greatest enemy—how did it come about that this man, after his death, triumphed over Voltaire, revived religion, transformed education, elevated the morals of France, inspired the Romantic movement and the French Revolution, influenced the philosophy of Kant and Schopenhauer, the plays of Schiller, the novels of Goethe, the poems of Wordsworth, Byron and Shelley, the socialism of Marx, the ethics of Tolstoi, and, altogether, had more effect on posterity than any other writer or thinker of that eighteenth century in which writers were more influential than they had ever been before?" (p. 3)

Although others might not evaluate the influence of Rousseau quite so highly, there is no question but that it has been very far-reaching. Yet the conditions of his early life might have been expected to prevent such development and such influence. This example highlights the multiplicity of variables that affect human development and the enormous difficulty of trying to relate particular environmental "causes" to particular effects. Often the most that we can say is that *under such and such conditions, with a child with these characteristics, variable A will probably exert an influence in direction B.* Our inability to make a more precise prediction is in part a reflection of our ignorance but, equally important, a reflection of the role of the individual in helping to shape his own development.

A further difficulty is added by the necessity of examining one variable or condition at a time (or at most a limited number), whereas the effect of any condition will depend on the total context in which it operates. We can say that the loss of a parent at an early age will tend to be an upsetting and disruptive experience, but its actual effects will depend on the particular child, on his previous relationship to the parent, on what relationships remain or are substituted for the lost ones, and upon whether his life situation is generally stable and supportive or unstable and nonsupportive. Thus the question about Rousseau highlights an exceedingly complex problem for which we do not yet have an adequate answer.

Despite limitations in our knowledge, however, several common conditions have been identified which typically influence development in unhealthy ways: (1) genetic and constitutional defects, (2) early deprivation and trauma, (3) pathogenic family patterns, (4) social pathology, and (5) faulty self-structure. Our primary focus will be on the effects of such conditions upon psychological development—in terms of arrested and distorted development and special vulnerabilities.

Genetic and Acquired Defects

The quality of our bodily equipment is of key importance in our personality development and functioning. Thus defects—whether of genetic or environmental origin—which impair our potential and/or create stressful adjustment problems may lead to faulty psychological development.

As we noted in Chapter 3, any disruption of the patterned sequence of early development may have damaging effects. From a highly simplified view, the sequencing of development can be likened to an assembly line in an automobile plant, except that in biological development there is no way to stop the assembly line. Thus a lack of essential materials or impaired timing may lead to irreparable bodily damage. In general, the time when a particular body part or sub-system is first being differentiated is the time of greatest susceptibility to damage. For example, biological development is most vulnerable to the effects of radiation or drugs during the first third of the prenatal period—the "dangerous 90 days" when body organs and subsystems are differentiating and becoming functional. Malnutrition or other harmful conditions occurring in infancy or childhood may also impair development, but the earlier a harmful influence is exerted the more vulnerable the organism is likely to be and the more irreversible any damage that takes place.

In this country an estimated 7 of every 100 babies who survive one month after birth have some birth defect. About a third of these defects are considered to be of hereditary origin, about a sixth are due to drugs or disease, and the rest—about half—result from unknown causes. Although many such defects are minor, congenital malformations and defects constitute one of the five leading causes of death during childhood (Department of Health, Education, and Welfare, 1965).

Mutant genes. Mutations may be caused by ionizing radiation, X rays, or other agents, including, apparently, some of the man-made pollutants in our air. As we have noted, the effects of gene mutations are usually detrimental. Often, however, such mutations result in relatively minor congenital malformations, such as six toes. But sometimes genetic deviations seriously impair development. In the biochemical disorder of phenylketonuria (PKU), for example, the lack of an enzyme needed for protein metabolism results in the building up of phenylalanine in the blood and serious damage to the brain. Fortunately, this genetic disorder can ordinarily be detected early and controlled by dietary or other medical procedures. In other instances genetic defects appear to make the individual especially vulnerable to particular physical or mental disorders. For example, genetic factors appear to be of significance in predisposing the individual to schizophrenic and other mental disorders under stressful conditions. Gross genetic deviations ordinarily lead to the death of the embryo.

The effects of gene mutations may be apparent at birth, as in various congenital malformations, or may become apparent later. For example, a mutant gene has been identified that causes *retinoblastoma,* or cancer of the eye in childhood; and the progressive nervous system affliction known as *Huntington's chorea,* apparently based on mutant genes, does not usually occur till middle or later life. Fortunately, new advances in genetics—particularly associated with the study of enzymes which carry out the orders genes give for growth—are gradually paving the way for the eradication of many disorders associated with mutant genes (Culliton, 1967).[1]

Prenatal and birth difficulties. Many growth abnormalities are the result of faulty environmental conditions rather than defective genes. Such conditions may operate before, during, or after birth.

Prenatal conditions that can lead to growth defects include nutritional deficiencies, drugs, radiation, disease, and emotional stress. Recent studies have pinpointed protein deficiency in the maternal diet as a cause of lower IQ and other impairments in the offspring. Various drugs, including LSD, and the excessive use of alcohol have been implicated in faulty fetal development, as have German measles, diabetes, tuberculosis, syphilis, and other illnesses of the mother during pregnancy. Ionizing radiations—which produce their effects by killing or maiming cells—may lead to fetal damage (Rugh, 1962).

Birth complications, including prematurity, anoxia, bleeding, and prolonged pressure on the head during difficult delivery, may result in a wide range of growth abnormalities. Damage to the brain is common in such conditions and may lead to mental re-

---

[1] An excellent study of factors associated with impaired development of premature infants is that of Braine, Heimer, Wortis, & Freedman, 1966.

tardation, epilepsy, hyperactivity, learning disabilities, and related difficulties. As one might expect, socioeconomic status has been found to be associated with the incidence of fetal and birth difficulties—the incidence being several times greater among lower socioeconomic class mothers (Pasamanick & Knobloch, 1960, 1961).

Interestingly enough, mothers who are subjected to anxiety and emotional stress during pregnancy appear to have a higher incidence of premature deliveries and complications in delivery (Davids & DeVault, 1962; Davids et al., 1961; Blau et al., 1963; McDonald et al., 1963). Severe maternal stress appears to cause a hyperactive state of the fetus during the later months of pregnancy, and after birth to be reflected in feeding difficulties, sleep problems, and general irritability of the infant (Davids et al., 1961, 1963; Hurlock, 1968).

It has also been shown that the more negative the mother's attitudes toward sex and toward her feminine role, the more likely she is "to experience a spectrum of psychological and physiological problems during pregnancy" (Heinstein, 1967, p. 234). As a consequence of such findings it would appear that the fetus is less well protected than many investigators formerly thought—that a variety of physiological and emotional stresses affecting the mother during pregnancy can have profound effects on the child's early development. Fortunately, the great increase in the public understanding of basic hygiene, the development and widespread use of immunization agents against communicable disease, the increasing attention being given to the care of pregnant women, and the development of more effective methods of diagnosis and treatment for disorders that occur have greatly decreased the incidence of congenital defects and helped to minimize the effects of such handicaps when they do occur.

Physical handicaps acquired after birth. It is estimated that almost a fifth of all youth under 17 suffer from at least one chronic physical handicap—such as allergy, sinusitis or other respiratory ailment, orthopedic impairment, hearing or speech defect, or heart disease (Department of Health, Education, and Welfare, 1965). Accidents, too, take a tremendous toll. An estimated 11 million persons suffer from some chronic defect or impairment resulting from accidental injury, and accidental injuries are the leading cause of death and physical mutilation during the first half of the life span.

Another major source of physical impairment is malnutrition during infancy and early childhood—which can lead to the stunting of physical growth, a lack of energy for normal learning, and lowered resistance to disease. A number of recent studies have also found lowered mental ability in children who were severely underfed during the early months of infancy (Dobbing, 1967; Bladeslee, 1967). The effects of malnutrition, occurring before or soon after birth, are often irreversible—as contrasted with those of malnutrition in adults, which can be in large part compensated for if the malnutrition has not been too severe and too long sustained. In view of the high incidence of malnutrition in many parts of the world—particularly protein deficiency—such findings give cause for serious concern.[1]

The effects of genetic and acquired defects on development vary considerably. Except in cases where the defect seriously lowers the individual's coping resources, the critical factor for development is not the handicap itself but the reaction of the individual and the group to it. A person's body as he perceives and evaluates it is highly important in determining his feelings of adequacy and esteem. The possession of physical traits considered desirable by one's family and social group fosters a favorable self-image while the possession of traits considered undesirable tends to lead to self-devaluation. Particularly during adolescence, physical deviations considered undesirable by the group are likely to create problems; in

---

[1] It is estimated that 60 per cent of the world's preschoolers lack sufficient protein food (*Science News*, 1967a).

fact, even minor deviations, such as freckles or a long nose, may be magnified out of all proportion by the individual.

Under reasonably favorable environmental conditions, even severe handicaps are often dealt with effectively. Helen Keller is a classic example. She became totally deaf and blind at the age of nineteen months but was able to become a highly educated, compassionate, and capable human being. After World War II, she helped blinded veterans to make the difficult adjustment to a useful life without sight. Thus despite the very real difficulties posed by physical handicaps, it is often possible to lead a productive and satisfying life.

Maternal Deprivation and Early Trauma

We saw in the last chapter that there are early critical periods during which certain kinds of stimulation are essential for normal development. When this stimulation is lacking, intellectual, emotional, and social development may be impaired. Similarly, noxious stimuli which inflict serious injury or damage upon the organism may impair physical and/or psychological development. The term *trauma* is used to refer to psychological as well as somatic injury or damage; in the present context, it is psychological trauma with which we are primarily concerned.

Since childhood is the foundation period of life, maternal deprivation and early psychic trauma may have long-range consequences for development. But children differ considerably in their vulnerability to such stresses. Some children are badly damaged by maternal deprivation or traumatic experiences, whereas others appear to survive such experiences with minimal damage and to achieve adequate adjustment as adults.

Although deprivation and trauma often go hand in hand—as when a child loses a parent—we will consider them separately for purposes of discussion.

Maternal deprivation. The effects of early maternal deprivation on children have been shown most dramatically in studies of infants in institutions. Even as late as 1919, approximately half the mortality rate for institutionalized infants under one year of age was attributed to *marasmus*—a condition in which, despite adequate physical care, infants seemed to "waste away." Since then, institutions have endeavored to provide more adequate personal care and stimulation, to arrange early foster-home placements where feasible, and to encourage long-term dependable relationships with individual adults for children who must remain institutionalized.

Institutions today vary considerably in their facilities, but even good institutional care is likely to fall short of a desirable home environment in the stimulation, guidance, and affectional relationships it can offer an infant during his early critical years. The effects of one modern institutional environment—as contrasted with a home environment—were studied by Provence and Lipton (1963). Among the effects manifested by these infants, as summarized on page 114, were apathy, lack of social responsiveness, a lag in language development, and failure to develop a normal sense of self. With more severe and pervasive deprivation, development may be even more severely retarded. In fact, Dennis (1960) found that over 60 per cent of the 2-year-olds in a Teheran orphanage—where stimulation was minimal—were not yet sitting up alone and 85 per cent of the 4-year-olds were not yet walking alone.

The long-range damage that may follow from early deprivation has been documented by many studies. One of the studies that first called attention to such long-term damage was a follow-up of 38 adolescents who had been institutionalized from three weeks to three years of age. At the time of the study, sixteen to eighteen years after discharge from the orphanage, 4 were diagnosed as psychotic, 21 as having a character disorder, 4 as mentally retarded, and 2 as psychoneurotic. Only 7 had achieved adequate adjustment (Beres & Obers, 1950). More recently Skeels' follow-up study of institutionalized children (1966), as reported

INFANTS IN INSTITUTIONS

Provence and Lipton (1963) compared a group of year-old infants in families with a comparable group who had spent their first year in an institution. The personnel had done their best to provide warmth as well as physical care, but the infants had not had personalized, loving care from one maternal figure. Provence and Lipton report:

"At the end of the first year of life the institutionalized infants who were studied were different in many ways from the babies reared in a family environment. The general impairment of their relationship to people and the weakness of their emotional attachments were prominent abnormalities in their development and behavior. They rarely turned to the adult for help, comfort, or pleasure. There were no signs of a strong attachment to any one person, nor any signs of the development of a sense of trust in the adults who cared for them. The capacity for anticipation of the future and the ability to defer immediate gratification of needs were impaired. . . .

"The retardation of speech and the meagerness of all forms of communication were striking. They used no words, had no names for people or objects, and used very few vocal signals to express a feeling or to indicate a need. Their play with toys was impoverished, poorly elaborated, and repetitive; it lacked the signs of pleasure, interest, and experimental zest seen in the family babies. Some aspects of their motor behavior were delayed or deviant, although in this area they looked relatively better than in other functions. . . .

"Their behavior did not indicate the normal development of a sense of self. They seemed to have a low investment not only in all aspects of the environment but in themselves as well. They did not turn to such autoerotic activities as thumb sucking or genital play, although all rocked excessively. They had difficulty in being active either in order to make a contact to obtain comfort or pleasure or in order to avoid an unpleasant situation. They appeared virtually defenseless when faced with a painful stimulation." (pp. 159-160)

Provence and Lipton then contrast this picture of deprivation with one of adequate "mothering" and general stimulation:

"In contrast to this picture, a baby who has adequate maternal care develops much and learns many things in the first year of his life. By the time he is a year of age he is upright and interested in walking; he has a spoken language of two or three words; he can communicate his wants and feelings in a variety of ways. He recognizes his mother as a person of special importance, can remember her for a brief time in her absence, and expresses his personal attachment to her. He has learned to know also a few other people whom he may accept as a substitute for the mother for brief periods of time. He enjoys various kinds of playthings and uses them for pleasure, for learning, and for expression of feelings. While he is still quite dependent upon others for many things, he has already developed ways of doing some things for himself, of being active about mastering anxiety, of solving simple problems, and at times of comforting himself when he is upset. He has some awareness of himself as distinct from others; he has a 'provisionally organized personality.'" (pp. 160-161)

in the previous chapter, found comparable results and showed dramatically how an enriched experience can change the final picture. In general, growing up in an institution, with restricted experience, results in lower intelligence, less capability in attending to tasks and coping with problems, and less adequate interpersonal relations in adolescence and adulthood.

By far the greatest number of infants subjected to maternal deprivation are not separated from their mothers but suffer from inadequate maternal care at home. Such "masked" deprivation can be as devastating as institutionalization (Prugh & Harlow, 1962; Bullard *et al.,* 1967). But whether the source of deprivation is actual separation from the mother or masked deprivation in the home, the end result is retardation in the overall development of the infant. The actual nature and extent of the damage appear to depend upon: (1) the age at which deprivation first occurs, (2) the extent and duration of the deprivation, (3) the substitute care, if any, that is provided, and (4) the constitutional make-up of the infant (Yarrow, 1965).

Early, intensive, and long-continued maternal deprivation may never be overcome, though good substitute care introduced early enough can go far to minimize or even reverse the damage, especially in a child with good resilience and constitutional balance.

Traumatic experiences. All children are exposed to crises and anxiety-arousing situations during the course of growing up. Some have serious accidents or suffer the loss of a parent. A few are grossly mistreated. Some undergo rejection, sexual attack, or other severely self-devaluating or frightening experiences. Usually the traumatic episode comes suddenly as an emergency. Unexpectedly, the child finds himself in a new situation in which he sees either the world or himself as unpredictable and dangerous because he does not understand what is happening or how to cope with it.

One form of traumatic experience that may befall a child is separation from or loss of parents. Though research on temporary separation has been limited, there usually seem to be no permanent detrimental effects from short-term separation, especially when the child is left in familiar surroundings or with familiar caretakers.

The effects of long-term or permanent separation from one or both parents are more complex. When the separation occurs as early as 3 months, the infant's emotional upset seems to be primarily a reaction to strangeness and environmental change, and the infant usually adapts readily to a surrogate mother figure. Once attachment behavior has developed, however, the emotional hurt may be deeper and more sustained, and the child may have greater difficulty in adjusting to the change in his life situation. It would appear that the infant is most vulnerable to long-term separation or loss occurring between about 7 months and 3 years of age (Yarrow, 1964; 1965). The long-term consequences of such loss appear to depend not only on the time of occurrence itself but also on the particular child, the intensity of his previous relationship with

the parent, and the nature of subsequent parental care. Where the child is then reared by one parent, further difficulties such as lack of an adequate parental model may occur.

The magnitude of the problem of separation from parents is indicated by the finding that some 10 million children in the United States have had the experience of losing at least one parent through separation, divorce, or death; this is approximately 1 child in 7 (Witmer, 1965). We shall deal with the consequences of divorce on children in Chapter 10.

Most traumatic experiences in childhood are probably of minor significance and transient in their effects, because the child finds adequate ways of dealing with setbacks and challenges. In fact, as we have seen, normal psychological development can take place only if there is stimulation and challenge from the environment. Often the after-effects of trauma depend in large part on the support given the child by significant persons in his world—"bad things can turn into good things." However, intensely traumatic experiences or a series of traumatic experiences that keep a child off balance are likely to bring disruption instead of growth and may have serious long-term consequences.

Pathogenic Family Patterns

Pathogenic family patterns may be approached in terms of either: (1) parent-child patterns, or (2) total patterns of family interactions and relationships—the family as a group system. Thus we can study the effects on the child of parental overpermissiveness or rejection; or we can study the effects of membership in a "disturbed" or "inadequate" type of family. A recent estimate concludes that 25 per cent of the nation's children come from homes in which the parents are inadequate (Joint Commission on the Mental Health of Children, 1968).

Although there is a good deal written about pathogenic parent-child patterns and pathogenic families, we have only fragmentary information concerning the long-range effects of various family and childrearing patterns. And as we have seen, the task of identifying predictable relationships is complicated by the fact that different children respond somewhat differently to the same conditions, so that we cannot expect to find invariable one-to-one relationships between particular family patterns and later personality characteristics of the child. The further fact that later experiences may either aggravate or counteract early damage also makes firm predictions hazardous at best.

In the discussion which follows we shall deal with some pathogenic family patterns found to be harmful in a number of studies. In view of the complexities involved, however, care should be taken in applying these findings to the understanding or prediction of particular cases.

Faulty parent-child relationships. Sometimes parents do too much, not letting the child do his own growing; sometimes they do too little, not providing him with a stimulating environment or with the love and guidance he needs; sometimes they encourage and inadvertently reward inappropriate and distorted behavior patterns. Whatever they do, their methods tend to be fairly consistent during the child's growing years (Schaefer & Bayley, 1960).

On a more specific level, several types of faulty parent-child patterns have been consistently found in the background of children evidencing emotional disturbances and other types of faulty development. These patterns are interrelated, and the effects of a given pattern depend upon the total family context.

1. *Rejection.* By rejection we refer to the negative end of the acceptance-rejection continuum—involving a basic nonacceptance of the child and the withholding of love. Rejection may be manifested in various ways— by physical neglect, invidious comparisons with other children, ridicule, refusing the child attention, denying him affection, not spending time with him, obvious lack of respect for him and his feelings, lack of interest

in him, covert or overt hostility, and coercive control techniques, such as intimidation. In a minority of cases it involves cruel and abusive treatment. Parental rejection may be partial or complete, passive or active, behavioral or verbal, and subtly or overtly cruel.

The effects of rejection vary considerably depending upon the degree of rejection, whether both parents are involved, the degree of acceptance and affection shown by the nonrejecting parent or other adults, the way the parent's behavior is perceived and interpreted by the child, and other aspects of the child's total life situation. In general, however, rejected children tend to be anxious, insecure, low in self-esteem, jealous, attention seeking, aggressive, hostile, lonely, and slow in conscience development (Pepitone & Wilpizeski, 1960; Sears *et al.,* 1957; Bandura & Walters, 1959; Siegelman, 1965; Jenkins, 1968). In later life many rejected children appear to have serious difficulty in giving and receiving love and affection.

Several of these characteristics merit further consideration. Since the child's self-concept is largely a reflection of the way "significant others" react to him, it is not surprising that parental rejection tends to foster a devaluated self-concept; or, as Coopersmith (1967) found, "feelings of personal insignificance." If his parents do not see him as being of worth, it is difficult for the child to view himself in a positive way and to develop the feelings of self-esteem needed for confident interactions with his world. Since the rejected child is not rewarded by praise and encouragement for desirable behavior, it is also more difficult for him to discriminate between approved and disapproved behavior. Nor does he have the motivation of wanting to imitate or please his parents because of admiring and identifying with them. Presumably for these reasons, rejected children have been found to be slower in conscience development than accepted children (Sears *et al.,* 1957).

In view of their low self-esteem, it is hardly surprising that rejected children tend to need constant reassurance and often try to obtain it by attention-getting behaviors, such as showing off; or that later, as young adults, they are much more sensitive to social censure than children coming from a background of acceptance (Heilbrun *et al.*, 1966). The frustration created by neglect and rejection may also lead to hostile, aggressive behavior; the most overtly aggressive and poorly controlled behavior seems to result when the rejecting parent is both hostile and permissive toward the child (Bandura & Walters, 1959; Becker, 1964).

Baldwin (1955) found that rejected children tended to be less alert mentally and to do poorer schoolwork. Exploring this theme further, Hurley (1965) has hypothesized that the common core of discourage-

ment and unpleasant emotional climate has a general inhibiting and suppressing effect on the child's curiosity and intellectual functioning. Whether or not we fully subscribe to Hurley's hypotheses, it is of interest to note that he found parental rejection associated with diminished intelligence during early school years, particularly for mother-daughter relationships. And we probably would agree with his conclusion that his findings tend to tie in with "many strands of evidence suggesting that punitive, coercive, and repressive interpersonal experiences have a brutalizing and intellectually impoverishing influence upon humans." (1965, p. 28)

Rejection is not a one-way street, and the child may reject his parents whether or

"BATTERED CHILDREN"

Although most parents try to protect their children from hurt, a minority are cruel and abusive. Estimates (based on federal, state, and local statistics) are that some 50,000 to 70,000 infants and young children each year in the United States are severely neglected, cruelly treated, or starved and that over 300,000 children are in foster homes for such reasons (Morris, 1966). In a two-year study of this problem, Earl (1965) found that each year hundreds of the victims die and many others are paralyzed, physically deformed, or made mentally retarded as a consequence of physical damage. The following are examples of the cases he found:

A 29-month-old boy whose mother claimed he was a behavior problem beat him with a stick and screwdriver handle, dropped him on the floor, beat his head on the wall or threw him against it, choked him to force his mouth open to eat, and burned him on the face and hands. After a severe beating the mother found the child dead.

A blond, blue-eyed four-year-old girl was admitted unconscious to a hospital in the nation's capital. Examination disclosed a fractured skull, and lacerations covering her back, face, arms, and legs. Later she reportedly told the doctors, "Mama kept hitting me with a big black stick."

Because her 2½-year-old daughter did not re-

spond readily enough to toilet training, the mother became indignant and in a fit of temper over the child's inability to control a bowel movement gave her an enema with near scalding water. To save the child's life a doctor was forced to perform a colostomy.

As one might suspect, the parents most commonly involved in such behavior appear to be emotionally unstable or mentally ill. Alcoholic fathers were found in the group, particularly in cases of rape and child beating, but disturbed mothers appeared to be the more common offenders. Some of the children were illegitimate, but the majority were not. Most of the parents had themselves been reared with neglect and brutality and without love and showed little or no evidence of remorse for their cruel behavior.

A hopeful note is sounded here by the findings of Kadushin and his associates (1967), who interviewed the adoptive parents of 91 children who had been removed from their parents by court order as a consequence of mistreatment. All the children had been 5 or older when placed for adoption. A majority of the adoptive parents (70 to 80 per cent) believed that the adoption had turned out quite well and that the children had not been seriously damaged by their earlier experiences.

not he is rejected by them. This sometimes occurs when the parents belong to a low-status minority group of which the child is ashamed. The results of such rejection have not been studied systematically but undoubtedly it tends to deny the child needed models, loving relationships, and other essentials for healthy development.

2. Overprotection and restrictiveness. Maternal overprotection or "momism" involves the "smothering" of the child's growth. The mother may watch over the child constantly, prevent him from taking the slightest risk, overly clothe and medicate him, protect him from others, and make up his mind for him at every opportunity. Usually the child is protected from exposure to any kind of family illness or other emergency. Often the parent spends too much time with the child, so that he has little or no exposure to other children. In the case of mother-son relationships, there is often excessive physical contact, in which the mother sleeps with the child for years and is subtly seductive in her relationships with him. Here it is of interest to note that the early study by Levy (1943)—which first drew attention to the problem of "momism" —found that 75 per cent of the abnormally protective mothers had little in common with their husbands. Apparently the mother attempted to gain satisfactions through contact with her son that should normally have been achieved in her marriage. In such cases, it is not uncommon for the mother to call her son "lover" and to encourage him in somewhat typical courting behavior.

Not surprisingly, children of overly protective mothers usually lack self-reliance and the ability to cope realistically with their problems. In a study of the family backgrounds of children referred to a child guidance clinic, Jenkins (1968) found that children characterized as "overanxious" were likely to have an infantilizing, overprotective mother. In shielding the child from every danger, the mother denies him opportunities for needed reality testing and for developing essential competencies. In addition, her overprotection tells him, in effect, that she regards him as incapable of fending for himself. It is not surprising that such children, as adolescents and young adults, often feel inadequate and threatened by a dangerous world. Although girls may also be the victims of parental overprotection, the effects seem to be more serious for boys, tending more to passivity, lack of initiative, and overdependency (Kagan & Moss, 1962).

Closely related to overprotection is restrictiveness. Here the parents exercise maximal control over the child, rigidly enforcing restrictive rules and standards and giving the child little autonomy or freedom for growing in his own way. Whether such complaints were justified or not, Douvan and Adelson (1966) found "parental restrictions" to be the most common complaint of adolescent girls against their parents.

The effects of severe restrictiveness appear to vary considerably, depending on the nature and duration of the restrictions, the age of the child when they are introduced, the sex of the child, and the family context in which the restrictiveness occurs. The effects may not be the same where severe restrictions are introduced early and maintained throughout childhood and into adolescence as where the parents have initially been rather permissive and later "slap on restrictions" because they think the child or adolescent is misusing his freedom. In a review of available research findings, Becker (1964) concluded that while restrictiveness fosters well-controlled, socialized behavior, it also tends to foster fearful, dependent, and submissive behavior, repressed hostility, and some dulling of intellectual striving. In a study of young adult college men, Keniston (1967) has also implicated severe restrictiveness, coupled with other parental inadequacies, as a major cause of alienation.

3. Overpermissiveness (indulgence). Where the home is overly permissive or indulgent, one or both parents may cater to the child's every whim and fail to teach or reward desirable standards of behavior. In essence, the parent surrenders the running of the home to an uninhibited son or daughter. Pollack (1968, p. 28) quotes a permissive father who finally rebelled at the tyranny of his 9-year-old daughter and in a near tantrum exploded with: "I want one thing clearly understood—I live here, too!"

Such overly indulged children have been found to be characteristically spoiled, selfish, inconsiderate, and demanding (Becker, 1964; Watson, 1965). Sears (1961) also found high permissiveness and low punishment in the home positively correlated with antisocial, aggressive behavior, particularly during middle and later childhood. Unlike the rejected, emotionally deprived child, who may find it difficult to enter into warm human relationships, the indulged child enters readily into such relationships but exploits them for his own purposes in much the same way that he has exploited his parents. In dealing with authority, such children are usually rebellious since they have had their own way for so long. Often they approach problems in an aggressive and demanding way and find it difficult to accept present frustrations in the interests of long-range goals. Also the overly indulged child often has little appreciation of goals or rewards because he has never had to work for them.

When he finds that his pampered and protected status in the home does not automatically transfer to the outside world, such a child may suffer confusion and adjustive difficulties, as "reality" forces him to reassess his assumptions concerning himself and his world. As a 25-year-old girl in psychoanalysis reflected:

"The worst mistake my parents made was giving me free rein. I was an only child, so my parents treated me like a queen. They made me think I could always have everything I wanted—not just money, but privileges. I wish they had set some limitation because when I got out in the world I found things different." (Pollack, 1968, p. 28)

4. *Unrealistic demands.* Some parents, particularly middle-class parents, pressure their children toward high-level performance and goals. Often they are extremely anxious for their children to excel in schoolwork, starting the race toward college entrance when the infant is still in the cradle and maintaining the pressure throughout childhood and adolescence.

Although high parental expectations are both common and desirable, they need to be realistic and to take into consideration the capabilities and temperament of the child. Too often such standards become a matter of what the parents value rather than what the child wants to do and achieve. A successful surgeon may have his heart set on having his son become a surgeon; or a father who did not quite make the football team may have his heart set on having his son become an all-American football player. In some instances parental demands are so incompatible with the child's make-up that he is not permitted to be himself but must constantly strive to be somebody that he is not and cannot be. Such instances have been referred to as *misidentification.*

Unrealistic demands may also focus around moral standards—particularly relating to sex. Thus the parents may instill in the child the view that masturbation or any other sexual activity is terribly sinful and can only lead to moral and physical degeneration. The child who has accepted such rigid parental standards is likely to face many guilt-arousing and self-devaluating conflicts. For despite attempts to control their thoughts and actions, many young adolescents engage in masturbation—even when they have been taught to regard it as harmful to their health and a sign that they lack moral strength and self-control. Such anxiety-arousing failures, of course, are devastating to feelings of self-esteem; and such unrealistic attitudes tend to foster rigid, restricted personalities.

Even though parental demands are unrealistic, the child often feels that he must not let his parents down and perhaps that they will not love him if he fails to live up to their expectations. Even if he has the ability to live up to their expectations, he may be under such sustained pressure that little room is left for spontaneity and for his own development as a person; more commonly, he suffers a series of self-devaluating failures and eventually resists or rebels.

In other cases, parental demands are unrealistically low, and the parents do not care what the child does as long as he stays out of trouble and has a reasonably good time. Coopersmith (1967) found that the children of such parents were significantly lower in both achievement and self-esteem than children whose parents had high but realistic expectations for them. Unrealistic standards and demands—either too high or too low—can be important causes of faulty development.

5. *Faulty communication.* Sometimes parent-child problems are rooted in faulty communication, perhaps reflecting the gap in viewpoints between the generations or ineptitude or pathology on the part of the parents.

Some parents are too busy with their own concerns to listen to their children and try to understand the conflicts and pressures they are facing. Others have forgotten that the world often looks quite different to a child or adolescent and that words may mean different things. Hayakawa (1965) cited the following experience with his small daughter:

"Once, when our little girl was three years old, she found the bath too hot and she said 'Make it warmer.' It took me a moment to figure out that she meant, 'Bring the water more nearly to the condition we call warm.' It makes perfectly good sense when you look at it that way."

Another problem is contradictory and inconsistent communications by the parent. For example, the mother who has baked her daughter a birthday cake may insist that the daughter show her appreciation by eating a large piece but later point out that boys don't like girls who are overweight and she should be more careful. Or

the mother may complain that her son does not show his love for her but testily reject his attempts to show affection with the statement that he is too grown up to be acting like a child.

This has been called a *double-bind* experience—one in which the child cannot win. No matter what he does, it is wrong. Although the double-bind phenomenon needs further study before its precise effects on development can be ascertained, it has been found to be more common in the background of emotionally disturbed adolescents and young adults than among those adequately adjusted (Bateson, 1960; Lu, 1962; Mishler & Waxler, 1965; Schuham, 1967).

The inadequate communication patterns which often characterize parent-child interactions in socially disadvantaged families will be discussed later.

6. *Faulty discipline.* Parents have been particularly baffled during recent years with respect to appropriate forms of discipline. Sometimes a misinterpretation of psychological findings and theories has led to the view that all punishment and frustration should be avoided lest the child be warped in his development. In other cases parents have taken the view of "spare the rod and spoil the child" and have resorted to excessively harsh discipline for what they thought was the child's good. And in still other cases, the parents seem to have had no general guidelines, punishing the child one day and ignoring or even rewarding him the next for doing the same thing.

As we have noted in our review of permissiveness, lack of discipline tends to produce a spoiled, inconsiderate, antisocially aggressive child. On the other hand, harsh or overly severe discipline may have a variety of effects, including fear and hatred of the punishing person, little initiative or spontaneity, and a lack of friendly feelings toward others (Watson, 1965; Becker, 1964). When accompanied by rigid moral standards, overly severe discipline is likely to result in a seriously repressed child who lacks spontaneity and warmth and devotes much of his energy to controlling his own unacceptable impulses. Such children often suffer severe self-recrimination and self-punishment for real or imagined mistakes and misdeeds. Overly harsh or severe punishment, combined with general restrictiveness, may also lead to socially deviant behavior (Winder & Rau, 1962) and to rebellion as the child grows older and is subjected increasingly to outside influences which may be incompatible with the views and practices of his parents.

In understanding the effects of punishment, it may be noted that punishment conveys to the child most emphatically the message, "You've failed." For this reason, it is considered important for a parent to make it clear that in disapproving the child's behavior, he is not disapproving or rejecting the child himself.

Inconsistent discipline, as would be expected, makes it difficult for the child to establish stable values for guiding his behavior (Azrin *et al.,* 1963). Also, intermittent punishment and permissiveness for comparable behavior tends to produce highly aggressive behavior on the part of many children (Sears *et al.,* 1957; Rosenthal, 1962). When parents threaten their children for misbehavior but do not carry out their threats, the child soon figures out that his parents do not mean what they say and proceeds to do what he wants to do (Pollack, 1968).

7. Sibling rivalry. When a child feels that more parental love and attention are directed toward a brother or sister than toward himself, or when a new arrival in the family replaces him as the center of attention, personality difficulties commonly ensue. In younger children these changes are typically of a regressive nature; thus the child may wet himself, resort to baby talk, show off, and evidence other behavior designed to elicit parental attention. Not infrequently the child threatens to injure the new baby and may actually pinch or hit him. However, the child soon learns that such open aggression leads to a further deterioration of parental relationships, and usually works out more indirect and covert methods of expressing hostility—such as belittling, tattling, teasing, or referring to the younger sibling with contempt.

Usually undesirable attitudes and reactions can be prevented or alleviated by preparing the child in advance for the advent of the new baby. Even without such preparation, most children make a fairly rapid adjustment to the new situation without apparent long-range damage. In some cases, however, parents do "play favorites" and focus their interest and affection on one child in preference to others. For example, the father may make it very clear that he identifies himself with the accomplishments and behavior of the older son or with the son and not the daughter. If one child is exceptionally attractive or has special talents which lead to accomplishment and recognition, the parents may tend to focus their attention and admiration on the more successful sibling. Such parental patterns, of course, are likely to lead to intense jealousy and to feelings of insecurity and self-devaluation on the part of the less favored sibling.

Although there is actually a dearth of research data on the long-range effects of sibling relationships, it is apparent that sibling interactions involve close interpersonal relationships over a sustained period of time and that siblings serve as close-range models for each other. Where such relationships are fraught with jealousy and hostility or take other undesirable forms—as where an older sibling is an undesirable model—they are likely to have an adverse effect on development. On the other hand, desirable sibling models and emotionally supportive relationships with them may have highly beneficial effects upon development—and even may go far toward compensating for other family deficiencies.

8. Undesirable parental models. Ordinarily, as we have seen, the child's key models are his parents, and their behavior can have a beneficial or detrimental effect on the way the child learns to perceive, think, feel, and act. When parental behavior is based on undesirable moral values

Does violence on TV teach children to be aggressive? The extent to which children imitate what they see was demonstrated in a study in which children saw a film in which an adult hit and kicked a large inflated doll and pounded it with a mallet. All three actions were observed in the children's play a little later, after they had undergone mild frustration (Bandura, Ross, & Ross, 1963a).

or is inconsistent, it provides a faulty model for the child. For example, the parent who sets unrealistic goals for himself or who refuses to face family problems and deal with them realistically provides an undesirable model for the child. Similarly, the parent who lies and cheats or espouses criminal values is an undesirable model, as is the parent who shows a discrepancy between the values he claims to hold and those reflected in his actual behavior. The latter, of course, sets a confusing model for the child as well as an undesirable one. Young people today often criticize their parents for such discrepancies between alleged values and actual behavior.

Parents may also serve as undesirable models when they are emotionally disturbed, mentally ill, addicted to alcohol or drugs, or otherwise inadequate personally and socially. In his extensive study of psychiatric syndromes in children and their relation to family background, for example, Jenkins (1966) found that nearly half of a group of children diagnosed as "overanxious-neurotic" had mothers who were described as neurotic because of extreme anxiety, nervousness, and related symptoms, while the children characterized by habitual delinquent behavior tended to come from a background combining poverty, parental neglect, a bad neighborhood, and an inadequate father figure. Undesirable parental models are undoubtedly an important factor in the tendency for mental disorders, delinquency, crime, and other forms of maladjustment to run in families.

It should be pointed out, however, that there is nothing inevitable in the effects of parental pathology on the child's development. The pathology of one parent may be compensated for by the wisdom and concern of the other; or an alcoholic parent may perhaps serve as a "negative model"—showing the child what he does *not* want to be like. In any event, Kadushin (1967) has cited a number of studies in which children coming from homes with undesirable parental models have grown up into successful and well-adjusted adults. In fact, Victor and Mildred Goertzel, in their book *Cradles of Eminence* (Little, 1962), looked back over the lives of 400 eminent people and found that only 58 had come from warm, supportive, and relatively untroubled homes; the remainder had come from homes that demonstrated "considerable pathology."

Although the reasons for such favorable outcomes are not clear, these findings should be borne in mind as we turn to a brief summary of types of pathological homes—homes characterized by pathogenic interactions in the family as a group.

Pathogenic families. As already indicated, our second approach to identifying the effects of family patterns upon child development focuses on the total family pattern of interaction rather than on specific relationships between the child and one or both of the parents. Again we have the problem of setting up criteria of "pathological," since, as in the case of the individual, we have no model of the "ideal" family.

Several investigators, however, have attempted a typology of disordered families which clearly have a pathogenic influence on child development in our society. For present purposes, we will briefly describe four such types of families.

1. *The inadequate family.* An inade-quate family is characterized by inability to cope with the ordinary problems of family living. It lacks the resources, physical or psychological, for meeting demands that most families can cope with satisfactorily. Consequently, the inadequate family relies heavily upon continued outside assistance and support in resolving its problems. Inadequacy may stem from immaturity, lack of education, mental retardation, or other shortcomings on the part of the parents. Sometimes, of course, demands are so severe that they overtax the adjustive resources of even highly adequate families; but we are concerned here with more typical, usually solvable family problems, such as earning a living, with which most families can deal.

A family that is floundering against odds too great for its resources, for whatever reason, cannot give its children the feeling of safety and security they need or adequately guide them in the development of essential competencies. Nor can financial or other outside assistance be counted on to meet the needs of such families, for families, like individuals, need to feel they are self-directing and basically in control of their own lives. Many socially disadvantaged families fall into this category—the parents often being uneducated, unskilled, and bewildered by the problems with which they are confronted.

2. *The disturbed family.* At all socioeconomic levels we find some parents who because of personal instability or warped development interact with other people in ways that are destructive to others and to themselves. Parents with grossly eccentric and abnormal personalities may keep the home in constant emotional turmoil. In his study of the homes of young schizophrenic patients, Lidz and his associates (1958; 1963) pointed to a type of *marital schism* in which the parents lived in a state of chronic disorder that constantly threatened the continuation of the marriage. Each parent tried to undermine the worth of the other parent in the eyes of the child and subjected him to irrational situations and demands. The mother in such a family, feeling unloved by her husband, might engage in seductive behavior toward her son, or the father toward his daughter. Often the child was made to feel that by showing affection or cooperation toward one parent he was betraying the other; sometimes he was given the thankless role of mediator between the parents. Another pathological pattern identified by Lidz *et al.* (1958) was named *marital skew*. Here the entire family was oriented around the pathology of one or both parents. The marriage was stable but at the expense of rationality in family interactions.

Disturbed homes may involve many other pathological patterns, but such homes appear to have certain characteristics in common: (1) parents who are fighting to maintain their own equilibrium and who are unable to give the child the love and guidance that he needs; (2) exposure of the child to a highly irrational home environment and faulty parental models; and (3) almost inevitably, the enmeshment of the child in the emotional conflicts of the parents at the expense of his own development. In general, it would appear that maladjusted parents who are able to establish a harmonious relationship with each other are less damaging to the child than are maladjusted parents who live in disharmony (Fisher *et al.*, 1959; Bowen, 1960).

3. *The antisocial family.* Here the family is characterized by undesirable moral values, usually leading to conflict with the wider community. In some families the parents are overtly or covertly engaged in behavior which violates the standards and interests of society and may be chronically in difficulty with the law. Such antisocial values usually handicap marital and other family relationships as well as providing undesirable guides for the development of the child.

Children in such families may be encouraged in dishonesty, deceit, and other undesirable behavior patterns; or they may simply observe and imitate the behavior of undesirable parental models. In some cases,

children may develop a high degree of courage, self-discipline, and loyalty to the family group at the expense of identification with the society as a whole. More often, however, the models they see are immature and self-seeking, and the social interactions they observe and take part in are shallow and manipulative—a poor preparation for mature, responsible adulthood. Here it is of interest to note that Langner and Michael (1963) in an extensive study of mental health and mental disorder in a congested urban area found a higher mental health risk for children who saw their parents' character negatively than for those who experienced a broken home.

4. *The disrupted family.* Disrupted families are families that are incomplete as a result of death, divorce, separation, or other conditions involving the loss of a parent. In the 1960 census, almost 17 per cent of the children under 18 in one large city—Los Angeles—were living with only one parent, and in some of the disadvantaged sections of the city the figure ran as high as 40 per cent (Stinson, 1965). This compares with an overall average for the United States of 12.5 per cent (Schlesinger, 1966). The effects of family disruption vary, depending upon a constellation of conditions before and after the disruption. Landis (1960) found divorce much more traumatic for children whose homes had been happy ones prior to divorce than for those who came from unhappy homes. Loss of a mother during the early critical period of socialization is likely to be more detrimental than the same loss at a later age, as we have seen; the loss of a father is likely to be more serious for a son than a daughter.

A number of studies have shown that a disproportionate number of juvenile delinquents and adult criminals come from broken homes. In California, for example, 75 per cent of juvenile delinquents and 50 per cent of inmates of adult penal institutions come from broken homes. However, a high proportion of broken homes are among the economically and socially disadvantaged, and many factors other than father-

or mother-absence in itself contribute to faulty development. In fact, the Langner and Michael study already mentioned (1963) did not find a high risk of later maladjustment associated with broken homes, even though loss of a parent or parents was a highly traumatic experience. In any case, the long-term effects of disruption may be minimized if the remaining family members are able to compensate in part for the missing parent or if the home is reconstituted by a successful remarriage that provides an adequate environment for child rearing.

The preceding categories are by no means discrete and a given family may show a wide range of "symptoms." The important point is that these family patterns have been labeled "disordered" or "pathogenic" because of the high frequency with which they are associated with problems in child development. It should be emphasized again that although healthy parents are more likely than emotionally maladjusted parents to have healthy children, this relation is not inevitable. As Chess, Thomas, and Birch (1965) found:

"We see loving mothers whose children have problems. And we see very sick mothers with healthy and well-adjusted children who are apparently immune to the mother's pathology and the erratic patterns of care." (p. 13)

Most children tend to be wonderfully resilient and able to survive and prosper despite parental mistakes. And often the school and other community agencies can do much toward counteracting faulty patterns in the home.

Social Pathology

When there are conditions in the community or larger society which have a pervasively detrimental effect on the development and behavior of people exposed to them, we speak of *social pathology* because a disordered society rather than a disordered organism is at the root of the trouble. Included here are a wide range of conditions, such as poverty, delinquency and crime, racial prejudice and discrimination, and social disorganization. In some instances an entire society may be considered pathological, as in the case of a military dictatorship which indoctrinates its youth in beliefs and values that lead to intolerance, cruelty, disregard for the rights of others, and glorification of force.

In this country attention has centered in recent years on the deprivations and other undesirable conditions experienced by children growing up in slum areas, especially in the ghetto areas of the big cities, where the effects of prejudice and discrimination are added to those of poverty and social instability. It is with these interrelated problems of low socioeconomic status and racial prejudice that we are concerned here.

Cultural deprivation: the socially disadvantaged child.[1] In 1968 almost 30 million Americans were estimated to be living below the "poverty line," as defined by the Social Security Administration. Although their income was far higher—in absolute terms—than that of the poor in many parts of the world, it was not enough to ensure a decent standard of living in America. As Miller et al. (1967) have pointed out, the term *inequality* is perhaps more applicable in general than *poverty,* for physical deprivation is compounded for the poor by the affluence they see around them and cannot share. This gap between advantaged and disadvantaged, made glaringly apparent through TV and other mass media, represents a major problem for which our society must find a solution.

Adults who are trapped in low-income areas, especially in the big cities, are apt to be chronically submerged in a whole complex of difficult and often insoluble problems, thus lacking both the material and the psychological resources for the

---

[1]The term *socially disadvantaged* has largely replaced the term *culturally deprived* because the children coming from these families do not lack a culture but rather come from a culture which fails to prepare them for competent performance in school and in our contemporary society.

MOTHERS' TEACHING STYLES

Although much has been written about "good" and "bad" parents, there is very little information with respect to the methods by which parents actually teach their children to approach problems and process information. In a study of mothers' teaching styles, Hess and Shipman (1965) made recordings of structured teaching situations in which the mother was to teach the child how to sort a number of small toys. Three examples are given below:

The first mother outlines the task for the child, gives sufficient help and explanation to permit the child to proceed on her own. She says:

"All right, Susan, this board is the place where we put the little toys; first of all you're supposed to learn how to place them according to color. Can you do that? The things that are all the same color you put in one section; in the second section you put another group of colors, and in the third section you put the last group of colors. Can you do that? Or would you like to see me do it first?"

Child: "I want to do it."

This mother has given explicit information about the task and what is expected of the child; she has offered support and help of various kinds; and she has made it clear that she impelled the child to perform.

A second mother's style offers less clarity and precision. She says in introducing the same task:

"Now, I'll take them all off the board; now you put them all back on the board. What are these?"

Child: "A truck."

"All right, just put them right here; put the other one right here; all right put the other one there."

This mother must rely more on nonverbal communication in her commands; she does not define the task for the child; the child is not provided with ideas or information that she can grasp in attempting to solve the problem; neither is she told what to expect or what the task is, even in general terms.

A third mother is even less explicit. She introduces the task as follows:

"I've got some chairs and cars, do you want to play the game?" Child does not respond. Mother continues: "O.K. What's this?"

Child: "A wagon?"

Mother: "Hm?"

Child: "A wagon?"

Mother: "This is not a wagon. What's this?"

The conversation continues with this sort of exchange for several pages. Here again, the child is not provided with the essential information he needs to solve or to understand the problem. There is clearly some impelling on the part of the mother for the child to perform, but the child has not been told what he is to do. There were marked social-class differences in the ability of the children to learn from their mothers in the teaching sessions. (pp. 881-882)

adequate rearing of their children. So it is hardly surprising that one study of 1414 children aged 4 to 6, enrolled in an OEO Head Start project in Boston, found 25 per cent of the children showing severe psychological difficulties ranging from serious behavior problems to psychoses (*Medical World News*, 1968). In general, studies have shown a higher rate and wider range of maladjustment problems for lower-class children, especially boys, than for middle-class children (Glidewell & Swallow, 1968).

Research studies of families in urban slum areas have delineated several prevalent conditions which are detrimental to child development:

1. A lack of many of the cultural artifacts commonly associated with intellectual development and school readiness, such as books, magazines, toys, objects of different sizes, shapes, and colors, and self-instructional materials. Opportunities for the normal development of fine perceptual discriminations and concepts of relation, size, position, and directionality are in short supply. Often such children have never been to a zoo or a museum or a library. They may live only a few miles from an ocean and never have seen it.

2. Limited parent-child communication and language usage. Parents typically speak in short, disconnected sentences and discourage their children from asking questions. There is a lack of the information and general intellectual stimulation which any child needs to interpret and represent his feelings, experiences, and environment as a basis for normal learning and intellectual development.

3. Physical and often arbitrary punishment rather than explanation and persuasion in child discipline, with predictable fear of the parents, often coupled with hostility and resentment. Children are not helped to appraise their own behavior rationally or to evaluate the probable outcomes of alternative courses of action.

4. Noise, overcrowding, and disorganization. Despite the close proximity of many people in such dwellings, there is often little coordinated activity. Only half of the children in one study regularly ate a meal with their parents (Keller, 1963). Constant noise and other stimulation apparently leads to an ability to "tune out"—a valuable protective device for the child in this setting but a habit that may carry over into inattentiveness at school. Family disorganization is also shown in the high incidence of broken homes: almost half of these families lack a father.

5. Inability of parents to serve as effective models and teachers. As Close (1965) has pointed out, "Being born to uneducated, unskilled and bewildered poverty-stricken parents could in itself be a major handicap for even the healthiest of babies." Such parents' own lack of education and constant struggle for survival keep them cut off from the mainstream of the society, and their children have no way of making contact with the many opportunities that society offers.

The adult models in such an environment are apt to try to solve their own problems in restricted, impulsive ways. They do not know how to help their children to meet the demands of school and the broader community. The inability of such parents to instruct their children is well brought out in the study by Hess and Shipman (1965), summarized on page 126. The children, in turn, do not look upon adults as persons to ask questions of or expect help from.

Studies of the results of such conditions,

as compared with typical development in middle-class homes, have revealed a number of limitations and distortions in development. Among these are:

1. Meager and poor-quality language development, with specific limitations in ability to discriminate, label, categorize, and conceptualize.

2. Deficiencies in ability to solve problems and to learn through communicative interaction with adults; slowness, excessive concreteness, and lack of flexibility in intellectual functioning.

3. Inadequate internal controls—reality and conscience controls—and continued dependence on external controls.

4. Motivational difficulties, such as apathy, inability to postpone immediate gratification for long-range goals, and no desire to improve.

5. Indifference toward or active rejection of school values as a result of a mismatch between home and school standards.

6. Self-devaluation, resentment, and no sense of one's ability to achieve or to exert any control over events. Expectation that hard work will not pay and that failure and rebuff in school are inevitable.[1]

The intellectual retardation of many children coming from parents of low educational and economic status is apparent in the preschool years, and by the time they begin kindergarten or first grade, these children, as a group, are about two years behind (Hess & Shipman, 1965). They are usually neither prepared nor motivated to adjust satisfactorily in the typical school environment and tend to fall proportionately farther behind during their school years. As a consequence, they are much more likely than socially advantaged children to become school dropouts. In fact, the great majority of the million or more students who drop out of school each year before completing high school come from socially disadvantaged families;

---

[1]These two summaries are based on several studies, including the following: Clark, 1967; Hunt, 1964; Stodolsky & Lesser, 1967; Miller *et al.*, 1967; Marland, 1965; Pettigrew, 1967.

for children in the Negro ghetto, the chances are that only about 1 in 3 will finish high school. Many of these dropouts then find themselves at a serious disadvantage in an increasingly technological society and forced to take low-paying menial jobs or to seek welfare, thus perpetuating the vicious circle.

Of course, not all disadvantaged families are pathogenic in structure, and a considerable number manage to rear healthy children. But the odds are not in their favor. For aside from their own influence, their children are also subjected to the broader pathological environment around them, with its high incidence of mental illness, delinquency, crime, drug addiction, venereal disease, illegitimacy, broken homes, undesirable models, and pervasive despair. This is especially true in a poverty-stricken area which is also a ghetto.

Prejudice and Discrimination. Discrimination against members of other racial or religious groups is an aspect of our culture decried in theory, yet apparently among our most ingrained habits. In his book dealing with the Negro ghetto, Clark (1965) described the combined effects of ghetto living and racial prejudice on development as follows:

"Human beings who are forced to live under ghetto conditions and whose daily experience tells them that almost nowhere in society are they respected and granted the ordinary dignity and courtesy accorded to others will, as a matter of course, begin to doubt their own worth. Since every human being depends upon his cumulative experiences with others for clues as to how he should view and value himself, children who are consistently rejected understandably begin to question and doubt whether they, their family, and their group really deserve no more respect from the larger society than they receive. These doubts become the seeds of a pernicious self- and group-hatred and the Negro's complex, debilitating prejudice against himself. . . .

"Many Negroes live sporadically in a world of fantasy, and fantasy takes different forms at different ages. In childhood the de-

lusion is a simple one—the child may pretend that he is really white. When Negro children as young as three years old are shown white- and Negro-appearing dolls or asked to color pictures of children to look like themselves, many of them tend to reject the dark-skinned dolls as 'dirty' and 'bad' or to color the picture of themselves a light color or a bizarre shade of purple. But the fantasy is not complete, for when asked to identify which doll is like themselves, some Negro children, particularly in the North, will refuse, burst into tears, and run away. By the age of seven most Negro children have accepted the reality that they are, after all, dark-skinned. But the stigma remains; they have been forced to recognize themselves as inferior. Few if any Negroes ever fully lose that sense of shame and self-hatred." (pp. 63-65)

One index of the toll such conditions take is Harlem's rate of admissions to mental hospitals, which is triple the rate for the rest of New York City (Clark, 1967). Instability, irrationality, and discouragement combine with deprivation of all kinds to give children in such a setting an almost impossible task in trying to learn what is predictable and how to cope with it. For such children, the key goal too often comes to be to justify one's existence rather than to fulfill it.

It is against this background that the movement toward black power has developed, with its emphasis on "Black is beautiful" and its insistence on educational, political, and economic equality for black people. It is essentially an attempt to replace self-hatred and a "victim image" with a sense of self-worth and dignity and of potential power over one's own destiny.

Through the centuries in most parts of the world, prejudice and inequality have usually been accepted blindly or regarded as inevitable. Despite our heritage, our own history is replete with examples of prejudice and discrimination against minority groups which, like other forms of cruelty and tyranny, have debased the victims, the practitioners, and those who have functioned as accessories by refusing to take a stand. But today the aspirations for equality and a better life have reached even the most isolated parts of the world, and we know that prejudice is not inevitable but learned and thus, in theory at least, subject to our control.[1] In our own country—as a consequence of both our democratic principles and our technological and economic progress—this awakening is particularly strong and the demand for basic changes increasingly insistent.

Faulty Self-Structure

We have seen that the self-structure is the center of the individual's world of experience, the reference point for evaluating and coping with his world, and an increasingly important determinant of his further development as he progresses from outer direction by parents and others to inner self-direction. We have also seen that though the self-structure is subject to some change, the individual tends to maintain his existing self-structure and to behave in ways consistent with it. Thus if the self-structure which emerges is faulty, it tends to steer subsequent development into increasingly distorted patterns.

The various unfavorable conditions that we have discussed tend to lead the individual to inaccurate answers to the three key questions: Who am I? Where am I going? Why? The answers are inaccurate because he has been taught defensive and distorted patterns of response and also because he has an inaccurate and distorted picture of both himself and the world around him. He is likely to have an unclear, distorted, and devaluated sense of his assets, liabilities, and general worth, with discrepancies between what he thinks he is and what he would like to be. He may bristle at nonexistent bogeymen and be unaware of real hazards. To the extent that his view is distorted, he is handicapped and almost inevitably makes miscalculations which lead to failure and further self-devaluation.

The effects of a faulty frame of reference can be clearly seen in the case of the child in the ghetto slum who has been subjected to rejection, irrationality, cruelty, discrimination, and poverty. He may see himself as inferior and powerless in a hostile world, and he may never learn to see the world as predictable and safe or himself as the initiator of his own actions. He may never learn to see himself as capable of solving problems or developing the competencies that would make him less helpless. He may never develop a clear sense of who he is and who he wants to be, for such considerations may seem irrelevant in a life that is so largely a struggle for physical and social survival. He may have little opportunity to learn to see his family or neighborhood as part of a larger society and himself as a member of that larger society.

In varying ways and degrees, the middle- or upper-class child who is subjected to rejection, overprotection, or other faulty conditions of development is also handicapped in answering the questions Who, Where, and Why. For he too is likely to develop a faulty frame of reference, inadequate self-differentiation, a lack of essential competencies, and negative feelings about his worth and ability. Where the slum child is likely not to adopt middle-class goals and norms because he is sure he cannot succeed, the middle-class child is likely to adopt them and then feel an acute sense of failure and self-devaluation when he falls short. In both cases, the individual is handicapped in achieving the healthy self-structure essential for mature and effective self-direction.

In a review of the literature relating self-evaluation to adjustment, Wylie (1961) found that a high degree of self-acceptance or self-regard usually was associated with good adjustment whereas a low self-evaluation tended to be associated with maladjustment of various kinds. She also found that individuals who were self-accepting tended to be more accepting of others. Apparently the individual who has a favorable evaluation of himself feels secure enough to be less defen-

---

[1]An excellent review of research on several forms of ethnic prejudice is found in Proshansky (1966).

sive toward others and more able to see their behavior objectively and with understanding. The individual who deprecates and rejects himself also tends to deprecate and reject others.

EARLY CONDITIONS FOSTERING HEALTHY DEVELOPMENT

Although the optimal conditions for healthy child development have not yet been identified, research has provided many important clues. In fact, the present generation has more adequate information than any previous one on how children develop and how various methods of child rearing influence this development.

Not surprisingly, the conditions that appear to foster healthy development are the reverse of those found to be associated with faulty development. Here too, of course, the influence of a particular condition cannot be evaluated by itself, because it always depends partly also on the particular child and on what other favorable and unfavorable conditions are operating. Each child has a different set of resources for coping with the problems and hurdles of his growing. As Murphy (1962) has noted in her intensive longitudinal study of infants and children, a newer viewpoint has emerged in which we think of the child:

". . . as a small human being, carrying on his own struggle to make sense out of life, to meet his own needs, to master the challenges presented by life—but differing from adults especially in the proportion of newness to which he is exposed." (p. 1)

The foundations of healthy development are laid in early life—in the physical care which the child receives, the love and acceptance he experiences, the degree to which his environment stimulates learning, the discipline and guidance he is given, and the recognition and reinforcement he receives for successful accomplishment. Fortunately, there seems to be a considerable margin of safety: Only when parental attitudes and be-

havior deviate markedly from established guidelines are they likely to have seriously detrimental effects on the child (Chess et al., 1965).

Infant and Child Care

The most obvious need of the human infant is for physical care, for he is completely helpless. But the parents who provide food, warmth, and safety can do it in ways that foster or prevent healthy development. The how and when as well as the what are of key importance.

Acceptance of the infant's own developmental plan. Recent studies indicate that good physical care requires an acceptance by the mother of the baby's own autonomy and developmental plan. It means a willingness to be guided by the cues the baby gives of his needs rather than an attempt to impose a predetermined pattern on him (Sander, 1962; Murphy, 1962; Chess et al., 1965).

In their longitudinal study of infant development, Chess and her associates (1965) found that most babies are "easy" to care for. Soon after birth they settle down to a regular schedule of eating and sleeping, their mood is predominantly pleasant, and they adapt well to changes in routine. However, some 7 to 10 per cent are "difficult" babies. They have irregular patterns of eating, sleeping, and bowel movements and tend to cry a lot and to show predominantly negative moods; they have difficulty in adapting to change and tend to withdraw from new stimuli. In her efforts to deal with such a baby's irregular functioning and frequent crying, the mother often tries first one method and then another so that she is highly inconsistent in her interactions with the infant. She does not gain the satisfaction from her infant that she expected and tends to have ambivalent feelings of helplessness, punitiveness, and guilt. The end result is often a disturbance in mother-infant relationships which may involve some measure of maternal deprivation for the infant.

Mothers, too, differ in personality make-up and in the types of child-care patterns they tend to establish. In an intensive study of 27 relatively "good mothers" Heider (1960) found marked differences in the mothers' awareness of their babies' needs, the compatibility of the mothers with their children, and the mothers' degree of acceptance of their infants. Here it is interesting to note Heider's conclusion that given procedures in infant care could be evaluated only in terms of the characteristics of both mother and infant and the total family context. A noisy home might be upsetting to a sensitive child, a source of enjoyment to another, and a matter of indifference to a third; likewise, the same maternal quality affected different children in different ways. The effect of any one factor could be known only by an examination of the whole picture. One factor that did seem of general significance, however, was the mother's awareness and acceptance of the infant's own developmental plan and growing autonomy.

Physical care. Adequate nutrition, exercise, rest, and other conditions essential to the maintenance of physical health and vigor are also of key importance for healthy personality development. Too many children are exposed to poor physical hygiene and thus suffer unnecessarily from lack of energy, irritability, virus infections, and related symptoms. Such conditions may interfere with the child's ability to learn, as well as complicating his relations with parents, teachers, and peers.

On the other hand, the child who has a healthy body and can operate at a high level of physical efficiency has an automatic advantage in dealing with other people, in exerting the effort needed for sustained learning, and in coping with whatever problems he encounters.

Love and Acceptance

The importance of love and acceptance in healthy personality development has been demonstrated in numerous research studies. In an intensive study of 261 well-adjusted children, for example, Langdon and Stout (1951) found the most important factor in their good adjustment to be parental love and acceptance. The children came from various socioeconomic levels and different-sized families and had been subjected to widely differing kinds of discipline and child-rearing procedures. The one factor they shared in common was that they were loved and accepted and made to feel wanted. Similarly, in their extensive study of patterns in child rearing, Sears *et al.* (1957) concluded that the most crucial and pervasive of all the influences exerted in the home were the love and warmth imparted by the parents.

Beneficial effects of love and acceptance. Other studies have corroborated the close relationship between parental love and acceptance and the development of such crucial traits as self-esteem, self-reliance, independence, and self-control (Coopersmith, 1967; Peck & Havighurst, 1960; Bandura & Walters, 1963). Evidently parental warmth and acceptance determine how readily a child identifies with his parents and accepts their values and standards. If they express warmth toward the child, the child can identify with them and use their behavior as a model for expressing his own feelings toward others (Sears *et al.,* 1957; Hetherington & Frankie, 1967). Pringle (1965) found that institutionalized children who had not experienced lasting love and loyalty from any adult were unable to develop feelings of love and loyalty in their own relationships. Hurley (1965) found intelligence can be enhanced by parental acceptance and affection and diminished by parental rejection, as we have seen.

As with proper physical care, parental love and acceptance pay many subtle dividends in personality development. Love and acceptance help the child to develop a basic sense of trust toward his parents and the world around him, which becomes a major safeguard against fear and anxiety—thus giving him the feeling of security he needs to be able to explore his environment confidently and accept its demands; only as he does so can he master developmental tasks and develop new competencies. Furthermore, for the child who feels loved and accepted, many conditions that might otherwise seriously impair development, such as a physical handicap, poverty, or unusually strict or harsh discipline, may be to a considerable extent neutralized.

Love and acceptance as part of a broader family pattern. Here it may be pointed out that love and acceptance usually form part of a broader pattern of positive family interrelationships. For example, love and acceptance tend to be accompanied by an interest in the child and what he is doing, by respect for the child as a person, and by displays of warmth and affection (Coopersmith, 1967). The child is typically encouraged to interact with his world—within limits essential for his protection —and is subjected to firm but not coercive controls (Hurley, 1965). Often, too, the parents encourage the child to meet high but realistic standards. Thus a whole cluster of attitudes and actions is usually involved in "love and acceptance." Farnsworth (1966) made this point very well in the context of the broader needs of the child:

"If a child encounters essentially friendly and accepting attitudes in the people around him during his years of helpless dependency, he has a reasonably good chance of growing up with basic attitudes of trust and a sort of optimism that enables him to make satisfying contacts with his fellows as he goes along. Every child needs affection, the feeling of belonging and being wanted, respect as an individual in his own right, a favorable setting for growth and the development of security, freedom from excessive domination, firm discipline from a respected source, and privacy enough to allow his active imagination to develop. He usually reacts more favorably to judicious praise than to indiscriminate fault finding; and he needs to feel that what he does has meaning. Most of these needs are met almost automatically when the mother and all other members of the family have a warm relationship with the child." (p. 44)

In summary then, it would appear that love and acceptance are important in:

1. Building self-esteem, confidence, and a sense of security which, in turn, foster general intellectual, emotional, and social development.

2. Fostering conscience development and self-control. Being loved appears to foster the child's identification with his parents, his desire to please them, and his vulnerability to their disapproval and thus to provide conditions under which he internalizes their moral standards.

3. Developing warm interpersonal relationships. The kind and depth of love relationships an individual can establish in later life with other persons appear directly related to the amount of love he has experienced in early life.

4. Fostering self-differentiation. The parents who love and accept the child tend to respect and appreciate him as a unique person and thus to encourage his growth and autonomy as a person in his own right.

A Stimulating and Responsive Environment

The infant does not have to learn to be curious. He is constantly exploring—touching, tasting, listening, and looking. As nerves and muscles mature and mental capacities develop, the scope of his exploration broadens; as soon as he can talk, he begins to ask questions. Good parents will provide an environment conducive to new but not overwhelming experiences and thus to enjoyable learning. For although the infant's tendencies toward curiosity, exploration, and learning are "built-in," they can be blocked either by lack of opportunity and stimulation or by early experiences which teach the child to regard curiosity as dangerous and nonrewarding.

In our earlier discussion of cultural deprivation we noted some of the common effects of an impoverished early environment

—such as inadequate language development, a paucity of information and concepts, and inability to use adults as sources of information. The latter is of particular significance, since the child needs not only a stimulating environment but also a responsive one—one in which he gets immediate and adequate "feedback." He needs to have his questions answered, to know what progress he is making, to have meaningful environmental interactions, and to be able to count on predictable effects from his actions.

"Enriched" early stimulation. Recently a good deal of interest has been expressed by psychologists and educators concerning the effects of an enriched early environment upon development. As we saw in the last chapter, rats exposed to a stimulating environment during their first month did better on learning tasks later and were found to have developed heavier and thicker brain cortexes. They also showed gains in growth rate, intelligence, and ability to withstand stress (Schultz, 1965). And McGraw's classic study of Johnny and Jimmy found that some skills could be learned much earlier than usual with special training. Likewise, we saw that preschool enrichment programs have shown encouraging results in preventing the progressive intellectual deterioration so often seen among institutionalized and socially disadvantaged children and that increasingly investigators are taking an interactional view of intelligence, believing that the child's intelligence grows as he processes information and that even the growth and maintenance of the underlying neural structures are dependent upon the functional demands made upon them by stimulation.

The concept of an optimal level of stimulation. It is generally believed that there is an optimal level of stimulation or input for an individual, determined largely by his early postnatal experience: an impoverished early environment is believed to lead to a low level and an enriched early environment to a high level of optimal stimulation (Hunt, 1961, 1964, 1965; Bronson, 1965). Thus

the concept of a responsive environment has been emphasized both in parent-child relations and in education.

In recent attempts to design ways of using computers in education, for example, not only drill-and-practice sessions but "dialogue" programs are being designed which attempt to provide the richest possible interaction between the student and the computer. Computers so used can provide enriched, individualized instruction with immediate feedback (Loughary, 1967).

Structure and Guidance

Children grow and function best in a clearly structured environment—one which is orderly and consistent and in which they know what is expected of them and what will be disapproved of or punished. With such structuring the child can experience the success and approval that come from living up to his parents' expectations, and he can avoid the unnecessary frustration of having to be continually testing reality in an attempt to find some order that he can count on in working out his coping strategies. As Murphy (1962) found:

"In a stable, homogeneous and circumscribed environment the child has the greatest opportunity to achieve mastery over the successive opportunities and demands to which he is exposed at his own pace and in a manner shaped by his own natural style; and accordingly, has maximal opportunity for harmonious integration of successive stages of mastery." (p. 113)

Key elements of structure. Three elements of structuring seem particularly important for healthy development: (1) clearly defined standards and limits—so that the child understands what goals, procedures, and conduct are approved, (2) adequately defined roles for both older and younger members of the family, so that the child knows what is expected of both himself and others, and (3) established methods of handling the child that encourage desired behavior, discourage misbehavior, and deal with infractions when they occur. The limits, roles, and methods of dealing with a child should, of course, be realistic and appropriate to his age, needs, and abilities. Treatment that helps one child to develop and maintain desirable behavior patterns may make another child rebellious and still another one insecure and withdrawn.

In recent decades psychologists, educators, and parents have argued the case for permissiveness in childrearing as opposed to "old-fashioned discipline." Although the trend has been toward increasing permissiveness in childrearing, there is general agreement today that a child can be just as handicapped—though in a different way—by a lack of discipline as by overly severe restraints. As we have seen, too much permissiveness tends to produce a spoiled, inconsiderate child—and often an insecure and unhappy one. In general, it would appear that freedom should be commensurate with maturity—with the child's ability to use it wisely—and that parents need to love their children enough to discipline them.

Need for guidance and assistance. Closely related to structuring is guidance—helping the child to select the paths and responses that will be constructive for him. We take it for granted that a child needs help in learning to read and work arithmetic problems, but we are less likely to realize that he also needs guidance in learning nonacademic skills—in developing emotional and social competencies, in acquiring a sound value system, and in learning independence and responsibility. For example, many discipline problems involve both angry feelings and angry acts, and the two parts may require separate handling. Feelings may have to be identified, clarified, accepted, and "worked through" whereas acts may have to be controlled, limited, or redirected. Without parental guidance in such matters, the child is handicapped in mastering essential developmental tasks.

Children in our society are exposed to many ideas, situations, and points of view before they are mature enough to evaluate them critically without help. Thus they need guidance in deciding what is true and real, what is morally right, and what is worth striving for—in building a reliable frame of reference. As we have seen, high but realistic parental standards and expectations help children develop such a frame of reference and in so doing foster self-esteem and self-confidence, whereas parents who set no standards for their children and just want them to enjoy themselves tend to have children with low self-esteem. Children with high self-esteem, in turn, are self-confident, make friends more readily, and show greater tolerance to minor rebuffs, whereas those with low self-esteem tend to think of themselves in adverse ways which hamper their adjustive efforts and school achievement (Coopersmith, 1967).

The need for competent and understanding adult guidance is often increased during critical periods of development—for example, when a child starts school or approaches adolescence, when he suffers failures and traumas, when excessive demands are made upon him. And throughout their development, children need extra help in handling such special problems as hostility and sexual desires and in dealing with new and complex situations. Although the child may be able to work out satisfactory solutions on his own, stressful experience may have a disintegrative effect which blocks normal growth. For example, the child who is having serious difficulty in learning to read may need an extra measure of parental guidance and support. Unfortunately, parents not infrequently react to such problems with anxiety and disapproval instead of encouragement, thus undermining the child's confidence in himself and complicating his adjustive efforts.

Guidance and assistance do not always take the form of direct instruction, although there are many times when it is necessary to point out details that a child might not notice, to give him information, and to help him see new relationships. Children also need regular times to be alone with the parents and to have parents who are willing to listen instead of saying "Can't you see I'm busy." For children, like adults, experience problems that they need to talk about and feelings that they need to express.

Parents and other adults may also guide a child by structuring his environment in such a way as to provide certain kinds of experiences and reinforcements. Democratic values, for example, are fostered by a democratic home environment where cooperation and personal responsibility are expected and rewarded.

Perhaps most important of all as a form of guidance are the behavioral models the child sees in his parents. Especially if he loves and admires them, he sees their behavior as a visible demonstration of how he should behave and tends to pattern his attitudes, opinions, approaches to problems, and relationships with other people on what he sees his parents do. In their efforts at explicit guidance, parents often fail to realize how much guidance they are unwittingly providing through their own behavior.

CHILDREN'S CHARACTERISTICS AND TYPICAL FAMILY BACKGROUNDS

ACHIEVEMENT MOTIVATION	*High:* Achievement-oriented parents who have high aspirations for children, are interested in and encourage them.
	Low: "Unconcerned" families, content if child keeps out of trouble; emotionally disturbed homes; socially disadvantaged homes.
AGGRESSION (BOYS)	Lack of consistent standards; punitive, restrictive, cold parents; aggressive personal models; physical punishment; family disharmony; broken home.
CONSCIENCE (SELF-CONTROL)	*Good:* Parental warmth and acceptance; clear-cut standards consistently enforced; love-oriented discipline; good parental models.
	Poor: Maternal coldness; rejection; unclear or shifting standards; inconsistency; overindulgence; poor parental models.
SOCIABILITY, LEADERSHIP	*Good:* Parental warmth and involvement, democratic climate in home, love-oriented discipline; greater salience of same-sexed parent without marked dominance of either parent.
	Poor: Overindulgence or parental restrictiveness; parental rejection, neglect, or absence; cold, demanding parents.
AUTONOMY	Parental warmth and acceptance, high parental standards strictly enforced; reinforcement of independent behavior without punishment of dependent behavior; parental guidance toward competence, parental support during special stress; chance for the child to share in formulation and enforcement of rules.
DEPENDENCY	Early severe social deprivation; rejecting, punitive parents or combination of warmth and restrictiveness; either reward or punishment for dependency.
SELF-IDENTITY, SELF-ESTEEM	*Good:* Parental love and acceptance, fostering identification and feeling of belonging; democratic home in which all members have roles and responsibilities commensurate with their maturity; stable, meaningful, supportive environment; mature, well-differentiated parental models.
	Poor: Rejection; parental dominance or overprotection; power-coercive discipline; lack of close, continuing ties to desirable adult model.

This summary is based on many studies, including Bandura & Walters, 1963a; Becker, 1964; Berkowitz, 1964; Douvan & Adelson, 1966; Hoffman, 1963; Kagan & Moss, 1962; Kohlberg, 1964; McCord, McCord, & Verdon, 1962.

Success and Recognition

One need only observe a child's eager request to "Watch me, Mommy," as he demonstrates some new achievement, to understand the importance of success and recognition. Bessell (1968) has concluded from extensive work with nursery school and kindergarten children:

> "Every child wants to succeed; every child has the same questions when he starts to school: 'Am I safe? Can I cope with this? Will I be accepted?' The child is not a cognitive machine. He will feel like a failure unless he perceives success, unless he really feels power and responsibility for what happens to him, and around him. If he feels strong, he can achieve far more in school and in life itself." (p. 34)

As Allport (1943; p. 466) pointed out many years ago, not only does human learning appear to proceed best under conditions of success and recognition or praise, but "the individual's *capacity* for learning actually seems to expand" under these conditions.

Keeping the balance in favor of success. Although it would be imprudent as well as impossible to protect a child from every failure, healthy development requires that the balance be kept on the side of success. Any child will have setbacks, rejections, disappointments, and other experiences that challenge his feelings of capability and worth. But if, on balance, he has more experiences adding to his self-esteeem than detracting from it, he can continue to grow in competence and self-confidence.

Parents and teachers can help a child to maintain a favorable balance both by not expecting more from him than he is capable of achieving and by anticipating future demands and furnishing the guidance and instruction necessary to ensure that he will be ready for them. Some hurt and some pain will be inevitable aspects of many new learning experiences. Parents strive to protect their children from severe and unnecessary trauma—which might lead to fear and withdrawal—but they handicap the child if they keep him from seeking out and coping with new experiences despite occasional bumps and defeats. The need for such experiences has been succinctly stated by Murphy (1962):

> "Over and over again we saw how the impact of a new challenge intensified the child's awareness of himself; his capacity to meet such a challenge enhances his pleasure, his sense of adequacy, and his pride. Through the successive experiences of spontaneous mastery of new demands and utilizing new opportunities for gratification the child extends and verifies his identity as one who can manage certain aspects of the environment. Through his coping experiences the child discovers and measures himself, and develops his own perception of who and what he is and in time may become. We can say that the child creates his identity through his efforts in coming to terms with the environment in his own personal way." (p. 374)

The child who sees the world as basically predictable and reasonable and himself as capable of making his way in it learns to see himself as the originator of his actions. He can develop a clear picture of who he is, where he is going, and why. If the problems he meets are within his ability to solve, he grows, through solving them, toward increasing competency and self-confidence. On the other hand, a child who continually fails—in schoolwork, in fist fights, in competition with other children, or in living up to his parents' expectations—is likely to begin regarding himself as personally inadequate and unworthy in the eyes of others. Such self-devaluating attitudes, in turn, tend to breed anxiety and fear and to discourage further effort. Sometimes, unfortunately, a child misses the experience of success even when his achievements are good, because his aspirations—or the standards set for him by others—are unreasonably high.

Constructive use of failure. Fully as important as experiencing success is learning to use failure constructively. Here again, parents and teachers can help—first, by giving the child enough acceptance and support to assure him that he still is a worthy person and that his failure is not catastrophic; second, by helping him to see the lessons his mistake contains so that his failure becomes a stepping stone to better achievement next time. To achieve such results, of course, the parent must be willing to listen to the child to see how he has interpreted the experience. Understanding and communicating meaningfully with him usually requires spending time alone with him so that he can talk about his problems and his feelings.

Early Detection and Correction of Defects

Even with the best intentions and the greatest skill, not all unhealthy development will be prevented. Thus in fostering healthy development, the early detection and if possible correction of defects is of key importance. Medical science now has many ways of guarding the infant during the prenatal period and of reducing birth injuries, and remarkable progress has been made in identifying the genetic origin of various birth defects as well as in identifying potential parents who may be carriers of the defective genes that cause them (Davis, 1968; Beck, 1968). Where defects do occur that would adversely affect intellectual and other development, early diagnosis and correction or amelioration are often possible.

In a similar way, modern psychology and psychiatry have made notable advances in the early detection and treatment of faulty personality trends. Although the symptoms of unhealthy psychological development are less clearly defined—particularly in early development—many have been delineated. For example, apathy, lying and stealing, rigidity and lack of spontaneity, and a seriously devaluated self-concept are danger signals.

"NORMAL" PROBLEMS

Chess *et al.* (1965) list the following as setbacks and symptoms that occur almost without exception among children under eight:

1. Sleep problems—*Wakefulness, climbing out of bed and wandering around house, wanting to get into parents' bed, frightening dreams.*

2. Fears—*Avoidance of a dog or cat or perhaps the vacuum cleaner or a room with a sculptured figure; may vomit every morning from fear of school.*

3. Excessive timidity—*Gives up place in line, or gives up toys too easily, remaining bereft and helpless instead of solving problem or finding substitute.*

4. Play problems—*Remains on sidelines even after long time in group, can join activity only with great effort by teacher; or too dependent on company but only uses them as space fillers.*

5. General dissatisfaction—*Nothing pleases, general sadness and discontent no matter how treated.*

6. Extreme negativism—*"No" on principle, tantrums, resistant to stopping anything he wants to do or to giving up anything he has.*

7. Clinging—*Refuses to leave side of mother or teacher to do anything on own (common among three-year-olds).*

8. Moving backward—*Relapses and regression.*

Three questions that help to distinguish such relatively "normal" disturbances from those of a more malignant nature are:

Is this like him? The problem is more likely to be serious if the new behavior is different in kind than if it is an intensification of the child's typical coping pattern.

Is there a reason? Was the difficulty precipitated by external strain, stress, or shock or unusual changes in routine or environment? Even if so, the problem behavior should be mild and temporary unless a deeper, already present problem has been heightened.

Is it spreading? The problem is usually less serious if it is an isolated behavior that does not interfere seriously with the child's normal activity.

In general, it is safe to say that parents should seek advice when they are worried for any length of time or when tension becomes the dominant theme in their interaction with the child.

On the other hand, some kinds of behavior that disturb both parents and children seem to be virtually universal. Some of these are summarized in the chart on p. 137.

Unfortunately, developmental defects that are not detected and corrected early tend to perpetuate themselves. The child who is overly sensitive and withdraws from social interaction, for example, will probably fail to master the competencies he needs for dealing effectively with people. This, in turn, will result in inevitable failures and further withdrawal—with further loss of opportunity for needed learning.

Although it may not be possible to undo early psychological damage completely— such as that caused by parental rejection or a socially disadvantaged environment—even serious personality damage can often be corrected or ameliorated by providing conditions that make possible relearning and change. Psychological assistance, such as psychotherapy, can often facilitate such relearning.

SUMMARY AND A LOOK AHEAD

In this chapter we have defined *personality* as the unique pattern of traits that distinguishes one individual from all others and accounts for his characteristic and relatively consistent ways of behaving. On most traits people tend to cluster around the midpoint of a continuum, with the cases falling off rapidly toward either extreme of the range. The influence of a particular trait depends on the pattern within which it occurs and on the individual's evaluation of it.

Approaches to the problem of defining *healthy development* have included (1) regarding health as absence of disease; (2) defining healthy development more positively, as optimal realization of potentialities; and (3) listing criteria generally agreed upon as components of psychological health, such as a realistic frame of reference. In specifying the meaning of such terms as "realistic," value judgments are inevitably entailed. There is more agreement about what constitutes *faulty* development. Three common types are (1) arrested development; (2) special vulnerability; and (3) distortions in development.

Early conditions conducive to faulty development include genetic or acquired defects, maternal deprivation or early trauma, pathogenic family patterns, social pathology in the environment of the growing child, and a faulty self-structure or inaccurate frame of reference. Early conditions that foster healthy development are good physical care based on acceptance of the infant's own developmental plan; unconditional love and acceptance; a stimulating and responsive environment; understanding and guidance within a clearly defined structure; a favorable balance of success over failure, with help in using failure constructively; and early detection and correction of defects to avoid a mounting spiral of difficulty. In both cases, however, the actual effect of these conditions will depend partly on the child and his evaluations, as well as on the larger context within which the particular condition occurs.

This chapter concludes our survey of "human nature" and the development of human personalities. In Part Two we shall be looking at what makes us do what we do and what happens when we encounter difficult adjustive demands.

Key terms used in this chapter include:

personality, traits (pp. 104-105)
normal distribution, skewed distribution (p. 105)
"healthy" and "unhealthy" development (pp. 106-107)
multiple criteria approach (p. 107)
arrested development, special vulnerabilities, distorted development (pp. 108-109)
genetic defects, mutant genes (pp. 110-111)
prenatal and birth difficulties (p. 111)
maternal deprivation, early trauma, marasmus (pp. 113-114)
traumatic experiences (p. 115)
pathogenic family patterns, faulty parent-child relationships (pp. 115-124)
misidentification (p. 119)
double-bind (p. 120)
inadequate family, disturbed family, antisocial family, disrupted family (pp. 123-124)
social pathology (p. 125)
cultural deprivation, socially disadvantaged (p. 125)
faulty self-structure (p. 129)
acceptance of infant's developmental plan (p. 130)
stimulating and responsive environment, optimal level of stimulation (pp. 132-133)
"normal" problems (p. 137)

Part Two

THE DYNAMICS
OF ADJUSTIVE BEHAVIOR

Development and behavior are integral aspects of a functioning and changing system. Consideration of one apart from the other is simply a matter of where we focus our attention. In Part One we examined the nature of the human system and showed how our human potentialities develop through maturation and learning. As we would expect, the traits which are built into the individual's structure during the course of his development constitute the resources he brings to each new situation. But they do not entirely account for his behavior. As we shall see in Part Two, human behavior results from a complicated interplay of inner and outer determinants.

Chapter 5 takes up the question of motivation. What moves an individual to act at all, and what determines the particular goals he will seek? What mechanisms provide the energy he uses in pursuing his goals and to what extent is his behavior determined by environmental demands?

Chapter 6 deals with the ways in which our behavior is complicated by frustrations, conflicts, and pressures—with problems of adjustment, or *stress*. Such problems interfere with the attainment of our goals and hence require special adjustive behavior.

Chapter 7 examines our reactions to stress—the ways in which we attempt to cope with problems of adjustment. What is the typical sequence involved in the "processing" of stressful situations and what factors make this process adjustive or maladjustive?

Chapter 8 examines faulty patterns of adjustment, ranging from minor self-defeating patterns of behavior to the complete breakdown of personality organization. We will look at the major syndromes of mental disorders, at the roles of both faulty development and excessive stress in their background, and finally, very briefly, at modern concepts of treatment and prevention.

Chapter 5

MOTIVATION:
HUMAN NEEDS AND GOALS

Ernest Hemingway (1955) introduced his story "The Snows of Kilimanjaro" with the following:

> *"Kilimanjaro is a snow covered mountain 19,710 feet high, and is said to be the highest mountain in Africa. . . . Close to the western summit there is the dried and frozen carcass of a leopard. No one has explained what the leopard was seeking at that altitude." (p. 52)*

This dramatic introduction implies two interesting points: (1) that the behavior of the leopard was purposive—that he was trying to find or achieve something by climbing to the top of a snow-covered mountain—and (2) that to understand the leopard's behavior we would have to understand his purpose—what he was seeking. Though no concept of purposiveness or inner motivation is needed to explain the behavior of atoms or oceans it seems evident that the behavior of living organisms, whether of lower animals or of man, cannot be accounted for without it.

WAYS OF VIEWING MOTIVATION

The view that motivation is a key determinant of a person's behavior is not a new one. In dealing with people and attempting to understand them, we give high priority to information concerning their motives. We ponder our own motives when we contemplate marriage; and we question the other person's motives when our proposal is turned down. The salesman is directly concerned with the needs and motives of his client. The police detective apprehending a murderer, the judge and jury who decide on the criminal's fate, and the sociologist trying to understand the origin of crime, are all vitally interested in the intent behind the behavior. And sometimes we have as hard a time trying to understand our own motives as those of other people.

Although we are often able to infer the motives underlying a given action, our understanding of human motivation is far from complete. Our research findings are spotty, and psychologists have advanced differing viewpoints which are often contradictory and confusing. A comprehensive and definitive psychology of motivation has yet to be constructed. However, there is an expanding body of research data and ideas which help us to understand many aspects of the problem and provide us with a general perspective for thinking about human motivation.

What Motivation Helps to Explain

The term *motivation* will be used here to include any inner condition of the organism that initiates or directs its behavior toward a goal. For example, a need for food sets in motion behavior aimed at meeting this requirement; a need for social approval may lead an individual to work hard to help his group achieve its goals; a desire for money may lead to an economically oriented marriage rather than a love-oriented one. The term *motive* has a more specific and limited connotation: a motive is a tendency to seek a particular kind of goal.

Viewed in this way, motivation is a broad concept which includes the inner needs, desires, and purposes of the organism. Specifically, it helps us to understand: (1) the directionality of behavior, and (2) the activation or energizing of behavior. Accounting for directionality and activation, in turn, will help us to understand both the common denominators in human strivings and their great diversity.

Directionality of behavior. Glickman and Schiff (1967) have suggested that each species of animal has built-in response propensities which tend to: (1) bring the individual into contact with stimuli relevant to its survival—*approach behavior,* and (2) remove the individual from stimuli which are threatening to its survival—*avoidance behavior.* For lower animals, such built-in tendencies may be highly specific. Snakes, for example, have built-in genetic information that enables them to recognize the exact prey normally eaten by their species— they know their prey by its odor and can make the identification at birth *(Science News,* 1967b).

Higher species, of course, become increasingly dependent on learning rather than built-in guides for their approach and avoidance responses. Through experience the individual learns to make fairly accurate appraisals of the reward or punishment aspects of objects and activities and on this basis builds a pattern of values, or preferences, which guides his choices. Thus we find, within the broad categories of approach and avoidance behavior, that the directions of our strivings are as varied as the things we have learned to value. Curiously enough, we can learn to value that which is actually harmful to us—as in drug addiction—as well as that which meets our biological and psychological needs. Sometimes our values change with new experience and learning— leading to changes also in the direction of our behavior.

Implicit in the concept of directionality is that of selectivity. Motives make us selectively sensitive to environmental stimuli which are perceived as relevant to the meeting of our needs or wants. Thus the hungry man is more sensitive to stimuli associated with food than is the man who has just eaten; the person striving for social acceptance may be more sensitive to his effect on others than is the person who has no worries about his popularity. In our later discussion we will examine ways in which such sensitivities, based on motivational conditions, can affect our perceptions and judgments.

Activation of behavior. Though stimuli can trigger behavior or act as cues in our search for particular conditions to meet inner needs, it is clear that stimuli do not provide the increased energy needed for goal-directed behavior. The mechanisms of activation will be discussed in a later section; for the present, we will note simply that the amount of energy that is made available, and hence the vigor and persistence of the behavior, depends on the importance of the goal to the individual. We all tire quickly of effort toward a goal we care little about, whereas we will work long and tirelessly for something we see as crucially important. Thus the strength of an individual's motivation is often gauged by the amount of effort he is willing to expend to achieve his goal, and stronger motivation gives him a better chance of reaching it by making more energy available to him.

Although motivation helps us account for the direction and selectivity of behavior as well as its vigor and persistence, it is not the sole determinant of what we do. Motivation is not enough to put a football player on the team: he must also have the requisite health, size, skill, intelligence, and opportunity. And field forces, too, help to determine what he does at a given moment. If no receiver can get clear, the would-be passer runs with the ball; and if he is knocked off his feet by a hard tackle from an opposing player, his fall cannot be explained solely in terms of his motives. Although motives are key determinants of behavior, they are always part of a larger pattern of inner processes and outer conditions which together determine what we do.

Similarities and differences in basic human strivings. Some motives, like hunger, start with a "wired-in" need; others, such as the desire for financial success, may be entirely learned. Since we can acquire almost any motive as a consequence of learning, it is inevitable that our motivational patterns should show almost infinite variety. Thus again we are confronted with the problem of finding order in the diversity of human behavior.

At first glance human motives appear to defy classification. Yet if we look closer, we see some common denominators. People everywhere are concerned about such matters as food, clothing, shelter, medical care, education, work, marriage, belonging, security, and approval. And if we look still closer, we can see that common to man's activities everywhere are strivings toward *self-maintenance* or survival and toward the *actualization of potentialities*—of both the individual and the group of which he is a part. In fact, all our specific strivings—toward food, shelter, security, and all the rest—are variations on these two basic themes.

Although man shares these two basic strivings with all living creatures, there is an important difference: the strivings that subserve maintenance seem less important to man than do the strivings that subserve actualization—at least under reasonably favorable conditions. For example, the college

freshman is likely to be much more concerned about getting good grades, having fun on dates, and improving his social skills than he is about his diet or his hours of sleep. In fact, it is in his attempts at creative expression, in his deliberate effort toward increasing his knowledge and ability, and in his quest for values and meaning that man reveals himself as most human and most distinct from other species.

The concept of basic strivings toward maintenance and actualization also gives us a basis for evaluating behavior. Just as the efficiency of a machine can be evaluated in terms of how well and at what cost it achieves the purposes for which it was built, the behavior of an individual is evaluated in terms of his efficiency in fulfilling his basic purposes—achieving his maintenance and actualization.

Motivational Models

Psychologists differ considerably in their views of motivation. Thus before attempting a systematic analysis of the concept of motivation, it will be helpful to consider briefly three divergent viewpoints which underlie much of the current thinking about motivation.

Primary and secondary motives. One popular view has maintained that there are a few basic, inborn, biological drives with which every member of the species begins life. The diversity of the motives in everyday behavior is regarded as the result of the conditioning of our inborn biological drives to new goals. Such conditioning is assumed to occur as follows:

The mother is usually present when the infant is fed; and she removes his cold clothing when he is wet. Thus she becomes a conditioned stimulus associated with relief from distress. And when she is not present, his distress is likely to continue. Because her presence is associated with relief of distress, he will learn many responses for which her presence is the only reinforcement. Then, as he discovers that her approval also signals rewards as well as relief from distress, he will learn to seek her approval. Later, seeking approval may come to be associated with honesty, academic achievement, athletic prowess, or whatever form of competence is valued by those around him.

Granting the reality of this conditioning process, it becomes apparent that a wide range of social behavior could be based upon motives developed in this way. Thus proponents of this view regard motives for affiliation, for power, and for achievement as extensions of more primitive physiological motive states. Any motives except the *primary*, physiological ones are considered *secondary* motives. Such a position has tended to belittle the relative importance of psychological and social motives in human behavior because of the assumption that behavior apparently powered by "higher" motives was, in fact, through conditioning, "really" still powered by hunger, sex, and other biological drives.

This position seems plausible but two of its assumptions are open to question: (1) that our only inborn motive states are those powered by hunger, thirst, sex, and other biological drives, and (2) that conditioning can in fact account for the diverse motives that seem to power human behavior.

The first assumption is open to question as a consequence of increasing evidence that whatever the neurological mechanisms may turn out to be, there is a substratum of inborn psychological needs and strivings comparable to the biological substratum. For example, no child must be taught to be curious. Nor does a child have to learn to need love in order for a deprivation of love to distort his psychological development.

The second assumption is open to question because there is nothing in conditioning theory to explain how a supposedly conditioned drive could become stronger than the original one or one antithetical to it. Monkeys can be taught to work for tokens which they can then exchange for food, but they never come to prefer the tokens to the food. Yet a man can choose to die rather than recant his

beliefs. The truth may be sought even though it leads to no biological satisfactions, and the striving to preserve one's self-esteem may take precedence over any and all biological needs.

Without minimizing the role of learning in motive development, the view that all psychological motives are derived from biological ones through conditioning not only is unproven but is contrary to a good deal of research evidence.

Motivation as tension reduction. Here the deprivation of needs, whether biological or psychological, is viewed as setting up unpleasant tension. When the deficit is remedied—as when the hungry organism obtains food—the tension is relieved and the organism returns to a state of equilibrium. Thus motives are viewed as devices for satisfying needs by reducing tension and restoring equilibrium.

Much of our biological and psychological functioning does obviously follow this pattern, and our homeostatic drives goad us into action when action toward maintenance is necessary. But human beings clearly are not concerned solely with removal of tension and restoration of equilibrium. We may put off eating and sleeping while we finish reading a book or watching television; and we may undergo a great deal of physical hardship and social disapproval in pursuing courses of action that we consider important for the maintenance of our freedom. Few people are content to live like vegetables. Instead they go out of their way to create, to explore, to build—to increase the complexity and meaningfulness of their lives. Such activities are often tension arousing rather than tension reducing. Thus the view of motivation as a matter of satisfying needs, reducing tension, and maintaining equilibrium is incomplete.

A variation of the tension-reduction model is the *pleasure-pain* model. Need deprivation and tension are unpleasant or painful, while the gratification of needs is usually pleasurable, and it has long been observed that man tends to seek that which is pleasurable and to avoid that which is painful. In recent years, techniques making possible the stimulation of specific brain areas have revealed so-called "pain" and "pleasure" centers—regions in which electrical stimulation seems to be unpleasant or pleasant and is actively avoided or sought by the subject. Such findings as these lend support to the old hedonistic doctrine that pleasure and pain—or in more modern terms, *reward* and *punishment*—are the key facets of human motivation.

It is apparent that people devote considerable effort toward making their lives more comfortable and pleasurable and that many cultural innovations—such as air-conditioning and exotic restaurants—are directed toward relieving the unpleasant and fostering the pleasant. But, as in the case of tension reduction, we also see people choosing to do things which are unpleasant. If we try to explain such behavior by saying that they must *really* be getting pleasure from these actions, we are retreating to an untestable hypothesis in which "pleasurable" is defined after the fact as whatever the individual does. There is insufficient evidence to indicate that the course of action a person chooses is always the one having the greatest pleasure potential for him.

For such reasons, achievement of pleasure and avoidance of pain are no longer considered the key to human behavior. Rather they are viewed chiefly as reinforcers of behavior directed toward other goals.

Push and pull models. Most approaches to motivation can be labelled as "push" or "pull" models. The push models emphasize man's inner purposes, strivings, and essentially active nature. Rather than being an inert protoplasmic mass whose actions are controlled by environmental stimuli, he is viewed as an active, purposeful agent who perceives and deals with his environment in accordance with his motives and values. The environment may provide what he needs or put obstacles in his way, but the action is initiated by his inner strivings to meet his needs and to find a meaningful way of life.

The pull models, on the other hand, emphasize environmental stimuli as the forces that induce and channel behavior. Behavior is conceived as a reaction to demands and pressures, rewards and punishments—in essence, the result of the patterning of stimuli in the environment. Society, by manipulating the rewards and punishments for given behaviors, can shape and channel the behavior of the individual in the directions which the given society deems desirable. Whereas the push models emphasize the purposes and strivings of the individual and provide him with some measure of choice, the pull models view man as a puppet manipulated by whatever incentives and stimuli are most potent.

In extreme form, pull models do not use the concept of motivation at all in explaining behavior. The concept of drive is replaced by that of response repertoires and habits built up by past reinforcement and called forth under appropriate stimulus conditions. In essence, motive power becomes externalized so that incentives in the environment take on the properties accorded to "drive" in the push theories. Thus according to these theorists when the buzzer sounds at the end of the class hour and we get up to leave the class, there is no necessity to talk about an acquired motive "to leave the class." Our available response of getting up to leave is simply called forth by the environment.

It seems evident that neither a push nor a pull viewpoint is sufficient by itself. Man is both active and reactive. His behavior, like that of other living systems, is the result of both: (1) his inner structural and integrative properties and (2) the conditions and forces of his field or environment. Some things we do primarily because of inner demands or conditions; others primarily because of environmental incentives and demands. So both the instigation of behavior and the form it takes must be seen as resulting from both our own make-up and the field in which the action takes place.

An eclectic approach. While we cannot confine ourselves to any of the approaches outlined above, we shall incorporate useful concepts from all of them. Although we do not accept the notion of primary and secondary motives as a full explanation of our motivation, it is clear that learning plays a tremendous part in shaping human motives. An understanding of motivation must thus delineate the role of conditioning and other learning. Although we do not accept a tension-reduction view or a pleasure-pain interpretation as the whole story, we will apply both concepts to the kinds of behavior where they seem to fit. For it is apparent that the individual does guide his choice of goals and activities on the basis of their anticipated reward or punishment value. And although neither push nor pull models are complete alone, the insights of both will be needed to show how inner strivings and field forces together direct our behavior.

STRIVINGS TOWARD MAINTENANCE AND ACTUALIZATION

Although we do not fully understand the processes involved, it is apparent that digestive, circulatory, and other bodily functions operate in such a way as to maintain the physiological equilibrium of the body. Whereas we may go several hours with no food and then eat a large meal, the concentration of sugar and other chemicals in the blood must remain relatively constant; a slight increase in acidity, for example, would result in coma and death. Similarly, body temperature must remain within a very limited range even though the temperature in the environment may go above a hundred degrees or below zero. Thus living systems endeavor to maintain *steady states*—to maintain their physiological variables within a range essential for survival—an endeavor referred to as *homeostasis*.

On the psychological level, we understand even less the processes involved in maintenance. However, they appear to be an extension of the strivings we see operating on the biological level. As we shall see,

for example, a certain level of meaningful sensory (information) input is essential for the maintenance of psychological integration. When sensory input falls below the minimal level, the individual strives to increase it; if the information input increases to the point of overloading the system, as when the individual is forced to deal with too many problems at once, he strives to decrease the input. Thus man also strives to maintain the steady states essential for his psychological integration—for thinking, feeling, and acting in organized and coherent ways.

In attempting to understand our strivings toward maintenance, we could take up various motives and show how they relate to these strivings. For example, we might show how the food motive or the social approval motive relates to maintenance. The great diversity of human motives and motive patterns, however, argues against this approach. A second and more economical approach is to think in terms of certain basic requirements or needs that must be met for biological and psychological maintenance—to delineate a basic core of requirements that appear to be characteristic of man.

Any such listing is, of course, somewhat arbitrary despite the increasing research data on which such a list can be based. And since individuals may live at different levels of efficiency, certain requirements on our list may not be met in given cases. In a concentration camp, for example, where the inmates receive only a few hundred calories a day and few psychological satisfactions, life may continue at a bare subsistence level. An individual may hang onto life for months or years even when many biological and psychological requirements are not being adequately met. The requirements we shall be discussing are those considered essential for normal functioning and growth, not for mere survival.

Our first task, then, will be to review some of the generally agreed-on requirements —biological and psychological needs—that must be met for normal development and functioning. Then we shall attempt to deal with the even more complex problem of ac-

SPECIFIC HUNGERS

Among animals, specific hungers often develop when some substance is especially needed. Rats given a choice have been shown to select foods containing needed vitamins; cattle deficient in minerals will eat bones; and sick dogs, as well as other animals, have been observed to seek out and eat specific plants or other foods that have medicinal qualities. Human infants also possess some of this "body wisdom."

In a classic study, Davis (1928) permitted three newly weaned infants to select from a wide variety of wholesome foods. Although the infants tended to go on "egg jags" or "cereal jags," they chose a reasonably balanced diet over a period of time. Of particular interest was the fact that one infant, who suffered from rickets, selected large quantities of cod liver oil which contains vitamin D-1, a specific for curing rickets.

Primitive people also appear to be adept in obtaining foods necessary for adequate nutrition. For example, Eskimos have been observed to eat the vegetable content of diving birds' stomachs to supplement their almost exclusively meat diet (Sinclair, 1954).

But although there appears to be a physiological wisdom related to food intake, it is not infallible. Babies may eat sufficient quantities of some foods, such as salt, to become seriously ill or even die. Even college students in appreciable numbers suffer from malnutrition due to unbalanced diets—too many cokes and hamburgers.

---

tualization strivings—particularly the forms such strivings take on the psychological level.

Biological Maintenance

For normal functioning the human body needs many substances, conditions, and activities ranging from vitamins to sexual release. Some needs, such as our needs for food and water, may be clearly felt and follow a cyclic pattern of deficit and gratification; others, such as that for air, are usually met automatically and enter our awareness only under unusual conditions of deprivation. Still other needs, such as our need for vitamin A, do not enter awareness at all, although there is some evidence of a "wisdom of the body" for seeking and choosing foods that contain the elements in which we are deficient.

In our present discussion, we shall not attempt to cover the gamut of biological needs. Instead we will summarize briefly the requirements which appear particularly relevant to an understanding of our behavior.

Visceral needs. Here we are concerned with bodily needs related to food, water, sleep, and other conditions essential for normal bodily functioning and survival—and for normal growth during our early years.

1. *Hunger and thirst.* In our society most of us have no first-hand knowledge of the far-reaching effects that severe hunger can have on psychological as well as physiological functioning. These effects were well illustrated in an interesting study carried out during World War II by Keys and his associates (1950).

Thirty-two conscientious objectors volunteered to serve as subjects in an experimental study of the effects of semistarvation. The men existed on about 1600 calories per day, which resulted in an average weight loss of 24 per cent during the six-month period of the study.

Dramatic personality changes took place during the experiment. The men became irritable, unsociable, and increasingly unable to concentrate on anything but the thought of food. By the end of the 25th week, food dominated their thoughts, conversation, and day dreams. The men even pinned up pictures of chocolate cake instead of pretty girls. In some cases, they went so far as to replan their lives in the light of their newly acquired respect for food.

In total starvation, hunger eventually disappears, but in this study, in which the men suffered prolonged semistarvation, their desire for food showed no lessening. In thirst too, the desire continues unabated. Men who have been deprived of both food and water over long periods of time have reported that feelings of hunger tended to decrease, whereas thirst remained intense and became almost maddening.

Although some people live in arid desert areas and subsist on a minimum of water, intense and prolonged thirst is probably relatively rare. Hunger, however, is a major problem in many areas of the world. Without going into the many side effects of malnutrition in stunting physical and intellectual growth, lowering resistance to disease, and producing chronic fatigue, it is apparent that hunger remains an urgent motive in our contemporary world. Where conditions are hard, the struggle for subsistence may take virtually all the individual's time and effort.

2. *Sleep.* Jouvet (1967) has estimated that:

"At sixty years of age a man has spent more than 20 years in sleep. Fifteen of these years are passed in the subjective emptiness of dreamless sleep, and about five in the imaginary and prodigiously rich life of dream activity. We thus spend more than a third of our life unconscious of the universe which surrounds us." (p. 105)

From the research findings summarized on page 151 it is apparent that both the amount and the kinds of sleep one gets are important. Laboratory studies have shown that with prolonged deprivation of sleep the individual becomes uneven in his adaptive responses—he may respond accurately to stimulation at one moment but miss it completely the next. This may explain some high-

The hierarchy of motives changes with the pattern of available satisfactions. During twenty-four weeks of semi-starvation, subjects in the Minnesota experiment (p. 148) were asked to rate the strength of their drives for food, sex, and activity on a scale from −5 (extremely less than normal) to +5 (extremely more than normal). As the graph shows, concern with hunger increased steadily and concern with sex and activity declined during the starvation phase; during the rehabilitation phase, when adequate food was again available, these trends were reversed. The increasing preoccupation with food during the starvation period was accompanied by a decline in table manners. Subjects also developed a new interest in cookbooks, which they collected and read avidly, making files of recipes and planning concoctions like candy bars with chocolate sauce (Keys *et al.*, 1950).

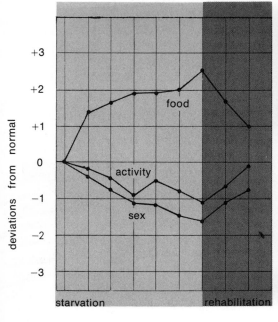

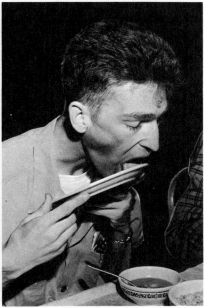

way crashes in which people fail to respond to signs or other visual cues; what apparently happens is described as a "sleep seizure" or "microsleep" when for a split second their brain waves are those of sleep (Segal, 1966). Sleep deprivation is also associated with increased irritability and impaired judgment, as well as with a marked decline in performance on complex learning and problem-solving tasks. Prolonged and severe sleep deprivation, like severe hunger and thirst, is a painful experience; both types of deprivation have been used in extracting information and confessions from prisoners.

3. *Warmth and cold.* Man has built-in homeostatic mechanisms which enable him to adjust to variations in heat and cold up to certain limits. For example, at a signal that the body is overheating, blood vessels on the surface of the skin dilate and circulation of the blood increases, thus exposing a greater amount of the blood to the outer surfaces of the body for cooling. At the same time, activities of the sweat glands are increased, and perspiration helps to cool the surface of the body. Such homeostatic mechanisms maintain body temperature at a fairly constant 98 to 99 degrees necessary for normal functioning and survival.

Man has shown great ingenuity in supplementing his body resources for temperature control by such innovations as clothing, shelter, air conditioning, electric fans, ice water, hot drinks, and blankets. Such innovations have enabled him to survive in both very warm and very cold geographical areas. Climate, of course, is an important factor in the popularity of some areas of our country, such as Arizona, California, Hawaii, and Florida.

Safety—pain avoidance. Very early an infant will withdraw from painful experience or try to avoid objects that have brought him pain or discomfort in the past. The threat or experience of pain is unpleasant and highly motivating as well as serving as a warning or indicator of bodily harm.

Pain differs from other biological drives, such as hunger and thirst, in that it is not aroused by deprivation and does not involve a cyclic pattern of occurrence and gratification but is an episodic condition of the organism that can be produced at any time by pain-inducing stimuli. Most forms of intense stimulation—such as light, sound, heat, cold, and pressure—as well as tissue inflammation and damage can produce pain. We have already noted that severe hunger, thirst, and fatigue can also be intensely painful. And certain emotions—particularly anxiety—are painful and highly motivating.

Pain-avoidance tendencies are so strong that even consummatory acts necessary for survival of the individual and the species can be seriously suppressed by painful stimulation. In male dogs and cats, for example, sexual behavior can be seriously suppressed by mildly painful electric shocks; even eating can be suppressed by moderately painful shock delivered through the feet or food dish when the animal is eating (Solomon, 1964). Such suppression can be permanent, leading to fatal self-starvation.

Since pain is usually produced by situations that are harmful to the organism, it is of crucial survival value in preventing bodily injury or damage. Unfortunately, even in our technologically advanced society, the basic need for safety and pain avoidance is by no means fully met. Accidents and painful diseases, such as arthritis and cancer, affect many people. However, we can see the motivation toward ensuring safety and pain avoidance in the many safety rules and precautions that society establishes and in the search for better anesthetics, drugs, and other methods for alleviating physical pain.

Stimulation and activity. Research studies have shown that a certain level of information input is essential for maintaining psychological integration. If the input level falls below the minimum, the individual strives to increase it; and if the information input increases to the point of overloading the system, the individual strives to decrease the rate. As Jones and McGill (1967) have described it:

"Human Ss appear to experience drive states whenever their rate of information transmission varies in either direction from some characteristic value. . . ." (p. 29)

Although individuals react somewhat differently depending on their personality make-up, a marked reduction of stimulation over a period of hours or days tends to be both disorganizing and uncomfortable. In an early experiment at McGill University, stu-

---

STAGES OF SLEEP AND SLEEP NEEDS

Recent studies indicate that it is not simply how much sleep the individual gets but also the type of sleep which determines whether he awakens refreshed or groggy. Recordings of brain waves, eye movements, and other measures have shown that there are four stages of sleep, extending from light sleep to progressively deeper sleep. Such recordings reveal that a normal adult spends about 20 per cent of his sleep in Stage 1 (probably the main stage for dreaming and characterized by rapid eye movements —REM); about 60 per cent in intermediary Stages 2 and 3; and about 20 per cent in the deep sleep of Stage 4. Typically, the individual goes through all four stages in about 90 minutes—from light through deep sleep and back again to light sleep and a repetition of the cycle (Hartmann, 1966).

Man has long been fascinated by his dreams, and more recently the systematic study of dreaming has shown that Stage 1 (REM sleep, or dreaming) is of key importance. In a most interesting experiment, Dement (1960) deprived 5 normal human subjects of most of their dreaming for 5 nights in a row. This was done by awakening the subjects whenever their brain waves and eye movements indicated that they were entering a REM period. This procedure reduced dreaming time some 80 to 90 per cent. Among the many interesting findings reported by Dement were:

1. An increasing number of awakenings were required to keep the subjects from having REM periods—from 4 to 5 the first night to 20 to 30 the fifth night.

2. During the recovery nights, the subjects showed a marked increase in REM time, often taking up 30 to 40 per cent of total sleeping time.

3. In the daytime, during the deprivation period, the subjects were observed to be unusually tense and irritable. Although they had slept 6 to 7 hours, they behaved as if they had been deprived of a great deal of sleep.

4. In a control study later, when the same subjects were subjected to the same number of awakenings but during non-REM sleep, none of the preceding findings were repeated.

5. When three human subjects were subjected to 15 nights of dream deprivation, the effects were accentuated. In fact, Dement (1963) concluded that where an individual is marginally adjusted, the prevention of REM sleep may trigger a breakdown.

Originally it was thought that the dreaming was what was needed but it now appears likely that it is the type of sleep that is essential, especially during early development, when REM sleep may provide stimulation essential for the developing central nervous system. Newborn babies spend at least half their sleeping time in the REM state, and for premature babies the REM state may involve as much as 80 per cent of sleeping time.

Recent research findings indicate that deep sleep, too, may be much more important to well-being than had been previously recognized:

In a study of three groups of poor sleepers—normal elderly persons, severe asthmatics, and patients suffering from insufficient thyroid hormones—it was found that all members of these three groups had a marked lack of deep sleep and in some cases almost none. When the thyroid-deficient patients were treated with thyroid hormone, the percentage of sleep in Stage 4 rose from 11 to 12 to 17 per cent (Jacobson & Kales, 1967).

Depressed patients, too, commonly suffer a deficit of deep sleep and show more Stage 4 sleep after therapy (Nelson, 1967; Jacobson & Kales, 1967). Vigorous exercise during the day or early evening has been found to lead to an increase of deep sleep. Apparently there is some validity to the old saying about "sleeping like a log."

These findings raise the question of possible long-range effects from sleeping pills and other drugs on the sleep cycle and hence on psychological functioning. For example, the barbiturates, the amphetamines, and also alcohol have been found to suppress the dream state (Hartmann, 1966).

EFFECTS OF SENSORY DEPRIVATION

In a study of the psychological strains engendered when small groups are isolated from others and confined to a limited space, as in undersea stations and space capsules, Haythorn and Altman (1967) concluded:

"People confined to dark, quiet chambers—the traditional 'solitary confinement' of the prisoner, or the sound-proof room used for training astronauts—often display bizarre stress and anxiety symptoms, including hallucinations, delusions, apathy, and the fear of losing sanity. Their performance deteriorates. In fact, recent evidence suggests that important changes may actually occur in the nervous system that will persist for some time after the isolate comes back to the normal world. Men in lonely military stations have shown similar reactions, if to a lesser degree. Men simply may not be built to adapt well to a world with too little stimulus or variety."(p. 19)

Here it may be pointed out that stimulus invariance as well as level of stimulation may be of crucial importance for adjustment to isolation and confinement (Weybrew, 1967). This is especially true in cases where the isolation or confinement continues over an extended period of time.

---

dents would remain lying quietly in a room by themselves no more than three days even though they were being well paid to do so (Heron, Doane, & Scott, 1956). They found the experience increasingly unpleasant and frightening and eventually intolerable. Under extreme conditions, studies have shown that there tends to be some measure of disorientation, impairment of problem solving, and other symptoms of lowered integration. Some subjects even develop delusions and hallucinations (Schultz, 1965; Haythorn & Altman, 1967). At the same time, the individual becomes increasingly eager for stimulation and is prone to accept any information that is "fed in," a tendency which suggests why brainwashing can be effective. Interestingly, a low level of unstructured stimulation, such as a continuous soft buzzer or a dim, suffused light, is more disruptive than total absence of stimulation.

Students who have attempted too many courses at once are well aware of the effects of information input overloading. Miller (1960; 1965a) has shown that when messages come in too fast, we cannot handle even the usual number effectively—resulting in a reduction in problem-solving ability and lowered psychological integration. Typically the subject attempts to "tune out" surplus inputs in an effort to maintain inner integration. Where such defenses are inadequate and the excessive input continues, psychological functioning may become disorganized.

Even in the less dramatic conditions of everyday life, there appears to be an optimal level of stimulation, which varies with the individual and with time. Under some conditions—as in boredom—we may strive to increase the level of stimulation by doing something different or engaging in activities that we find "exciting." On the other hand, when we feel under excessive pressure or "overloaded," we strive to reduce the level of input. Thus we may drop a course or otherwise restrict our activities. Each individual apparently develops techniques for maintaining the level of stimulation within the limits essential for his integrated functioning.

Sex. Sexual motivation is probably second only to the hunger motive in its far-reaching implications for social living. The family is based upon a sexual union as well as on enduring emotional and other ties. And sex is a dominant theme in much of our music, art, drama, and literature.

Although the meaning and importance of sex vary greatly from one person to another, sexual tensions, fantasies, and experiences, as well as problems centering around sexual gratification, are usually important facets of a young person's life in our society. Depending on his attitude toward his sexuality and the part he assigns it in his overall life plan, it can be an important channel for self-actualization and intimacy or a source of anxiety and self-devaluation.

Although the sex drive has a hormonal basis and stimulation of the genitals is innately pleasurable, the strength of the sex drive clearly depends upon the individual's experience (Hardy, 1964). For example, the girl who is indoctrinated with the view that sex is evil and dirty may develop little sexual motivation and may even find sexual intercourse unpleasant or repugnant. As a consequence of differing cultural viewpoints and individual life experiences, there are widespread differences in the strength and perceived significance of the sex drive among adolescents and young adults. Approved patterns of sexual gratification also vary considerably from one society to another although, interestingly, incest is forbidden by all major social groups. In our own society sexual codes seem to be becoming more liberalized. We shall deal with this trend and other aspects of sexual adjustment in a later chapter.

Now, as we turn to a consideration of psychological motives, it may be pointed out that in general our biological motives tend to foster uniformities in human behavior. Although the expression of hunger, sex, and other biological motives is influenced by differing patterns of socialization, our biological motives do not, in general, lead to the marked variations that distinguish the members of one culture from members of another.

Psychological Maintenance

Despite the almost unlimited differences in motive patterns that we can develop, there seems to be a common core of psychological needs which must be met for normal development and functioning. These needs appear to represent a common psychological substratum comparable to our basic biological needs. Although failure to meet them may not threaten the individual's survival, it leads to feelings of dissatisfaction and can result in lowered psychological integration.

As we have noted, any attempt to delineate basic needs is at best arbitrary and any list must be considered tentative. In addition, basic psychological needs are by no means distinct from each other: our need for love cannot be entirely separated from our need for security or social approval. We are dealing with a complex spectrum of interrelated psychological requirements which operate together in varying combinations.

Curiosity. An early and unmistakable characteristic of the healthy infant is his preoccupation with exploring the sights, sounds, tastes, and feel of objects around him. He is tireless in his explorations and will pursue them despite considerable pain and inconvenience. As mothers are quick to testify, the infant is "all over the house" and "gets into everything."

Berlyne (1960) has suggested that there are three types of exploratory behavior:

1. *Orienting responses*—various automatic changes in posture or sensory adjustment in response to a novel or striking stimulus.

2. *Locomotor exploration*—active exploration of an unfamiliar environment by moving about in it and noting its details.

3. *Investigatory responses*—active manipulation of objects in the environment, including picking them up, examining them, and taking them apart.

Undoubtedly a child's need to explore and manipulate is related to his physical need for stimulation and activity, but the child is doing more than simply being active and exercising his sense organs and muscles. He is finding regularities that he can use to understand his world and to establish expectations. Gradually he learns that certain motions produce interesting noises and certain acts bring punishment or service from his mother. He thus finds patterns that give consistency and predictability to his world from one day to the next and make it possible for him to improve his adjustments to it on successive encounters.

Since children encounter diverse reinforcements in relation to their curiosity mo-

CURIOSITY IN THE INFANT MONKEY

Curiosity is by no means limited to man. The lowly rat will learn to solve problems or even cross an electrified grid when the only reward is the opportunity to explore a maze; and the curiosity of cats is legendary. The following description by Harlow (1963) indicated the strength of the infant monkey's motivation to explore as soon as it is able to respond to visual stimuli:

"At this time the monkey begins to show a compulsive need for visual exploration, which leads to manipulation. It can see and it must see; it can manipulate and it cannot keep itself from manipulating. It searches its cage for anything to explore: some mechanical part of the cage or any toy or plaything that is introduced. This is a strong, powerful compulsive motive. If the best plaything available is only a piece of chain hanging down into the cage, the infant will bat it back and forth or pull it or climb it or swing from it dozens or hundreds of times a day. If a more intriguing plaything such as a mechanical puzzle . . . is placed in the cage, the monkeys will work on it again and again and will, after a time, learn how to solve it for no other reward than the sheer satisfaction of making the proper movements. Once visual exploration, curiosity, and subsequent manipulation appear, they are never lost, and monkeys both in their cages and in the wild spend a large part of their day engaging in such activities." (p. 590)

As we go up the phylogenetic scale, we find not only more exploratory behavior but a greater proportion of active investigatory behavior in which the organism goes beyond finding out about the environment to looking for ways to influence and control it. For man, science is an enterprise in which these investigations are carried out in a systematic and cumulative way.

tive, it is not surprising that there are wide differences among adults in the strength of this need and in the ways it is met. Given favorable conditions, however, adults continue to show a high level of curiosity. In fact, through history men have repeatedly risked their lives to learn about their world —and now their universe. As Phenix (1964) has pointed out, the feeling of obligation to discover and tell the truth is one of the most insistent and perennial aspects of human behavior. Most of us want to know about reality even when the knowledge is painful or unpleasant.

Order and meaning. Man cannot act effectively until he has built up an orderly view of his world and himself which enables him to evaluate new situations and anticipate the effect of his actions. To be effective, the frame of reference that he builds up must be accurate. But accurate or inaccurate, man develops a frame of reference because he must. Unless he can see regularity and predictability in his environment, he cannot work out an intelligent response to it.

Man's striving to achieve an orderly and meaningful picture of his world is shown by his dislike of ambiguity, lack of structuring, chaos, or events which seem beyond his understanding and control and which place him at the mercy of alien forces. Even the most primitive peoples develop explanations for lightning, thunder, death, and other events which they do not understand. Accurate or not, such explanations provide order and meaning and a sense of potential prediction and control. Modern science is simply a more sophisticated attempt to meet the same need.

Our striving for order and meaning is also evident in the tendency to maintain the consistency and stability of our frame of reference. Festinger (1962) has shown that when new information is inconsistent with our existing ideas, we are uncomfortable until the conflict is resolved. For example, if we were to walk bareheaded in the rain and not get wet, we would be uncomfortable until we could resolve the *cognitive dissonance*— the discrepancy between our existing assumptions and the new information. Trying to get along with contradictory pictures of our world would be like trying to drive on a highway with incompatible pictures of on-coming traffic. When new information is at variance with accepted assumptions, we strive to reduce the dissonance, often by denial, rationalization, or reinterpretation.

To say that man strives for order and meaning in his world does not mean that he always acts rationally. But curiously enough, he strives to prove to himself and others that his actions are rational. As Fromm (1955) has pointed out: "However unreasonable or immoral an action may be, man has an insuperable urge to rationalize it—that is, to prove to himself and to others that his action is determined by reason, common sense, or at least conventional morality." (p. 65) To face the fact that one's behavior may be irrational arouses anxiety, for it implies a lack of order and dependability in oneself, comparable to what one would experience in a world lacking in order and stability.

Adequacy, competence, security. Each person needs to feel basically capable of dealing with his problems. When we see our resources as inadequate for coping with a stressful situation, we tend to become anxious and disorganized, for we anticipate failure and painful consequences. This pattern is dramatically illustrated in the disor-ganization that occurs in panic reactions, but felt inadequacy in any situation can interfere with integrated, effective behavior.

Feelings of adequacy are heavily dependent upon the development of competencies for dealing with life's problems—in fact, adequacy and competence appear to be opposite sides of the same coin. White (1959) has pointed out that strivings for competence are evident even in the early playful investigatory behavior of children. Through exploration, "reality testing," and play, the child tries out different kinds of transactions with his environment and practices many basic skills. Later, these early foundations of knowledge and competence are greatly expanded by the processes of formal education. In a broad sense, it would appear that our strivings toward competence are part of our human tendency to grow toward autonomy, independence, and self-direction.

The need for security develops with and is closely related to our need for adequacy. In a general sense, security is assurance of adequacy in the future. Because we soon learn that failure to meet our needs is acutely unpleasant, we strive to establish and maintain conditions that will ensure future as well as present need gratification. Our need for security is reflected in the common prefer-

IS THERE AN INNATE TERRITORIALITY MOTIVE IN MAN?

Many species of animals show a possessiveness about specific areas of land which has been called "territoriality." Early in the spring, for example, a male robin establishes an area for receiving his mate and will fight other males who try to enter this area. Lions stake out certain hunting grounds and fight off intruders. Little research has been done on territoriality in humans, but attachment to homeland has always been a strong motivating force—as has ownership of land and home. Throughout history, nations, groups, and individuals have often fought to maintain their "territorial rights." In his book *Culture Against Man,* anthropologist Jules Henry (1963) makes a strong case for territoriality as a basic motive for man as well as many other animals.

However, Ashley Montagu (1968) has pointed out that whereas some peoples are addicted to their territories and jealously defend their boundaries, others, like the Eskimo, show no sense of territorial rights and welcome anyone who chooses to settle among them. Other tribal groups peacefully adapt themselves to those who encroach on their lands or move elsewhere. And still other groups appear to have little difficulty in giving up their homelands for other lands more favorable to their purposes. In short, some peoples are territorially minded and others are not—apparently learning rather than biological tendencies playing the key role in determining how they have come to think and feel about their homeland.

ence for jobs with tenure, in social security legislation, in insurance against disability and other contingencies, and in the establishment and maintenance of law and order. When an individual chronically has a deep and pervasive sense of insecurity, it is likely to lead to fearfulness and apprehension and failure to participate fully in his world.

The more adequate we feel, the less aware we are of our need for security. Thus the person who feels confident of his powers may value the exploration of unfamiliar paths—leaving the safe security of the known to look for richer experiences and more fulfilling ways of life. On the other hand, the more inadequate we feel, the more need we feel for security and the more we cling to the known and familiar. Undoubtedly many people continue in an uncongenial job because the challenge of starting anew is too frightening.

Love and affiliation. The need to love and be loved appears to be crucial for both healthy functioning and normal personality development. Its role in development was discussed in the preceding chapter. Human beings appear to need and strive to achieve warm, loving relationships with others and suffer from loneliness and a sense of deficit when such relationships are lacking. The longing for intimacy with others remains with us throughout our lives, and separation from or loss of loved ones usually presents a difficult adjustment problem.

The general tendency to relate to others in a warm, positive way has been called the *affiliative* motive. Affiliative behavior takes many forms; it is seen in the normal infant-mother relationship, in companionship and friendship, and in the devotion and love of happily married couples. The extent to which the affiliative motive develops appears to depend heavily upon the quality of early relationships with others. As we have seen, if a child fails to establish a social attachment during his early months or if he is treated with coldness, rejection, or brutality in his early years, he is likely to experience later difficulties in establishing warm relationships.

Often the need for love and affiliation is thought of simply as a need to receive love and affection from others, but our need to love is fully as great. We need to relate to and care about other people if we are to grow and function properly as human beings. Christianity and other great religions see such an outgoing love as basic to man's fulfillment. Although we ordinarily meet our needs for love and affiliation in marriage, family, and friendships, we are capable of "brotherly love" which goes beyond the love of family and particular individuals to a basic orientation of concern for all mankind. Individuals who lack such "psychological roots" often feel alienated from the mainstream of humanity—somewhat like strangers in a foreign land.

Belonging and approval. The growing infant is completely dependent on assistance from others. As we have seen, he soon learns that such assistance may be tied to approval—that socially approved behavior is rewarded, while socially disapproved behavior is punished. At first, this pattern involves only the family group, but with time it becomes necessary to be accepted and approved by others in order to meet many of his physical and psychological needs. So he learns to strive for positive regard from other persons who play an important role in his life, and he strives to become and remain an approved member of the social groups with which he identifies himself.

Man's need for social belonging and approval was well brought out many years ago by William James (1890):
"No more fiendish punishment could be devised . . . than that one should be turned loose in society and remain absolutely unnoticed by all the members thereof. If no one turned around when we entered, answered when we spoke, or minded what we did, but if every person we met 'cut us dead,' and acted as if we were non-existing things, a kind of rage and impotent despair would ere long well up in us, from which the cruelest bodily tortures would be a relief. . . ." (pp. 293-294)

Failure to gain interpersonal and group acceptance and the loneliness that results are particularly difficult and painful problems in the group-conscious society in which we live. Especially is this true for the person who depends heavily upon the regard of others as a basis for his feelings of self-identity and worth.

Self-esteem and worth. As we learn society's values and standards concerning education, physical appearance, economic status, and moral behavior, we begin to apply these standards in evaluating ourselves. We come to need not only other people's approval, but our own approval of ourselves. Only as we measure up to the standards we have accepted do we feel good about ourselves and worthy of the respect of others. If we see ourselves as falling short, we tend to feel unworthy, devaluated, and anxious. Thus we come to place a high value on the situations and activities that bring us evidences of our own worth.

Self-esteem has its early grounding in parental affirmation of our worth and in our mastery of early developmental tasks; it receives continued nourishment from the development of new competencies and from achievement in areas that we think are important. Being a football star or earning a Phi Beta Kappa key or simply doing a competent job in our studies can contribute to our self-esteem. We also tend to depend for continuing confirmation of our worth on others' esteem for us. Most of us try to ensure such esteem by making ourselves attractive to others, conforming to their norms, and seeking acceptance in respected groups. The esteem of the people most important to us is especially crucial. It is difficult to maintain a conviction of our own worth when those we admire look down on us.

Although self-approval and social approval usually result from the same kinds of behavior, this is not always the case, especially in a complex and heterogeneous society like ours. If the individual rejects the standards of the larger culture or of particular groups, then their approval will not bolster his self-esteem but may actually undermine it. For example, members of Students for a Democratic Society would not be reassured by approval from middle-class groups, and members of the Young Republicans League would be disturbed if the Communist party endorsed a program they had undertaken. On the other hand, members of both groups gain self-esteem from the approval of their own members.

Values, goals, plans, and hope. We have emphasized man's need for values as a guide to his choices and for providing meaning for his existence—for answering the question "Why?" In Chapter 16 we shall deal with man's quest for values in some detail; here we may simply reiterate their central importance as a basis for his choices and actions.

Closely related to and guided by his

SILENT TREATMENT AND THE "LONG EYE"

Eloquent testimony to man's need for feelings of belonging and approval was provided by the experience of small groups of scientists, officers, and enlisted personnel who voluntarily subjected themselves to isolated antarctic living for the better part of a year (Rohrer, 1961). During this period, troublesome individuals were occasionally given the "silent treatment"; the man was completely ignored by the group as if he did not exist. This "isolation" procedure resulted in a syndrome called the "long eye," which was characterized by varying combinations of sleeplessness, spontaneous bursts of crying, hallucinations, a deterioration in habits of personal hygiene, and a tendency for the man to move aimlessly about or lie in his bunk staring into space. These symptoms cleared up when he was again accepted by the group and permitted to interact with others in it.

values are the individual's goals and plans. For man lives in the future as well as in the present: his goals and plans—and his hope of achieving them—are the focus not only of his dreams but of much of his present behavior.

Young adults in our society who "drop out" often appear to do so because they see nothing worth making an effort for; "apathy" in the ghetto often reflects not lack of desire but hopelessness about achieving anything worth while. In more extreme situations, reports of prisoner-of-war camps tell of cases in which prisoners who had lost hope simply pulled their blankets over their heads and waited for death to come (Nardini, 1952). Lazarus (1966) reports that shipwreck victims who lose hope may die after a few days even though physiologically they could have survived many days longer.

Surprisingly, there has been little research on the need for goals and for hope. But like the need for love, we can infer such needs from observations of the typical results when people are "planless" or lack hope. Plans and hope appear to act as catalysts: in their presence energy is mobilized, effort is undertaken and coordinated, skills are developed and used, and satisfactions are achieved. Without them, life is meaningless and we drift; and neither we nor our society gain satisfaction from our existence.

Forms of Actualization Strivings

Motivation theory, as we have seen, has long been dominated by the concept of maintenance of steady states—with the emphasis on overcoming deficits, reducing tension, and returning to a state of equilibrium. But maintenance strivings do not explain the behavior of the explorer, the scientist, the artist, the composer, the dramatist, or the astronaut. Man strives to grow, to improve, to become more capable, to express himself—to actualize his potentialities and fulfill himself as a human being. Huxley (1953) has made this point with dramatic clarity:

"Human life is a struggle—against frustration, ignorance, suffering, evil, the madden-

ing inertia of things in general; but it is also a struggle for something . . . . And fulfillment seems to describe better than any other single word the positive side of human development and human evolution—the realization of inherent capacities by the individual and of new possibilities by the race; the satisfaction of needs, spiritual as well as material; the emergence of new qualities of experience to be enjoyed; the building of personalities." (pp. 162-163)

Actualization strivings are aimed not at restoring the equilibrium or status quo but at some sort of improvement. Achievement of one goal usually opens new vistas and creates new incentives for further growth. By contrast, the achievement of maintenance goals is likely to end the activity in that direction until or unless deprivation occurs again or is anticipated.

Our actualization strivings, like our maintenance strivings, seem to be initiated from within. They "come naturally" without having to be learned and are characteristic of human beings in widely differing cultures. Yet prevalent as this growth motivation is, growth is not universal. The person who must struggle hard for mere survival may have little time or energy left for social or spiritual growth; the neurotic is too busy defending himself to be free to grow. Because man is a creature of choice rather than instinct, he can choose stagnation instead of growth.

Our strivings toward actualization take different forms depending upon our abilities, values, and life situation. On a simple level, we see attempts at self-enhancement in the use of cosmetics and other ornamentation to make oneself attractive; on a more complex level, fulfillment strivings may take the form of learning new skills, being a good wife and mother, or writing poetry—any activity that contributes to personal growth or that adds meaning and richness to one's life.

We have described our needs for meaning, love, and relatedness as maintenance needs, since they must be met for normal growth and functioning. However, they are also forms of actualization striving, since

The actions and adornments that bring us self-enhancement depend on what we have learned to regard as attractive—which, in turn, are strongly influenced by what we know others around us will admire and regard as attractive. The many kinds of dress and adornment that have made girls feel "chic" are only an especially visible demonstration of the variety in styles of speaking, thinking, and behaving that can bring us social approval and a confirmation of our attractiveness. For such approval and self-enhancement, people have been willing to undergo considerable physical discomfort—from bound feet to laced-in waists to copper coils that stretch the neck, like those worn by the Burmese girl above which tell her world that she is a girl of wealth.

much of our actualization takes place as we broaden our scope of knowledge, form loving relationships with others, and expand our relatedness to our world.

Finding increased satisfactions. Our capacity to see value in our experiences results in our coming to expect a certain level of satisfaction from everything we do. When we go out to dinner, we expect the food to meet certain standards in quality and variety. When we go to a movie, we expect it to meet certain standards of plot, character portrayal, and photography. The norms that we use in evaluating new experience as "worth while" or "disappointing" are based on our standards and expectations. We also use such standards in deciding which new experiences to choose and which ones to avoid. We plan a trip because we expect certain values from it. We avoid a party, a television program, or a lecture if we think it will not make a sufficient return in value received on our investment of time and participation.

But this is not all. We seem to suffer from what the poets call "divine discontent." What was perfectly satisfying yesterday seems a little flat today, and we are constantly trying to improve the quality of our experience. We wait in line to see the movie that the critics have given a top rating, excitedly watch championship football games, read interesting new novels, and attend outstanding art exhibits. The increased satisfaction that we find in any new experience becomes a part of our new standard for judging the value of subsequent experiences.

As our standards become higher, increments of satisfaction may become increasingly hard to achieve and may entail struggle and sacrifice. Yet one of our most persistent urges seems to be to build, to improve, to go beyond previous achievements and understandings, to reach just a little higher and farther than we did before.

Enhancing self-worth. The concept of self-enhancement is so broad as to be almost a substitute for the term actualization though the term is often used in the more limited sense of enhancement of one's attractiveness. The forms such enhancement takes are, of course, heavily influenced by sociocultural standards: the large, stretched lips that enhance a Ubangi woman's feeling of worth would not have that effect for us.

On a relatively simple level, this striving toward self-enhancement can be seen in the use of cosmetics, the wearing of stylish clothes, the joining of exclusive clubs, and the driving of prestige cars. This type of behavior (though of course taking different forms) is common to people all over the world. The striving toward self-enhancement is also seen in our attempt to improve our performance, to make a better showing. Our efforts in this direction may range from learning to dance or ski to make ourselves more attractive to members of the opposite sex to becoming proficient in tennis or golf for the sheer satisfaction we gain from outstanding performance.

Many of these attempts at self-enhancement result in real self-improvement, but because of the importance we attach to improving our worth in other people's eyes, the means we choose may improve our attractiveness to other people without actually changing us "inside" or improving our capabilities. Some psychologists find the source of much of modern man's anxiety in precisely this problem: in trying to develop the traits and behavior and appearance that will please other people, we often are untrue to ourselves. As Fromm (1955) has pointed out, we tend to develop a "marketing" orientation, in which we gauge the worth of a trait by its market value, instead of a "productive" orientation, in which we prize our own capacities for creative functioning regardless of what others are currently rewarding. We are afraid to be ourselves and to grow in the directions our inner natures dictate. When self-enhancement strivings are limited to externals, they do not carry us far toward actualization.

Developing and using potentials. The most obvious form of developing potentials is seen in our physical growth, in which, without conscious effort, our bodies move toward the fulfillment of the pattern inherent in the original genes. Most of our psychological potentialities get no such automatic fulfillment. Yet intellectually, emotionally, and socially, as well as physically, there is an urge to grow, to improve, to become more capable.

One of the chief ways in which this urge is evident is in the common attempt to make better sense of our world. We listen and read to find out what is going on and what has gone on and what others have thought about it. We try to broaden our viewpoint, to get a more complete picture, to expand our basic assumptions and generalizations about what is true, what is important, and what is possible. We also try to improve our understanding by redefining and reorganizing the ideas and assumptions we already have, looking for new relationships, and trying to reconcile contradictory elements.

Another important way in which we fulfill our potentialities is through building new competencies and improving old ones, developing whatever capacities we have into greater actual abilities, and using these abilities creatively. If we have special talents for music or writing, we may be quite miserable if prevented from developing and expressing them. We may persist in working at what we have a special bent for even when it is a skill not especially prized in our group. Continuing growth is satisfying in its own right. In current terminology, we all have a need to "do our thing."

Building rich linkages with the world. One of the ways we seek to grow is through the associations we form with our world, and especially with other people. We have a deep capacity for caring for others, for protecting, encouraging, and teaching others, and for helping *them* grow and find meaning and satisfaction in their lives. Unless we use this capacity we feel incomplete, unsatisfied. This is a particularly human characteristic, and caring deeply for something outside oneself is one of the most gratifying and self-fulfilling of human experiences.

Many of the experiences we value most highly are those we have shared with others close to us. Sharing a crisis or a joy or even just an hour of silence with those dear to us is an enriching thing that broadens our base of self. We treasure our family anecdotes, triumphs, and traditions. Louise Rich, in her autobiographical novel, *Happy the Land* (1946), said:

"Of Plymouth Rock, I may tell my children: 'This is where the Pilgrims landed.' Of the rock by the side of the road, halfway up Wangan Hill, I say 'Right here is where your father found the little deer that time.'" (p. 19)
Throughout our lives we build landmarks of this kind which enrich our lives and add to their meaning and value by increasing our sense of relatedness to the world around us.

Self-centeredness or narrow concern with self leads to a restriction of energy and

Developing a high degree of skill and precision in an art highly valued in one's society is an important way of satisfying one's needs for both social approval and self-actualization.

an impoverishment of meaning in one's life. By contrast, the person who can lose himself in a "cause" and feel himself part of a movement that will someday enrich life for many other people may experience exhilaration and a deep sense of fulfillment even though the gains he works for do not come to him personally or even materialize during his lifetime.

Becoming a person. Closely allied with the striving to develop one's potentials but not quite the same thing is the striving to become a person—to achieve a clear-cut sense of one's identity and to be one's "real self." As Rogers (1958) has put it:
"As I follow the experience of many clients in the therapeutic relationship which we endeavor to create for them, it seems to me that each one has the same problem. Below the level of the problem situation about which the individual is complaining—behind the trouble with studies, or wife, or employer, or with his own uncontrollable or bizarre behavior, or with his frightening feelings lies one central search. It seems to me that at bottom each person is asking: 'Who am I, really? How can I get in touch with this real self, underlying all my surface behavior? How can I become myself?'" (pp. 9-10)

The Danish philosopher Kierkegaard described this search for self more than a century ago. He pointed out that the most common despair is in being unwilling to be one's self, but that the deepest form of despair is choosing to be other than one's self.

This sense of who we are comes partly from the way others perceive us and partly from looking inward—but even more from measuring ourselves against challenges. We may learn that we are good at manipulating ideas but clumsy with our fingers, that we work best under pressure, that we can usually get people to cooperate with us, that we can usually keep our head in an emergency and figure out a solution to a new problem. The person we become is the cumulative result of countless experiences of trying to cope with particular demands; our perception of what we do well and what we do

poorly is important in the development of our sense of identity.

Each of us develops an inner nature in part uniquely his and in part common to the species. When this essential core is denied expression, the individual becomes physically or mentally ill—sometimes in obvious ways, sometimes in devious, subtle ways. As Maslow (1956) has pointed out:
"This inner nature is not strong and overpowering and unmistakable like the instincts of animals. It is weak and delicate and subtle and easily overcome by habit, cultural pressure, and wrong attitudes." But ". . . though weak, it never disappears in the normal person—perhaps not even in the sick person. Even though denied, it persists underground forever pressing for actualization." (p. 233)

Becoming a person seems to be bound up with a striving toward wholeness, toward integration and self-direction.

Activation—Drive Forces

Living systems, as we have seen, are equipped to process both energy and information. By *activation* we mean the energy mobilization required for the organism to pursue its goals and meet its needs.

The physiological mechanisms in energy mobilization, or activation, are not yet fully understood, but we know that they involve a complex combination of neural, glandular, and motor systems. In man, the nervous system—particularly the brain—seems to exercise ultimate control. Both a general arousal system and specific energizers seem to be involved.

General arousal system. Since many different external and internal stimuli (pain, loud noises, and hunger, for example) can lead to the arousal of the organism, it is evident that some central neural structure plays the primary coordinating role.[1] All the variations in intensity of behavior, whether involving simply an increase in alertness or extensive energy mobilization, appear to be mediated by this central arousal system.

In the activation of behavior, two distinct functions are performed by the central arousal system. First, it appears to "turn down" some incoming messages while letting others through, thus enabling the individual to attend selectively to particular stimuli from among the barrage of stimulation assailing him. Second, in response to certain incoming information from both internal and external receptors—information originating both inside and outside the body—it alerts the organism and sends command information for the mobilization of energy.

The stimuli to which the general arousal system responds are determined both through genetic programing and through learning. For example, a sudden loud noise or oxygen deprivation (usually, an excess of carbon dioxide) leads to arousal innately, whereas stimuli that have in the past been associated with reward or punishment also lead to arousal, but in this case through learning. Thus the general arousal system appears responsible for regulating the energy mobilization required for both biological and psychological maintenance and actualization.

Specific activating mechanisms. Other mechanisms which influence the level of activation are biological drives, emotional states, and pain and pleasure. Although these specific activators work through the general arousal system, they merit brief mention in their own right.

When biological needs are not being adequately met, equilibrium is disturbed and various internal changes take place in the organism. For example, when the individual is deprived of water for a period of time, the thirst drive comes into operation, involving both the unpleasant sensation of dryness of the mouth and throat tissues and changes in the salt concentration of the blood, which, through hypothalamic centers, trigger the

mobilization of energy. The unpleasant sensations of thirst, and the tension associated with increased activation, together appear to "drive" the organism toward meeting the need and restoring equilibrium. Our biological drives thus provide for both direction and activation of behavior; they are provisions nature has made to ensure the satisfaction of certain basic bodily needs.

Emotions, too, play an important role in both energizing behavior and influencing its direction. But whereas biological drives are initially activated by tissue needs, emotional arousal depends upon the perception of significance in a present or anticipated situation. Thus the individual may experience fear, anger, anxiety, or other emotions depending upon the way he interprets events around him. While certain emotions, such as fear, anger, and anxiety, increase the level of arousal, others, such as dejection or depression, lower it.

Our emotions also serve as important sources of emergency power in dealing with crisis situations. In a situation of great danger, for example, the mobilization of bodily resources enables the individual to exert more strength than he normally could muster as well as to sustain effort over a longer period of time. For example, in a disastrous explosion and fire aboard the aircraft carrier U.S.S. *Forrestal,* a seaman weighing only 130 pounds picked up a 250-pound, fully armed bomb and dropped it overboard (*Wingo,* 1967). The literature records many other examples of such unusual feats.

Pain or pleasure may influence the level of activation as well as the direction of behavior. For example, when the sensation of thirst becomes intense, the discomfort and pain may increase energy mobilization and drive strength. Similarly, intense anxiety is acutely painful; this in turn augments general activation as well as adding to the drive forces aimed at alleviating the anxiety. And in high degrees of energy mobilization there is unpleasant tension which adds to the drive forces already in operation. It need hardly be pointed out that anticipation of pleasure can serve as an energizer.

[1] Until recently it was thought that this central arousal system consisted of nerve nuclei and fibers in the brain stem and parts of the thalamus and hypothalamus known collectively as the *reticular activating system.* Conflicting findings have cast doubt on the adequacy of this view and have made it clear that we still have much to learn about the exact mechanisms responsible.

Levels of activation. Activation or arousal can vary in degree from very low to very high—from deep sleep to intense excitement. At any moment our level of activation is influenced by a wide range of individual and situational factors. It is affected by the way we perceive our situation and evaluate its potential satisfactions and frustrations; it is affected by many inner conditions ranging from memories and fantasies to food deprivation, illness, and fatigue; and it is affected by stimuli of the moment such as sudden loud noises, strange or novel stimuli, and conditions which inflict pain and arouse emotion.

With accumulating experience, most of us learn to respond to most situations with an appropriate level of activation. However, unfamiliar situations or situations to which we are especially vulnerable may lead to over-reaction. Or special conditions, such as severe fatigue, intense inner conflict, chronic anxiety, or illness may lead to inappropriate levels of activation as well as to extreme fluctuations in activation and slow recovery from the effects of prior activation.

There seems to be a changing relationship between level of activation and efficiency of task performance, with both low and very high levels of activation resulting in decreased efficiency. At a low level there is inadequate expenditure of energy and effort; at very high levels, as in panic reactions, there is impulsive and poorly coordinated activity. A moderate level of activation is associated with optimum alertness, flexibility, and coordination (Duffy, 1962; Lacey, 1967; Malmo, 1959).

Among the problems of modern living are those of maintaining alertness or vigilance while performing under monotonous conditions, as when driving an automobile for a sustained period of time. Maintaining arousal or activation for effort toward long-range goals such as professional degrees may also be a problem, especially when some of the courses and other steps along the way are not particularly interesting. In general, the more we see a particular goal as being related to our essential purposes and satisfactions in

living, the more energy we will have for pursuing it. For this reason, confidence in the importance of one's goals in life is a critical factor in achieving them.

MOTIVE PATTERNS AND BEHAVIOR

We have been talking about various motives as if they were independent of each other and of other psychological processes, but of course they are not. Nor are they independent of the social field in which they develop and are expressed.

Since individual motives subserve more basic strivings toward maintenance and actualization, it is helpful to view them in relation to these strivings. Thus a child shows off not because he has developed a special motive for showing off but because he is trying to gain the affection he needs for psychological equilibrium.

In keeping with whatever we learn to see as most valuable, we usually develop key, enduring motives that greatly influence our whole life style. For one person, such key motives may focus on personal achievement and the gaining of power; for another, on love and affiliation; for still another, on working toward social justice.

In this section we will briefly examine the role of social forces in motivation, the patterning of our motives, the effects of motives on other psychological processes, and the nature of motive change.

Social Forces in Motivation

Just as we found the environment to be an important force in shaping overall personality development, so we find it shaping and channeling our motives in important ways. Social standards and opportunities, social pressures and demands, and the needs of others all have an effect on our motive patterns—by influencing the goals and means we choose and by encouraging us to develop certain motives and not others. This channeling is made possible through society's ability to control how far and under what conditions our needs are met.

Goals and means. Our goals and the means we choose for achieving them are heavily influenced by social standards and opportunities. For example, as a consequence of the standards of those around us, we learn to eat certain types of food and not others, to partake of certain drinks and not others, and to satisfy our hunger and thirst under certain conditions and not others. We ordinarily reject worms and bugs as food except under conditions of severe deprivation. A devout Hindu would rather die than eat meat from the cow; devout Moslems will not eat pork. Thus satisfaction of our need for food entails far more than just finding something to eat and eating it.

Since social conditions and standards vary markedly from one group to another, the goals that are highly valued in one group may have little or no value in another. Charms to protect the individual from witchcraft would be considered of little value in our society; the monetary goals with which most Americans are preoccupied would inspire little effort among the members of a monastic order; in some societies the members try to avoid rather than to seek leadership.

Some cultures offer rich opportunities for psychological satisfactions and the fulfillment of potentialities. Others are limiting, repressive, and rigid. Some provide fulfillment opportunities for certain groups but not others—the leaders but not the followers, the wealthy but not the poor, the men but not the women. But in any group, the goals which the individual seeks and his means for trying to achieve them depend on the opportunities, rules, and standards provided by the group.

Social inhibition and facilitation of motives. Social groups, like individuals, strive for maintenance and actualization. To maintain themselves and grow, they too must meet certain needs, such as the maintenance of law and order and defense against attack by other groups.

A crucial aspect of the group's maintenance and actualization is the exercise of some measure of control over the motive patterns of its members. By its system of values and by its manipulation of rewards and punishments, society encourages certain motives and not others. In our own society there are strong incentives to develop motivation for athletic prowess, academic excellence, creative accomplishment, financial success, and leadership. Although the particular motives encouraged vary greatly from one society to another, most societies try to bring the expression of aggression and patterns of sexual gratification under social regulations—usually in ways that tend to inhibit these motives.

Hopefully, the needs and goals of the group will be compatible with those of the individual, but there is no guarantee that this will be so. Where it is not, the needs of society may sometimes take precedence over those of the individual. The government may ask us to pay high taxes and to accept austerity for the long-term good of the country; or a young man may be asked to devote several years of his life to military service. In an emergency, we may even have to risk our lives for group goals—as when the soldier is called upon to risk and, if need be, sacrifice his life in combat. In general, the needs of the individual and of the group are less likely to conflict in a democratic society than in an autocratic one.

Of course, social demands and pressures are perceived and evaluated by each individual in terms of his own frame of reference. If an individual sees social demands as threatening his own purposes and values or as detrimental to the long-range welfare and progress of the group, he may resist or reject them. When a sizable number of persons in any society perceive themselves as being in conflict with the values and goals of the rest of the group, there are likely to be severe repercussions affecting both the individuals and the larger group.

NEEDS, GOALS, AND MOTIVES

ONE NEED MAY BE SATISFIED IN MANY WAYS

Need	Examples of motives through which adequacy need might be met	Possible means for carrying out motive
Need for adequacy	to be rich	marry a rich man
	to have status	gain membership in socially elite groups
	to be commended	conform to current standards of dress and action
	to manage by oneself	earn one's way through school
	to be chosen as a wife	try to meet good prospects and attract them
	to make a contribution to society	prepare for "helping" professions

ONE GOAL CAN MEET MANY NEEDS

Goal	Possible means of reaching	Needs that might be met
College degree	pick easy courses in popular college	status, security, approval
	choose college and courses to expand competencies and prepare for challenging life work	self-fulfillment, rich linkages with world

It is clear that the same psychological need can be met through many kinds of behavior and that the same behavior, in different people, can be meeting quite different needs. In most behavior, several needs are being served at once, often in disguised form. Because learning plays such a large role in psychological motivation, we differ widely, both individually and culturally, in the strength of different psychological needs and in the motives and goals through which they are met.

Needs of others. An individual's motives and purposes derive not only from his own personal maintenance and growth needs but also from his role in the group or suprasystem (Miller, 1965a). Social living involves a constant give and take among individuals, with mutual efforts to help one another.

To the extent that we identify with other persons and with groups, we extend our motivation to concern for their maintenance and actualization as well as our own. A wife may work hard to help her husband achieve political success, and when the goal is achieved she may be as pleased as if the success were her own. An honor awarded to a son may be a source of great pride to the father. When our football team wins the big game, we may be as elated as if we had accomplished the whole thing by ourselves. This same quality of identification even makes it possible for the needs of others to take precedence over our own needs. Parents may go hungry to feed their children; a young wife may give up or postpone her own schooling to help her husband through medical school; a soldier may risk his life to rescue a wounded friend. The ability of the individual to identify with others, feel their needs as his own, and make sacrifices for them is apparent in all societies.

Sometimes, of course, our own needs and motives are in active conflict with those of others close to us. An immature mother may have a need to prolong her child's dependence; an ambitious and status-oriented wife may place excessive pressure on her easygoing husband. Often the demands and responsibilities of marriage lead to a conflict of motives between the marital partners—especially when they are not compatible to begin with. But whether or not our motives are compatible with those of others, we can meet many of our own needs only through social interaction: those near to us are dependent on our efforts and we on theirs. The chances for cementing relationships and avoiding conflict are best where there is commonality of purpose and a reasonable congruence of needs.

The individual's simultaneous existence as an individual organism and as a part of a larger social whole gives a *duality* to his motivational base. He is concerned not only with himself as a person but also with filling a meaningful role in his social context. Young people's search for something worth while to be involved in—to give their allegiance to, and to work for—attests to the significance of our social motivations in our search for self-fulfillment.

Hierarchy of Motives

Maslow (1954) has suggested that our needs arrange themselves in a hierarchy from the basic biological needs to the need for self-fulfillment or actualization, which represents the higher development of the human personality. With slight modification for our present purposes, Maslow's hierarchy may be envisaged as involving five levels of needs:

1. *Physiological needs*—basic bodily needs including the needs for food, sleep, stimulation, and activity.

2. *Safety needs*—needs for protection from bodily harm or injury and for security from threat.

3. *Love and belongingness needs*—including needs for acceptance, warmth, affection, and approval.

4. *Esteem needs*—including needs for adequacy, worth, status, and self-respect.

5. *Self-actualization (fulfillment) needs* —needs for personal growth and the realization of potentialities.

Relative strength under deprivation. According to Maslow's formulation, the lowest level of unmet need is ordinarily the one that is prepotent—the one that commands the individual's attention and efforts. For example, unless the needs for food and safety are reasonably well met, behavior will be dominated by these needs. With their gratification, however, the individual is free to devote his energies to meeting his needs on higher levels.

This concept of shifting prepotency is supported by observations of behavior in extreme situations. Both in the Nazi concentration camps and in the Japanese prisoner-of-war camps in World War II, it was a common pattern for prisoners subjected to prolonged deprivation and torture to lower their moral standards, take food from each other, and in other ways surrender the loyalties and values they had held under more normal conditions (Bettelheim, 1943; Nardini, 1952). Under conditions of extreme deprivation, most individuals will sacrifice their higher-level, actualization needs to meet acceptance, belonging, and other psychological maintenance needs—and will sacrifice the latter, in turn, for personal safety and survival.

This pattern does not always hold, however. Many creative people have pursued the development and expression of their special talents despite great physical hardships and social ridicule. Social reformers have continued their struggles despite harassment, jail sentences, and other punishment and deprivation. Every great human catastrophe has had its heroes who sacrificed their own welfare for the good of others and every age its martyrs who remained faithful to their principles and beliefs despite social ostracism, physical deprivation, torture, and often certain death. Through learning and experience, our beliefs, values, and self-esteem may become more important to us than our needs for social approval and security or even our need for safety. The extent to which safety and physiological needs dominate our behavior even under extreme conditions is an individual matter.

Deficiency vs. growth motivation. Maslow has emphasized the distinction between *deficiency* and *growth* motivation. Behavior motivated primarily by maintenance needs—hunger, safety, social approval, and so on—is deficiency motivated; that is, it is motivated by the lack of something the individual needs for stability—as compared with behavior like learning to sing or developing proficiency in athletics, which is aimed at increasing one's long-term capabilities. It is the gratification of maintenance needs that releases the individual from domination by them and frees him for self-actualization.

People who remain dominated by maintenance strivings despite adequate resources or who have not found anything else worth striving for tend to be maladjusted and unhappy. Maslow (1954) has summarized it this way: "I should say simply that a healthy man is primarily motivated by his needs to develop and actualize his fullest potentialities and capacities. If a man has any other basic needs in any active, chronic sense, he is simply an unhealthy man." In a study comparing deficiency-motivated with growth-motivated people, Maslow (1954) discovered that the latter showed a more efficient perception of reality and more comfortable relations with it; could tolerate uncertainty better; were more spontaneous and creative; were more accepting of themselves and others, were more problem-centered and less ego-centered; had deeper than average relationships with other people; had a philosophical, unhostile sense of humor; and felt kinship with and concern for all humanity.

Here the conclusions expressed by Helson (1966) appear particularly relevant: *"Men who have been creative, whether in science, the arts, literature, politics, or industry, have often been excited to a far greater degree by ideas than by food, sex, and sleep. The satisfaction of so-called basic needs is necessary but not suffcient for a full and truly satisfying life. . . . Let us there-*

fore get on with [the experimental study of] those sources of motivation, which are responsible for man's unique position among all living things." (p. 179)

Only as lower-level needs receive some minimum level of gratification are higher-level needs likely to become dominant; but only through efforts to meet higher-level needs can the individual actualize his potentialities as a human being.

Motives and Other Psychological Processes

Just as a man's various motives are related to each other, so his motivational processes and other processes are interrelated in many ways. Man, like other organisms, functions as a unit, and the primary business being attended to at the moment determines how all processes operate. During physical exertion, digestive processes cease so that more resources can be diverted to the needed physical activity. Perception and cognitive processes also subserve both the dominant activity in progress and the individual's long-term motivational patterns.

Motivational selectivity. For good or ill, our motives exercise a continuing influence over what we notice, how we see and think about it, and what we learn from it, as well as what we have fantasies and dreams about. This influence of motivation on cognitive processes is called *motivational selectivity.*

1. *Attention and perception.* Perception is an active process by means of which we select, organize, and give meaning to the information we receive from both external and internal sources. Our attention and perception may be influenced in several important ways by the motive states which predominate at the moment.

First, we are more sensitive to information related to our needs and wishes. A student scanning a bibliography to find entries on "dreaming in young children" would be selectively sensitive to titles on this subject while tending to ignore those dealing with other topics. On a more dramatic level, a man lost in the desert and suffering from intense thirst would be searching for some indication of water and probably would not notice the beauty of the sunset. In such situations the stimuli that are relevant to the active motive tend to stand out focally, while irrelevant stimuli tend to fade into the background (Leeper, 1965). People also pay more attention to information about themselves and to information they know they will have to act on later (de Sola Pool & Kessler, 1965). This tendency of an organism to single out what it considers most relevant to its purposes is called *selective vigilance.*

Second, we try to screen out information that would make us uncomfortable. Thus we tend to see only the aspects of a situation that are consistent with our expectations, assumptions, and wishes. The critical, punitive teacher spots every incipient infraction of the rules; the one who loves children sees their efforts to do the right thing. The proud father may selectively perceive the desirable traits of his son while tending not to recognize undesirable ones.

This latter form of selectivity, in which one actively resists certain perceptions, is referred to as *perceptual defense.* Numerous laboratory studies have demonstrated this phenomenon. For example, words associated with failure have been found to be less readily recognized than neutral words (Eriksen & Browne, 1956), and rude words less accurately identified than neutral words (Bootzin & Natsoulas, 1965). Evidently we try to prevent or reduce cognitive strain by not recognizing things that would make us anxious.

Third, we make perceptual errors in the direction of what we want or need to be true. If we need to see our leader as noble and strong, we resist evidence that he has feet of clay. If we mistrust a person, whatever he does "looks suspicious" and must have some nefarious motive behind it, whereas the same act performed by someone we trust would be perceived as reasonable and righteous. In a classic study, subjects were briefly shown pictures of a Negro-white conflict in which the white person was brandishing a knife;

prejudiced white viewers "saw" the knife as being in the hands of the Negro (Allport & Postman, 1945). When we encounter information that does not fit in with what we have already accepted, our need for an orderly, meaningful, predictable view of the world evidently leads us to try to change it in such a way as to produce greater consistency.

2. *Thinking and learning.* Much as we prize our ability to reason and need it for solving problems, it is all too easily subverted to a justification of what we want to do or to believe. The slogan "There are no atheists in foxholes," which became famous in World War II, is not so much a proof of God's existence as evidence of the force of the need for safety, which believing helps us to satisfy. It is notoriously difficult to think objectively about a situation when our own needs and purposes are directly involved. A marriage counselor can be more objective about the problems of other couples than he can about his own marital problems; a mother can reason more objectively about the child-rearing problems of other mothers than she can about her own. When evidence first began to appear on the relation of smoking to lung cancer, heavy smokers, as a group, were slower to accept it and more ready to argue that a causal relation had not yet been proved.

Learning, too, subserves our motivational requirements. It is hard and uninteresting to learn things that appear unrelated to our key motives, whereas we willingly devote time and energy to learning things that we see as important and useful to us. As our effort "pays off" and we begin to experience the anticipated satisfaction from learning, our incentive for further similar learning is increased. Where learning requires changing what we have already learned rather than simply acquiring new information, motivation also plays an important role, for we actively resist learning new information which is contradictory to our existing beliefs, particularly when these beliefs are central to our needs and purposes (Abelson & Carroll, 1965). A white individual who believes that dark-skinned peoples are genetically inferior to whites may find it very difficult to give up his belief despite scientific evidence to the contrary if the belief is important in bolstering his feelings of adequacy and worth. Thus what we learn, how rapidly, and how much are all influenced by our motivation.

3. *Remembering and forgetting.* Psychoanalytic models of forgetting have emphasized the relationship between unpleasantness of a memory and inability to recall it. Likewise several early experiments found that pleasant memories—particularly memories favorable to the self-concept of the individual—are more amenable to recall than unpleasant ones. Incidents which reflect adversely upon the adequacy and worth of a person are less likely to be remembered—or at least recalled (Eriksen, 1954; Glixman, 1949; Rosenzweig, 1933).

In more dramatic form, the effect of motives on recall can be seen in cases of psychogenic amnesia where the individual is unable to recall large segments of his experience which have become intolerable to him. In such cases, the material has not been forgotten but is simply inaccessible to recall; later it may be recalled again.

4. *Fantasy and dreams.* The chains of thoughts and images which occur when we are not busy responding to current demands may also reflect what we are most concerned about. According to Frankl (1959), for example, fantasies of starving prisoners of war in German concentration camps in World War II most often were of things like bread, cake, cigarettes, and warm baths. Children who live in orphanages commonly dream—both in daydreams and during sleep—about being adopted into a happy family. We have probably all experienced both fantasies and dreams concerning sexual activities, revenge, self-enhancement, and other matters in which we could readily see the influence of motivational factors. In psychotherapy, therapists often use the patient's dreams in an attempt to understand his motives and problems better.

Of course, cognitive processes are influenced by factors other than motivation; in addition, our cognitive processes may lead to changes in our motives. What we strive for is directly influenced by our assumptions concerning reality, value, and possibility—and by the feedback we obtain in terms of whether the outcome of pursuing given motives turns out to be satisfying or not. Often we must trim our motivational sails in keeping with new information.

Levels of awareness. Although writers and dramatists have long portrayed the influence of unconscious motives—motives of which we are unaware—on our behavior, Sigmund Freud was the first to study this phenomenon systematically. He noted that unconscious motives may express themselves in several forms of behavior: (1) dreams, in which desires unknown to the dreamer may appear, (2) slips of the tongue and "forgetting" names or appointments that we do not want to remember, and (3) certain neurotic reactions, as when the individual feels compelled to wash his hands many times during the day but is unaware of why he feels this compulsion. Freud concluded that such motives were not admitted to consciousness because they were unacceptable to the individual. He saw a key goal of psychoanalysis as helping the individual to identify and learn to accept this unconscious part of himself.

Although there is still considerable controversy among psychologists concerning the nature and importance of unconscious processes in human behavior, there is abundant evidence that we are often unaware or only partially aware of the motives underlying our behavior. Sometimes we are unaware of even key motives, and others may be able to infer our motives more accurately from observing our behavior than we can from introspection. Thus it may be apparent to others—but not to us—that we continually contrive to lean on someone else, or maneuver to keep people from getting too close to us, or constantly try to build ourselves up by belittling other people. Similarly, we may show off, wear expensive clothes, even marry for reasons which are unclear to us. Of course, we may think of good reasons to justify our behavior, but these may be only partially accurate, or they may not be real reasons at all.

It would appear that awareness of one's motives varies considerably from one behavior pattern to another and from person to person. Most of us are probably puzzled at one time or another by some of the things we do and think, while feeling quite certain about our motives in other cases. Usually individuals who are seriously maladjusted have only a fragmentary understanding of their motivation.

Changes in Motive Patterns

As we have seen, the developing self-structure of each person leads to a fairly consistent life style which others recognize as characteristic of him and which makes his behavior relatively predictable from one situation to another.

A central part of the individual's life style is his motive pattern—particularly his key motives, which encompass the goals of greatest worth to him. Such key motives may focus around affiliation, achievement, power, or other goals depending upon the person. Since they tend to be relatively enduring, they contribute to the continuity and consistency of his behavior. However, our motive patterns are also subject to change—both short-term and long-term changes; and these changes are important in understanding our behavior.

Short-term change. Our motivational pattern is continually changing as given needs are gratified and others come into operation. On the biological level, this process is based on

UNCONSCIOUS MOTIVATION

That unconscious motives can guide behavior has been shown experimentally by means of hypnosis. Such demonstrations are especially revealing because here we know the motivational pattern underlying the behavior. The following is a classic illustration (Erickson, 1939).

"During profound hypnosis the subject was instructed to feel that smoking was a bad habit, that he both loved and hated it, that he wanted to get over the habit but that he felt it was too strong a habit to break, that he would be very reluctant to smoke and would give anything not to smoke, but that he would find himself compelled to smoke; and that after he was awakened he would experience all of these feelings.

"After he was awakened the subject was drawn into a casual conversation with the hypnotist who, lighting one himself, offered him a cigarette. The subject waved it aside with the explanation that he had his own and that he preferred Camels, and promptly began to reach for his own pack. Instead of looking in his customary pocket, however, he seemed to forget where he carried his cigarettes and searched fruitlessly through all of his other pockets with a gradually increasing concern. Finally, after having sought them repeatedly in all other pockets, he lo- cated his cigarettes in their usual place. He took them out, engaged in a brief conversation as he dallied with the pack, and then began to search for matches, which he failed to find. During his search for matches he replaced the cigarettes in his pocket and began using both hands, finally locating the matches too in their usual pocket. Having done this, he now began using both hands to search for his cigarettes. He finally located them but then found that he had once more misplaced his matches. This time however he kept his cigarettes in hand while attempting to locate the matches. He then placed a cigarette in his mouth and struck a match. As he struck it, however, he began a conversation which so engrossed him that he forgot the match and allowed it to burn his finger tips whereupon, with a grimace of pain, he tossed it in the ash tray. . . .

"This behavior continued with numerous variations. He tried lighting a cigarette with a split match, burned his fingers, got both ends of one cigarette wet, demonstrated how he could roll a cigarette, kept stopping to converse or tell a joke, and so on. Several cigarettes were ruined and discarded. When he finally got one going successfully, he took only a few good puffs with long pauses in between and discarded it before it was used up." (pp. 342-345)

DEVELOPMENT OF NEW MOTIVES

From his pilot studies attempting to develop greater achievement motivation in adults, McClelland (1965) has drawn a number of generalizations. The following are illustrative of the conditions which appear to foster the development of new motives in general. Development of a new motive is most likely when:

1. *The individual has reason, in advance, to believe that he can, will, or should develop the motive.*

2. *The individual perceives that developing the motive is consistent with the demands of reality (and reason).*

3. *The individual can conceptualize the motive clearly and relate it to events in his everyday life.*

4. *The individual can perceive and experience the new motive as an improvement in his self-image.*

5. *The individual feels warmly and honestly supported and respected by others as a person capable of directing his own future behavior.*

Although these generalizations are based upon motive changes in an educational setting, they would appear to be applicable to our broader life setting as well.

---

the periodic intensification and reduction in the strength of physiological drives—a phenomenon referred to as *drive cycle* or *periodicity* of drive. This rhythm of many biological drives can be readily seen in the case of the hunger drive; with deprivation, it comes into operation; with satiation, it is replaced by other motives.

A periodic rhythm on the psychological level is not apparent—either in maintenance strivings, such as those for adequacy and self-esteem, or in strivings for growth and fulfillment. Yet here too, deprivation is followed by an increase in motive strength, while with gratification, the salience of a given motive tends to be reduced and other motives take precedence. Thus however well off we are, we always seem to find some new dissatisfaction on which to focus our energies. This is often dramatically illustrated when we achieve some long-sought goal in life, such as college graduation or marriage, which does in fact gratify important needs, only to find that instead of feeling relaxation and peace we become aware of a whole new set of motives.

Short-term changes in motives may also occur as a result of unexpected events. A person who wins a two-week vacation trip to Hawaii in a contest may interrupt his other plans long enough to take advantage of this opportunity; a person watching television interrupts his viewing in a hurry when he discovers that the room is on fire. Many of the unpredictable opportunities and threats which occur in our lives lead to short-term motive change.

To take advantage of unexpected opportunities and to protect itself from sudden threats, the organism has *interrupt mechanisms* which enable it to cease its ongoing activity and respond to more urgent needs (Simon, 1967). Sudden "loud" stimuli which warn of danger as well as internal stimuli apprising us of some critical need can bring the interrupt system into operation—as can a re-evaluation of the worth of a goal we have been avidly pursuing or the sudden apparent availability of a more attractive one.

Long-term changes. Our motive patterns may undergo considerable change over time. We may develop important new motives, show a shift in the priorities of existing motives, or discard motives that have formerly been of significance. Some of these long-term changes are the result of experience and learning; others seem to come about from new requirements at different life stages.

There are some predictable changes in motive patterns as we go through life. The key motives of the child are not those of the adolescent; nor are those of the adolescent the same as those of the adult or older person. Changes in the environment and in our life situation may lead to modification of our motive pattern. The college beauty queen may show a considerable shift in motives and behavior when she becomes a mother and full-time homemaker.

A classic example of changed motives with new environmental demands is that of young King Henry of England, as portrayed by Shakespeare in *Henry V*. Before he became king, he had been a fun-loving young man without apparent interest in anything but the next riotous party. After he became king, he developed a deep concern for the welfare of his country and disciplined himself for responsible service to it. Less dramatic but equally basic changes in motivation may occur in any one of us if we see our environment making new demands on us.

Unfortunately, we know comparatively little about the development of particular motives. One motive which has received a good deal of research attention is the achievement motive; research is also in progress on the development of other motives, such as those for affiliation and power.

One important contributor to motive change is feedback. If we realize that a motive has been unrewarding or even punishing, we may re-evaluate its significance. Thus the carefree bachelor may take a different view of marriage when he realizes that he is not building lasting relationships, is denied a normal family life, and in general finds his existence unrewarding and unfulfilling. A sizable number of young people today are rejecting the widely accepted motives of power, achievement, and financial success in favor of what they consider more growth-oriented and self-fulfilling motives. All of us develop standards of evaluation, and when a particular motive yields little satisfaction, we are likely to make changes.

To help them better understand their own motives and to make motive changes in a more systematic manner, many people participate in intensive group experience or obtain professional counseling or psychotherapy. We shall examine these resources for change in Chapter 12.

SUMMARY AND A LOOK AHEAD

By *motivation* we mean conditions within the organism that *activate* behavior and influence its *direction*. Despite the diversity in the goals we seek, our behavior can be seen as directed toward the broad goals of maintaining our safety and wholeness and developing our potentialities. Motivation has been variously conceived in terms of primary and derived drives, the reduction of tension, and either inner forces or environmental stringpulling. Since both inner and outer conditions arouse behavior and influence its direction, both must be taken into account.

Among our requirements for optimal biological maintenance are food, water, and sleep; stimulation and activity; safety; and sexual expression. Among our requirements for psychological balance and efficient functioning are knowing about our world and seeing order and meaning in it; feeling adequate, competent, and secure; experiencing love and affiliation, feeling that we belong and are approved; seeing ourselves as being of worth; and having a sense of direction, with hope for success in our efforts. Actualization strivings include attempts to find increased satisfactions, to enhance our self-worth, to develop and use our potentials, to build rich linkages with the world, and to become a person.

Energy for the pursuit of our goals is made available through a general arousal system, as well as by means of a number of specific mechanisms associated with particular drives. Emotions, aroused by the perception of significance, are also energizers, as are pain or pleasure (present or anticipated) and muscular tension. Moderate levels of activation are associated with more efficiency of behavior than either very low or very high levels.

Social demands and rewards limit the goals we seek and the means we use for meeting our needs; they also encourage the development of certain motive patterns and discourage the development of others. To the extent that we identify with other individuals and with groups, we regard their maintenance and growth as part of our own; sometimes we even work toward others' welfare at the sacrifice of our own.

There is a hierarchy of human motives, encompassing physiological needs, safety needs, love and belongingness needs, esteem needs, and actualization needs. Under conditions of deprivation, the "deficiency" needs usually predominate, but when they are met, human beings become restless and more concerned with meeting actualization needs. Human beings may choose to meet psychosocial needs at the expense of biological ones.

Man functions as a unit, and attention, perception, thinking, learning, and other cognitive processes all tend to subserve both the dominant activity of the moment and the individual's long-term motivational patterns. We may be aware, partially aware, or unaware of our motives.

Key motives, encompassing the goals of greatest worth to an individual, are a continuing, central part of his life style. However, there are both short-term changes in motives—as a result of drive periodicity and "interrupt mechanisms"—and long-term changes, some predictable at different life periods, others learned in response to experience or changed environmental requirements.

In this chapter we have been concerned with inner conditions that arouse us and influence the directions of our strivings. In the next chapter we will examine what happens when our strivings are blocked or when inner or outer conditions place us under stress.

Key terms used in this chapter include:

motivation, motive, directionality and activation of behavior (p. 143)
approach behavior, avoidance behavior (p. 143)
primary motives, secondary motives (p. 144)
motivation as tension reduction, pleasure-pain model (pp. 145-146)
push and pull models of motivation (p. 146)
steady states, homeostasis (p. 147)
biological maintenance needs (pp. 148-152)
psychological maintenance needs (pp.153-157)
cognitive dissonance (p. 154)
forms of actualization strivings (pp. 158-162)
drive forces in behavior (pp. 162-163)
social inhibition and facilitation of motives (p. 165)
hierarchy of motives (p. 167)
deficiency motivation, growth motivation (p. 168)
motivational selectivity, perceptual defense (pp. 168-170)
levels of awareness (p. 170)
short-term motive changes, long-term motive changes (pp. 171-173)

Chapter 6

PROBLEMS OF ADJUSTMENT
(STRESS)

Types and Sources of Stress
Severity of Stress
Other Key Aspects of Stress

Life would be simple indeed if our needs could always be satisfied. But as we know, there are many obstacles—both environmental and internal—which interfere with gratification of our needs and complicate our strivings toward our goals. We all encounter delays, lacks, failures, losses, restrictions, obligations, illnesses, conflicts, and pressures. Such events place adjustive demands or *stress* on us. They require effort and action on our part if we are to meet our needs.

Most of the stress situations we encounter in everyday life are minor and relatively easy to cope with. When we feel hungry, we may stop what we are doing and go to the cafeteria for lunch; when we feel cold we put on a sweater or coat. Such adjustive demands require adaptive action, but they produce minimal *strain* within the organism—that is, they do not lead to serious disequilibrium of physiological or psychological steady states. From time to time, however, most of us face stress situations which are difficult to cope with and result in considerable inner strain. A serious illness requiring major surgery, a broken engagement, marital discord or divorce, the death of a loved one, flunking out of college, being arrested, financial pressures or losses, social disapproval, severe guilt feelings, and value conflicts are examples of such stressful situations. For many

people, the pressures and worries of modern living are continuing sources of severe stress, exacting a cumulative toll in wear and tear on the organism. In some cases, the strain is so severe that the coping resources of the individual are overtaxed and he breaks down.

Stress may involve biological- or psychological-level processes. Pneumonia viruses produce stress on a biological level, and the basic adjustive reaction involves defenses on the biological level. Guilt, on the other hand, is stressful chiefly on the psychological level, and self-defense mechanisms are the chief means of coping with it. We may also speak of stress on group and societal levels. Thus the loss of the father constitutes a stressful situation for the family; economic depressions and wars are examples of stress situations which place adjustive demands on the society as a whole as well as on the individuals and groups within it.

In our present discussion, we shall be concerned primarily with psychological-level stress as experienced by the individual although some consideration of both biological- and sociological-level stress will inevitably be entailed. We shall consider: (1) the basic types of stress we encounter and some of the particular stresses that characterize our time and place in history, (2) factors influencing the severity of stress, and (3) other key aspects of stress including its cost to the organism. Then in the chapter which follows, we shall deal with our reactions to stress—with the ways in which we attempt to cope with stress situations.

TYPES AND SOURCES OF STRESS

Problems of adjustment can be classified as frustrations, conflicts, and pressures. Elements of all three may of course be present in the same situation, but for simplicity we will discuss them separately.

Frustration

Frustration is the result of the thwarting of a motive—either by some obstacle that blocks or impedes our progress toward a desired goal, or by the absence of an appropriate goal object. Overly restrictive parents would be a source of frustration to an adolescent who wanted to go to a school party, while a lack of water would be a source of frustration to a man lost in the desert. Frustrations may be minor and inconsequential, or they may represent serious threats to our welfare or even survival.

Sources of frustration. Frustrations may arise from *outer* (environmental) or *inner* (personal) sources.

There are a wide range of environmental obstacles, both physical and social, which can lead to the frustration of our needs. Earthquakes, famines, fires, accidents, and the death of loved ones are major sources of thwarting in the physical environment. Pens that refuse to write, traffic congestion when we are in a hurry, rain when we want to play golf or tennis, advertisements that make us want things we cannot have, red tape that prevents us from taking a desired course, and long years of study before we can enter a professional field—are examples of the countless environmentally caused frustrations that plague us in everyday life.

Personal characteristics can also keep us from getting what we want. Physical handicaps, disease, low intelligence, lack of special talents, inadequate competencies, and lack of self-discipline are sources of frustration that result from our own limitations. Many frustrations arise out of psychological barriers in the form of reality and ethical controls. The young adult may refrain from premarital sexual relations because of fear of pregnancy or social disapproval—or because of moral values which make such behavior unacceptable. And if reality and ethical restraints break down, self-recrimination and guilt may follow. Of course, faulty assumptions and values may lead to unnecessary frustrations.

Common frustrations in our culture. In our relatively prosperous and literate culture, few of us suffer from the material privations and limitations to fulfillment that still are realities for over half the world's people. Most prevalent among us are frustrations stemming from delays, from discrepancies between what we have and what we would like, from the lack of satisfying values or meaning, from the loss of someone or something precious to us, from failure, guilt, discrimination, and limitations. A complete list, of course, would be endless, but a few of those that cause us special difficulty warrant some discussion.

1. *Delays.* In our time-conscious culture, where we feel we must make every minute count, delays are especially galling. Yet with our concentrations of population, our specialization, and our high degree of interdependence, many delays are inevitable. We cannot all get through the intersection at the same time but must take our turn. Literally and figuratively, we are continually standing in line waiting for something we would like. We cannot marry when we are physiologically ready but must wait until we have the skills we need to earn a living. Few of us can buy the new car or the house we want the moment we decide we would like it.

Many of our delays—especially those related to material possessions—are made especially difficult by the constant barrage of advertising that keeps stimulating our desires. Necessary as this aspect of modern marketing may be for creating broader markets and greater productivity, it creates a stress for those who cannot keep pace in their purchases with the desires and standards thus created. This stress is often further intensified by our tendency to ignore what we *do* have and preoccupy ourselves with the things that are still lacking.

2. *Lack of resources.* Although most of us do not lack the basic necessities of life, probably few of us are satisfied with what we have. We would like to have more money to buy and do the things we want—perhaps to buy a more elaborate home or a newer car, or to provide freedom to travel. Many people feel that they lack adequate opportunity for realization of their potentials. There always seem to be lacks in our material resources.

Personal limitations can be especially frustrating in our society. A lack of dates or other indications that men find her unattractive is frustrating to a girl; lack of requisite ability to compete for grades in college may be highly frustrating to an ambitious student;

and physical handicaps which limit our achievement and personal attractiveness are apt to be highly frustrating. Couples who are eager to have children may feel deep frustration if they find they are unable to do so. Similarly, feelings of inadequacy and inferiority are debilitating frustrations.

3. *Losses.* Loss of anything that we have possessed and valued is frustrating because it deprives us of a source of gratification or a resource for meeting our needs. Loss of money or time may mean we must forego a cherished dream. Loss of friendship or love may not only deprive us of satisfactions we had come to depend on but also threaten our self-esteem. The death of someone close to us upsets our previous pattern of giving and receiving love and leaves us feeling incomplete. The losses that come with aging—loss of loved ones, loss of financial independence, loss of valued status in the group, and gradual loss of one's abilities—are all highly frustrating.

Losses are especially frustrating because so often they are beyond our control, and once they have occurred there is nothing we can do about them. They often seem to

---

DEFINITION OF TERMS

Stress is a term which the biological and social sciences have taken over with only imperfect success from the physical sciences. In engineering usage, a force directed at an object is said to place it under *stress*. The resulting distortion or deformation caused in the object by the stress is called *strain*. For example, a small amount of weight placed on a bridge would create a mild stress and the resulting strain would be minimal. Increasing the weight, and hence the level of stress, would cause increasing levels of strain; depending on the materials of the bridge and its construction, there might be buckling or sagging or perhaps eventually even a breakdown of the bridge.

We shall follow a similar usage in discussing stress on the human organism. Any condition that makes an adjustive demand on the organism places

it under some degree of *stress*. Mild stress usually causes little or no *strain*, for the individual has ample resources for coping with it and is not likely to see it as a threat. Very severe stress, however, resulting from a very difficult adjustive demand, may cause severe strain or may even overtax the individual's coping resources and lead to a breakdown of integrated functioning. Sarbin (1968) has suggested the term *cognitive strain* to refer to the effects of adjustive demands that arise in connection with problems of choice, conflict, interference, overloading, and related aspects of the human condition.

Living systems—particularly human beings—have advantages over nonliving ones in meeting stress, for they can anticipate and prepare for it, change their strategies for coping with it, and sometimes leave the field when it is too severe.

represent the whim of a cruel and capricious fate.

4. *Failure.* Even if we did not live in a competitive society, we would sometimes be bound to fail in our endeavors; the competitive setting in which we operate increases the frequency of failure and frustration. No athletic team is likely to win all of the time, nor can all who have aspirations become movie or television stars or achieve high political office. For each one who succeeds, there is an inevitable crop of failures. Even when we do well in the light of our own ability, we may feel we have failed if we have not done as well as someone else. Any failure is frustrating, even though we may learn to live with and profit from it.

A special type of failure which is often highly frustrating is *guilt*. Either doing something we feel is wrong or failing to do something we feel we should can lead to self-recrimination and guilt. Guilt is a source of frustration because it thwarts our needs for feelings of self-esteem and worth; and since we have been taught that wrongdoing leads to inevitable punishment, we may also feel insecure and fear that we will somehow be punished. As in other types of failure, guilt may be particularly frustrating if there is nothing we can do to rectify our error.

5. *Meaninglessness.* A serious cause of frustration stems from an inability to find and lead a meaningful and fulfilling way of life. Apparently a somewhat new phenomenon in our generation is the inability of large numbers of our young people to accept and identify with the goals and values of our culture. They are repelled by the "phoniness," hypocrisy, and materialistic status-seeking they see in the adult world; yet they see no constructive alternatives or more valid goals to substitute. Emptiness, meaninglessness, and a sense of alienation are the result. If they "drop out" or just drift, this brings frustration too and is not a satisfying long-term answer. Of course, meaninglessness and despair are by no means the sole prerogatives of our young people; many older people too suffer from a frustrating sense of meaninglessness and lack of fulfillment.

In addition to the common sources of frustration already mentioned, several others may be briefly noted. Having to interrupt one's education or career to serve in the military forces is a serious frustration for many young people. Although widely decried in principle, racial and ethnic prejudice is still a serious source of frustration for many of us. Inflation is a source of frustration to many older persons living on fixed incomes. Even with adequate income, many of us suffer the frustration of being stuck in jobs in which we are misfits. The frustrations that result from an unhappy marriage are especially severe since they permeate one's whole "home base" and threaten one's basic anchorages. And finally, of course, the knowledge that we are living in a world of nations armed to the teeth with weapons capable of destroying all human life is not conducive to feelings of security and faith in man's ultimate future.

Conflict

Often the stress comes not from a single obstacle but from a conflict of motives. You want to go home for the weekend, but you also want to stay for the dance; you are interested in taking a certain course, but you want to avoid Saturday classes; you would like to get married but feel you would have to quit college and take a job.

As a citizen in a democracy, we also have many value decisions to make concerning courses of action that we feel will contribute to or impair social progress. When we hear about "the struggle for men's minds," the speaker is usually referring to the conflicting ideologies of communism and democracy on the world stage. But within our own society the struggle for men's minds goes on too. We are propagandized by reactionaries and radicals, by liberals and conservatives, by "doves" and "hawks," by black and white power advocates, by those who believe needed changes can come through reform and those who believe existing social structures must first be swept away. As citizens, we are responsible for choosing the most promising goals and means for the welfare and progress of our society and of the individuals in it; yet it is often difficult to decide which courses offer the most promise.

Although it is convenient to make a distinction between frustration and conflict, it is the underlying threat of frustration that makes a conflict stressful. In a conflict you are threatened with frustration regardless of which course you choose to follow. You have to give up the dance or the weekend at home, the course you want or your free Saturdays, college or getting married now.

Implicit in the concept of conflict is the assumption that the contradictory alternatives are approximately of equal attractiveness or unattractiveness and that some decision is required. Since the selection of one alternative involves frustration with respect to the other, such a decision is often difficult to make. It is not surprising that the person in conflict often hesitates, vacillates, and goes through agony trying to make up his mind.

Types of conflict. Conflicts are usually classified in terms of the reward or punishment value the alternatives have for the individual. Thus the conflicts we all meet may be conveniently classified as approach-avoidant, double-approach, and double-avoidant conflicts.

1. *Approach-avoidant conflicts.* In an approach-avoidant conflict there are strong tendencies both to approach and to avoid the same goal. A woman may feel trapped and denied fulfillment by an unhappy marriage and yet place a high value on the security and status it gives her. A person may want to marry for sexual, social, and security reasons, while at the same time fearing the responsibilities and loss of personal freedom. He has tendencies both to approach and to avoid marriage. In a similar way one's desires may conflict with his moral principles or with fear of failure. Perhaps he can join a high status group only by indulging in behavior contrary to his ethical standards; or he feels intensely attracted to a beautiful and intelligent girl but recognizes that her scale of values would

almost inevitably lead to the failure of their marriage.

Approach-avoidant conflicts are sometimes referred to as "mixed blessing" conflicts, because some negative and some positive features must be accepted regardless of which course of action we select. Since many approach-avoidance conflicts involve multiple alternatives—rather than just one either-or choice—the term *multiple approach-avoidance* is sometimes used here also. Thus the individual may be in conflict not only about whether to get married but also about which girl would make the best wife; or he may be in conflict about whether to focus on physics, law, or psychology, each of which he sees as offering both advantages and disadvantages.

2. *Double-approach conflicts.* As the name implies, double-approach conflicts involve competition between two or more desirable alternatives. On a simple level, a decision may have to be made between two courses we would like to take, between playing tennis or going swimming, between going to a movie or watching a special program on television, or between two invitations for the same evening. To a large extent, such simple "plus-plus" conflicts result from the inevitable limitations in our time, space, energy, and personal resources. We cannot be in two places at once, we do not have the time and energy to do all the things we would like to do, and most of us have limited funds.

Although even simple decisions—such as whether to have steak or stroganoff for dinner or to buy a blue or brown sweater—may be hard to make, they do not ordinarily upset us greatly because we are assured of reasonable gratification at the moment and because we are often able to obtain the other desired alternative at a later time. In more complex cases—as when the individual is torn between loyalty to his mother and to his wife, between careers in law and medicine, between faithfulness to his absent fiancée and sexual attraction toward another girl, or between present and future satisfactions—decision making may be very difficult and stressful.

3. *Double-avoidant conflicts.* In a double-avoidant conflict we are caught "between the devil and the deep blue sea" and must try to choose the lesser of two evils. The unskilled young person may have to choose between unemployment and a disagreeable job; a middle-aged woman may have a choice between a loveless marriage and the possibility of no marriage at all. An employee may have to choose between using sales techniques which he feels are unethical and giving up a lucrative job which he needs. For some young people, both conformity to the "establishment" and membership in some nonconforming group in which they do not fully believe present difficult alternatives. In wartime, the individual may have to choose between military service, with the possibility of killing others or being killed, and refusal to serve, with the possibility of social disapproval and punishment. When such "minus-minus" conflicts are severe, they can bring about serious adjustment problems because even resolution of the conflict will bring frustration rather than relief.

It can be readily seen that this classification of conflicts is somewhat arbitrary and that various combinations among these different types are the rule rather than the exception in everyday life. Thus a "plus-plus" conflict between marrying one of two desirable persons may also have its "plus-minus" aspects growing out of the responsibilities and loss of personal freedom entailed in marriage.

Common conflicts in our society. Most of the conflicts in our society are *value conflicts.* They are especially common and disturbing because to a greater extent than ever before individuals must choose what they are to become, both as individuals and as participants in our society. Is it better to be manipulative or honest, to refrain from premarital sexual intercourse or to follow one's impulses, to give of one's self to others or to play it cool, to stay in a competitive society or to "drop out," to take "mind-expanding" drugs or to follow more conventional methods of self-

exploration and growth? Each of us experiences many such value conflicts—often accompanied by considerable pressure in one direction or another from family or friends—and such conflicts are often major sources of confusion, indecision, and stress.

Although our value patterns and conflicts will be dealt with in later chapters, some of the more troubling ones will be mentioned briefly here.

1. *Self-direction vs. outer direction.* The insecurities of our anxious age and the lack of a clear pattern for young people to follow make the development of self-direction and acceptance of personal responsibility especially difficult today. Often we are torn between contradictory demands and values advocated by parents, peers, and public officials; and, of course, rapid social change including change in traditional values adds to the problem. Thus it is no easy task to construct a value system and chart a course of action that will meet our needs for both security and growth and for both self-esteem and social approval.

Several writers of our time—Riesman, Fromm, and Whyte, to name a few—have pointed to the tendency of many people in our anxious age to surrender the risks and pains of independence for the security of authority. Sometimes this authority is tradition; sometimes it is a peer group; sometimes it is a corporation; sometimes it is an autocratic form of government. When we are unsure of our values or lack the courage to live by them, we may find ourselves choosing clothes, political viewpoints, courses of action, and even friends and mates because they conform to the values advocated by the group. By ignoring or going counter to our own experience or values, we are likely to become a stranger to our real feelings and to suffer a sense of deep frustration—for we are violating a central part of our nature.

On the other hand, standing up against group standards—as when one's conscience demands actions strongly at variance with generally accepted behavior or even legal requirements—can also be highly stressful. Here the individual runs the risk of losing status in his group or even of being expelled from it and perhaps given harsh punishment. Thus the young man conscientiously opposed to war may have to choose between self-respect and social approval, and perhaps between freedom and prison. The conflict between remaining faithful to one's values and giving in to group standards is a difficult and inevitably frustrating one.

2. *Commitment vs. noninvolvement.* The conflict between commitment and non-involvement vividly confronts Americans each time we hear of incidents such as the stabbing of Catherine Genovese:

In March, 1964, a young woman returning from work late at night to her apartment in Kew Gardens, Queens, was attacked on a well-lighted street within a hundred feet of her apartment. It was later established that her screams awakened 38 of her neighbors; and twice, as apartment lights went on, her attacker scurried away. Each time he came back and finally stabbed her to death. Although Miss Genovese kept yelling "Please help me!" "Please help me!" not one of the 38 neighbors called the police during the 35 minutes between the first and last attack.

Although most religious and social philosophies emphasize the ideal of helping others, the impersonality and anonymity of modern urban society are not conducive to a feeling of commitment to the welfare of others. The individual in such an environment often feels part of an impersonal series of events over which he has no control. The risk of involvement and its possible repercussions seem too great a price to pay when one is dealing with "strangers." As Seeman (1966) has put it: "Often it seems painful but realistic to conclude that, in the last analysis, you and your family are alone, and the only ones you can really count on for help and support are yourselves. No one else cares." (p. 35)

The conflict between commitment and noninvolvement is by no means confined to relationships with strangers. Even in close interpersonal relationships the individual may choose noninvolvement rather than care or love. All caring has hazards, since one who is involved is vulnerable to being hurt and a painless outcome can never be guaranteed. But noninvolvement also exacts a price in terms of lost satisfactions, feelings of estrangement and alienation, and a lack of meaning in one's existence. In a general sense, it would appear that the person who does not get involved does not really live.

Commitment also includes the espousal of positive values and causes and a feeling of responsibility for working toward maintaining and improving the quality of life in the society as a whole. Every generation has had its "dropouts," who felt no responsibility for the welfare of anyone but themselves and their own families and friends; today's dropouts include also a sizable segment of idealistic young people who have taken seriously the principles of love, honesty, and open sharing and feel that to enter the adult society they see would be to surrender their integrity. Many other young people, who feel a responsibility for doing what they can to bring improvement and believe that their effort can make a difference, attempt to work for constructive change within established social structures.

3. *Avoiding vs. facing reality.* An approach-avoidant conflict familiar to all of us is the conflict between wanting to know the truth and wanting to be comfortable, especially about ourselves. Yet a central requisite of personal maturity is the ability to be objective about ourselves and the world around us and to acknowledge reality even when it is unpleasant. This is not easy because unpleasant reality makes us anxious and we defend ourselves against anxiety as automatically (and often as unconsciously) as we defend ourselves against invading germs. We have already seen the ease with which our cognitive processes are subverted to the service of making us see what we want to see and believe and preventing us from seeing inconsistencies between our professed beliefs and our actions.

To face the reality that our failure in some important venture, such as a close personal relationship, has resulted from stupid-

THE EXPERIENCE OF CONFLICT

Perhaps no one has better described the experience of being in conflict—of being confused and torn in different directions—than Shakespeare in Hamlet's famous soliloquy:

To be, or not to be: that is the question:
Whether 'tis nobler in the mind to suffer
The slings and arrows of outrageous fortune,
Or to take arms against a sea of troubles,
And by opposing end them? To die: to sleep;
No more; and by a sleep to say we end
The heart-ache and the thousand natural shocks
That flesh is heir to, 'tis a consummation
Devoutly to be wish'd. To die, to sleep;
To sleep: perchance to dream: ay, there's the rub;

For in that sleep of death what dreams may come
When we have shuffled off this mortal coil,
Must give us pause: . . .
For who would bear the whips and scorns of time, . . .
The oppressor's wrong, the proud man's contumely,
The pangs of despised love, the law's delay, . . .
When he himself might his quietus make
With a bare bodkin? . . .
But that the dread of something after death,
The undiscover'd country from whose bourn
No traveller returns, puzzles the will
And makes us rather bear those ills we have
Than fly to others that we know not of? . . .

Hamlet, Act III, Scene I

ity on our part would be self-devaluating, and we are likely to look for some other explanation. So perhaps we rationalize or project the blame onto the other person or onto "circumstances beyond our control." In the same way, we may underestimate or close our eyes to social injustices that might otherwise make us uncomfortable; or we may be unwilling to listen to responsible persons in public life who hold political views and values somewhat different from our own.

Facing reality not only may be uncomfortable but may confront us with the necessity for taking positive action that we fear will be hazardous and disagreeable. The unwillingness to respond to a stranger's call for help may represent an attempt to avoid possible unpleasant consequences as much as a lack of concern for others' welfare. The ways of avoiding reality are legion and the conflict between facing and avoiding reality is not a new one, though some of the forms it takes may be novel in our time.

4. *Integrity vs. self-advantage.* We all experience times when it appears that our needs might be best served by actions that would conflict with our ethical values. We may be tempted to cheat on examinations, to be devious in business transactions, to lie or

otherwise practice deceit in our attempts to get something we need, or to be silent about our beliefs because of possible social disapproval. We appear particularly prone to such behavior when we observe that others engage in it with seemingly successful results.

Of course, individuals with very limited conscience development or with values consistent with such behavior will experience little conflict in such situations, nor will they have guilt feelings later if they choose expediency over principle. In fact, they may believe that the successful completion of their objective is justification for any means used in achieving it. One has only to read the daily paper to observe the frequency with which self-advantage takes priority over what most of us have been taught to consider "fair play."

The idealistic young person in our society may find it particularly disillusioning to learn that the adult world does not always abide by the standards it proclaims and that he himself is tempted to act in ways inconsistent with his own principles. Thus he may experience considerable conflict in adhering to his ethical standards and considerable guilt if he violates them. Throughout human history we have seen examples of men wrestling with their consciences as they tried to be true to their values and to stand up for what they believed in—even though the path of personal gain lay in the other direction. It often takes great courage to follow one's convictions under such conditions. Such courage is well portrayed in the characterization of Thomas More in the play *A Man for All Seasons.*

5. *Sexual desires vs. restraints.* Current investigators do not consider sexual conflicts the inevitable problems that Freud judged them to be. Yet they are common enough in our society to cause considerable stress, especially among young people. The earliest sexual conflict often centers around the practice of masturbation, so long condemned as a vile, enfeebling, immoral habit. Even present-day knowledge of its physical harmlessness and of its prevalence during certain stages of development does not always prevent a sense of fear and guilt concerning it. Often, too, a child's early sexual development is complicated by an overattachment to the mother or father, accompanied by strong sexual desires and fantasies. Freudian theory has placed great emphasis on the "Oedipal conflict" as a source of stress. According to this theory, the situation is usually resolved as the little boy comes to identify with the father and the girl with her mother, and latent sexual desires give way to harmless tender affection. However, ambivalence or sexual feelings toward parents can be a source of considerable guilt and conflict while they endure.

With later adolescence and young adulthood, sexual conflicts are likely to be aroused by questions of petting, premarital sexual relations, and infidelity after marriage. The individual may find his desires or even his behavior at variance with established social mores and perhaps with his own moral convictions. Conflicts of conscience and values may be further complicated by reality considerations, such as the possibility of disease or pregnancy.

Adding to young people's difficulty is the confusion and disagreement they see around them concerning what is acceptable and unacceptable, right and wrong, in sexual behavior. In general, our society appears to be moving toward a view of sexual behavior as a natural and acceptable source of enjoyment and toward decreasing restraints on permissible patterns of sexual behavior. But guidelines are not clear, and sexual values may differ markedly for different racial, socioeconomic, and religious groups. As a consequence, many young people experience intense conflict as they try to work out a code of sexual ethics which is acceptable to them.

6. *Other conflicts.* Many of our most difficult conflicts are those in which our basic value assumptions are in conflict and we have to choose one at the sacrifice of another. For example, it is assumed that loyalty to a friend is a good thing. Does this mean that you must lend him money? Does it mean that you stand up for him in public if you think he has committed a wrong? Should sex only occur for purposes of procreation or is it a proper human pleasure? Is it one's duty to remain with a wife one despises in order to help bring up the children, or is divorce a valid solution to such a problem? Must one be "his brother's keeper" or is it justified to pursue one's own interest and happiness? Is it wrong to use unethical means in the pursuit of worth-while and important goals?

In many ways conflicts are the most severe type of stress we experience, for the type of person we become depends on the way we handle them.

Pressure

Problems of adjustment come not only because our own strivings are frustrated or in conflict but also because of pressures that complicate our journey toward our goals or provide additional demands for us to meet. For example, if our parents have made sacrifices to send us to college and expect us to do well, we may feel under great pressure not to let them down. Such pressures may force us to intensify our effort and speed up our activity—often to an uncomfortable degree.

Sources of pressure. Pressures, like frustrations, may stem from inner or outer sources.

Inner sources typically center around our own aspirations and ego-ideal. Where we have a high level of aspiration in terms of standards to be met and goals to be achieved, the pressure may be continuous and severe. Many of us drive ourselves mercilessly and strive to live up to unrealistically high standards of ethical behavior, courage, and social responsibility in order to conform to a picture of ourselves as we think we *should* be. We may feel we should get along with everyone, should show more concentration and self-control, should not feel the way we clearly do feel, and in general should do much better than we are doing. Pressures like this, stemming from unrealistic assumptions about ourselves and our world, have been referred to as the "tyranny of the *should*."

A combination of inner aspirations and outer demands often intensifies the pressure. Ambitious high-school seniors, expected to show excellence in grades, athletics, and extracurricular activities, often feel that colleges are looking for paragons rather than immature human beings. A young salesman anxious to distinguish himself may find himself up against quotas he thinks are unrealistically high and competition from veterans who already have outstanding records of success.

Common pressures in our society. Although each of us faces a unique pattern of demands and pressures, there are several pressures that most of us share by virtue of our membership in our particular society. Prevalent among these are pressure to achieve in a competitive society; pressure to put forth sustained effort, often at an uncomfortably fast pace; pressure to keep adjusting to constantly changing conditions; and pressures from family and other close personal relationships.

1. *The pressure for competitive achievement.* Many of our pressures stem from demands for academic and occupational achievement. Although such demands are more pressing for men than for women in our society and for middle-class than for lower-class members, they subject many of us to considerable strain. We realize that the high status and the financial rewards will go to those who do well in school, who get advanced training, and who manage to get promoted on the job. To fail or even to do poorly in school is to close the door to teaching, law, medicine, engineering, and other desirable occupational fields. Out of school and on the job, the pressure continues as we move up the ladder, and each advance makes additional demands on our time and competence.

In our highly competitive society we compete for grades, athletic honors, leadership, jobs, financial advantages, social status, marital partners, and almost everything else we want. Although we endorse certain rules for playing the game and may give grudging credit for effort, it is success that gains the rewards. The losing football team does not attract crowds or gain plaudits for its performance; the company that fails to gain contracts in competition with other companies may go bankrupt. It is the students with superior records who win the competition for college entrance and later the competition for selection for advanced training on the job or in graduate school. We all are encouraged to "hitch our wagon to a star"—to "think big." Yet not everyone can come in first, and striving to do the impossible invites frustration and self-devaluation.

Competitive pressures have been acclaimed as leading to greater productivity, an increased sense of purpose, higher standards of excellence, and the "feel of life." Yet inappropriate or indiscriminate competition may be harmful to the individual and devisive for the group. If it leads to a constant "overloading" of the individual's capacities, both his health and his long-term productivity may suffer. The need for mutual help and support among the members of any social group suggests that cooperation is at least as much a "law of life" as is competition.

2. *Sustained concentration of effort.* Since Sputnik, there has been a shift in American schools away from "life adjustment" and toward pressure for ever higher levels of academic excellence. With our contemporary "information explosion" this trend can be expected to continue and increase, with ever more material to cover and more ideas to comprehend and assimilate in the same amount of time. Too many demands are made at once, and students must be always in a hurry, with no chance to go slowly, dig deeper, and savor one experience at a time. Increasingly, then, most students—particularly those who go beyond high school—are subjected to considerable strain by the long hours of study, the tension of frequent deadlines and examinations, and the fear of doing poorly or flunking out. For many, this steady concentration of effort, with its attendant strain, continues over a period of many years.

The sustained concentration of effort involved in educational achievement is stressful not only in its own right but also because it thwarts and delays action to subserve other motives. Many students delay marriage long after they are physically and emotionally mature because they feel it essential to complete their education and have a job before undertaking the responsibilities of marriage and possibly children. And despite opportunities at college and in the broader community for leisure activities and creative pursuits, many students have little time or energy available after meeting the demands of their study programs.

Nor does the strain of sustained concentration at an uncomfortable pace cease when the individual leaves school. One who finds himself on the bottom rung of the occupational ladder is under pressure to prove himself, to make a good showing and to advance. Interestingly, Packard (1962) found in one survey that the greatest pressure was felt not among the top executives, whose decisions could advance or wreck the company, but at the lower echelons among the ambitious, ulcer-ridden junior executives, whose status was still dependent on competitive success.

3. *Complexity and rapid change.* All life involves change: we grow up, marry, have children, face the death of parents, undergo illnesses, and adjust to numberless other major and minor changes as we go

through life. Change *per se* need not cause difficulty. In fact, we are so used to continuing change that we all expect next year's cars, TV sets, building construction, and so on to be different and generally assume that they will be better. We expect to adapt to new standards of excellence, new gadgets and innovations, and continuing new methods and concepts in our field of specialization. We also expect that next year's problems will be somewhat different from this year's and that we will have to keep developing new insights and new skills to keep up. It is hard for us even to imagine living in a situation in which the same values and patterns would continue unchanged for generation after generation.

The rate and pervasiveness of change today, however, are different from anything our ancestors ever experienced, and all aspects of our lives are affected—our education, our jobs, our family life, our leisure pursuits, and our beliefs and values. Constantly trying to keep up with the new adjustments demanded by these changes is a source of considerable stress. In medicine, psychology, and other scientific and technical fields it is a constant problem to keep up with new findings and techniques. In one survey, 89 per cent of a group of engineers admitted having difficulty in keeping pace with the new information relevant to their jobs (*Science News,* 1967b). Whole businesses become obsolete as new products and processes appear. No value or custom or social institution is exempt from the challenge to justify itself or give way to a replacement.

And besides the constant and far-reaching changes within our own society, technological innovations have made the world so much smaller that many complex social problems are superimposed upon the personal problems of the individual and require his attention as a citizen. Whether we like it or not, we have to be concerned with what happens in China, Africa, and other parts of the world—for these happenings may directly affect our own security and well-being. There is increasing evidence that chronic "overloading" from our need to make complex adaptations to constantly changing conditions is an important factor in our high incidence of heart attacks, diseases of adaptation, and psychological breakdown.

Murphy and Leighton (1965), studying the effects of the rapid influx of new ideas from outside cultures, found that stress and personality damage were most likely under the following circumstances: when the tempo was so rapid that major dimensions of change occurred within the life span of a single generation; when a pervasive reorientation of basic assumptions was involved, especially if it involved new roles or values that did not fit into the previously existing system; when the people were unprepared for the changes, did not see where they were leading, and were encouraged in unrealistic expectations; and when the new conditions created a sense of overloading by increasing the number of adjustive demands made on the members of the group rather than simply substituting new demands.

4. *Pressures from family and other relationships.* Although many of our deepest needs are satisfied through family relationships, such relationships can also place difficult pressures on us. Marriage makes many demands on an individual—demands that may be quite stressful if either partner is immature or if the external situation is not favorable. Marriage calls on the individual to adjust to an intimate relationship with another person, to help work out a mutually satisfactory approach to problems, and to resolve value conflicts. With the arrival of children there are new demands on time and patience as well as on one's ability to love. Child-rearing problems may enhance marital strain. Ill or aging parents may also need our financial and emotional support.

Relationships with those outside our families can also be sources of pressure. We are constantly being called on by other individuals or groups to help advance their concerns. Our friends may need our help at inconvenient times. Organizations to which we belong may need long hours that we cannot easily spare. Community problems may cry out for time and effort from us as con-cerned citizens. All these demands add to the pressures that complicate our lives.

Many other frustrations, conflicts, and pressures could, of course, be mentioned in our discussion. Disappointments in love are probably experienced at one time or another by most of us and can be terribly hurtful. Terrifying accidents, major surgery, loss of social status, and arrest and imprisonment are highly stressful situations for those who have to face them. To one whose feelings of worth are largely dependent upon physical attractiveness, the deterioration of aging may present a particularly difficult problem. Finally, the prospect of our own inevitable death is a traumatic reality with which we must all come to terms.

SEVERITY OF STRESS

In reviewing the major types and sources of stress it becomes apparent that stress involves transactions between individuals and situations. Thus in discussing the severity of stress we shall be concerned with the contributions of the adjustive demand itself, the individual's personality characteristics, and the presence or absence of external resources and supports.

The *severity of stress* is the degree of strain or disequilibrium produced in the organism. In mild stress there is little disturbance in equilibrium and adjustive action is usually relatively simple; in moderate and severe stress, there are proportionately greater degrees of strain imposed on the organism and adjustive action may be difficult; and in excessive stress, severe disequilibrium occurs and the adaptive capacities of the organism are overtaxed. Thus we may think of severity along a continuum from mild through moderate and severe to excessive stress.

The severity of stress depends partly upon the characteristics of the adjustive demand, partly on the characteristics of the individual, and partly on the cultural and situational context in which the stress occurs.

On a biological level, for example, the severity of stress created by invading viruses depends partly on the strength and number of the invaders, partly on the organism's ability to resist and destroy them, and partly on available medical resources for implementing body defenses. On a psychological level, individual factors usually play a more crucial role. For here the severity of the adjustive demand depends not only upon the stress situation and the individual's resources —both personal and situational—but also upon how he evaluates the stress situation.

Characteristics of the Adjustive Demand

Several characteristics of the demand affect its severity regardless of the make-up of the individual or the situational context in which it occurs.

Importance, duration, and multiplicity of demands. The severity of the stress depends first of all on the relative importance of the need being deprived or threatened with deprivation. Frustration of a central, key motive is more stressful than frustration of more peripheral desires. Thus failing one's bar exams would be more stressful than having to give up a desired vacation trip.

Ordinarily, the longer a stress situation continues, the more severe will be the strain on the organism. An individual can easily afford to miss a meal or two, but continued hunger brings severe strain. Often, too, stress appears to have a cumulative effect. A hen-pecked husband may maintain composure through a long series of minor irritations and conflicts only to explode in the face of the final straw. The wife may be quite dumfounded by the suddenness and violence of this seeming overreaction, not realizing that it represents the culmination of a long series of minor frustrations.

The number of demands made upon the individual at the same time also has a direct relationship to the degree of strain he experiences. In a high-pressure managerial job, any single problem or decision may be easily within the individual's ability to handle, but the sheer number of problems and decisions to be coped with each day may lead to a serious strain. If a student loses his fiancée, flunks a course, and is drafted, all within a few days, the stress will be more severe and harder to handle than if such events are spaced further apart and he has time to cope with one before being confronted with the next.

In their study of life stresses and mental health in midtown Manhattan, Langner and Michael (1963) found that it was the number of stress factors—past and present—rather than any particular stress factor or combination of factors that best predicted the subjects' mental health. Fourteen stress factors, including health status, work worries, socioeconomic worries, social isolation, marital worries, and parental worries were rated individually on a scale from 1 to 10. The higher the score for the list as a whole, the poorer the subject's mental health was found to be.

Strength of the conflicting forces. Conflicts between weak or peripheral motives produce minimal strain for neither choice entails serious loss. For example, deciding between a dance and a movie is not usually a severe problem. On the other hand, conflicts between important motives—such as having to choose between self-esteem and social approval—subject the individual to much greater strain.

The comparative strength of the opposing motives is also a factor. If an individual finds guilt feelings over sexual behavior far more stressful than sexual frustration, his conflict is readily resolved. If both inner restraints and sexual desires are strong, the situation is much more stressful since either alternative will lead to serious frustration. The picture is complicated further by the fact that the attractiveness of a given goal is not static and unchanging. The closer we get to a highly desired goal, the more we tend to want it. But if there are negative aspects, they loom larger too. Thus, if a young man is ambivalent about getting married, both his eagerness and his fear will become more intense as the wedding date approaches. Stress mounts accordingly.

Interestingly enough, the approach and avoidance trends do not increase at the same rate in such a situation. Typically, the avoidance gradient increases more sharply as the goal draws near (Miller, 1959). This helps to explain why many people experience a feeling of anxiety or near panic on their wedding day. Suddenly, all the underlying doubts seem to well up out of proportion to the positive values, which have also increased in attractiveness but not so rapidly. Where a goal has appreciable negative as well as positive aspects, it may become essentially negative as it comes within reach.

Unfamiliarity and suddenness of the problem. The frustrations, conflicts and pressures that we have coped with successfully before may cause little strain when we meet them again, for usually we can see a relatively painless way out on the basis of our past experience. But new problems which we have not anticipated, for which we have no ready-made coping pattern, and in which the requirements of the situation may not be clearly understood can put us under severe strain.

One reason major catastrophes are so overwhelming is that all one's usual "props" have disappeared and one's knowledge and skills seem totally inadequate and irrelevant to the task at hand. Any problem we do not know how to cope with may pose a serious difficulty. By contrast, if we can anticipate and prepare for a stressful event, even a potentially catastrophic one, it loses much of its power to throw us "off base." The training of firemen, policemen, and soldiers in exactly what to expect and what to do makes it possible for them to function effectively in highly stressful situations.

The same sense of adequacy and control may be achieved when the stress has been chosen voluntarily rather than having been imposed by others or having come unexpectedly from an accident. A scientist who decides voluntarily to spend a year in the Antarctic to make observations that will test an important hypothesis is likely to find the physical rigors and loneliness less stressful than an enlisted man who is assigned to the mission against his wishes. Seeing meaning in a stressful experience, knowing it is coming, preparing for it, and knowing how long it will last all lessen the severity of the stress when it comes.

The presence of a threat. Threat is the anticipation of harm. Many stress situations do not carry any major threat to biological or psychological needs. A cold is not the threat that pneumonia is; nor is social disapproval usually the threat that would be posed by the "silent treatment" administered to wayward members of antarctic expeditions, described on page 157. But stress situations which we see as physically damaging or threatening to our survival—such as having a limb amputated or being given a diagnosis of cancer—carry a high degree of threat. Similarly, stress situations which threaten the adequacy and worth of the self—such as failing in one's chosen occupation or having desires which one considers immoral and incompatible with his self-concept—involve a strong element of threat. The individual is also likely to feel threatened in stress situations which place demands on him that he feels inadequate to meet.

In general, a situation perceived as threatening is much more stressful than one perceived as presenting a difficult but manageable problem. And, as we shall see, threat arouses anxiety, which further augments the severity of the stress.

Imminence of an anticipated stress. Anticipation of stress is itself stressful, especially as the event becomes more imminent. For example, Mechanic (1962), observing graduate students, found that although the students thought about their examinations from time to time and experienced some anxiety during the three months beforehand, they were not seriously worried until near exam time.

"As the examinations approached and as student anxiety increased, various changes

occurred in behavior. Joking increased, and while students still sought social support and talked a great deal about examinations, they began specifically to avoid certain people who aroused their anxiety. Stomach aches, asthma, and a general feeling of weariness became common complaints, and other psychosomatic symptoms appeared. The use of tranquilizers and sleeping pills became more frequent." (p. 142)

"When the examinations are nearly upon the student, anxiety is very high, even for those rated as low-anxiety persons, although students do fluctuate between confidence and anxiety. Since studying is difficult, the student questions his motivation, interest, and ability in the field." (p. 144) Probably many undergraduate students undergo similar experiences as final exams or comprehensives approach.

Characteristics of the Individual

Situations that one person finds difficult may be mildly stressful or even nonstressful for another. The individual's level of competence, his perception of the problem, the presence or absence of threat, and his level of stress tolerance all help determine the severity of the stress he experiences.

Degree of competence. Whatever the problem we face, its severity for us will depend partly on the degree to which we have the particular competence it requires. The greater our competence, the less severe the stress. The well-trained debater can organize an eloquent rebuttal while his opponent is speaking, whereas one less well trained may not be able to keep track of all the points he wants to answer and may become hopelessly flustered. In most situations, the higher the individual's level of psychological differentiation—overall intellectual, emotional, and social development—the greater his adaptive potential (Phillips, 1968).

But the individual's actual level of competence is not the whole story: the way he views his capabilities is important too. If he feels generally self-confident and expects to solve a problem successfully, he will not experience severe stress even if the demand is a difficult one. By contrast, if he lacks self-confidence and is convinced he will bungle an important job, he will experience severe stress even if he actually possesses ample competencies for dealing with the situation.

Perception of the problem. Another crucial factor in determining the severity of stress is the way in which the individual per-

SELF-CONFIDENCE AND THREAT

The attitude of the Mercury astronauts shows that the individual's confidence in his own competence can prevent even a dangerous situation from being seen as a threat. The astronauts were convinced that their experience and intensive training had prepared them for any emergency.

"In the days and hours before flight, all of the men felt ready to go and competent for the job. Conscious thoughts of danger and possible death were infrequent, and suppressed as they arose. The men were preoccupied with operational details and showed little anticipatory anxiety. . . .

"Considering every eventuality and doing all possible to prepare for it, they saw little point in worrying further. When thoughts of danger did arise, they were displaced by review of the flight plan or other technical aspects of the flight. In one man's words, 'Whenever I think of something that may go wrong, I think of a plan to take care of it.'

". . . In the period just before lift-off . . . there was excitement, anticipation, and readiness to go, of the sort athletes describe before the race, but no instances of severe or potentially disabling anxiety." (Ruff & Korchin, 1967, p. 306)

Because they believed that their inner and outer resources were adequate for the task, these men felt confident in a situation that most of us would see as highly traumatic and threatening.

KINDS OF ANXIETY

objective—appropriate to the degree of threat	vs.	*nonobjective*—not in proportion to threat, influenced largely by individual's frame of reference
situational—present only in reference to particular situations	vs.	*general*—present in most situations
acute—sudden, intense reaction	vs.	*chronic*—continuously high enough to be uncomfortable
conscious—anxiety clearly felt	vs.	*unconscious or partially conscious*—vague uneasiness or unawareness of anxiety or of one's defenses against it

Based in part on Arkoff, 1968

ceives the problem and defines the demand being made on him. For example, one girl may view a broken engagement as a humiliating and self-devaluating failure, while another girl may view it as hurtful but also fortunate, in that the incompatibility became apparent before rather than after the marriage.

An individual's evaluation of a particular problem depends on his whole belief system. If he views the world as a dangerous and hostile place, each new stress is evaluated in this context and seen as adding one more element to the burden he is already bearing. If he sees the world as basically friendly and supportive, specific stresses will be viewed in this context. In the case of the Mercury astronauts, for example (page 189), they had been living for years in a situation where they had relied successfully on teamwork and backup systems to take care of any problems that arose; they were used to trying one plan and shifting to another if necessary. They believed that if one had the necessary knowledge and did what he should, things would turn out right.

One's appraisal of a particular threat is also affected by his general evaluation of himself. If he sees himself as generally helpless and inadequate, a stress that would look minor to someone else may look seriously threatening to him. Thus a failing grade that might spur a generally self-confident student to study harder might be seen by a less confident student as proof of his inability to do acceptable college-level work. The same failing grade would have different effects because it was seen differently as a result of different self-evaluations.

This last example highlights the difficulty of predicting the effects of any environmental condition and the lack of any one-to-one correlation between stimulus and response. We all react not to the situation as it exists objectively but to the situation as we perceive, define, and evaluate it. Often an outsider sees no stresses in a person's life situation severe enough to account for his discouragement or maladjustive symptoms—or perhaps even mental breakdown. Yet to him the situation may have been intolerable.

Stress tolerance. By *stress tolerance* we refer to the individual's capacity for withstanding stress or, operationally speaking, the amount of stress the individual can tolerate before his integrated functioning is seriously impaired. Tolerance for stress is fairly constant for a given individual although there are minor fluctuations with special conditions.

Both biologically and psychologically, people differ greatly in the amounts and the types of stress they can withstand. Prolonged exertion and fatigue that would be only mildly stressful to a young person may prove fatal to an older person or someone with a heart defect. Emergencies, disappointments, and other life problems that a competent, confident individual can take in stride may prove incapacitating to one who is (or believes he is) inadequate. Some people can continue to function well in very complex and difficult situations and even in the presence of strong and disturbing emotions. Others are so marginally adjusted that even minor stress can precipitate a serious disorganization of biological or psychological functioning.

Sometimes, as we have seen, early traumatic experiences leave the individual especially vulnerable to certain types of stress situations. The hurt felt by a little girl whose home has been broken by divorce may later make it difficult or impossible for her to accept the possibility of divorce as a solution to her own unhappy marriage. If her husband leaves her, she may be unable to cope with the situation. Even without such early traumas, each of us has our special vulnerabilities. We may be able to cope with failure but not with social rejection; with prejudice and discrimination but not with disappointment in love. Thus the individual's tolerance for a general type of stress may play an important role in determining the severity of a particular stress situation.

External Resources and Supports

Usually we are not alone when we meet severe stress situations. If we have to undergo crucial surgery, we can count on the emotional support of our families and friends—and health insurance may be available to cover the cost. Lack of external supports—either personal or material—makes a given stress more severe and weakens our capacity to cope with it. A divorce or the death of one's mate is more stressful if one feels alone and unloved than if one is still surrounded by people one cares about and feels close to (Fromm-Reichmann, 1959).

Even pressures toward conformity are less stressful and more easily withstood when one has an ally than when one is alone (Asch, 1955). It is hardly surprising that studies have found a tendency for individuals exposed to highly stressful situations to turn to others for support and reassurance (Schachter, 1959).

Environmental supports are a complex matter, however, and behavior by one's family or friends which is intended to provide support may actually increase the stress. In this connection, in the study cited earlier of graduate students facing crucial examinations, Mechanic (1962) compared the effects of different types of behavior on the part of the spouses:

"In general, spouses do not provide blind support. They perceive the kinds of support the student wants and they provide it. The wife who becomes worried about examinations also may provide more support than the spouse who says, 'I'm not worried,

FACTORS IN THE SEVERITY OF STRESS

In general, stress is more severe:
1. The more important the motives being blocked and the needs deprived
2. The longer the stress situation continues
3. The greater the number of adjustive demands placed on the individual at once or during a short interval of time
4. The more unfamiliar and unexpected the problem
5. The less adequate the individual's resources, including personal resources and social supports

6. The stronger and more equal the opposing forces in conflict situations
7. The closer one gets to the goal in approach-avoidance conflict
8. The greater the perceived threat and the more imminent the threat
9. The less tolerance the individual has for this type and degree of stress
10. The more the individual sees the threat as imposed on him and beyond his control

you will surely pass.' Indeed, since there is a chance that the student will not pass, the person who is supportive in a meaningful sense will not give blind assurance. Rather, she will seek to find the realistic limits of the situation, the weaknesses of the spouse, and the anxieties and tensions that are being experienced; and then she will attempt to help reduce these. Often a statement to the effect, 'Do the best you can' is more supportive than, 'I'm sure you are going to do well.' The latter statement adds to the student's burden, for not only must he fear the disappointment of not passing, but also the loss of respect in the eyes of his spouse." (p. 158)

Often the culture provides for specific rituals or other courses of action which support the individual in his attempts to deal with certain types of stress. For example, most religions provide rituals which help the bereaved through their ordeal; and in some religions, confession and atonement may help people to deal with stresses pertaining to guilt and self-recrimination.

OTHER KEY ASPECTS OF STRESS

In addition to type, source, and severity of stress, three additional aspects of stress are of immediate interest. First is the individual nature of our stress patterns, however similar our life situations may appear. Second is the finding that, as in the case of motives, we may be only partially aware or even unaware of stress. And third is the problem that adaptation to stress may be expensive both physically and psychologically.

Stress Patterns Are Unique

Stresses, like motives, usually do not come singly or operate independently of one another. The total stress pattern at any time determines the part any one stress will play and has much to do with how skillful we will be at resolving it. If a student's stress pattern includes fatigue, pressure toward winning a

scholarship, a chemistry assignment that he cannot understand, and new competition for the affections of his best girl, he may decide to concentrate on winning back his girl and disregard his fatigue and his schoolwork in a way he would not do if all were well with his love life. At the same time, however, his fatigue may make him more irritable than usual and that plus his uneasiness about his undone schoolwork may make him seem moody and unappealing to his girl, so that his stress load is increased rather than lessened.

Stress patterns are unique and changing. To understand any person's behavior, it is important to understand the unique stress pattern with which he is confronted. This pattern will vary in relation to his age, sex, occupation, economic status, special interests and talents, group memberships, and other personal and cultural conditions. The stress pattern of the child is different in many respects from that of an adult; that of the patient with an incurable illness differs from that of a healthy person. The soldier in combat has a different stress pattern from that of the civilian; the woman executive has somewhat different problems from those of a man. But even two people faced with the same stressful situation—for example, two middle-aged executives whose firms have gone bankrupt—may be affected quite differently, for each will perceive the situation in his own way and will have his own unique pattern of resources for meeting it.

Changes in the individual, in his immediate life situation, and in the broader society all contribute to a continual change in the patterns of stress that he experiences. Some of these changes bring only minor stress, as when a new business venture compels him to be away from his family from time to time; other changes, such as the death of a son or a technological development that makes his skills obsolete, may place him under severe stress. In any case, stress patterns, like motive patterns, change both from day to day and from one period of life to another. Your stress pattern is somewhat different today from what it was a week ago, and as a whole is quite different this year from what it will be when your oldest child is about to be married.

Key stresses in a person's life. Often there is one key stress—or a limited number of key stresses—that permeates the life of an individual, particularly his adult life. Sometimes such key stresses reflect a continuing difficult life situation. For example, an individual may be stuck indefinitely in a distasteful job from which he seemingly cannot escape; or he may suffer for years in an unhappy and conflictful marriage; or he may be severely limited by a physical handicap or a chronic health problem. In other instances, the continuing stress derives from a traumatic experience from which the individual has never fully recovered. A college student who fails his premedical program may always thereafter feel a sense of frustration that he was not able to become the physician that he wanted to be. For many people the unexpected death of a loved one—particularly a daughter, son, wife, or husband—makes a major and lasting impact on their lives.

In some cases the key stresses in a person's life center around what might be called "crisis" situations. Although there is some confusion concerning what we mean by a "crisis," Lazarus (1966) has pointed out that:

"Crisis seems to imply a limited period in which an individual or group is exposed to threats and demands which are at or near the limits of their resources to cope.

"In threat the emphasis is on a particular harm, while in crisis, the focus is on a period of the person's or group's life in which major threats and frustrations that tax adaptation are prominent." (pp. 407-408)

A crisis might center around a traumatic divorce, or an episode of depression in which the individual sees no hope and seriously considers suicide, or the aftermath of serious injuries or disease which force difficult readjustments in the individual's self-concept and way of life, or other events which force a mobilization of all the individual's adjustive resources. The outcome of such crises has profound significance for the individual's subsequent adjustment.

If we succeed in discovering the key stresses, past and present, in a person's life —and how he has dealt and is attempting to deal with them—we have gone a long way toward understanding his behavior.

Stress Patterns May Be Unconscious

Since we are so often unaware of our underlying motives and assumptions, it is not surprising that stress, too, is often not clearly perceived. Although we are acutely aware of many of the frustrations, conflicts, and pressures that beset us, there are others of which we are only partially aware or even unaware.

Partial awareness of stress. Sometimes we feel threatened or anxious but do not know just why. For example, an individual may experience a feeling of not being fully accepted

---

UNCONSCIOUSNESS OF THREAT

In a stress situation, we may be unaware or partially aware of any or all of the following:

   1. What the adjustive demand is.

   2. What fears or motives in ourselves make this demand seem threatening; what goals are being threatened.

   3. The connection between the outer situation and our feeling of being threatened.

   4. What resources and alternatives are available for meeting the adjustive demand.

   5. The fact of having reacted emotionally or of having defended oneself against threat.

Based in part on Lazarus, 1966.

or appreciated by his supervisor yet not be able to put his finger on just what gives rise to these feelings. Or a girl may sense that her fiancé is losing interest in her and become anxious yet be unable to pinpoint the reasons for her apprehension. In both cases the individual is reacting to cues in the situation that he cannot identify.

In other cases where the individual feels vaguely anxious, it turns out that unacceptable motives of which he is unaware are responsible. For example, a youth who has felt threatened when another male has stared at him in a warm way may discover that he has homosexual tendencies of which he has been unaware.

Lack of awareness of stress. Just as the body may be invaded by microörganisms and may take defensive action against them without our awareness, so psychological needs may be frustrated and defensive behavior undertaken with no awareness or conscious choice on our part. For example, show-off behavior and negativism are usually defensive reactions to the frustration of needs for adequacy, social approval, and acceptance, but in some cases, not only the defensive tactics but even the feelings of inadequacy that prompt them are below the level of consciousness.

Even when conflict rather than simple need frustration is the problem, we find the same principles operating. The individual may be clearly aware of the nature of his conflict, as when he is trying to decide between two jobs, or the conflict may involve lesser degrees of awareness or actually be unconscious. He may feel vaguely uncomfortable or uneasy or even acutely anxious without being able to identify the source of his anxiety. In fact, the presence of such "free floating" anxiety is often taken as evidence that ego-defenses are preventing a painful stress situation from entering our consciousness.

The example of hypnotically induced conflict given in the last chapter shows dramatically how behavior may be affected by stress of which we are quite unaware. In this case the subject's artificially induced attitudes toward his smoking functioned on an unconscious level in much the same way as do many of our assumptions and attitudes. Many of us have unconscious attitudes toward sexual behavior, authority demands, marriage, and other life situations that conflict with our conscious wishes and ideas. The recognition of unconscious conflicts makes intelligible much behavior that on the surface seems irrational or incomprehensible.

Adaptation to Stress Is Expensive

Stress is inevitable in life, though not all stresses are imposed on us by others or by conditions in our life situation. Some are of our own creation and even deliberate choosing. We all have choice points when we can choose security or risk. We choose whether we will compete for a college education, accept a job or a promotion that will increase the pressure on us, and take on the responsibilities of marriage and a family. To say "No" to all such stresses would be to say "No" to life.

Mental health and effective adjustment result not from lack of stress but from learning how to cope with stress. All adaptation has costs, however, in energy, resources, and time. For severe or long-continued stress, these costs can be great.

Lowering of adaptive efficiency. Under severe stress there is a narrowing of the perceptual field and an increased rigidity of cognitive processes. The individual tends to withdraw his attention from other parts of the field and to concentrate on the particular stress, thus limiting the field to which he is responsive. At the same time his perceptions and frame of reference seem to become more rigid, thus making it difficult or impossible for him to reinterpret the situation or see new possibilities and relationships in it.

Experiments with both animal and human subjects have demonstrated this rigidity.

Rats, given an unsolvable discrimination problem, developed a stereotyped response, perhaps always jumping toward one side; later, when food was placed in full view on the other side, they continued to jump to the nonrewarding side (Maier, 1949). Similarly, college students were given a series of verbal mazes to solve, half of the students working under threat of academic failure, the other half not. Part way through the series, the initial method of solution became incorrect and a new method was necessary. The threatened subjects were significantly slower than the others in seeing the need for change and making it (Maher, 1957). Many other studies have shown that people working under stress and anxiety tend to be rigid and inflexible and to approach new problems in a stereotyped way (Lazarus, 1966).

The narrowing of the perceptual field and the increased rigidity of cognitive processes under stress probably explains why people in the throes of a difficult conflict are often unaware of much that is going on around them. They have focused their major attention and energies inward on their conflict and in this sense have withdrawn from the surrounding world. In extreme form, this process can be seen in psychotic patients who become so completely preoccupied with their inner world that they literally lose contact with the world around them.

Our cognitive efficiency may also be impaired by the emotions that typically accompany severe stress. For example, acute stage fright may disrupt the performance of a public speaker; "examination jitters" may lead to poor performance despite adequate preparation; in a sudden catastrophe, intense fear may cause the individual to panic or freeze. In fact, high levels of fear, anger, or anxiety may lead not only to impaired performance but to actual behavior disorganization. When stress increases beyond a moderate level, the efficiency of perception, problem solving, and decision making progressively decreases.

In using its resources to meet one severe stress, the organism may suffer a lowering of tolerance for other stresses. The Canadian physiologist Hans Selye (1956) found that mice exposed to extremes of cold developed increased resistance to the cold but became unusually sensitive to X rays. Similarly, soldiers who develop resistance to combat may show a lowering of tolerance to other stresses, such as bad news from home. A father who has learned to handle his difficult boss tactfully all day, may find when he gets home that he has no patience left for trying to understand and help his thirteen-year-old son.

It appears that the coping resources of the system are limited; if they are already mobilized to capacity against one stress, they are not available for coping with others. This

STRESS MAY HAVE POSITIVE EFFECTS

Although severe stress may lead to lowered adaptive efficiency and to wear and tear on the system, stress can also have positive consequences. The following are some of the possible positive effects of stress:

1. *New self-understanding.* Through his experience in a very difficult situation, an individual may get a clearer picture of his assets, liabilities, and adaptive potential.

2. *Increased competencies.* After flunking a test, an individual may find more effective methods of study and learn to put more effort into his work.

3. *New approaches to problems.* If he acknowledges that past approaches have not worked well, an individual may find more effective strategies.

4. *More realistic goals and expectations.* Persistent failure or frustration may lead an individual to a more realistic appraisal of the alternatives actually open to him.

5. *Increased stress tolerance.* By success in adapting to and "living with" difficult stresses, an individual may increase his ability to meet stress—as well as his confidence in his ability to do so.

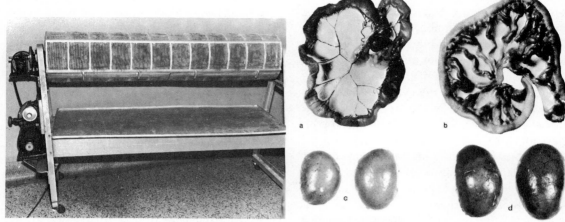

Rats repeatedly subjected to stress by being turned in the revolving drum above developed many signs of pathology. Blood vessels in the intestine (a) became greatly thickened (b), contributing to high blood pressure. The adrenal glands, normally small and yellow (c), became enlarged and brown (d). Other changes included a wasted thymus and stomach ulcers (Constantinides and Carey, 1949).

helps to explain how sustained psychological stress can lower biological resistance to disease, and how sustained bodily disease can lower resistance to psychological stress. Interestingly, prolonged stress may lead to either pathological over-responsiveness to stress—as illustrated by the "last straw" response—or to pathological insensitivity to stress, as in loss of hope and extreme apathy. In general, sustained stress of any kind may lead to a serious reduction in the overall adaptive capacity of the organism.

Wear and tear on the system. Probably many people believe that even after a very stressful experience, rest can completely restore them. In his pioneering studies of stress, Selye (1956) found evidence that this is a false assumption.

"Experiments on animals have clearly shown that each exposure leaves an indelible scar, in that it uses up reserves of adaptability which cannot be replaced. It is true that immediately after some harassing experience, rest can restore us almost to the original level of fitness by eliminating acute fatigue. But the emphasis is on almost. *Since we constantly go through periods of stress and rest during life, just a little deficit of adaptation energy every day adds up—it adds up to what we call* aging.

". . . Due to the great advances made by classic medicine during the last half century, premature death caused by specific disease producers (microbes, malnutrition, etc.) has declined at a phenomenal rate. . . . [But] an ever-increasing proportion of the human population dies from the so-called wear-and-tear diseases, or degenerative diseases, which are primarily due to stress." (pp. 274-275)

More recent findings on the role of stress in cardiovascular and other degenerative diseases have strongly supported these earlier findings.

After coping with stressful situations, the neurophysiological mechanisms associated with activation and emotion return the body to normal levels. And although successive stresses may leave us gradually less resilient, there may not be a serious reduction in adaptive resources. But when stress is severe and long-continued, physiological mobilization may become chronic and may in time lead to actual tissue damage and irreversible pathology in bodily organs. Sustained emotional tension associated with identifiable life stresses has been shown to lead to a wide range of psychosomatic disorders, from peptic ulcers and high blood pressure to heart attacks and cerebral accidents (strokes). In fact, it has been estimated that over half of the patients who consult physicians have difficulties caused largely by emotional tension.

Breakdown under excessive stress. As we have already noted, each individual has his level of stress tolerance. When this level is exceeded, he breaks down. In Chapter 7 we shall examine the process of decompensation under excessive stress and in Chapter 8 the forms of abnormality that may result.

SUMMARY AND A LOOK AHEAD

In this chapter we have examined some of the frustrations, conflicts, and pressures that place difficult adjustive demands on us and complicate our path toward our goals. We have seen that the severity of stress depends on (1) characteristics of the situation itself, such as importance, duration, and multiplicity of demands, the strength of conflicting forces, unfamiliarity or suddenness, the presence of threat, and the imminence of an anticipated stress; (2) characteristics of the individual, such as his degree of competence, his evaluation of the problem and of his ability to meet it, and his general level of stress tolerance; and (3) the presence or absence of external resources and supports. Stress, like a motive, may be partly or wholly unconscious, though the presence of uneasiness or anxiety may be a clue that stress is present. Each person experiences a unique and changing pattern of stress though often there are key, continuing stresses in one's life that provide a focus for his adjustive efforts.

Stress is inevitable and sometimes chosen voluntarily; mental health results not from lack of stress but from ability to cope with it satisfactorily. Severe stress has costs, however, in lowered efficiency and in wear and tear on the system, and too severe or long-continued stress may lead to the breakdown of the system.

In Chapter 7, which follows, we shall examine the usual sequence in our processing of adjustive demands, the ways in which feedback may be used, and the three general types of reactions that we may make.

Key terms used in this chapter include:

adjustive demand, stress, strain (pp. 175, 177)
biological-level stress, psychological-level stress (p. 175)
frustration, conflict, pressure (pp. 176, 178, 183)
approach-avoidant, double-approach, double-avoidant conflicts (pp. 178-180)
value conflicts (p. 180)
commitment vs. noninvolvement (p. 181)
severity of stress (p. 186)
importance, duration, multiplicity of demands (p. 187)
threat (p. 188)
stress tolerance (p. 190)
external resources and supports (p. 191)
levels of awareness of stress (p. 193)

Chapter 7

REACTIONS TO ADJUSTIVE DEMANDS

An Introduction to Adustive Behavior
Processing Adjustive Demands
Types of Psychological Adjustive Reactions

All behavior—successful, unsuccessful, wise, foolish, flexible, rigid—is an attempt by the organism to meet the demands facing it, or perceived as facing it. The requirements we try to meet may stem primarily from within (demands for food, rest, affection, self-esteem, achievement) or from without (demands for cooperation with others, obedience to law, adherence to expected role behavior). Depending upon the nature of the demand and our resources for coping with it, we may solve the problem easily and effectively or we may experience considerable strain and, even after sustained effort, meet it with only partial success. In some cases, as we have seen, a demand may exceed our adaptive potential.

Unfortunately, problems of adjustment do not stand in line and present themselves one at a time. They crowd in upon us, competing for our attention and our adaptive resources. Thus a student may be trying to cope with the emotional hurt of a broken engagement, under heavy pressure from upcoming final examinations, and harrassed by financial problems all at once. Even though some of our problems are solved or simply disappear with time, others persist, and new problems are constantly arising. Thus coping with stress is a never ending venture for all of us.

AN INTRODUCTION TO ADJUSTIVE BEHAVIOR

Since stress—beyond a certain level—endangers the well-being of the organism, it leads us to persistent attempts to resolve it; it forces us to do something about it. What we do depends upon a host of factors including our frame of reference, motives, competencies, and stress tolerance, as well as our environmental resources and the demands and expectations of others.

The emphasis that psychologists place on meeting adjustive demands—on *adjusting*—is sometimes misunderstood as implying conformity, in which one achieves harmony between self and environment by surrendering one's own individuality. But adjusting does not imply surrender or denial of self, because many of our most insistent demands are inner demands for personal integrity and growth. If they are ignored, our adjustment is incomplete and inadequate. Adjustment involves transactions with one's environment which change both the environment and the self; it is rarely simply a matter of adapting oneself to meet environmental demands.

In the chapter which follows we will examine the criteria by which we decide whether an individual's mode of adjusting is effective and healthy or ineffective and unhealthy. For the moment, the point to be made is that all behavior is an attempt to adjust—to meet inner and outer demands. Human behavior becomes intelligible only when seen in this context.

Some General Principles of Adjustive Behavior

Before looking more closely at the actual dynamics of adjustive behavior, it will be helpful to broaden our perspective by examining some generalizations that can be made regarding reactions to stress. We shall see that our adjustive actions are "holistic" and economical, that they may have diverse emotional reinforcement, and that they may be relatively conscious or automatic.

Reactions to stress are holistic. An organism develops as a unit and behaves as a unit. Just as arms and legs develop not at random or independently but in keeping with a centrally controlled pattern, so individual psychological processes—perceiving, remembering, learning, reasoning, desiring, feeling—are coordinated with the organism's efforts to meet adjustive demands. The behavior of a healthy organism is not a jumble of disconnected activities but a coordinated and integrated sequence of steps directed toward definite goals.

Since all our adjustive behavior must use the same bodily equipment—sense organs, nervous system, glands, muscles, and so on—the overall adjustive demands of the moment will determine how it is used. If there are several competing demands, the one that is most important, or is perceived as most important, commandeers the organ-

ism's adjustive resources, and some functions or actions will be *inhibited* while others are *facilitated.*

This coordination is readily illustrated by the emergency reaction, in which digestion and other bodily processes that are not immediately essential to survival stop or slow down while the organism's resources for increased activity and effort are mobilized—muscle tonus increases, stored sugar goes into the blood stream, adrenalin is secreted. Similarly, on a psychological level a certain desire or impulse may be given immediate and direct expression, or may be inhibited until a more appropriate time, or may be suppressed and pushed out of consciousness each time it appears. If a desire seriously threatens the individual's sense of psychological well-being—as, for example, sexual desires sometimes do—it may be entirely screened out of consciousness by the mechanism of repression. In general, facilitating and inhibiting controls provide the organism with the flexibility it needs for dealing with stress, enabling it to mobilize its resources to meet the most crucial demand of the moment.

Only under unusual or pathological conditions does the organism function "segmentally" rather than as an integrated unit. A person threatened with starvation may steal to obtain food, though this may violate his self-concept and pattern of values. Segmental actions may also occur as a consequence of interference with the integrating functions of the higher brain centers by alcohol, drugs, or brain damage. Under normal circumstances, however, the organism functions as an integrated unit in its pursuit of overall maintenance and actualization. The alternative would be disorganized behavior which would disable the individual just as surely as a football team would be disabled if each player did as he pleased instead of functioning as a member of a team.

Reactions to stress are economical. Not only does the individual react to stress as an integrated unit, but he reacts in a way which is economical—which involves an economical expenditure of his resources.

Since the individual's resources are limited, it is not surprising that he tends to deal with the business of living in economical ways. In fact, J. G. Miller (1965b) has pointed out that organisms that survive—whether lower or higher on the evolutionary scale—tend to employ the least expensive defenses against stress first; if these are ineffective, additional and more expensive resources are brought into operation. For example, if acid is injected into a dog's veins, the first defense which appears is overbreathing; if this does not prove effective, more drastic protective mechanisms, such as biochemical changes in the blood, are brought into operation. Similarly, if a general finds a squad too small to achieve a military objective, he may commit a company or a regiment—at an increasing cost in resources.

The same sequence may be observed on the psychological level. For example, a student who gets an F instead of the A or B he expected on an examination may feel self-devaluated and anxious. As a consequence, he may curtail his social life, increase his study hours, and redouble his efforts. If he still obtains a low grade in the next examination, he may lower his level of aspiration and hope to get through the course with a C or D. This is a relatively inexpensive defense, at least for the moment. However, if he then fails the course and feels increasingly inadequate and anxious, he may blame his failure on an unqualified and unfair instructor. This is a more expensive and self-defeating defense, since he cannot now profit from whatever mistakes he has made or see himself more realistically as a consequence of his failure experience. In extreme cases, self-devaluating and anxiety-arousing stress may lead to the development of psychotic reactions—in which the individual denies the reality of the situation—an extremely costly defense.

Some of the defenses that people use are so self-defeating that it is hard for an outsider to see why they are not abandoned. We can only assume that for the individual, they represent the most economical way he knows for coping with the stress situation. Since he has no objective way of checking his perception and assumptions, he is usually doing the best that he knows how in relation to his view of the stress situation. But even if he is aware that other coping patterns would be more effective, they would require effort and change, which is difficult and threatening and might not be successful. Thus his present approach looks (to him) most economical and least risky, all things considered.

The tendency to resist change is referred to as *inertia* on the individual level and as *cultural lag* on the social level. The relative comfortableness and ease of the familiar and habitual and the effort, anxiety, and uncertainty entailed by change lead to a tendency to persist in established behavior patterns long after the situation calls for different responses.

Reactions may be automatic or planned. Just as we may be fully aware, partially aware, or totally unaware of our motivations or of being under stress, we may respond to stress automatically and with little or no thought, or with awareness and in a planned way.

On a biological level, the repair of damaged tissue, immunological defenses against disease, and other corrective and defensive processes take place automatically. Some psychological tension-reducing mechanisms, such as crying, repetitive talking, and fainting in the face of a highly traumatic situation, also take place automatically. Even if the individual is aware of what he is doing, these responses are not consciously thought out and decided upon.

Automatic functioning is also seen in the form of habitual behavior in which situations that once required our conscious coping efforts no longer require our attention. Still another kind of automatic functioning involves the use of rationalization and other unconscious mechanisms for avoiding or defending oneself against threats to one's worth. Thus we may rationalize our failures or repress painful and devaluating experiences without realizing we are doing so.

Automatic functioning is potentially of great value in helping us to deal with routine stress situations without taking our attention from more important events which cannot be dealt with routinely but require thought. It is apparent, however, that automatic functioning may be used when a problem actually requires conscious thought and planning, as when a marital problem needs our most concerted efforts if it is to be resolved. In such cases, automatic functioning may lead to irrational and ineffective behavior.

In our complicated and changing environment, automatic functioning must be continuously reassessed and supplemented by conscious processes involving reasoning, imagination, and learning of new behavior. As we have seen, man's advantage over lower species rests largely on his ability to reflect, to recognize new requirements, to consider alternative actions, and to take intentional, preplanned action appropriate to changing conditions. To the extent that unconscious processes take over the direction of anything but the most routine behavior, the individual's flexibility of response—and hence his ability to make effective adjustments—is reduced.

Stress arouses emotion. The particular emotional states accompanying reactions to stress vary greatly. In a contest of skill or other stressful situation where the individual feels he has a good chance of coming out on top, he may experience exhilaration. More often, however, stress brings negative emotions and some measure of emotional mobilization for emergency action. Three emotional patterns are of special significance here: anger, fear, and anxiety.

The organism tends to react to frustration with anger. And anger, in turn, tends to lead to attack or aggressive action. Where the frustration continues or the individual is confronted with a succession of frustrating situations stemming from the same source, feelings of anger at being blocked gradually blend into hostility directed toward the person or object viewed as the source of frustration with a tendency to destroy, damage, or hurt him or it (Buss, 1961).

Specific dangers tend to arouse fear; and fear, in turn, tends to lead to withdrawal or flight. However, the nature of the stress situation and the degree of fear elicited will have much to do with the direction and quality of the behavior that is induced. The individual who fears he has cancer may go in immediately for a medical checkup; or he may put it off because he fears the possibility of a positive diagnosis. In the face of dangers which elicit intense fear, the individual may panic or freeze and become unable to function in an organized manner. Such behavior can be readily observed in fires and other disasters.

As we have noted, threat arouses anxiety, which is a subjective warning of danger as well as an acutely unpleasant condition that forces us to undertake some action to relieve it—much as physical pain drives us to action. Many stress situations—such as the threat of global atomic warfare—may give rise to both fear and anxiety. But in general, we may conceive of fear as related to perceived dangers, whereas the nature of the threat eliciting anxiety may or may not be clearly perceived. For example, if repressed hostility threatens to break through existing defenses into violent action, the individual may become anxious even though he may not be clearly aware of the source of the threat. As we shall see, we have many defenses for coping with anxiety.

Anger, fear, and anxiety may be aroused singly or in various combinations. Where fear or anxiety is aroused, anger and hostility often follow, for the things we fear are actual or potential sources of frustration. Of course, these so-called negative emotions of anger, fear, and anxiety may be intermeshed with more positive emotions such as love—as when an individual feels both love and hostility toward a mate who has subjected him to a series of frustrations. In general, our perception and appraisal of the stress situation determine the specific emotional patterns that are elicited.

Levels of adjustive action. Adjustive behavior can be viewed in terms of biological, psychological, and sociological levels of defense and action. Thus we have cellular or immunological defenses against disease; we have psychological resources, including defensive mechanisms for coping with stress and protecting the self from devaluation; and on a sociological level we have interpersonal and group resources, such as family, friends, labor unions, and police forces.

Failure on any of the adjustive levels may seriously impair our adjustment on other levels. For example, failure of our immunological defenses against disease may impair not only bodily functioning but psychological functioning as well; chronic failure in our psychological adjustive actions to cope with stress may lead to peptic ulcers or other "diseases of adaptation"; and failure of groups on which one depends—such as failure of the lawmakers and courts to maintain justice or failure of the police to maintain order—may lead to harmful consequences for the individual. In fact, failure on any of these adjustive levels may lead to impaired overall functioning of the individual or even to his death. Thus again we see the integrated and holistic functioning of the human organism in its complex and continuing transactions with its environment.

Reactions Are Shaped by Inner and Outer Determinants

The ways in which we attempt to adjust are determined both by our structural and integrative personality characteristics and by the nature of the surrounding field. Sometimes *inner* determinants, such as our unique frame of reference, play the predominant role; at other times *outer* determinants, such as social expectations or environmental resources, are of primary importance. But any adjustive action reflects the interplay of a combination of inner and outer determinants.

Since we have encountered most of the determinants of behavior in our discussion of development, motivation, and stress, we need only summarize their role in the present context.

Inner determinants of stress reactions. Inner determinants which help to shape our reactions to stress include our frame of reference, motive patterns, competencies, stress tolerance, and momentary physiological and psychological conditions.

1. *Frame of reference—cognitive map.* Our assumptions about reality, possibility, and value influence the way we appraise stress situations, the alternative courses of action we consider, and what we decide to do. As we have noted, one individual may feel threatened in a situation which another person can deal with easily. Similarly, in a situation of risk with many unknowns, some of us will choose to play it safe, others will take moderate chances, and still others will "go for broke."

It is probably safe to say that we are rarely aware of all the possibilities of action that a situation leaves open to us. The ways that we see to act are the ones consistent with our assumptions about ourselves and our world, and the alternative we choose is the one most comfortable for us—or least uncomfortable—and most in keeping with our view of the kind of person we are. Unfortunately, our frame of reference can interfere with effective adjustment to the extent that lack of information or inaccurate assumptions distort our perceptions, lead to faulty decisions, and blind us to promising courses of action.

2. *Motive patterns.* The strength of the motive or motives endangered by the stress situation influences the amount of energy we are willing to expend, the obstacles we are willing to try to surmount, and the persistence of our efforts.

Our motives, as we have seen, may be conscious or unconscious, may push us in harmonious or contradictory directions, and may change considerably with time. And sometimes they are based upon "false" values, so that the achievement of our goals does not bring us the satisfaction we anticipate. But whatever their pattern at a given time, they are chief determinants of the direction and energizing of our behavior and of our adjustive action.

3. *Competencies.* Our skills and abilities are a crucial part of our adaptive potential in determining what action we can take and how successful it is likely to be. If the situation calls for competencies we do not have, we are not likely to meet its demands successfully.

Both our capacity and our learned skills are important here. Our level of intelligence and other capabilities will set limits on the range within which we *can* function, but even high capacity will not ensure that we *will* function at a high level. Even with great musical talent, one does not reach the concert stage without long hours of instruction and practice. Fortunately, most of us start with potential more than adequate for our needs; it is the extent to which we develop it into physical, intellectual, emotional, and social competencies that largely determines what doors will be open to us as we go through life and what ones will be closed.

4. *Stress tolerance.* A person's ability to tolerate stress is another important resource for dealing with problems of adjustment—and hence another important determinant of behavior. As we noted in Chapter 6, each of us is more vulnerable to some types of stress than to others, and each has his own breaking point—the point at which he can no longer function in an integrated way.

The individual's level of stress tolerance, whether high or low, seems to be based upon his constitutional make-up, the general degree of success with which he has been able to meet his biological and psychological needs, his intellectual and other competencies, his overall degree of self-confidence, and the development of traits such as patience, courage, and flexibility.

5. *Momentary conditions.* Many momentary conditions can affect our reactions to stress. A problem encountered when we feel generally optimistic may be seen in perspective and solved with dispatch; the same problem encountered on a day when we are discouraged may "send us into a tailspin." Illness, fatigue, a recent failure or jolt, or preoccupation with another difficult stress can make us less able than usual to deal with a new problem, whereas good health, feeling rested, or having just had the satisfaction of public recognition of our ability can make us better able to cope with a new stress. What we have been doing, thinking, and feeling always provides the background against which we see and evaluate a new problem and helps to determine how much of our resources and attention we will devote to it and with what skill.

Outer determinants of stress reactions. Determinants in our environment that help to shape our reactions to stress include environmental resources, social supports, social expectations and restraints, the individual's general life situation, and the conditions and events of the moment.

1. *Environmental resources.* The alternatives open to us inevitably are limited by the available resources in the environment. We cannot call a doctor if there is none in the vicinity; we cannot call the police if we live in a frontier area where government has not yet been established; and we cannot go to school if there are no educational facilities in our community and we lack the means to go elsewhere. Although we live in an affluent society, few of us have all the financial and other resources we would like to have; for our poor and for people who live in underdeveloped countries, there are severe limitations placed on their adjustive behavior by lack of educational, health, occupational, and other facilities.

2. *Social supports.* We saw in the last chapter that a problem seems less stressful when we can meet it with the support of our friends, family, and/or other groups; that an individual is most vulnerable when he is isolated and alone; and that people under stress tend to seek the support and assistance of others to give them strength and bolster their own resources. The presence, encouragement, and emotional support of others make a stress seem less threatening and enable the individual to meet it more rationally; conversely, criticism, nagging, or abandonment by family and friends may make a stress much more difficult to cope with.

3. *Social expectations, demands, and constraints.* Whereas social supports help us to cope with stress and meet our needs, social expectations and constraints complicate our behavior by: (1) specifying the channels through which we may move in pursuit of our goals, and (2) demanding certain behaviors of individuals occupying given positions in the group. Many means of coping with stress situations—such as robbing a bank when we are in financial straits—are excluded from serious consideration because of social constraints. Similarly, role expectations and demands may take precedence over personal desires and judgments, as when an army officer who wants to retreat is ordered by his superior to hold his position or attack. Throughout our lives, the social structures in which we operate influence the ways in which and the extent to which we are able to meet our needs.

4. *Life situation of the individual.* Each individual has a unique life situation, usually characterized by a particular balance of stresses and resources, successes and failures. A common factor in the early lives of the Mercury astronauts (see page 189) was that they went to schools where they did well and showed smooth growth patterns with a favorable balance of success, confidence, and rising levels of aspiration (Korchin & Ruff, 1964). If the life situation of an individual, taken as a whole, has shown a favorable balance of resources and success experiences in coping with adjustive demands, he will have steadily increased his ability to cope effectively with new problems; if not, or if the present balance is decidedly unfavorable, he may be unable to cope effectively with a difficult adjustive demand.

5. *Momentary and unusual events.* Just as momentary inner conditions may influence our adjustive actions, so momentary and unusual environmental conditions may also act as determinants. Unusual stresses that come when we are in an unstable, transitory situation may be harder to cope with; two critical examinations scheduled the same day and conducted in a noisy building after an evening when we must work late at an outside

job provide an unusually difficult demand, and our performance may well be different from what it would be if the examinations were on different days in a quiet room after a good night's sleep.

The Perspective of Time and Learning

In our brief review of the behavioristic model of man in Chapter 1, we noted some of the principles of learning which account for the acquisition of responses and their modification over time. However, the perspective that we are trying to achieve here goes beyond the principles established for the learning of isolated, easily delineated responses to the concept of living as a process of learning to cope with adjustive demands and meet our needs—learning to overcome frustrations, resolve conflicts, alleviate pressures, assess changes, and repeatedly work out appropriate ways of meeting changed requirements. This is a never ending process in which we try out and abandon various responses in keeping with long-term goals, deal in new and creative ways with recurrent situations instead of simply repeating responses that have been reinforced in the past, and attempt to improve our general competence over time.

Although we shall sometimes discuss a bit of behavior as if it were an isolated act, it is usually impossible to pinpoint the beginning or end of an adjustive action. And ongoing, combined actions to meet a pattern of requirements may be so interrelated that they cannot be separately identified. Adjustive behavior is both complex and continuous, with evolving insights and skills, new discoveries and adaptations, and variations on recurrent themes. There is never a point when we can say we have reached adjustment—as long as we live we are adjusting.

PROCESSING ADJUSTIVE DEMANDS

In spite of a great deal of research, we know relatively little about how the human brain processes stress situations. At one time the brain was thought of as a "switchboard" where stimuli and responses were connected. Present-day computer-simulation studies support the notion that it is more like an elaborate communication center where incoming information is continuously evaluated, alternative responses are formulated and weighed, decisions are made and implemented, and feedback is checked.

Our self-aware "human computer" is at once more and less efficient at handling problems than is the electronic computer. It is more inventive and creative, but it is much slower and more subject to error. We often come up with wrong answers not only because of a lack of accurate information but because of time pressures, the need to defend ourselves from devaluation, emotional involvement in the stress situation, and other limiting conditions that are peculiarly human. Furthermore, our thought machinery operates on more than one level of consciousness; the problems we deal with consciously and thoughtfully tend to be processed more rationally than those to which we react without awareness. For the moment, we are concerned primarily with the conscious processing of stress rather than with habitual or automatic responses.

Although we can do no more than make tentative assumptions about what actually happens as the human brain processes an adjustive demand, the sequence of events can be described in terms of three basic steps: (1) appraising the stress situation—including available resources for coping with it, (2) formulating alternatives and deciding on a course of action, and (3) taking action and checking on feedback—with a view to correcting possible error.

Appraising the Stress Situation

We are continually scanning our environment—both external and internal—to see what opportunities or dangers may be present. When we become aware of a new adjustive demand, our first task is to define it and evaluate its degree of threat. Here it is important that we make an accurate evaluation of the problem, for an incomplete or distorted picture would place us at a disadvantage in coping with it.

Categorizing the stress situation. The vast volume of new information continuously being received is quickly assigned to categories on the basis of similarities to and differences from previous experiences. Our tendency to classify and categorize is such an important integrative characteristic that it deserves a little elaboration. As Bruner, Goodnow, and Austin (1956) have stated it:

"We begin with what seems a paradox. The world of experience of any normal man is composed of a tremendous array of discriminably different objects, events, people, impressions. There are estimated to be more than 7 million discriminable colors alone, and in the course of a week or two we come in contact with a fair proportion of these. . . .

"But were we to utilize fully our capacity for registering the differences in things and to respond to each event encountered as unique, we would soon be overwhelmed by the complexity of our environment. Consider only the linguistic task of acquiring a vocabulary fully adequate to cope with the world of color differences! The resolution of the seeming paradox—the existence of discrimination capacities which, if fully used, would make us slaves to the particular—is achieved by man's capacity to categorize. To categorize is to render discriminably different things equivalent, to group the objects and events and people around us into classes, and to respond to them in terms of their class membership rather than their uniqueness. . . . In place of a color lexicon of 7 million items, people in our society get along with a dozen or so commonly used color names. . . ." (p. 1)

It thus becomes apparent that our natural tendency to simplify by categorizing is a highly useful one, making our environment simple enough to evaluate. However, this tendency is also a possible source of error since our categorization of a new situation depends so heavily upon the characteristics it shares with past situations of a similar nature rather than upon its own unique characteristics. Simplification too often becomes oversimplification. This can be readily seen, for example, in overly simplified stereotypes of communists, Democrats, Republicans, labor leaders, liberals, conservatives, politicians, "hawks" and "doves," and so on. All those labeled *liberals,* for example, are assumed to be unrealistic and bad, or idealistic and humanitarian, depending on the perceiver's political and social orientation. As Miller (1962) has pointed out:

"It makes the world a great deal simpler when the good guys are always smart, honest, beautiful, and brave, while the bad guys are always stupid, crooked, ugly cowards." (p. 274)

Although we are not usually as naïve as Miller's statement might imply, our natural tendency to simplify by categorizing and our further tendency to protect our existing frame of reference make it doubly easy for us to see things in black and white and often very difficult to see shades of gray.

Of course, when we face a stress problem for which our categories are obviously inadequate, we are forced to analyze it as a unique situation and to try to discern its key dimensions. Sometimes further information enables us to classify it in one of our established categories, but sometimes we must form a new category which in turn may be used in categorizing subsequent experiences.

Through our categories or "coding patterns" we thus group and organize information about our world. To the extent that our coding patterns are too simplified or otherwise inaccurate, we are handicapped in dealing with stress problems. But accurate or inaccurate, our first step in coping with stress is to define the stress situation as best we can.

Appraising the threat. An integral part of evaluating the stress situation is identifying the degree of threat which it poses. As we have seen, *threat* refers to anticipated harm, the degree of threat depending upon the magnitude of anticipated harm, and what is highly threatening to one person may be only mildly threatening or even nonthreatening to another.

If the individual judges the stress situation to be nonthreatening or only mildly threatening, he is likely to cope with it in terms of established patterns which require little thought or effort. On the other hand, if he interprets the adjustive demand as a serious threat, he is likely to experience anxiety and to interrupt other ongoing activities in order to focus his energies on coping with it (Simon, 1967).

Of course, the individual's appraisal may be in error, and he may perceive threat where none exists or fail to perceive threat where it does exist. But accurate or inaccurate, threat appraisal is an extremely important aspect of the appraisal of the stress situation as a whole, for the degree of threat perceived will markedly influence the way the further processing of the stress situation will proceed.

Deciding on a Course of Action

Having defined the problem and its degree of threat, the individual must next decide what he will do about it. This involves formulating alternative courses of action that might solve the problem and selecting the one most promising. Both these steps involve extremely complex processes which we can study only by inference.

Formulating alternative courses of action. Often in defining the problem we have already begun some formulation of possible alternatives. The categorization of the problem provides what some investigators have called a "search model" by setting the requirements that will have to be met by a suitable course of action.

In a familiar situation the whole process of definition, formulation of alternative actions, and choice of action may take place automatically with little or no conscious involvement. An example of this would be our almost instantaneous reaction to a car stopping suddenly ahead of us on a freeway. At the other extreme, a stress situation with many unfamiliar elements may not be amenable to immediate categorization, and no appropriate response pattern may be evident even when the problem has been defined. Here we may have to use reason, imagination, and other conscious processes to work out possible solutions.

The processes by which people formulate possible solutions and decide on their relative suitability vary considerably. Some of us avoid coming to grips with a difficult problem as long as we can—perhaps hoping that time will resolve the situation; some of us seek advice or help from presumably stronger or wiser persons; some of us tackle a stress situation head-on as if we were knights of old and the problem a dragon to be slain. Most of us, of course, approach different kinds of problems in somewhat different ways. A scientist may be very objective in coping with pressures and problems in his work but irrational and emotional in dealing with a family problem.

In general, the more threatened and less confident we feel, the less rationally we tend to envision and weigh the possibilities and the more we tend to look for safety and reduction of anxiety instead of a long-term, well-worked-out, constructive solution.

Balancing probability, desirability, and cost. Once the individual has formulated alternative solutions to the stress situation that appear feasible—having rejected those which are obviously imcompatible with reality, his standards and values, or the requirements of the adjustive demand—he must assess the relative merits of these alternatives and make a choice. In so doing, he will weigh such considerations as his probabilities of success, the degree of satisfaction he will accept, and the cost he is willing to pay.

1. *Playing the probabilities.* Peterson and Beach (1967) have concluded from their research on problem solving and decision making that man seems to be an "intuitive statistician." Other things being equal, an individual tends to select the course of action that seems to offer the greatest probability of

success—as he defines success. In figuring the odds, he not only examines the relevant information at his disposal but tends to assess—often unconsciously—the likelihood that chance factors will upset his calculations or that events beyond his control will interfere to prevent him from carrying out a given course of action and reaching his goal. Although man dislikes uncertainty, his world confronts him only with probabilities and he has to make the best of it and keep betting on life's contingencies.

"And man gambles well. He survives and prospers while using the fallible information to infer the states of his uncertain environment and to predict future events." (p. 29)

Being forced by life to bet on probabilities, however, does not mean that we always calculate the odds rationally. Wishful thinking may lead a person to take untoward risks or disregard danger signs. He may even keep betting on responses which have failed consistently in the past, like the gambler who continues despite heavy losses over a period of time. If we knowingly choose to go against the odds, the element of strain is likely to be increased.

2. *Deciding on an acceptable level of satisfaction.* Though we may take bigger risks for bigger potential gains, we do not automatically choose the course which, if successful, would yield the greatest satisfaction. If the most gainful course of action also carries with it the risk of losing everything if we fail, we may settle for an alternative that is less appealing but more sure of bringing us *some* level of satisfaction. We are willing to date a girl less attractive than the much sought-after campus queen and to accept a good job rather than wait for the better one that may never come through. How high we aim—how much we demand from ourselves and our world—is an important part of our whole life style and helps make the processing of stress the individual matter that it is.

Although individuals differ in the standards of satisfaction they are accustomed to and insist on, most of us are usually content to find a course of action that we feel is "good

ADJUSTIVE BEHAVIOR: ANALOGY TO A COMPUTER

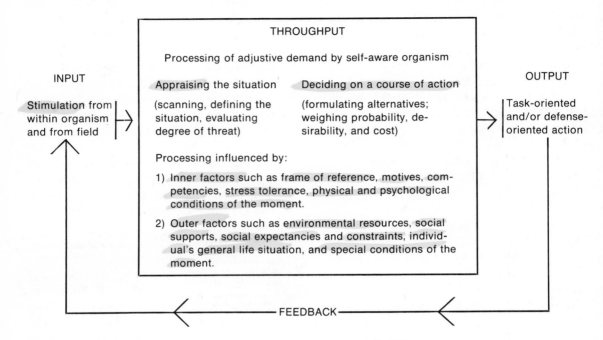

During ongoing behavior, the individual's actions and their effects are part of the input on which he bases further action and evaluation. The analogy of human adjustive behavior to information processing by a computer is useful but far from perfect. For example, the stimulation which initiates human action—unlike the input of a computer—does not have an unvarying effect: as the diagram suggests, responses to it vary with changes in the individual's frame of reference, motivational state, and other inner factors as well as with momentary and long-lasting factors in the environment. A computer, furthermore, cannot set its own goals or discover ways of processing information for which it has not previously been programed.

enough"—that *satisfices* rather than *optimizes* the outcome (Simon, 1957). In coping with the problem of selling our automobile or our home, for example, we may not insist on obtaining the maximum price that could possibly be obtained but rather settle on a price which we consider "fair" and satisfactory. We tend to select the first alternative that meets our criteria and has a high probability of success. Rarely do we attempt to ascertain every possible course of action and ferret out the one that promises to yield maximum returns.

People differ in the extent to which they are willing to take risks for higher possible return and also in the extent to which they are willing to adapt their requirements to accept a moderately satisfactory bird-in-hand instead of holding out for the more alluring bird they had hoped to catch. People who are content with moderate satisfactions in some areas may insist on the very best in others. The man who is content to cope with financial pressures by economizing in his clothes, automobile, and home may not be willing to take the same approach when it comes to selecting a wife. We demand a greater return on our investment and may take a higher risk when we care deeply about the results.

3. *Weighing the costs.* All behavior has its costs in effort, material resources, time, and the surrender of other possibilities. Some behavior also exacts costs in unpleasantness or pain or subsequent loss. Thus staying in school may require such long hours of study that a student must give up hobbies or social life, but dropping out of school might cost him future opportunities for professional advancement.

In selecting between alternative courses of action, we balance the risks and the costs —the amount of effort, anxiety, or other cost —against the possible satisfactions. For high stakes and good odds we may be willing to work hard and undergo considerable pain and sacrifice; but if the returns look small and the risk of losing is considerable, we are usually reluctant to exert much effort. Although we often weigh the factors differently, we all look for what we regard as the best balance of probable gains and costs.

In balancing risk, satisfaction, and cost we must also consider the relationship between a single decision and our ultimate goals. Although some choices are likely to arise only once and to have a continuing influence on our lives—for example, whether we go to college and whom we marry—others are relatively unimportant in the long run, even some that seem immensely important at the time, such as whether we buy a new or used car, a provincial or modern home.

The mature person realizes, too, that since he has only probabilities to judge he cannot hope to win every time. Small losses must be balanced off against overall gains. As the Overstreets (1956) have pointed out:

"After all, we live by batting averages, not by perfect scores. The research scientist does not expect that every hypothesis he sets up will prove out. The teacher does not expect every day's lesson to set aflame the minds of youth. We live by making plans and by making efforts that are, so far as we can see, in line with the results we want; by improving our plans and efforts as experience dictates; and by believing that a fair batting average constitutes enough success to justify our staying on the job." (p. 24)

Sources of error in our calculations. Just as wishful thinking may distort our calculation of the odds or lead us to disregard

them against our better judgment, error may occur in any part of the sequence in processing an adjustive demand. Faulty assumptions, desires, emotions, lack of adequate information, inability to foresee outcome, time pressures, and many other factors may lead us to wrong answers. Even when we have all the facts we need, we can make a self-defeating choice. Problems of self-defense may enter into the way we see and define a problem, the alternatives we find acceptable, and the particular course of action we select. At a particular moment we may need safety or recognition or belonging more than we need to solve the "objective" problem, and our choices and actions may reflect this need.

Thus although the human organism tends to process problems rationally, there are many possible sources of error. Shubik (1967) put it this way:

"Man lives in an environment about which his information is highly incomplete. Not only does he not know how to evaluate many of the alternatives facing him, he is not even aware of a considerable percentage of them. His perceptions are relatively limited; his powers of calculation and accuracy are less than those of a computer in many situations; his searching, data processing, and memory capabilities are erratic. As the speed of transmission of stimuli and the volume of new stimuli increase, the limitations of the individual become more marked relative to society as a whole." (p. 772)

In some stress situations where conditions permit, we can take our time, get more information if we need it, weigh and balance all factors carefully, and emerge with a choice in which we have considerable confidence. But in other situations we may be experiencing so much stress that *any* decision seems better than none. In this case we may take the first possible way out even though it promises little in positive satisfaction or even in freedom from later risk and strain. When we must act but have not yet identified a course of action in which we have confidence, we tend to become disorganized and to act on impulse.

GOAL-TERMINATING MECHANISMS

A course of action undertaken to meet an adjustive demand may continue until the goal is achieved or may be terminated at some intermediate point judged "good enough." For example, a man in his thirties who is anxious to marry and have a family may start in search of an "ideal wife." His quest is likely to continue until it is terminated by one of the following:

1. *Goal achievement.* He achieves the goal he set for himself and resolves the adjustive demand: he finds someone he thinks will make an "ideal wife."

2. *Satisficing.* He ceases his search when he finds someone that he thinks is "good enough" even though not the "ideal wife" he had hoped to be able to find.

3. *Impatience.* After a certain amount of time and effort have been expended in his search without finding the ideal wife, he ceases his search, perhaps settling on the alternative that "seems best so far."

4. *Discouragement.* He stops looking because he concludes that he is getting nowhere—that his strategy and tactics have not worked out. In this case, he may work out a different strategy and launch a new effort or give up the search permanently.

Taking Action and Using Feedback

Once a decision has been made, the next step is to implement the decision—to put the chosen alternative into action. And once a course of action has been embarked upon, the individual can keep checking on whatever feedback information is available to see if corrections or adjustments in ongoing action are called for.

Taking action. The action we take is the transaction with our environment by which we attempt to meet the adjustive demand. It is the test of the definition and appraisal we have made of the situation and of the decision we have made about probabilities and costs. As the action is proceeding, we use feedback to gauge the wisdom of our decision and the effectiveness with which we are carrying it out.

Once a course of action has been undertaken, it is usually continued until the stress situation has been resolved and/or the strain resulting from it has been relieved. There are several "goal-terminating mechanisms," however, which may come into operation sooner (Simon, 1967). Some of these are summarized in the chart above.

Utilizing feedback. As we have seen, homeostatic mechanisms maintain steady states in the human body by constant response to chemical and neural cues. For example, changes in temperature or chemical balance in the blood trigger automatic corrective mechanisms which keep the body at a relatively constant temperature or chemical composition. Comparable feedback mechanisms are employed in mechanical *servomechanisms* like target-seeking missiles. These missiles are sensitive to stimuli—such as heat—coming from the target; such information is used for continuous checking and, if necessary, correction of the missile's course.

A human being taking action to reach a goal is also able to make adjustments in his behavior if he has feedback information concerning the progress or outcome of his actions. Grades in college, for example, are one type of feedback which can be used as a basis for continuing or modifying our present study patterns. Similarly, the happiness of our marriage, the promotions we receive at work, the success of our financial ventures, and the way others respond to us as persons are all types of feedback information that we use to evaluate the progress of our adjustive efforts.

Here it may be noted that "feedback" also involves what Richards (1968) has called "feedforward." That is, when an individual embarks on a course of action he has certain expectancies about what is going to happen

—about the outcome of his action. There is a forward reference in his action patterns, and it is against this "expectation of outcome" that the individual evaluates feedback to see how he is doing.

The type and amount of feedback we receive and the way it is utilized in maintaining or modifying our course of action are of immediate interest.

1. *Convergent and divergent feedback.* Feedback may indicate that we either are on or off the beam. *Convergent* feedback is information telling us that we are making satisfactory progress toward our goal or that the goal has been achieved. If the adjustment problem is highly stressful and/or if we are uncertain about the course of action we have chosen, convergent feedback usually alleviates anxiety, builds self-confidence, and leads to increased effort for it is a signal that the stress will be resolved and our needs met.

Feedback is rarely altogether favorable. When an action is not progressing as satisfactorily as we had anticipated, we get *divergent* feedback, indicating that—perhaps because of unforseen complications or a wrong choice of action—we are not progressing toward our goal as well as we might or perhaps that our action is ineffective or even making the stress situation worse. A young person who talks too much in an effort to gain attention and approval may be informed, by the negative reactions of other people, that he is not succeeding in his efforts. Besides signaling the need for a modification of behavior, divergent feedback indicates that stress is likely to be prolonged or intensified.

In general, we interpret pain, punishment, and discomfort as cues that we are not doing well—as divergent feedback, while rewards, pleasure, and satisfying experiences are interpreted as confirmation that we are on the right track.

2. *Amount of feedback.* In some situations we receive relatively complete information concerning the progress and outcome of our actions. In other situations we may receive only partial or even zero feedback. The amount of feedback is determined not only by the information available but also by our

ability to perceive it. A child may not associate a stomach ache with having eaten green apples; an adult may ignore or misinterpret frowns or other signs of social disapproval.

Zero feedback usually means that the individual receives no information until his action is complete. For example, a student may not be given any grades on his lab reports until several have had to be submitted. In general, the delay of feedback until after the completion of an important action tends to foster worry and anxiety.

Often we receive prompt but only partial feedback. A student who gets a low grade on a test may have little information as to why he received such a low rating or "what he is doing wrong." Or we may notice that people seem to be avoiding or reacting negatively to us but not have any clues as to the reason. Limited feedback is often ambiguous and difficult to interpret; especially in important situations it makes us anxious and uncertain.

In some situations we receive relatively complete feedback and can modify an ongoing course of our action to make it more effective. A football player receives a great deal of feedback—both during and after a game—and can improve both immediate and later performance. Programed instruction is based on the demonstrated principle that learning is most efficient and improvement most rapid when precise feedback is given immediately. In general, immediate and complete feedback is followed by both improved performance and increased confidence—except, of course, where it is highly divergent and the individual sees no way of improving his course of action.

3. *Using feedback to change course.* It is in using feedback to monitor our progress toward our goal that the servomechanism analogy is most apt. Having decided on a course of action, we use divergent feedback to get us back on course, whereas convergent, congruent feedback assures us that we are on the right track and should continue as we have been going.

But the human "computer," unlike its inanimate counterpart, uses feedback not only to monitor its progress in carrying out a course of action but also to check on the validity of its goal and the wisdom of its current "program." Thus if the situation changes or if feedback tells the individual that his goal is going to be too expensive or not worth achieving, he can abandon one course of action in midstream and embark on another.[1]

It thus becomes apparent that once an action is begun, the feedback that becomes available is an important part of the overall situation to which we then respond. For example, if we undertake a course of action in an attempt to repair a failing marriage, the feedback we get from our marital partner's reaction to our efforts becomes an integral part of the total situation with which we are coping. In fact, such feedback may be as important as the original adjustive demand in shaping later parts of the action sequence.

When we have enough feedback and use it in such a way as to correct behavior in progress, we develop greater skill for meeting other stress situations later. The processing of stress is thus potentially a learning experience during which we can improve both present and future performance. For this reason, man is referred to as a "self-correcting energy system."

TYPES OF PSYCHOLOGICAL ADJUSTIVE REACTIONS

Three general types of reactions to stress can be delineated: (1) *task-oriented* reactions, aimed primarily at meeting the adjustive demand; (2) *defense-oriented* reactions, aimed primarily at reducing the strain and discomfort resulting from the stress; and (3) *decompensatory* reactions, signalling that the stress has become too great.[2]

An example of a task-oriented response would be reacting to a failing examination grade by improving one's study habits, getting a tutor, and perhaps taking other measures to ensure better preparation and performance in the future. A defense-oriented

reaction in the same situation would be blaming the failure on an unfair teacher or rationalizing that the test was not a very important one, so why worry about it. Many reactions involve both task-oriented and defense-oriented components, but it is usually possible to characterize an action as principally one or the other.

When we feel competent to handle an adjustive demand, our behavior tends to be task oriented—aimed primarily at meeting the requirements of the situation. This holds true even if the problem is a difficult one and whether we actually are competent or only think we are. But when we feel inadequate in the face of a stress situation, our behavior tends to be defense oriented—aimed primarily at lessening the strain and protecting the self-system from devaluation and disorganization.

In the face of continued stress that exceeds our adjustive resources, our behavior undergoes progressive disorganization. As we shall see, this disorganization, or *decompensation* as it is called, tends to follow certain well-defined stages, culminating in the exhaustion and breakdown of the system.

Task-Oriented Reactions

Task-oriented reactions, being aimed at realistically meeting the demands of the stress situation and undertaken by an individual who has confidence in his ability to solve his problem, tend to be based on an objective appraisal of the stress situation and on a conscious, rational, and constructive course of action.

The action itself may involve making changes in one's self or one's surroundings or both, depending upon the situation. The action may be overt—as in improving one's study habits—or covert—as in lowering

[1]For an account of computer simulation of belief systems, see the article by Colby starting on page 484.
[2]For a good account of some of the indirect ways in which task-oriented and defense-oriented strategies are converted into behavior, see the article by Bruner on pages 476-483.

one's level of aspiration or changing one's attitudes. And the action may involve attacking the problem, withdrawing from it, or finding a workable compromise.

Although we shall consider attack, withdrawal, and compromise reactions separately, a given action may embody components of all these reaction types. For example, a student who is going to college to prepare for a career in science (basically an attack approach) may avoid courses which he feels are particularly difficult for him (basically a withdrawal or avoidance reaction), and he may be content to work less hard and make adequate rather than outstanding grades in order to take part in campus activities (basically a compromise approach). Often, too, the same action may be an attack reaction in one context and a withdrawal or compromise reaction in another. For example indecision in a conflict situation might represent an attempt to avoid the further stress of making a decision, or it might be part of an attack reaction in which the individual was delaying his decision in order to study the situation further so as to ensure a wise decision. Attack, withdrawal, and compromise reactions are not all-or-nothing patterns but rather convenient categories for ordering our discussion of stress reactions.

Attacking the problem. A western hero, seeing the "bad guy" starting to draw his gun, may handle the situation by beating him to the draw. This is a simple attack reaction and is the prototype of much of our action. We size up the requirements of the stress situation and try to meet them by direct action.

Attack responses usually take somewhat different forms, depending on whether the stress involves frustration, conflict, or pressure. Three common task-oriented attack responses are: (1) aggression, in response to frustration; (2) choice, as a resolution of conflict; and (3) resistance, as a response to pressure.

1. *Aggression in response to frustration.* According to a well-known hypothesis formally advanced by Miller and Dollard (1941), aggressive behavior is a logical and expected consequence of frustration. When our efforts toward reaching a desired goal are blocked, our first reaction is often one of attacking and attempting to remove or surmount the obstacle. Research has shown that this is particularly likely to be our reaction when the obstacle is viewed as arbitrarily imposed (Pastore, 1952; Lazarus, 1966).

If we believe, for example, that we have a good case for getting a C raised to a B but

TASK-ORIENTED ATTACK REACTIONS

Despite their diversity, task-oriented attack reactions usually share the following characteristics:

1. *Focusing of coping resources on the problem.* The individual musters his forces, increases his effort, and undertakes a course of action to deal with the problem.

2. *Inhibition and suppression of disruptive emotion.* A task-oriented reaction to stress, particularly a threatening stress, requires an ability to keep calm, to remain sehsitive to changes in the environmental situation, and to move ahead toward a rational solution despite fear or anger.

3. *Flexibility in mode of attack.* The individual chooses the most promising course of action but shifts his approach if it does not seem to be working out or if a better possibility presents itself. He attempts to avoid the narrowing and rigidity of thinking which often accompany severe stress.

4. *Development of new resources and competencies.* The individual attempts to increase his coping resources by such means as searching out new information, developing new competencies or improving existing ones, and obtaining professional assistance when indicated.

5. *Affiliation for group action.* The individual may join with others so that the resources of the group can be added to his own in dealing with the stress situation.

meet with blunt refusal from our instructor, we are likely to experience anger and an impulse to remove or circumvent his interference with our achieving our goal. In a more primitive world, our impulse might have been to attack and destroy such an obstacle to our goal; and many studies have documented the close relationship between frustration and aggression even in our more "civilized" society.

Although aggression may well be a task-oriented response to frustration, an aggressive reaction to frustration tends to occur only in cases where it is seen as a possible way of removing the obstacle without undue cost to the individual (Buss, 1963). Usually, we cannot physically attack and destroy or remove the source of our frustration—or even if we could, would lose more than we would gain by doing so. Thus a physical attack on our instructor would likely complicate our problem rather than resolve it. Consequently, we are more likely to take indirect action, such as "going over his head to the dean" or taking our grievance to a student committee. Although our basic tendency may be to respond to frustration with aggression, we learn many other ways—both task-oriented and defense-oriented—for dealing with frustration.

2. *Choice to resolve conflict.* Since even wise decisions bring frustration, it is hardly surprising that people in conflict situations tend to vacillate and to be indecisive in an effort to avoid the frustration of either choice. The girl who is trying to choose between two eligible suitors—one exciting and fun to be with but sometimes irresponsible and immature and the other steady and dependable but a bit dull—may find herself deciding on first one and then the other, perhaps not even seeing the possibility that neither one would make her a satisfactory mate.

The more equally matched the alternatives, the harder the decision. And when the conflict involves serious consequences—where the outcome is very important to us, as when we are considering marriage or an investment of our life's savings—we may try to delay a decision until we are quite sure of the consequences. Sometimes, of course, we may even carefully keep the alternatives open indefinitely—contriving *not* to make a decision and thus gaining some of the attractive features of both alternatives. Thus a girl may strive to maintain a relationship with two suitors and avoid making a decision as long as she can. This may represent a task-oriented reaction—keeping her options open until she is better prepared to make a sound decision—or a defense-oriented reaction—avoiding unpleasantness and getting ego satisfaction indefinitely at others' expense. But in most cases, sooner or later, a choice must be made if a conflict is to be resolved.

3. *Resistance in response to pressure.* Usually the individual resists pressures on him—especially when he sees them as arbitrary or unwarranted. Children often develop highly effective techniques of resistance in coping with perfectionistic parents or teachers. Defiance and rebellion are active forms of resistance, but there are passive forms too, such as inattention, dawdling, helplessness, and deliberate underachievement. Resistance to pressure may be important in helping the individual to maintain his integrity and in protecting him from excessive demands or overloading.

Pressures on a group also tend to elicit resistance, active or passive. Workers may resist demands for a speed-up by petition to the management, by union grievance committees, or by a strike, a slow-down, or excessive absenteeism. A class of fourth-graders may resist pressures toward unrealistic quietness and attention to uninteresting subject matter by apathy, by flagrant disregard of rules, or by hiding a snake in the teacher's drawer. Gandhi's India used passive resistance tellingly in its struggle against English rule.

The possible ways of attacking problems in task-oriented ways are legion and include patience, cunning, cooperation, long-range planning, increased effort, restructuring one's view of the situation, and many other patterns. When appropriate to the situation and the resources of the individual, an attack response usually offers the best strategy for resolving stress. However, attack behavior may be inappropriate and destructive, as when the individual resists pressures to do something that would actually benefit him, makes impulsive choices in dealing with conflicts, or engages in physical assault or destruction of property.

Withdrawing from the problem. Sometimes it is the better part of valor to avoid or withdraw from a difficult situation that is exerting demands we cannot or prefer not to meet.

1. *Escape.* Although many animals are capable of fairly well-coordinated withdrawal or flight reactions shortly after birth, the human infant has no such complex built-in patterns. He can withdraw a hand or foot from a painful stimulus, however, and he soon learns to withdraw physically from situations that are unpleasant or dangerous. He also learns to withdraw in various psychological ways, such as by admitting defeat or reducing his emotional involvement in a situation.

Although many stress situations cannot be escaped, others can be successfully dealt with in this way. For example, an unpleasant job or one without a future may offer so little reward that we can better meet our needs for achievement and growth by looking elsewhere. Sometimes students get half way through medical or law school only to realize that it is not for them. A realistic, task-oriented solution then usually involves admitting their error, writing off the lost time as perhaps not entirely lost, and switching to another field. In the same way an individual

may withdraw his membership from an organization when he finds that he does not agree with its principles and realizes that continued membership would only be a source of frustration.

When a person has invested a great deal of time and effort in the pursuit of an important goal, it is often difficult to face the situation squarely when the goal turns out to be unattainable or inappropriate. A satisfactory resolution of many stress situations, however, depends upon knowing when to take one's losses and change one's direction.

Although most conflicts can be resolved only by a choice from among the available alternatives, some can be terminated by withdrawal from the conflict situation. Thus, for example, a girl unable to choose between two suitors may decide that she is not ready for marriage and should broaden her field of choice even if it means losing her two immediate prospects. Although she may be taking a chance in hoping to find others as eligible as those she is turning down, she manages to escape from the immediate stressful decision.

Although we cannot cope with most pressures satisfactorily by withdrawal—as in the case of pressures stemming from final examinations, being interviewed for jobs, or dealing with severe competition—there are other sources of pressure from which withdrawal is possible and may be a task-oriented reaction. If a student finds that he has registered for too many courses and his work load is excessive, he may withdraw from a course to lighten his load. Similarly, a housewife may withdraw from participa-

TASK-ORIENTED WITHDRAWAL REACTIONS

Characteristics which commonly underlie the diversity of task-oriented withdrawal reactions are:

1. *Admitting defeat.* The individual admits that the situation is too difficult for him or that he has chosen an inappropriate goal which he no longer wishes to pursue.

2. *Leaving the field.* This may involve actual

physical or psychological withdrawal from the stress situation or both—as in the case of leaving an uncongenial profession.

3. *Establishment of a new direction.* Instead of drifting or indefinitely "nursing his wounds," the individual redirects his efforts toward a new and hopefully more appropriate goal.

COMMON CHARACTERISTICS OF TASK-ORIENTED COMPROMISE REACTIONS

Task-oriented compromise reactions are often characterized by:

1. *Accepting substitute goals.* When it becomes apparent that you cannot attain the exact goal you are seeking, you may settle for the best substitute or approximation. This may mean lowering your level of aspiration to a more achievable level.

2. *Accepting substitute means.* If you cannot get through college in 3½ years as you had hoped, you take longer. If you cannot afford to fly, you go by bus. Sometimes people lower their ethical standards to get what they want; such a reaction, though task-oriented, is maladjustive in the larger view because it meets their needs at others' expense.

3. *Assuring minimum essentials.* If no available solution meets all your hoped-for requirements, it is important to know what you can and cannot do without. For example, a young wife who maintains harmony by always giving in to her husband's wishes has chosen a compromise that she probably cannot live with indefinitely. Sometimes we make bad compromises that complicate rather than resolve our problems in the long run.

4. *Taking time to deliberate.* When we are in doubt and a decision does not have to be made right away, we do well not to let ourselves be rushed into action. With a wait-and-see response we can let the situation unfold and avoid precipitous action that we might later regret. Circumstances may change, and the problem may even solve itself. In some cases, of course, the convenient option of delay may not be open to us.

---

tion in various civic organizations when she finds that she has "too many things going at once."

2. *Avoidance.* As a result of learning, the individual anticipates and avoids getting into many situations that he views as potentially dangerous or threatening. Such behavior is shown by the student who avoids taking courses that he thinks will be too difficult for him or by the businessman who refuses a promotion because he feels that it would entail increased pressures that he prefers not to undertake. Young people often avoid emotional involvement in situations where they are afraid of being hurt.

Once again we see that the individual is not a passive recipient of stress: often he can exercise considerable control over the nature and degree of pressure to which he is exposed and thus keep stress from becoming excessive.

Attack and withdrawal—fight and flight—are fundamental forms of coping with stress found in all animals. They appear to be part of the organism's built-in evolutionary heritage. Attack helps the organism to overcome obstacles and attain goals relevant to its survival; withdrawal serves to remove the organism from threatening situations which it cannot overcome. Anger is the most common emotion accompanying attack, fear the most common emotion accompanying withdrawal. In severe stress, anxiety is usually prominent also.

Compromise. Most task-oriented behavior is neither entirely attack nor entirely withdrawal but a compromise. You may change what you can in yourself or the stress situation, avoid confrontation with certain aspects of it, perhaps by limiting your field of operations, and live as best you can with what cannot be changed or escaped or with what you decide is, on balance, worth the trouble. Two common compromise reactions are substitution and accommodation.

1. *Substitution.* In a situation of sustained or seemingly quite inescapable frustration, the individual often tends to reduce the stress by accepting whatever goals and satisfactions he can attain in the situation. For example, a young man who is consistently turned down by the girl he would really like to date finally takes out someone else; a young woman compromises with the "dream image" husband she has always

imagined and marries the young man who is actually available.

In more severe stress situations, compromises may be rather extreme in degree. A prisoner-of-war may collaborate with his hated captors in an effort to ensure survival and better treatment. An individual who has been subjected to prolonged semistarvation may eat insects, the bark off trees, and practically any other substitute that has nutritional value or tends to assuage his hunger. One of the men in the ill-fated Greeley expedition to the arctic (see page 19) ate his sealskin boots. In a somewhat similar way, a frustrated person may find symbolic satisfactions, such as staring at pin-up pictures in lieu of the real thing; or he may gain some satisfaction from fantasies of desired goals.

Of course, the extent to which the individual will accept such substitute and symbolic goals will depend on the character and strength of the barrier and on his motivation, values, and ability to withstand stress. He is particularly likely to accept substitute goals when the barrier seems insurmountable or would require more effort and sacrifice than he thinks the original goal warrants.

2. *Accommodation.* The term *accommodation* has various meanings but here is used to refer to compromise behavior in which we settle for part of what we wanted. And since the resolution of so many of our problems is dependent on the action of others as well as ourselves, *mutual accommodation* is often needed, in which both parties give a little and get a little. For example, the resolution of a problem in marital adjustment usually involves mutual give and take, with some adaptation on the part of both partners.

Many problems on both interpersonal and intergroup levels are solved through negotiating, bargaining, and concessions on one or both sides—in essence, compromise behavior in which the participants accommodate their requirements and get part of what they wanted but not all. We see such patterns in labor-management disputes, student-faculty conflicts, and relationships between nations, as well as in our relationships with friends and family members. We shall elabo-

rate further on interpersonal accommodation in our later discussion of marriage and other social relationships. Suffice it here to note the importance of such compromise patterns in dealing with stress problems.

If the compromise reaction succeeds in meeting the essential requirements of the situation, the stress problem is satisfactorily resolved and the individual can devote his energies to other matters. Often, however, we make compromises which we cannot fully accept or live with because important needs continue to go unmet. In such instances, additional adjustive action is required.

Although a task-oriented approach usually has the best chance of resolving our problems, even a task-oriented approach can fail. If our choices are based on faulty values, we may meet the immediate demand but may lay the basis for more serious problems later. If, because of limited knowledge, we choose an unsuitable course of action, it may even compound our problem. And even when we choose well and act with skill, factors beyond our control may tip the balance in preventing our action from solving the problem. As the poet Burns put it so succinctly:

> *"The best-laid schemes o' mice an' men,*
> *Gang aft a-gley."*

Defense-Oriented Reactions

The individual who faces severe stress has two problems: (1) to meet the adjustive demand, and (2) to protect himself from psychological disorganization. In defense-oriented behavior the individual is concentrating on the latter—choosing actions aimed chiefly at lessening or avoiding self-devaluation or emotional hurt and alleviating his anxiety.

Three types of defense-oriented reactions may be distinguished. The first consists of such reactions as crying and "talking it out," which seem to function as "wired-in" reparative mechanisms. The second type consists of the ego-defense mechanisms—learned means of protecting the self-system from devaluation and disorganization. The third type consists of the use of drugs to alleviate tension and anxiety. All three are directed toward maintaining psychological equilibrium and integration in much the same way that homeostatic mechanisms maintain physiological steady states. But they meet only half of the adjustive demand.

"Wired-in" reparative mechanisms. These defense reactions appear to operate on a relatively conscious level although they usually come into operation automatically rather than as a result of choice on the part of the individual. Although they do not help the individual with a solution to his problem, they are basically constructive in being a means of repairing psychological damage and restoring psychological equilibrium. Among the more important of these mechanisms are the following:

1. *Crying.* A built-in defense mechanism which is useful in relieving emotional tension and hurt is crying. This mechanism is commonly seen in the behavior of children who have been frustrated or hurt. And although we are often taught that "grown-ups don't cry," crying is not uncommon among adults and may serve as an important means of relieving tension and hurt and restoring inner equilibrium.

The basic purpose of "crying it out" seems to be release of emotional tension. This release is apparent in grief reactions, in which crying appears to be an essential part of the "grief work" that one must go through in the gradual regaining of emotional equilibrium. The individual may discover, however, that crying gains him sympathy, which also reduces his emotional pain. He may then develop a pattern of "crying on someone's shoulder"—of sharing his miseries with others and gaining some emotional support from their expressions of sympathy and recognition of how difficult things must be for him. This pattern is known as *sympathism.*

2. *Talking it out.* Another built-in way of relieving emotional tension is talking it out. This mechanism is so simple and so widely used that we often overlook its great reparative value.

We probably all have had friends who

enjoyed telling us in gory detail about their operations or accidents or other traumatic experiences. Much of the talk teen-agers have with each other seems to be an effort to analyze and put into words new feelings that are troubling them. Individuals who have survived highly traumatic experiences, such as disasters or other catastrophes, often show a compulsive need to tell others of the experience. Gaining emotional relief through putting one's feelings into words is an important part of most psychotherapy; in that context the process is known as *catharsis.*

Besides relieving emotional tension, talking it out may help the individual to see his situation more clearly, new ideas and viewpoints may emerge, and there may be a constructive sharing of views. In such a case talking it out may be considered as both a task-oriented response and a defense-oriented one.

3. *Laughing it off.* Trying to view one's problems with a sense of humor and laughing off setbacks and hurts is a widely used means of tension reduction. Probably we have all heard the phrase "Everything happens to me"—delivered with a shrug, indicating an attempt to see the humorous side of hurtful experiences.

In essence, this mechanism seems to be directed toward keeping things in perspective, toward an acceptance of inevitable hurts and setbacks, and toward not taking oneself too seriously. Perhaps its basic pattern can be seen in the role of the clown who laughs to cover his inner sadness and hurt. In fact, it is an interesting aspect of this defense mechanism that when it fails, the individual often bursts into tears.

Humor is also frequently used to reduce the tension associated with aggressive impulses and hostility toward others. Such humor tends to be hostile (Singer, 1968).

4. *Thinking it through.* After an emotional hurt, some people want to get away, as it were, to retreat to their own private mountain top and "think things through." Often a hurtful failure leaves the individual not only damaged but somewhat confused as to what went wrong and as to the nature of his values and actions that may have contributed to the catastrophe. He may need to think about how to salvage what he can from the situation and perhaps to restructure the situation in his own mind so that he can see it more clearly and evaluate its actual significance to him more accurately.

Sometimes thinking it through is the only action available for dealing with a hurtful situation. In searching for the true meaning and significance of the situation to him, the individual becomes able to assimilate it into his cognitive structure and reduce the tension and hurt associated with it.

5. *Leaning on others.* We have noted that in times of stress people often want to be with others and may seek emotional support. Thus in going through a hurtful emotional experience—such as an emotionally damaging divorce or the loss of a loved one—the individual may temporarily need to lean on others for emotional support and assistance until he can regain his equilibrium.

This pattern can be readily seen in children who turn to their mothers for comfort and solace when they have been hurt. In adulthood, too, "misery loves company" and we like to be with and talk to others who care. As a habitual defensive reaction, leaning on others may be complicated by identification, in which the individual gains strength by identifying with a strong, admired person.

In some cases, however, leaning on others can be a task-oriented reaction, as when the individual is stymied in his efforts to solve a problem and turns to a professional for help.

Other built-in mechanisms which appear helpful in repairing psychological damage are sleep, dreams, and efforts toward self-control. People who have undergone severely traumatic experiences—such as combat experiences in wartime or severe earthquakes or other catastrophes—often have repetitive nightmares in which they re-enact their experience and apparently are eventually desensitized to it so that they can assimilate it into their cognitive structure without undue strain.

Most people seem to have difficulty sleeping when they are under emotional tension and strain, but when sleep is possible it appears to have a healing function. In fact, Bateson and Mead (1942) reported in an early study that on the island of Bali, accused prisoners often escaped from the stress of their trial by falling asleep.

Finally, in a stressful situation we may lecture ourselves about not giving up, or not "letting things get us down," and in other ways try to keep ourselves from giving way to panic. This seems a built-in tendency—part of our automatic striving to maintain our inner stability, both physiological and psychological.

COMMON EFFECTS OF STRESS

EFFECTS OF FRUSTRATION	EFFECTS OF CONFLICT	EFFECTS OF PRESSURE

If goal seen as reachable:
  Greater effort toward goal
  Attack, aggression
If goal seen as unreachable:
  Acceptance of substitute goals
  Lowered aspiration
  Restricted field of operation
  Anxiety, depression
  Apathy, regression
  Fantasy, symbolic satisfactions
	Vacillation, indecision
	Anxiety, discouragement
	Postponement of decision
	Inability to accept either alternative whole-heartedly
	Escape through sickness or divertive activities
		Increased effort
		Overloading, physical and psychological strain
		Fear, anxiety
		Defensive reactions such as resistance, defiance, destructiveness, dawdling, helplessness, apathy, fantasy

Ego-defense mechanisms. There are a number of defense mechanisms which protect the self from threat and alleviate anxiety. These mechanisms are heavily dependent upon learning but tend to operate on habitual and unconscious levels. For the most part they lead to some measure of self-deception and reality distortion and thus are not adaptive in the sense of realistically coping with the stress situation.

Despite their drawbacks, however, all of us make some use of such defenses. They are essential for softening failure, reducing cognitive dissonance, alleviating anxiety, repairing emotional hurt, and maintaining our feelings of adequacy and worth. Thus we must consider them normal coping mechanisms unless they are used to such a degree that they impair the individual's ability to meet his life problems. Like a nation devoting its major energies to armaments, too heavy a load of defensive activities can be self-defeating, making the individual less strong instead of more so.

Ego-defense mechanisms protect the self from both external threats—such as devaluating failures—and internal threats—such as unacceptable desires and impulses or guilt resulting from actions we have already taken. They protect us in one or more of the following ways: (1) by denying or restricting our experience, (2) by cognitive distortion, (3) by reduction of emotional involvement, and (4) by counteraction of the threat. Often, of course, a given defense mechanism may offer more than one kind of protection.

1. *Denial of reality.* A primitive defense mechanism for restricting experience, observable even in young children, is to deny reality. We evade many disagreeable realities simply by ignoring or refusing to acknowledge them. Very few of us, for example, accept the full inevitability of death. Even if we act as if we were quite resigned to the idea, the full realization of our own inevitable death is usually mercifully obscured by vague feelings of omnipotence—everybody else dies but not us—or by religious convictions about life after death.

Our tendency toward perceptual defense, already discussed, is part of this tendency to avoid or deny unpleasant reality. We turn away from unpleasant sights, refuse to discuss unpleasant topics, ignore or deny criticism, and refuse to face many of our real problems. Under extreme conditions, such as imprisonment, the individual may experience the feeling that "This isn't really happening to me." Here, at least temporarily, the denial appears to protect the individual from the full impact of the traumatic experience.

By ignoring or denying unpleasant reality, we do protect ourselves from a great deal of stress. But like the proverbial ostrich who buries his head in the sand when danger approaches, we may fail to take cognizance of many realities that we need to know about for effective adjustment.

2. *Repression.* This is a defense mechanism by means of which threatening or painful thoughts and desires are excluded from consciousness. This mechanism is illustrated in a dramatic way by the soldier who has undergone an extremely traumatic battle experience and is brought to an aid station suffering from amnesia. He does not remember the situation or his name or anything about himself. He may be nervous and depressed and show other signs of his ordeal, but the intolerable battle situation itself is screened from his consciousness, and he is thus protected from overwhelming stress. The repressed experience is not forgotten, however, and may be brought into consciousness by means of hypnosis or pentothal interviews. Such repressive defenses operate on a temporary basis until time and other conditions have desensitized him to the point where he can recall the event without serious psychological disorganization.

In a less dramatic situation, a boy with strong feelings of hostility toward his father may have these feelings so well repressed that he is unaware of his hatred. Similarly, sexual desires that the individual considers immoral may be blocked from his consciousness by means of repression. But repression is not always complete, and repressed memories and desires may be revealed in dreams and reveries and under the influence of alcohol or drugs. When repressive defenses are in danger of failing, the individual becomes extremely anxious, for he is again placed under threat. And if his defenses actually do fail, as when repressed homosexual desires enter consciousness, the individual's psychological functioning may be seriously disrupted.

Repression is an important means of helping the individual to cope with the potentially disorganizing effects of painful experiences and desires regarded as dangerous and unacceptable. In fact, in varying degrees repression enters into most other defensive patterns. However, repression may screen out stressful experiences that could better be met by realistically facing and working through the situation. We cannot solve and learn from a problem that we do not see.

Repression is an unconscious device and thus not subject to conscious evaluation and control. In this it differs from *suppression,* in which one decides not to express a feeling or not to act on a desire or even not to think about a disturbing event. Suppression is a healthy process, necessary for mature functioning in a social context; repression is a pain-softening but potentially very dangerous process.

3. *Regression.* This is a reaction involving a retreat to the use of reaction patterns which were appropriate at an earlier level of development. For example, when a new baby in the family has seemingly undermined his status, a child may revert to bedwetting, baby talk, and other infantile behavior which once brought him parental attention. But regression is a more comprehensive reaction than merely trying out older, formerly successful modes of response when new ones have failed. For in regression the individual retreats from present reality to an earlier, less demanding personal status— one which involves lowered aspirations and more readily accomplished satisfactions.

On a simple level regression is illustrated by the new bride who goes home to the protective arms of her mother at the first sign of trouble in her marriage; and by the husband who becomes "childish" and demands to be waited on when he gets the flu. A more dramatic example of regressive behavior under stress is provided by Bettelheim's description (1943) of the general "regression to infantile behavior" seen in nearly all the prisoners at the concentration camps of Dachau and Buchenwald in Nazi Germany:

"The prisoners lived, like children, only in the immediate present; . . . they became unable to plan for the future or to give up immediate pleasure satisfactions to gain greater ones in the future. . . . They were boastful, telling tales about what they had accomplished in their former lives, or how they succeeded in cheating foremen or guards, and how they sabotaged the work. Like children they felt not at all set back or ashamed when it became known that they had lied about their prowess." (pp. 445-446)

Most people do not rely heavily on regression as a defense against stress. However, the emergence of developmentally lower levels of functioning is frequently seen among persons suffering severe mental disorders. Dinello (1967) has described the case of a seventeen-year-old youth who had regressed to the point of wearing a diaper. In extreme cases, such persons may become unable to dress or feed themselves or to take care of their eliminative needs. These examples of regression, of course, are clearly beyond the range of the "normal."

4. *Escapism.* Here the individual avoids experiencing unpleasant reality by some form of physical or psychological escape. Common methods include getting sick, "not being in the mood," and "dropping out." Although the behavior of the hippies and other similar groups may be task-oriented to the extent that it represents a searching for new values, it often comes to be an escape from the responsibilities and stresses of modern life. Through labored nonconformity, they manage to escape, at least temporarily, from the conventional problems and commitments of living.

5. *Fantasy.* Besides screening out unpleasant aspects of reality, we also tend to

use fantasy to picture things as we would like them to be. Fantasy is stimulated by frustrated desires and grows out of mental images associated with need gratification. In fantasy, the person achieves his goals and meets his needs in his imagination.

Two common varieties of wish-fulfilling fantasy are the "conquering hero" and the "suffering hero" patterns. In the first, the individual pictures himself as a great athlete, a renowned surgeon, a distinguished and courageous soldier, a man of immense wealth, or some other remarkable figure who performs incredible feats and wins the admiration and respect of all—the basic idea being that he is respected and powerful. James Thurber used this theme in his popular *Secret Life of Walter Mitty*. The conquering hero dissipates his hostility safely by fantasied punishments and destruction of all who stand in his way. Such fantasies act as safety valves and provide some measure of compensatory gratification.

Another common fantasy pattern is the "suffering hero" type. Here the individual imagines that he is suffering from some horrible affliction or handicap or is an adopted and abused child; when people find out about the difficulties besetting him, they will be sorry for the way they have treated him and give him the attention he deserves. By such fantasies, the individual avoids the admission of personal inferiority or lack of worth and to some extent also avoids the necessity of striving more strenuously toward his goals. He has actually demonstrated remarkable courage and is highly successful considering the handicaps under which he has labored. In short, he merits the sympathy and admiration of all.

Escaping temporarily from the stresses of everyday life into a more pleasant fantasy world is often helpful in adding the dash of excitement and encouragement that enables us to return to the struggle. But fantasy becomes maladjustive if we substitute the easier accomplishments of make-believe for real-life endeavors. This mechanism can be seen in extreme form in the case of mental patients who develop delusions of grandeur and retreat from reality into a fantasy world of their own construction.

6. *Rationalization.* This is a defense mechanism in which we justify our behavior by imputing logical and admirable or at least acceptable motivation to it. If we decide to go to a movie when we know we should study, we can usually think up various reasons to justify our decision: we only live once, everyone needs a change of pace, and the relaxation will brush away the cobwebs and make us able to think more clearly. Or we may try to justify cheating by pointing out that others cheat, that there is no virtue in being a sucker, and that in real life society doesn't ask too many questions as long as you are successful. By rationalizing, we can usually justify about everything we have done, are doing, or propose to do and hence can alleviate the devaluating effects of failure, guilt, and irrational behavior.

Rationalization is also used to soften the disappointment of thwarted desires. A common example of such rationalization is the "sour grapes" reaction—stemming from Aesop's fable of the fox who, unable to reach a cluster of delicious grapes, decided he did not want them anyway because they were probably sour. If we have little money, we may emphasize that the really important things in life—such as love and friendship—are free; if we are turned down for a date, we may decide the evening probably would have been dull anyway. The opposite of the sour grape type of rationalization is the "sweet lemon" mechanism; not only is what we cannot have not worth having, but what we do have is remarkably satisfactory. Not only are the most important things in life free, but it is actually better to be poor because money is the root of all evil.

Rationalization is a very complex mechanism and one that is often difficult to detect because rationalizations frequently contain elements of truth. We may suspect that we are rationalizing when we: (1) hunt for reasons to justify our behavior or beliefs, (2) are unable to recognize inconsistencies that others see, and (3) become emotional when the reasons for our behavior are questioned.

The questioning of our rationalizations is, of course, a threat to the defenses we have constructed against frustration and self-devaluation, and anxiety is aroused when these defenses are jeopardized or destroyed. The price of this defensive reaction, however, is self-deception, for we accept reasons for our behavior which are not the true ones. Like repression, rationalization enters in varying degree into a number of other defense mechanisms.

7. *Projection.* This is a reaction in which we blame others for our own mistakes and shortcomings or ascribe to others our own unacceptable motivations. The erring husband blames his extramarital affairs on his unsympathetic wife or on "girls who lead him on"; the boy punished for fighting protests, "He hit me first—it was his fault." The dishonest person may insist that you can't trust anybody.[1]

Projection appears to be a common mechanism among individuals with rigid moral values and conscience development. Their rigid standards make it impossible for them to accept unethical desires as part of their own make-up. Such desires are highly threatening and self-devaluating and usually cannot be adequately handled by rationalization or other defense mechanisms. As a consequence, they are projected to someone else who now becomes the offender while the individual himself remains conveniently "pure." The individual with guilt-arousing homosexual leanings may accuse other men of trying to seduce him—while he remains unaware of his own homosexual inclinations. In extreme form, such projections are evidenced by mental patients who accuse others of "pouring filth into their minds."

Rationalization and projection probably develop from our early learning that advancing socially approved reasons for our behavior or putting the blame on others helps us to avoid disapproval and punishment. And as we learn and accept society's values, such defense reactions protect us from self-devaluation and anxiety. However, we may pay an exorbitant price for such defensive maneuvers.

8. *Reaction formation.* Here the person protects himself from dangerous desires by not only repressing them but actually developing conscious attitudes and behavior patterns directly opposed to such desires. Thus he may conceal hate with a façade of love, cruelty with kindness, or desires for sexual promiscuity with moralistic sexual attitudes and behavior. These new feelings or attitudes help the individual to keep his real but dangerous desires from entering consciousness or being carried out in action.

On a simple level, reaction formation is illustrated by the joke about the old maid who looks hopefully under her bed each night for fear that a man may be lurking there. On a more complex level, reaction formation may be manifested by people who crusade militantly against loose sexual morals or the evils of alcohol or gambling. Often such people have a background of earlier difficulties with such problems themselves, and their zealous crusading appears to be a means of safeguarding themselves against a recurrence of such behavior.

Self-appointed protectors of the public morals who devote their lives to ferreting out obscene passages in literary works or drawing attention to the inadequate attire of nightclub dancers can even gain a certain amount of vicarious satisfaction of their own repressed desires without endangering their self-concepts. In some cases, reaction formation is more subtle, as when a juror demands the most severe penalty that the law provides for an infraction that he himself has been tempted to commit. By such condemnation and punishment, he is attempting to hold his own dangerous impulses in check.

Reaction formation helps to maintain socially approved behavior and protects a person from the knowledge that he has antisocial or unethical desires. But the self-deception is based on an inability to accept himself as he is. Preventing an accurate self-picture, it also keeps him from realistically

---

[1]Holmes (1968), in an excellent summary of the dimensions of projection, emphasizes the lack of research relating to it, despite its frequent appearance in the clinical literature.

working through his problems and leads to rigidity and harshness in dealing with others.

9. *Identification.* As we have seen in our earlier discussion, identification takes place in imitative learning—as when a boy identifies with his father and uses him as a model. Identification may also operate as a defense mechanism in enhancing feelings of worth and protecting the individual against self-devaluation.

The growing child soon realizes that other people's evaluation of him is to a large extent dependent upon his family and other group memberships. His father's occupation and the family's financial status and position in the community are important in determining the way other people evaluate him; and his own sense of personal worth and identity may come to depend heavily upon these family characteristics. During adolescence and adulthood, the mechanism of identification is expanded to include a wide range of personal and group identifications.

Most of us identify strongly with being "an American"; some of us also identify ourselves with some region of the country and think of ourselves as Southerners, New Yorkers, or Texans. College students bask in the reflected glory of their football teams —"We won today"; fraternity and sorority members feel personally enhanced by the social prestige of their groups. An adult's sense of identity includes the prestige accorded his occupation, the size and address of his home, his memberships in clubs or other organizations, and the accomplishments of his children. He enhances his own feelings of adequacy and worth by associating himself with respected individuals and groups either through actual activity or through name-dropping. Particularly for an individual who feels basically inferior, such identifications may have important defensive values.

Although identification may help us to feel more adequate and secure, it also has its dangers. The individual who relies too heavily on his identifications with others for his feelings of adequacy and self-worth develops an inaccurate and unrealistically favorable self-image and is highly vulnerable in stress situations in which his identifications cannot help him or in which those with whom he identifies suffer humiliation. In the latter case, his identifications may lead to self-devaluation rather than enhancement. This is one reason why it is difficult for a coach to hold his job if his team loses consistently.

10. *Introjection.* Introjection is closely related to identification. It means acceptance of others' values and attitudes as one's own as a safety measure, even when they are contrary to one's previous values. After revolutions leading to dictatorial forms of government, for example, many people introject the new values and beliefs as a protection against behavior which might get them into trouble. By internalizing the socially prescribed values as their own, they can then trust themselves to avoid behavior that would bring social retaliation and punishment.

The use of introjection under extreme conditions, was well described by Bettelheim (1943) in his report of experiences in Nazi concentration camps. Under the insidious camp experiences, previous values and identifications were broken down and new norms were introjected—Nazi norms.

"A prisoner had reached the final stage of adjustment to the camp situation when he had changed his personality so as to accept as his own the values of the Gestapo . . . old prisoners were sometimes instrumental in getting rid of the unfit, in this way making a feature of Gestapo ideology a feature of their own behavior." (pp. 447-449)

Though introjection may have defensive value in protecting the individual from hopeless frustrations and enabling him to maintain some control over his fate, it is obviously a primitive and potentially destructive defensive pattern.

11. *Emotional insulation.* Here one reduces his degree of emotional involvement in potentially hurtful situations. Since we all undergo many disappointments in life, we usually learn to keep our hopes and anticipations within bounds until a hoped-for event actually occurs. We are careful to avoid premature celebrations or to let our hopes get too high. The student who is looking forward to a date with a very attractive girl may not let himself get too emotionally involved for fear that something will go wrong or that she may not like him. Such reactions are well expressed in the common saying, "I didn't dare to hope."

In extreme conditions of long-continued frustration, as in chronic unemployment or prison confinement, many persons lose hope and become resigned and apathetic. Such "broken" individuals protect themselves from the hurt of sustained frustration by reducing their involvement—they no longer care and hence deprive the stress situation of much of its power to hurt them. In chronic schizophrenic reactions, to be examined in the next chapter, there is often an extreme use of emotional insulation, which protects the individual from further hurt by a world he has found unbearably painful.

Up to a point, emotional insulation is an important mechanism for defending ourselves from both unnecessary and unavoidable hurt. But life involves calculated risks, and most of us are willing to take our chances on active participation. Although we may get badly hurt on occasion, we have the resiliency to recover and try again. Emotional insulation provides a protective shell that prevents a repetition of previous pain, but in so doing it also prevents the individual's healthy, vigorous participation in living.

12. Intellectualization. This mechanism is related to both emotional insulation and rationalization. Here the emotional reaction that would normally accompany an event is avoided by a rational explanation which divests the event of personal significance and painful feeling. Grief over the senseless death of a child may be softened by pointing out that "the good die young"; catastrophes are interpreted as "the will of God"; failures and disappointments are softened by pointing out that "it could have been worse." Cynicism may become a convenient means of preventing or reducing remorse over not living up to our ideals. Or we may reduce our guilt feelings over unethical behavior by arguing the cultural relativity of

everyone's ideas of right and wrong. Even the verbalizing of good intentions as in a glib admission that "we should be less selfish and more interested in the welfare of others" seems to cut off a good deal of guilt and relieve us of the necessity of mending our ways.

Intellectualization may be utilized under extremely stressful conditions as well as in dealing with the milder stresses of everyday life. Bluestone and McGahee (1962) have found that this defense mechanism is often used by prisoners awaiting execution. They describe the pattern as follows: "'So they'll kill me; and that's that'—this said with a shrug of the shoulders suggests that the affect appropriate to the thought has somehow been isolated." Or they may feel as though it were all happening to someone else and they are watching, impersonally, from a distance. In such reactions, denial, rationalization, and other defense mechanisms may also play a prominent role, but it is the cutting off of normal affective (emotional) charge by means of intellectualization that concerns us here.

In some instances intellectualization takes the form of *isolation,* in which contradictory ideas are sealed off from each other in "logic tight" compartments. For example, the individual who believes firmly in democracy and is willing to fight for it if necessary may also believe firmly in racial segregation. The ruthless and dishonest businessman may be a kind and understanding father and a "pillar" of his church. The individual may resort to rationalization to make his views seem more consistent and often he is unaware of their inconsistency. By keeping such incompatible ideas isolated from each other in our minds, we avoid painful emotional conflicts.

13. Compensation. In compensation the individual defends himself against feelings of inadequacy by disguising or counterbalancing a weak or undesirable trait while emphasizing or developing a desirable one. Compensatory reactions take many forms and actually have considerable adjustive value. For example, a physically unattractive boy or girl may develop a pleasing personality and become an interesting conversationalist. As a consequence, the physical unattractiveness is no longer a major obstacle to social acceptance and success.

Unfortunately, not all compensatory reactions are desirable or useful. The child who feels insecure may show off to try to get more attention and raise his status in the eyes of others and himself; the boy who feels inferior and unpopular may become the local bully; and the person who feels unloved and frustrated may eat too much. Some people build themselves up by bragging about their own accomplishments; others do it by criticism or innuendoes in an attempt to cut other people down. In extreme cases, the individual may become markedly eccentric in an attempt to win interest and admiration from others.

In the main, compensatory reactions are ineffective because the activities engaged in are aimed not at a positive goal but at balancing a deficit. They tend not to be constructive—as in the case of eating too much as a reaction to frustration. Or they incur social disapproval—as in showing off—which only increases the person's sense of failure and inferiority.

14. *Displaced aggression (displacement).* In this mechanism there is a redirection of hostility toward some object or person other than the one actually causing the frustration. Unable for practical reasons to express his feelings directly, the individual is able to find some relief by expressing it toward a less dangerous target. A child who has been spanked or thwarted by his mother may kick his little sister or break up his toys. A common subject for cartoons is the office clerk who has been refused a raise. Instead of expressing his hostility toward his employer —which would be dangerous to his job—he goes home and snaps irritably at his wife because dinner is a few minutes late. His frustrated wife, in turn, takes out her hostility on their son, who displaces his anger onto the dog or cat.

Displaced aggression may also take other forms. One is swearing, commonly used as a means of discharging feelings elic-

ited by frustration. Another is to find a scapegoat[1] who can be blamed for one's problems and cannot fight back. In Hitler's Germany the Jews were blamed for the country's ills, and pent-up feelings of frustration and hostility were discharged against this group. The scapegoating mechanism is common in dictatorships, where hostility is likely to be aroused by the stern, repressive measures of the government but where any opposition or direct expression of hostility is extremely dangerous. Throughout the history of the world, racial, religious, and political prejudices have often been intertwined with displaced aggression and scapegoating.

In some instances, the individual is either afraid or unable to direct his hostility toward others and may turn it inward upon himself. In such cases, he may engage in exaggerated self-accusations and recriminations and may feel severe guilt and self-devaluation. Such intropunitive reactions may lead to depression and to suicide or threats of suicide.

Displacement may be of adjustive value, since it is a means of discharging dangerous emotional tensions without the risk of retaliation. It may also enable the person to avoid ambivalent feelings toward some powerful or loved figure. By displacing his hostility onto his wife, the clerk may maintain relatively pure feelings of respect and cordiality toward his domineering boss. Unfortunately, however, this achievement may be at the expense of harmony in his marriage; likewise, the use of minority groups as scapegoats is not likely to contribute to social progress. And turning one's hostility inward gains feelings of safety at the expense of feelings of self-respect. So displacement may enact a high price for its benefits. In most cases it is much more healthful and less painful in the long run to face and work through painful or hostility-arousing situations than to avoid them through displacement.

---

[1]Among the ancient Israelites, the priest ceremoniously heaped all of the sins of the people upon a pure white goat—a *scapegoat*—which was then driven into the wilderness to die (English & English, 1958).

15. *Undoing.* This is a mechanism designed to negate or atone for some disapproved thought, impulse, or act. It is as if the individual has spelled a word wrong and then uses an eraser to clear the paper and start over. Apologizing for wrongs against others, penance, repentance, and undergoing punishment are some of the common forms that undoing may take. The opportunity for confession and the assurance of forgiveness in some religions meet a deep human need to be able to get rid of guilt feelings and make a new beginning.

Undoing, as a defense mechanism, apparently develops out of early training in which we are punished or forced to make restitution for our misdeeds. Once the restitution has taken place, our misdeed is negated and we can start with a clean slate. By returning his sister's toys with alacrity and saying he is sorry, Johnny may make sufficient restitution to avoid being punished and to re-establish parental approval and affection. Such early lessons relating wrongdoing to punishment and undoing to escape from punishment are not lost on us; in adult life the same techniques of atoning may help to alleviate the guilt we feel when we violate values that we have accepted. Thus the unfaithful husband may have a sudden impulse to bring his wife flowers; an unethical business-man may give unusually large sums of money to some charitable organization; and the rejecting mother may shower her child with material indications of her alleged care and concern.

Sometimes people feel so uncomfortable with their guilt that they confess their misdeeds in order to be punished as atonement for their sins. Not infrequently, individuals who have committed minor crimes years earlier will confess to the police in order to "pay their debt to society" and start afresh.

Since undoing promotes ethical human relations and helps us maintain our feelings of self-esteem and worth, it is one of our most valuable defense mechanisms. Again, however, we may rely on it too much—at the expense of understanding and improving our behavior. In fact, some individuals even appear to undertake unethical behavior with the expectation that they can make atonement for it later and emerge without guilt. Rationalization and projection may, of course, help make such a course seem attractive and safe. However, undoing does not always enable the individual to escape from the consequences of his actions. Even though he apologizes for lying to a friend on an important matter and attempts to atone for it, their relationship may never be the same again.

TYPICAL PATTERNS OF DEFENSE MECHANISMS

STRESS CENTERING AROUND:	COMMON EGO-DEFENSE MECHANISMS:
Failure	Rationalization, projection, compensation
Guilt	Rationalization, projection, undoing
Hostility	Fantasy, displacement, repression, reaction formation
Inferiority feelings	Identification, compensation, fantasy
Disappointment in love	Insulation, rationalization, fantasy
Personal limitations	Denial of reality, fantasy, compensation
Forbidden sexual desires or behavior	Rationalization, projection, repression

16. *Acting out.* One may reduce the tension and anxiety associated with forbidden desires by acting out—by permitting their expression. Instead of trying to deny or repress or change immoral sexual or hostile desires or hold strong aggressive impulses in check, he simply engages in the behavior. For example, an individual in conflict over his homosexual desires may go ahead and engage in an overt homosexual act; or one who has helplessly nursed a long history of grievances may finally lash out verbally or physically and may damage property associated with those he considers responsible for his frustration. Vandalism around school property often seems to be motivated by pent-up anger and frustration. Much acting out is to some degree violent and antisocial.

All of us have probably experienced times of acute conflict or stress when tension and anxiety have built up to such a level that we welcomed almost any action that would "get it over with." Soldiers, under the stress of waiting, have been known to leave their relatively safe shelter and blindly attack the enemy. Although such acting-out behavior may momentarily reduce tension and anxiety, it is obviously not well designed to deal effectively with the demand creating the anxiety.

Under most circumstances acting out is not feasible except for those who have very weak reality and ethical controls; most people are deterred not only by their own values but also by the likelihood of social disapproval or perhaps punishment. Although acting out may reduce emotional tension, it does not usually cope with the adjustive demand but only lessens the individual's anxiety temporarily.

In the preceding discussion we have examined the major defense mechanisms that we use in coping with the stresses of life. Although we have dealt with them singly, they are often used in combination, as when intense hostility toward an autocratic and feared father is handled by a combination of repression, reaction formation, and displacement. They may also be combined with more task-oriented behavior. It is worth re-emphasizing that defense mechanisms are in the main learned; that they are designed to deal with inner hurt, anxiety, and tension and to protect the self from threat or devaluation; that they operate on relatively habitual and unconscious levels; and that they typically involve some measure of self-deception and reality distortion.

Dependence on drugs. A great deal of concern has been expressed by health authorities concerning the increasing use and abuse of drugs by large numbers of people. The use of drugs in the United States is unequalled in the history of man. We take pills to calm us down, pills to pep us up, pills to make us sleep, pills to keep us awake, pills for "mind expansion," and pills just for kicks.

In many instances these pills serve a useful defensive function—as in the use of tranquilizers given under medical supervision for alleviating unhealthy levels of anxiety and tension. Many people use alcohol in moderate quantities for reducing tension as well as for social reasons. However, drugs are a two-edged sword which can help us cope with stress or can wreck our lives. For the most part such help as they give us is in lessening our experience of stress rather than in helping solve the stressful problem. We shall deal with drug problems in more detail in the next chapter. For the moment we are simply pointing to the use of drugs as one pattern of defense-oriented behavior.

Decompensation Under Excessive Stress

If stress proves excessive and cannot be escaped, there is lowered integration and eventually a breakdown of the system. A model which helps to explain the course of decompensation under excessive stress has been advanced by Selye (1956) in his formulation of the *general-adaptation-syndrome.* Selye found that the body's reaction to sustained, severe stress occurs in three major phases: an *alarm reaction,* a *stage of resistance,* and a *stage of exhaustion.* Although he was concerned chiefly with physiological breakdown, as summarized in the chart below, psychological decompensation seems to follow similar stages.

Alarm and mobilization. As in the case of biological stress, the first stage in reactions to psychological stress involves the alerting of the organism and the mobilization of resources for coping with the stress. Typically involved here are emotional arousal and increased tension, heightened sensitivity and alertness (vigilance), and determined efforts at self-control. At the same time, the individual undertakes various coping measures —which may be task-oriented or defense-oriented or a combination of the two—in his efforts to meet the emergency. In this stage, the individual may show symptoms of maladjustment, such as continuous anxiety, gastrointestinal upset or other bodily manifestations, and lowered efficiency—indications that the mobilization of adaptive resources is not proving adequate to cope with the stress.

THE GENERAL-ADAPTATION-SYNDROME

Selye (1956) found that the body's reaction to a wide range of stressors—such as trauma, infection, toxic substances, and so on—followed the same three stages: an *alarm reaction,* a *stage of resistance,* and a *stage of exhaustion.*

1. *The alarm reaction.* The alarm reaction is a call-to-arms of the body's defense forces in the face of stress. It involves a complex series of physiological changes which help the body to cope with the stressor. These changes focus around the pituitary-adrenal system and interestingly enough, usually follow the same general pattern regardless of the exact nature of the stressor. For example, animals subjected to starvation, infections, extreme cold, extreme heat, poisoning, and surgical hemorrhage all showed much the same pattern of physiological change. This finding helps account for the similarity in symptoms—such as fever, fatigue, and loss of appetite—seen in people suffering from different illnesses.

2. *The stage of resistance.* If exposure to the stress continues, the alarm reaction is followed by a stage of resistance. Here the organism stabilizes its defenses against the stress, and the symptoms that occurred during the alarm reaction disappear. The development of resistance to the stress appears to be achieved in large part by the increased activity of the pituitary and the adrenal cortex, though more specific adaptations may also be made in blood chemistry, nutrition, and other processes. For example, continued exposure to low oxygen content in the air gradually results in an adaptation that permits the individual to perform work at high altitudes which would have been impossible at the beginning. If successful adaptation is achieved in this stage, the organism may be able to cope with the stress over a sustained period of time.

3. *The stage of exhaustion.* If the stress continues too long or increases in severity, body defenses break down and further exposure leads to a stage of exhaustion. The anterior pituitary and the adrenal cortex are no longer able to continue secreting their hormones at the increased rate, and the organism can no longer adapt to the continuing stress. Many of the physiological dysfunctions or symptoms which appeared during the alarm reaction begin to reappear. If the stressor continues to act on the organism after this time, disintegration and death occur. Usually, of course, severe stress is relieved before the stage of exhaustion is reached.

The concept of the general-adaptation-syndrome (GAS) has been helpful in explaining peptic ulcers and other psychosomatic disorders associated with adaptation to sustained stress—disorders which Selye has referred to as "diseases of adaptation." In these diseases physiological changes induced by stress overshoot their mark or continue so long that pathology develops.

Other investigators have identified specific patterns of response to specific stresses, pointing out, for example, that responses to noxious conditions such as anoxia are somewhat different from responses to cold or heat (Lazarus, 1966). Both the general and the specific approaches appear of value in understanding stress reactions, but it has been Selye's concept of nonspecific adaptation to stress that has provided a broad framework for understanding the similarity of stress responses to different kinds of adjustive demands.

DECOMPENSATION UNDER STRESS

The following excerpts are taken from the diary of an American soldier during a tour of duty at Guadalcanal during World War II. They provide an unusually graphic demonstration of the progressive disruption of functioning that may occur with continued exposure to very severe stress. Although this example involves a reaction to the stress of combat, a similar sequence could occur in response to continued, severe stress in civilian life.

These excerpts cover a period of six weeks (Stern, 1957):

"Aug. 7, 1942. Convoy arrived at Guadalcanal Bay at approximately 4 A.M. in the morning. Ships gave enemy a heavy shelling. At 9 A.M. we stormed the beach and formed an immediate beachhead, a very successful landing, marched all day in the hot sun, and at night took positions and rested. Enemy planes attacked convoy in bay but lost 39 out of 40 planes.

"Aug. 8, 1942. Continued march in the hot sun and in afternoon arrived at airport. Continued on through the Jap village and made camp for the night. During the night, Jap navy attacked convoy in battle that lasted until early morning. Enemy had terrific losses and we lost two ships. This night while on sentry duty, I mistook a horse for a Jap and killed it.

"Aug. 19, 1942. Enemy cruiser and destroyer came into bay and shelled the beach for about two hours. The cruiser left and the destroyer hung around for the entire morning. We all kept under shelter for the early afternoon a flying fortress flew over, spotting the ship and bombed it, setting it afire we all jumped and shouted with joy. That night trouble again was feared and we again slept in foxholes.

"Aug. 21, 1942. The long waited landing by the enemy was made during the night 1500 troops in all and a few prisoners were taken and the rest were killed. Bodies were laying all over beach. In afternoon planes again bombed the Island. [Here the writing begins to be shaky, and less careful than previously.]

"Aug. 28, 1942. The company left this morning in higgins Boats to the end of the Island, landed and started through thick Jungle and hills. It was hot and we had to cut our way through. In afternoon we contacted the japs. our squad was in the assault squad so we moved up the beach to take positions the enemy trapped us with machine gun and rifle fire for about two hours. The lead was really flying. Two of our men were killed, two were hit by a hand greade and my corporal received a piece of shrampnel in back,— was wounded in arm, out of the squad of eight we had five causitry. We withdrew and were taken back to the Hospital.

"Sept. 12, 1942. Large jap squadron again bombed Island out of 35 planes sent over our air force knocked down 24. During the raid a large bomb was dropped just sevety yards from my fox hole.

"Sept. 13, 1942. At on o'clock three destroyers and one cruiser shelled us contumally all night. The ships turned surch lights all up and down the beach, and stopped one my foxhole seveal time I'm feeling pritty nervese and scared, afraid I'll be a nervas reack be for long. slept in fox hole all night not much sleep. This morning a 9:00 we had a nother air raid, the raid consisted of mostly fighter planes. I believe we got several, this afternoon. we had a nother raid, and our planes went out to met them, met them someplace over Tulagi, new came in that the aircraft carrier wasp sent planes out to intersept the bombers. This eving all hell broke lose. Our marines contacted enemy to south of us and keep up constant fire all night through.

"Sept. 14, 1942. This morning firing still going on my company is scaduted to unload ships went half ways up to dock when enemyfire start on docks, were called back to our pososeion allon beach, company called out again to go after japs, hope were lucker than we were last time [part of this illegible]. Went up into hills at 4:00 P.M. found positions, at 7:00 en 8 sea planes fombed and strifed us, 151942 were strifed biy amfibious planes and bombed the concussion of one through me of balance and down a 52 foot hil. I was shaking likd a leaf. Lost my bayanut, and ran out of wathr. I nearves and very jumpy, hop I last out until morning. I hop sevearly machine s guns ore oping up on our left flank there going over our heads

"Sept. 16. this moring we going in to take up new possissons we march all moring and I am very week and nerves, we marched up a hill and ran in to the affaul place y and z company lost so many men I hardly new what I was doing then I'm going nuts.

"Sept. 17. don't remember much of this day.

"Sept. 18. Today I'm on a ship leaving this awful place, called Green Hell. I'm still nearves and shakey." (pp. 583-586)

Stage of resistance. If the stress situation continues, the individual usually reaches a stage of resistance in which his coping efforts are relatively successful in restoring his psychological equilibrium. Temporarily this may be achieved by task-oriented coping measures —such as learning to handle a difficult boss "with kid gloves" or making an extra effort to stabilize a shaky marriage. Usually, however, defense mechanisms are brought into operation and their use is intensified.

If exposure to the stress continues, new and more deviant defensive measures may be brought into operation. These usually include the exaggerated use of defense mechanisms such as rationalization and projection and may involve the gradual introduction of neurotic defensive patterns (to be discussed in the next chapter). Neurotic patterns usually enable the individual to consolidate his defenses on this level, although at a relatively high cost in efficiency and happiness. During the stage of resistance, defenses tend to become rigid and the individual clings uncritically to his defensive patterns. It is difficult or impossible for him to examine and try out alternative, possibly more adaptive, ways of coping with the stress situation.

Disorganization and exhaustion. In the face of continued severe stress, neurotic defenses also prove inadequate, and the individual is forced to even more deviant measures in the form of more severe neuroses or psychotic reactions. These reactions may be characterized by a "break with reality" and the introduction of delusional and hallucinatory defenses, which represent attempts to salvage some measure of psychological integration and self-integrity by restructuring reality.

By these deviant psychotic defenses, he may escape from feelings of anxiety, but at a high price, for he becomes disorganized and incompetent to deal with the everyday problems of living. In much the same way that exaggerated physiological defenses may lead to tissue damage or even the death of the organism, these exaggerated psychological defenses involve serious distortion and breakdown of psychological functioning. In this sense "an organism may be injured or destroyed by its own defenses." (Lachman, 1963, p. 247)

If the stress continues to be excessive despite such defenses, the process of decompensation continues to the stage of exhaustion with complete psychological disintegration—perhaps involving continuous uncontrolled violence, apathy, or stupor.

Occasionally acute neurotic and even psychotic reactions may be precipitated by sudden and extreme stress, but psychological decompensation is more often a gradual, long-range process. Typically, of course, treatment measures are instituted before decompensation runs its course. Such measures may increase the individual's adaptive capacities or alleviate the stress situation so that the process of decompensation is reversed—*recompensation*. The various neurotic and psychotic disorders to which psychological decompensation may lead are discussed in Chapter 8.

Although we shall not pursue the matter here, the concept of decompensation under excessive stress appears as applicable on the group level as on the biological or psychological levels.

SUMMARY AND A LOOK AHEAD

Reacting to adjustive demands—*adjusting*—means acting to meet both inner and outer demands. All behavior can be viewed as an effort to adjust.

Reactions to adjustive demands are holistic and economical, may be automatic or planned, may be accompanied by emotion, and may occur on biological, psychological, or sociological levels. They are influenced by inner determinants, such as one's frame of reference, motives, competencies, stress tolerance, and physical and psychological condition of the moment, and by outer determinants, such as environmental resources, social supports, social expectations and constraints, the individual's general life situation, and special conditions of the moment. They form a changing pattern by which we try to meet our goals in increasingly effective ways.

The processing of an adjustive demand occurs in three basic steps: (1) appraising the situation, including categorizing it and assessing its degree of threat; (2) deciding on a course of action, including formulating alternative possibilities and balancing probability, desirability, and cost; and (3) taking action, using feedback to correct or improve our actions.

Psychological reactions to stress include: (1) task-oriented reactions, aimed primarily at solving the problem; (2) defense-oriented reactions, aimed primarily at reducing anxiety and bolstering self-esteem; and (3) decompensatory reactions, in which integrated functioning breaks down. Task-oriented reactions include attacking the problem (most often through aggression in the case of frustration, choice in the case of conflict, and resistance in the case of pressure), withdrawing (through either escape or avoidance), and compromising (often through substitution or accommodation). Defense-oriented reactions include built-in tension-reducing mechanisms, learned ego-defense mechanisms, and dependence on drugs.

If stress is severe or long-continued, there may be *decompensation*—a breakdown of integrated functioning. This may occur in three stages (alarm and mobilization, resistance, and exhaustion) similar to those observed in the general-adaptation-syndrome in cases of excessive or long-continued physiological stress.

In the next chapter we will examine the criteria by which we assess the normality and effectiveness of our adjustive efforts and will summarize the main maladjustive patterns.

Key terms used in this chapter include:

adjusting (p. 198)
holistic nature of reactions to stress (p. 199)
economical nature of reactions to stress (pp. 199-200)
inertia, cultural lag (p. 200)
automatic reactions (p. 200)
levels of adjustive action (pp. 201-202)
inner and outer determinants of stress reactions (pp. 202-204)
categorizing the stress situation (pp. 205-206)
balancing probability, desirability, and cost (pp. 207-209)
satisficing (p. 208)
servomechanism, feedback, feedforward (p. 210)
convergent and divergent feedback (p. 211)
task-oriented, defense-oriented, decompensatory reactions (p. 212)
task-oriented attack in response to frustration, conflict, pressure (pp. 213-214)
task-oriented withdrawal: escape, avoidance (p. 215)
task-oriented compromise: substitution, accommodation (pp. 216-217)
"wired-in" reparative mechanisms (pp. 218-219)
learned ego-defense mechanisms (pp. 220-228)
general-adaptation-syndrome (p. 228)
psychological decompensation, recompensation (pp. 228-231)

Chapter 8

FAULTY PATTERNS
OF ADJUSTMENT

Nature of Effective and Ineffective Adjustment
Major Maladjustive Patterns
Introduction to Treatment and Prevention

We have seen that behavior is an attempt by the organism to adapt to inner and outer demands. This is as true of maladjustive behavior as it is of smooth, effective, successful behavior. Both represent answers to the same questions—how best to protect one's well-being, develop one's potentialities, and meet social demands. Thus the same basic principles which underlie effective behavior also underlie ineffective or maladjustive behavior.

In the present chapter we shall attempt to (1) gain a perspective concerning the nature of effective and ineffective behavior; (2) achieve a basic understanding of the major types or patterns of maladjustive behavior; and (3) briefly review modern approaches to treatment and prevention. Although science and clinical experience have provided us with much information concerning maladjustive behavior and its significance to the individual and to society, there are still many important questions to be answered.

NATURE OF EFFECTIVE AND INEFFECTIVE ADJUSTMENT

There is no mysterious difference between effective and ineffective adjustment. Rather we are dealing with a continuum of adjustive-maladjustive behavior, with most people clustering around a central point or average. Thus the majority of persons achieve an average or moderate level of adjustment, while a few at one extreme lead unusually effective and fulfilling lives and a few at the other extreme are severely maladjusted. A given individual may fall anywhere on this continuum of effective-ineffective adjustment, and his position on the continuum may change with time. For example, his adjustment may deteriorate under severe and continued stress, or may improve when his life situation improves or when he learns to cope more effectively with problems. Some people adjust well in certain areas of living but poorly in others.

In the present section we shall look briefly at the criteria we use for evaluating specific patterns of behavior, and at differing models for viewing maladaptive behavior.

Criteria of Effective Adjustment

The particular actions or coping patterns that are judged effective vary greatly in different cultural and situational settings. Nevertheless, it is possible to make some generalizations about effective and ineffective adjustive behavior that apply to human beings in any setting—from Madison Avenue to the tropical rain forests of the upper Amazon.

Does the action meet the demands of the situation? Some actions, as we have seen, do not help resolve the stress situation but merely provide temporary relief. Thus the individual who uses tranquilizers as a means of alleviating tension and anxiety is not likely to be solving the adjustive demands which led to his difficulty. In some stressful situations, of course—such as the death of loved ones or disappointment in love—the wounds tend to heal with time, and temporary defensive measures may be of value.

But when defense-oriented behavior is relied upon as the major means of coping with stress, it usually only puts off the day of reckoning. Indeed, in the long run it may even increase the stress and the difficulty of meeting adjustive demands successfully. For example, the individual who escapes from an unhappy home situation by resorting to alcohol not only fails to solve his problem but usually makes his situation worse. One criterion of effective adjustment, then, is that it meets the objective requirements of the situation.

Does the action meet the overall needs of the individual? Sometimes an action seems to meet the demands of the situation but fails to meet the maintenance or actualization needs of the individual. The boy who wants to be a teacher but gives in to his father's wish for him to go into the family business may relieve the stress of parental pressures at the expense of frustrating his need for self-fulfillment. Far from being an effective adjustment, such a decision is likely to create inner conflict and cause more difficult problems of adjustment later on.

Another factor to consider in determining whether behavior is effective or ineffective is how much it costs in relation to the satisfactions it yields. A high-pressure executive job may offer a man rich rewards in money, prestige, and fulfillment of his potentialities, but if he is constantly anxious and his long hours at work make him a stranger to his wife and children, the cost may be too great and his behavior pattern may be ineffective from the point of view of his overall ad-

justment. Likewise, defenses like repression —though they may relieve anxiety—are costly because they inevitably impair the individual's ability to cope realistically with his problems. And as we saw in Chapter 6, any long-term and costly adjustment to one stress tends to lessen a person's ability to cope with other stresses.

Is the action compatible with group welfare? Ideally, effective adjustment means that the individual copes with his problems in such a way as to be in harmony with his environment and also maintain his own integrity and well-being. If he satisfies his needs at the expense of other people, his action cannot be considered truly adjustive. And if it is harmful to others, it is likely in the long run to lead to the frustration of his needs too.

The ability to maintain both inner harmony and harmonious relations with one's surroundings presupposes a "normal" environment in which the same acts *can* forward both individual and group goals. But where the group is repressive or otherwise pathological, it may be impossible for an individual to maintain his own integrity and meet his needs without running counter to group demands. Thus while freedom fighters in a dictatorship might be regarded as enemies of the state, from a broader perspective of human welfare they might be behaving in an adaptive way. Any ultimate definition of effective and ineffective adjustment must take into consideration both the optimal development of the individual and the fostering of social conditions which are compatible with group welfare.

Models for Understanding Maladjustment

During the Middle Ages and until relatively recent times, individuals evidencing mental disorders were usually thought to be possessed of devils or evil spirits and were often treated with unbelievable cruelty. Sometimes they were burned as witches. Gradually, however, they came to be viewed as sick persons in need of treatment and were referred to as "mentally ill." With this change in viewpoint came the development of mental hospitals expressly for the purpose of treating the mentally ill. The first such hospital in the United States was founded in Williamsburg, Virginia, in 1773.

The medical model. This view of the mentally disturbed as "ill" followed the medical model of disease. Just as fever and internal pain indicate some bodily ailment resulting from a virus or other causative agent, so mental disorders were assumed to reflect underlying brain pathology. This "organic viewpoint" of mental illness received a great deal of impetus during the nineteenth century with the discovery of the syphilitic basis of general paresis (syphilis of the brain resulting in severe mental disorder, deterioration, and death) and other organic conditions associated with mental disorders. As a consequence, it became the generally accepted view that mental disorders were based on some underlying brain pathology, and a great deal of research was initiated with a view to finding the precise pathology in schizophrenia and other mental disorders. Despite extensive research, however, the supposed brain pathology underlying many disorders continued to evade detection.

Diagnosis plays an important part in the medical model, for the symptoms are assumed to be clues to underlying organic or psychological causes. Treatment, in turn, is aimed at altering the causes as well as at getting rid of the immediate symptoms. For example, the treatment of alcoholism with drugs that make a drinker nauseated when he drinks even a small amount of alcohol would not be considered complete therapy, since the underlying causes that presumably led to the alcoholism have not been cleared up. Denied alcohol, the patient might become depressed or develop some other maladjustive reaction in his desperate efforts to cope with his underlying difficulties and anxieties. The latter process is referred to as *symptom substitution.*

The medical model, with its concept of

symptoms, mental illness, and underlying causes has largely dominated contemporary thinking about personality maladjustment. It has been particularly utilized in dealing with disorders associated with brain pathology, in alcoholism and drug addiction, and in other mental disorders severe enough to require hospitalization. The use of various medical procedures—such as antipsychotic drugs and electroshock—and the medical supervision of patients in hospital settings have both stemmed from and tended to maintain the medical model.

The psychological model. By about 1900 a new current of thought concerning the causation of mental disorders was introduced by the clinical findings of Sigmund Freud, who showed that one form of mental disorder—conversion hysteria—was clearly the result of psychological rather than organic causes. This, in turn, led to a psychological model of mental disorders, emphasizing the view that some mental disorders could be caused by the exaggerated use of ego-defense mechanisms in the individual's efforts to cope with his problems and lessen his anxiety. While some mental disorders were unquestionably disease entities—based on underlying brain pathology—other disorders might result from anxiety and exaggerated ego defenses. Thus the medical model of organic causes was broadened to include the concept of anxiety-defense causes for certain kinds of mental disorders.

Both the medical and the psychological models were further extended by the work of Selye on the general-adaptation-syndrome, which we reviewed in Chapter 7. Here we can see maladaptive behavior resulting from decompensation—biological or psychological—occurring under excessive stress on either level. From the standpoint of the psychological model, the stress-decompensation view of maladjustive behavior was added to the anxiety-defense view formulated by Freud.

More recently still, during the last decade a number of investigators have concluded that the next great step forward in dealing with personality maladjustment—aside from the minority of cases associated with brain pathology—will come when mental disorder is viewed simply as maladaptive learning and "mental illness" is seen as a myth. As Szasz (1961) has insisted, the adversary is neither demons nor "illness" but inability to cope with the problems of living.

This further extension of the psychological model is based on behavioristic learning theory, summarized in Chapter 1. Maladaptive behavior is seen as resulting from (1) a deficiency of prior learning and lack of needed competencies for coping with everyday problems, or (2) the learning of maladaptive behavior which has then been maintained through reinforcement—it has "paid off" for the individual, who has seen no methods more effective for meeting his needs. This general viewpoint is well stated by Ullmann and Krasner (1965):

"Maladaptive behaviors are learned behaviors, and the development and maintenance of a maladaptive behavior is not different from the development and maintenance of any other behavior. There is no discontinuity between desirable and undesirable modes of adjustment or between "healthy" and "sick" behavior. The first major implication of this view is the question of how a behavior is to be identified as desirable or undesirable, adaptive or maladaptive. The general answer we propose is that because there are no disease entities involved in the majority of subjects displaying maladaptive behavior, the designation of a behavior as pathological or not is dependent upon the individual's society." (p. 20)

These investigators regard maladjustive behavior as important in its own right. No behavior is considered as simply a symptom of underlying difficulties. Maladaptive responses are themselves the problem—simply patterns of behavior, learned through unfortunate contingencies of reinforcement and subject to modification by further learning. In addition, any pattern of behavior is considered maladaptive only in a given social setting. And since no behaviors are considered maladaptive in all societies, maladaptive behavior becomes simply a failure to live up to social roles and other expectations and demands in one's own culture.

The learning-theory view of maladjustive behavior has had important implications for assessment and treatment. Assessment is concerned not with underlying causes but with (1) identifying the maladaptive behavior which needs to be changed and (2) identifying the reinforcing stimuli in the individual's social situation which are maintaining the maladaptive behavior. The emphasis in therapy is then placed on techniques of behavior modification and control. If the individual is handicapped by irrational fears, obsessive thoughts, or the excessive use of alcohol, it is assumed that these reactions can be extinguished and more effective reactions can be learned. By means of negative reinforcement or related techniques, maladaptive behavior can be extinguished; by means of positive reinforcement, more effective patterns can be established.

As we have noted in Chapter 1, models are simply analogies and approximations and do not have to be entirely accurate or all embracing. Thus it would appear that both the medical model and the psychological model are useful in dealing with certain kinds of maladjustment. Few would deny the validity of the medical model in dealing with mental disorders associated with organic brain pathology, and few would deny the validity of the psychological model in explaining conversion hysteria, phobias, sexual deviations, combat reactions, and other maladjustive patterns in which an anxiety-defense, stress-decompensation, or straightforward learning approach seems to offer the best explanation.

There is still a "no man's land," however, in which there is dispute as to which model best applies. For example, the causes of schizophrenia still baffle modern science and both organic and psychological models have their champions. Here it may be emphasized that both the medical model and the several variants of the psychological model take account of the important role of sociocultural influences in the development of mental disorders.

In the brief review of faulty adjustive

patterns which follows, we shall have occasion to see the usefulness of these models. For convenience, we shall use certain terms borrowed from the medical model—such as *mental disorders, symptoms, treatment, etiology,* and *prognosis*—without implying any assumptions about organic or psychological determinants except as discussed in relation to a particular disorder.[1]

MAJOR MALADJUSTIVE PATTERNS

Many classifications of maladjustive behavior have been attempted—based on similarities of observed behavior (symptoms) or on theories of causation or both. None have been entirely satisfactory, and some workers have rejected classifications altogether, pointing out that any set of categories tends to set up arbitrary groupings which obscure both similarities and differences among maladjusted persons. The same symptoms may have very different causes; likewise, the same original problem can lead to many different patterns of symptoms in different individuals.

Despite these difficulties, the use of broad categories of maladjustive behavior has been helpful for purposes of understanding, treatment, and research. In our present discussion we shall utilize six categories that have been reasonably well delineated: (1) transient personality disorders brought about by acute or special stress; (2) neurotic disorders, such as conversion hysteria; (3) psychotic disorders, such as schizophrenia; (4) psychosomatic disorders, such as peptic ulcers; (5) character disorders, including sexual deviations and crime; and (6) alcoholism and drug addiction.

In reading about the symptoms of various mental disorders, students often come to the conclusion that they have many of the same symptoms and begin to wonder if they

are neurotic or perhaps even schizophrenic. Medical students, too, are notoriously prone to find in themselves symptoms of the various diseases they are reading about. But since many maladjustive reactions are observed to some degree among normal individuals, there is usually no cause for alarm. In the more seriously maladjusted person, the reactions are exaggerated and form part of a broad pattern of serious difficulties in adjustment. Of course, any of us may experience serious adjustment difficulties if the going gets tough enough; in such a case it is wise to seek professional assistance.

Transient Situational Personality Disorders

Under conditions of overwhelmingly severe stress—such as terrifying accidents, imprisonment, physical mutilation, or military combat—temporary mental disorders may develop even in previously stable personalities. The personality decompensation may be sudden, as in the case of a fire or other catastrophe, or it may be gradual, as in a prisoner-of-war camp or even a very difficult life situation in civilian life. Usually the individual shows good recoverability once the stressful situation is over, though in some cases there is residual damage to the self-structure and an increased vulnerability to certain types of stress.

Transient personality disorders are commonly grouped into three categories: (1) reactions to combat, (2) reactions to civilian catastrophies, and (3) reactions to chronic situational stress.

Combat exhaustion. Warfare places tremendous stress upon men. As might be expected, reactions to combat involving personality decompensation have been common throughout the history of warfare though it is only recently that such reactions have been studied systematically.

Most of our present information stems from studies made during World War II and the Korean War, in which about 10 per cent

---

[1]For a further examination of the medical vs. psychosocial model problem, the reader is referred to Ullmann & Krasner, 1965; and Sarason & Ganzer, 1968.

of the men in combat developed severe enough disorders to render them temporarily or permanently unfit for combat duty. In Vietnam, very few cases of combat exhaustion have been reported (Tiffany & Allerton, 1967). This low incidence has apparently been due in large measure to the brief, intensive, and sporadic nature of the fighting followed by periods of relative calm and safety —as contrasted with the weeks and months of prolonged combat in World War II and the Korean War. In Vietnam, too, there has been a policy of rotation after about a year; it has apparently been easier for soldiers to tolerate combat stress for a known and relatively brief period of time. Since the study of combat reactions has contributed to our understanding of other disorders, a brief review of the nature of such reactions will be useful.

The clinical picture in combat reactions varies somewhat depending upon the branch of the service, the nature and duration of combat experiences, and the personality make-up of the individual soldier. In some cases the personality decompensation is sudden, but usually it occurs after months of combat duty. Among infantry soldiers, hypersensitivity, irritability, and sleep disturbances commonly signal the first stage. Often the personality decompensation goes no further unless or until some particularly traumatic experience upsets the already unstable equilibrium.

In the full-blown combat reaction, the clinical picture typically involves weariness, dejection, hypersensitivity, sleep disturbances, tremors, and overwhelming anxiety:

"In the majority of cases they followed a stereotyped pattern: 'I just can't take it any more'; 'I can't stand those shells'; 'I just couldn't control myself.' They varied little from patient to patient. Whether it was the soldier who had experienced his baptism of fire or the older veteran who had lost his comrades, the superficial result was very similar. Typically he appeared as a dejected, dirty, weary man. His facial expression was one of depression, sometimes of tearfulness. Frequently his hands were trembling or

jerking. Occasionally he would display varying degrees of confusion, perhaps to the extent of being mute or staring into space." (Menninger, 1948, p. 143)

In very severe cases, the clinical picture often included amnesia for the combat experience that had precipitated the breakdown. The defense mechanism of repression is clearly demonstrated in these cases, for such experiences could be brought to consciousness under hypnosis or drugs like sodium pentothal.

A number of predisposing factors may lower the overall stress tolerance of the soldier and pave the way for possible breakdown. Among these are severe fatigue, increased feelings of personal vulnerability resulting from seeing friends killed or wounded, disturbing letters from home, and lack of faith in the immediate objectives or long-range goals for which he is fighting. The most common precipitating event usually involves a highly traumatic combat experience, leaving him with the feeling that his "number is up." Particularly where a soldier has almost completed the number of missions or duration of duty necessary for rotation is he likely to feel that his "luck has run out." Factors that tend in the other direction—toward increased stress tolerance to combat—are a feeling of *esprit de corps* and pride in being a part of an efficient combat unit, confidence in his commanding officers, and belief in the worth and importance of the war goals.

In most cases combat reactions are quickly reversed when the men are temporarily removed from combat. Treatment has been found to be most effective when it is provided as near the combat unit as possible, and when there is a "duty-expectant attitude," in which everyone makes it apparent that the soldier is expected to perform his combat duties despite his anxieties and that his symptoms will not justify permanent removal from combat (Bell, 1958; Tiffany & Allerton, 1967).

Reactions to civilian catastrophes. In civilian life, people exposed to sudden terrifying experiences, such as tornadoes, fires, explosions, earthquakes, ship disasters, and other accidents, may show varying degrees of personality decompensation. Such reactions, like combat reactions, occur even in previously stable personalities and are usually temporary.

Victims of such terrifying experiences typically show a "disaster syndrome," in which three stages have been delineated (Raker *et al.*, 1956): (1) a *shock stage*, during which the victim is stunned, dazed, and apathetic, often unaware of the extent of his injuries and unable to make more than minimal efforts to help himself or others; (2) a *suggestible stage*, during which the victim tends to be passive and willing to take directions from rescue workers or others less affected by the disaster; and (3) a *recovery stage*, during which the individual gradually regains his equilibrium.

During stage 3, the individual at first tends to talk repetitively about the catastrophe. Often, too, he suffers from tension, apprehensiveness, and difficulty in concentrating and sleeping. In cases where loved ones have been lost in the catastrophe, intense feelings of grief, depression, and sometimes guilt may complicate the picture. There may also be recurring nightmares which typically re-enact or are closely related to the traumatic experience. Such symptoms usually clear up rapidly, however, especially if he receives supportive psychotherapy at a hospital or aid station. In some cases a syndrome involving anxiety, tension, irritability, and repetitive nightmares may continue for weeks or even months, but this reaction pattern is not typical.

In civilian shock, the individual has not been prepared for the situation and also lacks such support as the soldier gets from being part of a fighting unit. The dynamics are similar, however, and such decompensation as occurs, though perhaps acute, is usually temporary.

Situational reactions. Sometimes a person finds himself in an intolerable life situation from which he sees no escape. He may feel trapped in an unhappy marriage which he feels he must maintain because of the children, or he may hate his work but feel he must stick to it because of heavy financial responsibilities or lack of training for any other kind of job. In the course of time, he may develop various symptoms, ranging from chronic fatigue and discouragement to serious inefficiency or excessive drinking.

Similar but typically more severe reactions are seen in individuals serving long prison terms or held as prisoners of war. Here the symptoms may include apathy, depression, a lowering of ethical standards, and an exaggerated use of defense mechanisms.

Commander Nardini (1952), an eyewitness and participant, has described the reaction of American soldiers to imprisonment by the Japanese following the fall of Bataan and Corregidor in World War II.

"Conditions of imprisonment varied from time to time in different places and with different groups. In general there was shortage, wearisome sameness, and deficiency of food; much physical misery and disease; squalid living conditions; fear and despair; horrible monotony . . . inadequate clothing and cleansing facilities; temperature extremes; and physical abuse. . . .

". . . hungry men were constantly reminded of their own nearness to death by observing the steady, relentless march to death of their comrades. . . .

". . . Men quibbled over portions of food, were suspicious of those who were in more favored positions than themselves, participated in unethical barter, took advantage of less clever or enterprising fellow prisoners, stole, rummaged in garbage, and even curried the favor of their detested captors. There was a great distortion of previous personality as manifested by increased irritability, unfriendliness, and sullen withdrawal. . . .

". . . most men experienced bouts of apathy or depression. These ranged from slight to prolonged deep depressions where there was a loss of interest in living and lack of willingness or ability to marshal the powers of will necessary to combat disease. An

*ever-present sign of fatal withdrawal oc-
curred 3 to 4 days before death when the
man pulled his covers up over his head and
lay passive, quiet, and refusing food." (pp.
242-243)*

Chronic stress conditions may involve
people of any age in highly diverse life situations. The child who has to deal with an indifferent father and a cruel and capricious
stepmother is in a chronic stress situation
and may show truancy from school, destruc-
tiveness, stealing, emotional withdrawal,
or other reactions. In old age, chronic poor
health and constant physical pain may lead
to personality decompensation with depression and suicidal tendencies. A crucial factor
in all chronic situational reactions seems to
be the individual's inability either to find adjustive patterns that meet his needs or to see
any hope for change.

Neurotic Disorders

Neurotic reactions involve the exaggerated
use of defensive patterns. Most contemporary investigators see these reactions as
learned maladaptive responses which are
maintained because they alleviate anxiety
and protect the self from danger or devaluation. They are considered maladaptive because they do not solve the individual's problems but instead tend to complicate them.
In addition, they usually occur in response
to stresses that most people could deal with
effectively and without undue difficulty. Although neurotic reactions may seriously
interfere with the individual's effectiveness,
however, they are not usually incapacitating,
nor do they ordinarily require that the individual be hospitalized for treatment.

Although there is no characteristic personality type which predisposes an individual to neurotic reactions, such reactions do
appear to have their roots in faulty personality development and early learning. As a
group, neurotics lack a clear-cut sense of
personal identity and show a discrepancy
between what they think they *should* be
and what they see themselves as being. Typ-

ically there is a pervasive feeling of inadequacy which may have considerable basis in
fact; for even though the neurotic may have
high intelligence and exceptional abilities in
specific areas, he usually suffers from various immaturities—often including an immature and rigid conscience—and from a lack
of some of the competencies necessary for
coping successfully with typical life problems (Cattell & Scheier, 1961). Such characteristics appear to render him especially vulnerable to threat from both inner and outer
sources and have been referred to as the
neurotic nucleus.

We shall examine the dynamics of neurotic reactions in our discussion of phobias
and other reaction types. In general, however, neurotic reactions appear to (1) represent relatively simple conditioned responses
—usually of the avoidance variety—to
anxiety-arousing stress, or (2) follow an
anxiety-defense pattern involving an exaggeration of ego-defense mechanisms in the
face of severe stress. Regardless of the precise origin, neurotic reactions do alleviate
anxiety and hence tend to be continually
reinforced.

The stress that precipitates a neurotic
reaction may be an inner conflict—perhaps
relating to the handling of hostility or sexual
desires—or an outer condition such as oppressive group demands. In either event, the
individual is face to face with an anxiety-
arousing stress situation which he sees as
threatening and with which he feels inadequate to cope. His neurotic reaction is essentially oriented toward defense, for his main
effort goes into measures to allay his anxiety
and maintain his feelings of adequacy and
worth rather than into efforts at more efficient
coping.

For this reason, a neurotic cannot readily give up his defenses, despite their ineffectiveness, for he would again be exposed to
the disruptive stress situation. This tendency for neurotic reactions to be both self-
defeating and self-perpetuating has been referred to as the *neurotic paradox.*

There are an estimated 10 million or
more neurotics in the United States. Neu-

rotic reactions are more common among females than males and occur more frequently in early adulthood than in other life periods. Langner and Michael (1963) found the incidence of neurotic reactions significantly higher among the upper third of the population in terms of socioeconomic level. The incidence and types of neurotic reactions also vary greatly from one culture to another.

Several neurotic reactions can be distinguished. Except for a relatively few classic cases, however, most neurotics show a combination of symptoms and cannot be pigeonholed as neatly as the following descriptions might suggest.

Anxiety reaction. In this type of neurotic reaction, which is the most common, anxiety is the chief symptom. Often the individual worries a great deal; as soon as one worry is proved to be unfounded, he finds another one to take its place. Although anxiety is a normal response to threat, the anxiety neurotic responds with anxiety which is not commensurate with the objective threat. As a consequence, he shows a chronic level of anxiety which appears to be a pervasive characteristic of his life style.

The neurotic's continuous but usually bearable level of anxiety and apprehensiveness may be punctuated from time to time by acute anxiety attacks in which he has feelings of foreboding and panic, accompanied by such physical symptoms as heart palpitations, profuse sweating, and dryness of the mouth. During an attack, he may be sure that he is about to die, that he is going insane, or that some other calamity is going to overtake him. Such attacks may last from a few seconds to a few hours and vary greatly in intensity but are likely to be very frightening to the individual.

Both personality and stress factors typically contribute to this particular reaction pattern. The anxiety neurotic tends to be introverted and oversensitive, to have a high

IS THERE AN EXISTENTIAL NEUROSIS?

In an interesting formulation Maddi (1967) has suggested the existence of a specific form of neurosis which is characteristic in twentieth-century United States—a neurotic pattern he refers to as the *existential neurosis.* The dominant characteristics are apathy, aimlessness, and a chronic sense of meaninglessness.

Unlike the asthenic reaction, with its lack of energy, the existential reaction is characterized by a moderate level of energy and activity—but the activities are not chosen by the individual. It is as if he were a social robot, who goes through the motions of playing the roles assigned to him; it seems to be immaterial to him what, if any, activities he pursues. When he exercises selectivity, it is in the direction of a minimal expenditure of effort and avoidance of decision making, picking the least demanding course of action.

The personality background of such a person usually reveals a lack of clear-cut personal identity, with a dominating view of the self as "an embodiment of biological needs and a player of social roles." (p. 311). Such a self-picture tends to separate him from deep and satisfying interpersonal relationships as well as from a feeling of his own personal vitality. In essence, he is alienated both from himself and from society. Instead of being a self-directing and growing person, pursuing a meaningful and fulfilling way of life, he leads an empty existence in which he plays his assigned roles and meets his bodily needs but with no clear sense of meaning or fulfillment. In existential terms, his is a state of *nonbeing.*

A person with such a sense of self-identity may go through life in a superficially adequate and even successful way—keeping his vague anxieties and dissatisfactions to himself. Occasionally stresses such as the imminent threat of death, gross disruption of the established social order and consequently of his social roles and status, or, more commonly, confrontation by others will reveal to him his existential failure as a human being.

level of aspiration, and to experience strong guilt feelings when he fails to live up to his high standards (Cattell & Scheier, 1961; Mowrer, 1967). By virtue of his temperament, he appears to be especially prone to the development of conditioned fear reactions (Eysenck, 1960). This vulnerability may in part account for the tendency he has developed to feel basically inadequate in a dangerous world and to be sensitized to both inner and outer sources of danger. In any case, it is not surprising that neurotics approach the problems of living with considerable apprehension, worry, and sustained anxiety.

In anxiety attacks, as in persistent chronic anxiety, the individual is usually unaware of the source of the threat. Often it appears to involve desires which the individual views as immoral and dangerous—usually centering around sex and hostility.

Mary _____, a pretty 19-year-old girl, had been brought up to believe that sex was evil and premarital sexual relations particularly so. Yet she found herself sexually attracted to a young man with whom she had been going steady and felt herself in danger of giving in to his overtures. About this time she began having periodic attacks of anxiety, usually occurring a short time before he was to pick her up in the evening. However, she saw no relationship between her anxiety attacks and her sexual conflict.

Repression is the primary defense in such anxiety reactions and operates in such a way as to screen out dangerous desires each time they arise. The anxiety attacks proper apparently signal the threat that such repressed desires are about to break through into consciousness and apparently lead to reinforcement of the repressive defense. Although this mechanism provides temporary relief from having to cope with a serious inner conflict, it is gained at the cost of the individual's continued unawareness of the source of his anxiety. Anxiety attacks may continue over a period of time, assuming that the conflict continues; but usually some solution is found to the conflict, or other defensive measures such as phobias are brought in

to bolster the person's defenses. Anxiety neurotics often resort to tranquilizers or alcohol in an attempt to alleviate their anxiety, but such patterns usually provide temporary relief at best and often further complicate the person's adjustive difficulties.

Phobic reaction. A phobia is persistent, excessive fear of something in the absence of any substantial danger. Common phobias include:

>   acrophobia—fear of high places
>   claustrophobia—fear of small closed places
>   pyrophobia—fear of fire
>   agoraphobia—fear of open places
>   mysophobia—fear of dirt, germs, and contamination

An individual with a neurotic phobia cannot account for his fear, is often seriously inconvenienced by it, and experiences intense anxiety if he is forced to face the phobic situation. And he usually suffers from a number of phobias rather than just one.

In most cases phobias appear to be based upon conditioned learning in situations eliciting strong fear reactions. For example, a child who has been attacked and terrified by a vicious dog may tend to have an irrational fear of dogs for a sustained period thereafter. And since he is likely to feel fearful when exposed to a dog, he is likely to avoid such exposures. The consequent avoidance reaction tends to reduce his fear and anxiety and is consequently reinforcing. Thus the irrational fear of dogs together with his avoidance reactions may continue indefinitely, since he never permits himself to extinguish his fear by experiences with friendly dogs. Also, of course, such fears may generalize to other animals—as we noted in the classic case of little Albert, who was conditioned to fear a white rat and subsequently was afraid of other furry animals too.

In many instances, it would appear that neurotic phobic reactions involve the displacement of fear from an anxiety-arousing source of stress to some symbolic object or situation associated with it. For example, a girl experiencing anxiety attacks associated with repressed sexual desires may develop a phobia of disease germs or of syphilis—so that she now becomes highly anxious if a boy attempts to kiss her. By driving her to avoid such intimacy, this phobia further protects her from the danger of what she considers immoral desires and behavior.

In essence, phobias represent attempts to cope with internal or external dangers by avoiding them. However, they restrict and interfere with one's life activities and do not prevent subjective distress, for the anxiety is not entirely escaped; in addition, the individual realizes that he is behaving irrationally and cannot control himself.

Conversion reaction (hysteria). In a conversion reaction the individual protects himself against some anxiety-arousing situation by developing the symptoms of a disease or disability. For example, a soldier may go blind just as he is about to be sent into combat, or an individual in ordinary life, facing a threat from which he cannot escape, may become deaf or paralyzed, develop coughing or sneezing spells, lose his sensitivity to touch and pain in some body area, or even show the symptoms of some disease like malaria. No organic pathology underlies such symptoms though occasionally the picture is complicated by the fact that the symptoms are superimposed on actual organic damage, as when an individual with a history of impaired hearing suddenly becomes totally deaf.

These reactions were named *conversion reactions* because it was once thought that the psychological conflict was somehow "converted" into physical symptoms. Although the neurophysiological mechanisms involved are still not fully understood, three characteristics usually make it possible to differentiate between conversion reactions and physical illness: (1) conversion symptoms can be changed, modified, or removed under hypnosis or drugs such as sodium pentothal, (2) the neurotic patient shows little apparent concern over his physical disability, and (3) conversion reactions often fail to follow medical fact; for example, in a condition called *glove anaesthesia* the neurotic loses sensitivity to touch and pain in approximately the area covered by a glove, which does not correspond with the nerve patterns in the area.

The conversion hysteric is not malingering or putting on an act. His symptoms are real, and he is as baffled by them as anyone else, though he typically does not show the concern one would expect to see in someone actually going blind or suddenly afflicted by a paralyzed limb.

Conversion reactions used to be common in both military and civilian life. Interestingly, the symptoms among military personnel were usually related to the type of job a man was doing. For example, in World War II fighter pilots who developed conversion reactions usually complained of visual difficulties such as night blindness, while paratroopers were more subject to leg paralyses (Grinker & Spiegel, 1945a). In an age and society which no longer believes in being "struck" blind or deaf and which has the medical facilities for determining the extent of physical pathology, conversion reactions have become understandably rare. For they no longer serve their defensive functions. Yet they still occur occasionally among Americans and remain common in less sophisticated societies.

Dissociative reaction. This is a relatively rare reaction in which certain aspects of reality are so painful that the individual represses entire episodes of his life from consciousness. Three subtypes of dissociative reactions are distinguished—amnesia, fugue, and multiple personality.

In an amnesic reaction, repression usually involves the screening out of some traumatic and anxiety-arousing event, such as a guilt-arousing homosexual episode, until time reduces the trauma. In a fugue reaction, amnesia generalizes to include whole areas of the individual's experience, and the amnesia is accompanied by actual physical flight—usually to escape from what the individual considers an intolerable life situation. He becomes amnesic and wanders away; then, days, weeks, or even years later, he may suddenly find himself in a strange place with no memory of how he got there or what he has been doing.

In an interesting example of fugue, a married salesman with four children disappeared from a Midwestern town and was recognized eight years later in another state. He had no recollection of his former life, but his identity was confirmed by means of fingerprints. In the meantime, he had remarried and become a successful sports announcer.

During the fugue period, the individual retains his basic skills and habit patterns but takes on a new identity and does not know who he is or where he has come from.

The most extreme form of dissociative reaction is multiple personality. Here the individual may develop two or perhaps several distinct personalities which alternate in consciousness—each functioning as the self-system for varying periods of time. Such reactions appear to be based on severe inner conflicts between contradictory sets of self-identities, motives, and roles. If a person is unable to reconcile the role he feels he must play with a contradictory role that he would *like* to play and that is also insistent in its demands on him, he may repress one pattern while he temporarily lives out the other—in effect achieving the gratification of both. Thus a moralistic, timid personality may alternate with an outgoing, promiscuous, fun-loving one. This type of reaction is extremely rare despite the celebrated "Dr. Jekyll" and "Mr. Hyde" and related dramatizations in literature, movies, and television.

As we have seen, many people suffer temporary amnesia for particularly traumatic events, such as soldiers may experience in combat episodes. In dissociative reactions, however, the individual is defending himself from stress that most people could handle in more effective ways.

Neurotic amnesia is also to be distinguished from amnesia associated with brain pathology—such as amnesia resulting from head injuries—which is usually permanent. In dissociative amnesia, the person's memory can be recovered under hypnosis or

sodium pentothal and usually returns spontaneously sooner or later.

Obsessive-compulsive reactions. In obsessive-compulsive reactions, the individual is seemingly victimized by persistent irrational thoughts or by a compulsion to carry out irrational acts. Obsessive and compulsive reactions may occur independently of each other, but typically they go together and are considered separate aspects of a single response pattern.

Often people under heavy pressure set up strict and unvarying procedures for maintaining order and predictability, thus ensuring that nothing can go wrong that would make additional or unforeseen demands on them. Many obsessive-compulsive reactions appear to be an exaggeration of these learned and normally adaptive patterns of orderliness. Typically they take place in a personality similar to that of the anxiety neurotic. The individual is sensitized to the dangers of living and allays his chronic feelings of insecurity and inadequacy by a ritualistic exaggeration of orderliness, often involving an overconcern with normal role behavior. Thus a young housewife may be constantly cleaning the stove, spraying the air with pesticides, going over every bill several times to be sure it is accurate, and otherwise preoccupying herself with extreme orderliness.

In other instances, obsessive-compulsive reactions appear to be associated with repressed desires relating to hostility or to immoral sexual desires. Here the obsessive thoughts appear to represent the breakthrough into consciousness of actual thoughts or desires simply as ideas, without emotional or motivational reinforcement. Thus the youth who has repressed resentment and hostility toward his father may experience fantasies of his father being killed—or even of killing him—but without any consciousness of a desire for such an event to come about.

In still other instances, obsessive thoughts may take the form of phobias—such as an obsessive fear of syphilis—which helps the individual to control sexual desires which he considers immoral. Despite their inappropriateness, such irrational thoughts cannot be banished voluntarily from consciousness; to the individual, they may seem not only irrational but horrifying. Although thoughts of immorality and violence are common in obsessions, the individual's rigid conscience usually prevents their being carried out in action.

Obsessive thoughts may lead to compulsive symbolic actions designed to counteract the immoral thoughts. A daughter who has persistent thoughts of her mother dying may feel compelled to make the sign of the Cross and say "God protect my dear mother" each time such thoughts enter her mind; similarly, a youth who cannot rid himself of thoughts of masturbating, which he considers terribly evil, may have a compulsion to wash his hands every few minutes—thus symbolically "washing away" his guilt feelings and cleansing himself.

All of us have probably experienced minor obsessive thoughts such as a persistent tune, thoughts of suicide, or fantasies of committing immoral sexual acts or acts of violence. Often too, we may experience a compulsion to check several times to make sure we have locked the front door or to see that the lights are off when we have parked the car. The background and personality make-up of the obsessive-compulsive neurotic seem to foster an exaggeration of such normal tendencies.

In general, individuals evidencing obsessive-compulsive reactions appear to come from a home background which rigidly indoctrinated the child in strict standards of right and wrong concerning sex, hostility, cleanliness, and related behaviors. Such standards were probably enforced with severe punitive measures, so that any transgression of the code—in thought or deed—tended to elicit intense anxiety on the part of the child. The end product of such training appears to be a young person with rigid and unrealistic standards, who is severely inhibited and lacking in spontaneity. Faced with the conflicts and other stresses of adolescence and young adulthood, his rigid defenses appear in danger of breaking down

and permitting immoral thoughts and desires to enter consciousness and perhaps even be carried out in action. When such forbidden thoughts do break through repressive defenses into consciousness, their motivational or affective base is cut off by the mechanism of isolation and they are not carried out in action. Compulsive actions are then introduced as a means of counteracting the obsessive thoughts and reducing guilt and anxiety via the mechanism of undoing. The individual's defenses are only partially successful, however, and he realizes that his behavior is irrational and is interfering with his ongoing activities.

Asthenic reaction. The neurotic reaction, formerly called *neurasthenia,* is characterized by chronic physical and mental fatigue. The individual feels tired most of the time, has difficulty in concentrating, and lacks the vigor required to carry activities through to successful completion. Even minor tasks seem to require a herculean effort. Although he may sleep a great deal, he typically feels "just rotten," and usually suffers as well from various somatic symptoms such as dizzy spells, stomach upset, hypersensitivity to noise, and palpitation of the heart. Often he is quite concerned about his health and physical condition and may have numerous medical examinations in an effort to find some somatic basis for his difficulties. In an actual asthenic reaction, however, the symptoms are the result of sustained tension and frustration of emotional needs.

The following excerpts are taken from an interview with a middle-aged married woman who felt with good reason that her husband no longer cared for her. Often he failed to come home for several days at a time and when home showed no interest or affection for her. The woman had no occupational skills and felt completely dependent upon her husband for support as well as for the meeting of her affectional needs.

Housewife: *Everything seems like such an effort . . . like I had an anchor tied to me or something. I no longer care to play cards or even talk to people any more. . . . Even the*

FACTS ABOUT SUICIDE

A great deal of recent attention has focused on the problem of suicide, which now ranks third among causes of death for those of student age. Each year over 200,000 suicide attempts are made in the United States, of which some 25,000 or more are successful. About three times as many males as females kill themselves. All the causes of suicides are not fully understood; they undoubtedly vary greatly. Most often they seem to be associated with feelings of inadequacy, hopelessness, and depression.

One major attempt to reduce suicides has been the establishment of Suicide Prevention Centers. These agencies encourage people contemplating suicide to call them and discuss their difficulties before attempting suicide.

The Directors of the Los Angeles Suicide Prevention Center have stressed that there are certain warning signs by which others can recognize the danger. The following generalizations are based on analysis of thousands of cases (Bell, 1967, p. 33):

"1. Some people who talk about suicide do commit suicide. Eight of 10 suicides give definite warnings. Suicide threats must be taken seriously.

2. Suicide does not happen impulsively. Studies show that the suicidal person gives many clues to his intentions, often over a long period of time.

3. Suicidal people are not fully intent on dying. It is wrong to say 'Why bother because we can't stop them anyway?' Most suicidal people are undecided about living, and any suicide attempt is usually also a cry for help to save a life.

4. People are not suicidal for life. Hundreds of case histories show that a person brought through a suicidal crisis can go on to live a long and useful life.

5. Improvement does not necessarily mean that the suicidal risk has passed. Many suicides take place in the three months following the beginning of 'improvement.' This is a time to be especially vigilant.

6. Suicide attacks all economic and occupational classes. Suicide is highly 'democratic' and is spread proportionately throughout all levels of society.

7. Suicidal people are not necessarily mentally ill. The suicidal person is extremely unhappy, but this may result from a temporary emotional upset or a complete loss of hope.

8. Suicidal tendencies are not inherited. Suicide is an individual matter and can be prevented."

Based in part also on Farberow & Shneidman, 1961; and Ehrlick, 1967.

---

simplest things are too much for me . . . sometimes I can just barely live . . . I mean just listen to the radio or read or eat . . . I mean just like being in a daze or something . . . I don't know . . . I just feel so horribly tired and sick. Two months ago I felt better than I had been . . .
Therapist: *Two months ago you felt better?*
Housewife: *Well yes . . . you see my husband's brother came to visit us . . . and he would talk to me and he had such a way of diverting me and he was very interesting, and you'd be amazed, within a few minutes or a few hours I'd be just different . . . and he took me to several shows and to the dance. I felt so much better and I had a really good time. So I can see it isn't sleeping or eating. I mean . . . I need someone who'd give me something different to think about . . . someone who'd show you some affection . . . enough interest in you so that you would improve. But my husband . . . well I just can't*

understand how he can treat a woman who is ill . . . and trying her best . . . well (tears) . . . I have just sort of withdrawn . . . he has really made me sick . . .

The asthenic reaction is similar in many respects to acute situational maladjustment. In both instances the individual finds himself in a stressful situation which is seriously frustrating and from which he sees no way out. However, the asthenic reaction usually involves a person who is immature, inadequate, self-pitying, and demanding. In the face of a situation which most people could find constructive ways to cope with, such an individual experiences sustained emotional frustration and tension, leading to chronic fatigue, dejection, and loss of hope.

Neurotic depressive reaction. Neurotic depressive reactions typically occur in response to situations that normally produce grief or depression, such as a death in the family, a severe financial reverse, a chronic illness, or the loss of social status. The neurotic depressive reaction differs from normal grief and sadness in two key ways: (1) It is disproportionate to the stress situation in intensity and duration, and (2) it occurs in an individual with certain predisposing personality traits—such as an immature but rigid conscience and a tendency to blame himself for setbacks. In most essential respects, the personality make-up of the neurotic depressive is comparable to that typically found among obsessive-compulsive neurotics.

Symptoms of depressive reaction commonly include sadness, listlessness, loss of appetite, fatigue, inability to concentrate, feelings of unworthiness, and vague tension and anxiety. Although the individual may have thoughts of committing suicide and may even do so, the danger of suicide is not usually as great as in the psychotic depressive reaction, which we will describe shortly. The depressive reaction may last for weeks or even months but eventually clears up with or without treatment.

In summary, it may be emphasized that there is a wide range of kinds and degrees of neurotic reactions, and that such clear-cut patterns as those we have described are not common. It is also apparent that there is no personality type associated with neuroses in general, although certain patterns of immaturity and inadequacy are associated with particular neurotic patterns. Finally, it may be emphasized again that the individual who behaves in such seemingly irrational and self-defeating ways is not doing so deliberately. Neurotic reactions are learned means of coping with stress and often involve the exaggerated use of various ego-defense mechanisms. Since they are not fully effective in coping with the stress, neurotic reactions tend also to be characterized by some degree of personality decompensation. Despite the ineffectiveness and often inconvenience and suffering involved in neurotic reactions, the neurotic clings to them because they help to protect him from anxiety and painful self-devaluation and hence are continually reinforced.

Psychotic Disorders

In psychotic disorders there are such severe disturbances in thinking, feeling, and behavior that the individual's contact with reality is seriously impaired, and hospitalization is usually necessary. The term *insanity* is sometimes used in referring to psychotic disorders, but this is a legal term rather than a clinical one, indicating that the individual is unable to manage his affairs, perform his social responsibilities, or be held accountable for his actions.

Psychoses associated with demonstrable brain damage are called *organic psychoses;* those without apparent brain pathology are called *functional psychoses*. It is still a moot question whether brain pathology will eventually be found in all psychoses. Abnormal brain chemistry has been found in some cases of functional psychoses, but it has not yet been established whether such biochemical abnormalities are causes, concomitants, or results of the psychosis.

Psychotic reactions may appear suddenly or emerge over a long period of time. They may be of brief or long-term duration. There are an estimated million or more persons in the United States suffering from psychoses, of whom about half are in institutions. Although there is an increasing trend toward treating psychoses—particularly functional psychoses—in the home and community setting, about 1 person in 12 is likely to enter a mental hospital if present trends continue (Eiduson, 1968).

Although several distinctive psychotic syndromes have been delineated, most psychotic persons share the following characteristics:

1. *Personality disorganization*. Psychotics show serious personality disorganization, though the degree varies greatly from one case to another and in the same case from time to time. There is a marked impairment of contact with reality, which may show itself in disorientation for time, place, and person. The person may know he is in a hospital but not realize why. Often the disorganization and lowering of cortical controls

bring inappropriate behavior—for example, profane language, indiscriminate sexual overtures, or physical or verbal attacks.

2. *Delusions.* Delusions are false beliefs that the patient defends despite their logical absurdity and all contrary evidence. There are several kinds of delusions, most frequent of which are:

> Delusions of guilt about having committed some unforgivable sin
>
> Hypochondriacal delusions about having some horrible disease
>
> Delusions of persecution, in which enemies are plotting against the individual, talking about him, or influencing him in some way
>
> Delusions of grandeur, in which the individual thinks he is some important and remarkable person, perhaps a great leader who has been appointed to save the world from destruction

These delusions may be transient and disorganized, or they may be organized into enduring, coherent logical systems.

3. *Hallucinations.* Hallucinations are perceptions of objects, smells, or other sensory phenomena without any appropriate sensory stimulation. The most common hallucinations are auditory ones, but other sensory modes are commonly involved. The patient may taste poison in his food, smell poison gas that his enemies are using to try to kill him, or feel small bugs running around under his skin. Not all psychotics have hallucinations, of course, and the same person may have hallucinations at one time but not at another.

4. *Emotional disturbance.* Some psychotic individuals become apathetic and emotionally unresponsive. Others show extremes of emotion, becoming unduly elated and euphoric or severely depressed without apparent external reason. In still other cases, emotional responses are distorted and inappropriate to the situation, as when the person laughs when informed that his son has been killed or his wife has died.

These symptoms may have either a psychological or a physiological origin. For example, a delusion may result from drug intoxication or from the exaggeration of an ego defense such as projection. Often both psychological and organic factors are involved. Unlike neurotics, who are usually aware of the abnormal nature of their symptoms, psychotics commonly fail to view their experiences and behavior as out of the ordinary.

For present purposes, we will briefly review four commonly distinguished types of functional psychoses—schizophrenic reactions, paranoid reactions, manic-depressive reactions, and involutional reactions; then we will comment briefly on psychosis associated with known brain pathology.

Schizophrenic reactions. The term *schizophrenia* refers to a split between thought and emotion and a general loss of contact with reality. The disorder affects about 1 person in 100 and is the most common of the psychoses. It accounts for about a fifth of all first admissions to mental hospitals and almost a third of readmissions. Since a considerable number of schizophrenics require prolonged hospitalization, they constitute about half of the resident mental hospital population at any given time. The sex ratio is about equal; the average age of first admission is about 34 years. Although the disorder typically occurs between late adolescence and the early fifties, it may occur in childhood or later life. Schizophrenic reactions occur in all societies. In our own society, they are most prevalent on lower socioeconomic levels.

Schizophrenic reactions usually develop gradually over a period of several years. The full-blown reaction is characterized by withdrawal from reality, delusions and hallucinations, emotional blunting and distortion, disorganization of mental processes, deterioration of personal habits and ethical controls, and peculiarities of gesture or speech.

Although symptoms are not always clear-cut, there are four main subtypes of schizophrenia, each seeming to involve a different strategy for coping with conflict and anxiety. In *simple schizophrenia* the individual solves his problem by withdrawing and insulating himself from life. He simply gives

COMMON SYMPTOMS IN MENTAL DISORDERS

SYMPTOMS REFLECTING THOUGHT DISTURBANCES

amnesia	total or partial loss of memory
phobia	fear which the individual recognizes as irrational
obsession	persistent idea that the individual considers irrational but cannot get out of his mind
compulsion	compelling impulse to perform some act even though the individual considers it irrational
delusion	false belief held despite contrary objective evidence
hallucination	false perception unwarranted by external stimuli; most often auditory
disorientation	inability to identify time, place, or person accurately

SYMPTOMS REFLECTING EMOTIONAL DISTURBANCES

pathological anxiety	anxiety out of all proportion to any realistic danger or threat
euphoria	exaggerated and irrational feeling of elation and well-being
depression	irrational state of dejection, with lowered initiative and gloomy thoughts
apathy	lack of feeling or interest in situations that normally evoke such reactions
pathological guilt	exaggerated guilt feelings out of all proportion to one's actual or imagined mis-doings.

SYMPTOMS REFLECTING DISTURBANCES IN MOTIVATION AND VALUES

anomie	a feeling of not really belonging or having any place in society
impulsivity	inability to restrain impulse; action without reflection
delinquency	antisocial or illegal behavior by a minor
crime	antisocial, illegal behavior
perversion	socially condemned deviation from ordinary conduct, especially in sexual behavior
immorality	behavior that violates accepted standards of right and wrong

SYMPTOMS REFLECTING DISTURBANCES IN PHYSIOLOGICAL PROCESSES

anesthesia	loss of sensitivity
hypesthesia	partial loss of sensitivity
hyperesthesia	excessive sensitivity
paraesthesia	unusual or inappropriate sensation
paralysis	loss or impairment of movement
tic	intermittent twitching or jerking of specific muscles
tremor	shaking or trembling
psychomotor retardation	slowing down of thought and movement
psychomotor excitement	rapidly shifting thought processes and overactivity

A variety of symptoms may, of course, be shown in a particular disorder.

up caring or trying to achieve anything. In *hebephrenic schizophrenia* withdrawal and decompensation reach their ultimate, and silliness, fragmentation of thought processes, delusions, and hallucinations attest to the complete disintegration of the personality. In *catatonic schizophrenia* the individual seems to be still struggling desperately to save himself. He typically alternates between periods of excited activity and periods of stupor, during which he may maintain odd postures and follow stereotyped ritualistic patterns. In *paranoid schizophrenia* the individual tries to maintain his feelings of adequacy by blaming his difficulties on others. He may assert that his impure thoughts have been elicited by others who control his mind with electronic devices, or that his failures are due to enemies who are plotting against him. But his delusions are poorly systematized and do not protect him from further self-devaluation and decompensation. This is the most common type of schizophrenia in our society. Interestingly, however, Carothers (1959) found that among rural Africans the hebephrenic type was most prevalent, with the paranoid type relatively rare.

Agreement has not been reached as to the causes of schizophrenia. A number of biological, psychological, and sociocultural factors have been implicated. Genetic factors are suggested in the fact that there is a much greater frequency of schizophrenia among the relatives of schizophrenics than among the general population and that the incidence increases with degree of genetic relatedness (Kallmann, 1953, 1958).

Relationship to schizophrenic patient	Per cent who develop schizophrenia
Identical twin (same genetic make-up)	86.2
Fraternal twin (same genetic relatedness as siblings)	14.5
Siblings	14.2
Half-siblings	7.1
General population	0.85

In a more recent and extensive study in Norway, however, Kringlen (1967) found less than 40 per cent concordance for identical twins and only 10 per cent for fraternal twins. Interestingly enough, in both identical and fraternal twins, the schizophrenic twin had been most often the lonely, submissive, reserved, dependent, and obsessive one as they were growing up.

Despite differences in the magnitude of the preceding findings, they both suggest that genetic factors may predispose certain individuals to the development of schizophrenic reactions under excessive stress. Under favorable life conditions, however, a psychotic breakdown would presumably not occur.

A great deal of research has been devoted to possible biochemical factors in schizophrenia. Much excitement was caused by the findings of Heath and his associates (1958) who injected taraxein, a substance obtained from the blood of schizophrenic patients, into the blood of two volunteer convicts from Louisiana State Prison. One subject developed a temporary catatonic reaction and the other a temporary paranoid reaction. Similar findings have been made in follow-up studies by these same investigators (Heath *et al.,* 1967) though other investigators have been unable to confirm their findings. Nevertheless, many investigators are convinced that the delusions, hallucinations, and other symptoms in schizophrenia are caused by a toxic substance in the blood of the patient which disturbs the functioning of the brain.

Many studies of psychological factors have shown that schizophrenic patients have been exposed to pathological family patterns, with training in faulty attitudes and response patterns and a general failure in socialization. Mothers of male schizophrenics have often been found to be rejecting, dominating, cold, overprotective, impervious to the feelings and needs of others; often they have been dependent on the son, rather than the father, for emotional satisfaction. Kaufman *et al.* (1960) found that the mothers of 80 schizophrenic children and adolescents almost uniformly showed psychotic-like defensive patterns in dealing with their own problems. Fathers of schizophrenics likewise reveal many pathological characteristics, typically being inadequate in their interpersonal relationships, indifferent, detached, humorless, and prone to the use of deviant defensive patterns in coping with their own problems; often they upset the mother's relationship with the children (Kind, 1967). Sometimes the father rejects his son while being seductive toward his daughter, making it clear that she means more to him than his wife, toward whom he is highly derogatory. This not only creates incestuous conflicts (Fleck, 1960; Fleck *et al.,* 1963) for the daughter but makes it hard for her to use her mother as a model for development as a woman. The mother's own inadequacies, in turn, make it impossible for her to correct the situation.

Studies of the overall interaction patterns in the families of schizophrenics have pointed to many pathological conditions (Mishler and Waxler, 1965). Family members have serious difficulties in relating to each other, and their intercommunications are often confusing and conflicting; they tend to play rigid and stereotyped roles and share in gross distortions of reality. Typically such families are isolated from others and view their own pathological interactions as normal while other people are seen as out of step. The children are thus constantly subjected to training in irrationality, often being caught in "double-bind" situations in which they are both induced to behave in certain ways and then made to feel guilty for doing so. In general, such studies point to pathological relationships between the parents—as well as between the parents and the child—which deprive the child of meaningful emotional relationships either in the family or outside it. A person coming out of such a pathogenic family background is likely to have serious difficulties in his interpersonal relationships and in dealing with typical life stresses even if he does not become psychotic. In fact, Laing (1967) has concluded that all schizophrenics show a disturbed and disturbing family life pattern, and that the schizophren-

ic reaction "is a special strategy that a person invents in order to live in an unlivable situation."

Schizophrenia is a highly complex disorder, as evidenced by differences among schizophrenics in their symptom pictures, personality organization before the disorder, precipitating stresses, defensive maneuvers, degrees of personality decompensation, duration of the disorder, and long-range prognosis. It may in fact be a group of disorders, with multiple and varying causes. It seems clear that biological, psychological, and sociocultural factors operate in varying combinations in different cases.

The prognosis in schizophrenia also varies greatly, but with newer methods of treatment approximately two thirds of such patients can be discharged from mental hospitals within six months, and about 80 to 90 per cent within a year (Yolles, 1967). In many cases, the effective use of drug therapy enables the patient to be treated in an outpatient or day hospital and thus to remain in his family and community setting.

Paranoid reactions. In a paranoid reaction the patient develops a set of delusions but otherwise shows no evidence of serious personality disorganization. Because paranoid individuals seem so normal in other respects, they are often able to avoid being hospitalized. Less than 1 per cent of first admissions to mental hospitals are classified as paranoiacs. Paranoid reactions usually develop during middle adulthood and generally involve persons of higher educational and socioeconomic level than do schizophrenic reactions.

Paranoid delusions are intricate and highly systematized. Usually they center around one theme, such as financial matters, a job, or an unfaithful wife. Typically, delusions of persecution predominate—the individual feels that he is being taken advantage of, lied to, mistreated, plotted against, or otherwise persecuted. Some paranoiacs develop delusions of grandeur, fancying themselves to be someone with an important mission to perform for the benefit of mankind.

Although the "evidence" on which the paranoiac bases his delusions is extremely tenuous, he is firm in maintaining his own interpretation of the facts. He may be convinced of his wife's unfaithfulness because she has suddenly taken to buying perfume guaranteed to make her attractive to men. When he tells his friends about her unfaithfulness and they question his assumptions, he is sure they have turned against him and gone over to his wife's side—have become his enemies. Thus with time, more and more of his world comes to be integrated into his delusional system. Eventually his delusions may lead to his creation of what has been called a "pseudocommunity"—an imaginary organization of persons whose purpose is to carry out some action against him.

Many people, of course, go through life brooding about real and imagined injustices. In the case of paranoid reactions this trend is exaggerated, gradually, into a delusional system with which the individual is intensely preoccupied. Often the behavior of the paranoid involves what is called a "self-fulfilling prophecy." He behaves toward others in such a way as to elicit behavior that confirms his suspicions. For example, his paranoid accusations of infidelity against his wife may lead to a rift in their marriage and to her actually becoming interested in someone else. Interestingly enough, Lemert (1962) found a number of cases in which paranoid individuals actually had been taken advantage of and mistreated prior to any vindictive behavior on their part. But whether the delusional system begins with real or imagined injustices, the eventual picture involves gross distortion of reality.

Personality characteristics that commonly foreshadow paranoid reactions include a high level of aspiration, hypersensitivity to criticism, craving for praise and recognition, an overly critical and aloof attitude toward others, formal adherence to socially approved behavior, and an almost complete lack of a sense of humor. Possibly as a result of his difficulties in adjustment, the paranoid also tends to be suspicious and hostile toward others and to suffer from in-

tense feelings of inferiority. Such characteristics are likely to lead to repeated failures in critical life situations. To defend himself against the anxiety and self-devaluation of chronic failure, he projects the blame for his difficulties to others.

Although paranoiacs are not always dangerous, there is the possibility that they may become desperate and decide to take matters into their own hands. Many people, including wives and husbands falsely accused of infidelity, have been killed by paranoiacs intent on righting the wrongs they feel have been done them. As one might suspect, the prognosis in paranoid reactions is not usually a favorable one.

Manic-depressive reactions. The central characteristic of manic-depressive reactions is an exaggerated elation or depression. Against this background, there are a variety of other symptoms in keeping with the prevailing mood. A person may show only the elated reaction *(manic type)*, only the depressive reaction *(depressive type)*, or an alternation between them *(circular type)* with a cycle of a few minutes to several months. These reactions may occur from early childhood to old age but are most common during middle adulthood. The depressive reaction is the most common type and occurs more frequently among women than among men. Jaco (1960) found manic-depressive disorders distributed fairly evenly among the different socioeconomic levels but more common in urban than rural areas.

In the manic reaction, the patient is elated and expresses feelings of well-being, optimism, and good humor. Initially he may give the impression of being an aggressive, witty, sociable, energetic individual who has many important projects under way. However, it soon becomes apparent that he is highly distractible, monopolizes the conversation, and does not follow through on any of his plans. As the disorder progresses, the clinical picture becomes increasingly exaggerated and the individual shows such symptoms as: (1) psychomotor overactivity—in which he is constantly talking and moving about under a "pressure of activity"; (2) flight of ideas—involving extreme distractibility and rapid shifts of thought; (3) delusions and hallucinations—usually of a transient and grandiose nature in keeping with his elated mood and excited state; (4) impaired judgment and lowered ethical restraints—which may lead to unwise financial investments, promiscuous sexual acts, and other behavior indicative of lowered inner controls. In extreme form, the manic reaction progresses to delirious ideation and disorientation, and the individual rapidly exhausts himself with his incessant activity.

In the depressive reaction the symptoms are essentially the opposite. The individual becomes discouraged and dejected and there is a slowing down of thought and activity. Feelings of failure, unworthiness, and guilt dominate his consciousness. As the disorder progresses, delusions and hallucinations centering around his guilt may be evidenced. He may feel that his unethical thoughts—often relating to immoral sexual behavior and hostility—are as sinful as if they had been carried out in action; and he may even be convinced that he actually *did* commit some horrible deed that he may have had fantasies of committing. He may insist that he is suffering from some horrible disease that gives him a bad odor or complain that his brain is rotting away. Apprehensiveness and anxiety are common, and such individuals often develop ideas of suicide, which they may carry out. In extreme form, the individual may lapse into a depressive stupor with an almost complete lack of response and a dangerous reduction in heart and circulatory action.

As in the case of schizophrenia, manic-depressive reactions show a higher incidence among the relatives of patients than in the population at large. It has also been noted in twin studies that if one twin develops a manic-depressive reaction it is extremely rare for the other to develop a schizophrenic reaction (Kallmann, 1953, 1958). As a consequence, the genetic predisposing factors in manic-depressive reactions are thought to be different from those in schizophrenia.

The possibility of faulty brain chemistry has also undergone considerable investigation. Particularly prominent has been the "catecholamine hypothesis," which relates both elation and depression to the level of catecholamines, particularly norepinephrine, in the blood. So far, the evidence is insufficient to warrant any general conclusions (Schildkraut, 1967).

From a psychological viewpoint, manic reactions appear to be a way of escaping from anxiety-arousing stress by becoming involved in a whirlwind of activities. In lesser degree this is not an uncommon defensive pattern in our society. Many people avoid facing their underlying conflicts and anxieties by keeping busy with an endless round of parties, club meetings, or work duties. In the case of the manic, however, the defensive maneuver gets out of hand. The manic reaction sometimes may also be a defense against depression, which may explain why many manic patients later become depressed. In depressive reactions the patient presumably gives up in defeat and no longer tries to escape from the stress situation. The orgy of self-blame that follows evidently serves two defensive objectives: (1) the self-punishment helps to atone for his "sins" and (2) his admission of complete worthlessness enables him to give up the struggle temporarily and regress to dependence. But these defenses appear to overshoot their mark.

Individuals who show manic-depressive reactions tend to be ambitious, outgoing, energetic, and often highly successful. Typically they hold conventional and somewhat authoritarian attitudes, place high value on what others think of them, and adhere to stereotyped achievement values. They usually evidence relatively rigid conscience development, blaming themselves rather than others when they fail and feeling guilt for hostile or other disapproved feelings and impulses. Often they show a history of exaggerated mood swings—becoming elated and enthusiastic when things go well and dejected and discouraged when they do not (Becker, 1960; Grinker, 1961; Spielberger *et al.,* 1963).

Interestingly enough, among rural Africans in the 1950's, Carothers (1959) found manic reactions common but depressive reactions rare—the exact opposite of their incidence in the U.S. He attributed the low incidence of depressive reactions to the lack of feelings of personal responsibility for failure in that society, the blame being automatically placed on forces outside the individual. If one is not responsible, there is no reason to feel guilt or devaluation, which appear to play a key role in depressive reactions. In a more recent study, Wintrob (1968) also reports a lack of depressive reactions in Liberia, West Africa—apparently as a result of culturally sanctioned ways of alleviating feelings of guilt and worthlessness.

With or without treatment, these disorders tend to run their course and clear up spontaneously; with modern methods of treatment, they can usually be cleared up in a matter of days or at most a few weeks. However, they tend to recur, and a given individual may have several episodes during his lifetime. The danger of suicide is a serious one: prior to the advent of more effective treatment procedures, an estimated 25 per cent of these patients died by their own hands (English & Finch, 1954).

Involutional reactions. An involutional reaction is a psychotic depressive reaction that develops during the "involutional" period—between about 40 and 55 years of age—without a prior history of manic-depressive reactions. Involutional reactions are more common among women than among men. In contrast to the depressed reaction of the manic-depressive, which involves a slowdown of thought and activity, the involutional reaction involves sustained agitation.

Involutional reactions usually begin with restlessness, insomnia, unprovoked spells of weeping, and excessive worry about minor matters. As the reaction becomes more acute, the individual becomes increasingly depressed and apprehensive and develops strong feelings of worthlessness and self-condemnation. He may become preoccupied with some real or imagined sin that he

feels can never be forgiven. He is in utmost despair and feels there is absolutely no hope. In his agitation he may pace the floor, weep, wring his hands, pull his hair, bite his lips, and cry aloud at fate.

Hypochondriacal delusions are common: the individual may insist that his stomach is rotting away or that his brain is being destroyed by some dread disease. Yet despite his depression and anxiety, he may not be disoriented and may realize he needs help.

Involutional reactions are often complicated by the glandular changes which take place during the involutional period in both men and women. These changes are dramatically illustrated in the menopause syndrome in women, characterized by hot flashes, nervous irritability, insomnia, and mild depression. This condition is apparently due to a decrease in ovarian hormone production and can be rapidly corrected by medical treatment. We do not yet know what role if any is played by other biochemical or genetic factors, though it is known that involutional reactions are more frequent among relatives of those who have shown the disorder than among the general population.

The primary emphasis in understanding involutional reactions has been placed upon psychological factors which predispose the individual to such reactions in the face of the severe stresses of this life period. Usually these individuals have a history of being overly conscientious, meticulous, perfectionistic, rigid, narrow in social interests, and compulsive. During the involutional period the individual comes to realize that his youth is over and that he is committed to a life pattern which he finds unsatisfactory, futile, and meaningless—and he places the blame squarely on himself. Although the painful self-recrimination may help him atone for his alleged shortcomings and misdeeds, his life situation remains so stressful that anxiety, depression, and personality decompensation remain. These reactions may have a prolonged course if not treated, but modern methods of treatment are highly effective and most reactions can be cleared up in a matter of days or weeks.

Cross-cultural studies indicate that involutional reactions occur in all societies; although interestingly enough, Carothers (1959) found no guilt in the involutional reactions of rural Africans but only feelings of futility and hopelessness. In our own society these reactions are decreasing in incidence, apparently as a consequence of early treatment before the disorder progresses to its characteristic symptomatology (Rosenthal, 1968).

In concluding our discussion of the functional psychoses, it should be emphasized again that: (1) psychotics often show mixed symptoms and do not fit well into any category, (2) exact symptoms may shift markedly over short-range periods, (3) persons in any given category differ greatly in personality make-up, and (4) the causal picture is unclear, but varying combinations of biological, psychological, and sociocultural factors appear to be involved.

Disorders associated with brain pathology. There are a number of conditions—such as injuries, tumors, infectious diseases, drugs, and the deteriorative changes of old age— which interfere with the functioning of the brain and result in psychological disturbances. Such disturbances may be mild or severe depending upon both the nature and severity of the brain pathology and the personality make-up and life situation of the individual. Disorders associated with brain pathology account for about a fourth of all first admissions to mental hospitals—about the same incidence figure as that for the functional psychoses as a group.

Depending upon the reversibility of the brain pathology, such disorders are often classified as *acute* or *chronic*. An acute disorder—as in drug intoxication—is likely to be temporary and reversible. Here the individual may show such symptoms as coma and stupor or disorientation and delirium, which clear up over a period of hours or days. A chronic disorder—as in syphilis of the brain—involves permanent damage to the nervous system; here the brain pathology is not reversible or only partially so. Where the

brain damage is severe, the symptoms may include a permanent impairment of intellectual functioning, emotional shallowness and instability, and a deterioration in conduct and behavior standards.

The chronic mental disorders associated with old age usually involve either (1) gradual deterioration and atrophy of the brain cells, with a lessening of mental alertness and adaptability, failing comprehension and judgment, and progressive personality deterioration; or (2) hardening of the arteries leading to the brain, with inadequate circulation, faulty nutrition of the brain cells, and in some cases, hemorrhages in the brain, with acute episodes of confusion and incoherence (Busse, 1967). The prognosis among older persons with brain disorders varies greatly. For hospitalized patients, the outcome is likely to be unfavorable unless the individual shows improvement during the first year after admission. The long-term progression of such disorders is in the direction of increasing personality deterioration, leading eventually to a vegetative existence and death.

Again however, personality and situational factors may play an important role. A number of studies have shown that individuals who are handicapped psychologically by undesirable personality traits such as rigidity, suspiciousness, and social inadequacy are much more vulnerable to the psychoses of old age. A mature and well-integrated person can usually cope with brain damage as well as other stress better than a rigid, immature, emotionally disturbed, or otherwise psychologically handicapped person. There are many cases involving relatively severe brain pathology in which behavior disturbances are relatively minor and many cases of mild brain pathology in which the individual becomes psychotic.

Similarly, a very unfavorable life situation may increase the individual's vulnerability. Unfortunately, older members of our society often face especially difficult stresses. In our youth-oriented society, we have little respect or reverence for age. Anyone who has led a busy, productive life finds it hard to be relegated to the sidelines where

PSYCHOSOMATIC REACTIONS

Psychosomatic reactions are classified according to the organ system affected, and no organ system appears to be immune. Among the more common psychosomatic reactions are the following:

1. *Gastrointestinal reactions,* including peptic ulcers, mucous colitis, and chronic gastritis.

2. *Respiratory reactions,* including asthma, bronchial spasms, and recurring bronchitis.

3. *Musculoskeletal reactions,* including backache, rheumatism, and arthritis.

4. *Skin reactions,* including allergic eczema and various so-called neurodermatoses.

5. *Cardiovascular reactions,* including high blood pressure, vascular spasms, and migraine headaches.

High blood pressure, certain arthritic reactions, and migraine headaches tend to be more common among females, while peptic ulcers, bronchial asthma, and eczema tend to be more common among males.

Based in part on Coleman, 1964; Lipton, 1966; and Treisman, 1968.

---

no one needs him or asks his advice. The death of a life partner and a narrowing circle of friends may lead to loneliness and loss of meaning. Chronic poor health may erode a previously cheerful outlook. And for most older people, an inadequate income is a reality.

During the past decade society has become increasingly aware of the problems confronting our senior citizens and has taken measures, such as Medicare, to reduce the stresses on older people. But although society can do much to improve the status of the older person, the individual can also do much to prepare himself for the problems typical of old age—to plan ahead for an active and useful life in his later years.

Psychophysiologic (Psychosomatic) Reactions

Emergency emotional reactions involve widespread changes in circulation, respiration, and other bodily processes. Normally such emotion-induced changes are short-lived, and our physiological activities return to normal levels. Sometimes, however, emotion-arousing stress situations continue over sustained periods of time—as with a soldier in combat, a person who hates his work, or a person in a conflictful and unhappy marriage. Over a period of time, such a chronic acceleration of physiological activ-

ities may lead to actual tissue damage in some bodily system—as in peptic ulcers. Such disorders are called *psychosomatic* or *psychophysiologic* disorders. There are an estimated 20 million or more persons in the United States suffering from such afflictions.

Some of the more commonly observed patterns of psychosomatic disorders are summarized in the chart. It should be emphasized, of course, that factors other than chronic emotion also may lead to physiological malfunction and subsequent damage or breakdown. For example, high blood pressure may be due primarily to physical disease, to chronic emotion-arousing stress, or to a combination of the two. As in the case of other faulty stress reactions, these disorders may be mild or severe.

Why one organ system rather than another is affected is not known. It may be that the one affected is constitutionally weak or has been made especially vulnerable by prior illness. A person who has had a serious respiratory infection, for example, may thereafter be especially prone to bronchial attacks or similar respiratory disorders when he is under emotional tension. Another partial explanation why one or another organ is affected may be that different emotional states have differing effects on visceral activity—for example, the physiological changes accompanying hostility and resentment are somewhat different from those accompanying fear.

It would appear that highly driven individuals who tend to react to any threat to their goals with anxiety and hostility—but suppress or repress their emotion instead of expressing it—seem prone to sustained emotional reactions and hence to psychophysiologic disorders. Within this general pattern, however, attempts to delineate more specific personality characteristics associated with peptic ulcers, eczema, and other psychophysiological reactions have not yielded definitive findings. For example, Mordkoff and Parsons (1968) have pointed out that there is little research evidence to support the concept of a "coronary personality"—someone especially prone to heart attacks. Wide differences in personality make-up have been found associated with the various types of psychosomatic reactions.

Situational factors have also come under scrutiny in psychosomatic disorders. For example, Wall Street and Madison Avenue have been referred to as "Ulcer Alley," because the particular stresses of these competitive, high-pressure settings seem conducive to the development of peptic ulcers. It would appear that the different occupational settings have somewhat characteristic stresses and psychosomatic hazards. But again a combination of factors is involved, for only a limited number of persons in such settings develop psychosomatic disorders.

Although most psychophysiologic disorders do not greatly interfere with the individual's ability to make adjustments in most areas of living, they are costly answers to stress. They often cause irreversible tissue damage and, as in severe cases of bleeding ulcers, occasionally result in death. Since they are the end result of emotional stress, medical treatment alone is usually not sufficient; often both psychotherapy and sociotherapy are also required for effective treatment.

Character (Personality) Disorders

The disorders lumped together as character disorders have little in common except that they seem to represent distorted personality development rather than decompensation under stress. Also they tend to involve a direct *acting out* rather than the indirect defense of the self seen in the various symptoms of the neurotic or psychotic. Individuals in this category experience little or no anxiety or sense of distress. Nor do they usually show symptoms of personality disorganization. Rather their disorder is manifested in deviant action, usually starting early in their development.

We shall restrict our present discussion to three of the more common reaction types included in the category of character disorders—antisocial (psychopathic) reaction, dyssocial reaction, and sexual deviation.

COMPULSIVE GAMBLING

There are an estimated 6 to 10 million compulsive gamblers in the United States who lose some $20 billion or more each year. Unlike persons who enjoy betting at the races occasionally or playing poker for small stakes, they are unable to stop gambling—often believing, despite continual and heavy losses, that they can become rich by gambling. In the process, they may use up their families' savings, go heavily into debt, and even embezzle in order to continue their gambling.

Limited studies of such persons indicate that

they usually are immature and unconventional, dislike regulations, and are prone to acting out their impulses. Typically, they see themselves as businessmen taking calculated risks. Often recrimination by family and friends leads to an intensification of their gambling as they try to vindicate themselves.

The effectiveness of psychotherapy with such persons has not been systematically studied. An organization which may be of help is Gamblers Anonymous, which is similar in many ways to Alcoholics Anonymous.

Based in part on Berry, 1968; Bolen & Boyd, 1968; and Rosten, 1961.

TRAITS ASSOCIATED WITH ANTISOCIAL PERSONALITY

The following traits are considered indicative of antisocial (psychopathic) personality although not all of them are necessarily found in a given case.

1. *Amoral, unreliable, irresponsible.* Often a marked discrepancy between intellectual level and conscience development. May deceive others by verbal endorsement of high standards, but does not understand or adhere to accepted moral values. Pathological lying, deceitfulness, and a callous disregard for the rights of others.

2. *Impulsive, hedonistic, unrealistic goals.* Prone to thrill-seeking, deviant sexual patterns, and unconventional behavior. Lives in present with primary concern for immediate pleasures and no long-range goals. Shows poor judgment and often engages in impulsive acts detrimental to his own well-being as well as that of others. Dislikes routine work and frequently changes jobs, moves from place to place, lives by his wits, or depends on others for support.

3. *Ability to impress and exploit others.* Often a charming individual with a good sense of humor and a generally optimistic outlook. Easily wins the liking and friendship of others but ruthlessly exploits the interpersonal relationships he develops. Often shows contempt for those he is able to take advantage of—the "marks." Unable to give or receive love.

4. *Lack of anxiety and guilt.* Tends to act out tensions rather than worry them out. Cynical, unsympathetic, and remorseless in his dealings with others, with little or no sense of guilt. Lack of anxiety combined with seeming sincerity often enables psychopath to lie his way out of difficulties. Undeterred by punishment.

5. *Disappointing and distressing to others.* Frequently a burden on friends and relatives. Unstable and disappointing in marital relationships. Often has history of difficulty with law enforcement agencies but not a calculating professional criminal.

Antisocial (psychopathic) reaction. One of the most baffling disorders is that in which an individual who otherwise seems normal is lacking in conscience development and in any feeling of warmth for or loyalty to other people. In this category we find unprincipled businessmen, confidence men, impostors, crooked politicians, prostitutes, and assorted delinquents and criminals. This reaction type is believed to be much more common among males than among females.

The dynamics in antisocial reactions are not fully understood and undoubtedly differ markedly from one case to another. There is some evidence that these individuals do not show normal fear and anxiety reactions or learn readily from punishment or noxious stimuli because of some constitutional peculiarity or malfunctioning of the autonomic system (Eysenck, 1960). Physiologically, such individuals would seem to be at the other end of the continuum from anxiety neurotics, who appear to be overly sensitive and to suffer from a surplus of conditioned

fears and anxieties. However, this possibility requires further investigation.

In many cases the primary determinants appear to lie in early sociocultural deprivation, with a lack of warm interpersonal relationships and other normal socializing experiences. We have examined the effects of such conditions in Chapter 4. In some cases, antisocial personalities come from families that are respected in the community and appear to provide a desirable environment for the child but actually provide a pathological family atmosphere in which the child is denied normal affection and lacks adequate models for ethical development. By precept and example, such parents often emphasize the importance of appearances rather than values and may encourage the development of personal charm and poise as tools for manipulating others. Children coming from such homes often feel rejected, hostile toward all authority, and prone to acting out their aggressive impulses without considering the rights of others or even their own long-range needs (Bandura & Walters, 1959; 1963).

Although the prognosis for antisocial reactions varies greatly from one case to another, it is generally considered unfavorable —in part due to our lack of adequate treatment or retraining facilities. With or without treatment, however, there appears to be a tendency for the reactions to be ameliorated with age. This is probably due in part to exposure to various socializing influences and in part to the individual's eventual realization that his behavior is self-defeating.

Dyssocial reaction. A child who grows up in the home of a professional criminal or in a slum area where antisocial attitudes are common may develop a personality that is fairly mature and well integrated but is built around values that the larger society regards as undesirable. Many delinquents and criminals fall in this category.

Unlike the antisocial personality, who is loyal to no one, the dyssocial personality is capable of strong loyalty to his group. He often shows courage, responsibility, imagination, and other desirable traits but unfortunately uses these assets to achieve socially undesirable goals. Since the dyssocial personality shows relatively strong conscience development and good inner control, he is not as impulsive, irrational, or self-defeating

as the antisocial personality. In addition, the dyssocial personality gains some measure of strength from his membership in and adherence to the predatory group. Although such individuals may show personality decompensation under the stresses typical of their way of life, their training in "toughness" and emotional insulation often results in high stress tolerance.

The long-term outcome in such cases again depends upon many factors. Since most of these individuals are eventually apprehended by the police and sentenced to time in penal institutions, the availability and quality of rehabilitative facilities in our jails and prisons can be of great importance—as can the type of life that is available to them upon their return to the community.

Sexual deviation. A sexual deviation is a method of achieving sexual satisfaction which is considered undesirable by society and for which there may be criminal penalties. Little is actually known about the incidence of sexual deviation since such behavior rarely takes place in public, and our sexual taboos make many people reluctant to discuss their sexual behavior even when they have been victims of sex crimes.

Sexual behavior may deviate from the normal with respect to: (1) intensity and frequency of drive and gratification—as in im-

DELINQUENCY AND CRIME

The incidence of delinquency and crime in the United States has shown a marked increase during the last decade, especially among teen-agers and young adults. In 1967 an estimated 3.75 million serious crimes were reported to law enforcement agencies; of these, almost half a million were crimes involving violence—murder, rape, robbery, and aggravated assault. Most of these crimes were committed by young males. If present trends continue, it has been estimated that at least 40 per cent of our male children will be arrested at some time in their lives for

nontraffic violations; for boys living in cities, the figure is closer to 60 per cent.

The causes of crime are both complex and diverse, and we shall not attempt to summarize them here. However, it may be noted that although antisocial and dyssocial personalities contribute their share of people who commit crimes, many criminal acts do not involve such personalities. Peer-group pressures, mental disorders, addiction to alcohol and drugs, social disorganization, and a wide range of family and community factors may be involved.

Based in part on Ennis, 1967; Federal Bureau of Investigation, 1968; Harms, 1967; and Short, 1966.

potence and nymphomania, (2) choice of sex object—as in homosexuality and incest, (3) mode of gratification—as in exhibitionism and peeping, and (4) context in which sexual behavior occurs—as in prostitution and rape. The most common deviations fall in the last three categories—relating to object, mode, and context. Although the specific factors that result in sexually deviate behavior vary greatly from one case to another, they all tend to involve some degree of faulty learning; many also reflect lowered inner controls associated with general personality decompensation or mental disorder.

There are many types of sexually deviate behavior. Four of the most common will be described briefly here.

1. *Exhibitionism.* Some deviates achieve sexual gratification by exposing their genitals in public or semipublic places, usually to members of the opposite sex or to children; sometimes the demonstrations are accompanied by suggestive gestures or masturbatory activity. The exhibitionist is eager for signs that his victim is impressed or shocked and is let down if his demonstration does not produce this effect. Typically, he is a quiet, submissive, "nice" young man who feels inadequate in personal and sexual relationships, has a very puritanical attitude toward the evils of sex, and has inadequate sex knowledge. Often he has serious doubts about his masculinity and is using this relatively safe way of proving himself. In most instances, exhibitionists respond quite well to treatment.

2. *Pedophilia.* In pedophilia the sex object is a child. Because of the possible damage to the child through manipulation, penetration, or other sexual abuse, pedophilia is a serious offense. Pedophiliacs are a diverse group in age and cultural background; most of the older ones are married, and many have children of their own. On the surface they are self-assertive and aggressive, and they often use force to carry out their sexual acts. They tend to be either (1) individuals who feel inadequate and inferior and focus their attention on children to avoid possible failure and self-devaluation in normal adult

relationships; (2) older men with fears about their potency, who have a basically psychopathic make-up; or (3) mentally ill individuals whose ethical restraints have been lowered by their mental disorder.

3. *Rape.* In some cases rape is attempted or committed by psychotics, but usually a rapist is a psychopathic personality who has failed to develop normal ethical controls and who has strong aggressive and hostile tendencies. He often has a record of other kinds of antisocial actions; sexual assault, for him, is just one of many ways of expressing hostility. Instead of money, he takes sexual satisfaction. Most rapists are in their twenties; about half are married and living with their wives.

A rapist usually shows no esthetic preference in his choice of victims and may simply decide to rape the first woman he can, regardless of her age or appearance. He may seriously injure or even kill his victim if she struggles against him.

4. *Homosexuality.* This category of deviation includes various types of sexual relationships between members of the same sex. Our society condemns such behavior, but it has existed throughout man's recorded history and has even been regarded favorably in some cultures. In fact, England has recently enacted legislation making it legal for adult males to engage in such behavior by mutual consent.

There is little information concerning homosexual behavior in our society. According to the early study by Kinsey *et al.* (1948), 4 per cent of American men were exclusively homosexual, 18 per cent revealed as much homosexual as heterosexual behavior in their histories, and about half of the male population had at one time had some homosexual experience. Whether these figures hold today is an open question. The incidence of homosexuality is considered to be much higher among males than among females, but here, too, there is a dearth of specific information.

In the past, considerable emphasis has been placed on the supposed femininity of homosexual men and masculinity of homosexual women, but such patterns are now considered the exception rather than the rule. It may be that constitutional factors can predispose an individual toward homosexuality, but such factors have not been demonstrated. Nor does endocrine balance seem to be the key. Some homosexuals reveal an endocrine imbalance, but so do some heterosexuals, and many homosexuals show no imbalance. The same individual may shift from one pattern of behavior to the other without apparent change in endocrine functioning, and treatment with sex hormones does not ordinarily influence the direction of sexual behavior. In general, homosexual tendencies seem more related to early experiences—early enjoyed homosexual seduction or a home situation in which the child has for some reason learned the wrong sex role. The latter can happen, for example, when a girl is brought up like a boy because the parents wanted a boy, or when there is an overly strong identification with the parent of the opposite sex (Bieber *et al.,* 1962; Apperson & McAdoo, 1968).

A study by Hooker (1962) on the "homosexual community" has shown that there tend to be clusters of homosexuals in certain residential areas of large cities, and that ho-

mosexuals as a group have established their own subculture with customs, value systems, and communication techniques in terms of language, dress, and gesture. Where the homosexual has become affiliated with an organized homosexual group, there is a tendency for him to think of his problem as a subgroup problem and therefore a social rather than an individual problem. In such cases, the individual may consider his homosexual behavior a normal pattern and even consider himself "emancipated" from conventional heterosexual morality. However, as a consequence of society's disapproval, it is usually difficult for homosexuals to make adequate occupational, sexual, and general social adjustments.

Alcoholism and Drug Addiction

Although many aspects of alcoholism and drug addiction are not yet fully understood, these reactions represent two more ways in which an individual who feels threatened and inadequate may respond. They are generally classified as character disorders but will be discussed separately here because of their seriousness in our society.

COMMON BACKGROUND FACTORS IN SEXUAL DEVIATIONS

Despite wide variations from case to case, the following conditions are commonly associated with sexual deviations:

1. *Faulty learning and differentiation.* Normal adult heterosexuality is the end result of a long process of development, and the sexual patterns reached in adulthood depend upon the individual's experience and learning. Homosexuality, for example, may result primarily from early seduction and training in homosexual patterns, while impotence and frigidity may result from a long process of aversive conditioning concerning the evils of sex.

2. *Prolonged heterosexual frustration.* Sexual deprivation is often difficult to withstand and may promote deviant sexual practices designed to reduce

sexual tensions and yield some measure of gratification. In prisons and other institutions where the sexes are segregated, for example, the incidence of homosexual behavior is usually much higher than in normal life situations (Huffman, 1960).

3. *Lowered controls associated with mental disorders.* Many serious sexual offenses involve individuals suffering from general personality decompensation. In an early study of 300 convicted sexual offenders in New Jersey, Brancale, Ellis, & Doorbar (1952) found only 14 per cent to be psychologically "normal"; the remaining 86 per cent were classified as either neurotic, pre-psychotic, psychotic, brain-damaged, psychopathic, or mentally retarded.

PSYCHOTIC REACTIONS ASSOCIATED WITH EXCESSIVE DRINKING

Chronic alcoholics may in time develop one of the following psychotic reactions:

1. *Pathological intoxication*—a condition in which a person with low tolerance for alcohol, perhaps because of exhaustion or emotional stress, overreacts to even a moderate amount and may become hallucinated, disoriented, and violent. In this case, the alcohol only touches off the reaction and is not the primary cause.

2. *Delirium tremens*—a reaction of disorientation, tremors, hallucinations, and intense fear. It occurs in the long-time excessive drinker largely as a result of dietary deficiency and metabolic upset and can usually be cleared up by massive doses of vitamins and a better diet.

3. *Chronic alcoholic deterioration*—an overall personality deterioration that may come with habitual excessive drinking and the disorganization of the individual's whole life pattern that this eventually involves.

Alcoholics now constitute about 12 per cent of all first admissions to mental hospitals.

Alcoholism. Contrary to popular belief, alcohol is not a stimulant but a depressant that numbs the higher brain centers and thus lessens their inhibiting control. Aside from this release, which may lead him to say or do things he would normally inhibit, the drinker may find that drinking gives him a sense of well-being in which unpleasant realities are minimized and his sense of adequacy is increased. When the alcohol content of the blood reaches 0.1 per cent, visual-motor and thought processes are impaired and the individual is assumed to be intoxicated. When the alcoholic content reaches 0.5 per cent, the neurophysiological balance is seriously disturbed and the individual "passes out."

It is estimated that 5 to 6½ million Americans drink excessively (Irwin, 1968). About three fourths are classified as *symptomatic drinkers,* or *controlled drinkers.* Although these individuals drink too much, they still manage to maintain some control over their consumption and to carry on their work. The others are the "alcohol addicts" and are called *chronic alcoholics* or simply *alcoholics.* They have lost control over their drinking, usually after a period of excessive drinking. Although alcoholism is considered more prevalent among men than among women, the actual incidence is difficult to estimate since women who do not work can often conceal their alcoholism.

In recent years the problem of alcoholics also addicted to tranquilizers, stimulant drugs, or barbiturates has increased greatly. Whereas most alcoholics over 50 are addicted only to alcohol, pure alcoholism is rarely found among alcoholics under 30 (*Science News,* 1968b). People under the influence of alcohol are more affected by a given dosage of these drugs and more easily addicted to them.

The dynamics of alcoholism are not fully understood but a number of biological, psychological, and sociocultural factors have been emphasized. On a biological level, attention has focused around the possibility of constitutional sensitivity or vulnerability to alcohol. Some individuals seem to have a much lower tolerance to alcohol than others —in terms of the amount required for intoxication—and may be more prone to physiological addiction.

A limited number of studies have dealt with the pre-alcoholic personality traits of alcoholics—traits shown before they became alcoholics. These studies have found a characteristic cluster of traits: impulsivity, rebelliousness, underlying dependency, overplaying of the masculine role, and a tendency to rely on denial as a defense mechanism (Jones, 1968; McCord & McCord, 1962).

Alcoholics, as a group, show somewhat similar characteristics: low frustration tolerance, inability to endure tension, a tendency to "act out" conflicts, and feelings of inadequacy and self-devaluation. Many alcoholics appear to be immature, dependent individuals who have an unrealistically high level of aspiration and an inability to tolerate failure. Although apparently sociable and outgoing, they often have deep problems in interpersonal relationships—frequently harboring a good deal of resentment and hostility toward the people closest to them. Sooner or later—often during adolescence and young adulthood—they begin to use alcohol for the temporary alleviation of their insecurities, anxieties, and tensions. Eventually the crutch becomes a master over which they have little or no control: once they start drinking, it usually leads to prolonged intoxication.

Sociocultural factors, such as family, peer group, and religious attitudes toward drinking may also enter into the etiological picture. Some ethnic, religious, and national groups have a much higher incidence of alcoholism than others. For example, the incidence of alcoholism is low among the Jews, Mormons, and Moslems whose religious values prohibit or severely limit the use of alcohol.

Although relatively effective methods for the treatment of alcoholism do exist, they are usually ineffective unless the alcoholic wants to be cured. Often this does not occur until he has suffered serious disturbances in his overall life situation—with his marriage, friends, employer, and often the police. An organization which has been of great help in coping with alcoholism is Alcoholics Anonymous; a related organization, Al-Anon, has proven helpful in assisting the family and friends of alcoholics.

Drug addiction. Drug use and addiction is an extremely complex problem and we cannot deal with it exhaustively in our present discussion. By way of introduction, however, it is of interest to note that the use of various mind-altering drugs has long fol-

STAGES OF ADDICTION TO ALCOHOL

INITIAL PHASE

The social drinker turns increasingly to alcohol for relief of tension, present or anticipated. Toward the end of this period, there are four warning signs of approaching alcoholism:

1. *Increasing consumption*—gradual or rapid. The individual may begin to worry about his drinking at this point.
2. *Morning drinking*—to reduce hangovers or get him through the day.
3. *Extreme behavior*—commission of various acts that leave the individual feeling guilty and embarrassed later.
4. *"Blackouts"*—the individual cannot remember what happened during his drinking. Not usually frequent until excessive drinking has continued for some time.

CRUCIAL PHASE

The individual loses control over his drinking: one drink seems to start a chain reaction, although he can still partially control the occasions when he will or will not take the first drink. In this phase, he frequently begins to rationalize and make alibis for his drinking and often encounters reproof from family and friends.

CHRONIC PHASE

The individual's control over his drinking completely breaks down and alcohol plays an increasingly dominant role in his life. At the same time, his physiological tolerance for alcohol decreases, and he now becomes intoxicated from far less alcohol than previously. He also begins to experience tremors and other symptoms while he is sober, leading to drinking to control such symptoms. During this period, his life situation usually undergoes serious deterioration and he becomes increasingly susceptible to alcoholic psychosis.

KINDS OF DRUGS

Drugs in use today can be classified in five somewhat overlapping categories, according to their effects (Jarvik, 1967):

Psychotherapeutics, including anti-psychotic, anti-anxiety, and anti-depressant drugs. Used in treatment of anxiety and mental disorders.

Psychotogenics, including LSD, mescaline, and others. Produce major changes in mood, thinking, and behavior. May lead to psychotic-like states.

Stimulants, such as amphetamine. Used to elevate mood, increase alertness and confidence, and alleviate feelings of fatigue.

Sedatives, such as the barbiturates. Have a calming effect and are used to alleviate insomnia, anxiety, and mental stress.

Narcotics, including opium, heroin, and morphine. Used for the alleviation of pain. These are the major drugs of addiction.

---

lowed a cyclic pattern, with rises during periods of heightened stress.

The particular drugs used have changed. For example, opium was popular among some of the most gifted and prominent people in nineteenth-century England; about the turn of the century, "laughing gas" had its dedicated "turned-on" clientele among college students in the United States. At other times and places, cocaine, chloroform, ether, and other preparations have had their enthusiasts. As Cohen (1968) has pointed out:

"During every epoch of discontent, despair, and directionlessness there have been those who sought the magic of a potion or a prophet that would provide quick answers, easy Utopias, or instant surcease." (p. 149)

At such times, new psychochemicals, or those new to a culture, tend to be overvalued and misused by those who feel that the world has never been in such a hopeless state.

In describing drug dependence in relation to the various drugs, it is useful to make a distinction between addiction and habituation. *Addiction* is characterized by: (1) an overwhelming desire or compulsion to continue taking the drug, (2) a tendency to increase the dosage because the individual's tolerance to the drug increases and he must take more of the drug to get the same effect, and (3) psychological and physiological dependence on the drug—the latter being manifested in withdrawal symptoms if the drug is discontinued. With *habituation* there is a desire but not a compulsion to continue taking the drug, little or no tendency to an increase in dosage, and psychological but not physiological dependence on the drug.

The major drugs of addiction have traditionally been morphine and other opium derivates and their synthetic counterparts. However, a number of studies have also shown that addiction to barbiturates and amphetamines is also possible. The drugs most commonly associated with habituation are cocaine and marihuana. Studies indicate that LSD and other hallucinogenic drugs are probably not addictive. In the present context, four drugs merit further mention—morphine and other opium derivatives, LSD, amphetamines, and marihuana.

1. *Morphine and heroin.* Like other derivatives of opium, these drugs lead to euphoria and contentment, together with pleasant reverie or daydreaming. Sexual desire, voluntary movement, and anxiety or pain—if any—are reduced. When the addict fails to get a dose of the drug within a few hours after the last dose—the interval varying with the stage of addiction—painful withdrawal symptoms make their appearance.

There are an estimated 60,000 or more individuals in the United States addicted to heroin or other opium derivatives. The great majority of these addicts are teen-agers and young adults who become addicted through thrill-seeking, curiosity, or peer-group pressures to conform. Typically these addicts come from lower socioeconomic areas in which drug addiction often tends to be condoned. In general, these addicts appear to be immature, passive, inadequate individuals who find in morphine a pleasant means of escape from a world which demands achievement. Once addicted, the individual needs ever increasing amounts of the drug to produce the same desired effect or merely to avoid the intense physical discomfort caused by his craving. To maintain a continuing supply of their drug, most addicts eventually engage in illegal activities. Male addicts most often turn to stealing; female addicts, to prostitution.

Addiction to drugs such as heroin and morphine can be broken by a painful process of withdrawal from the use of the drug—usually in a hospital setting. Typically addicts have become so *psychologically* dependent on the drug, however, that they go back to its use when they are released.

2. *LSD.* Much popular and research interest has focused on the alleged "mind-expanding" effects of LSD. The limited available findings from controlled experiments do not always apply to effects of its use outside the laboratory, where both dosage and purity of the drug may be quite dissimilar.

Under LSD most subjects in one study experienced a feeling of being detached from the outer world, a sense of increased perceptual sharpness but with the external world having an unreal quality, a feeling of loss of control over their emotions and thoughts, and the occurrence of strong but opposing emotions or sometimes emotions with no cognitive counterpart, such as anger with no object (Katz, Waskow, & Olssen, 1968).

These investigators point out that such profound alterations of consciousness appear to create a bizarre experience for most persons in our culture—an experience that may not be easy to assimilate. Perhaps for this reason, factors like previous experience, expectation, social setting, and personality make-up play an important part in determining the meaning of the experience to the individual and the overall effects of the drug.

The profound and contradictory effects of LSD also make it apparent why it is considered an extremely dangerous drug. Its effects in changing consciousness are produced by changes in the delicate chemical balance of the brain, and neither the precise biochemical changes nor the long-term results are yet known. In some cases it has precipitated serious personality disorders; sometimes the effects recur days or weeks later. Tolerance builds up rapidly, leading to its use in quantities which sometimes have serious organic side effects (McGlothlin & West, 1967).

3. *Amphetamine.* Amphetamine is the active ingredient in "pep" pills. Effects include an elevation of mood, increased alertness and confidence, and reduced feelings of fatigue. This drug has been prescribed by physicians for counteracting fatigue, depression, and excessive weight.

In recent years a considerable number of young people, particularly of high-school age, have used "speed" out of curiosity or for "kicks." Often the drug is injected by needle, exaggerating its effects. Large doses of amphetamine lead to hallucinations and paranoid states and to disorientation for time and place (Griffith, 1966). Affected individuals are usually amnesic for these events after the drug wears off.

Continued use of amphetamine—either alone or in conjunction with barbiturates (often used to regulate the effects of amphetamine)—leads to addiction. It can also produce permanent brain damage and serious personality changes, including chronic psychoses (Lemere, 1966). For such reasons, amphetamine is considered a very dangerous drug which should be used only under medical supervision.

4. *Marihuana.* Like alcohol, marihuana characteristically produces a mild euphoria, an increased feeling of well-being and self-confidence, and decreased tension and anxiety. In large amounts, the effects of marihuana resemble those of the hallucinogens and may include depersonalization and hallucinations. However, marihuana has a sedative effect like alcohol and in large amounts tends eventually to produce sleep rather than the long periods of wakefulness characteristic of LSD and other hallucinogens.

As yet no conclusive evidence has been found for long-term detrimental physical effects; however, there is a good deal of clinical evidence that the regular use of marihuana may lead to an "amotivational syndrome" characterized by passivity, inward-turning, and inability to concentrate for sustained periods of time or to pursue long-term plans of an achievement-oriented nature (McGlothlin & West, 1968; Allen & West, 1968). Contrary to much popular opinion, marihuana does not lead to acts of violence but tends in the opposite direction.[1]

Many people who use alcohol and drugs today apparently do so less because they are seeking ways to reduce stress than because it is regarded in their social group as the "in" thing to do. Such social sanctions, of course, make it easier for the immature, anxious individual to use this means of stress reduction. But whether their early contact is for reasons of social conformity or stress reduction, those who become dependent on drugs usually do so from personality need.

INTRODUCTION TO TREATMENT AND PREVENTION

In concluding our review of faulty patterns of adjustment, it is pertinent to note the nature of modern methods of treatment and prevention of the serious mental disorders. In Chapter 12, we shall deal in more detail with counseling as well as with psychotherapeutic and other techniques for improving self-understanding and opening pathways to personal growth.

The United States today seems to be undergoing what has been called "a third revolution" in mental health care (Smith, 1968). The first mental health revolution unshackled the mentally disordered and treated them in mental hospitals as human beings; the second revolution involved the introduction of individual and group psychotherapy and of psychotherapeutic drugs; the third and current revolution is focusing on a community approach to mental health, relating treat-

ment not only to the individual but to his family and to his life situation in the community.

In our brief review of modern approaches to treatment and prevention, we shall again find it helpful to think in terms of biological, psychological, and sociological levels.

Modern Approaches to Treatment

Treatment procedures may vary greatly depending upon the nature of the mental disorder. In the case of drug intoxication, for example, immediate medical measures may be indicated, whereas in dealing with a neurotic reaction psychotherapy may be indicated.

Usually the first step in treatment involves an assessment or diagnosis of the disorder. On a biological or medical level, this assessment is concerned with any physical pathology which may be a factor. Also important are conditions which contraindicate the use of tranquilizing drugs or other physical treatment procedures. On a psychological level, assessment usually focuses on the individual's present mental state and on delineating the role of personality and emotional stress in the development of the disorder. Assessment procedures may include interviews and the use of psychological tests. On a sociological level, we are concerned with marital, occupational, and other data pertaining to the individual's general life situation. Such data are usually obtained from family and other sources as well as from the person seeking help. All the facts then are integrated into a total picture of the individual in relation to his life situation, providing a basis for understanding the disorder and for planning appropriate treatment.

Treatment may also involve a wide range of medical, psychological, and sociological procedures. Medical treatment is di-

---

[1]A more detailed overview of the personal and social problems associated with the use of marihuana—which also has implications for other types of drugs as well—is provided in the article by McGlothlin and West, reproduced on page 488.

rected toward the correction of organic pathology, if any, and the alleviation of mental symptoms. Of great importance are the newer psychotherapeutic drugs, which have largely revolutionized modern treatment. These drugs essentially fall into three categories: (1) "minor" tranquilizing drugs, such as Miltown or Equanil, which are used primarily for alleviating anxiety and tension, (2) "major" tranquilizing drugs, such as chlorpromazine, which also have an antipsychotic action and are used to alleviate delusions, hallucinations, and other psychotic symptoms, and (3) energizing drugs which have an antidepressive action and are used to alleviate depressive reactions. Antidepressant drugs are often supplemented by electroshock therapy, which has proved very effective in depressive reactions. Although drug therapy is remarkably effective in alleviating severely neurotic and psychotic reactions, it does not lead to the resolution of inner conflicts or personality change and of course does not change the person's life situation.

Psychological treatment, or *psychotherapy,* may be aimed primarily at alleviating the patient's symptoms or maladjustive behavior or at achieving personality changes which foster more effective adjustment. For convenience, we can think in terms of three types of psychotherapy: (1) supportive psychotherapy, aimed at helping the person feel more adequate and better able to face his problems, (2) behavior modification, aimed primarily at modifying the individual's maladaptive behavior and achieving more effective coping techniques, and (3) re-educative psychotherapy involving insight, aimed at changing faulty assumptions and attitudes and bringing about fundamental changes in personality organization. Behavior modification—based upon learning-theory principles involving the extinction of maladaptive reactions and the acquisition of adaptive reactions through systematic use of reinforcement—is currently receiving a great deal of emphasis. Psychotherapy may employ a wide range of techniques and may be carried out with one individual at a time or in a group setting. In Chapter 12 we will discuss psychotherapy in some detail.

In sociological treatment, or *sociotherapy,* the attempt is made to modify stressful conditions in the individual's life situation which are interfering with his adjustive efforts. In many cases, sociotherapy is of crucial significance in the treatment program. For example, little progress may be made in treating an emotionally disturbed child or adolescent unless changes can be made in the family situation which will make a more effective adjustment possible. Similarly, it may be difficult or impossible to help an emotionally disturbed adult until his marital or family adjustment can be improved. As a consequence, increasing attention has been directed toward the alleviation of pathogenic family conditions, often involving the treatment of family members as a group.

For purposes of clarity we have dealt with medical, psychological, and sociological treatment separately. Modern treatment, however, involves the integration of different procedures as determined by the needs of the individual and available treatment facilities. Frequently drug therapy is coordinated with psychotherapy and sociotherapy for achieving the most effective program.

The Problem of Prevention

The prevention of mental disorders has proven to be a most difficult problem. However, a good deal of progress has been made in the early detection and correction of various types of organic pathology associated with mental disorders. For example, syphilitic infection of the brain, which used to be a major cause of mental disorders, is now of rare occurrence because of effective methods of diagnosing and treating syphilis. Similarly, with the availability of procedures for the early detection and correction of PKU, this condition no longer need lead to mental retardation. Increasing emphasis is also being placed on general health measures, including adequate maternity services for all mothers, regardless of socioeconomic level, and aid for dependent children in inadequate family and community settings.

Psychological preventive measures have focused in the main on public education concerning the nature of mental disorders and on the early detection and correction of pathological trends. As a consequence, older views of mental disorders as a disgrace have largely been dispelled, and people are more understanding and accepting of the idea of therapy. Psychologists have also taken an active role in the establishment of child guidance facilities, suicide prevention centers, and other community resources for mental health. Of particular importance, psychologists have been and are in the forefront of research into the conditions which result in mental disorders.

Sociological preventive measures include a wide range of programs centered primarily on the family and the community. We have noted the role of the Head Start program in dealing with socially disadvantaged children; and other programs are directed toward community organization and development in an attempt to alleviate social disorganization and other conditions that breed mental disorders. Of key importance, as we have noted, is the trend toward establishing community facilities for the treatment of mental disorders. These facilities enable many individuals to function in their family and community setting who might otherwise have to be hospitalized—often a long distance from their families and homes; they can often prevent incipient disorders from becoming more serious and can also be of great help in the rehabilitation of individuals who have received institutional treatment.

Despite many advances, however, the problem of preventing mental disorders is far from solved. In fact, one might say that the real fight has just begun. Currently, the most promising approach appears to be intensified and continued research into the role of biological, psychological, and sociocultural factors in the development and amelioration of mental disorders. As we learn more about the role of genetic and physiological processes, the acquisition and modification of maladaptive reactions, and the effects of particular sociocultural conditions on mental health, it will be possible to formulate and carry out more effective preventive programs.

SUMMARY AND A LOOK AHEAD

In this chapter we have identified *effective behavior* as behavior that (1) meets the demands of the situation; (2) meets the needs of the individual; and (3) is compatible with the welfare of others. We have seen that both effective and ineffective patterns are attempts to meet inner and outer demands, that ineffective behavior represents various kinds of "error" in the process of coping with these demands, and that there is a continuum from effective at one end to seriously ineffective, or maladjustive, at the other. Current researchers vary in the extent to which they use a medical or a psychological model in attempting to understand and deal with maladjustive behavior; in some cases one seems more appropriate, in some cases the other. They are not mutually exclusive and may both apply in some cases.

Seriously faulty adjustive reactions, or *mental disorders,* include (1) *transient reactions* to acute or special stress; (2) *neurotic reactions,* which may be viewed as learned maladaptive responses to anxiety-arousing stress usually not requiring hospitalization; (3) *psychotic reactions,* disorders with severe personality decompensations in which emotional distortion, hallucinations, and delusions may occur and in which brain damage and biochemical abnormalities sometimes play a role; (4) *psychophysiologic (psy-*

chosomatic) reactions, in which chronic emotional mobilization leads to actual tissue damage; (5) *character (personality) reactions,* which are "acting out" disorders reflecting distorted personality development rather than decompensation under stress and which include antisocial (psychopathic) reactions, dyssocial reactions, and sexual deviations; (6) *alcoholism and drug addiction,* technically categorized as character disorders.

Diagnosis and therapy include biological, psychological, and sociological procedures since all three kinds of factors may be involved in a given case. Contemporary psychotherapy—psychological procedures for therapy —can be divided into (1) *supportive therapies,* which are largely aimed at reducing anxiety; (2) *behavior therapies,* which change particular responses by the use of reinforcement; and (3) *insight therapies,* which attempt a basic change of the individual's frame of reference and self-system. Preventive measures, too, may be biological, psychological, and/or sociological and include both providing conditions in which ineffective patterns will not develop and spotting errors in the early stages before they become serious.

We have now filled in our picture of the development, motivation, and adjustive behavior of individuals in our society. In the next few chapters we will be examining the extent to which groups, too, have structural and integrative properties and the problem of meshing individual and group purposes.

Key terms used in this chapter include:

criteria of effective adjustment (pp. 233-234)
medical model, psychological model (pp. 235-236)
transient situational personality disorders (p. 237)
neurotic disorders (p. 240)
anxiety reaction (p. 241)
phobic reaction (p. 242)
conversion reaction (hysteria) (p. 243)
dissociative reaction, amnesia, fugue, multiple personality (pp. 243-244)
obsessive-compulsive reaction (p. 244)
asthenic reaction (p. 245)
neurotic depressive reaction (p. 246)
psychotic disorders (p. 247)
delusions, hallucinations (p. 248)
schizophrenic reactions (pp. 248-249)
paranoid reactions (p. 251)
psychophysiologic (psychosomatic) reactions (pp. 256-257)
character (personality) disorders (p. 258)
antisocial (psychopathic) reaction (p. 258)
dyssocial reactions (p. 259)
sexual deviation (pp. 259-260)
alcoholism (p. 262)
addiction, habituation, psychological dependence (p. 264)
medical treatment, psychotherapy, sociotherapy (pp. 266-267)

Part Three

PROBLEMS IN GROUP LIVING

In Parts One and Two of this text, we have dealt with personality development and adjustment, and until now our focus has been on the individual. Now we shall expand our focus to include both the individual and his natural habitat—the group setting in which he is embedded and in which he lives and functions. In Chapter 9 we shall apply some of the concepts developed in other chapters—perception, learning, maintenance and actualization needs, adjustive demands, and reactions to stress—to the development and functioning of groups as living systems, examining some of the ways in which groups and individuals influence each other. This chapter also treats the special problem of conformity and provides a brief introduction to interpersonal relationships within group settings.

Chapter 10 applies the principles of individual and group functioning to the special setting of premarital and marital relationships. Included here is a discussion of changing premarital patterns and views of marriage; the role of the quest for romantic love and other factors in the choice of a mate; some of the different styles and interactions that characterize modern marriages in our society; and factors in good marital adjustment. The chapter concludes with a consideration of marital unhappiness and divorce and the problem of remarriage.

Chapter 11 parallels Chapter 10, applying many of the same concepts to the work setting. Included here is a discussion of our changing views of work and leisure; personality traits and other considerations in career choice; common problems in occupational adjustment, such as "the first-job dilemma"; and some special problems, such as those faced by working women. The chapter concludes with a brief view of some present and probable trends in the world of work.

Chapter 12 surveys three kinds of resources for personal growth and change. Included here is an examination of intensive group experiences, including sensitivity training (T-groups) and encounter groups; a brief review of psychological assessment and counseling for help with educational, occupational, and marital problems or plans; and the nature and use of individual and group psychotherapy in dealing with personality maladjustment and thereby opening avenues for personal growth.

Chapter 9

THE INDIVIDUAL
IN THE GROUP

How Groups Develop and Function
Group-Individual Interaction
Interpersonal Relationships

In talking about individual behavior, we have been confronted again and again with the importance of its social context. The ways we develop, our attitudes and values, our goals and means, the problems we encounter, our characteristic reaction patterns, and the satisfactions we achieve—all of these are influenced by our group memberships and the roles we play in these groups. The extent to which we are "group creatures" has been well described by Cartwright and Zander (1968):

"If it were possible for the overworked hypothetical man from Mars to take a fresh view of the people of Earth, he would probably be impressed by the amount of time they spend doing things together in groups. He would note that most people cluster into relatively small groups, with the members residing together in the same dwelling, satisfying their basic biological needs within the group, depending upon the same source for economic support, rearing children, and mutually caring for the health of one another. He would observe that the education and socialization of children tend to occur in other, usually larger, groups in churches, schools, and other social institutions. He would see that much of the work of the world is carried out by people who perform their activities in close interdependence within relatively enduring associations. He would perhaps be saddened to find groups of men engaged in warfare, gaining courage and morale from pride in their unit and a knowledge that they can depend on their buddies. He might be gladdened to see groups of people enjoying themselves in recreations and sports of various kinds. Finally he might be puzzled why so many people spend so much time in little groups talking, planning, and being 'in conference.' Surely he would conclude that if he wanted to understand much about what is happening on Earth he would have to examine rather carefully the ways in which groups form, function, and dissolve." (p. 3)

Following the more customary perspective of Earth's inhabitants, psychologists have traditionally studied the individual—how he perceives, feels, thinks, and acts—as if he were a self-contained unit. Only comparatively recently have they studied systematically the structure and behavior of groups and the ways an individual's behavior varies in different group settings. Yet simply placing man in his "social habitat," in terms of the groups to which he belongs and his position in these groups, takes us a long step forward in understanding his behavior. And as we probe into interactions between a group and its members we add indispensable information to our understanding of man's behavior.

One of the most significant outcomes emerging from the study of groups has been the realization that there are many parallels between individual and group functioning—that groups face stresses and attempt to cope with them in ways that closely resemble the behavior of individuals. The behavior of a group, like that of an individual, depends on both its inner structure and its setting, including the nature and demands of larger groups of which it is a part. To understand the behavior of husband and wife in a family unit, for example, we need to know the individuals involved but also whether the family is in a society that practices polyandry, polygamy, or monogamy.

Thus many of the concepts developed in our discussion of individual behavior apply also to group behavior. But since we are dealing with a different level of system, we shall also find some characteristics that are different. For example, groups usually form to meet the needs of individuals, whereas an individual organism could hardly be said to be formed to meet the needs of its constituent organs. Similarly, there is no unitary "group mind" parallel to an individual's consciousness.

In the present chapter, then, we shall be concerned with the social setting of behavior. This will lead us to: (1) a brief excursion into the nature of groups—how they develop and function, (2) a glimpse at the ways in which individuals and groups interact and influence each other, and (3) an introduction to the nature of interpersonal relationships in group settings.

HOW GROUPS DEVELOP AND FUNCTION

In a general sense the word *group* refers to persons who are bound together by specific relationships which set them apart from others. Usually they have come together to work toward certain common goals. Thus the term is applied to such diverse cases as members of a family, participants in a mob, adherents to Buddhism, and citizens of a nation. Groups vary in size—from two persons to millions—in their degree of organization, and in the degree to which the members function together in a coordinated way. Families and military groups are examples of organized groups; while audiences and mobs are examples of relatively unorganized groups, often referred to as *collectivities*.

In general, it is organized groups rather than collectivities which have the greatest influence on our lives and behavior. Thus our discussion in this section will focus on organized groups, particularly with respect to: (1) group formation and membership, (2) group structure, and (3) group effectiveness and change.

Group Formation and Membership

As already indicated, the needs of individuals are ordinarily the basis for the formation of groups. Groups may be developed to provide security for their members, to carry on economic activities, to furnish opportunities for social experience, to educate the young, or to achieve any of countless other goals.

How groups form. Many groups form more or less spontaneously by the mutual agreement of people who share common interests or are faced with a common threat. Thus bridge fans may form a bridge club, or property owners may band together to protest the proposed route of a new freeway. Such spontaneously formed groups are often loosely organized and may quickly dissolve if they do not seem to function well or if the immediate need for them passes. In other instances, however, such groups may serve continuing and changing needs and may expand in size and organization.

Sometimes groups are formed largely through the activities and persuasive powers of a particularly articulate person. Mary

Baker Eddy was the founder of Christian Science, and Martin Luther King, Jr., was the guiding spirit behind the nonviolent civil rights movement in this country. On a less dramatic level, perhaps, a young man may persuade the girl he has selected to marry him and start a family. New groups may also be formed through election or appointment by larger groups already in existence. In such cases, the new group is set up to perform functions considered essential to the parent body. A club may set up a committee to handle the details of its annual charity ball; the mayor of a city may appoint a group to study traffic congestion.

The way a group is formed will strongly influence the role expectations, freedom of action, and behavior of its members. For example, members of an appointed group may have their goals and functions laid out for them; members of leader-formed groups may expect the leader to take most of the initiative; members of groups formed by mutual agreement are likely to feel more personal responsibility in determining the goals and actions of the group.

Group membership. Individuals attain group membership in several ways: by birth, by choice, by invitation, and by mutual consent. Most of us belong to a family or a national group because we were born into it; we belong to a political party because we chose to join; we belong to a sorority or fraternity because we were invited to join (and accepted the invitation); and we become a partner to a marriage by mutual consent.

In some instances failure to achieve group membership or even group membership itself may be highly frustrating. A girl who is not invited to join a sorority may be very disappointed; a youth born into a poverty-stricken slum family may feel frustrated and trapped; and a person who is unhappily married may feel disillusioned and hurt.

Although we all belong to groups, not all of us place the same value on group memberships. At one extreme are the so-called "joiners," who are active in a variety of groups; at the other extreme are the "loners," who avoid participation in groups whenever possible. Often a person is uncertain as to whether or not he wishes to join or retain his membership in a given group. The extent to which he perceives the group as related to the meeting of his needs is likely to be a key consideration in such membership decisions.

The composition of the group—in terms of the age, sex, interests, capabilities, values, and other characteristics of individual members—is important not only in determining the interpersonal and other satisfactions the individual finds in the group but also in determining the performance and effectiveness of the group.

Group Structure (Organization)

As a new group develops and achieves some stability, it becomes structured. Positions of authority and responsibility emerge, social roles are delineated, and group norms and standards develop which help to regulate the actions of group members. In the broadest sense, the structure of the group includes all these relatively stable characteristics of the group's organization.

Power. In the animal kingdom there typically emerges a hierarchy of power based on physical prowess. On a simple level this can be seen in the order established when cats or other animals are placed in a situation where only one animal can eat at a time. A sequence is soon established in which the strongest animal eats first and so on down the line to the weakest or most passive animal, who eats last. The term *pecking order* derives from the hierarchy of dominance established in any barnyard.

Human groups, too, develop power hierarchies—usually on some basis other than physical prowess. Thus we find hierarchies of power in large corporations, governmental agencies, military organizations, school systems, neighborhood gangs, and families. In human groups *power* refers to the ability to control some aspect of the behavior of other persons—for example, to compel their obedience or induce some action from them. Typically such power derives ultimately from the ability to control reward and punishment; *reward power* is the ability to deliver rewards to persons who comply with demands or expectations, and punishment or *coercive power* is the ability to deliver punishment to or withhold rewards from persons who fail to comply. The social bases of power are summarized below.

We are continually seeking things from people in power positions—we may try to get a teacher to change our grade, a counselor to permit us to skip a course requirement, or a supervisor to recommend us for a promotion. In approaching power figures, our behavior is likely to be courteous and deferential in contrast to the way we may deal with those on a par with us or below us in the power hierarchy. Our position in the power structure will determine what we can do and how autonomous we can be.

The arbitrary and capricious use of power may result in its being taken away by other group members. Even without misuse, power is notoriously impermanent.

Leadership structure. Closely related to the power structure, but not synonymous with it, is the leadership structure of the group. Whereas the person with power has actual ability to influence or determine the fate of others, the person in the leadership role is more concerned with mobilizing group effort and with planning and coordinating group action, and he may have much or little power for doing so.

Although the leader usually occupies the highest power position in the group, sometimes there is a "power behind the throne." For example, a subgroup may delegate the leadership responsibility to others but keep the real power in its own hands. Political machines often operate in this way. Thus the leader may be a "figurehead" who is subject to control by others occupying higher power positions in the group.

Groups differ greatly in their leadership structure. In loosely organized groups, leadership may be virtually nonexistent or constantly shifting. A different person, for example, may assume the leadership role in organizing successive meetings of a bridge club; in a family, the father may exercise leadership in some situations and the mother

SOCIAL BASES OF POWER

The individual or group in power is in a position to dispense reward and punishment (and promises thereof) to those below as inducement to desired behavior and as a consequence of complying or failing to comply. Rewards include commendation, material benefits, and higher status; punishments include physical harm, social isolation, demotion, and disgrace. Although a common basis for maintenance of power, once attained, is the ability to control rewards and punishments, power may be attained and held through other routes:

1. *Expert power.* Power may be granted a person or group regarded as possessing essential knowledge or abilities; an example is the physician-patient relationship. Ultimately, of course, his expert-ness is expected to bring benefits (rewards) to the followers.

2. *Legitimate power.* Power may be gained through channels recognized as "legitimate," such as election, appointment, or inheritance. An example is the power of a lieutenant over a private or the power of a king over his subjects by "divine right."

3. *Assumed power.* Power may simply be taken by one who can persuade or force others to follow his wishes. This may occur in an unstable situation or in a situation still undergoing structuring.

4. *Usurped power.* Power may be usurped by an individual or subgroup and then maintained by force—by reward and punishment power. An example is the military coup.

Based in part on French & Raven, 1958; McDavid & Harari, 1968.

KEY FACETS OF SOCIAL ROLES

ROLE EXPECTATIONS | The behavior prescribed for an individual occupying a given position in the group.

ROLE CONCEPTION | The way the individual perceives his role, which may be different from the way it is perceived by others.

ROLE ACCEPTANCE | The degree to which the individual finds his role compatible with his values, needs, and self-concept.

ROLE PERFORMANCE (ROLE BEHAVIOR) | The way in which the individual actually plays or performs his role in the group.

ROLE CONFLICT | The contradictory role demands resulting from multiple group memberships, as when the role of mother conflicts with that of an active participant in community and civic organizatons.

A serious discrepancy between the individual and other group members in terms of role expectations, role conceptions, or role behavior is likely to create problems. Typically, however, such problems appear to be resolved through accommodation rather than by rigid role enforcement by the group.

in others. In highly organized groups, however, leadership usually becomes a more pervasive characteristic of group structure. Such groups may be led by an individual or by a committee or other subgroup; and the methods of leadership may be autocratic, democratic, laissez-faire, or somewhere in between. In groups with autocratic leadership, the individual who does not belong to the "power elite" may have few rights and little autonomy or freedom.

We shall examine the qualities of leaders and the effects of different methods of leadership in a later section of this chapter. Suffice it here to point out that the leadership structure of the group may be of crucial importance in determining the satisfaction of individual members, the effectiveness of group performance, and the direction of group change.

Role structure. As we noted in Chapter 2, a social role is the pattern of behavior expected of a person occupying a particular position in the group. Thus certain responsibilities and behaviors are explicit in the roles of husband and father or wife and mother. A clear delineation of social roles is useful in:

(1) providing the individuals in a group with general guidelines as to what is expected of them and what they may expect of others, and (2) ensuring necessary specialization of function as well as coordination of group activity. Since we all belong to more than one group, we may learn to play several different social roles—sometimes fitting into a consistent and comfortable pattern, sometimes inconsistent with each other.

Some roles must be followed more rigidly than others. If the organization of the group is flexible, members may have considerable leeway in interpreting their roles or in working out roles that are suitable for them. For example, husband and wife roles in American marriages tend to evolve as a consequence of each partner's accommodating to the characteristics and needs of the other; in some instances conventional role behavior may even be largely reversed—as when the wife works and the husband does the cooking and other housework. In other situations there may be little leeway afforded in role behavior, as in the case of a waitress serving at a formal diplomatic function. In general, however, it would appear that most social roles leave ample room for individuality and creativity in role behavior (Turner, 1962).

It is not only individual members of a group who have roles to play. Subgroups also take on specialized functions and roles in the larger society—as exemplified by the police department, the Supreme Court, and the American Red Cross. Subgroups, like individuals, may promote the goals and welfare of society or may play roles detrimental to the larger group. Criminal gangs are a clear example of the latter type of subgroup.

Communication structure. Communication is essential for transmitting information and coordinating the activities of individuals and subgroups. In any group there tends to be a stabilization of particular lines of communication which are referred to as *communication nets.* Thus a group member does not communicate equally often with each other member; rather power and role relationships, personal likes and dislikes, subgroup cleavages, and other conditions tend to result in the establishment of particular communication nets.

In small groups, two-way communication, as between family members or between teacher and students, gives the group as a whole the benefit of each member's ideas, provides individual members with a sense of involvement, and gives group leaders important feedback. As the size and complexity of the group increases, however, problems of communication multiply and restrictive patterns of communication become typical. A private in the army who has what he considers a worth-while idea for improving the combat efficiency of his unit does not communicate his idea directly to the commanding general of the division but places it in the proper channels. Similarly, in business organizations and universities there are established channels for handling particular types of communication—which may or may not function well for group effectiveness and for the personal satisfaction of individual members.

The established channels of communication in any group reveal a great deal about its power and leadership structure. Usually the individuals occupying high positions are at the top or hub of the communication net.

Autocratic leaders typically attempt to control the communication system in order to maintain their position of power. Thus they may censor the information that goes to group members, or they may deliberately fabricate misinformation that they think will enhance their power position. Even in a democracy, there must be continual vigilance to see that information is not withheld or manipulated by those in power positions.

Where the existing information channels are restricted by autocratic leadership or are so poorly organized that the members of the group are not kept informed about events of importance to them, informal channels of communication called "grapevines" tend to develop. Sometimes the information carried by these grapevines is amazingly accurate, but more commonly it consists largely of rumor and conjecture. Central members of the group, who have access to communication channels, tend to have higher morale, a stronger desire for the group to succeed, and a greater feeling of responsibility for the outcome of group action (Medow & Zander, 1965).

Sociometric structure. The sociometric structure is the pattern of personal attractions within the group. This pattern can be determined by having each person in the group name the two or three other members whom he likes best or with whom he would most like to perform some specified task. This way it is possible to find out where the friendship links are, which members are well liked generally, and which members are "isolates."

A diagram of sociometric structure—called a *sociogram*—will also often reveal clusters, or cliques, within the larger group. The members of these cliques are joined to each other by mutual friendship bonds but generally remain aloof from other members of the group. Often their attitudes and behavior are influenced more by the clique than by the larger group. For this reason teachers, supervisors, and others in positions of au-

CARGO CULTS

As in the case of the individual, unrealistic or distorted assumptions by a group interfere with effective behavior and can result in the failure and eventual disintegration of the group. An extreme example of how an unrealistic ideological structure can lead to unadaptive group behavior is provided by the curious "cargo cults" of Melanesia (Worsley, 1959). From occasional contacts with white missionaries and traders, the primitive people who belong to these cults have been impressed with the white man's "magic." They have seen the "cargo" (pidgin English for trade goods) that the white man gets by some unknown means and have interpreted the Christian message of the returning Messiah as a promise that a "cargo" would eventually come to them, bringing a millennium. Knowing nothing about modern production and merchandising, they have concluded that the white man does not work but gets his cargo simply by writing "secret signs" on scraps of paper. In attempting to discover the white man's secret, the cultists usually work out rituals "in imitation of the mysterious European customs which are held to be the clue to the white man's extraordinary power. . . . The believers sit around tables with bottles of flowers in front of them, dressed in European clothes, waiting for the cargo ship or airplane to materialize; other cultists feature magic pieces of paper and cabalistic writing" (p. 121). During outbreaks of religious frenzy the cultists may kill their pigs, destroy their gardens, and break their most sacred taboos. Although the hoped-for cargo never arrives, the cults live on—attributing their failure to some error in ritual rather than to an unrealistic premise.

thority often find it necessary to break up cliques in order to keep them from undermining the program and purposes of the larger group.

An individual's position in the sociometric structure of a group will largely determine the gratification he will receive from membership in that group. The individual who is valued and receives warmth and acceptance is likely to gain much more satisfaction from his group membership than is the "isolate." Studies of classroom groups have shown that the isolate is usually the first to give up when the group encounters difficulties—for example, when a class project is not going well; he is also more likely than are other class members to become ill or to create disciplinary problems (Redl & Wattenberg, 1951). It is probable that such characteristics apply to isolates in other groups as well.

Group norms and ideology. Groups tend to develop characteristic ways of doing things and, concurrently, strong feelings that these are the ways things *should* be done—that these are the "normal" ways, the "right" ways. Typical patterns of speech and other behavior and typical attitudes and values not only become characteristic of a given group but acquire a mandatory character. Political parties expect all loyal members to support the party platform. Church groups issue official statements concerning approved beliefs and disapproved behavior. The workers in a plant may exert considerable pressure on ambitious members not to speed up beyond the established norm. An adolescent girl may find it necessary to dress and behave in certain ways if she wants to belong to the crowd.

The norms of larger social groups are usually embodied in laws, customs, and traditions. In small groups, norms may appear in formal rules and regulations, or they may be unwritten laws learned by all members through participation in the group. In one way or another, however, the group communicates its norms to its members, so that the individual is usually well aware of what the group norms are—whether or not he accepts them. Whether formal or informal, the group's standards serve as criteria of conduct for the members of the group and specify the range of tolerable behavior for members in good standing.

Whereas group norms focus on the social rules for individual behavior, group ideology focuses more on group purposes and on group assumptions about reality, possibility, and value. Groups develop a frame of reference—assumptions about themselves and their environment—in much the same way that individuals do. These assumptions incline them toward certain goals, and toward characteristic ways of coping with problems and evaluating themselves and others. Thus one group will prize novelty and excitement; another, tradition and custom. Different societies have prized honesty, chicanery, extravagance, frugality, religious revelation, experimental evidence, spiritual values, material values, graciousness, bluffness, individualism, and conformity.

In some small groups—such as a bridge or chess club—the ideology of the group may not be explicitly formulated or even relevant; in the family group, the ideology is important although it may not be explicitly formulated; in larger organized groups, the ideology of the group is usually clearly formulated in official documents—an example being the Constitution of the United States.

In some cases, of course, groups formally profess one value orientation but implicitly accept another. Thus a group may profess to believe in human equality but actually practice discrimination, or a nation may profess democratic ideals but "railroad through" its leaders' decisions in autocratic or even brutal ways. As in the case of the individual's assumptions, group assumptions about reality, value, and possibility may be accurate or inaccurate; faulty assumptions can interfere with effective performance or even result in the disintegration of the group. Often it is both interesting and revealing to examine the ideological structure of the groups to which one belongs, including one's family.

Group atmosphere and cohesiveness. Small groups, such as families, have a prevailing climate which may be one of harmony or dis-

harmony, love or hostility, discouragement or optimism, and so on. In the family group, the attitudes of individual members both contribute to the family climate and are influenced by it. For example, an emotionally supportive member with a good sense of humor helps to establish a positive, cooperative climate and induce integrative behavior from others, whereas an irrational, immature member is a disruptive force, inducing defensiveness and resentment in other members. And depending on the climate established by the contributions and interactions of all the personalities, any one member may find the family climate attractive and personally satisfying or unpleasant and frustrating.

The *cohesiveness* of a group is gauged by the members' identification with and desire to remain in the group. It is a rather intangible characteristic of the group, associated with feelings of common purpose, attraction of group members to each other, the importance of the group's activities and goals to the individual members, and the competence and success of the group. *Esprit de corps* is a characteristic of a highly cohesive group.

Conditions that promote group cohesiveness include clear-cut and agreed-upon goals, an effective group organization in which members have confidence in each other to do what is required, and successful past achievement by the group. Cohesiveness also appears to develop from—as well as lead to—group traditions, symbols, ceremonials, and sometimes a special jargon. Shared experiences—whether crises, recreational activities, or everyday routine—further tend to strengthen the ties between group members. Perhaps inevitably, large groups with a complicated organization and with few opportunities for personal contact tend to be much lower in cohesiveness than most smaller groups, such as families or athletic teams.

The more cohesive a group, the more personal loyalty its members feel and the less likely they are to abandon it when "the going gets tough." A cohesive group tends to have high morale—a prevailing mood of confidence in its ability to cope with its problems. Faced with the same external demands, a cohesive group with high morale may maintain and even strengthen itself, whereas a low-morale group may suffer disintegration.

The importance of morale and *esprit de corps* in determining the effectiveness of combat units under stress was shown dramatically in the story of the famous Carlson's Raiders of World War II (Sherif & Sherif, 1956):

"In this unit, reciprocal expectations were stabilized among men in terms of the functions necessary for an explicitly formulated goal. This stabilization process involved minimizing or eliminating those traditional distinctions between officers and enlisted men which did not seem essential for coordinated action and clear outlining of the plans followed and their purpose. Officers were expected to demonstrate their worth as leaders of activity. Carlson, in particular, made himself the model in consistently meeting high expectations for his behavior.

"The result of these efforts to foster an in-group structure in which high expectations for behavior were standardized and consistently met was astounding group solidarity, even under terrible combat conditions of Guadalcanal and other battles which broke down many other units and individuals in them. It became virtually unnecessary for Carlson to exert formal disciplinary measures. Modes of behavior were standardized and internalized by members of the units. Thus, activities toward group goals were carried out with zeal and enthusiasm stemming from the men themselves and not from direct external compulsion." (p. 166)

Cohesiveness and morale are not static qualities; they may change greatly with successes, setbacks, or changes in the environment. Such a change in cohesiveness and morale is dramatically demonstrated in the report of what eventually happened to Carlson's Raiders:

"There came a time when the men were weary of combat and expecting a rest period, when Carlson could not fulfill the high expectations that his role demanded. Appar-

ently this was beyond his control; his outfit was ordered back into combat and his requests for material comforts for the men were denied. Being a loyal Marine officer, he answered the men's questions and complaints evasively, refusing to put the blame on the higher echelons. As far as the men were concerned, he was 'letting them down.' His previous behavior seemed like trickery; he was just another 'brass hat.'

"As a result of this breakdown in stabilized expectations, morale was low. In contrast to the earlier period of solidarity, there was 'hell in the ranks.' Carlson and the values emphasized in the Raiders became objects of ridicule and resentment." (pp. 166-167)

Group Action

Group structure and function are so interdependent that it is difficult to separate them even for discussion. In this section, however, we are less concerned with the organization of the group and more concerned with its functioning, including its goals, the means it uses, and the results of its efforts in terms of effectiveness or ineffectiveness.

Task and maintenance goals. It is apparent that group goals may vary widely. For a football team, the winning of games may be the primary goal; in a planning group, the key objective may be to formulate strategies for dealing with a specific problem such as air pollution; in a "brainstorming" group, the goal may be the gathering of new ideas; in a therapy group, the goal is the personal growth and more effective adjustment of the individual members.

The primary objectives of the group—for example, the winning of games by a football team—are referred to as *task goals*. But whatever its primary goals, the group must also take measures to maintain its organization and integration if it is to function effectively or even survive. Thus the group must also be concerned with *maintenance goals*. Usually maintenance goals center around resolving conflicts among group members and meeting their emotional-social needs; for conflict, dissension, and dissatisfaction among group members are major sources of disorganization in groups. The replacement of group members lost as a result of death or other causes is also a major maintenance goal of many groups; if such members cannot be replaced, the group may work out a new organizational equilibrium, based on different relationships and responsibilities for the members who are left.

This tendency to restore organizational equilibrium can be seen in dramatic form when a military leader is killed during an enemy attack and a new leader emerges to head the unit as it strives to regain its functional effectiveness. Similarly, the loss of the mother or father in a family may lead to changed roles and responsibilities as the family attempts to regain its organizational equilibrium.

Thus group goals and strivings are roughly analogous to those of individuals. Like individuals, too, some groups are highly task oriented, with the predominance of their effort directed toward their task goals, while other groups are more concerned with main-

taining themselves as an organized entity—for example, by making the group attractive to the members or to possible new members.

Group pressures toward conformity are often decried today; yet they develop inevitably as a group tries to maintain itself and achieve its goals. In fact, no group could long function as a unit without some uniformity and discipline of its members. A football team without training rules or an established practice time would probably not win many games, and a political party would suffer if its candidates openly supported greatly differing positions. Uniformity of opinion also can increase efficiency when a group must act quickly. A group with one voice can determine its direction and reach its goal faster than a group with many voices urging different actions.

Group pressures toward uniformity thus serve basic needs of the group. If the pressure to conform is too strong, however, it can stifle individual creativity and lead to rigid, unadaptive behavior on the part of the group as a whole—for a group's fundamental resources are the initiative and enthusiasm of its individual members. The special problem of maintaining the opportunity for varia-

GROUP FORMULATION OF GOALS

Studies show that one way to get maximal personal involvement in the group's goals is to have the members participate in their formulation. For example, in one study (Ziller, 1957) military aircraft crews were put into situations where a decision was required, and four different techniques of decision making were compared: (1) authoritarian—the leader's decision was the group's decision and there was no discussion; (2) leader-suggestion—the leader stated his opinion first and then permitted group discussion; (3) group-leader census—the leader stated his opinion but only after group discussion and a census of the opinions of the group members; (4) leader-chairman—the leader guided a discussion without revealing his own opinion.

The reactions of the crews indicated that they felt most satisfaction with the group-leader census technique and least with the authoritarian technique. It was also found that when the decision-making process was group-centered rather than leader-centered, the crews were willing to make greater sacrifices to achieve group goals—for example, to undertake more dangerous combat missions.

Thus even in a traditionally autocratic situation like a military group, member participation in goal-setting may be more "practical" than direction from above. Many other studies have shown that decisions in which members participate are more effective in changing behavior than decisions made by leaders and passed on as orders.

FACTORS IN GROUP EFFECTIVENESS

GROUP MEMBERS
A group's effectiveness depends heavily upon the individuals within it, since ultimately it is individuals who actually make and implement group decisions. Members with serious personality weaknesses, immaturities, or lack of essential skills may disrupt or prevent group progress, just as mature, competent, and dedicated members help to ensure group effectiveness and success. Characteristics of members—especially in terms of the possession of essential competencies and commitment to group goals—are especially important when the group is under severe stress. A group's loss of dedicated and capable members, particularly those with outstanding leadership skill or other key abilities needed by the group, can be seriously disruptive to group performance and effectiveness.

GROUP ORGANIZATION
AND PERFORMANCE
Group effectiveness is influenced by each of the major dimensions of group organization discussed in the text. Effectiveness is enhanced by a type of power and leadership structure appropriate to the group's tasks; clear-cut, realistic, and agreed-upon goals; clear and appropriate social roles compatible with the self-concepts and values of group members; sound group values and an accurate frame of reference; and efficient communication.

The group's record of past successes and failures, its level of cohesiveness and morale, the efficiency with which it uses its human and material resources, and its ability to meet the needs of group members also play key roles in group effectiveness.

ENVIRONMENTAL
(FIELD) CONDITIONS
Group effectiveness is fostered by a reasonable correspondence between the group and its environment—between what it is trying to accomplish and the resources and possibilities provided by its setting. In many underdeveloped countries, the lack of material resources, made more acute by overpopulation, makes it well-nigh impossible for individual and group needs to be met effectively.

Intergroup relationships are also often of great importance. Where groups cooperate in the interests of common goals, their effectiveness may be enhanced. Even intense competition among groups may lead to greater group effectiveness. However, if the relations go beyond competition to hostility and conflict, the achievement of group goals may be made more difficult, and group effectiveness may be reduced.

---

tion and dissent—for the society's benefit as well as the individual's—will be discussed in a later section of the chapter.[1]

Solving problems and making decisions. Groups process problems in much the same way that individuals do. The problem is assessed, alternative solutions are formulated, and a given alternative is chosen on the basis of such factors as probable outcome, risk, and satisfaction of needs.

In comparisons of the performance of groups and of individuals working alone on problem-solving tasks, it has been found that groups have advantages and disadvantages. Groups can often assess a problem more ac-

curately because several perceivers are able to compare their impressions; the pooling of individual resources may lead to the formulation of a wider range of alternative choices; and the varied past experiences of group members may lead to a more accurate prediction of probable outcome, risk, and satisfaction in selecting a given alternative. In one study dealing with problems in which a

---

[1]For an article spelling out the implications of regarding social groups as energy systems, see "Society as a Complex Adaptive Mechanism" by Walter Buckley, reprinted on pages 495-506. Buckley compares the mechanisms of adaptation in simpler organisms, individual human beings, and societies and emphasizes societies' need for maintaining both organization and variation.

high degree of inference and judgment were called for, group solutions were found to be better than the average individual solution but not better than the best individual solution (Hall, Mouton, & Blake, 1963). Thus though the less able members may reap benefits they could not earn by themselves, the more able members may be held back or inhibited by the requirement of functioning in a group.

A group's ability to solve a problem is heavily dependent upon its composition—upon the abilities and characteristics of its individual members. Where no one in the group is qualified to deal with the problems at hand, group action is not likely to have the advantages mentioned above. Sometimes, too, the members of a group are operating on the basis of different information or assumptions; in such cases, they may have serious difficulties in communicating with each other and may work at cross purposes. Members may also have conflicting needs or belong to other groups which pull them in opposing directions.

Sometimes group members irritate each other, and emotional conflicts and tensions arise which distract attention from the task at hand and interfere with objective consideration of the problem. And, of course, as in the case of individuals, groups may become more concerned with the safety and prestige of the group than with carrying out their original goals.

Group action and feedback. As in individual action, action taken by groups may be primarily task oriented or defense oriented. A football team trying to perfect new plays for an important game is task oriented in its behavior; the same team trying to explain a defeat erroneously as due to "poor refereeing" would be defense oriented.

Like an individual, a defense-oriented group may rationalize, project blame, indulge in "scapegoating," or utilize other defense mechanisms. Such defensive patterns are commonly initiated by group leaders and communicated to members through established communication channels; their intent

is to maintain the adequacy and worth of the group in the eyes of its members—and hence to maintain or improve group cohesiveness and morale.

As in individual behavior, task-oriented action by the group varies greatly in strength and persistence. For the big game a football team may outdo itself, showing great effort and determination; for a less important game, the players may neither try as hard nor perform as well. In general, the amount and persistence of group effort depend heavily on the degree to which group goals are perceived as relevant to the members' needs and accepted as their own. One of the key problems faced by leaders—from football coaches to presidents of companies or countries—is that of mobilizing group effort toward key group goals.

Like individuals, groups also utilize feedback concerning the outcome of their actions as a basis for making possible changes—whether in a task-oriented or a defense-oriented way. When feedback is used in a task-oriented way, the group becomes a "self-correcting" energy system. When not, it may become so concerned with its "image" or its good name that its efforts go into defensive maneuvers instead of into more effective efforts toward its goals.

Thus group action appears to follow the same basic principles as individual coping behavior. Groups have certain potential advantages, such as the potential for specialization of function of individual members, the ability to handle multiple tasks at the same time, and the capacity to deal with problems that are beyond the range of any one individual. At the same time, groups are often at a disadvantage compared to the individual with respect to such factors as communication, decision time, and coordination of action.

Factors in group effectiveness. In recent years there has been extensive research on the variables that are related to group effectiveness —the success of the group in achieving its goals and meeting the need of its members. Three sets of factors play a role in determining how effective a group will be: (1) characteristics of the group members, (2) the group organization and manner of functioning, and (3) the setting in which the group functions. Some of the most important conditions in each of these three general categories are summarized on page 282. These conditions contribute not only to the level of group effectiveness but also to the level of stress tolerance of the group—to the difficulty of adjustive demands with which the group can cope without undergoing serious disorganization—and hence to the quality of the group's performance under sustained stress and in crisis situations.

Patterning of Group Change

With time, group structure and functioning may undergo marked changes. Changes may take place in group goals, leadership, roles, values, membership, and other aspects of the group's structure. Similarly, the group may show improvement or deterioration in its level of performance and in its ability to achieve its goals. Such changes result from a combination of inner and outer determinants, including changes in the composition of the group.

Life-cycle changes. Many groups appear to follow a pattern of change somewhat comparable to the life cycle of the individual—with an early period of growth, a middle period of maturity, and a later period of deterioration or atrophy. The historian Toynbee (1947) has described the characteristic stages of this pattern as: (1) a formative, youthful period, during which the group is vigorous, dedicated to its aims, and highly productive; (2) a period of conservative middle age, during which initiative and dedication are reduced and the group rests on its laurels, content with the progress it has made; and (3) a period of old age and disintegration, during which internal conflicts and inconsistencies within the group gradually lead to its decline and fall. Rome, for example, had its period

of youth and vigor, during which it conquered most of the known world and made remarkable technological and cultural advances, its period of middle age, during which it tended to maintain its gains rather than to implement them or show further creativity, and its period of old age, during which it suffered corruption, decline, and eventual fall to the barbarians some five hundred years after its founding.

But group change does not always follow this pattern. Many conditions within the group or in its environment can influence the direction and rate of change—or even keep the group from changing appreciably. Many groups remain small and ineffectual for the entire period of their existence; others have a sudden spurt in growth and effectiveness because of favorable changes in their environment. Certain types of groups also appear to follow their own characteristic patterns. For example, the family group follows a clear-cut pattern from its inception with marriage, through the rearing of children and their eventual leaving of the family, to the dissolution of the marriage with the death of the marital partners. But here too the pattern is not always followed, as when a family is prematurely disrupted by divorce or the early death of family members.

As we have noted, rapid change in group customs, beliefs, and values may pose a threat to group integration. If old anchorages are torn away before the foundations for new ones can be laid, group members tend to become confused, uncertain of their roles, and "alienated" from the group. Thus the rate as well as the patterning and quality of social change may have far-reaching effects on individuals as well as on the survival and effectiveness of the group.

Group decompensation. Groups generally try to change in ways that will further the attainment of their goals and improve their effectiveness, but they are not always successful. In some cases, under severe and sustained stress, a group shows changes in the direction of disorganization or decompensation rather than increased effectiveness.

The course of group decompensation follows stages comparable to those we traced for individuals: (1) alarm and mobilization, (2) resistance, and (3) exhaustion—the end of the group as a unit. The sequence of group decompensation is vividly illustrated in the case of the Xetas, described below.

Sometimes a group undergoes some measure of decompensation but manages to stabilize itself during the stage of resistance. Thus a threatened marriage may be stabilized sufficiently to continue, though without adequately meeting the needs of the marital partners or fulfilling its initial promise. On the other hand, a failing marriage may recompensate as a result of the determined efforts of the marital partners to make the necessary readjustments.

Group Pathology

Short of actual group decompensation and breakdown, there are many conditions in groups that can be considered pathological. Serious dissension and conflict among group members, repressive or dishonest leaders, faulty assumptions and values, and subgroups who disregard the general group wel-

fare are representative of conditions that can cripple a group and keep it from achieving its goals and meeting the needs of group members. As we have noted, rapid changes in group customs, beliefs, and values may also pose a threat to group integration.

In Chapter 4 we noted some of the characteristics of family interactions which appear to be pathological and detrimental to family members. It is perhaps also appropriate to note that our own society has been criticized as pathogenic on a number of scores—prominent among which are its racism, both black and white; its failure to solve the problems of poverty and the deteriorating cities; its overemphasis on material values; and the prevalence of crime and violence. Often such characteristics have been cited as symptoms of our group pathology.

But there is another side to the picture. We can point to the remarkable degree of personal freedom and opportunity that Americans as a group enjoy; to our acceptance, in principle, of the worth and dignity of each individual; to our general feelings of responsibility for trying to eradicate conditions in which there is injustice or inequality of opportunity; to the concern of our young people for seeking out what is genuine; and

GROUP DECOMPENSATION

The Xetas were an Indian tribe discovered in southwestern Brazil in the 1950's and believed to be the most primitive humans in existence.

"They have no agriculture, know no metal, make no pottery. They sleep on the ground instead of in hammocks as most Brazilian primitives do. Their weapons are bows and arrows and stone axes. Their knives are sharp flakes of stone. They eat everything that they can find or kill in the jungle: fruit, insects, snakes, roots too fibrous for white men's stomachs." (*Time*, 1959, p. 62)

The alarm and mobilization period had evidently begun for this tribe when it was driven back into rugged mountain country by stronger tribes and the white man. This pattern of resistance was successful

to the extent that the Xetas managed to hide from the civilized world for several hundred years, but the weaknesses within the group and its inhospitable environment doomed it to eventual exhaustion. Eventually they were flushed out of hiding by starvation and the wooings of an anthropology professor (who hoped the surviving members of the tribe would be given government protection in a jungle preserve).

By 1959 only about 250 remained, and for a time they lived in small bands, shifting camp every few days. Now they have left their forest retreats and the survivors have become largely scattered, working on the farms of the area. As a tribe, they no longer exist (Crocker, 1968).

to many other fundamental strengths of our society.

In any event we can agree that conditions which interfere with the achievement of our primary goals—and hence lead to a failure of need fulfillment for many group members—are pathological. Perhaps we can also agree that progress and good adjustment for our society will consist in correcting these conditions, and moving ahead toward realizing the growth potentials of all our citizens and of our nation as a whole—and letting other societies do the same.

GROUP-INDIVIDUAL INTERACTION

In the preceding discussion we have attempted to sketch a broad picture of the group setting of behavior, looking at groups as energy systems having structural, integrative, and field properties and striving toward maintenance and enhancement somewhat as individuals do. In this section we will be concerned with more specific effects of the group upon the individual and, since this is not a one-way street, with some of the effects of the individual upon the group. We cannot begin here to deal with all the effects in both directions but will focus on three features of group-individual interaction which appear especially pertinent: (1) the effects of the individual who is the leader; and (2) some effects of group membership on the individual; and (3) the special problems of conformity, independence, and rebellion.

The Individual As a Leader

Groups differ greatly in their leadership structure. In informal or loosely organized groups, especially where there is unanimity of purpose, leadership may be virtually nonexistent or constantly shifting. In highly organized groups, on the other hand, leadership becomes an important characteristic of group organization. Such groups may be led by an individual or by a committee or other subgroup. Two leaders will often emerge—a task specialist and a social specialist, the first concerned with directing the group toward its primary goals and the second with maintaining the functional harmony of the group itself (Bales, 1958). Most leaders, however, are concerned to some extent with both maintenance and task goals.

Leadership is a highly complex phenomenon, and despite a great deal of research many aspects of leadership are not well understood. Our present focus will be on the functions leaders perform, the personal characteristics typically associated with leadership, and differences in types or styles of leadership. As we will see, the leader both creates and is created by the situation: the demands, expectations, and cooperation or resistance of the followers, as well as the setting in which the group is functioning may be as important as the individual's personal characteristics in determining whether he becomes a leader and how successful a leader he can be.

Functions of the leader. The responsibilities of a leader will vary from one group to another, but some functions are common to most leaders. Ruch (1967) has delineated four such functions:

1. *Structuring the situation.* A key function of the leader is to set the climate and to define the situation so that all the members will have the same picture of where the group is and what it is trying to do. He also makes it clear when choices must be made and what the alternatives are; as effort proceeds and conditions change, he is alert to new demands or conditions which may require new planning. In a democratic group, he helps to clarify differences in viewpoint among the members and helps the group to understand and resolve disagreements or conflicts that may arise.

2. *Controlling group behavior.* It is the leader's responsibility to prevent individuals from exploiting the group, and the group from exploiting individuals. This means enforcing the rules that have been established and in

some cases making or helping to make new ones. He is responsible for keeping the group's energies and efforts directed into the channels decided on as well as for coping with members who get out of line.

3. *Speaking for the group.* The leader is responsible for translating the group's feelings into words and actions. He is the spokesman for the group, helping to articulate to the members what Quakers call "the sense of the meeting" and to interpret to outsiders what the group's objectives and desires are. He must be sensitive to differences within the group and skillful in finding and delineating areas of agreement.

4. *Helping the group achieve its goals and potential.* Included here are the functions of planning, coordinating, decision making, and mobilizing the energy of group members. Included here also is the responsibility for ensuring the active participation of all the group members and the utilization of their diverse capabilities—in short, for providing whatever help the group may need to develop and utilize its resources effectively.

Since these functions are essential for group achievement, individuals soon emerge as leaders in groups which initially have no formal leadership as well as in groups which have lost their leaders. The leader, in turn, is enabled to accomplish many of his functions by virtue of the power vested in the leadership role by the other group members.

Qualities of leaders. An early view which has persisted into contemporary times is "the great man" view of leadership. This is the view that certain individuals possessing outstanding abilities are destined to emerge as leaders and to influence whatever groups they participate in. Often the term "charismatic" is used to refer to leaders presumably endowed with the gift of leadership.

During the early part of the twentieth century an alternative view came into popularity—the view of leadership as a product of situational conditions. Rather than being destined to lead by virtue of great ability, the leader was viewed as an individual who possessed the abilities needed by the group in a given situation. Different situations might call for quite different qualities in leaders; and if the situation changed, the group might change leaders.

Although the pendulum has swung in the direction of the situational view of leadership, certain personality traits appear to be related to leadership. In a review of the research evidence, Berelson and Steiner (1964) concluded that the exercise of leadership, at least in small, voluntary groups, is related to the following personal qualities: (1) physical size, (2) physical appearance and dress, (3) self-confidence and self-assurance, (4) sociability and friendliness, (5) will, determination, and energy, and (6) intelligence, so long as the individual is not too much more intelligent than the rest of the group. Most effective leaders also appear to be perceptive of the needs, feelings, and attitudes of group members; to be flexible and responsible; and to have superior communication skills. But although these traits tend to be associated with leadership, there are marked differences among leaders in the degree to which a particular leader will possess them.

All these qualities appear also to be widely distributed among nonleaders as well as leaders, thus highlighting the importance of situational demands in determining what particular mix of these general qualities and what special qualities will be sought when a particular leader is being chosen. In selecting a university president, for example, high intelligence and other characteristics among those listed above may be considered essential, but "fund raising" ability may be the deciding consideration.

In large groups, campaigns using modern methods of persuasion and "image making" may make it difficult for members to assess accurately the qualities of persons they are choosing as leaders. And in some instances, people do not select the ablest leader, especially when there is no opportunity to know him personally. Uninformed people who are frustrated and discouraged by social conditions may fall prey to a demagogue who exploits the situation for his own ends.

EFFECTS OF AUTOCRATIC, DEMOCRATIC, AND LAISSEZ-FAIRE LEADERSHIP

In a classic study of the effects of different kinds of leadership, clubs were formed of 10-year-old boys matched as to age, intelligence, economic background, and so on, and three different types of adult leadership were practiced in the various groups. In the *authoritarian* groups the leader set the group goals, controlled all activity with step-by-step directions, and evaluated the boys' work. In the *laissez-faire* groups the leader simply stood by and answered when spoken to: the groups were entirely on their own in planning and assigning work. In the *democratic* groups members and leader discussed and determined policies and assignments together. The factor of possible personality differences was controlled by having each leader and all the boys operate in at least two different climates.

Differences in performance and other reactions were striking. In the autocratic groups performance was fairly good, but motivation was low and the boys worked only when the leader was present to direct them. The laissez-faire groups did less work and work of a poorer quality. The boys in the democratic groups showed more interest in their work and more originality and kept on working whether the leader was present or not. There was more destruction of property and more aggressiveness and hostility in the autocratic groups, but the hostility tended to be channeled toward a scapegoat member or toward the working materials rather than toward the leader. Members of autocratic groups were also more dependent and more submissive, showed less individuality, and gave less friendly praise to each other. Morale and cohesiveness were lowest in the laissez-faire groups, highest in the democratic groups. The democratic leaders were liked best by the boys (Lewin, Lippitt, & White, 1939).

Sometimes, too, people will follow a particular leader out of sentiment or loyalty despite clear evidence that the best interests of the group are not being served. Thus research on ways of predicting success in leadership is now focusing on the interaction of the leader, the group, and the situation.

Types or styles of leadership. The methods used by leaders in exerting their influence and control appear to depend upon the characteristics of the leader, group, and situation. Some leaders are prone to autocratic, others to democratic, and still others to laissez-faire methods of leadership. Similarly, some groups will respond favorably to one kind of leadership and not another, often depending upon what they are used to or what the larger culture expects. For example, individuals may accept autocratic leadership in a military setting which they would not countenance in a civilian setting; or they may accept laissez-faire leadership in a neighborhood group which they would not countenance in a business organization. The general nature and effects of autocratic, democratic, and laissez-faire methods of leadership were demon-

strated in the classic study by Lewin, Lippitt, and White (1939) described above.

In assessing the effects of different styles of leadership on group members, it is now realized that past socialization experiences also play an important role: individuals with different past social experience may respond differently to the same kind of leadership. In general, Americans and Western Europeans are reared under conditions which lead to a preference for democratic methods of leadership—whether in the family or in a larger group setting. But in a society where leaders are expected to be autocratic, a democratic leader may be perceived as weak and inept and may elicit noncooperation instead of better member participation. Thus it is risky to predict the effects of a given method of leadership without knowing something of the experience and expectations of the particular group.

In general, it can probably be said that autocratic leadership may be efficient for meeting immediate and temporary crisis situations—as in the fighting of wars—but will tend to defeat its own purposes if maintained over a long period of time or used in situations that do not require it. For it usually reduces the initiative and creativity of individual members and subgroups, thus eventually reducing the adaptive potentiality of the group.

On the other hand, democratic leadership appears to have greater long-range survival value for a group because it elicits member involvement and places minimum restraints on their initiative and creativity, thus tending to promote the adaptability so necessary for meeting changing conditions and demands. Democratic leadership is often more difficult to achieve, however, because it demands more of the leader as well as of the group members.

The influence of leaders. The actual role of leaders in shaping human affairs is a subject of some dispute. Many social psychologists and sociologists attribute great powers to leaders and consider them key influences in shaping history. Others believe that the leaders merely symbolize what their followers want and exert influence over the group only insofar as they go in the direction that the group desires. They point out that the leader who tries to guide his followers in a direction they oppose will either lose his position of leadership, be unsuccessful, or cause the group to disintegrate.

History gives examples which seem to support both these contentions. A particular social situation must usually exist before a particular kind of leader can emerge and be accepted; a leader like Mao, for example, could come to power only during a period of great social unrest and change. Yet often a group could be led in any of several directions by a strong leader—for example, toward innovation and experiment with new ways of solving the group's problems, or toward efforts to maintain the status quo, or toward preoccupation with problems of secondary importance and denial of the reality of a major demand to be met. Also the leader can deploy the group's resources wisely or inefficiently; he can inspire dedication and enthusiasm or dissension and discontent; and he can raise or lower members'

sights in terms of their collective goals and purposes. Different leaders can move the same group toward reasoned action, emotionalism, apathy, or violence. Thus individual leaders may have a potent influence on the group.

But what the group achieves depends on the quality of "followership" as well as on the leader. As we have seen, the motives, capabilities, attitudes, and commitment of individual members are of key importance in determining how a group functions. In fact, in an interesting study of men working in small groups during a twelve-month period of isolation in Antarctic scientific stations, several of the same personality traits were consistently found to be characteristic of both effective leaders and effective followers; these included a high degree of satisfaction with work assignments, acceptance of authority, and motivation to be part of the group and work as a team (Nelson, 1964).

Again it becomes apparent that we must have adequate knowledge of group members as well as of the leadership and of the situation in which the group is functioning—and the interaction among these three sets of factors—if we are to understand the behavior of the group and of individuals in it.

Some Effects of Group Membership on the Individual

The specific effects on an individual of being in a group depend, of course, on many factors, including the size, purpose, organization, ideology, prestige, power, and effectiveness of the group; the individual's actual position and role in the group and his length of membership; his age, sex, motives, intelligence, and frame of reference; and what other groups he belongs to or would like to belong to. Often the group's influence on the individual's behavior at a given moment is determined largely by what it means to him to be in that particular group setting. For example, the senior speaking at graduation ceremonies may feel jittery and frightened, not because of anything members of the group are doing to him, but because he feels "on the spot" and fears he may not live up to their expectations.

In addition to—or in spite of—the influences of specific factors in a particular case, there are certain typical effects of being in a group that merit brief attention.

Satisfactions, frustrations, and personal growth. An individual's group memberships may bring a large proportion of the satisfaction or frustration he feels with his life situation. The man who has a responsible job, a close-knit, happy family, and responsibilities in community organizations has continuing sources of satisfaction and confirmation of his worth as well as several areas for further personal growth. The man who has an uncongenial job and an unhappy marriage and lives in a deteriorating community finds these three group settings sources of frustration, dissatisfaction, and blocked growth.

In general, such characteristics as high status, effective performance, and harmonious relationships among group members are likely to be associated with a high level of member satisfaction, whereas such characteristics as low status, ineffectiveness in goal achievement, and conflict with other group members are likely to be associated with fewer satisfactions and more frustrations for group members. Membership in groups which are subjected to severe stress and threat or which are in the process of disintegrating are also likely to provide proportionately fewer satisfactions and more frustrations.

Groups differ in the extent to which they provide opportunities for continuing personal growth. In general, it would appear that a democratically organized group tends to foster personal responsibility, involvement, and growth, whereas an authoritarian setting tends to block personal growth except in limited, approved directions. Whether an individual devotes his major efforts to maintenance or actualization often depends more on the limitations and opportunities provided by his group memberships than it does on personality factors.

In-group and out-group attitudes. Membership in a group which is important to the individual may strongly influence his attitudes and behavior toward other members as well as toward "outsiders." For example, individuals who closely identify with a group and its status tend to perceive the group and other members—the "in-group"—in a highly favorable light, as generally more intelligent, well-intentioned, and worthy than outsiders. Fellow in-group members get the benefit of the doubt. Outsiders are regarded with suspicion and may be assumed to be dangerous until proved friendly. Often the individual enhances his own status by building up in-group members and downgrading members of an out-group.

Apparently the same kind of perceptual distortion that makes an individual less aware of his own failings than of other people's operates to make him less aware of the shortcomings of his own group than of the failings of other comparable groups. In direct proportion to the extent that he identifies with a group, the group member tends to defend it from attack or threat and to try to maintain a favorable view of it, calling on the same defense mechanisms he uses to protect his personal self.

Many of our biases are thus a consequence of our group identifications. National groups disparage their neighbors; one religious or political group may take a "holier than thou" attitude toward another. Students in one school may feel superior to those in a nearby school.

Fortunately, however, such in-group and out-group attitudes are not inevitable, and members who are genuinely concerned about a group's welfare and progress may take a critical and evaluative attitude in the hope of improving its effectiveness. And often a suggestion or criticism coming from a member is accepted as helpful and constructive, where the same criticism from an outsider would arouse defensiveness or resentment.

Social facilitation. A number of early studies demonstrated that the presence of others influenced the behavior of the individual, usually eliciting greater effort or improved performance. This influence was referred to as *social facilitation.*

In a dramatic way, social facilitation can be seen in the interstimulation and "social contagion" of crowd behavior, as in a riot or in the panic reactions of individuals attempting to escape from a burning building. Apparently, especially in emotion-arousing situations, individuals respond to and, in turn, further contribute to heightened emotionality in those around them. This phenomenon of social contagion helps to account for both the tremendous force and the irrationality of much crowd behavior (Broom & Selznick, 1963; McDavid & Harari, 1968). For as the individual becomes increasingly influenced by the prevailing mood and behavior of the crowd, he becomes less influenced by reality, ethical, and other restraints.

Social facilitation and contagion can also be observed in smaller and more highly organized groups. In a classroom, the restlessness or defiance of a few students may quickly spread to the rest. Members of a football team with good morale and *esprit de corps* often feel buoyed up by each others' presence and exert greater effort in competitive play against another team; and team members may exuberantly hug a player who

has made a brilliant run leading to a crucial touchdown.

Conversely, members of a losing football team may become demoralized and less effective as they lose confidence in their ability and respond to each others' discouragement. Depending on the circumstances, social facilitation may thus lead to either an improvement or a deterioration in individual performance and consequently to increased or decreased group effectiveness.

Distortion of perception and judgment. A child learns very early that many of his needs will be met only through social interactions in which he maintains the approval of those with power. Thus he learns to conform—at home, in school, and in his peer group. The need to conform in a group situation, in order to gain group acceptance and approval—and the related need to avoid group disapproval—can lead to remarkable distortions in judgment and even perception. Such distortion was shown dramatically in the classic study summarized on page 292. Peer and other group pressures in real life are probably even stronger than those generated in this experimental situation. In the following section we shall examine conformity pressures as a potential problem for both individuals and groups.

GROUP ATTRACTIVENESS TO THE INDIVIDUAL

A number of rational and irrational considerations influence a group's attractiveness to an individual.

1. *Commonality of interests, values, and goals.* The individual tends to join and participate in groups whose purposes and values are congruent with his own; conversely, he is likely to avoid or drop out of groups lacking such characteristics.

2. *Success and status of group.* Individuals tend to be attracted to groups which have a demonstrated record of competence and success and which have high status among their peer group.

3. *Difficulty of gaining entrance.* Individuals often place a high value on membership in a group to

which it is difficult to gain entry—such as a group with exclusive membership or one requiring the performance of difficult tasks to establish eligibility for membership.

4. *Security and anxiety reduction.* An individual may be attracted to a group that provides some measure of security and/or anxiety reduction, as in homosexual organizations or therapy groups.

5. *Antidote to loneliness and alienation.* An individual may be attracted to a group because he feels alone and confused and the group provides him with ready-made purposes, values, and norms and something to give allegiance to.

EFFECTS OF CONFORMITY PRESSURES

In the classic experiment by Asch (1952, 1955), groups of seven to nine college students were asked to say which of three lines on a card (right) matched the length of a standard line on a second card (left). One of the three lines they could choose from was actually the same length as the standard line; the others differed from the standard by anywhere from three fourths of an inch to an inch and three fourths. It had been determined in advance that these differences were clearly distinguishable.

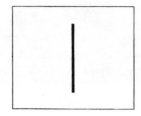 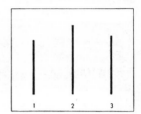

In each group all but one of the "subjects" were actually stooges, previously instructed to make a *unanimous wrong* choice on most of the trials after the first two. The actual subject was always in such a position that he would not announce his own judgment until after most or all of the others had announced theirs. Thus, after hearing the false judgment given by the planted majority, the minority subject had to choose between denying the evidence of his senses and contradicting the judgment of the group.

Under such pressure, minority subjects accepted the majority's wrong selections in 36.8 per cent of the trials. Some individuals, however, were able to stand up to such pressure better than others: about a fourth of the 123 naïve subjects clung consistently to their minority judgments, while a few subjects yielded to the majority decision on almost every trial.

When the test subjects were interviewed after the experiment, it was found that some had yielded out of fear of "seeming different," even though they continued to believe in the correctness of their own judgments. Others assumed that, although their own perceptions clearly *seemed* correct, the majority could not be wrong. In a few cases perception itself had apparently been distorted: the subject was apparently unaware of having yielded to group pressure.

Even subjects who consistently maintained their independent judgments tended to be considerably disturbed by their disagreement with the majority and reported that they had been seriously tempted to go along with the group in order to avoid seeming inferior or absurd. In fact, in a later study utilizing the same experimental setup, Bogdonoff *et al.* (1961) found that students "who called them as they saw them" suffered more anxiety, as indicated by physiological changes. One subject who consistently disagreed with the group was dripping with perspiration by the end of the session even though his judgments were right in each instance.

The Special Problem of Conformity Pressures

As we have seen, group pressures toward conformity serve a basic need of the group for self-maintenance. Thus they develop to some extent in any organized group, although the strength of such pressures—and the degree of conformity actually needed for a group's maintenance—vary greatly from one situation to another. For example, the conformity demanded and actually needed in a military organization during wartime is much greater than the conformity sought or needed in the sensitivity-training groups described in Chapter 12. Even in the latter case, however, certain ground rules are established and members are under some pressure to conform to them.

Not all nonconforming behavior meets with group sanctions. Sometimes nothing happens to the nonconformist—for example, if the norm he breaks is unimportant or if he is considered an important member of the group. In some cases, group leaders are allowed ·more latitude in behavior than are other members of the group (McDavid & Harari, 1968). The immediate situation of the group is also important. If the group is not under threat and is generally performing effectively, it is likely to permit more latitude on the part of its members than if it is struggling to establish itself or survive.

In this section we shall examine (1) some of the techniques groups use for inducing conformity; (2) the individual's problem of maintaining his integrity in the face of pressure to conform, and (3) society's need to temper its pressures toward conformity with provisions for variation and even dissent.

Techniques for inducing conformity. The techniques and pressures that groups exert to achieve conformity take many forms. Often there are role definitions that set limits to permissible behavior and thus tend to induce conformity. Group members may be subjected to a continual barrage of factual information and/or propaganda in an effort to convince them of the validity of group goals and values—and hence to elicit their cooperation and support. In small groups, the participation of members in setting goals and making decisions helps to create and maintain the involvement of group members and some measure of conformity. In special cases, extreme measures such as "brainwashing" may be utilized in an attempt to change basic thought patterns.

Usually group pressures toward conformity rest heavily upon the manipulation of rewards and punishments. The recognition and approval of other group members, advancement to a higher position in the group, and chances for awards and honors are common incentives for inducing conformity behavior, whereas members who create difficulties for the group by their deviant behavior may suffer social disapproval, loss of position, expulsion from the group, or a wide range of other punishments. Some English labor groups practice an organized ritual of "sending to Coventry" in which a norm violator is completely ignored by his fellow workers—never spoken to or included in group activities (Suedfeld, 1966).

In larger groups, sanctions may follow codes of law, in which norm violations and their attendant penalties are formally prescribed. In small face-to-face groups, sanctions are usually informal but may be even more influential in controlling the behavior of group members since so many personal psychological needs are normally met through close social interaction.

Conformity, independence, and personal integrity. Exposure to different values and memberships in different groups often result in conformity demands from one group that are in conflict with the demands another group is making on us or at variance with our own convictions. Usually we are most susceptible to the influence of demands by the group in which we most value membership, for they have the greatest power to give or withhold approval—and hence the satisfaction, affection, belonging, and self-esteem that we need. Thus it is easier for most teenagers to violate adult standards than to go against the dress, speech, and mannerisms expected by their peers—and their parents may feel equally reluctant to go against the expectations of *their* peers.

Despite the pressures we feel to conform to others' expectations, we all tend to condemn blind conformity because it is a giving up of self-direction—using others' values instead of one's own. But blind nonconformity is equally self-defeating. Rebelling for the sake of being "against" is an exaggerated assertion of independence and autonomy that fails to meet either individual or group needs.

Either conforming or nonconforming behavior may be "blind" or may be based upon rational thought and decision. A student may follow a school rule because he believes such cooperation will enable more people to work effectively, or because it has not occurred to him to question it, or because he is afraid to protest although he feels it to be unfair. Protest and rebellion, for a given young person, may represent a search for valid standards and an attempt to live by them, or it may be a slavish following of whatever is currently "in," or it may be simply an attempt to escape and destroy. Living in accordance with

our own convictions will sometimes lead us to behavior that others expect and value, but sometimes it will mean standing alone.[1]

An individual who rejects the established norms and values may move in any of several directions. Thus he may (1) continue to conform outwardly but become bitter and cynical; (2) withdraw from the mainstream of life, with alienation, anomie, and lack of direction; (3) embrace some new ideology, as represented by a political, religious, or social movement; or (4) work for changes within the normal channels of the existing social framework.

Society's need for deviation. Although some measure of conformity appears essential for coordinating group effort, some measure of nonconformity also appears essential for maintenance of the group's adaptability. If a group is to adapt effectively to changing conditions, it must be capable of making needed changes within its own structure and functioning. This means that someone in the group must recognize the new conditions, propose new approaches, and make other

group members aware of the need for change.

This point has been well elaborated by Buckley (1968) in his concept of "requisite deviation":[2]

"A requisite of sociocultural systems is the development and maintenance of a significant level of non-pathological deviance manifest as a pool of alternative ideas and behaviors with respect to the traditional, institutionalized ideologies and role behaviors. Rigidification of any given institutional structure must eventually lead to disruption or dissolution of the society by way of internal upheaval or ineffectiveness against external change." (p. 495)

In spite of pressures toward conformity, every large group has its share of people who do not conform. Some of these deviants—like our criminals—are emotionally immature or have learned distorted values that make them unable or unwilling to conform to the norms of society—though they may be

---

[1]The article on "Anonymity, Dissent, and Individual Integrity" by Mulford Sibley, reprinted on pages 506-512, is relevant here.
[2]Buckley's article is reprinted on pages 495-506.

The strongest pressures to conform—in dress, behavior, attitudes, and even mannerisms—are the pressures exerted by those in our peer groups, whether these be clubs, boards of directors, or social groups. Our typically high degree of conformity to such pressures helps to explain why the members of a group tend to look so much alike to outsiders.

conforming to the norms of their own deviant subgroup and be reaping the usual rewards of conformity from it. But many nonconformists in man's history have been men and women of maturity and vision—individuals like Columbus, Galileo, Roger Bacon, Billy Mitchell, Jane Addams, and Joan of Arc. Nonconformists like these perform lasting services to their society by initiating necessary or desirable changes in group norms, even at the cost of great personal sacrifice.

Unfortunately, it is often difficult for society to evaluate its nonconformists accurately. Even when there is an honest attempt to weigh historical and scientific evidence in judging new ideas, our perspective is always limited and the decision of contemporaries may be different from that of later generations. Thus it will be interesting to see how today's nonconformists are assessed 20 or 50 years from now. Sometimes history shows that nonconforming behavior has been divisive and detrimental to the group; in other instances, nonconformists who were roundly condemned in their time, like Jesus, were the prophets and founders of new ideas and

movements and the instigators of needed social change.

The problem for any group is how to maintain a necessary measure of conformity, while also maintaining the degree of deviance essential for flexibility and adaptability of the group. In the long run, individual and group interests appear to be best served when conformity pressures are limited to those areas where unanimity is essential for coordinated group functioning and effectiveness. Ideally, a group concerns itself explicitly with setting up ways of fostering requisite deviation and identifying it when it occurs.

INTERPERSONAL RELATIONSHIPS

Interaction among group members leads to the formation of social bonds or relationships. Such interpersonal relationships may be intimate or impersonal, harmonious or conflictful, supportive or destructive, or a combination of these and many other qualities as well. Interpersonal patterns can be extremely complex, and they keep changing. The quality of the interpersonal relationships we establish in groups to which we belong can be a source of great satisfaction or frustration, of personal growth and self-fulfillment or stultification.

The larger setting, as well as the structure of the immediate group, may foster one pattern rather than another among its members. Some cultures foster warm and intimate relationships; others foster aloofness, suspiciousness, and even hostility.

Three facets of our interpersonal relationships in group settings are of immediate interest here: (1) our goals in establishing and maintaining them, (2) our perceptions and mutual feelings of attraction, and (3) our accommodations to each other. In Chapter 15 we shall extend our discussion to include a consideration of factors that contribute to competence in relationships with other people.

Interpersonal Goals

Goals in establishing relationships with others are not always explicit and fully recognized by those concerned. However, any relationship that exists over a period of time usually must satisfy needs of the individuals involved; otherwise the relationship is likely to be terminated.

According to Bennis *et al.* (1964), individuals may establish group relationships with others to meet one or more of the following goals: (1) to satisfy needs for love, warmth, approval, and relatedness—as, for example, in a marriage; (2) to gain a realistic and orderly view of oneself and/or the world —as in associations of scholars which meet for the exchange of ideas and research findings; (3) to change oneself or the other(s)— as in a therapy group or a sensitivity-training group; or (4) to pool resources to achieve some common goal—as in a business partnership or a social action group.

Most relationships between individuals are complex and subserve more than one

goal for those taking part. For example, a marriage may subserve all the goals listed above. And with time, the goals or other characteristics of a relationship may change. Thus a marriage which started out primarily as a source of emotional need fulfillment may continue largely as an instrument for child rearing.

Interpersonal Perception and Attraction

In perceiving another person, we tend to look at and assess three related aspects (McDavid & Harari, 1968):

1. *Physical dimensions*—whether the observed person is male or female, young or old, attractive or unattractive, and so on.

2. *Behavioral dimensions*—the habitual and seemingly stable behavior patterns of the other person, such as whether he is quiet or talkative, honest or dishonest, friendly or aloof.

3. *Interactional dimensions*—the ways he can affect us, dependent on a variety of factors such as whether the person is our spouse or a friend, a peer or a subordinate or superior, and in a position to help or hurt us.

A perception of another person usually is an amalgam of all three—what he looks like, how he acts, and what potentials we see him as having for affecting us.

As in all perception, the motives and frame of reference of the perceiver help to determine what he sees in other people. A man may see the same girl quite differently depending on whether he is looking for a wife or a bridge partner or a secretary. And in assessing any unknown person, one inevitably uses his own experience and information, however limited or accurate, as a reference point.

The differential perception of in-group members and outsiders has already been mentioned. One of the most common mistakes is to assume that all members of a group, especially a group to which one does not belong, will be like the examples one has known or has heard about. *Prejudice* literally means "prejudgment" and implies that the perceiver has formed judgments in advance about the characteristics and behavior of all members of a given group. Any member is then "seen" as having these characteristics whether, in fact, he does or not. Such over-simplified stereotypes, as we have seen, are quite common. A familiar stereotype of the Irishman, for example, usually includes a keen sense of humor, a gift of "blarney," a fondness for alcohol, and a readiness to fight at the slightest provocation. Conservatives tend to have stereotypes of liberals and radicals; new leftists tend to have stereotypes of conservatives; black militants tend to have stereotypes of members of the white power structure. Stereotypes are often grossly inaccurate and at best fail to discriminate individual differences among the members of given groups. Often they reflect the motives and personality needs of the stereotype holder.

Studies of characteristics associated with interpersonal attraction have identified various traits generally regarded as socially desirable, such as superior intelligence, high socioeconomic status, a good sense of humor, sincerity and integrity, and physical attractiveness and health. Obviously

such a list will vary somewhat from group to group and individual to individual. In general, interpersonal attraction is closely related to commonality of interests, attitudes, values, and purposes and to the degree to which individuals experience or anticipate need satisfaction in their interactions with each other.

Proximity is also an important factor, especially at the beginning. Newcomb (1956) found three conditions that seem to be predictive of mutual attraction between people just getting acquainted: (1) frequency of interaction, (2) similarity of the new person to someone already liked, and (3) the potentiality for a relationship of reciprocal reward.

Thus it would appear that the old adage "Birds of a feather flock together" is closer to reality than the saying that "Opposites attract." Apparently individuals are attracted to both groups and individuals who have congruent values and purposes and can be instrumental in helping them meet their needs. It also then happens that their values and purposes tend to become increasingly alike if the association does in fact bring the anticipated satisfactions. There is even evidence that the mere act of committing oneself to a group membership tends to result in

FACTORS IN EFFECTIVE INTERPERSONAL ACCOMMODATION

In a review of his own and related research, Kelley (1968) has suggested that the success of attempts at interpersonal accommodation depend largely on the following factors:

1. Whether there is conflict or commonality of goals (interests)—accommodation being facilitated when individuals have purposes and goals in common.

2. How much incentive value the relationship has for both partners—the greater the incentives or consequences anticipated, the more important the relationship to the partners and the better the accommodation.

3. How well they can communicate—explicit communication about goals, needs, and problems facilitating accommodation. Without explicit communication, the individuals are forced to infer the

intent and meaning of each other's actions and may get an inaccurate picture.

4. How well reciprocal actions and moves are timed—whether, for example, quarreling lovers feel like making up at the same time. If not, accommodation may be difficult or impossible to achieve.

5. What strategy and tactics are used by the partners—cooperation, honesty, trust, and openness, for example, facilitating accommodation and competitiveness, deceit, distrust, and secrecy working against it.

Accommodation may also be influenced by other factors such as whether the individuals have learned appropriate patterns of accommodation in former relationships and are able to apply them to the new situation.

a change of one's values in the direction of those prized by the group even in advance of the satisfactions of participation (Kiesler, 1968).

Interpersonal Accommodation

Interpersonal accommodation is the process whereby two partners in a relationship evolve patterns of interaction which permit mutual need satisfaction. This process of accommodation or adjustment is necessary for an effective, enduring, harmonious interpersonal relationship.

If accommodation leads to maximal (or at least adequate) satisfaction of both partners' needs, the relationship is likely to stabilize and continue. If the relationship leads to frustration or minimal need gratification for one or both partners, there is likely to be a re-evaluation of goals or means or a disruption of the relationship. Dissatisfaction with or disruption of bonds between individual members of a group is likely to cause difficulties for the rest of the group—particularly a small group like a family. On the other hand, mutually satisfying interpersonal relationships are likely to lead to increased cohesiveness and commitment of the individual members to the group.

SUMMARY AND A LOOK AHEAD

Groups, like individuals, have structural and integrative characteristics and operate in physical and social settings. Like individuals, they strive to maintain themselves and resist disintegration and to grow and develop their potentialities. Like individuals, too, they may solve their problems in either task-oriented or defense-oriented ways, and if their problems are beyond their resources—or believed to be—they may show evidences of strain, decompensation, and pathology.

Groups have power structures, leadership structures, role structures, communication structures, and sociometric structures. They develop norms and ideologies and characteristic atmospheres and degrees of cohesiveness and morale. Different types of organization are appropriate for different groups; as they have greater or lesser success in meeting their primary goals and as their external situation changes, group organization may change in appropriate or inappropriate ways. Many groups show a "life cycle" not unlike that of individuals.

Group-individual relationships and mutual responsibilities are a perennial problem for both groups and individuals. Most groups have leaders, who perform various structuring and coordinating functions. They become leaders through various mechanisms and show differing styles. The qualities needed in a leader are determined in large part by the group values and goals and by the environmental demands and resources; thus even effective leaders are not all alike.

Many of our satisfactions and frustrations grow out of our participation in groups and our strivings, with others, toward group goals. Identification with a group and its goals leads to in-group and out-group attitudes—different perceptions of and feelings about insiders and outsiders. Our judgments, attitudes, and even perceptions can be distorted by our need to feel a part of the group and to feel approved by other group members. On the social level, as on the individual level, some variability is needed for health and growth and for potential for adaptation to changing environmental demands.

Society's problem is to encourage and recognize useful deviance; the individual's problem is to maintain his integrity and openness to his own experience in the face of conformity pressures.

Relationships among individuals are also an important medium through which we try to meet our needs and thus are potential sources of satisfaction and growth or unhappiness and frustration. Our goals in such relationships, the bases for attraction to others, and the mechanisms by which we accommodate ourselves to others' needs are currently subjects of active, systematic research.

The basic dimensions of group dynamics, group-individual interaction, and interpersonal relationships have been sketched in this chapter. The use of these concepts in the study of two particular types of social adjustment—marital adjustment and occupational adjustment—will be the focus of the next two chapters.

Key terms used in this chapter include:

group, collectivity (p. 273)
power hierarchy, reward power, coercive power (p. 275)
leadership structure (p. 275)
role structure, role expectation, role behavior, role conflict (p. 276)
communication structure, communication net (p. 277)
sociometric structure, sociogram (p. 277)
group norms, group ideology (p. 278)
group atmosphere (p. 279)
task and maintenance goals for groups (p. 280)
factors in group effectiveness (pp. 282-284)
group decompensation (p. 284)
functions of a leader (pp. 286-287)
autocratic, democratic, laissez-faire leadership (p. 288)
social facilitation, social contagion (pp. 290-291)
society's need for deviation (p. 294)
interpersonal accommodation (p. 298)

Chapter 10

PREMARITAL AND MARITAL ADJUSTMENT

Changing Premarital Patterns
Marital Relationships and Adjustment
Marital Unhappiness and Divorce

The relationship between the sexes is of key importance in human behavior. This relationship varies considerably from culture to culture and among the individuals and subgroups within a given culture. Among some cultures, for example, women are accorded an inferior status and denied the rights which women in Western societies have come to take for granted; often in such cultures the daughter is considered the property of her father and later of her husband and has little control over her own life. In some cultures relations between the sexes are fraught with suspicion, ridicule, and even contempt. Although such extreme patterns are changing, there are still great differences in the relationships between the sexes in different societies both before and after marriage.

In our brief overview, it is not our intent to cover the myriad forms or details of marital interactions and relationships but rather to delineate some of the key variables involved in marital adjustment. We shall also concern ourselves with the impact of contemporary social change upon premarital and marital patterns in our society. For sex roles, relationships between the sexes, and

other aspects of premarital and marital behavior are caught up in the turmoil and change of our contemporary world.

Although we shall find ourselves again handicapped by inadequate data from research, we can point to certain changes in premarital patterns which are influencing the marriage relationship itself, to some key marital styles and accommodations, and to problems in marital adjustment, including divorce. In the main, our discussion will focus on middle-class patterns and trends in our own society.

CHANGING PREMARITAL PATTERNS

Although the establishment of satisfactory male-female relationships has probably never been easy, there have usually been rules and standards and clearly defined sex roles to guide young people. Today such rules, standards, and roles are in disarray, and the young person has to rely increasingly on himself in achieving workable and satisfying heterosexual relationships prior to marriage.

Sex Roles and Relationships
Before Marriage

The much-discussed "sexual revolution" pertains largely to relationships between unmarried teen-agers or young adults. Young people's sex roles and relationships with each other before marriage, however, provide the experience and the attitudes that they carry with them into marriage. Thus if we are to understand the factors affecting marital adjustment, we need to start by looking at the changes in the social preparation our young people are receiving for it.

Convergence of sex roles. Traditionally in our society, male and female sex roles have been clearly differentiated, with clear differences in expected appearance, dress, interests, responsibilities, aggression, and other characteristics and behavior. Such traits as aggressiveness, competitiveness, logicality, and ability to restrain the show of emotion were part of the male role, while the female was supposed to be intuitive, submissive, emotional, and often clever and guileful. Now, however, there is a trend toward convergence of the sex roles. This "new look" is described by the sociologist Winick (1968) as follows:

"*A modishly dressed couple might be walking along with the woman in hip-length boots, "basic black" leather coat, a helmet, and a pants suit or straight-line dress of heavy fabric. Her male companion might be wearing a soft pastel slack suit, mauve hat, and a frilled and cuff-linked pink shirt. He could sport a delicate tie and jewelry, exude fragrance, and wear tapered shoes with stacked heels. Both could have shoulder-length hair, and their silhouettes would be quite indistinguishable.*" (p. 21)

Admittedly this example is an extreme one, but there does appear to be a blurring of traditional differences in male and female sex roles—not only in appearance and clothing but in interests, work roles, recreational activities, sexual behavior, and marital responsibilities.

The depolarization of sex roles appears to be one aspect of the rebellion of youth against the establishment; it also reflects the broader breakdown and confusion in our social norms and a groping toward new sexual identities and new dimensions in heterosexual relationships. Although it is presently impossible to predict with any assurance how far such role changes will go or what effect they will ultimately have on individuals and society, they are unquestionably modifying both premarital and marital patterns.

More permissive attitudes toward sex. A key problem for the adolescent and young adult prior to marriage is the gratification of sexual needs. Although the sex drive greatly increases in strength following puberty, the young person is not usually in a position to marry until several years later. In the meantime traditional standards for sexual behavior in our society have emphasized abstinence from sexual relations prior to marriage. Such standards are somewhat confusing and contradictory, however, because they have been applied to females more stringently than to males. In fact, sexual prowess at an early age on the part of the male has often been viewed as a sign of masculinity and tacitly approved. Thus there has been a general ambivalence in our society toward sexuality. As Eisenberg (1965) has pointed out:

"*The ambivalence of Western society toward sexuality—manifested by the conflicts between official attitudes and private behavior, and the pervasive emphasis on sex side by side with sanctions against its expression—accounts for the difficulty, so common in adolescence, of attaining the basis for a sense of competence, freedom, and pleasure as a sexually functioning adult.*" (p. 134)

As in the case of converging sex roles, marked changes appear to have taken place in the last decade in attitudes toward premarital sexual practices. These changes seem to be generally in the direction of abandonment of the double standard and extreme restrictiveness in favor of greater freedom of individual choice. Rebellion against the traditional standards and alleged hypocrisy in actual behavior of adults has undoubtedly played a part, as has the decline of parental controls and community scrutiny over adolescent premarital behavior. And of course availability of "the pill" has greatly reduced the fear of pregnancy. In any case, it is becoming apparent that many factors which in the past inhibited premarital sexual involvement are disappearing, with a concomitant change in attitudes toward premarital sexual relations.

Some students of the subject believe that the supposed sexual revolution is largely a myth and that actual sexual practices have changed little though attitudes clearly have changed (Reiss, 1968). However, in a survey of the sex practices of 2200 unmarried juniors and seniors in colleges and universities in the United States, Packard (1968) found that 43 per cent of the 21-year-old females and 57 per cent of the 21-year-old males reported having had sexual intercourse. This contrasts with figures of 27 and 51 per cent, respectively, for college-educated subjects in the earlier Kinsey studies. Although today's figures are higher for both sexes, the increase is considerably greater for females.

In a sample of married college students, half the wives and three fourths of the husbands admitted to premarital intercourse (Chilman, 1966). Aside from a reduction in social restraints and more permissive attitudes toward sex, the latter finding may also be related to the trend toward equal rights for the sexes and toward considering men and women as basically similar in their emotional and sexual needs (Winick, 1968).

The double standard is apparently not completely dead, however. Packard (1968) found that while the majority of college women said they would not be troubled by the knowledge that their marital partner had had premarital sexual experiences with one or more other persons, more than two thirds of the college men indicated that they would be troubled to some extent.

Despite apparent changes in attitudes toward premarital sexual practices, many of the perennial deterrents remain—including religious beliefs and the maintenance of tra-ditional values and standards on the part of many parents and youth. Whatever the deterrents, however, it is apparent that American youth are assuming an increasing amount of choice and responsibility for their own premarital sexual behavior.

Changing goals of premarital behavior. In a sense, life starts anew with each generation, and the lessons of living must be learned anew by each young person. A key developmental task of adolescence is achieving an adequate heterosexual adjustment in preparation for marriage and the starting of a new family. Thus the basic and continuing long-term purpose in the interaction of teen-age boys and girls—both from their point of view and that of society—is to prepare them for adult sex roles and relationships.

In our society social contacts between the sexes prior to marriage range from casual dating to more serious heterosexual commitments, such as those involved in "going steady" and formal engagement. Dating and going steady appear to be particularly important in preparing the young person for his adult sex role and serve at least three key purposes: (1) they provide experiences in which the young person can learn about and practice getting along with members of the opposite sex, (2) they provide an important means of meeting psychological as well as sexual needs, and (3) they enable the individual to establish standards by which a marriage partner is eventually chosen.

In the context of these three traditional and continuing purposes, there appears to be a shift in emphasis and specific practices which again reflects the broader social scene. Intimate sexual relations for the gratification of sexual and psychological needs seem to play an earlier and more important role. This is encouraged by the more permissive attitudes toward premarital sexual behavior, already discussed; it is also an attempt to counter feelings of anonymity and alienation in an impersonal mass society (Dreyfus, 1967). Aloneness, openness, alienation, and authenticity are by-words of the younger generation; beneath them is a striving for companionship, intimacy, and relatedness in heterosexual as well as other relationships. Sometimes this striving for intimacy and relatedness appears to take relatively superficial forms, as when a young person plunges into indiscriminate sexual practices or goes through meaningless group activities with a hope of "getting in touch."

Problems in premarital adjustment. In his experiences of dating, the young person may discover that his attitudes and values pose problems for him in adjusting to the demands of a heterosexual relationship; sometimes the attitudes, values, and behavior of other young people raise moral problems for him. Particularly is this likely to be true for dating couples coming from dissimilar social backgrounds. Although couples can sometimes get along amicably with quite different frames of reference and value orientations, such differences are likely to create serious problems in their relationship.

Disapproving parents or friends can also cause difficulty for a dating couple. Often parents intervene actively when a dating relationship crosses religious, social-class, or racial boundaries. Usually a dating couple spend some time with each other's friends; where such interactions are unpleasant or conflictual, they may pose adjustment problems for the couple. A girl may resent the influence her date's friends exert over him, or he may resent the influence of her friends. And as in marriage, financial problems or differences of opinion about the use of money can be a divisive factor.

Although the dating system can foster personal growth, it can also be damaging. Being popular with members of the opposite sex helps a young person to gain self-confidence, but the youth who is unattractive or unpopular may experience intense feelings of loneliness, isolation, and self-devaluation. Often he feels that a social stigma has been placed on him and that he has been evaluated and found wanting by his peers.

Even the youth who is popular with the opposite sex may use his new-found power for purposes of conquest and exploitation rather than for communicating and learning to understand and care about others. Sometimes, too, young people become emotionally involved with others who have a detrimental rather than constructive influence on their further development—as when a girl is inducted into delinquent behavior by a boy for whom she cares a great deal. Finally, termination of a relationship in which there has been intense sexual and emotional involvement can be painful and leave a residue of hurt and self-devaluation. The needs that premarital relationships can satisfy are many, but the actual patterns such relationships take may be either constructive and rewarding or unhealthy and destructive.

Expectations of Marriage

Marriage is an important goal for most people, and over 90 per cent of us do marry at some time in our lives. Married Americans now number about 90 million, or 66 per cent of the population over age 14. The median age at time of marriage is about 23 for men and 20.5 for women (Bureau of the Census, 1967). For college students, however, the median age is somewhat higher. Neubeck (1964) found that for students who complete 4 or more years of college the median age of marriage is 26 for men and 24 for women.

Monogamy is the only acceptable form of marriage in the United States today and has been so for many decades. In most other aspects, however, the institution of marriage is a varied and changing phenomenon. Like most other social institutions, it has become considerably different from what it was even a few years ago. The general nature of marital relationships, the reasons for marrying, the skills needed for success, and the criteria for evaluating marital adjustment are all in the process of change.

Changing marital relationships and expectations. Marriage was formerly an institution in which the partners' roles and relationships were largely prescribed by tradition and by the economic and social context of the family unit. Increasingly, in recent years, marriage has become a special form of companionship in which the partners' roles and relationships are expressions of their own motives and personalities rather than a fulfillment of prescriptions from their environment.

"With all the variations among American families, it is apparent that they are all in greater or lesser degree in a process of change toward an emerging type of family that is perhaps most aptly described as the 'companionship' form. This term emphasizes the point that the essential bonds in the family are now found more and more in the interpersonal relationships of its members, as compared with those of law, custom, public opinion, and duty in the older institutional forms of the family." (Burgess, 1964, p. 196) Burgess does not imply that companionship, affection, and happiness are absent in the institutional marriage but points out that these are not its primary objectives. In the United States today, society's stake in the family as a stable economic and social unit is regarded as somewhat secondary in importance to what the marital experience provides for the individuals involved.

A key consequence of the changing emphasis has been a change in the expectations and meaning of marriage to those undertaking it. Marriage is anticipated today chiefly as a means to personal fulfillment and happiness in a close relationship of love and sharing.

Reasons for marriage. People marry for many reasons. Probably the most common and important of these relate to sexual satisfactions, to economic considerations, and to the meeting of psychological needs. The relative importance of these factors varies greatly, of course, from one person to another.

1. *Sexual satisfaction.* In probably every society, marriage is the most acceptable way of achieving sexual satisfaction. It is still true in modern America despite the apparent relaxing of some restrictions governing sexual behavior. There still are social sanctions discouraging sexual relations prior to marriage, and young people are encouraged to guide their sexual impulses into marital channels. After marriage, there are even stronger social and legal pressures on the individual to limit his sexual expression to the marital relationship. Although it is probably easier now than in the past to find sexual satisfaction outside of marriage, most people view the intimate and socially sanctioned marital setting as the most adequate basis for such satisfaction.

2. *Economic considerations.* In the past, especially when marriages were arranged by the parents, marriage choices were often made on the basis of economic considerations. Families often achieved or maintained status according to the families with whom they could establish marital relationships. And in our earlier rural economy, the partners in a marriage made an efficient economic team, with the wife caring for the home and children and the husband farming the land. A single man or woman often had no choice but to live with relatives or friends.

Although this kind of economic teamwork is not essential in today's family, many individuals, especially women, still look to marriage as a way of gaining financial security. With increasing occupational opportunities for women, however, the seeking of economic security appears to be a less significant and compelling reason for marrying than in the past.

3. *Meeting of psychological needs.* In contemporary America, most people do not marry primarily for sexual or economic reasons but to gain psychological satisfactions. In part, this change reflects the fact that in our generally affluent society maintenance needs are generally of less concern than actualization needs. Marriage is anticipated more as a means of gaining companionship, mutual emotional support, a secure "home base," and most of all an intimate relationship in which one can share all aspects of one's life. And since the rearing of children also constitutes a key facet of the actualization strivings of most people, marriage is sought as the most adequate and acceptable setting for family life.

Many other psychological needs—healthy and unhealthy—may influence an individual's decision to marry. Thus a person may marry to escape from loneliness or from the parental home, to be protected, to gain notoriety or social position, or to please or spite someone. When an individual sees most of his friends and other age-mates getting married, he may feel that it is "the thing to do" and even try to convince himself that he is in love with the person he is currently dating. A related phenomenon is the panic experienced by some people, especially women, when they reach an age considered to be old for marriage and fear they will end up as "old maids." Under these circumstances, the individual may be less selective in his choice of a mate because he feels that time is running out and the field is narrowing.

Why some people never marry. One of the questions Packard (1968) asked in his survey of sexual attitudes and practices of college students was, "Can you visualize a happy, satisfying life for yourself that might not include marriage?" Only 15 per cent of college females and 24 per cent of males answered "Yes." And his data do not indicate how many of these preferred life with marriage and were hoping to marry. Undoubtedly the great majority of young people plan to marry; but a minority never do.

Just as there are many reasons why people marry, there are many reasons why some people do not marry. Some do not find the right person; others are unwilling to give up their personal freedom to share their lives with someone else. With the availability of "the pill" and the greater permissiveness toward premarital sexual relations, a small group of young people—especially men—are reluctant to commit themselves to the rigors and mixed blessings of family responsibilities. This attitude seems to be part of the broader attitude in our culture of "playing it cool," and not becoming committed to anything or anyone. However, by the age of 35 to 44, only about 5 per cent of women and 8 per cent of men are never-marrieds (Bureau of the Census, 1964).

The accepted viewpoint has been that women have more difficulties, both psychologically and socially, in adjusting to the unmarried state than do men. It is usually assumed that the woman has not remained single by choice and that she is likely to feel somewhat devaluated and unfulfilled. In a recent study of 38 never-married women and 38 married mothers, however, Baker (1968) found no support for this viewpoint. The two groups of women manifested equivalent adjustment, and it was concluded that through creative activities that contribute to society the never-married woman may achieve a satisfactory adjustment and self-fulfillment even though denied a husband and children.

On the other hand, a survey of single men found them to be more maladjusted than either single women or married men (Knupfer et al., 1966). It was also found that the single men in the study had experienced a higher level of childhood stress than the other groups and that their current lives were more socially isolated and antisocial than those of the single women. In view of men's greater freedom of choice in the marriage market, it seems likely that men who do not marry are, as a group, more psychologically impaired to begin with and then continue to increase their maladjustment through isolation or transient and superficial relationships.

In general, it would appear that many single individuals are able to establish meaningful relationships with others, engage in constructive work, and lead fulfilling lives. Marriage is not the only channel for intimacy, meaningful communication and sharing, or even for care and guidance of the young. The old assumption that "only in pairs are people persons"—which is often the basis for ill-prepared and unhappy marriages—does not seem to be borne out by research.

New standards for assessing marital success. With the changes in the functions served by marital relationships and in the reasons for marrying, new standards have evolved for evaluating marital success. On the frontier, the survival of the family members depended on the competence of both husband and wife in many specialized skills; for example, wifely responsibilities included spinning, sewing, baking, cooking, doctoring, and teaching of the children. The demands to be met were specified largely by the environment and the success of the marriage required that both partners handle their responsibilities adequately.

Today, although economic maintenance and childrearing are still important functions of the family, they are not usually the main criteria by which its success is judged. In fact, there is no clear pattern of external demands on a marriage against which we can measure its success. With marriage increasingly seen as a means of meeting personal needs and achieving self-fulfillment and happiness for those entering into it, we tend to evaluate marriages on the basis of the adjustment between the marital partners along such dimensions as sexual compatibility, common interests and values, emotional closeness, and mutual need satisfaction. If a marriage is providing an intense, intimate, and mutually satisfying experience which contributes to the personal adjustment and growth of both marital partners, we tend to regard it as a healthy marriage regardless of whether it has produced children or advanced the economic well-being of the participants. But if these aspects of mutual satisfaction are missing and the partners are disappointed and unhappy, the marital relationship is considered deficient. And such a deficiency is often viewed as sufficient justification for ending the marriage.

Initially it might appear that these new standards for marital success place less stressful demands on the marital relationship, but this does not necessarily follow. For a mark of our times has been the gradual disappearance of the extended family—usually comprising two or three generations—which is still characteristic in many parts of the world. In the United States today, marriage increasingly involves a breaking away of both husband and wife from their respective families and the establishing of a nuclear family unit with only themselves and their offspring. Instead of being a merger with a larger group, such a marriage involves the formation of a new small group which is socially self-sufficient in terms of meeting the psychological needs of its members. Its lack of strong ties with and responsibilities to a larger family unit accentuates the demands that are made upon the relationships within it; increasingly family members are thrown back upon each other for feelings of belongingness, security, emotional support, and a sense of meaning. Thus modern marriage is subject to expectations and demands which require a high level of interpersonal competence and personal maturity on the part of the marital partners.

Selecting a Mate

Questions pertaining to how people select their mates and to who marries whom are of perennial interest. In many societies, complex rules guide mate selection, and often the selection is made or heavily influenced by parents. In our own society the individual makes the choice largely on his own, often without obtaining the consent or even approval of parents.

What are the bases on which this choice is made? How important is romantic love? What do young people say they are looking for, and what other factors enter into the choices they finally make? And how accurately can the results of a given choice be predicted?

The quest for romantic love. Many years ago the anthropologist Ralph Linton (1936) pointed out that:

"All societies recognize that there are occasional violent, emotional attachments between persons of opposite sex, but our present American culture is practically the only one which has attempted to . . . make them the basis for marriage." (p. 175)

Since this observation was made, romantic love as a basis for mating has become common in the Western World and is taking hold in Japan and other parts of the Orient (Rosenblatt, 1968).

Although romantic love is a dominant theme in novels and in movie and television dramas, we actually know very little about its actual nature or role in modern marriage. This is a particularly curious fact since romantic love is generally not only accepted as the most desirable basis for choosing a partner but also assumed to be the basis on which most marriages in our society are contracted.

In Chapter 14 dealing with problem emotions, we shall compare romantic love with infatuation. For the moment let us simply note that romantic love appears to involve strong feelings of physical attraction and affection, respect for the other person, a desire to be with the other person, and a concern for the welfare of the other person. Not all people appear capable of experiencing romantic love: as we have noted, early family relationships appear important in determining our later ability to love and be concerned about the welfare of others.

According to a study by Kephart (1960), the female probably has more control over her romantic inclinations than the male. While the female experiences more romantic attachments than the male during adolescence, a kind of "matrimonial directedness" expresses itself during her young adulthood which tends to include an ability to ignore or reject some of her earlier romantic notions in the interests of achieving matrimony. Presumably the male, who is generally less matrimonially oriented, retains his notions of romantic love as of central importance and makes sure that this criterion is met before seriously considering marriage.

Without the support of a good interpersonal relationship between the partners, romantic love forms an unstable base for a love relationship in marriage and usually does not long endure. There is some evidence that the pendulum may be swinging back gradually to a more pragmatic and sophisticated middle ground in which romantic love and the quality of the relationship with one's proposed mate are both seen as important in choosing a partner and committing oneself to marriage.

What do young people look for? Young people have definite ideas about what they are looking for in a mate and about what categories of persons are "eligible" or "ineligible." Certain individuals tend to be excluded automatically on the basis of age, education, race, body type, and social orientation. The strength of such ideas usually leads to a screening of dating partners to a considerable degree and to the screening of potential marital partners to an even greater extent. In addition, a whole array of personal and social factors—such as special personality needs and social pressures—may enter into the selection process. A girl may consistently look for men who are strong and masterful, or socially facile, or sensitive and introvertive; members of certain sororities may be expected to date only members of certain fraternities.

Studies of what young people are looking for in a marital partner have been generally in agreement about objective criteria like age, education, and social class, as well as on less easily measured characteristics like character, emotional stability, and a pleasant disposition. In a summary of studies extending into the early 1960's, Cavan (1963) concluded that:

"... the college man desires a wife who has an attractive and dependable personality, who is healthy, well groomed, and affectionate, whose intelligence and education preferably are not greater than his own, who is several years younger, and who is a good homemaker. The college woman prefers a husband who is dependable and mature, in love with her, well groomed and mannered, whose intelligence and education preferably are greater than her own, who is older, and whose financial prospects are good and probably will be improved through his ambition and industriousness." (p. 325)

According to the comparison summarized on page 308, the relative importance of different qualities in prospective marriage partners, as seen by college men, seems to have remained remarkably stable over a span of almost 25 years. Although there is some minor shifting within the lists, the same four

RANK ORDER OF QUALITIES SOUGHT IN A WIFE

COLLEGE MALES, 1939	COLLEGE MALES, 1956	COLLEGE MALES, 1963
Dependable Character	Dependable Character	Dependable Character
Emotional Stability	Emotional Stability	Emotional Stability
Pleasing Disposition	Mutual Attraction, Love	Mutual Attraction, Love
Mutual Attraction, Love	Pleasing Disposition	Pleasing Disposition
Good Health	Desire for Home and Children	Refinement and Neatness
Desire for Home and Children	Good Health	Desire for Home and Children
Refinement and Neatness	Refinement and Neatness	Education and Intelligence
Good Cook and Housekeeper	Good Cook and Housekeeper	Good Cook and Housekeeper
Ambition, Industriousness	Ambition, Industriousness	Good Health
Chastity	Similarity in Religion	Sociability
Education and Intelligence	Education and Intelligence	Ambition, Industriousness
Sociability	Sociability	Similarity in Religion
Similarity in Religion	Chastity	Good Looks
Good Looks	Similarity in Education	Chastity
Similarity in Education	Good Looks	Similarity in Education
Favorable Social Status	Favorable Social Status	Favorable Social Status
Good Financial Prospect	Good Financial Prospect	Good Financial Prospect
Similar Political Background	Similar Political Background	Similar Political Background

Based on McGinnis, 1958; Hurley, 1963.

traits are at the top in each of the three studies, which were carried out in 1939, 1956, and 1963. The three traits ranked at the bottom also remain the same.

Such findings may be somewhat misleading, however, for when respondents are asked to formulate their own list of desired characteristics instead of ranking traits suggested to them, there is a somewhat different listing and ordering of traits (Winch, 1955; Williamson, 1965). In such lists, for example a sense of humor is ordinarily given a high rating by both sexes, and males tend to rank physical attractiveness or good looks as more important than is indicated by the rankings in the chart.

In general, there seems to be agreement for both men and women that "physical attractiveness" and "personality" are important, with the details dependent upon both the individual's own views and the current standards of his cultural group. The physical characteristics and personality traits that "turn on" one generation may seem outmoded and irrelevant to the next.

There is a lack of adequate research data concerning the effects of recent social changes upon the qualities which young people are looking for in a mate. If one were to speculate, one might hazard a guess that increased importance is being given to such traits as emotional maturity, affection, common interests and values, a sense of humor, and the ability to communicate openly.

Other key factors in mate selection. In addition to the search for romantic love and for an individual with certain desired characteristics, a number of other key factors enter into the choice of a mate.

1. *Propinquity.* Until recent decades a girl tended to fall in love with and marry a boy with whom she had grown up and who lived within a mile or so of her (Kephart, 1961). Usually their families had known each other. Today, however, with urbanization, a high rate of family mobility, consolidated schools, and the automobile, falling in love with the boy next door appears to be an exception. Most young people today are exposed to a far wider range of acceptable dates as well as a wider range of potential mates from which to choose. Often, too, they give considerable thought to ways of improving their chances of meeting qualified potential mates. For example, girls may consider the romance-potential of colleges or jobs or careers.

Since social interactions take place in space and time, however, propinquity is still important—perhaps not so much residential propinquity as propinquity in one's general school or work environment. In fact, Catton and Smircich (1964) found physical proximity the most important single determinant of mate selection in a group they studied. Parents, of course, have often used this principle by encouraging a period of separation to test the endurance of an "unfortunate" love interest.

2. *Homogamy.* Romantic folklore has it that "opposites attract," but numerous studies have indicated that while persons of different background and unlike outlook may have a short-term appeal, young people tend to choose mates of a similar background and orientation when it comes to marrying. This tendency for "like to marry like" is called *homogamy.* It is shown especially in relation to social background factors, such as social class, education, religion, and race. It would also appear that common interests and values are conducive to the formation of a serious relationship that can, in turn, lead to marriage.

Evidently, however, homogamy in mate selection applies more often to social background than to personality characteristics (Troost, 1967; Udry, 1967). Wishful thinking may lead a couple to perceive similarities rather than differences in each other, but studies fail to show marked similarities in the personality characteristics of those planning to marry. And with greater social mobility, the lowering of parental influence, and changing cultural norms, there is much greater freedom for young people to marry across color, religious, ethnic, and social-class lines —and such marriages are becoming more common.

Our ideas about attractiveness in the opposite sex depend on when and where we live. The epitome of masculine attractiveness in one period may have no appeal at all to the ladies of another period.

3. *Complementary needs.* While research indicates that people most often marry someone of similar social background, it tells us little about how the selection takes place within the group of those socially eligible. Winch (1963) attempted to explain the process of selection by the hypothesis of complementary needs: ". . . within the field of eligibles, persons whose need patterns provide mutual gratification will tend to choose each other as marriage partners." (pp. 606-607) For example, he believed that a person with a strong need to be protected would be likely to marry someone with a compelling need to protect and nurture others; that a person with a strong need to dominate would be gratified by and would tend to choose a marital partner with a strong need to be submissive; and that a person who lacked achievement motivation might be particularly attracted to a person with strong achievement motivation. In essence, this approach is a sophisticated way of saying that a person will tend to fall in love with and marry someone whose traits complement his own and hence meet his needs by supplying what he lacks.

Despite the plausibility of the complementary need hypothesis, it has received uneven support by other investigators. After wrestling with the problem, Udry (1963, 1966) has concluded that partners may derive satisfaction from similar rather than complementary traits, that prized traits are not necessarily opposite sides of the same coin. And in a recent review of his hypothesis, Winch himself (1967) has suggested the advisability of adding the concept of role compatibility to that of need complementarity in predicting mate selection.

4. *Bargaining power.* Goode (1964) has suggested that the process of mate selection functions fundamentally like a market system and that variations from one society to another are variations in who controls the transaction, in the rules of exchange, and in the relative evaluation of various qualities. Similarly, the Swedish sociologist Boalt (1965) has advanced the view that whatever attributes a husband and wife bring to a marriage, the exchange usually represents a fair bargain between the two parties involved. When a person's family or friends feel that he could achieve a better match than the one he is making, they try to discourage the match as a poor bargain.

In our society, competition for desirable mates is intense, and undoubtedly the bargaining concept has some grounding in the realities of mate selection. In any event, it is apparent that in terms of age, physical appearance, intelligence, education, financial standing, and other characteristics, a given individual may be at an advantage or a disadvantage in his ability to attract and choose among eligible members of the other sex.

Though these various factors may be important in given cases, none is an adequate account by itself; even in combination they do not explain all mate choices. Selecting a mate is a complex process, and a whole pattern of inner and outer factors will usually determine the outcome. And typically the individual is probably unaware or only partially aware of many of the personal and social factors that influence his selection. As Stagner (1961) has pointed out:

"A girl may be attracted to a man on the basis of cues which have little validity for revealing inner personality patterns; she may be influenced much more by a physical similarity to her father than by evidence of motivations and temperament. Further, we must recognize the operation of needs at different levels of consciousness; a girl may say that she wants a husband who will let her work and treat her as an equal, when unconsciously she prefers to be dominated and protected. Thus, lacking insight into her own deeper impulses, she may think she is choosing a "complementary" mate when in fact she is not. And finally we must recognize that, even if she has correctly diagnosed her own inner motives, she may be in error about him." (p. 429)

In general, it would appear that growth-oriented motives are more likely to lead to a stable and satisfying marriage than are maintenance-oriented motives. The girl who is looking for someone to lean on will take her immaturities and inadequacies into the marital relationship, where they are likely to pose serious problems in marital adjustment. On the other hand, the mature person who views marriage in terms of mutual need satisfaction and actualization appears more likely to create an enduring and happy marital relationship.

Predicting marital success. It is evident that while marital partners may choose each other largely on the basis of qualities or traits they see in each other, these personal qualities are not the sole determinants of whether the marriage will be a "success." Other important factors—that may not be taken into account at the time of marriage but can be expected to influence its course—are (1) the interaction of the two personalities, including the changes in this interaction brought about by the addition of children; (2) the ability of both partners to fill the new roles that will be called for—to be husband or wife, parent, provider, housekeeper, nurse, hostess, and so on; and (3) the demands, pressures, and resources of the physical and social environment in which the couple live.

Attempts to predict a couple's marital success on the basis of personality and situational variables have produced only modest results. Premarital counseling usually utilizes tests to measure or assess (1) the quality of the interaction; (2) the attitudes of the partners toward marriage and toward each other; (3) personality differences, such as marked differences in interests and values; and (4) various background data and situational considerations. Although single indices from these tests have low predictive ability, it is possible, by combining many such indices, to achieve a modest level of accuracy in prediction, especially of marriages likely to fail (Udry, 1966). Such tests are particularly useful in spotting likely sources of difficulty in the marital relationship. The evidence regarding the relationship of several personality and background factors to marital adjustment is summarized later in the chapter.

MARITAL RELATIONSHIPS AND ADJUSTMENT

"I, John, take thee, Mary, to be my lawful wedded wife, to love and to cherish . . . till death us do part."

Each year some 2 million young Americans make these or similar wedding vows. This commitment involves one of the most important, if not the most important, decisions the individual will ever make. For it will affect his frustrations and satisfactions, his opportunities for personal growth, and almost every other aspect of his life. And if the marriage endures, young people today can expect the commitment to last some fifty years—to the celebration of their golden wedding anniversary.

In the present section we shall briefly view some of the patterns or "styles" which marriages in our society commonly take, how the coming of children affects marital roles, and factors related to happiness in marriage.

Marital Styles and Interactions

Not only is the individual pretty much on his own in selecting a mate, but it is also up to the marital partners to decide what kind of marriage they want to build and what they want their marriage to mean and to achieve. Modern marriages have been substantially freed from parental and societal surveillance, and even the model of one's parents' marriage may seem inadequate or irrelevant as a basis for patterning one's own. Nor are the "idealistic" marriages portrayed in the movies and on television likely to prove very realistic as models.

Marital styles. Packard (1968) has suggested three marital styles which seem to exemplify many contemporary marriages.

1. *The fun marriage.* This style of marriage is based upon preoccupation with having a good time. Usually what constitutes a good time is defined by the glamorous new "good life," as fostered by the mass media and the more restless and hedonistic members of the peer group. There is a concern with parties, trips, holiday outings, and weekends at ski-lodges and other popular recreational spots. Both enjoy being on the go in search of exciting activities, and their marriage adds to the convenience and fun since they can do all this together in a socially approved way. Often they show little interest in a home which might tie them down, rather tending to live in posh apartments much like those that appeal to young single persons. In essence, this style of marriage is the embodiment of the youth-oriented, fun-loving, romantic cult of our time.

2. *The colleague marriage.* Packard considers this to be a relatively new style of marriage which has achieved popularity among more serious, thoughtful, and achievement-oriented couples. The most important theme is the partners' interest in each other's careers. Such marriages may be planned in college or graduate school and the marital partners prepare for careers in related occupations or perhaps even the same one. Thus there are many married couples who are both lawyers, teachers, doctors, psychologists, and so on. The term *colleague marriage* was apparently first advanced by two sociologists (Miller & Swanson, 1958) to refer to the marriage of co-workers with equal but distinct and mutually recognized competencies.

Many business and educational organizations frown upon husbands and wives working in the same company and particularly in the same occupational area; thus such husband-and-wife teams may encounter difficulties. Such marriages are most often found in large metropolitan areas, where there are the widest employment opportunities for both partners.

3. *The nestling marriage.* The central theme of this type of marriage is that of finding a shelter where the marital partners can be close and snug with each other. The man may enter such a marriage in order to find a haven; the woman may enter it in search of protection. For both it represents a source of support, nurture, and protection in a confusing and turbulent world. Although such a

pattern appears to be common to some extent to most married couples, the nestling marriage makes it a primary theme. As one might suspect, having children is typically a key aspect of this style of marriage; the marital couple in essence create their own little world in which they find refuge from the world around them and fulfillment in the close ties of marriage and family.

Each marital style appears to have its advantages and disadvantages as well as its strengths and vulnerabilities. And, of course, there are many marriages in which these styles are found in varying degrees and combinations—as well as marriages which change in style over the years and marriages which do not conform to any of these styles.

Patterns of interaction and relationship. Although closely related to marital styles, the focus here is on the nature and quality of marital interactions and relationships—particularly in marriages which are fairly stable. The following categories—based on the work of Udry (1966) and Packard (1968)—appear to be relevant here.

1. *The conflict-habituated marriage.* In this type of marital relationship there is a great deal of tension and conflict—although it is controlled in such a way as to permit the continuance of the marriage. Often the marital partners feel trapped, embittered, and resentful, living their lives in an atmosphere of hostility, recrimination, and perhaps despair. Usually an attempt is made to conceal the conflict and tension from children and outsiders, but such attempts are rarely completely successful. The marital partners have adjusted to the tension and incompatibility, but the marriage is neither satisfying nor fulfilling.

2. *The minimal-interaction marriage.* Here the marital relationship may take a variety of related forms. Often it becomes a devitalized relationship in which there is no serious conflict or tension but simply apathy and lifelessness. The marriage seems to continue because of inertia and "the habit cage." The partners may assume that all marriages are like this. They may tiptoe

around various frustrations and resentments and learn to live with them instead of trying to resolve them. Often talk is perfunctory, and although the partners may enjoy certain activities together—such as playing bridge—they tend to go their own ways. Packard (1968) considers this form common among lower-class marriages as well as among many achievement- and power-oriented business executives and government leaders.

3. *The vitalized companionship marriage.* This form of marital relationship is in marked contrast to the two forms just discussed and is characterized by a sharing of life experiences, enjoyment of each other's companionship, and a lively, growth-type pattern of interaction. The marriage is considered of central importance to each partner, and they both try to make it a vital and successful relationship. Here husband and wife plan their lives together, strive to be with each other as much as possible, and find gratification in sharing both intellectual and physical intimacies. Typically they are "friends as well as lovers" and tend to resent anything beyond their ordinary occupational demands that keeps them from being together.

Marital relationships in stable marriages may thus run the gamut from a frustrating, embittered, and conflictful relationship through a relationship of withdrawal and apathy to a vitalized and deeply fulfilling relationship.

Change in marital patterns with time. Marital styles and relationships may fluctuate markedly over the years. Such fluctuations may result from changes in attitudes and values on the part of the partners, or they may be induced by situational factors such as the advent of children. Thus a fun marriage may be modified considerably by an unexpected pregnancy, or a nestling marriage may change to more of a fun marriage after the children have grown up and left home.

The marital partners' relationship and happiness in the marriage may also change with time. Many unhappy or precarious marriages are weeded out by divorce during the

first few years, but even a marriage of long duration is not immune to ending in the divorce court. Marital happiness is not something that once achieved can be counted on to continue indefinitely; rather the couple have to keep achieving it. Unfortunately this does not appear to be an easy task, and a number of researchers have found a tendency for many marriages to decline in satisfaction and happiness with the passing years (Blood & Wolfe, 1960; Pineo, 1961).

The Advent of Children

The advent of a child, particularly the first child, launches the married couple on a new career—that of parenthood—which may last for some twenty years. This new career brings changes in living routines, social roles, and the husband-wife relationship.

Reasons for having children. The great majority of married couples appear to want and do have children. In 1962 slightly over 85 per cent of married women in the age group 15 to 44 had children; for women in their 30's the figure was 90 per cent (Williamson, 1966). The number of children parents most often regard as "ideal" is four (Udry, 1966).

There are many reasons why a couple may desire to have children. Ackerman (1958) has suggested that a woman may want to have a baby in order to counteract anxiety about sterility, to please or punish her husband, to hold her husband, to gain the approval of her parents and friends, or to conform to the cultural stereotype of the "proper" family. For many women, bearing and rearing children appears to provide a sense of creativity and fulfillment; for both men and women parenthood can be a way of achieving a measure of personal significance and meaning as one sees oneself important to others (Packard, 1968). The desire to offer life to a new human being or to bequeath a part of oneself to posterity may also be an important reason for having children.

In the past, married couples often felt obligated to have children in order to perpetuate family blood lines; with the decline of the extended family and the current population explosion, this reason appears to be decreasing in importance. As with motives for getting married, reasons for having children seem to reflect increasingly the personal desires and choices of the marital partners.

Of course, not all people want to have children; and a husband and wife may disagree about having children or may have quite different reasons for wanting children. If they do have children, their motivations will influence the way they perceive the child, how they respond to him, and how the advent of the child will influence their lives together.

Shift in adult roles. With the birth of the first baby, husband and wife are faced with new social role demands. To the role of spouse, each mate adds the role of "parent," with its attendant satisfactions and responsibilities. As we saw in Chapter 4, parental roles in our society are rather loosely prescribed, though the trend is toward a democratically oriented family structure.

For the mother in particular, the advent of the baby is likely to lead to a drastic change in everyday activities, and she may feel that she has suddenly undertaken a new 24-hour-a-day job. If she had expected to fit the baby into an already full schedule, she may find that caring for a baby is far more time consuming than she realized and that she has little time or energy for anything else. If her husband does not help her and see that she gets "out from under" occasionally, she may feel both harassed and isolated. Most mothers, however, seem to adjust to and derive considerable satisfaction from the care of their infants.

In some cases the most difficult adjustment may be that of the father, in facing the reality that his wife now has less time and energy to devote to meeting his needs—that he must now share her love and attention while giving her extra emotional support. Where the husband feels that he is being neglected and left out, a considerable strain may be placed on the marital relationship.

How the husband and wife perceive their new roles as parents will be of key importance to their approach to child rearing as well as to their personal adjustments to parenthood. Duvall (1962), for example, has compared two types of roles that parents may take: a *traditional* role and a *developmental* one. The traditional role focuses on the physical care of the child, matters of discipline, and efforts to see that his behavior conforms to social norms and standards. A developmental role focuses on the fostering of healthy personality growth and optimal realization of the child's inherent potentialities; it is concerned with the more subtle psychological aspects of parent-child relationships. Thus a father who follows the traditional role may view himself primarily as the provider for the family and leave the details of childrearing to the mother; whereas a father who takes a more developmental role spends a good deal of time with his children to provide guidance and help and to encourage their personal growth.

Children and marital stability. The desire for and acceptance of children is positively correlated with happiness in marriage, although the actual presence or absence of children in the marriage is not. The timing of the birth of the first child also shows a relationship to later marital stability. Those whose first baby comes right away—including cases in which the wife is pregnant prior to marriage—tend to have more adjustment difficulties (Dame et al., 1966).

In the early months of marriage a couple is faced with many adjustive demands, and the advent of a child often appears to increase the stressfulness of such demands. Pregnancy may cause a wife to feel unwell or may bring financial worries. Whether or not they wanted the child, husband and wife usually find that they have less time to be alone together, less time for joint adult activities, and less money for their own enjoyment. In one early study, about a fourth of a group of married college couples with children felt that the early pregnancy had had a negative influence on their sexual adjustment (Landis *et al.,* 1950). In a study of couples representing three cultural groups—the sexually restrictive Mormons in Utah, an intermediate group in Indiana, and the more sexually permissive Danes of Copenhagen, Christensen (1963) found that the shorter the interval between marriage and the birth of the first child, the higher the divorce rate.

Interestingly enough, Feldman and Rogoff (1969) found that in some cases where husband and wife were especially close and dependent on each other, the advent of a baby led to a decrease in marital happiness, while in other cases, where a couple's interests were dissimilar before childbirth, the arrival of a baby strengthened

their relationship. In the first situation, three appeared to be "a crowd"; in the second, the sharing of parental responsibilities brought the partners closer together.

For most couples the new responsibilities and role changes that come with the advent of children are taken in stride, though with differing degrees of enthusiasm and sophistication. In general, the better adjusted the husband and wife are to each other, the less stress they experience in adjusting to their new roles as parents and the more likely they will be to find that parenthood adds significance and satisfaction to the life they are building together. On the other hand, if the husband and wife are maladjusted in their

---

A FAMILY AS A SMALL GROUP

ORGANIZATIONAL (STRUCTURAL) REQUIREMENTS

Role	Members need similar concepts as to what husband, wife, and children should be like, and what the duties, responsibilities, and rights of each should be; they also need flexibility, ability to change roles in changing conditions. Divorced couples often show wide discrepancies in role expectations.
Communication	Clear, two-way communication is needed. If any member feels unable to express negative feelings, closeness is threatened; unvoiced feelings, commonly expressed indirectly, may be more disruptive than those directly expressed.
Leadership and Power	Our society tends to expect partnership between husband and wife and alternation of leadership role in different types of situations; children are usually given more voice in family affairs as they grow older. In successful marriages, wives look to husbands for leadership more often than husbands to wives.
Ideological	Agreement on chief values, goals, priorities, strategies, overall organization of household is essential if family is to function as a coordinated unit and use its resources effectively. Without such commonality of purpose, there is likely to be conflict, dissension, and dissatisfaction.

INTEGRATIVE TASKS

Meeting Maintenance Needs	Maintenance needs include: (1) emotional support, security, and encouragement for all members; (2) mutual honesty, consideration, loyalty; (3) techniques for handling inevitable conflicts constructively; (4) resources for meeting physical needs.
Meeting Actualization Needs	Actualization needs include: (1) establishment of climate for satisfaction and growth of individual members; (2) establishment of family as a responsible, participating unit in community and larger society; (3) preparation of the children to meet challenges of their world; (4) implementing and passing on cultural and other values.

marriage, parenthood is usually a poor solution in terms of both the success of the marriage and the happiness of the child. Thus although there is a higher incidence of divorce among childless couples, having children does not appear to be a preventative of divorce. This point has been well elaborated by Jacobson (1959):

"... It is likely that in most cases both divorce and childlessness result from more fundamental factors in the marital relationship. Moreover, while children may hold some marriages together, in others pregnancy itself and the traditional strains involved may disintegrate rather than cement the marriage. It is also probable that some unsuccessful marriages are not legally dissolved until the children are grown up. However, their number is undoubtedly less than is popularly believed in view of the small difference in the divorce rate between the two groups at the later years of marriage." (p. 135)

Factors in Good Marital Adjustment

Like personal adjustment, marital adjustment can be viewed on a continuum from satisfactory to unsatisfactory. And here, too, it is harder to agree on what constitutes a good adjustment than on what constitutes a poor one. In fact, what one person or couple considers a good adjustment may be quite unsatisfactory to another.

One common test of marital adjustment is *permanence*. This is a useful criterion since the end of a marriage in separation or divorce is an objective indication of its failure. But permanence has limitations as a criterion of marital adjustment, because many marriages persist despite intense and sustained frustration and conflict. And as we have noted, we tend to expect considerably more of modern marriage than simply permanence.

A more critical test of marital adjustment has become that of *happiness*. The old ending to many a fairy-tale romance, "And they lived happily ever after," has become an actual criterion by which modern marriages are evaluated. Although happiness is a highly subjective term, husbands, wives, and objective observers show fairly good agreement in their evaluations of marital happiness, and happiness does correlate with other indices of effective family functioning. So marital happiness is a useful criterion of marital adjustment—and also is an important factor in the permanence of the marital relationship.

Why one marriage is happy and another unhappy is by no means fully understood. A number of factors have been delineated, however, which have some degree of correlation with marital happiness. Included here are factors relating to (1) the premarital background of the marital partners; (2) the personality make-up of the marital partners; (3) sexual adjustment; (4) the degree to which the partners can accommodate to each other and function as a group system; and (5) environmental resources, limitations, and demands. Interestingly enough, though girls seem more likely than boys to have marriage on their minds when dating, after marriage the husbands appear to be more generally content than the wives (Packard, 1968).

Premarital background factors. A number of premarital background factors correlate well enough with marital adjustment to be used for predictive purposes. Among the most important of these are:

1. *Family background.* A number of investigators have found that both good and bad marital adjustment and happiness tend to run in families (Burgess, Locke, & Thomas, 1963; Kirkpatrick, 1963). An individual's chances for marital happiness are greater if his parents were happily married than if they were unhappily married or divorced. Warm, loving relationships with one's parents and siblings also make more likely the establishment of such relationships in one's own marriage, and the young person who remembers his childhood as a happy one appears to have a greater chance for happiness in his own marriage.

2. *Social class, religion, and race.* In general, the lower the social class of the marital couple the less stable and happy the marriage is likely to be—possibly reflecting in part the lack of economic and social stability in the environment on lower socioeconomic levels (Komarovsky, 1964; Udry, 1966). Cross-class marriages—which typically involve a middle-class husband and a lower-class wife—also show a higher incidence of maladjustment and unhappiness than do middle-class marriages but may be happier than lower-class marriages. It is important to note that such studies deal with social class at the time of marriage; our society is a mobile one, and social class is not necessarily a fixed characteristic.

Interfaith marriages, although once frowned upon and considered a major source of marital conflict and unhappiness, are becoming more common and apparently more stable as well (Udry, 1966; Packard, 1968). Though findings are somewhat inconsistent, it would appear in general that Catholic-Protestant marriages are slightly less stable than Catholic marriages but not less stable than Protestant marriages. The general stability of interfaith marriages seems to result partly from the fact that individuals with strong religious convictions are not likely to enter into an interfaith marriage; those who enter such marriages are more likely to resolve later conflicts by a change of religious convictions than by a breaking up of the marriage.

A number of older studies also indicate that couples in which neither spouse has a religious affiliation are less stable than interfaith marriages, perhaps because most organized religions have discouraged divorce. With changing concepts both of religion and of marriage, it is difficult to predict the role of religious affiliation or of differing faiths in future marital adjustment.

Interracial marriages also appear to be increasing in frequency and to be meeting with less social disapproval than in the past (Udry, 1966; Packard, 1968). The greatest incidence of Negro-white marriages is in the state of Hawaii; in 1960 the proportion of Negro grooms marrying white brides was 14.7 per cent and of Negro brides marrying white grooms 12.5 per cent (Heer, 1965).

Although interracial marriages often pose additional problems for the marital couple, the stability and happiness of such marriages appear to depend on the couple involved, and studies so far have not found such marriages to be less stable or less happy than other marriages. Some investigators suggest that the existence of racial differences may increase the challenge to make the marriage successful (Udry, 1966; Packard, 1968).

In general, it would appear that marriages which are "mixed"—in terms of culture, religion, social class, or race—are likely to make additional adjustive demands on the couple but that the outcome will depend primarily upon the persons involved. Some of the earlier findings of greater hazard no longer seem to apply.

3. *Courtship.* Traditionally the courtship period has been regarded as very important in paving the way for later success in marriage for it is during this period that the couple try to get to know each other and have an opportunity to test their ability to get along together. In an early comparison of happily married and divorced or divorce-contemplating couples, Locke (1951) found that both length of acquaintanceship and engagement and absence of conflict before marriage were positively related to later marital adjustment and happiness. Later evidence also supports the view that couples who get to know each other well during dating and courtship are more likely to make a wise decision about marrying and to achieve a happy marriage than those who marry on brief acquaintance (Landis, 1965; Udry, 1966).

4. *Sex experience before marriage.* Several investigators have attempted to clarify the relationship, if any, between premarital sexual relations and later marital adjustment. In general, there would appear to be a low positive relationship between premarital virginity for girls and later sexual adjustment and happiness in marriage; this relationship is probably dependent in part on personality characteristics such as greater conventionality and ego strength among the premarital virgins rather than on intercourse or lack of it *per se* (Schope & Broderick, 1967). In any

TRAITS FOSTERING MARITAL HAPPINESS

1. *Large capacity for affection.* First prerequisite for enjoyment of marriage seems to be ability to give and receive love.

2. *Emotional maturity.* Needed for meeting stressful demands; emotional immaturity, such as selfishness or irresponsibility, likely to damage marriage.

3. *Capacity to communicate thoughts and feelings.* Needed for problem solving and mutual enjoyment; inability to communicate considered major source of misunderstanding, suspicion, and marital maladjustment.

4. *Zest for life.* Fosters positive enjoyment, rather than simply "adjustment."

5. *Capacity to handle tensions constructively.* Especially important if marriage is to provide climate for affection, companionship, and life-long personal growth.

6. *Playful approach to sex.* Relaxed attitude toward sex as a channel for tenderness and fun.

7. *Capacity to accept another person fully as he is with shortcomings.* No selective acceptance of some traits and rejection of others or expectation of changing the partner.

Based in part on Packard, 1968.

---

event, studies where intercourse has been restricted to the person's future spouse have found no correlation either way (Burgess *et al.*, 1963; Kirkpatrick, 1963).

5. *Age at time of marriage.* In a number of studies, early marriages—with grooms under 21 and brides under 18 years of age—have revealed more maladjustment and a higher-than-average incidence of divorce. An interpretation of this finding is far from simple, for a high proportion of early marriages are among those of lower socioeconomic status and lower educational attainment and involve premarital pregnancy—estimates indicating that from a third to a half of teen-age marriages involve a premarital pregnancy (Williamson, 1966). Thus early marriages are especially likely to be plagued by financial as well as other problems. In addition, couples who marry later and are unhappy are less likely to get a divorce than are younger people. Thus it seems likely that the higher incidence of maladjustment and divorce among those who marry early is related to personal and social characteristics rather than to the time of marriage *per se.* Although one might expect that marked discrepancies in age between marital partners would also lead to greater marital instability, present evidence does not bear out this prediction (Udry, 1966; Blood, 1962; Blood & Wolfe, 1960).

Personality factors. Studies of the role of personality factors in marital adjustment and happiness have focused on (1) identifying characteristics that appear to foster good adjustment in most marriages; (2) delineating characteristics that appear to have a negative influence on most marriages; and (3) analyzing the patterns of husband-wife traits—the "fit" of the two personalities.

1. *Characteristics having a positive influence.* On the basis of his four-year study of male-female relationships in our society, Packard (1968) has listed the seven traits above as likely to foster marital happiness. There is research support concerning the importance of some of these traits, such as emotional maturity, the capacity to communicate thoughts and feelings effectively, and the capacity to handle tensions constructively (Dean, 1966; Mudd, Mitchell, & Taubin, 1965; Blood, 1962). One component of emotional maturity—a clear sense of personal identity—appears of particular importance in helping the marital partners relate to each other. Wilson (1967) has also found that a generally happy person tends to be a happy mate which, in turn, is likely to foster a happy marriage.

2. *Characteristics having a negative influence.* Although common sense would tell us that certain personality traits—such as selfishness, deceit, stubbornness, and ir-

responsibility—would lead to marital difficulties, there is actually little research data to go on. The importance of such negative traits in a marriage probably depends on the style of the marriage and the type of relationship the marital couple is trying to establish. For example, in conflict-habituated marriages, where the partners are simply coexisting, such traits may not have the same significance that they would in a more vital companionship-type marriage.

Serious personality maladjustment, including excessive drinking, has been demonstrated to be correlated with adjustment difficulties in marriage (Crago & Tharp, 1968; Hurlock, 1968). Probably this is often a circular relationship in which personal pathology leads to conflictual and unsatisfying marital relationships which, in turn, intensify the personality difficulty.

Unfortunately, negative personality traits which were not evident in the premarital relationship may show up after marriage, or traits which seemed exciting or interesting in premarital relationships may not weather well in the marital setting. It would appear, however, that the hazards of an unhappy marriage can be reduced by a thoughtful consideration during the courtship period of both the personality traits that are apparent on both sides and the patterning of interests, needs, and values that is apparent in the relationship.

3. *Personality "fit" of marital partners.* We have probably all known individuals who were reasonably mature and well adjusted but whose personalities clashed when they were together very long. Not surprisingly, the patterning or "fit" of the two personalities involved is important in determining whether the marriage will be a happy one.

Several studies have pointed to similarity of values and interests as a factor in marital adjustment. Basic values and marital goals need to be in harmony if the interaction between the partners and their activities in the larger social setting are to be harmonious and satisfying to both.

Common goals and values provide a field for joint endeavors—both for emotional-social interaction and for the achievement of task goals—areas in which the partners can work together as a team and in which successes will bring satisfaction to them both. On the other hand, if they have basically different goals and values, they will find at best that they tend to operate as individuals rather than as a team—and at worst that they are working at cross-purposes, perhaps undercutting each other's efforts and each disparaging what is important to the other. It would appear that similarity of strongly held values helps to promote a marital fit (Coombs, 1966). Agreement on major values also makes many of the decisions in marriage much simpler (Price, 1968).

Several studies have shown that marital happiness is related to shared *familistic* interests—interest in the children and the home and in demonstrations of affection (Benson, 1952, 1955; Frumkin, 1954). The husband need not share his wife's interest in cooking or interior decoration, but it is important that they have some interests which ensure the sharing of enjoyable activities together.

The role of complementary needs in marital adjustment is far from clear, but it is apparent that the ability of each partner to satisfy the needs of the other is of key importance in marital happiness. Marked differences in motives or temperament or other characteristics that lead partners to react to problems in discrepant ways are likely to be sources of conflict. If either spouse has strong needs which are unacceptable to the other, some adaptation must be made if the marriage is not to suffer (Clausen, 1966). If one partner's needs are seriously and chronically unmet, the marriage is likely to encounter difficulty; in the long run, the other partner, too, is likely to find it an unsatisfying relationship.

Sexual adjustment. Sexual intercourse in marriage is the chief mode of sexual expression for most adults and is an important part of the marital relationship. However, the relative importance of marital intercourse varies greatly from one couple to another—again probably depending in large measure upon the marriage style. For example, Cuber and Harroff (1965) found that a substantial number of happily married couples did not view the sexual aspect of marriage as particularly important. For most young couples, however, an adequate sexual adjustment is probably considered of great importance.

The change in male and female sex roles, together with the waning of Victorian views of sex as lustful and evil, has been paralleled by a corresponding change in the expectations of both marital partners. It is usually assumed today that both partners should find satisfaction in their sexual relationship, and the attitude of women in particular has changed from one of repression and inhibition of sexual desires to one of seeking and even demanding sexual satisfaction in marriage. In fact, with the blurring of traditional masculine and feminine roles, some observers have noted a tendency for the sexual roles of men and women to be reversing themselves, with women becoming more aggressive and demanding and men more passive in their sexual behavior (Greenson, 1967). Whether or not this changeover is widespread, women today generally take a positive attitude toward sexual relations as an enjoyable experience and something that should add to the happiness of their marriage for them as well as their husbands.

Although it is risky at best to make generalizations about differences in male and female sexuality, it would appear that men are more susceptible to sexual arousal by many sensory and imaginal cues and tend to be prone to elaborate sexual fantasies, whereas women are less easily aroused sexually by sensory cues other than direct physical stimulation and much less prone to sexual fantasies. Women's sexuality also appears to be more closely bound up with affection, love, and "meaning." And although women find orgasm intensely pleasurable, many also appear to enjoy sexual relations without orgasm—an experience that is usually frustrating to a man.

Masters and Johnson (1966) found that given proper conditions and stimulation, women could achieve orgasm as rapidly as men, tended to respond longer and more intensely, and were more capable of multiple orgasms than men. Contrary to much popular opinion, Packard (1968) found that most of the students of both sexes in his study who had experienced coitus did not consider simultaneous orgasm necessary to a good sexual relationship.

Difficulties in sexual adjustment may arise if the marital partners have different attitudes toward the importance of sex in their marriage or show marked differences in sex drive and satisfaction from sexual behavior. In the early 1950's, Kinsey *et al.* (1953) found that husbands desired intercourse more frequently than their wives during the early years of marriage, but that later the situation was reversed, with the wives desiring intercourse more often than their husbands. Presumably it took the wife longer to adjust sexually in the marital relationship. With the increased knowledge and sophistication of young people, however, it would appear unlikely that this pattern is characteristic of marriages today.

Although sexual adjustment may markedly influence marital happiness, the reverse is also true. In fact, the degree of sexual adjustment is usually a good barometer of marital adjustment in general. If the day-to-day communications and interactions between the marital partners are characterized by conflict and hostility, it is likely that their sexual adjustment will be hampered. A deep and continuing resentment on the part of either partner is likely to be reflected in maladjustment in sexual behavior as well as in their other interchanges and relationships.

Roles and mutual accommodation. Each marital partner brings to the marriage certain ideas about how a husband and wife should behave and how problems and disagreements should be worked out. A marriage may succeed or fail depending on the ability of the partners to deal constructively with discrepant expectations.

1. *Marital roles.* The expectations with which couples enter marriage have to do not only with *what* should be done by each partner but also *how* it should be done. For example, there may be agreement that the wife should prepare the meals, but disagreement as to the kind of meals that should be prepared. Difficulty arises if there is a discrepancy in the role concepts and expectations of the two partners or if either one's behavior fails to come up to the other's expectations (Dyer, 1962).

As we have noted, there has been a considerable shift in male and female roles with respect to both premarital and marital behavior. Traditionally the husband played the role of provider, thinker, and doer, while the wife was the keeper of the home. As more women work outside the home, however, the role of economic provider is shared increasingly by both husband and wife, and often when the wife is working, the husband

has to assume various domestic responsibilities. In any event, modern marriage is becoming more of a partnership in which both partners share most of the functions to be performed, including decision making. And in our mobile society, where a family may move several times, the partners are increasingly dependent on each other for mutual emotional support and continuity of companionship and friendship, as other friendships come and go (Blood & Wolfe, 1960).

Where the marital partners come from similar backgrounds, compatible role expectations are more likely, and the problem of role accommodation may be minimal. On the other hand, couples from very different backgrounds are likely to enter a marriage with differing role expectations and to have

SOCIAL CLASS, SHARING OF INTERESTS, AND ENJOYMENT OF SEX IN MARRIAGE

Rainwater (1966) interviewed 409 men and women about their interest and enjoyment of sex in marriage, tabulating their responses by social class and by degree of sharing of their interests in their marital relationship as a whole. Their responses showed a higher level of interest and enjoyment of sex: (1) for men than for women; (2) for middle-class than for lower-class individuals of both sexes; and (3) for those who shared more interests and duties in their overall marital relationship: for both men and women, a higher percentage of this group than of the group with few or no shared interests checked "great" interest and enjoyment of sex.

	SOCIOECONOMIC CLASS			SHARED INTERESTS	
	Middle	Upper-Lower	Lower-Lower	Intermediate	Low
Husbands' interest and enjoyment					
great	78%	75%	44%	81%	56%
mild	22	25	56	19	44
Wives' interest and enjoyment					
great	50	53	20	64	13
mild	36	16	26	9	27
slightly negative	11	27	34	25	34
rejection of sex	3	4	20	2	26

greater difficulties in changing to achieve a better "fit."

Role concepts and expectations are usually not too rigid to undergo considerable change in the course of the marital interaction—particularly during the early phases of the marriage as the marital partners try to work out who is responsible for what and what the "ground rules" of their relationship should be in sexual, emotional, intellectual, and social realms. There is evidence that the husband's role definitions and expectations are more influential than those of the wife during early marital accommodation (Stuckert, 1963).

While the role relationships are still somewhat fluid, there may be a considerable sense of personal disorganization, especially if the individual has to make rather drastic changes from his previous role (Rapoport & Rapoport, 1967). In a happy marriage, roles are eventually worked out which are comfortable for both partners. If conflicting role expectations and concepts cannot be satisfactorily reconciled, however, continuing frustration and marital unhappiness can be expected unless the partners can work out some arrangement whereby they agree to disagree, respecting but not sharing the other's point of view.

2. *Communication.* Interpersonal accommodation in marriage depends heavily upon effective communication—open communication lines and the ability and willingness to use them. Without good communication, information cannot be exchanged, efforts cannot be coordinated, the other person's feelings and reactions will not be understood, incipient misunderstandings can become major sources of resentment and conflict and role accommodation will not take place.

In a study of communication patterns in marriage, Navran (1967) found that happily married couples, as compared with unhappily married couples: (a) talk to each other more; (b) convey the feeling that they understand what is being said to them; (c) communicate about a wider range of subjects; (d) preserve communication channels

and keep them open; (e) show more sensitivity to each other's feelings; (f) personalize their language symbols; and (g) make more use of supplementary nonverbal techniques of communication.

The feeling that it is safe to be open and honest about one's feelings, both positive and negative, is necessary if open communication is to take place between the partners.

"... *in a healthy relationship, each partner feels free to express his likes, dislikes, wants, wishes, feelings, impulses, and the other person feels free to react with like honesty to these. In such a relationship, there will be tears, laughter, sensuality, irritation, anger, fear, babylike behavior, and so on.*

"*The range of behavior, feelings, and wishes which will be brought out into the open is not arbitrarily limited. In fact, one gauge to the health of a relationship is the breadth of topics of conversation, the range of feelings which are openly expressed, and the range of activities which are shared. In each case, the broader the range, the healthier the relationship.*" (Jourard, 1963, p.343)

Levinger and Senn (1967) found that disclosure of one's feelings to one's spouse correlated positively with general marital satisfaction. They also found strong evidence of mutuality of disclosure: that is, the higher one partner's proportion of disclosure, the higher the other partner's tended to be. And in a study of happily married couples, sensitivity to the needs of the partner and the ability to communicate feelings and emotions were regarded by the couples as vital to their marital success (Mudd *et al.,* 1965).

3. *Coping patterns.* Even happily married couples have their share of problems, woes, and headaches. And from time to time most marriages undergo crises—periods of severe stress resulting in marital disequilibrium and the necessity of making changes in marital roles and relationships. Such crises may stem primarily from problems in the relationship or from environmental pressures and demands. Marital success depends in large measure on the pattern of approach

that the couple develops for coping with whatever problems arise.

Couples may approach their problems in task-oriented or defense-oriented ways. A task-oriented approach usually involves such steps as: (1) admitting that a problem exists and agreeing to work on it; (2) analyzing the problem—with each partner free to express his feelings and ideas concerning the dimensions of the problem and the possible solutions; and (3) deciding on a course of action, putting it into effect, and evaluating feedback. The importance of task-oriented coping patterns to marital adjustment is shown in the finding that happily married couples rarely taunt or threaten their partners with divorce, slap their marital partners, or slam doors or throw things. Although 20 per cent of one sample admitted that they got pretty angry, their responses indicated that they usually tried to discuss their problems in a fair-minded way and that many were able to be critical of themselves as well as of their partners (Mudd *et al.,* 1965).

By contrast, unhappily married couples appear far less task oriented and less effective in coping objectively with their marital problems. A defense-oriented approach may take various forms including quarreling, blaming each other for the problem, or even refusing to acknowledge its existence in the hope that it will somehow resolve itself. A common method of escaping from marital problems is to become heavily engaged in activities outside the marriage. Here it is of interest to note the finding of Scanzoni (1968) that dissolved marriages—as contrasted with existing ones—had been characterized not only by greater conflict but also by very little compromise on the part of husbands.

Where value conflicts exist, the partners have to decide how or even whether they can accommodate themselves to the discrepancies. Sometimes such decisions are made explicitly in open discussion. Decisions so made are more likely to provide a compromise that both members can live with than are decisions made by default—by how things happen to turn out. In one way or another, the partners "need to learn how to assert

their thoughts, wishes, feelings, and knowledge without destroying, invading, or obliterating the other, and while still coming out with a fitting joint outcome." (Satir, 1964, p. 13)

In general, it would appear that partners who place a high priority on the success of their relationship with each other will not let conflicts or other demands assume central importance. Instead, they will be sensitive to each other's needs and seek task-oriented solutions that will strengthen rather than weaken their relationship. On the other hand, when the partners are disappointed or resentful and perhaps have given up hope of a mutually satisfying relationship, they will find it harder to cope objectively both with problems in their relationship and with problems posed by the environment.

Environmental resources, limitations, and demands. No marriage is lived in a vacuum, and the setting may either support and strengthen the marriage or undermine its stability and happiness. Like individuals, families are open systems, requiring favorable physical resources as well as chances for effective transactions with both physical and social environment. If a family's values are at odds with the values of surrounding families, its members will feel a strain. A family that never has enough to eat and must live in a tumble-down, rat-infested, crowded building has a more difficult task in maintaining healthy interactions among its members than a family that lives in pleasant surroundings with chances for privacy. If the father cannot find work and the welfare laws provide for assistance only to families without fathers, as is true in some communities, he may leave home rather than let his family starve. Thus the adjustment and even the continuance of a family may be determined by conditions outside the family itself.

Whereas in some societies an extended family, a stable social structure, and clear, consistent expectations for husbands and wives all help to bolster the stability of individual marriages, a couple in our society have few such external supports and are

In some societies, a wedding is very much a community affair. In St. Sauvant-Poiton, a small village in France, there is a wedding procession through the village with several prescribed stops for various symbolic rituals. Along the way the bride lights piles of branches to symbolize that a new way of life has begun. Such shared rituals provide important social supports for a marriage.

largely on their own. In a shifting, rapidly changing society where contradictory values vie for acceptance, husband and wife may have a hard time finding and maintaining accord themselves and an even harder time helping their children to develop sound values and healthy personalities. In giving up externally prescribed rituals and roles we have also given up external standards of success and the comfort that external props and assurances can give.

MARITAL UNHAPPINESS AND DIVORCE

The divorce rate in the United States increased steadily from the beginning of the century until 1946, when it reached a peak as many World War II marriages were abandoned (Carter & Plateris, 1963). In recent years it has approximated about 1 out of every 4 marriages. An equivalent number of separations are also estimated to occur each

year, representing a grand total of about 1 million marital breakups each year (Packard, 1968). Even if the figure for separations is too high, it is apparent that seemingly insurmountable obstacles beset a large number of American marriages each year and that our rate of marital dissolution is considerably higher than that for other nations (Goode, 1964).

Of course, divorce and separation statistics do not tell the whole story about the incidence of unhappiness and maladjustment in marriages. Many marital couples stay together, though unhappy, because of considerations other than happiness—such as religious or financial considerations, reluctance to disrupt the lives of their children, fear of not being able to do any better on a second try, or simply habit or lethargy. Thus many of the marriages which end in divorce have probably been as happy as or happier than some of those which endure.

Causes of Divorce

Many factors undoubtedly combine to account for our high divorce rate. These factors include conditions in the social setting as well as characteristics of the two personalities and of the pattern of interaction between them.

General social change. As we have seen, there has been a challenging and loosening of most of our traditional values and social structures in recent years. Mobility, instability, and change appear to be both commonplace and expected—both in our society and in our own personal lives. And our high standard of living has raised our expectations for satisfactions of all kinds—including those by which we measure the acceptability of a marital relationship. It is also possible that marriages based on love and emotional need fulfillment are inherently more hazardous than those based on economic and other pragmatic considerations, where the conditions that give rise to the marriage help to maintain it.

Modern urbanization and the rise of the nuclear family have removed many of the environmental supports and the kinds of help with marital problems that tend to be available in the extended family living in a less hurried, less impersonal, more stable social network. At the same time, occupational opportunities for women have given dissatisfied wives an alternative to continuance that was lacking in the past; better opportunities for remarriage may also influence their decision. And with less stringent divorce laws and less stigma attached to divorced people, there is wider acceptance of divorce as a viable choice in an unsatisfactory marital situation. All these factors in our social setting make stable, satisfying marriages more difficult and separation more attractive when expectations are not being fulfilled.

Unfortunately, the rate and complexity of social change, with all its implications for mate selection and marital happiness, have not been matched by preparation of our young people in realistic expectations or in the attitudes and skills needed for a stable and satisfying marriage in this kind of society. It is often easier to obtain a marriage license than a fishing or driver's license. It would appear that a great deal of misery and many wasted years could be avoided by more adequate preparation of young people for both choosing and living with a mate.

In any case, American marriages today are undertaken against a cultural background which places an increasingly heavy burden on the marital partners for establishing stability and meeting each other's psychological needs. And as society's stake in stable family units has come to be regarded as secondary to the individuals' happiness—in marked contrast to the priorities established in many other cultural groups—the way appears to be paved for a continued high incidence of marital failure.

Reasons given for divorce. Harmsworth and Minnis (1955) surveyed the opinions of lawyers on the *actual*—as contrasted with *legal* —causes of divorce. They found adultery cited in 18.6 per cent, financial problems in 16.8 per cent, and incompatibility in 15.6

BACKGROUND FACTORS RELATED TO DIVORCE

EDUCATIONAL LEVEL	The lower the educational level, the higher the divorce rate.
OCCUPATIONAL STATUS	Divorce more common among lower socioeconomic groups than among professional groups.
FAMILY BACKGROUND	Higher divorce rate among children coming from unhappy homes and/or divorced parents.
RACIAL BACKGROUND	Nonwhite marriages more divorce-prone than white marriages at all educational and occupational levels.
RELIGION	Higher divorce rates among nonchurchgoers.
LENGTH OF COURTSHIP	Divorce rates higher for those with brief courtships.
AGE AT TIME OF MARRIAGE	Divorce rates very high for those marrying in their teens.
FACTORS NOT RELATED TO DIVORCE RATE	Interracial, mixed religion, sexual experience prior to marriage, age difference between spouses.

Based on many studies, including Bernard, 1966; Goode, 1961, 1964; Merrill, 1959; Udry, 1966, 1967.

per cent of the cases, with irresponsibility, cruelty, immaturity, cultural causes, in-law problems, and desertion each accounting for more than 2 per cent of the remaining cases. Although these findings are interesting, they are limited by the accuracy with which lawyers can gauge their clients' reasons for seeking a divorce.

In a more recent and comprehensive study of the counseling records of 600 couples applying for divorce, Levinger (1966) compared the complaints of husbands and wives and of middle-class and lower-class couples. Husbands cited half as many complaints as wives; most frequently mentioned by the husbands were mental cruelty, neglect of home and children, infidelity, and sexual incompatibility. Complaints most often made by the wives were of physical and mental cruelty, financial problems, and drinking. In general, the middle-class couples were more concerned with psychological and emotional satisfactions while the lower-class couples were more concerned with financial problems and the physical actions of their partners. Again we are reminded of Maslow's hypothesis of a hierarchy of needs in which maintenance needs must be adequately met before the individual will become concerned about and will actively seek for the satisfaction of actualization needs.

Effects of Divorce

Divorce can have far-reaching effects on both the spouses and the children. Effects vary greatly, however, depending upon such factors as the emotional involvement of the marital partners, the happiness and duration of the marriage prior to the divorce, the opportunities for remarriage, and the stress tolerance and other personality characteristics of all concerned.

Effects of divorce on the marital partners. Divorce is a sign of failure, and divorced persons often feel that they have failed in one of life's most important tasks. Following a divorce, many persons experience a sense of personal inadequacy, disillusionment, and depression. Often they are torn by self-recrimination and thoughts of "what might have been"—of what they might have done that would have made their marriage a success.

Divorced persons, as a group, show a consistently higher rate of drinking problems and other signs of maladjustment (as well as a higher rate of actual hospitalization for mental disorders) than do nondivorced persons (Blumenthal, 1967). Whether these problems have caused or been caused by their marital difficulties we do not know; in many instances a vicious circle is probably involved. We do know that a divorced person is likely to face difficult adjustments brought about by the changes in his life situation: he may have to cope with loss of security, guilt and self-recrimination, the cessation or disruption of sexual satisfactions, and financial problems. Feelings of alienation and loneliness may add to the stress, and where the divorce was sought by the other partner, a sense of having been rejected usually leads to feelings of hurt and self-devaluation. Even for the partner who sought the divorce, the stress of divorce and re-adjustment may bring more severe problems than those from which he was trying to escape.

Divorce and children. The strongest arguments against divorce have usually emphasized the undesirable effects of divorce on children, and a number of studies have found children of divorced parents to be more emotionally disturbed, delinquent, and maladjusted than children of intact marriages. As a consequence, many unhappy parents remain together "for the sake of the children."

Although no one would suggest that the dissolution of a marriage is a desirable experience for a child, there is evidence that children from broken homes fare as well as or better than children from intact but unhappy homes. For example, Nye (1957) found better emotional adjustment and less delinquency in a group of children from broken homes than in a group from unbroken but unhappy homes. And when Burchinal (1964) investigated the effects of divorce on emotional adjustment and school achievement of adolescents—matching the broken and unbroken homes for social class—no support was found for the alleged detrimental effects of divorce. Similarly, Langner and Michael (1963) in their extensive Midtown Manhattan Project found that adults who had experienced a broken home in childhood had only a slightly greater risk of psychiatric symptomology than those from unbroken homes.

The foregoing conclusions do not deny the common observation that children may be severely traumatized by the breakup of their home, particularly if the home was formerly happy and if they are emotionally close to their parents. Often the child is torn by dual loyalties and is hurt by emotional involvement in the marital entanglement. Some parents are too caught up in their own bitterness and unhappiness to be concerned about helping to ease the pain for their children.

"They fail to shield their youngsters from the confusion, pain and shock which darkens so many broken homes. They shortsightedly neglect to subordinate their real or imaginary grievances against each other by failing to work together for their children's best interests." (Pollack, 1967, p. 17)
In such cases, the children may carry emotional scars that tend to handicap them in all close relationships thereafter.

The Problem of Remarriage

In colonial times nearly all remarriages were of widows or widowers, but in recent decades there has been a gradually swelling tide of remarriages of those who have been divorced. The chance of remarriage after a divorce has greatly increased, especially for those in lower age groups; overall, about two thirds of divorced women and three fourths of divorced men eventually remarry (Packard, 1968). Remarriages occur, on the average, about two and a half years after the divorce.

Reasons for remarriage. Both societal pressures and individual needs steer divorced persons toward remarriage. The divorced mother may be encouraged to remarry because, she is told, the children need two parents in the home. Divorced persons often feel awkward in the company of married friends. A divorced woman may find herself incapable of handling all the responsibilities of maintaining a household for herself and her children. Factors such as these, together with the need for affection, adult companionship, and sexual intimacy lead many divorced persons to seek new marital partners.

In considering remarriage, there are often new factors to be weighed: a woman who has children from a previous marriage may be concerned about how her children will accept their prospective stepfather and how he will relate to them. A man considering remarriage may have financial responsibility for children of a former marriage; if he pays alimony and child support, he may not be in a position to assume the financial responsibilities of another family. The individual may be strongly motivated by a need to overcome the emotional hurt and self-devaluation from the prior divorce. The possibility that one is "marrying on the rebound" may be a factor to be considered carefully.

How successful are remarriages? Do second marriages have a better chance of success than first marriages? Has the divorced person's past experience taught him how to avoid the common pitfalls in marriage, or should his earlier failure be taken as a sign that he is a poor marital risk? The research evidence is both scanty and contradictory. In terms of statistics, first marriages, as a group, are the most stable, followed by remarriages in which one partner has been divorced, followed by remarriages in which both partners have had previous marriages. Marriages in which one or both of the spouses has had multiple prior marriages are probably least stable of all, though adequate statistics are not available.

About one third of those who remarry find themselves in the divorce mill again

(Packard, 1968). This figure is not surprising since obtaining a divorce in the first place signals the individual's willingness to break up an unhappy marriage by divorce. He may also have immaturities or other personality characteristics that make him divorce prone. However, divorce is usually a powerful learning experience.

Although more remarriages than first marriages end in divorce, remarried persons in general find that their second marriages are happier than their first (Bernard, 1956; Goode, 1956). Udry (1966) has suggested several possible reasons:

"There are many factors which contribute to the satisfaction which people find in second marriages after divorce. The divorced person has probably learned something about marriage from the first failure. If age contributes anything to maturity, he should be able to make a more mature choice the second time. The significance of sex is transformed, since it can be more taken for granted in the approach to second marriage. Second marriages have the advantage of being compared with a marriage which recently ended in bitterness and conflict. The second time around, the first-time loser has probably readjusted his expectations of marriage and is simply easier to please than those without previous marital experience." (p. 521)

Whether or not the divorced person has learned from his failure, and regardless of the odds against him, the potential rewards of the marital relationship appear to lead most divorced persons to try again.

SUMMARY AND A LOOK AHEAD

In marriage, as in other areas, modern Americans have greater opportunities than ever before to set their own goals and standards of success—with correspondingly greater opportunities for either satisfaction or failure. Increasingly we view marriage chiefly as a relationship providing for companionship, personal satisfaction, and growth for the participants rather than as an institutional arrangement serving economic and childrearing needs, among others. This new view has changed the expectations of those entering it and the criteria by which the success of a marriage is judged.

Dating and other social interaction between the sexes before marriage help young people learn to get along with each other and develop a basis for choice of a mate, as well as offering an important avenue for the meeting of psychological and sexual needs. Sex roles seem to be converging, and attitudes toward sexual activity before marriage have become more permissive; attitudes may have changed more than actual behavior.

Many needs may be met by marriage, and there are many motivations for marrying—also for staying single. In general, unmarried men seem to show a higher-than-average rate of personal maladjustment; unmarried women, as a group, do not. Young people tend to agree on the qualities they are looking for in a mate, but other factors consistently enter into the actual selections they make and increase or decrease their chances of success; some of these are similarity of background, propinquity, complementarity or congruence of needs and other personality characteristics, and bargaining power. Factors related to marital adjustment also include age and length of courtship, emotional maturity, similarity in values and interests, sexual adjustment, the ability of a couple to find comfortable roles and task-oriented techniques for solving problems and accommodating to each other's needs, open communication between the partners, and a supportive physical and social environment. Several marital "styles" can be delineated.

Divorce has become more common and more widely accepted, reflecting both the broader social changes in our society and the higher expectations for personal happiness with which people enter marriage. Divorce and separation can be painful for both the partners and their children, though an intact, unhappy home may be worse for children than a broken but happy one. The rate of remarriage has increased; though more second marriages than first marriages end in separation or divorce, remarried persons, as a group, report greater happiness in their second marriages.

In this chapter we have examined the factors related to adjustment and maladjustment in one important area of social living. In the next chapter we will look at another such area—the world of work.

Key terms used in this chapter include:

the "sexual revolution" (p. 301)
convergence of sex roles (p. 301)
extended family (p. 306)
new expectations in marriage (p. 306)
matrimonial directedness (p. 307)
propinquity in mate selection (p. 308)
homogamy (p. 309)
complementary need hypothesis (p. 310)
marital styles (p. 311)
criteria of marital adjustment (p. 316)
role accommodation (pp. 320-322)

Chapter 11

THE WORLD OF WORK

Career Choice: An Opportunity and a Problem
Problems in Occupational Adjustment
The Future World of Work

In 1967 the population of the United States reached and exceeded 200 million people. Of these about 103 million were between the ages of 20 and 64 from which the main work force in the United States is drawn. The work force itself constituted 78 million Americans, 49 million men and 29 million women. Three fourths of these worked for private employers; one seventh for local, state, or federal government; and one ninth were self-employed (Bureau of the Census, 1968).

The census data further showed that white-collar professionals, managers, clerks, and salesmen were the largest and fastest-growing group numbering over some 34 million persons; blue-collar craftsmen, foremen, machine operators, and laborers numbered only some 28 million. Service workers numbered slightly over 9 million, and farm workers approximated 3 to 4 million. The median family income was $7000, with nearly 15 million families enjoying incomes over $10,000. These figures reflect our dramatic shift from an agricultural to a technological society—and a generally affluent one. In fact, in 1967 we had almost three times as many engineers and professional people as farm workers. The need for unskilled and semi-skilled workers in our society continues to decrease while the demand for better-edu-

cated and more technically skilled personnel is greater than ever.

These statistics provide useful background data as we turn to a consideration of our changing concepts of work, problems in career planning and occupational adjustment, and new horizons in the world of work.

CAREER CHOICE:
AN OPPORTUNITY AND A PROBLEM

Most adults spend one third to one half of their lives in work and work-related activities—more time than they devote to any other activity. Work not only determines our income and standard of living but influences our social status and sense of identity and worth; satisfaction or dissatisfaction in our work can add up to frustration and lack of meaning or contribute to personal growth and self-fulfillment. Thus the choice of a career is of vital significance.

Career choice, of course, is something relatively new. In earlier times—as well as in many societies today—most young people had their choices made for them or were at best severely limited in what they could choose. Of necessity, most followed what their fathers had done or entered whatever apprenticeship training was available to them in their communities. Most young people today have an almost unlimited choice of careers; as in other life areas, however, having to choose provides both greater opportunities and new problems.

As in the case of marriage, our views of "work" are undergoing major changes—leading inevitably to some confusion. Often, too, the individual does not know enough about himself or about what various occupations are like. And even after a choice is made, career planning may entail a long and difficult preparation.

Changing Views of Work

As we saw in the case of marriage, we find that the reasons for working, the nature and meaning of work, and the criteria for evaluating occupational adjustment are all changing.

Decline of the Puritan work ethic. The Puritan concept of work both as necessary for survival and as a duty and virtue in and of itself has dominated our culture since Captain John Smith presumably told the early settlers that "he who will not work shall not eat." Today, however, the Puritan work ethic is on the decline.

Much as we have come to view marriage as far more than a simple economic necessity and basis for raising children, so we are coming to demand more of work than simply "filling a slot" or "doing a job." Young people are no longer content with only money as a return for their investment of time and energy.

Perhaps this change is more understandable if we note that at the turn of this century machines did some 6 per cent of the work in our society, as compared with over 90 per cent of it today and an even higher per cent expected in the decade to come. With machines taking over production of the necessities of life and relieving us of the drudgery and monotony of routine work, we are beginning to see the need for integrating

our working hours with our increased leisure into a meaningful way of life.

Just as we no longer view childhood as simply preparation for adulthood, we no longer think of education as simply preparation for work, or work as simply a means of earning a living. We see childhood as part of living, and both education and work as vehicles for personal growth, creative self-expression, and self-fulfillment.

Changing criteria of success. With this change in the meaning of education and work, the criteria by which we evaluate adjustment in these areas are also changing. No longer is a man necessarily considered a success because he is a bank president, or a failure because his paintings do not provide an adequate income. Occupational success is being evaluated far more by whether or not the individual's work brings him satisfaction and fulfillment.

This new view of work places a heavy responsibility on the individual. For out of the wide range of possibilities open to him, he must choose a career which will be meaningful and fulfilling and, hopefully, one in which he can contribute to the welfare of others and the progress of society. In choosing a career, the individual is acting as an architect of a major portion of his own life as well as delineating a role for himself in the wider society. It is in part for this reason that young people today are demanding an increasing voice in the educational and social programs planned for them in college.

Converging occupational roles for the sexes. Compulsory free education through grade school and high school has virtually eliminated illiteracy in the United States and has led to increasing equality between the sexes in educational achievement. Between 1940 and 1965 the proportion of high-school graduates who went on to college increased from 35 to 55 per cent, and in 1965 approximately 39 per cent of those in college were women.

The increasing trend toward equal education, combined with the lessening of dis-

Any "work world," besides involving a certain kind of setting and characteristic activities, also offers a particular cluster of associates, social opportunities and restrictions, and probable satisfactions and dissatisfactions. The particular work

crimination and prejudice against women in many occupations, has led many women in our society to combine occupational roles with those of child rearing (Johnstone, 1968). In fact, one of the most remarkable social changes in our society has been the startling increase in the number of married women working outside the home. In 1966, a survey of nearly 6000 women who had graduated from college seven years before revealed that 41 per cent of those presently married were working outside the home, including 28 per cent of those who had children under 6 years of age (Department of Labor, 1966). The new opportunities are leading many high-school and college women to plan for interesting careers in teaching and other fields.

The advent of women on a large scale into the occupational field has led to a blurring of traditional sex roles with respect to occupations. Women have entered such fields as medicine, law, psychology, physics, and so on in increasing numbers. We also find women astronauts, military officers,

real estate brokers, and professional athletes. No longer is it considered unfeminine for women to enter fields requiring courage, strength, and objectivity—or unmasculine for men to enter fields requiring a high level of sensitivity and creativity.

Factors in Career Planning

Although the young person has a wide range of career choices, the very abundance of opportunities often makes for confusion. Often he does not know enough about his own interests and capabilities or about the specific demands and characteristics of given occupations to ask the right questions or make the wisest choice. Many job fields are changing along with technological and social change, and the young person has the problem of anticipating how such change will affect the occupation he chooses. Thus it is not surprising that many young people today are uncertain about what career is right for them; yet it is the individual who must make the choice and live with the consequences.

world we live in, in turn, strongly influences our sense of identity and worth. Thus in choosing a job or a job field, we are choosing far more than something to do for eight hours a day.

Stages in career planning. An occupational choice may not be made until the individual reaches adolescence or early adulthood. But prior to this time, he makes many decisions that lead him toward or away from given occupations. And long before his first job he has developed ideas about the function of work and attitudes about different kinds of work. Thus career choice is a developmental process: the groundwork for it has been laid in many kinds of experiences long before the final, explicit choice is made.

One group of investigators found three stages in the development of vocational choice among middle-class students (Ginsberg *et al.,* 1951; Ginsberg, 1966).

1. *Fantasy period.* For most children this period extends until about age 11. In this stage the child does not relate an occupational choice to his intellectual and personal qualifications or to realistic opportunities but makes the assumption that he can become whatever he wants to become—whether it be a policeman, a scientist, an astronaut, or a physician. Children often try out many oc-

cupational roles in their play—identifying with the occupation of their father or other adults they know or have seen on TV.

2. *Tentative period.* From about 11 to 17 years, the young person recognizes the need to decide sometime on a future occupation. Now he makes tentative choices based on whatever awareness he has of his interests, abilities, and values as well as on his environmental opportunities. At first, he presumably considers compatible interests as the primary consideration in career choice. Later he begins to consider ability and training prerequisites, and still later personal values become an important consideration. By the end of this period, he recognizes that it is necessary to integrate his interests, abilities, and values and to allow for the realities his environment provides in making a tentative vocational choice.

3. *Realistic choice stage.* By about the age of 17, the young person tries to work out a suitable occupational plan by translating his own desires into what the external world has available. This process of synthesis is

often very difficult, especially for the young person who finds that his occupational dreams are unrealistic. At this stage comes the realization for many that there must be a compromise between their hopes and desires and the opportunities and realities of the external world. This stage, in turn, involves *exploration,* as the individual acquires information and possibly work experience; *crystallization,* as he narrows his range of alternatives and prepares to make a career choice; and finally, *specification,* with commitment to a given occupational goal.

Of course, these stages are no cut-and-dried matter. Some young people make a choice in childhood or early adolescence and stick to it with great confidence and persistence, while others have great difficulty in deciding what they want to do and may reach their early 20's still not knowing. Also a study of lower-class students might show a somewhat different sequence from the one outlined above. The stages found by Ginzberg, however, serve to show the developmental nature of career choices.

In the development of career choice, Nelson (1963) found negative choices of great importance. In a study of the occupational preferences of elementary and secondary school students, he found both children and adolescents better able to delineate occupations they would not like to enter than those they would. He suggests that the negative responses, besides limiting the occupations from which choices are later made, also form points of reference against which new possibilities are evaluated. Thus he sees the young person facing a narrowing field of choices as he grows older.

Personal characteristics. Three questions appear of particular significance from the standpoint of personal characteristics:

1. *What does the individual want to do?* The answer to this question concerns itself with interests, motives, and values. Does he like to work with people or with ideas or with things? Is he more interested in helping others or in making money? Does he thrive under pressure or does he prefer a more leisurely pace without deadlines? Relevant too are questions centering around what he would like to be doing ten or twenty years hence and what he would like his occupational experience to help him become.

2. *What can he do—or learn to do?* The answer to this question concerns his abilities and aptitudes. What is his general level of intelligence? What knowledge and skills does he have, and what is his potential for acquiring further competence in particular areas? Does he have any outstanding special abilities, such as unusual musical or athletic ability?

3. *How do his abilities and resources limit his choices?* The answer to this question concerns both the individual's present qualifications and the resources available to him for further needed training. For example, some occupations, such as psychology and medicine, require extensive undergraduate and graduate preparation; where the student is not in a position to meet the requirements for admission to an occupation, he may have to eliminate that occupation from serious consideration. Relevant here, too, are questions about how his age, sex, and health might affect his potential for success in a given occupation.

Astin and Nichols (1964) found that a person's choice depends largely on the relative importance he places upon six basic factors: (1) having a good self-concept—for example, being popular and influential; (2) being personally comfortable; (3) enjoyment of artistic and creative tasks; (4) having prestige; (5) enjoyment of scientific and technical tasks; and (6) being able to help others and to become personally mature. For example, students majoring in business placed a high value on personal comfort, while students planning to become clergymen stressed the value of helping others. These six factors, of course, cover various aspects of an individual's motives, interests, abilities, and values.

Psychologists have devised a number of assessment instruments for obtaining information about interests, abilities, values, and other personal characteristics and matching it against the requirements of given occupations. Such assessment information may be useful, but must be used with caution. A person's interests and key motives may undergo marked change with experience and learning, and, as we have seen, occupations are undergoing many changes under the impact of technological advances. We shall elaborate further on psychological assessment in the chapter which follows.

Occupational information. Here, too, three general questions appear to be relevant:

1. *What are the requirements and working conditions of the occupation under consideration?* What training and skills are needed for admission? What general personal qualities—such as initiative, social competence, a particular temperament, or physical endurance—are required? What would the individual be doing from day to day and in what kind of setting? Equally important, how do these requirements fit what he has to offer and what he enjoys doing?

Here it may be emphasized that different positions within a broad occupational category may vary greatly in work activities and conditions. For example, a clinical psychologist working primarily with marital problems might engage in quite different daily activities and live in quite a different world from a physiological psychologist who was doing research on endocrine function in rats. Even the requisite knowledge and skills differ greatly, depending on the area of specialization and the particular job within it.

2. *What does the occupation have to offer?* What rewards and satisfactions can be expected in terms of income, social status, and opportunities for advancement and personal growth? Are the rewards and satisfactions of the kind the individual most wants? Will the individual find the work interesting and personally fulfilling? What can he expect to contribute? In the long run, he is likely to find his work more meaningful and fulfilling if he feels he is making a contribution to his chosen field.

3. *What changes are likely to occur in this occupational area?* Since many of to-day's college students will be working beyond the year 2000 A.D., the question of future trends in their chosen occupational area is a relevant one. With the accelerating rate of technological and social change, major shifts in many occupations are taking place even in relatively short periods of time. Thus it is important for the individual not only to gain a clear view of given occupations as they now exist but also to know about probable changes in the near and distant future which might affect his work. If vocational guidance is available, it can often be extremely helpful in delineating the choices that are available and the probable "fit" of the individual's abilities and interests with the various occupations under consideration.[1]

Family and other influences. We noted earlier that the positive attitudes and achievement orientation of middle-class families toward school and work are not necessarily shared by lower-class families. However, the relationships between family, social class, and career planning are not as simple as might be expected.

1. *Parents and other significant figures.* Burchinal, Haller, and Taves (1962) concluded from a review of several studies that male and female students most often credit their parents with the greatest influence on their career plans. Next in influence were teachers, friends, and vocational counselors. Despite the "generation gap" parents still appear to be influential today.

Parental influences on career choice may be exerted directly or indirectly or both. As American society becomes more urbanized and complex and educational opportunities become more available to all, pressure

---

[1]An excellent resource for young people looking for information about career opportunities is the *Occupational Outlook Handbook,* published every two years by the Department of Labor. Besides a summary of general trends in various kinds of employment, details about over 700 occupations are given, including nature of the work, where workers are employed and how many, training and other qualifications for admission and advancement, the employment outlook, earnings and working conditions, and sources of more information.

on the son to take over a family business or succeed his father in a particular occupation seems to be on the decline. Yet in a study of over 76,000 male college freshmen, Werts (1968) found that sons tended to choose the same or similar occupations as their fathers in three areas: the social sciences, the physical sciences, and medicine. For example, teachers' sons "overchose" the occupation of college professor; scientists' sons overchose mathematician, physicist, and geologist; and the sons of physicians overchose medicine as a career. Thus Werts concluded that these broad types of occupations still appear to be passed from father to son.

2. *Social class, ethnic, and race factors.* Young people's vocational choices are also influenced by their social-class and ethnic background.

Krauss (1964), studying the aspirations of high-school seniors, found that in general middle-class students had higher educational aspirations than lower-class students, as a group. However, for lower-class students whose mothers were engaged in nonmanual work, 53 per cent were planning to attend college, as compared with only 29 per cent for those whose mothers were performing manual work. He also found a high relationship between the educational level of the parents and the educational and occupational plans of their children: the higher the parental educational level, the higher the aspirations of the children.

Of course, Krauss dealt with high-school seniors and hence did not adequately sample the lower extreme of the socioeconomic scale. Where children grow up in circumstances of poverty and cultural deprivation, they have much less chance of either becoming high-school graduates or attending college. Such children usually show low levels of aspiration and achievement—in keeping with their absence of opportunity. Their background of experience makes it far less likely that they will internalize the value orientation of sacrificing immediate satisfactions for long-range achievement, nor could they afford the sacrificing of present income for an extended period of education

for a better job in the future. Thus for many reasons, the social-class level of the father is a good predictor of the son's aspiration and career choice (Blau, 1965; Duncan, 1965; Werts, 1968).

Lower-class young people also tend to marry younger and so usually have the least education and the lower-level jobs that go with it. Usually they have no choice but to take the first job they can get without considering its long-range potential. They may change jobs often; rarely do they progress beyond minimal earning capacity. Yet more than a million young people—most of them from lower socioeconomic level families—drop out of high school each year and effectively lose whatever choice they might have had.

Membership in an ethnic or racial group may also be a limiting influence on career choice. The Negro American has undoubtedly been subjected to the greatest discrimination in occupational opportunity and hence in career choice. However, varying degrees of discrimination have also been directed toward Americans of Mexican, Indian, and Asian ancestry; Jews and Catholics, too, have been subjected to discriminatory educational, hiring, and promotional practices. Our society is taking determined steps toward providing equality of educational and occupational opportunity, and it .is to be hoped that prejudice and discrimination will be overcome.

Educational Preparation

The increasing demand for skilled technicians and professional personnel—engineers, computer programmers, physicists, chemists, psychologists, teachers, and so on—has brought an awareness of the importance of post-high-school education, reflected in the increasing proportion of young people who are entering college and continuing to graduate school. Two outcomes of the college experience are of key importance in preparing the student for entrance into the world of work—his educational achievement and his personal growth.

Academic achievement. The specific educational preparation required for different occupations varies greatly, but for most middle-class students the path of entrance is only through formal higher education.

Although teaching, medicine, psychology, law, and other professions have their own specific requirements, they also call for certain common educational denominators: (1) an extensive general education which

COLLEGE STUDENTS' STEREOTYPES OF OCCUPATIONAL GROUPS

Although any student knows that "students" as a group are not nearly so much alike as newspaper reporters and other outsiders tend to assume, there are many oversimplified images of other groups commonly held by students. One study of students' images of fifteen occupational groups found clear stereotypes for each one with little variation from one student group to another (Beardslee & O'Dowd, 1962). Such stereotypes, however inaccurate, inevitably influence a student's choice of a "suitable" occupation for himself. They also influence both the role behavior he tries to learn after he makes a choice and the expectations he has in regard to the behavior of students preparing for various occupations. Several of the student stereotypes found by Beardslee and O'Dowd are summarized below:

DOCTORS

Highly intelligent, personally and socially attractive, cheerful and optimistic, unselfish, calm and confident, realistic, strong, adaptable. Richly rewarded by social status, wealth, and success. No negative characteristics in stereotype.

LAWYERS

Highly intelligent, like doctors in many ways and in high status and wealth but less service-oriented, less happy. More self-assertive and a hint of a selfish, manipulative attitude.

COLLEGE PROFESSORS

Highly intelligent, also highly sensitive esthetically. Individualists, colorful, interesting with some rashness, emotional difficulty, and lack of adaptability. Not well-to-do, lacking in opportunities for advancement. Radical, have some power in political affairs.

SCIENTISTS

Highly intelligent, lacking in artistic sensitivity and social skills. Lack of interest in people, a shallow personal life. Self-sufficient, rational, persevering, emotionally stable. Satisfied with work, reasonably well rewarded with wealth and status.

SCHOOL TEACHERS

Intelligent, sensitive, moderately interested in art, attentive to people, unselfish. Lacking in confidence and poorly rewarded in wealth, social status, and opportunity for advancement.

BUSINESS EXECUTIVES

High in social status, wealth, success. Have power in public affairs, good opportunities for advancement. Very conservative, have good taste. Sociable, confident, assertive, responsible, persevering, basically selfish.

ACCOUNTANTS

Low-status, not well-to-do, little power in public affairs, little opportunity for advancement, little personal satisfaction in work. Conformists, with limited intelligence, minimum social skills, inadequate sensibilities. Cold, submissive, unsure of selves, cautious, conservative.

ARTISTS

High sensitivity coupled with violent emotions and impulsiveness. Intuitive, rash, excitable, attention-demanding, irresponsible, uninterested in people, and unwilling to contribute to society in a disciplined way. Moody. No rewards from work other than high sense of satisfaction.

provides the individual with a broad background of information; (2) the learning of a code of ethics and social obligations which membership in the profession will entail; and (3) satisfactory completion of the curriculum required for admission to the profession. The latter requirement often poses problems in view of the intense competition for admission to college and later for admission to specialized programs of training leading to professional status.

In general, prior academic success in high school is used as a primary criterion for gaining admission to college and is a good predictor of academic achievement in college (Panos & Astin, 1968). Interestingly enough, however, college grades have not been found to be good predictors of later professional achievement (Hoyt, 1965; Martin, 1968). Assuming the requisite intellectual capability and training, one's actual degree of success in the field seems to be determined by factors like creativity, competence in interpersonal relationships, and all-around personal maturity.

Personal growth. Since personal maturity, as well as intellectual and professional training, is so important to occupational success, it is important that the college years foster all-round personal growth as well as academic achievement.

A number of studies indicate that several changes in the direction of personal growth typically take place in college students (Boyer & Michael, 1965; Freedman, 1965; Webster, Freedman, & Heist, 1962):

1. *Independence and autonomy.* Students become more independent and autonomous and more critical of authority and established values.

2. *Decreased dogmatism.* Students become less rigid in their beliefs and more open-minded and receptive to new ideas.

3. *Decreased authoritarianism.* Students tend to become more democratic and less anti-intellectual but not less critical and evaluative.

4. *Decreased ethnocentricism.* Students become less prejudiced and less likely to resort to the use of stereotypes in evaluating others.

5. *Shift in attitude concerning civil liberties.* Students become more committed to the ideals of personal, intellectual, and academic freedom.

The amount of change varies, of course, from student to student and from college to college. But generally speaking, it would appear that college experience tends to facilitate these kinds of growth and change, and that such personal growth is important for later professional achievement and success.

PROBLEMS IN OCCUPATIONAL ADJUSTMENT

As we have noted, young people today expect a great deal of their occupation. In addition to meeting basic economic needs, they expect to meet needs for self-esteem, personal achievement, and self-fulfillment. Consequently the individual's occupational adjustment is of vital significance to him as well as to his family. But he is not the only one concerned about his job adjustment and satisfaction. Industrial and business employers are also interested in providing working conditions that maximize individual satisfaction, promote group morale, and increase the productive efficiency of the worker. Job dissatisfaction, reflected in low efficiency and high employee turnover, is expensive to the employer, especially if a long on-the-job training period is required for new employees. Thus both employee and employer are concerned with the meshing of individual and job—with successful occupational adjustment.

Transition from School to Work

". . . the confrontation of the young person with the world of work is a major change in the environment. The world of work is a new world of meanings. Generally, family does not enter here, nor do peers." (Tiedeman & O'Hara, 1963, p. 49)

In making the transition from school to work, the young person now enters the "adult world of reality." Although this world differs markedly from one job setting to another, it is a world which differs in many ways from the world of high school or college. The change may not be so abrupt for the student who has had summer jobs or worked part-time while going to school, but the complete transition from school to work not only represents a major milestone in the person's life but often poses a difficult transition problem.

Common fears and concerns. In moving from the competitive but relatively protected setting of school to the more demanding and often less supportive job setting, a young person may feel that he has entered an unknown new world whose dangers and pitfalls he does not know how to anticipate. Thus it is not surprising that many young people are somewhat fearful and apprehensive concerning their ability to make the shift successfully.

One common fear is of failing—of not being able to do the work satisfactorily. Even when the individual has adequate ability, he may still fear that he will be confronted with tasks for which he has not been adequately trained. A second common fear is of not being accepted or not getting along well with one's colleagues and superiors; in the case of a young person taking a supervisory position a common fear is of not gaining the respect and cooperation of subordinates.

Other fears and concerns may focus around whether he has made the right choice and whether the new endeavor will live up to his hopes and expectations and meet his needs. If he is unsure about his own abilities and needs as well as about the demands of the job, he may feel doubly insecure in this new setting.

The dilemma of the first job. Schein (1968) has used the phrase *first-job dilemma* to refer to the problems which the college graduate commonly encounters on his first job. *"The new graduate comes from college to his first job in industry prepared to be a company president. He is ambitious, enthu-* *siastic and ready. Then come the realities of the business world. Within a year, he is very likely to suffer a serious loss of motivation, to find himself facing the thought of quitting the job that once seemed so promising as a career opportunity, or to stop trying so hard, to ease off and lapse into a kind of apathy. What is wrong?"* (p. 27)

The fact that the first job often presents problems is reflected in the high incidence of job change among college graduates. In a study of the work records of graduates from the MIT business management program, Schein (1968) reported that half of the graduates of one class had already left their first job roughly 3 years later; within 5 years of graduation almost three fourths of another group had changed jobs at least once, and some were on their third or fourth jobs. Although these findings may not apply to all college graduates, it would appear that something happens early in the careers of many college graduates that causes them to change jobs.

In analyzing the reasons for such early job changes in the case of these graduates of the management program, Schein pointed to several factors, including the following:

1. The graduate's views of industry and business had been shaped by what he had been taught in his classes; often this involved learning to look at problems from the perspective of a high-ranking executive. Thus he thought in terms of general concepts, rational principles, and a long-term overview. He was prepared to deal with basic long-range problems rather than with day-to-day operational problems.

2. While his education had taught the graduate advanced management principles, day-to-day problems required that he put such principles into Deep-Freeze and develop a sort of common-sense wisdom which he unfortunately had not acquired in his formal training.

3. Most of the graduates stated that their education had prepared them very well technically but had been deficient in providing them with the psychological techniques for dealing and working with people in an occupational setting. In essence, they lacked the skills for coping with and managing other people.

4. The graduates gave evidence of certain needs of which they were not always aware: the need for an opportunity to test themselves, to learn and grow, to retain their individuality and integrity, and to make a meaningful and worth-while contribution. Often the new employee found that his "good ideas" were not accepted; common, too, was a lack of adequate feedback concerning his job performance.

5. Often unrealistic expectations had been built up by company recruiters who had made promises and painted glowing pictures of challenging work and opportunities for personal growth and advancement that turned out to be quite remote from reality. Thus the graduate often found that his job fell far short of what he had been led to expect.

On the basis of his findings, Schein pointed to the need for a more effective dialogue between the university, the student, and the business organization. These recommendations apply equally well when other kinds of special training are involved.

Unfortunately, the individual's decision to leave his first job and look for another one is often a self-devaluating experience in that he feels that he has "failed" in his first venture into the world of work. However, the first job can be seen as a training experience and an opportunity to analyze oneself and one's fitness for a certain type of job. If one finds that this is not the right job, then he can make a change, knowing more about both himself and the world of work than he did before.

Meshing of Individual and Job

In describing the first-job dilemma, we have noted some of the conditions that lead to job dissatisfaction—particularly on the first job. Now let us glance briefly at some of the factors in good occupational adjustment and job satisfaction.

Although *occupational adjustment* is a meaningful and widely used concept, criteria for judging it are by no means fully agreed upon. Objective criteria can be used, such as ability to hold a job, advancement in one's occupational field, and size of remuneration or degree of prestige of one's job; subjective criteria can be used, such as job satisfaction and happiness. Since we are focusing our discussion on middle-class college students, who generally look to their life work as an important source of personal growth and fulfillment, we shall be primarily concerned here with job satisfaction. As in the case of marital adjustment, the individual-job fit is as important as particular characteristics in either the individual or the job, and the perception is as important as the objective reality.

What the job offers. The satisfactions found in work are often described as being either *intrinsic* or *extrinsic*. Intrinsic satisfactions are found in the work itself—in its ability to satisfy one's needs for self-esteem, relatedness, meaning, and personal growth and fulfillment. Many workers find their jobs so interesting and meaningful that they work at them longer and harder than is required. Extrinsic satisfactions are extraneous to the work itself and involve rewards such as money, fringe benefits, and working conditions.

A number of studies have found that intrinsic satisfactions—which meet the higher-level psychological needs of the worker—are more important to most workers than working conditions or even monetary compensation. In a study of engineers and accountants, for example, Wernimont (1966) found that intrinsic factors were mentioned more often than extrinsic factors in describing the satisfactions and dissatisfactions in past jobs.

Herzberg (1968), reporting on an earlier study of engineers and accountants, found that five factors stood out as strong determiners of job satisfaction: achievement, recognition for achievement, the work itself, responsibility, and advancement. All of these were considered to be factors intrinsic to the work activity. In contrast, he found that the chief causes of job dissatisfaction were company policy and administration, supervision, salary, interpersonal relations, and working conditions. All of these were considered to be extrinsic factors. Herzberg also noted that a worker can be both satisfied and dissatisfied with his job.

In general it would appear that both employers and union leaders have tended to overemphasize the importance of money and other extrinsic factors and to underestimate the importance of intrinsic factors in job satisfaction. For example, Herzberg (1968) has pointed out that:

"One example of the striking lack of success of the present money motivation system is portrayed in the case of today's computer programmers. The cause of dissatisfaction is not the pay, for these men receive high salaries and excellent fringe benefits. Rather, the problem is boredom; after the initial challenge, most companies allow their com-

---

FACTORS IN JOB SATISFACTION

Many intergroup and interpersonal problems in the world of work, as in other social settings, stem from the failure of one party to understand what is important to the other. Such lack of understanding was demonstrated clearly in a study comparing the opinions of labor and management about the job factors most important to workers. From a list of seventy-one items, employees at several companies were asked to choose the five job factors that were most important to them personally. Fifty executives from the companies and forty-two union officers were asked to rank the same items in the order they thought the workers would rank them. Ranks for the ten items most frequently mentioned by the employees and the ranks given them by the other two groups are shown in the table below. (A rank of 40+ means that the item was not among the first forty items as ranked by the employees.)

JOB FACTORS	EM-PLOYEES	EXEC-UTIVES	UNION OFFICERS
Job security—employment stabilization	1	2	2
Opportunities [in the company] for advancement	2	4	18
Compensation—base pay	3	1	1
Employee financial benefits (pensions, etc.)	4	8	19
Practice of informing you of your job status (successes and failures)	5	40+	40+
Type of work	6	7	39
Vacation and holiday practices	7	3	8
Profit-sharing plans	8	13	40+
Physical working conditions (on the job)	9	5	4
Company's attitude toward employees (liberal or conservative interpretation of policies)	10	6	6

In general, both employers and union officials overemphasized the importance of economic factors in determining worker satisfaction and morale. The workers' desire to be kept informed of their job status—fifth in their rankings—was not even included in the first forty items listed by either the executives or the union leaders. Surprisingly, company executives were considerably more accurate than union officers in judging the importance of some of the factors—for example, advancement opportunities and type of work (National Industrial Conference Board, 1947).

WHAT ARE "GOOD WORKING CONDITIONS"?

The degree to which our standards of good working conditions have changed in a little over a hundred years is well illustrated by this Code of Office Staff Practices issued by a British company in 1852:

1. GODLINESS, Cleanliness and Punctuality are the necessities of a good business.

2. THIS FIRM has reduced the hours of work, and the Clerical Staff will now only have to be present between the hours of 7 A.M. and 6 P.M. on weekdays.

3. DAILY PRAYERS will be held each morning in the Main Office. The Clerical Staff will be present.

4. CLOTHING must be of a sober nature. The Clerical Staff will not disport themselves in raiment of bright colours, nor will they wear hose unless in good repair.

5. OVERSHOES and topcoats may not be worn in the office, but neck scarves and headwear may be worn in inclement weather.

6. A STOVE is provided for the benefit of the Clerical Staff. Coal and wood must be kept in the locker. It is recommended that each member of the Clerical Staff bring 4 pounds of coal each day during cold weather.

7. NO MEMBER of the Clerical Staff may leave the room without permission from Mr. Rogers. The calls of nature are permitted, and Clerical Staff may use the garden below the second gate. This area must be kept in good order.

8. NO TALKING is allowed during business hours.

9. THE CRAVING FOR TOBACCO, wines and spirits is a human weakness, and as such is forbidden to all members of the Clerical Staff.

10. NOW THAT THE HOURS of business have been drastically reduced, the partaking of food is allowed between 11:30 A.M. and noon, but work will not, on any account, cease.

11. MEMBERS OF THE CLERICAL STAFF will provide their own pens. A new sharpener is available, on application to Mr. Rogers.

12. MR. ROGERS will nominate a Senior Clerk to be responsible for the cleanliness of the Main Office and the Private Office, and all Boys and Juniors will report to him 40 minutes before Prayers and will remain after closing hours for similar work. Brushes, Brooms, Scrubbers and Soap are provided by the owners.

13. THE NEW INCREASED WEEKLY WAGES are as hereunder detailed:

Junior Boys (to 11 years) 1s. 4d.
Boys (to 14 years) 2s. 1d.
Juniors 4s. 8d.
Junior Clerks 8s. 7d.
Clerks 10s. 9d.
Senior Clerks (after 15 years with the Owners) 21s.

14. THE OWNERS RECOGNIZE the generosity of the new Labour Laws, but will expect a great rise in output of work to compensate for these near-Utopian conditions.

---

puter programming to turn into routine drudgery. This need not happen: certainly it would not be difficult to build some true motivational factors into a job with as much potential challenge as this." (p. 67)

Good salary and working conditions are important, but in our affluent society these are taken pretty much for granted, at least for occupations requiring a higher education. Of course, individuals differ in their motives and values and hence in the satisfactions or dissatisfactions they find in certain types of work. In any case, a good deal of current emphasis is being placed on making jobs more

meaningful and fulfilling to the worker.

In discussing job satisfaction, it is also of interest to note the finding of Morse and Weiss (1962), who asked a sample of 401 employed men the question:

"If by some chance you inherited enough money to live comfortably without working, do you think you would work anyway or not?" Although only 9 per cent of the men stated that they enjoyed their work, 80 per cent said they would continue to work. Apparently the men felt that work would continue to be worth while as a means of keeping busy and avoiding boredom and feelings of uselessness

---

even though they did not feel committed to a particular type of work.

What the individual brings to the job. As in marital adjustment, there are certain aspects of maturity that tend to foster occupational adjustment. Among these are a realistic view of oneself, tolerance for delayed gratification, and a willingness to make realistic compromises.

In an occupation, as in any other life task, a person often must endure hardships and wait for rewards which may be forthcoming only after long periods of concentrated effort. Beginning jobs, being usually low in the organizational hierarchy, are especially likely to bring frustration and dissatisfaction unless the individual realizes that they are necessary stages to go through and that promotions will come as he acquires more skill, maturity, and judgment.

Some persons are able to establish themselves in an occupation with seeming ease; although they may change jobs, they show an orderly progression of advancement in their chosen field. Other persons have a great deal of difficulty in finding a job which satisfies them; "taking hold" is a term which is commonly used when the individual finds a suitable job and becomes committed to it.

It is unlikely that all the individual's needs and expectations will be satisfied in any occupation even at more responsible levels. The young person looking for the "ideal job" may well find that it does not exist. Often it becomes necessary to compromise—that is, to lower one's expectations and desires to a realistic level. This is a relative matter, or course; making a compromise with which one cannot live comfortably may lead to more problems than it resolves. Here, as in other areas of adjustment, one needs to be able to work on what can be changed, accept what cannot, and be able to recognize the difference.

Occupational adjustment and the individual's life situation. Occupational adjustment both affects and is affected by the individual's life situation. Job satisfaction or dissatis-

faction can influence an individual's personal adjustment and be reflected in marital and other relationships. In fact, if the individual attaches a great deal of importance to his work, his satisfaction or dissatisfaction at work may be critical in shaping his whole personal adjustment. Particularly when he is frustrated and unhappy in his work he is likely to be irritable and depressed and to "bring his problems home."

The reverse also is true: the supports and stresses in the individual's life situation can influence his level of competence and performance on the job. If things are going well at home, he can bring zest and concentration to his work, whereas if he is emotionally upset by marital problems, he may find it difficult to concentrate on his work or to gain satisfaction from it. Any stressful situation outside the job may make adjustive demands on him which deplete his adjustive resources and leave him less flexible and resourceful in coping with the demands and pressures of his work.

The meshing of the individual and the job thus involves both his personality and his general life situation as well as the nature and demands of the job.

Special Problems in Vocational Adjustment

Many special problems in occupational adjustment might be mentioned. For present purposes, however, we are concerned with certain broad categories of problems, namely, those related to working women, disadvantaged workers, older workers, and military service.

Working women. We have noted the tremendous increase in the number of women who work outside the home; by 1970, 30 million of the 80 million working Americans are expected to be women.

The employment of women tends to be related to certain significant stages in their lives. There is an initial employment peak at about ages 18 and 19 after completion of high

WOMEN'S PREJUDICE AGAINST WOMEN

Despite women's clamor for equal rights, there is evidence that young women in America still see themselves as inferior to men. College girls were given six professional articles to read (on art history, dietetics, education, city planning, linguistics, and law). No mention was made of the authors, but for each girl half the articles were attributed to a male author and half to a female author. Thus for half the girls a given article was written by "John T. McKay"; for the other half, by "Joan T. McKay." All six articles were seen as more valuable when attributed to a male author than when purportedly written by a female author. Even in the traditionally "feminine" fields of teaching and dietetics, men's articles were evidently expected to be better (Goldberg, 1968).

The investigator concluded: "Women—at least these young college women—are prejudiced against female professionals and, regardless of the actual accomplishments of these professionals, will firmly refuse to recognize them as the equals of their male colleagues." (p. 31)

school and prior to marriage and the advent of children. After this the proportion of working women decreases (as childrearing responsibilities increase) until about age 30. After the age of 30 (following the birth of the last child, and when older children start attending school), the proportion of working women begins to rise again. And there is a final peak around 40 to 50 when the children are grown up and move away from home.

Family status and circumstances may also determine whether or not a woman seeks employment. Single women are more likely to work than married women; women who have been or are married but have never had children are more likely to work than those with children. Among mothers, those with younger children are less likely to work than those with older children. In his survey of college students, Packard (1968) reported that about half of the women approaching college graduation—in the last half of their undergraduate college training—were seriously planning a career.

With these trends in mind, let us glance at some of the findings with respect to women college graduates and also with respect to the occupational problems that women commonly encounter. Rossi (1964), in a study of 3500 female college graduates out of school three years, found that they could be divided into three groups in terms of occupation: (1) the homemakers; (2) the traditional careerists in fields where women have long been strong, such as teaching; and (3) the pioneers, who had entered occupations long dominated by males, such as engineering, architecture, and the natural sciences. Almost all of the homemakers were married by this time, as compared with two thirds of the traditional careerists and half of the pioneers.

Working women usually also have to shoulder household responsibilities and often childrearing ones too. The question is often raised as to whether employment outside the home interferes with a woman's role as wife and mother. Although evidence is somewhat contradictory, there do not appear to be insurmountable problems, providing the husband is willing to give her additional assistance. In fact, Mudd and her associates (1965) found that in successfully functioning families, the percentage of wives working outside the home was above average, that the woman usually derived considerable satisfaction from her work, and that the husband usually approved of the arrangement.

Besides the many problems a woman faces in managing her time so as to do an adequate job as wife, mother, and worker, she faces many difficulties on the job that are related to her status as a woman. Bloustein (1968) points out that on the one hand the modern woman is told that she can combine marriage and family life with a career, but that on the other hand, "she encounters at every turn obstacles of prejudice and discrimination and lack of institutional supports." For example, hours of work are rarely made flexible for the working mother, nor is she likely to receive comparable pay for the same position or comparable opportunities for advancement. In fact, Bloustein has pointed to what he considers a "marriage-career hoax":

"... the present marriage-career hoax is that women who might otherwise lead rich, fulfilling lives in the home—in the leisure that our affluent society provides—are being deprived of this opportunity by the American compulsion to achieve and to produce, something women are told they can and should do." (p. 38)

He concludes that we should either tell women that their place is in the home or alter our social institutions to make a meaningful career for the wife and mother possible and compatible with her other duties and responsibilities.

At the same time it may be noted that a woman's career, especially if she is married, does not usually have the same meaning for her as a career does for a man. Traditionally a man's role is that of wage earner and provider, and the man's status in the socio-economic hierarchy stems largely from his job—while that of the woman is derived largely from her husband's position. In addition, the woman's success is usually judged by her competence as a wife, mother, and home manager rather than by her achievements in the occupational world. Probably for such reasons, many women are willing to settle for subordinate jobs and are more accepting of discrimination in pay and promotional opportunities. In fact, they have an advantage over their husbands in that the family's status and standard of living are not usually dependent on their job success. Thus working wives often do not suffer from the pressure their husbands feel to persevere and get ahead.

Disadvantaged workers. The term *disadvantaged worker* is commonly used to refer to individuals who are disadvantaged socially and to those who are handicapped.

Although we live in an affluent society that shows a high degree of upward mobility, the poverty cycle of those on the lower rungs of the socioeconomic ladder tends to be self-perpetuating. Schorr (1966) has pointed to five critical stages in the life cycle of the poor when decision points are reached and the individual usually takes the direction toward life-long poverty:

1. *The family begins* usually with couples marrying and having their first child while still in their teens. Putting off marriage and parenthood until later would enable the young people to secure a better education and subsequently a better job.

2. *Occupational choices* are limited because the youth who marries young usually drops out of school and enters the world of work while still in his teens. He is forced to take the first job he can get whether or not it affords adequate monetary compensation, security, or potential for advancement. As a result, his earning potential remains meagre.

3. *Too many children.* Of all the poor families in the United States in 1963, only 12 per cent had small families; 49 per cent had 6 children or more. The size of the family, in turn, increases the economic pressures and makes it more difficult to provide adequate care for each child.

4. *Family breakdown.* Early marriages tend to end in divorce. Probably less than half of the women who marry at age 17 or younger will still be living with the same husband twenty or thirty years later. The shortage of money and the large number of children from these lower-class teen-age marriages tend to intensify the problems that ensue when the husband leaves. As we saw in Chapter 4, children growing up in such families are likely to suffer many distortions in their development, leaving them ill-prepared for productive adult life.

5. *The cycle begins again.* As the children in the poor families enter adolescence, they too tend to marry early, drop out of school, and take whatever employment they can find. Thus the poverty cycle is perpetuated. If one is also unlucky enough to belong to a disliked ethnic or racial minority, preju-

dice and discrimination are added to the crushing burden of poverty.

The occupational difficulties encountered by the handicapped—including the mentally retarded—depend on a number of factors, including the nature and severity of the individual's disability, his level of education, and the particular occupation to which he aspires. In general, our society has tried to individualize educational and vocational training for the handicapped in such a way as to enable them to develop and utilize whatever capabilities they have.

Sometimes the factor with the greatest influence on the handicapped person's occupational adjustment is his own attitude toward his handicap and toward himself. His success depends on his accepting his handicap while still seeing himself as a person of worth. This may be especially difficult if he has made a successful occupational adjustment and then suffers a physical disability which bars him from continuing in his chosen occupation and necessitates acceptance of lower occupational status.

In the past decade there has been a new focus by both government and industry on the problems of the disadvantaged worker. An increasing number of physically and mentally handicapped persons are being served by rehabilitation agencies and helped to make good occupational adjustments. And many private and governmental organizations are attempting to meet the special needs of the socially disadvantaged youth for better general education and job training as well as employment opportunities.

Older workers. Estimates of the Bureau of the Census (1968) have predicted that by 1970 there will be over 60 million people in the United States aged 45 or over, of whom a third will be over 65. Wolfbein (1964) has pointed out a major problem of the older worker:

"At the upper end of the age spectrum (e.g., men 45 years old and over) unemployment rates are relatively favorable; but once out of a job, older men encounter difficulty in becoming re-employed as many find their skills obsolescing in the face of technological change." (p. 170)

Often older workers are discriminated against by potential employers who consider them to be less capable both physically and mentally than younger workers. In a study of young as contrasted with middle-aged workers, however, Thumin (1968) failed to find evidence to support the common notion that middle-aged workers are risky prospects for employment because of being more rigid, defensive, easily threatened, and less alert mentally.

Factors other than expected capacity to work may also make it harder for older workers to find satisfactory employment. Some industries are less willing to hire and train older workers because of the reduced length of the worker's probable work life and hence smaller return on the company's investment. Middle-aged women entering the labor market for the first time after their children are reared or after their husbands have died often encounter similar difficulties in finding satisfactory employment.

The relation of age to loss of occupational effectiveness appears to depend heavily upon the occupation involved. In professional sports, for example, a person may be "old" by the time he reaches 30; whereas in other occupations, such as law, politics, and the arts, older men have often made outstanding contributions. In a report on ten famous men (including Michelangelo and Churchill) who continued their careers into their 80's and two groups of professional people past 70, Pressey and Pressey (1967) found several factors which they considered of key significance: a continuing strong and usually socially significant purpose, mellowed wisdom, and a status and role in which continuance of their careers was encouraged.

The problem of the older worker becomes more acute as he faces retirement. Each day in the United States over 3000 persons cross the invisible barrier of age 65 and by custom and law are forced into retirement. They have become "oldsters" or "senior citizens" and are benched for the remainder of the game. But with our increasing physical health and life span, the individual at 65 may still be at or near the peak of many of his abilities.

The older person facing retirement is usually subjected to new stresses, including a marked reduction in income and the problem of finding social contacts and meaningful activities to replace those he is leaving. As Pressey and Pressey (1967) have pointed out, these stresses could probably be greatly reduced and the potentialities for productive social effort better utilized if people's occupational lives could be selectively tapered off rather than arbitrarily cut off by retirement. Although some occupations do make room for such tapering off and find niches for their "elder statesmen," this is the exception.

How the older person reacts to his changed status and to the difficult stresses commonly associated with retirement will depend upon the adequacy of his preparation. Successful retirement usually involves planning ahead for a program of part-time work or meaningful nonwork activities which fit in with his energies and abilities. Given reasonably good physical health and adequate planning, retirement can be a productive period. Freed from the encumbrances of a fixed work schedule and the commitments of childrearing, the older person can devote his time to leisure activities that make for challenge and satisfaction and contribute to personal growth.

Military service. Many countries, including the United States, confront the young eligible male with compulsory draft into the armed services for a specified length of time. For young men who have well-laid career plans that include a long period of educational preparation, military service is a disruptive element in the pursuit of long-range goals. In such instances, military service may be regarded as merely a period of marking time until they can get back to civilian life and resume education and career activities. And for young men conscientiously opposed to war, conscription presents a moral dilemma.

For some individuals, however, especially those with little formal education or those from socially disadvantaged backgrounds, military service may represent an unusual opportunity for training and career advancement. The Defense Department operates a huge educational complex which provides diverse types of training and returns over half a million men to the nation's skilled manpower pool each year. Even while in service, some individuals can be placed in positions related to their educational background and interests. Thus many young people can and do make constructive use of the period of time they are required to serve in the armed forces. In these cases military service may represent a meaningful vocational experience that will help prepare them for later civilian work. Some, of course, decide to continue in military service as a career.

In recent years, too, a large number of young men who have failed to qualify for service under existing fitness standards have been permitted to enlist and participate in intensive short-range programs designed to bring them up to fitness standards. Such programs cover a range of services from diet and minor medical attention to instruction in reading and other school subjects. As Janowitz (1967) has pointed out, military service thus often represents a second educational chance for young people coming from disadvantaged sectors of our society.

THE FUTURE WORLD OF WORK

Much as the Industrial Revolution amplified and largely replaced man's muscle power and freed him from the drudgery of physical labor, the new Cybernetics Revolution is implementing man's intellectual capabilities and freeing him from the bonds of routine and repetitive work. New occupations are coming into being, and many traditional occupations are becoming obsolete. In concluding our discussion of the world of work, it is thus relevant to note some of the occupational trends in our society and the relation of these trends to educational change. Then we will speculate briefly on future possibilities and horizons in the world of work.

Computers and Occupational Trends

Cybernetics in industry means control of machines by machines instead of by people. As the Cybernetics Revolution has gained momentum, we read about "the wonderful world of computers"—computers making up payrolls, checking income tax returns, controlling air and auto traffic, operating factories, diagnosing disease, keeping track of insurance premiums, guiding spacecraft, and learning and teaching. There are even computers to help design better computers. In short, computers are having an increasing impact on almost every aspect of our society, including government, industry, banking, insurance, defense, agriculture, medicine, science, and education.

The effects of cybernetics on the world of work will be tremendous, for cybernetics makes possible a large increase in productivity with fewer and fewer workers. Computer robots appear capable of reducing man's work week to some 10 hours or less by the year 2000. Not only will they give him more leisure time; they will also influence the types of work that will be needed and available and hence the kinds of training that he will need for his career.

Based in part on a report to the Department of Health, Education, and Welfare concerning the prospects ahead for the youth of today and tomorrow, Michael (1965) concluded that the trend is toward a three-level occupational system comprising professionals, technicians, and the unskilled. The professionals will require a long and rigorous education and will be concerned with high-level decision making and future planning; the technicians will be concerned with research and with programing, monitoring, and servicing the computers and other automated equipment. The unskilled are portrayed as a disturbingly distinct group—at least through the next generation—who will be relegated to relatively menial and low-paying jobs by their lack of education and training. The psychological and social problems such a situation could entail are obviously both important and complex.

Meshing of Educational and Occupational Trends

"Education is repeatedly identified as the primary means for preparing individuals to participate in the changing society and for helping society itself to develop and maintain dynamic stability. As the key importance of education for all persons is recognized, new educational goals are articulated, new problems in achieving these goals are identified, and new power centers emerge—power centers seeking to influence the development and control of schools and colleges." (Tyler, 1968, p. vii)

Education will surely take on even more significance in the life of the worker of tomorrow. As the need for unskilled and semiskilled jobs declines and the work force shifts into more skilled and service occupations, young people are already needing more training both before and after they enter the work world. Borow (1966) has pointed to three trends that are likely to intensify in the future: (1) the trend toward raising the formal educational requirements for qualifying for many occupational fields, (2) the increasing difficulty in securing a good job without a relatively advanced level of education, and (3) the increasing use of education—refresher courses, evening classes, workshops, and so on—throughout the person's career.

Such continued education will be necessary for both the technician and the professional. As jobs change or become obsolete, retraining for new work will become commonplace and a man may be retrained several times during his work life. It has been predicted that by the mid-1970's the average working engineer will have to spend the equivalent of one day a week in some kind of formal study for the duration of his career (Kincaid, 1968).

Education itself will need to change both to make use of the new teaching technologies that are becoming available and to prepare individuals for a world in which they will be increasingly on their own to make their lives meaningful.

The Futurists: Looking Ahead

"Suppose instead of being about five billion years old, our planet, Earth, had come into being only 80 days ago.

"On this time scale, the first living creatures would be about 60 days old. But man would have come upon the scene about an hour ago.

"Similarly, significant numbers of modern men appeared less than a minute ago and agriculture came into being just 15 seconds ago. The use of metals would be 10 seconds old and the idea of a money-economy occurred to someone three-fourths of a second ago.

"The industrial revolution that replaced man's muscles with power-driven machines began three-tenths of a second ago, and the introduction of the electronic digital computers—machines that extend the capacity of the human mind—only about one-fifteenth of a second ago." (Bengelsdorf, 1966)

With the coming of computers, the rapid pace of social change has accelerated still further. As a result, concern with "things to come" is far more than a passing fad and has even given rise to a new group of experts —the "futurists"—who have made prophecy and prediction an organized and relatively scientific enterprise. If their predictions are correct, the world of tomorrow will be different in basic ways from the world of today.

Perhaps the biggest change they predict is a diminishing of work as a chief source of status and material benefits. By the year 2000 automated machines are expected to be producing so much that the average family will have a yearly income (in terms of 1966 dollars) of $30,000 to $40,000 (*Time*, 1966; Kalachek, 1967). As a consequence, a person's status and worth will be evaluated not by his "line of work" or his material possessions but by his involvement in the drama of living.

The great increase in time free from earning a living could bring serious new problems. Our traditional ideas of leisure as "time to kill" will have to change, for we will have to use leisure-time activities to meet many of the needs that we now meet through our work. Man, with his developed brain and sensitivity, should not have to waste his time doing routine work that a machine can handle. Leisure combined with lifelong learning could give man at last a chance to "realize the awesome potential of his brain, the creative capacity of which is, for all practical purposes, infinite." (Leonard, 1968) Thus the previously separate worlds of work, education, and leisure could merge into an integrated and meaningful way of life.

The work an individual sees to do reflects in part the needs of the larger society. Even if machines bring us unprecedented abundance, we still will have three herculean tasks to tax our ingenuity and call for our best effort: (1) completing our unfinished business of achieving our goals of equal opportunity for all and freedom from all kinds of discrimination; (2) coping with the new and pressing problems which have arisen in the course of our technological advances, such as air pollution, the population explosion, and the danger posed by national rivalries among those who possess thermonuclear and biological weapons of warfare; and (3) planning for the future—shaping a world which will offer resources and inducements for full, creative living and encouragement for the fullest development of the human potentials for meaning, value, and significance.

Perhaps our greatest need at this moment is to learn to predict and control the effects of the new forces that we are unleashing. Too often in the past our technological miracles have enslaved and dehumanized man instead of serving him and contributing to a fuller life for him. Never has so much of our world been of our own making. We are confronted with choices and decisions of enormous consequences; even our survival may depend on our ability to foresee the effects of the choices we make.

We have tended to take for granted the inevitability of continued technological development, proficiency, and control—have assumed that when a new, more effective technology appeared, *of course* it should replace the old one. But when we change a technology we also change psychological and social relationships; in solving an economic problem, we may create a psychological or social one that, on balance, leaves us worse off.

Can we provide economic security for all without either regimenting the whole society in the service of economic utopia or depriving people of the satisfaction that comes from achievement, overcoming obstacles, and contributing to the welfare of the group? Conceivably, for example, a guaranteed annual income could be provided in such a way that an increasingly large segment of the population would be cut off from sharing in the society except as consumers; this could be a frustrating, self-devaluating role to have to play; yet the time might even come when this disgruntled, excluded group would have the majority vote—without the training or inclination to use it wisely. Our best creativity is needed to devise and bring into being social arrangements that will take into account man's deepest psychological and social needs as well as his more obvious physical ones.

SUMMARY AND A LOOK AHEAD

In the world of work, as in marriage, expectations and criteria of success have changed. We expect our work not only to feed and clothe us but to give us satisfaction and an avenue for personal growth. Thus in our choice of a career—in itself a fairly new opportunity—we look for a type of activity that will add meaning and value to our lives.

Perhaps fortunately, this change in expectations has come at a time when machines are taking over more and more of the routine jobs; those that are left will require more skill and longer preparation. There is a blurring of traditional sex roles as more women work outside the home and enter formerly "masculine" fields.

Preparation for one's career starts early, and the final choice is influenced by many earlier choices, both positive and negative, along the way. Factors influencing career choice include personal characteristics and resources, occupational information and opportunities, and family and social-class attitudes. Vocational counseling may play an important role in clarifying the choices available to the individual. Educational preparation for work includes both the knowledge and skills needed in the particular field and general personal growth. In general, the experience of college seems to produce greater independence and autonomy; less dogmatism, authoritarianism, and ethnocentrism; and a greater commitment to the ideals of personal and intellectual freedom.

Early occupational maladjustment often reflects fears of inadequacy and faulty expectations regarding the responsibilities that are possible to those on the lower rungs of the organizational ladder. Ultimately, occupational adjustment depends on a meshing of what the job offers and demands with what the individual brings. The individual's life situation both affects and is affected by his adjustment at work. Four groups of workers who may have special problems in achieving good occupational adjustment are women working outside the home, culturally or physically handicapped workers, older workers, and those called for military service.

With machines bringing shorter working hours and perhaps forced leisure to many, we will need to find other ways of meeting the physical and psychological needs that work now meets. Hopefully, the now separate worlds of education, work, and leisure will be merged into an integrated and meaningful way of life which will contribute to the maximal fulfillment of the human potential.

In the last three chapters we have looked at group-individual relationships—first in general, and then in the two particular contexts of marriage and work. In the final chapter of this section we shall see how intensive group experience is being used to foster personal growth and what kinds of help counseling and psychotherapy can give to people with special problems of adjustment in order to enable them to develop and use their potential.

Key terms used in this chapter include:

Puritan work ethic (p. 331)
changing criteria of occupational success (p. 331)
converging occupational roles (p. 331)
"work world" (pp. 332-333)
stages in career planning (p. 333)
the first-job dilemma (p. 339)
occupational adjustment (pp. 340-341)
intrinsic and extrinsic satisfactions (p. 340)
Cybernetic Revolution (p. 348)

Chapter 12

RESOURCES FOR PERSONAL GROWTH AND CHANGE

Intensive Group Experience
Psychological Counseling
Psychotherapy

The problems of the twentieth century are problems of human relations quite as much as problems of technology. Contemporary living requires enhanced social sensitivity and greater skill in human relationships than ever before. Thus the quest for greater self-knowledge and for more meaningful ways of relating to others has become a pressing concern for many people today. Here the resources of modern psychology are proving of great assistance.

In modern life many professional resources are available to the individual who needs assistance in solving his problems. He can go to a lawyer for legal advice, consult a medical doctor for physical ailments, have an architect design his home and an interior decorator furnish it, and obtain the services of innumerable other specialists for other special problems. As psychology has come of age, people have turned increasingly to professional psychologists and other qualified counselors for help with marital, occupational, and educational problems.

Psychological resources available to the individual can be classified into three major types: (1) intensive experience in special small groups aimed at increasing participants' self-understanding and ability to relate to

others in meaningful ways, (2) counseling, for educational, occupational, and marital planning or help with problems, and (3) psychotherapy, directed toward the treatment of personality difficulties and maladjustment. All three can contribute to personal adjustment and growth as well as to the solution of particular problems.

INTENSIVE GROUP EXPERIENCE

The last two decades have seen a great deal of experimentation in the use of groups to increase the awareness and effectiveness of essentially normal people and to find pathways to enriched and more meaningful human relationships and "ways of being." This potent new cultural phenomenon is referred to as the *intensive group experience*. Groups vary considerably in goals and methods: a particular group may focus on training in human relations skills, on resolving personal problems, on developing creative imagination, or on other goals and may have an existential, humanistic, psychoanalytic, or other theoretical orientation. Groups have functioned in universities, industries, churches, clinics, and resort settings, and participants have been students, business executives, delinquents, priests, dancers, educators, philosophers, police officers, youth leaders, married couples, and entire families.

Despite their differences, most such groups are small and relatively unstructured, with the group having considerable freedom in choosing its goals and direction, and with a nondirective leader whose main responsibility is usually to facilitate the expression of thoughts and feelings. And central to all is the focus on the intensive experience of interacting with each other under conditions which differ from those in ordinary life in the degree to which honest exploration of feelings is encouraged. Unlike most therapy, they do not attempt to help their members come to terms with the past but focus on the "here and now," trying to get people to confront what they are feeling and doing at the moment and to try out new ways of feeling and communicating.

In the present section we shall review the nature and functioning of the common types of intensive experience groups and then examine briefly some of their apparent effects. The two main kinds of groups that have developed are (1) sensitivity-training groups (also called T-groups) and (2) encounter groups. "Workshops" and "training laboratories," in which additional resources and activities are built around the common intensive group experience, are also common.

Sensitivity training (T-groups)

Sensitivity training is an outgrowth of a research effort begun shortly after World War II by Kurt Lewin and his colleagues. They were concerned about the dangers of autocratic leadership and hoped, through research on group processes, both to identify the skills needed for effective democratic group functioning and to learn how these skills could be taught. The impetus of the original work led to the establishment of the National Training Laboratories at Bethel, Maine, associated with the National Education Association and now titled the NTL Institute for Applied Behavioral Science. The Institute and its affiliates continue to combine research aimed at establishing basic principles with practical help to various groups through intensive group experience. These "training groups" have been nicknamed "T-groups." Such training has been directed especially toward groups of professionals concerned with helping people in various ways, such as clergymen, youth leaders, nurses, psychologists, teachers, and social workers.

"Labs" are held each year for various groups of professionals. Here lectures, problem-solving exercises, and other activities are added to the basic T-group experience. A main thrust has been with business groups, especially executives, in whom attempts are made to develop human relations skills and an awareness of the need for them. One popular annual session is a "Presidents' Conference" for presidents of businesses. Recently there has been increased emphasis on training for community leaders.

There continues to be considerable experimentation with both the format and the focus of T-groups. Training labs are now offered on organizational growth, relationships between (as well as within) groups, and "personal growth." A number of university institutes and other organizations also conduct T-groups for students. In some cases college courses in group dynamics are being taught as T-groups, meeting once or twice a week throughout the college term, reading case examples of human relations problems and other source materials as varied as existential theory and Golding's *Lord of the Flies,* and using their class time to analyze their interactions and discuss their reading and whatever else is of concern to them.

Group format and goals. Sensitivity-training groups usually consist of 10 to 15 persons with one or two leaders called *trainers.*[1] A group usually meets for a total time of 20 to 50 hours, either on consecutive days or

[1]The NTL Institute and its affiliates have a well-worked-out procedure for training T-group leaders and issue certificates to those who have taken the training.

spaced over a period as long as several weeks. Recently, two new approaches have been introduced: (1) the *marathon* group, which may meet for an entire weekend without breaking for sleep, and (2) a combination of spaced and massed approaches, in which the initial session may begin with a live-in weekend (often some distance away from home), continue with weekly meetings, and then conclude with a final live-in weekend.

The ultimate purpose of greater effectiveness in the participants' relations with others requires the achievement of several subgoals, including:

1. Increased awareness of what one is doing and how others are reacting to it, with an examination of the values and assumptions behind his actions.

2. Increased sensitivity to what others are thinking and feeling and to the subtle ways in which people communicate with each other by voice inflections, facial expressions, and bodily postures.

3. Increased awareness of how individuals affect groups and how groups affect individuals, of what behavior inhibits or facilitates group functioning, and of how subgroups form and conflict with each other.

4. Increased skill in identifying what is happening in a group and what is helping or interfering with openness.

5. Increased competence in helping oneself and others achieve more effective interactions and in helping to make a group function more effectively in different kinds of situations.

Although these goals may be only partially achieved in the brief time a T-group meets, it is hoped that a direction will be established and new channels opened up for "learning how to learn." In essence, sensitivity-training groups are an institutionalized setting for social learning.

Group process. In the small face-to-face T-group there are usually no planned topics or activities, and the trainer does not take a leadership role. Often he simply specifies the amount of time the group will meet and points out that the major concern is to try to understand one's own behavior and that of other group members. The focus is kept on what is happening or being felt or communicated at the present moment, how the participants are portraying themselves to and affecting each other.

The lack of structuring often leads initially to feelings of frustration and expressions of hostility and discontent. Then, as the group interaction gets under way, the process of feedback becomes of crucial importance.

"Given the unstructured group as the vehicle and the behavior emitted in the group as the principal topic of conversation, the success of the venture depends on the crucial process of feedback. Thus, the participants must be able to inform each other how their behavior is being seen and interpreted and to describe the kinds of feelings generated. This is the primary process by which the delegates 'learn.' They must receive articulate and meaningful feedback about their own behavior . . . and their efforts to interpret group processes." (Campbell & Dunnette, 1968, p. 76)

For the desired new learning to occur, it is considered necessary for a certain amount of tension or anxiety to be generated—particularly near the beginning (Campbell & Dunnette, 1968). This anxiety arises when the individual discovers that his previous role-bound methods of interacting are seriously deficient for functioning successfully in this new type of group. Anxiety may also be aroused when the individual's self-image and defense mechanisms come under scrutiny by the group. Such anxiety apparently helps to jar him loose from his preconceived notions and habitual ways of reacting so that the feedback can have maximal effect in helping him to learn new and more effective ways of perceiving and interacting. Unless such "unfreezing" occurs, the feedback he gets may be ineffectual (Schein, 1964).

To ensure effective feedback, there must be a climate of "psychological safety" (Bradford, Gibb, & Benne, 1964). Each member must feel that it is safe to drop his defenses, to express his feelings, and to try out new ways of interacting. Unless the group is nonevaluative and supportive concerning whatever is revealed, this feeling of safety cannot be achieved and group progress is likely to come to a halt.

The establishment of such a climate is largely the responsibility of the trainer. Although he makes it clear that the group members are responsible for setting their own goals and making their own analyses, he sets the pace by expressing his own feelings openly and honestly, by supporting the honest expression of feeling by others, and by serving as a helpful model in absorbing expressions of hostility and frustration without becoming defensive. He also gives—and encourages others to give—descriptive rather than evaluative feedback: for example, not "You're being bossy" but "It made me uncomfortable when you said that."

The trainer may help the group to concentrate on either group-level or individual-level learnings. Thus he may raise questions about group factors, such as how the norms are being established or how decisions are being made, or he may call attention to feelings being expressed or perhaps being felt but expressed only in indirect and nonverbal ways. Through such a group experience, members can become much more aware of what they are really doing and how it is making other people feel, as well as what kinds of interactions are fostering or interfering with the functioning of the group. To a greater or lesser extent, depending on the trainer and the context, the experiences in awareness and in trying out new modes of interaction in the safety of the group may be supplemented by "cognitive handles" of theory and terminology.

Encounter Groups

Although some encounter groups are indistinguishable from sensitivity-training groups, others are considerably different in rationale, goals, and methods. Both are aimed at increased self-understanding, improved effectiveness in relating to others, and exposure to new channels of personal growth. In general, however, encounter groups put a greater emphasis on individual growth than on group interaction or group skills. Where the T-group member tends to direct his attention to how he is affecting others, the encounter-group member tends to focus on how others are affecting him and on the meaningfulness of an encounter between two human beings.

Format and goals. The basic encounter group is usually directed toward helping individual members gain insight into particular personal or social problems and learn to cope with them more effectively. For example, Stoller (1967) reports on the use of videotapes to help group members to see themselves in action:

"In one group, a wife had spent considerable time complaining bitterly that her husband 'behaved like a child' with her. On video tape, I was able to show her that she used many of the mannerisms of a scolding mother with him—she would glare, shake her finger, and when pleased, pat his head. 'I couldn't believe it,' she said. 'It was worth a thousand words.'" (p. 32)

There is even greater flexibility and experimentation in encounter groups than in T-groups, and a variety of formats have emerged. One interesting type is the workshop devoted to a particular topic or to personal or community problems. Of particular interest here is the family workshop, in which three or four families remain together for several days—usually a weekend—with the goal of gaining insight into their interactions and relationships and finding new and more effective ways of family functioning.

A center at which leaders conduct many different kinds of encounter groups is the Esalen Institute at Big Sur, California. Body awareness, nonverbal communication, creative imagination, and numerous other topics have formed the focus of weekend or week-long workshops. The typical sequence of interaction in such workshops is summarized on page 356.[1]

---

[1] A chronicle describing the progress of one such group is given in the article beginning on page 513.

EVENTS IN ENCOUNTER GROUPS

Rogers (1968) has delineated certain patterns which tend to occur in encounter groups. Although there is no clear-cut sequence in which one pattern ends and another begins, some patterns are likely to occur early and others later in the group process.

Milling around. As the leader makes it clear that the group is responsible for the direction of the group, there tends to be an initial period of confusion, frustration, awkward silences, and "cocktail-party talk"—polite surface interaction. Concern centers around such questions as "Who is responsible for us?" and "What is the purpose of the group?"

Resistance to personal expression or exploration. Initially it is the public self which members tend to present to each other. The individual is fearful and resistant to revealing his inner self and inner world. However, some members may reveal rather personal attitudes, which receive a very ambivalent reaction.

Expression of feelings. Despite doubts about the trustworthiness of the group and the risk of exposure, expression of feeling does begin to occur. Initially such feelings are likely to concern events outside the group, such as circumstances in a member's life situation which frustrate him; then gradually there is an expression of "here-and-now" feelings which often take the form of an attack upon the leader for insufficient guidance. Negative feelings usually predominate at first.

Expression and exploration of personally meaningful material. Criticism and anger having been expressed and accepted, a climate of trust begins to develop, and a member decides to gamble on revealing some deeper facet of himself to the group. Usually again, the information focuses on events outside the group.

The expression of immediate interpersonal feelings in the group. The next event is usually the expression of feelings being experienced toward each other. Such feelings may be negative or positive: "I like you less each time you speak out," or "I like the way you call a spade a spade." The attitudes underlying such feelings are explored in an increasing climate of trust.

The development of a healing capacity in the group. A fascinating aspect of the intensive group experience is the spontaneous way in which a number of group members are able to give help with a spirit of concern and caring that then helps other group members to reveal their true feelings.

Self-acceptance and the beginning of change. The individual comes to perceive himself as he really is and to feel that it is all right to be himself, with both strengths and weaknesses. As he learns to accept and be himself, he can drop his defenses, and he becomes more open to experience and to change.

The cracking of façades. One of the threads which overlaps and interweaves with what has gone before is the increasing impatience with defenses. The revealing of their deeper selves by some group members begins to make it clear that a more meaningful encounter is possible than one of surface interaction. Thus the group demands that each individual remove his mask, reveal his current feelings, and be himself—as the group strives toward the goal of a deeper and more basic encounter.

The individual receives feedback. In the interaction of group members, the individual receives a good deal of feedback concerning how he appears to others. In some instances the feedback is warm and positive; in others, it can be negative, as other members tell the individual what he does that annoys or irritates them. Through such feedback the individual may gain significant new insights.

Confrontation. The term confrontation is used when one member confronts another directly and "levels" with him. Such confrontation is a form of feedback and may be negative or positive in nature, but it is often an intensely emotional event. It is considered to be one of the most important and change-producing aspects of the intensive group experience.

The expression of positive feelings and closeness. As group sessions progress, there tend to be increasing feelings of warmth and group closeness; such feelings are considered to be of therapeutic value for the individual members.

Behavior changes in the group. Gestures and tonal inflections may change, the member may show greater ease and spontaneity in expressing his feelings, greater depth of feeling toward others, and so on. There may be increased understanding of oneself and others, new insight into problems, and the working out of more effective ways of relating to others.

A basic theme which runs through the group sessions is the concept of the basic encounter, in which members come into more direct and closer contact with each other than is customary in everyday life.

Another format for encounter groups is the marathon group which, as we have noted, usually stays together for a whole weekend without breaking for sleep. The events in a marathon encounter group that focused on the problem of racial discrimination are summarized on pp. 358-359.

Group process. In achieving group goals, emphasis is placed on the honest expression of thoughts and feelings, including anger and hostility, the breaking loose from habitual perceptions and role behaviors, and acceptance of responsibility for one's own acts and values. There is an encouragement of "constructive aggression" and a deliberate instigation of group pressures on individual members to change their behavior.

The intensity of the encounter group is at its height when the marathon format is used. This format is based on the view that the "opening up" process will be hastened by such intense, continuous contact, as well as by the lowering of inhibitions that comes with fatigue. Presumably also, there will be a more truthful expression of feelings since the participants are likely to be too tired to play games. Finally, being separated from any other environment for a sustained period of time, it is thought that they become more involved in the group experience and more susceptible to its pressures toward change.

The marathon encounter group has been called a "pressure cooker" because of the emotional tensions it builds up. And like a pressure cooker, it seems capable of compressing the amount of time required to do its work.

Effects of Intensive Group Experience

In both T-groups and encounter groups, a new reference group is established which exposes the individual to new norms concerning what is desirable, helpful, and authentic and supports him in his attempts to change in accordance with these new norms. In both instances, people have a chance to confront the degree to which they are playing rigid roles and doing what they think is expected

of them—and hence have been blind to alternative ways of perceiving and meeting their problems. In such following of prescribed roles and expectations, labels are especially rigidifying:

"When a person is labelled—neurotic, psychotic, executive, teacher, salesman, psychologist—either by himself or by others, he restricts his behavior to the role and even may rely upon the role for security. This diminishes the kind of experiences he is likely to have. Indeed, it is those groups whose members have shared labels—be it schizophrenic or executive—which are hardest to help move into intimate contact." (Stoller, 1967, pp. 29-30)

In the intensive group experience, people may discover with real shock the many rigidifying things they are doing to themselves. In the safety of the group they can begin to discard their facades and learn to become more honest and flexible in their perceptions and responses.

Some outcomes and issues. Expectation of change from T-groups or encounter-group experience rests on the assumption that most people lack adequate self-understanding and interpersonal competence at the start, that psychological freedom to "open up" can be achieved in a short time, even among strangers, that members can give each other the feedback they need for new learning, and that the behavior changes can transfer to the "back home" situation. Most of those who participate in such groups feel that the experience has changed them and has been useful and meaningful (Campbell & Dunnette, 1968). Objective data regarding behavioral change have been harder to come by.

Most of the research concerning the outcome of intensive group experiences has centered on T-groups. In a comprehensive review of these research findings, Campbell and Dunnette (1968) have concluded that the evidence is reasonably convincing that T-group experience induces behavior changes which carry over to the "back home" setting. Rather than a "typical" effect of T-group training, however, it appears that in-

A MARATHON ENCOUNTER GROUP

The following excerpts are taken from the report of a marathon encounter group that focused on the problem of racial discrimination. The meeting was held at Esalen Institute on a July weekend in 1967 at a time when many of our cities were torn by riots in the ghetto areas. The group consisted of mixed-race, predominantly middle-class participants under the leadership of a Negro psychiatrist and a staff member (Leonard, 1968).

The first evening was devoted to preliminary exercises such as trying to communicate without words. Participants were told to expect that they would soon be relating on levels generally unknown in the outside community and were directed to try to be completely honest and open, relating on the level of present feelings, not theorizing or rationalizing, not escaping into past events or future worries—and forgetting about politeness.

The next morning the first confrontation occurred, not between black and white but among the blacks, with bitter name-calling and accusations. For a time there was accusation but not encounter or change. Then a young Japanese-American named Larry, who had been cool and cynical, suddenly began to talk.

. . . He had not realized how deeply he had felt racial prejudice or how much it had ruled his life. But now he knew he was a yellow man, a "Jap," and was ready to admit it. He declared himself to be a soul brother. With this declaration, all of his reserve collapsed and he "burst" into tears. The dikes were down then, and several of the Negroes poured out their hurt. "How many of you people can realize," a mother asked, "what it's like to send your children off to school and know they'll probably be called 'nigger' or spat on? And there's nothing, nothing you can do about it?" (p. 204)

Soon after, Larry's Negro friend Cliff became locked in a bitter encounter with a beautiful young white schoolteacher named Pam:

She had told him she wanted his friendship, and he had responded scathingly, denouncing her "pitiful condescending" overtures. Now her eyes were filled with tears.

"Please. What can I do? I'm trying. Please help me." Cliff rocked his chair back and forth, looking across the room at her with contempt.

"No, baby, I'm not going to help you. I'm not going to take you off the hook. I want you to feel just what I feel. I want you to feel what I've felt for twenty-one years. Go on. Cry."

"Please," she begged. Tears streamed down her cheeks. Cliff kept rocking back and forth, his eyes fixed on hers. No one came to her aid. Somehow it seemed right that this interval in time should be fully realized by everyone in the room. The silence intensified, became in itself a powerful medium of communication. (pp. 204-205)

A number of different topics came up during the hours which followed but the main theme through dinner and later into the evening was the hurt and anger of the Negroes and their despair and absolute distrust of all whites. After darkness fell, the group was split into two sections for the night; and about this time an episode occurred that was to occupy one group for most of the night.

We had let a newcomer join the group at dinnertime. Chuck was in his early twenties, almost jet black, with a wary face and a body as taut as a steel spring. He began telling the group how he had successfully "transcended" the entire matter of race. He was utterly lacking in bad feelings against whites. He disliked the system, but not the man. He thought that racial incidents were extremely rare, especially in his own life. He never felt anger or hostility.

No one believed him. "It makes me nervous just to hear your voice," I told him. "That singsong way you have of talking, like there's no relation between what you're saying and what you feel. It puts me on edge. I feel like yelling at you." Someone suggested that I do so, and I did. Others followed me, cursing, yelling and cajoling as they expressed their feelings

dividual participants are affected in different ways. Clear evidence is lacking on whether people who have been in a T-group tend to show a higher general level of "sensitivity" or increased accuracy in their interpersonal perceptions, as judged by others.

Intensive groups are not without risk. Among these are: (1) short-term change and subsequent discouragement; (2) the risk that the individual may in revealing himself become deeply involved in problems which are not worked through; (3) the revelation of toward him and his professed attitude. But nothing moved Chuck. His face became a mask of stone. He had nothing but love for all mankind, the stone said. The group united in trying to get through to him. Black and white worked together. Cliff and Pam, the afternoon's bitterness forgotten, operated like a team. There was an unspoken accord among the eighteen people in the group that somehow no matter how long it took, we would get through to Chuck. . . (p. 206)

At this point an incident occurred which struck the group as funny and the resulting laughter served to release the tension of group members and to take the pressure temporarily off Chuck. It may be pointed out here that if Chuck had asked the group to take the pressure off him, they would have; or he could simply have left the group which would have been considered an honest and appropriate response. However, Chuck seemed to be fascinated by the confrontation.

Another hour passed. At last, Chuck's voice was beginning to sound more natural. He was talking about his sexual prowess. "I could take any woman here," he said, his eyes flashing around the room.

"How would you take Pam?" I asked him.

"I'll tell you."

"Tell her."

He turned toward the teacher. "All right. First I'd rap you, then I'd take you."

"Rap?"

"Talk. You know, establish rapport. I'd rap you, then I'd take you."

Pam looked at him with scorn. "You'd never take me. I wouldn't let you touch me. Ever."

"I'd take you, all right, baby." A fury lay just beneath his words.

Voices broke out around the group as various women denied or affirmed his sexual attraction. The Negro house-wife leaned over toward him.

"You could never take me, and I'm going to tell you why." Something in her voice reduced us all to silence. "Because you're just a dirty little black nigger."

Chuck almost leaped from his chair. Clenching his fists on the armrests, he loosed his hidden fury in a savage and frightening tirade. Finally, he caught himself, looked around the room with dazed eyes and covered his face with his hands. He sat that way as members of the group comforted him. Then he looked up and smiled. His face was different.

A little later, after a surprisingly tender interchange, he said, "I want to thank all of you. I've learned more in the last two hours than in the last two years." (pp. 207-208)

The following morning—Sunday—the group took an unexpected turn in that the whites began revealing themselves and baring the most tragic and painful moments in their lives. After one particularly tragic revelation:

Almost everyone in the room was crying. We were unashamed of our tears. We were not Negroes or whites or Orientals. We were human beings joined in a very precious, fragile awareness of our common plight, of the waste and loss in every life, and of hope for something better. For many of us, that morning was transcendental, a space in life when ordinary objects seem to shimmer, when all faces are beautiful and time can be taken at the crest like a great onrushing wave. That was the way it was for me.

Noon came and passed, but we wouldn't leave. At one-thirty, the dining-room crew came and told us we would have to go. We rose and moved, without a word, to the center of the room in a mass, moist-eyed embrace. (p. 209)

marital tensions which have been kept under cover, placing an absent spouse at a disadvantage later; and (4) the development of loving feelings between group members which have a high degree of sexual involvement—which, if not worked through in the group, may pose a threat to participants' marriages (Rogers, 1968). Especially with immature or unstable participants or an untrained or unskillful leader, the hazards of such unsettling experiences are obvious.

It would appear that the long-term effects

HOW PARTICIPANTS FEEL ABOUT INTENSIVE GROUP EXPERIENCE

In one follow-up study in which 481 individuals were queried about the results of their basic encounter-group experience from two to twelve months later, Rogers (1968) obtained the following responses:

PER CENT	RESULT REPORTED
5	Mostly damaging, annoying, or confusing
4	Neutral
19	More helpful than unhelpful
30	Constructive in its results
45	A deeply meaningful experience

Per cents who found the experience damaging or neutral are approximations. The figures add up to more than 100 per cent because some respondents checked more than one answer.

of intensive group experience depend on both the avenues to personal growth that are opened up in the group experience and the extent to which the individual continues to find support for his new ways of feeling and acting in the life setting to which he must return and in which he must function and perhaps earn his livelihood. An interesting development in this connection has been that whereas individuals were originally urged to come to T-groups and encounter groups without their associates, so as to be completely free of their usual role restrictions, work teams and family groups are now being encouraged to take training as groups so that they can continue to support each others' changes after the training session ends.

The need for a great deal more research on the effects of intensive group experience on both individuals and groups can hardly be overemphasized. Even though only a small per cent of participants appear to find the experience a damaging or negative one, it is an important concern if such an experience is potentially damaging to anyone. We need to know more about the effects of these groups on different kinds of people, more about the relation of such learning to other kinds of learning, and more about just what kinds of behavioral objectives can reasonably be expected from such experiences.

Potential of intensive group experience. Perhaps the most significant function of the intensive group experience is the unusual chance it offers members to explore new avenues to the greater realization of human potentials. For this reason, the various experimental formats utilizing intensive group experiences have been referred to collectively as the "human potential movement"; probably it is for the same reason that this movement has elicited the interest and often active participation of many distinguished clergymen, philosophers, writers, historians, educators, and scientists.

There is a widespread belief that in our preoccupation with scientific and technological advances we have glorified the development of intellect at the expense of emotional and social development—that we seem bent on achieving a society in which people are alienated from their own feelings, from each other, and from the broader society.[1] The "human potential movement" has stemmed in part from concern over this trend. By providing a tool for humanizing education, government, and industry, it represents a

[1]For an analysis of the relationship between the prevalence of alienation and meaninglessness in our society and our overemphasis on provisions for meeting biological needs at the expense of psychological ones, see the article by Von Bertalanffy beginning on page 530.

counterforce in the direction of greater self-understanding, enriched emotional experiencing, and more intimate and fulfilling personal relationships.

As Rogers (1968) has pointed out, encounter groups also raise the final issue of the type of person we want to develop in our society:

"It seems evident from our review of the group process that in a climate of freedom, group members move toward becoming more spontaneous, flexible, closely related to their feelings, open to their experience, and closer and more expressively intimate in their interpersonal relationships. If we value this type of person and this type of behavior, then clearly the group process is a valuable process. If, on the other hand, we place a value on the individual who is effective in suppressing his feelings, who operates from a firm set of principles, who does not trust his own reactions and experience but relies on authority, and who remains aloof in his interpersonal relationships, then we would regard the group process, as I have tried to describe it, as a dangerous force." (p. 275) Although we might not all agree on the answer, most of us probably would agree on the importance of the issue.

PSYCHOLOGICAL COUNSELING

Counselors help people to make plans and solve personal problems. Many work in schools or colleges and are particularly concerned with helping students to gain a better view of their motives, values, interests, and capabilities so as to make wise educational, occupational, and marital plans. Other counselors work in rehabilitation agencies and hospitals and are primarily concerned with helping persons with physical, mental, or emotional handicaps to make vocational and other adjustments. Still another group of counselors work in industrial settings, assisting with such problems as the development of managerial talent and the placement of employees to the best advantage, and with

various personal problems of employees. Finally, there are some counselors primarily concerned with child-rearing, marital, and other family problems.

In general, psychological counseling is directed toward one or more of the following objectives: (1) to assist the individual in gaining a more realistic picture of himself—particularly in relation to his assets and liabilities, interests, values, modes of adjustment, and related personality traits; (2) to assist him in achieving a better understanding of some problem which is bothering him—for example, by supplying information, by posing the problem from different points of view, and by delineating the key dimensions of the problem; and (3) to assist him in working out an effective solution to his problem—a solution which he can put into effective operation.

Psychological Assessment

In a broad sense, psychological assessment represents a systematic attempt to collect, organize, and interpret relevant information about a person and his life situation. This information is then used as a starting point in planning whatever help he needs.

Types of assessment information. Although the information obtained in psychological assessment varies considerably depending upon the specific goals of the assessment in a given case, the assessment usually includes four types of information concerning the individual and his life situation:

1. *Personal resources*—information concerning the individual's general level of intelligence, educational achievement, interests, special abilities, personal maturity, and other traits.

2. *Frame of reference*—information concerning the individual's reality, possibility, and value assumptions, including his self-concept and his motives and plans.

3. *Coping patterns and adjustment*—information concerning the individual's coping techniques, self-defenses, competencies,

level of anxiety, inner conflicts, and possible neurotic or other maladjustive patterns.

4. *Life situational factors*—information concerning interpersonal relationships, environmental resources and supports, group memberships, and stresses in the individual's life situation.

It is also important to include medical data in the overall assessment. For example, a heart condition of which he is unaware may make it impractical for him to enter a particular occupational field; in psychotherapy, it is essential to rule out the possibility that an organic condition—such as a brain tumor—is causing the maladjustive behavior. In short, a total picture of the individual includes medical, psychological, and situational or sociological assessment information.

Methods of assessment. In gathering information about the individual and his life situation, psychologists may use a wide range of assessment methods. For our purposes we may divide these various procedures into five general categories:

1. *Maximal performance tests.* This type of test challenges the individual to make the best response he can to certain standard tasks. For example, in an intelligence test this might include the solving of certain problems by reasoning, defining the meaning of certain words, and accurately identifying certain analogies. The main intent of this type of test is to demonstrate the full extent of the existence of a given trait such as intelligence.

Maximal performance tests are extensively used—particularly in measuring intelligence—and, on the whole, are easy to score and highly accurate. However, these tests require the subject's full cooperation if they are to provide accurate assessment data.

2. *Rating scales.* The rating scale is most often used for assessing traits that are difficult to measure by performance on set tasks. Aggressiveness, honesty, and sympathy are examples of traits that may be most easily measured by ratings made either by the subject himself or by someone who knows him well. A rating scale item for

aggressiveness, for example, might be as follows:

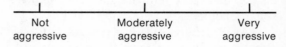

| Not aggressive | Moderately aggressive | Very aggressive |

One of the great advantages of rating scales is their simplicity, but such scales are subject to many sources of error. For example, the individual may be influenced by whether he thinks a high or low rating on a given trait is good or bad; when other people do the rating, their impression of the individual may be in error or they may be anxious to help him. However, well-designed rating scales, in the hands of trained interviewers or people who know the individual well, can yield accurate and useful assessment data.

3. *Personality inventories.* An inventory is usually made up of a series of direct questions that a subject is required to answer for himself. Inventories are widely used to measure traits relating to temperament, interests, attitudes, coping patterns, and the like. Usually the subject is required to answer "true" or "false" (or "yes" or "no") to given questions or statements, although some inventories include an intermediate category of "uncertain" or "cannot say." Examples of possible inventory items are:

I often feel as if things were unreal	Yes	No
When I am disappointed, I like to talk about my hurt with someone else	Yes	No
I have engaged in deviate sexual behavior about which I feel guilty	Yes	No

Personality inventories are usually easy to score and often provide accurate data. Some inventories even have provisions for correcting intentional distortions by the subject. For example, one commonly used personality inventory has several subscales whose sole purpose is to give the examiner an indication of the test-taking attitude of the subject. If the subject is very defensive and has been distorting his answers, this tendency will show up in a high score on one of these special subscales.

4. *Projective tests.* A projective test consists of an unstructured stimulus situation to which a subject is required to give meaning. For example, he may be shown an ink-blot and asked to tell what he sees in it; he may be shown a picture and asked to make up a story about it; or he may be given an incomplete sentence and asked to complete it. In performing such tasks, the subject is forced to organize and interpret the ambiguous stimuli, thereby revealing a great deal about his cognitive patterns, conflicts, self-defenses, and other aspects of his personality make-up.

Projective tests are widely used in the assessment of personality adjustment, but they have serious limitations with respect to scoring. Accurate interpretation of the subject's responses requires a high degree of training and skill, and the meaning of given responses is not always apparent to even highly trained psychologists. Their primary advantage seems to be in revealing personality characteristics of which the individual himself is not aware—which thus would not show up adequately in inventories or other assessment procedures.

5. *Interview assessment.* The interview technique is probably the oldest of the methods for making judgments about personality traits. For centuries men have assumed that they can "size up" another person by talking to him for a period of time.

The interview is usually defined as a face-to-face conversation between two people, conducted so that one person can obtain information from or evaluate the other. This description of the interview, however, belies the wide range and complexity of interview situations. For example, the interview may vary from the *simple interview,* in which a simple set of questions is asked, designed to gather certain information, to the *stress interview,* designed to see how a given subject will function intellectually and emotionally in a difficult situation, to the technically complex *therapeutic interview,* which may involve both assessment and therapy.

Although interview assessment is widely used and of undoubted value for obtaining certain types of information, distortions often stem from the interviewer's biases, values, motives, and limited range of experience; for example, a discrepancy of social class between interviewer and interviewee may change considerably the kind and extent of information that the interviewer obtains.

Other psychological assessment procedures include activity assessment, in which the subject's performance is observed in a real life situation or one that simulates a real life situation as closely as possible, and evaluation of expressive behavior—as exemplified in handwriting, painting, or literary productions, such as a brief autobiography written by the subject. The five assessment methods summarized above, however, are those most commonly used in psychological counseling.

Evaluation and integration of assessment data. In evaluating the significance of assessment data, psychologists are vitally concerned with the *validity, reliability,* and *standardization* of their tools. An intelligence test, for example, is *valid* if it actually measures intelligence and *reliable* if it gives consistent results at different times; if it has been *standardized,* the individual's score can be compared with the scores of a representative group of subjects and one can say whether it is a high, low, or intermediate score.

It is risky to draw conclusions from single items of information—such as a single test score or a single childhood memory. The psychologist feels more confident if he has "interlocking evidence" from independent sources. Even when the reliability of single scores is limited, as in the case of projective test scores, the probability that a conclusion is accurate is increased if several more or less independent sources of information point in the same direction. Since the overall goal of psychological assessment is to formulate a reasonably accurate "working model" of the client in relation to his life situation, it is essential that the assessment data not only be carefully evaluated but also be integrated into a coherent picture.

The Counseling Process

The counseling process actually begins with the first contact between client and counselor and continues with the establishment of a relationship which is suitable for the achievement of counseling goals. A key aspect of this relationship is the existence of *rapport*— feelings of trust, confidence, respect, and understanding. The client must feel free to respond honestly and completely during the assessment and later in discussions of his problem. Once rapport has been established, counseling may follow either of two general directions—directive or nondirective.

Directive counseling. In directive counseling the counselor will size up the client's problem, work out a "good" solution, and then concentrate on getting the client to accept it. The counseling sessions will center around explaining the problem and its solution to the client and considering the possible results of applying the solution offered.

This procedure is often criticized by counselors who use a nondirective approach. They insist that instead of helping the client to organize his own resources and teaching him to make his own decisions, the directive method tends to reduce his sense of responsibility and his confidence in his own adequacy for dealing with his problems; with the directive method, these critics feel, a type of father-son relationship is established in which the counselor assumes the role of an authoritarian father.

Such objections do not necessarily invalidate a directive approach for certain types of problems. For example, a directive approach would often appear indicated when the client's chief need is for information or reassurance or when lack of time dictates an immediate decision and the client is too immature or emotionally upset to get over this particular hurdle on his own. In the latter case, however, once the emergency is past, the counselor may encourage the client to take more responsibility for his decisions or to obtain psychotherapy to overcome deep-seated personality problems.

Where the counselor has a strong commitment to certain values—for example, the sanctity of certain social institutions, such as marriage, the style of counseling tends to be directive. Many persons seeking help prefer this type of counseling because it arouses less anxiety and gives them an authority to lean on for advice and guidance. Other individuals, however, resent attempts on the part of a counselor to force his own value system upon them.

Nondirective counseling. In nondirective counseling the counselor places the primary responsibility on the client for working out a solution to his own problems. The counselor largely restricts himself to supplying information the client may need—concerning job opportunities and the availability of certain kinds of training, for example, or the results of tests as to the client's own interests, values, and abilities. He then further helps the client clarify his thinking about himself in relation to the problem—helping him to see the key dimensions of the total situation in which he finds himself. The nondirective counselor tries to avoid suggesting decisions and solutions so that the final responsibility for the outcome of the counseling rests on the client himself.

In actual practice, of course, few counselors are entirely directive or nondirective. For example, the nondirective counselor may give the client reassurance in regard to his ability to solve the problem, may supply information concerning assessment data or life problems, and so on; similarly, the directive counselor may encourage the client to utilize his own resources in thinking through the problem, in exploring various ways of coping with it, in selecting the solution which seems most appropriate, and in putting this solution into operation and taking the responsibility for the outcome. Some clients need direction at first but later can be expected to take greater responsibility for dealing with their own problems; others have sufficient maturity and resources that the counselor can take a much more nondirective role from the start.

In general, it would appear that the most effective counselor, regardless of his general orientation, is the one who utilizes the client's resources to the fullest extent and modifies his own approach to ensure that the counseling will be a growth experience for the client, helping him to become more competent and self-reliant.

Stages in counseling. Although there are often variations, the counseling process appears to follow a basic pattern involving three general stages (Sundberg & Tyler, 1964).

In Stage 1, as already indicated above, rapport is established, laying the foundation for mutual participation of client and counselor in the counseling process. It is important here for the client to feel that he has come to the right place for assistance, and that he will be understood, accepted, and helped. A second step in Stage 1 is encouraging the client to express his feelings and attitudes toward other people, school, work, and other life matters that may be relevant to dealing with his problem. Here the presence of the counselor helps to reduce the anxiety that is often associated with facing one's fears, conflicts, frustrations, and concerns. This may help the client to recognize and discuss impulses and attitudes that he would ordinarily be unwilling to face or might not be fully aware of—for example, concern over whether he is mature enough to get married, whether he is sexually adequate, or whether he has homosexual inclinations that might interfere with his marriage.

Stage 2 involves helping the client to understand and organize into a meaningful pattern the information he needs for making choices and decisions. This usually means providing him with assessment information concerning his interests, abilities, and goals. Stage 2 goes considerably beyond this, however. In educational and occupational counseling, it involves the provision of information concerning various occupations and occupational opportunities and trends; in marital counseling, it may involve the provision of information concerning legal matters, the probability of finding compatibility with a particular mate, and so on. Often the counselor does not dispense such information himself, but rather makes it available to the client and later answers questions and helps the client to organize and assimilate what he has found.

The third and final stage of the counseling involves the actual making of choices and decisions. Using the information assembled in Stage 2, client and counselor discuss various alternatives; here, with a knowledgeable person to help him see clearly, the client can try out alternatives hypothetically and gain some familiarity with their probable consequences without having to actually put them into operation in a real life situation. This enables him to avoid premature crystallization of his thinking. Eventually, he "makes up his mind" and undertakes a course of action which seems necessary and appropriate.

At the conclusion of Stage 3 the counseling is terminated—the client no longer needs counseling, at least for the present. However, it is often helpful for the client to report to the counselor concerning the outcome of his action and to receive further assistance—if indicated—concerning minor problems that may arise.

PSYCHOTHERAPY

Psychotherapy is directed primarily toward helping the client to achieve a more adequate personality adjustment. It is usually assumed that the difficulty lies within the person himself and that in order to improve his adjustment there will need to be a change in him rather than simply in his life situation.

Although many people think of psychotherapy as a rather mysterious process, newer psychotherapeutic approaches are based upon the relatively straightforward application of learning concepts and other psychological principles to difficulties in adjustment. Among the personnel who are qualified to practice psychotherapy are clinical psychol-

PERSONNEL IN PSYCHOTHERAPY

	PROFESSIONAL REQUIREMENTS	TYPE OF THERAPY
PSYCHIATRIST	M.D. degree plus specialized training in mental hospitals or clinics	Medical therapy (drugs, shock, etc.) and/or psychotherapy
PSYCHOANALYST	M.D. degree plus extensive training in theory and practice of psychoanalysis	Intensive system of psychotherapy based largely upon Freudian theory
CLINICAL PSYCHOLOGIST	Ph.D. in psychology plus internship training in psychological assessment and psychotherapy	Psychological assessment, psychotherapy, and research
COUNSELING PSYCHOLOGIST	Essentially the same as for clinical psychologist but with training emphasis on counseling rather than psychotherapy	Educational, occupational, marital, and other counseling
BEHAVIOR THERAPIST	Ph.D. in psychology and special training in behavior modification techniques	Desensitization and other conditioning techniques to change particular behaviors
SOCIAL WORKER	M.A. degree in social work plus supervised experience in clinics or social service agencies	May work with spouse or other family members of clients, with groups in community, and with individuals
OCCUPATIONAL THERAPIST	B.S. plus clinical internship	Therapy with children and adults suffering from physical handicaps, helping them to make the most of their resources
INTERDISCIPLINARY TEAM	In both clinics and mental hospitals personnel from several disciplines may function as a treatment team—for example, psychiatrist, clinical psychologist, social worker, psychiatric nurse, and occupational therapist	

ogists, psychiatrists, psychoanalysts, and social workers. The chart summarizes the training of such personnel and their role in therapy. It is important when seeking help with adjustment problems that the individual go only to a qualified psychotherapist, for psychotherapy is an exceptionally complex process and requires the highest degree of professional competence and responsibility.

Setting goals in psychotherapy. Regardless of why a person seeks psychotherapy or what he expects it to accomplish for him—and often his expectations are unrealistic—there are certain goals toward which psychother-

apy is geared. In general, these goals involve: (1) increased understanding of self and environment—a more realistic frame of reference, (2) the elimination of maladaptive patterns and the learning of more effective coping techniques and competencies, and (3) personality growth toward maturity and self-actualization. As we shall see, however, different systematic approaches to psychotherapy place different emphases on the relative importance of these goals.

Specific goals in therapy vary considerably from one client to another, depending upon his resources, his immediate needs, the severity of his problems, the nature of his life situation, and other considerations. For one client the goals may be very limited—for example, to get rid of a phobia; for another they may be quite comprehensive and involve major personality changes. In some instances the goals are primarily supportive: the aim is to help the client cope with his immediate life situation by strengthening his existing adjustive patterns. In other instances, therapy goals may be little concerned with the immediate problems of the client but be focused on achieving self-understanding and long-range personal growth. In some instances, therapy may be aimed at alleviating marital problems or other stressful conditions in the client's life situation and may require counseling or therapy with other persons in addition to the client.

Often the psychotherapist has to work within severe limitations. He cannot suddenly cancel out the entire past history or even the present life situation of the client, nor can he expect major changes in the client's competencies and frame of reference in a short time. Rigidities and other personality traits of the individual may also severely limit the possible goals of therapy. Sometimes the client's life situation is so unfavorable that he operates under a continual load of anxiety and discouragement, making it almost impossible for him to profit from anything but the most superficial form of supportive therapy.

Here it is relevant to note the finding of Reiff (1966) that different goals are often involved for middle-class as contrasted with lower-class clients. The middle-class patient, having a more favorable environment, is likely to be concerned with improving self-understanding and personal adjustment, while the lower-class client, with a typically less favorable and often highly stressful environment, is more likely to be concerned about immediate specific problems.

Major Systematic Approaches to Psychotherapy

Although there is considerable overlapping, the various systematic approaches to psy-

chotherapy tend to conceptualize the process in somewhat different ways. Some view psychotherapy primarily as growth of the self; some see it as acquiring insight and undergoing emotional re-education; some see it as cognitive restructuring, involving a change in assumptions and values; some see it as changed patterns of interaction and communication with others; some regard it simply as habit change. In this section we shall briefly review five of the major systematic approaches to psychotherapy.

Psychoanalytic therapy. As developed by Sigmund Freud, psychoanalytic therapy has emphasized (1) the important role of irrational and unconscious processes in maladjustive behavior, (2) the origin of personality difficulties in early childhood experiences, and (3) the conflict between social prohibitions and basic instinctual drives such as sex and hostility. Psychoanalysis is a lengthy and intensive therapy which may involve several sessions a week over a period of years.

During the initial phase of therapy, the patient is taught the method of *free association*. Its purpose is to surmount his defenses and to bring his repressed feelings and thoughts into consciousness. These thoughts and feelings have presumably been "pushed down" into the unconscious because they were socially disapproved and anxiety arousing to the patient. And since the roots of a person's behavior are assumed to go back to his early years of life, free association often involves a "tracing back" into early life experiences. In the process of free association, however, the patient usually continues for some time to repress certain feelings and thoughts which he finds too threatening to talk about even in the accepting atmosphere of therapy. The process of bringing such emotions into consciousness and expressing them is known as *catharsis*.

Gradually, the psychoanalyst helps the person to overcome these blocks, known as *resistances*, through the technique of *interpretation*. Initially, the therapist's interpretations may be confined to pointing out that the patient is still repressing something; later they are directed toward helping him to understand the significance of what he has been saying—to develop *insight*. Another technique often used to provide a point of departure for the free-association process is *dream analysis*—the assumption here being that a person's dreams often have symbolic meanings and hence reveal much about his unconscious desires and conflicts.

As the patient and psychoanalyst interact in the process of therapy, the relationship between them becomes complex and emotionally involved. It is expected that the patient will re-enact in the therapy situation the same kind of emotional relationships that he had with his parents—emotional relationships which played a key role in shaping his personality development. Thus he may relate to the therapist in a way that he formerly related to his father, perhaps carrying over attitudes of dependency or fear of disapproval which are inappropriate and irrational when applied to the therapist. This phenomenon is known as *transference*. Once the transference is firmly established, an important part of psychoanalytic treatment is helping the patient to understand its irrational nature in the present therapeutic situation and its relevance to early experiences with some important person in his life. When the transference is handled in this way, the patient matures in his ability to deal with important figures in his present life situation, to see them more objectively without carrying over a residue of irrational attitudes from the past.

In general, psychoanalytic therapy is presumed to follow an orderly sequence beginning with the free expression of thought and feeling, continuing with the gradual achievement of insight and understanding, and terminating with the working through of conflicts and the achievement of emotional re-education and reorganization. It is a form of therapy which attempts major personality changes—in which unconscious and irrational processes which have been disruptive in the individual's life are brought into consciousness where they can be understood and dealt with so that a more mature and integrated personality structure can be developed.

A number of Freud's early disciples found themselves differing with him on various points and founded their own schools of psychology and approaches to psychotherapy, with various modifications of psychoanalytic concepts and procedures. Prominent among these are Adlerian and Jungian therapy, which emphasize insight and the growth of self in psychotherapy.

Another departure from psychoanalytic therapy is that of Sullivan (1953), who emphasized the social context of the individual's behavior and the importance of faulty interpersonal relationships and communications in personality difficulties. Here psychotherapy is directed toward trying to understand what is happening between the individual and "significant others" in his life and helping him to remove stumbling blocks and achieve more effective relationships. In a general sense, Sullivan's approach represented a rebellion against the individualistic and biological emphasis of psychoanalysis. It was an attempt to show the importance of the individual's ways of relating to others in determining his life style and adjustment. This broadening of the context of psychotherapy has had an important influence on the thinking of many contemporary psychotherapists.

Client-centered therapy. Most closely associated with the name of Carl Rogers—whose contributions to a humanistic model of man we briefly outlined in Chapter 1—client-centered therapy is essentially directed toward growth of the self. The primary objective of therapy is to help the client develop the ability and willingness to be *himself*. Although the therapy process may lead to the relief of symptoms and maladaptive behavior, these are byproducts rather than primary aims or effects.

Client-centered therapy, though viewing man as essentially good and rational, recognizes that the individual may be hampered in achieving his inherent potentialities for self-growth by irrational processes which lead to conflict and anxiety. Often, feelings, thoughts, and events which would threaten the individual's sense of adequacy and worth are screened from consciousness or given distorted symbolization. This process of self-defense, it is thought, ultimately leads to an incongruence between reality and the individual's experience and hence to a lack of integration of the self, with maladjustment and unhappiness.

For those who accept this viewpoint, the basic function of the therapist is to provide a situation in which the client can lower his self-defenses and look objectively at his real thoughts, feelings, and conflicts. Thus the therapist tries to create an atmosphere in which the client feels unconditionally accepted, understood, and valued as a person. In such a climate, the client becomes increasingly free to explore his real feelings and thoughts and increasingly able to accept them as part of himself. As his self-concept becomes congruent with his experience, he achieves integration and wholeness and the blocks to growth are removed. His natural tendencies toward actualization again assert themselves, and he becomes less defensive, more open, more self-accepting, and more effective as a self-directing person.

In the actual therapeutic process, as in nondirective counseling, the primary responsibility rests upon the client. The therapist plays a relatively passive role, since he assumes that the client is inherently able to solve his own problems. Approaching the client with as few preconceived notions as possible of what his problems may be or how they can be resolved, the therapist works with the material presented by the client, repeating or reflecting the client's feelings and thoughts, and helping him to clarify them but confining himself as much as possible to the client's own words and avoiding interpretation of what the client is saying or attempts to force insight on him.

As a consequence of extensive observation and research, Rogers has found that client-centered therapy follows an orderly and predictable sequence: (1) creation of the therapeutic relationship; (2) expression by the client of feelings and thoughts which had formerly been denied or distorted, including many negative feelings; (3) insight and increased self-understanding; (4) positive steps toward resolving his conflicts and more positive feelings about himself and others; and (5) termination of therapy. The last step is left to the client, who arrives at a point where he feels he no longer needs the support of the therapeutic relationship. The duration of therapy is typically short in comparison with psychoanalysis.

Existential psychotherapy. Existential approaches to psychotherapy were developed by a number of European philosophers and psychiatrists who were dissatisfied with orthodox psychoanalysis. As we have noted in Chapter 1, the existential philosophers are very much concerned about the predicament of modern man. They emphasize the breakdown of traditional faith, the alienation and depersonalization of man in our mass society, and the loss of meaning in human existence.

Despite his predicament, however, man is viewed as being essentially free. Unlike other living creatures, man has the ability to be conscious of himself as a self and to reflect on his own existence. He is aware that it is he who is in a situation and that he can do something about his problems through *his choices.* Man's freedom confronts him with the responsibility for *being*—for deciding what kind of person he shall be and for defining and actualizing himself.

Central to *being* is the problem of meaning. This is primarily a matter of finding satisfactory values. Frankl (1955) has distinguished three sets of values: (1) *creative values,* which relate to the achievement of tasks, (2) *experiential values,* which adhere in experiencing the good, the true, and the beautiful and in understanding and loving another human being, and (3) *attitudinal values,* which involve courage and the facing of inevitable suffering without flinching. Since some of these values can be realized regardless of the hopelessness of the objective situation, it is always possible to find some meaning in one's existence. However, each individual is unique; each must find the pattern of values capable of giving meaning to his life. As Nietzsche put it, "He who knows a Why of living surmounts almost every How." But to find values and meaning, the individual must have the courage to break away from his old defenses and escapes, make choices, and take responsibility for his own life.

Existential therapists do not follow any prescribed procedures but believe that a flexible approach is necessary in therapy. Their primary concern is with helping the client to clarify his values and work out a meaningful way of "being-in-the-world." They stress the importance of *confrontation* —challenging the individual directly with questions concerning the meaning and purpose of his existence—and the *encounter*— the relationship which is established between two interacting human beings in the therapeutic situation. They also strongly emphasize the individual's responsibility to his fellow man and his need to relate positively to and participate with other human beings. The individual's life can be meaningful and fulfilling only if it involves socially constructive choices and values.

While existential psychotherapy is similar in many ways to client-centered psychotherapy—both approaches viewing psychotherapy as growth of the self—the existential approach places less emphasis on discovering the true self behind the façade and more emphasis on taking the responsibility for one human life—for shaping one's self into the kind of person one wants to be and living in a socially constructive and meaningful way.

Cognitive change therapies. Recently there has been a good deal of experimentation with relatively brief but potent approaches to psychotherapy which minimize the importance of unconscious processes and are directed toward changes in concepts, assumptions, and values.

Historically these approaches owe a debt to Alfred Adler, an early follower of Freud who founded his own school of Indi-

vidual Psychology and developed his own approach to psychotherapy. His approach focused on the individual's *life style*—his own characteristic ways of perceiving and solving the problems of living. Interwoven in the individual's unique pattern of interpreting and responding to experiences are likely to be mistaken premises or assumptions which may lead to neurotic or other difficulties. Adler believed that the task of psychotherapy was to uncover these mistaken assumptions and help the client to understand them so that he could modify his life style to make it more congruent with the facts of life.

Two more recent cognitive change approaches merit brief mention.

1. *Rational psychotherapy.* This approach stems from the work of Ellis (1958), who has pointed out that in our society we are brought up to internalize and keep reinforcing many beliefs which inevitably lead to ineffective and self-defeating behavior. For example, Ellis (1957) compiled an interesting list of "mistaken ideas" that he found commonly involved in neurotic response patterns. Among these were:

That it is necessary to be loved and approved by everyone.

That one should be thoroughly competent and adequate.

That it is horrible or catastrophic when things are not as one would like them to be.

Such faulty assumptions are presumably maintained by a process of "self-talk"—a sort of dialogue with oneself in which the individual continually affirms his own faulty assumptions. For example, the individual may continually remind himself that it is essential to be approved by everyone, or that it is tragic not to be highly successful. Essentially the task of psychotherapy thus becomes one of unmasking the client's self-defeating verbalizations, helping him understand their role in causing and maintaining his difficulties, and helping him to change his faulty assumptions and verbalize more constructive ones to himself.

2. *Reality psychotherapy.* In reality therapy, as formulated by Glasser (1965), the assumption is made that very early in life the individual develops a basic sense of right and wrong which provides the basis for his later values, and that such values are remarkably similar for most people in most cultures. Early in therapy, the client is helped to clarify and acknowledge the set of values in which he believes. Then his behavior is evaluated in terms of whether he thinks he is doing right or wrong in terms of these values. Presumably there is little difficulty in helping a client to arrive at a clear set of values; the most difficult problem in therapy is helping him to learn to live responsibly in accordance with his values. The latter is achieved largely by helping him to perceive the deep satisfactions that accrue from living by one's values and the dissatisfactions that accrue from living irresponsibly in contradiction to them. It is interesting to note that Glasser has reported good results with this therapeutic approach in dealing with delinquents.

Behavior therapy. In the therapies so far discussed, the focus is upon the client's gaining insight into the underlying motivations, assumptions, and feelings that may have given rise to his symptoms; hence such forms of therapy are classified as *insight* therapies. *Behavior* therapy, by contrast, is a planful attack on the client's symptoms without much concern for their origin and without regard to whether the elimination of symptoms is accompanied by increased self-understanding; thus behavior therapy is also referred to as *action* therapy.

Behavior therapy stems from the work of Pavlov and Watson and represents a systematic attempt to apply the principles of stimulus-response learning theory to the treatment of personality maladjustment. Basic to behavior therapy is the assumption that maladaptive behavior results from (1) deficient conditioned reactions—failure to acquire needed adaptive responses, or (2) faulty or surplus conditioned reactions—maladaptive habit patterns, such as alcoholism or phobias. Therapy, then, becomes a matter of providing corrective experiences in which missing responses will be learned and maladaptive responses will be eliminated. In action therapy the primary responsibility for the content of therapy is placed on the therapist, who is considered to be a "reinforcement engineer."

Three major current methods of action therapy are: (1) *extinction techniques*, aimed at eliminating maladaptive responses, (2) *counterconditioning techniques*, in which an existing response is replaced by one that is antithetical to it, and (3) *operant conditioning techniques*, in which behavior is shaped by the manipulation of reinforcers. Extinction and counterconditioning techniques are commonly used in treating maladaptive habit patterns, such as irrational fears and anxieties, while operant conditioning is commonly used for fostering the development of desired new habit patterns. Extinction and operant conditioning may be used together, in combination—one to decrease undesirable present behaviors and the other to increase desirable behaviors. We

SHAPING IN THERAPY

In an interesting example of the use of shaping in therapy, a man who had been mute for 19 years was first given a stick of gum when he focused his eyes on it. After several sessions, the therapist began to give the gum only after the man made a small mouth movement; later, he had to make some sound. Soon he was making a croaking sound; next he had to say "gum" before receiving it. By the end of the sixth week (three sessions per week), he said "Gum, please," and began to answer questions but spoke only to the therapist.

Gradually, when the nurse and others insisted on verbalizations before complying with his wishes, he began to ask verbally. However, he still continued to use nonverbal requests whenever people would respond to them.

Based on Isaacs, Thomas, & Goldiamond, 1960.

cannot deal with these methods in detail, but a few examples may be of interest.

We have previously noted Watson and Rayner's early experiment in which they conditioned little Albert to fear a white rat by striking an iron bar behind him to make a loud noise each time Albert reached for the animal. The fear then generalized to other furry objects. Later, Mary Cover Jones (1924) succeeded in eliminating such fears by presenting a white rabbit at a distance when the infant was reacting positively to food—an anxiety inhibitor. By bringing the animal closer and closer—but avoiding over-balancing the positive tendency by the strength of the fear tendency—the boy's fear was finally eliminated and replaced by pleasant feelings toward the white rabbit and other furry animals.

This same concept lies at the heart of a method of therapy developed by Wolpe (1958). Wolpe considers neurotic behavior to be a learned habit, usually involving conditioned anxiety. This reaction is not subject to voluntary control and is not likely to extinguish automatically, nor does it do any good to try to talk the individual out of it. But incompatible responses can decrease it. As Wolpe (1958) has stated it:

"If a response antagonistic to anxiety can be made to occur in the presence of anxiety-evoking stimuli so that it is accompanied by a complete or partial suppression of the anxiety responses, the bond between these stimuli and the anxiety responses will be weakened." (p. 71)

In therapy, Wolpe formulates a list of the stimuli that elicit anxiety in the individual, arranging them in order from weakest to strongest. Then, during an anxiety-inhibiting response, such as relaxation, the individual is asked to imagine a situation in which the weakest anxiety stimulus on his list is present. If relaxation is unimpaired, he is told to imagine the next item in the hierarchy.

This process is continued through a series of sessions until even the strongest anxiety-evoking stimulus can be thought about without anxiety. Often hypnosis is used, both for helping the client to relax and

for having him imagine the anxiety-provoking stimulus. The extinction of anxiety has been found to generalize from the therapy situation to real life situations, and symptoms eliminated through this technique of *systematic desensitization* are not ordinarily replaced by other symptoms (Eysenck, 1967).

Another specific technique—essentially the opposite of desensitization—is *aversion therapy*. Perhaps the classic example of aversion therapy is the use of drugs in the treatment of alcoholism. Here the patient is repeatedly given an alcoholic drink together with a drug which causes nausea and vomiting. Eventually the mere sight of a drink will presumably evoke the conditioned response of nausea. Behavior therapists prefer to use electric shock as the aversive stimulus rather than drugs; they have utilized such aversion therapy in the treatment of a wide range of maladaptive behaviors from facial tics and persistent sneezing to alcoholism, homosexuality, and other deviant sexual patterns.

Although behavior therapy is not aimed at increasing self-understanding, changing assumptions and values, or fostering personal growth, the removal of maladaptive behavior patterns may alleviate deep feelings of discomfort and inadequacy and thus lead to an improvement in the individual's overall life adjustment. Whereas insight therapies generally assume that behavior changes as a result of new thought patterns, behavior therapists have given us evidence that the reverse may also be true—that changing a person's behavior may lead to a change in his thought patterns.[1]

Group Psychotherapy

Traditional methods of psychotherapy have focused primarily on the one-to-one relationship between the therapist and the client. In this relationship the therapist usually plays a central role, manipulating rewards and

[1]For a discussion of some of the issues and trends with respect to behavior therapy, the reader is referred to Rachman, 1967; Wilson, Hannon, & Evans, 1968; Murray, 1968; and Ullmann & Krasner, 1965, 1969.

punishments, acting as a sounding board, providing feedback, and otherwise influencing change on the part of the client. Group therapy, on the other hand, enables the therapist to see several clients simultaneously and reduces his role by enlisting the forces of the group in the therapeutic process.

Group therapy came into prominence during and after World War ii, when there were not enough therapists for individual therapy. Its great effectiveness in dealing with certain types of problems led to an exploration of group approaches to the treatment of a wide range of personality difficulties.

Types of group psychotherapy. One result of this search has been the proliferation of various kinds of group approaches designed to elicit behavior changes in participants. Many of these, such as T-groups and encounter groups, are not ordinarily presented as group therapy, although in fact they often constitute a form of psychotherapy. Similarly, the concept of the mental hospital clinic or correctional institution as a *therapeutic community* is essentially a form of group therapy although it is not usually classified as such.

Of the many forms that group approaches have taken, five have received considerable emphasis: (1) didactic groups, relatively large, educationally oriented groups in which a leader presents material and encourages discussion of it by group members; (2) inspirational or service groups, such as Alcoholics Anonymous, which stress group identification, the sharing of experiences, and mutual help among group members; (3) activity groups, such as special children's clubs, which provide opportunities for self-expression and interaction through arts and crafts or other group activities; (4) psychodrama, in which the individual acts out his problems on a stage with other persons; and (5) interview or interaction groups, which are organized and directed by a psychotherapist toward therapeutic goals for the group members. It is the latter which represent the usual group therapy situations and with which we are primarily concerned here.

Group format and process. The interview or interaction group typically consists of 5 to 10 members and meets once or twice a week for a period of several weeks or months. Usually the seating arrangement is circular to allow each member to see and talk with all the others. Ordinarily the members are selected to be similar enough in background to provide a common ground for the sharing and working out of problems. Often they have not been previously acquainted, though in some cases therapy groups are composed of married couples or several members of the same family.

The goals of group therapy are comparable to those of individual therapy but often focus more on behavior changes which will help members adapt more successfully in the social contexts in which they live. Toward this end, group therapy has proven particularly effective in removing feelings of isolation as members see that other people have problems similar to theirs, in providing mutual support and help to each group member in working through his particular problems, and in providing a miniature "laboratory of life" where members can gain insight into their own behavior, see its impact on others, and practice more effective modes of behavior. Where the therapy involves members of a family, of course, the goals of therapy may include not only individual change but also more effective functioning of the family as a group.

The role of the therapist and the kinds of activities that go on in group therapy vary greatly. Some therapists play a directive role, but more typically the therapist focuses on encouraging communication among group members and structuring the flow of the interaction so that it will be therapeutic rather than damaging. Beyond this, he usually plays a relatively nondirective role calculated to make the most of the forces generated as the group becomes an organized social system and develops a therapeutic potential of its own. In general, the sequence of events and the processes in group therapy are similar to those described on page 356 as characteristic of encounter groups.

How Effective Is Psychotherapy?

The question of effectiveness is one which evokes a wide range of response, with strong opinions on both sides.

One of the major criticisms leveled against the insight therapists in particular is that they have neglected to do the kinds of research studies—concerning processes and outcomes—which could provide solid evidence as to how effective they are. Often, on the basis of their experiences, psychotherapists are so convinced that they are being successful that it seems unnecessary to prove it. Skeptics, however, believe that the psychotherapist may be a victim of wishful thinking: he wants to believe that psychotherapy is helping the client, often manages to get the client to agree with him, and terminates the therapy when things are at a good point in the cycle of ups and downs which characterize the lives of most of us. Also, and perhaps more crucial, the psychotherapist may be taking credit for improvement that might have come without help.

There is considerable evidence that many neurotics and others who are unable to obtain psychotherapy do work out their problems and improve their adjustment (Eysenck, 1967). On the other hand, there is also considerable evidence that psychotherapy—whether insight or behavior therapy—often helps people to cope better with their immediate problems and opens channels for further growth. Particularly in group therapy, when the members of the group are properly selected and the group interaction is handled by a sensitive and skillful psychotherapist, the results seem impressive.

Systematic research on the effectiveness of therapy must ultimately answer such questions as: "What kinds of changes can be brought about, with what procedures, and with how high a degree of probability? What kinds of people can be helped and in what ways? Can psychotherapy produce changes that are worth the investment?" As contemporary psychotherapy focuses its research interests on the effects of various methods for achieving particular goals, we shall have more specific information concerning how and to what extent psychotherapy is effective in treating personality problems and fostering personal growth.

SUMMARY AND A LOOK AHEAD

In this chapter we have looked at three of the resources modern psychology offers through which individuals can be helped to achieve greater fulfillment of their potentialities and a richer and more satisfying life: intensive group experience, psychological counseling, and psychotherapy.

Intensive group experience is a comparatively new resource, still undergoing much experimentation. Through intensive interaction in a small group, individuals become more aware of their feelings and their effects on each other and are encouraged to confront what they are feeling and doing at the moment and try new "ways of being." Sensitivity training through T-groups is aimed at the development of greater emotional and social sensitivity and improved human relations skills, especially group-work skills. Encounter groups aim more at self-understanding and personal growth through openness and sharing and often are planned to focus on a particular topic.

Psychological counseling is a resource for helping individuals make plans or solve particular personal problems. Thus it is task-centered and usually of comparatively short duration. Typically it begins with assessment of the individual's needs and resources, continues with a clarification of the alternative courses open to the individual, and terminates when a decision is reached, perhaps with a follow-up report session.

Psychotherapy is aimed at personality change and more effective methods of coping with problems. It may take the form of individual or group therapy or a combination of the two. Specific goals vary, depending on the client's problem and life situation.

Among the numerous systematic approaches used today in psychotherapy are: (1) *psychoanalytic therapy,* a long-term therapy based on the Freudian model of man, aimed at uncovering repressed conflicts and achieving self-understanding and emotional re-education; (2) *client-centered therapy,* based on the humanistic view of man and designed to create a setting in which the individual's own tendencies toward growth will lead to a healthier and better integrated self; (3) *existential therapy,* based on the existential model of man and stressing the need for the individual to take responsibility for his own life, including searching out and committing himself to values that are personally and socially constructive and fulfilling; (4) *cognitive change therapies,* in which the focus is on changing faulty assumptions or inconsistencies between avowed values and actual behavior; and (5) *behavior therapy* (also called *action therapy*), based on the behavioristic model of man, in which maladaptive habits and responses are eliminated and desired ones substituted or added, without any attempt to affect the individual's values, assumptions, or self-concept.

Group therapy is helpful for people with many kinds of problems. It provides a miniature laboratory of life where the group members can gain insight into their own behavior and try out new and more effective coping patterns. Where the group consists of family members, the focus may also be on achieving more effective functioning of the marital or family group.

In the last four chapters we have been looking at the group settings in which we live—first outlining the general principles of group functioning and group-individual relationships, then focusing on the problems of adjustment in two areas of group living in which most of us become deeply involved, and finally reviewing resources for interaction with others through which we can achieve greater self-understanding and fuller use of our potentialities. At several points throughout the book so far we have mentioned the need for basic intellectual, emotional, and social competencies and sound values. Those will be the focus of the chapters in Part Four.

Key terms used in this chapter include:

intensive group experience, sensitivity training (T-groups), encounter groups (pp. 352-355)
psychological assessment, psychological counseling (p. 361)
maximal performance tests, interview assessment (pp. 362, 363)
projective tests, personality inventories, rating scales (pp. 362-363)
simple interview, therapeutic interview (p. 363)
validity, reliability, standardization (p. 363)
directive and nondirective counseling (p. 364)
psychotherapy, psychoanalytic therapy, client-centered therapy (pp. 365-368)
free association, catharsis, resistances, interpretation, dream analysis, transference (pp. 367-368)
existential psychotherapy, cognitive change therapies (pp. 369-370)
rational therapy, reality psychotherapy (pp. 370-371)
behavior therapy, action therapy (pp. 371-372)
extinction techniques, counter-conditioning techniques, operant conditioning techniques (p. 371)
systematic desensitization, aversion therapy (p. 372)

Part Four

TOWARD PERSONAL
EFFECTIVENESS AND GROWTH

In Parts One, Two, and Three we have emphasized the view of man as a unique creature with the capacity to assign value and meaning to his experience, to select and evaluate incoming information in terms of his needs and purposes, to think creatively, and to delay his reactions to stimuli and choose from alternative courses of action. We have noted the importance of the individual's sociocultural environment as well as his own unique genetic and learned make-up in shaping his development and behavior. We have examined some of the stresses of contemporary life and the nature of adjustive and maladjustive responses to them. And we have seen that man strives not only to maintain his physical and psychological well-being but also to grow and fulfill his potentialities as a human being.

In our discussion we have emphasized that man, being self-aware and lacking most of the "wired-in" controls that guide the behavior of lower animals, must develop for himself both the know-how and the know-why for successful living. Now as we come to Part Four, we shall take a closer look at just what this involves and try to see how the concepts and principles we have developed can be applied to achieving more effective adjustment and personal growth.

Assuming an adequate level of physical health, an individual's success in coping with both usual and extraordinary problems of life depends to a great extent upon his abilities to (1) make the best use of his intellectual resources in learning, solving problems, and making decisions; (2) direct, control, and find meaningful expression of his emotional resources; and (3) establish and maintain satisfying relationships with other people. Thus in Chapters 13, 14, and 15 we shall examine the factors that contribute to— or detract from—intellectual, emotional, and social competencies as basic resources for effective living.

Ultimately the directions we move, the energy and enthusiasm we put into what we do, and the meaning we see in the whole enterprise of living depend on our assumptions—of reality, of possibility, and especially of value. In Chapter 16 we shall examine the bases on which these assumptions are made, the criteria by which we can judge their soundness, and the role of a continuing search for values in personal growth throughout our lives.

Chapter 13

INTELLECTUAL COMPETENCE

Learning
Solving Problems and Making Decisions
Creative Thinking

Man's greatest adjustive resources are his intellectual gifts—his superior capacity for learning, reasoning, and imagining. It is largely by virtue of these resources that he has been able, as a species, to master so many facets of his environment and establish his supremacy over other members of the animal kingdom. And on the individual level, the person who develops and learns to use his intellectual capacities effectively has a decided advantage in adjusting to life problems; also he is likely to enjoy greater material and psychological benefits—high earning power and status and the feelings of adequacy and worth which come from being able to handle a wide range of problems. In the present chapter we shall discuss the development of intellectual resources under three categories: (1) learning, (2) problem solving and decision making, and (3) creative thinking.

LEARNING

In the preceding chapters we have outlined the general role of learning in development, noting that practically everything a person strives for, thinks, feels, and does is influenced by his past learning. We also noted the distinction between simple conditioning and complex learning involving reasoning, imag-

ination, and abstraction. In our present discussion we shall be concerned primarily with complex learning and its contributions to personal maturity and self-direction.

In analyzing the factors in effective learning, it is helpful to consider the characteristics of the person who is learning, the nature of the task to be learned, the way the individual goes about learning it, and the use of feedback in learning.

The Learner

What the individual brings to a learning situation in terms of personality traits, motivation, and general background has an important influence on what he is *willing* to learn, what he *can* learn, and how *efficiently* he will learn it.

Previous learning and resources. What an individual is capable of learning is always limited by what he already knows. He cannot learn algebra without some prior mastery of arithmetic, and he cannot understand psychopathology without having learned the basic principles of normal behavior. It is in recognition of this principle that, in teaching, so much emphasis is placed on introducing new skills and concepts in systematic fashion, in order to build upon what has been learned before. Many students get into difficulty in their college studies because they ignore the suggested prerequisites for the courses they want to take.

Competence in learning presupposes a level of intelligence adequate for mastering the task at hand. In general, the higher the individual's intelligence, the more capable he is of mastering a complex task and of doing so with a minimum of time and effort. Other resources that facilitate learning are good health and a high level of energy, adequate time to devote to the task, good study skills, and special talent or interest in the area.

Motivation. The basic motivation for learning is found in the human organism's normal tendency to explore and make sense of its environment. With time, this general tendency is differentiated in terms of specific needs, interests, and goals, so that we are motivated to learn things that tie in directly with our purposes while remaining relatively uninterested in learning other things. If curiosity is disapproved or punished, as it is by some parents and by some societies, the natural incentive for learning is greatly dulled.

Learning is encouraged when it is rewarded by material or psychological satisfaction. In a school situation, where the subject matter to be learned may bear little relationship to the learner's immediate interests and purposes, motivation must sometimes be induced by the manipulation of rewards and punishments. In general, however, the successful teacher is the one who manages to relate learning tasks to the experiences and purposes of his students—to get them ego-involved in the learning situation. The mature college student can do much to improve his own learning efficiency by making his studies as meaningful as possible and relating them to both his present interests and his long-range purposes and goals.

Motivation for learning is usually increased, too, by association with people who value intellectual competence and take a positive approach to the discipline of study. The approval of intellectual achievement by those we like and admire is a powerful incentive to our own learning.

Frame of reference. As we have seen, the assumptions and attitudes that comprise an individual's frame of reference determine in large part what he sees and learns. The range of information that will be meaningful to him, the way he will interpret new material, and whether he will perceive the learning task as a challenge, a threat, or of no importance, will all depend on his picture of himself and his world. Faulty assumptions or negative attitudes in relation to a particular task will obviously hamper effective learning.

Of special importance is the relation he sees between the learning task and his needs and capabilities. Usually an individual is eager to tackle learning tasks he sees as related to his needs and purposes and within his competence to handle. On the other hand, he usually tries to avoid those tasks which appear of little value to him or with which he feels inadequate to cope. Most of us fail to realize our learning potential in many areas—perhaps in art or music, playing bridge, or math or science—because we falsely conceive ourselves to be lacking in aptitude in such fields. Thus we may insist that we cannot "draw a straight line," "sing a single note," or "add two and two." Often a vicious circle develops in which the learner, feeling inadequate, forces himself into a learning situation with anxiety and trepidation; he expects to do badly and does, and the negative feedback then reinforces his concept of himself as inadequate in that area. Thus the individual's frame of reference influences not only the way he perceives a task but also the way he attempts to deal with it and the probable outcome of his strivings.

Personal maturity and adjustment. Efficient learning is also related to personal maturity and the ability to concentrate one's efforts on a particular learning task, to look at new information and ideas objectively, and to tolerate immediate frustration in the interest of achieving long-range goals.

Immaturities that often hamper learning —in everyday life as well as in academic situations—are overdependence on others, lack of self-discipline, uncertainty about goals and values, and lack of motivation toward achievement and personal growth. Preoccupation with inner conflicts, a high level of anxiety, feelings of discouragement and depression, and other maladjustive patterns can also seriously impair one's ability to learn. Personal immaturity or maladjustment—or a combination of the two —can be fatal to educational achievement even for the individual with good intellectual capabilities and a favorable setting.

The Task

Four characteristics of the learning task itself influence how the learner should approach it and how easily he can master it. These are the type of task, its size and complexity, its clarity, and the conditions under which it must be learned.

Type of task. The type of task influences both how easy it will be to learn and the method of approach that will be most suitable. Whereas the learning of motor skills usually requires time and practice over a considerable period to train the muscles to function with the desired skill and coordination, a verbal task can often be mastered at a single sitting. With verbal learning, meaningful material is much easier and quicker to learn than material which must be learned by rote. For meaningful material, intensive sessions with a focus on relationships leads to the quickest learning and the best retention; for unrelated data that must simply be memorized, spaced drill is usually best.

In our rapidly changing world our learning often includes "unlearning" what we have learned before. This may be relatively easy or very difficult depending upon our frame of reference and general flexibility, how much must be unlearned, and what social conflicts or pressures may be involved.

Size, complexity, and familiarity of task. In general, the smaller the amount of material to be learned, the easier the learning task. The extent to which difficulty is increased by additional material depends very largely, however, upon the kind of material to be learned. With any kind of verbatim or rote learning, an increase in the amount of material brings an increase not only in the total learning time but also in the average amount of time required for learning each unit. A list of seven nonsense syllables, for example, is within the memory span of the average college student and can be learned in a single presentation; but a list of ten syllables might require as many as eight or nine presentations. With meaningful material that does not require verbatim memorization, increased length has a relatively small effect on rate of learning.

The complexity of material and its familiarity are other factors that influence learning difficulty. Although added complexity tends to increase the time required for study and understanding, this factor may be offset if the learner is familiar with the material in a general way and has an adequate background for organizing and understanding it. Familiarity tends to encourage learning even when motivation to learn is relatively low—a principle which teachers apply by trying to relate new concepts to what their students already know.

Clarity. The clarity with which a learning task is defined seems to be an important variable in the learning process, although it has not been extensively studied. Probably every student has had the frustrating experience of listening to a teacher who failed to make clear the points he was trying to communicate or whose assignments were vague and ill-defined. In general, it would appear that the less clear the learning task, the more time and effort the learner will have to spend in mastering it—if he can master it at all.

One reason we often fail to learn what we should from our everyday experiences is that the essential elements are never pointed up clearly, either because they are too complex and interrelated or because we are too ego-involved to see them for what they are. One function of professional counselors and psychotherapists is to clarify the key dimensions of the problems the individual is trying to deal with.

Task environment. The conditions under which learning takes place represent another important variable of the learning task. If the learning is disapproved by one's associates, if conditions of study are unfavorable, if essential tools or resources are lacking, if time pressures are severe, or if other life demands are distracting, the difficulty of the learning task is increased over what it would be in a more favorable environment.

Other aspects of the task environment that may be important are its general climate (whether authoritarian or democratic), the individual's relationships to others in the learning situation, the quality of instruction available, and the social pressures and reinforcements associated with the learning task.

Procedure

If the student has the motivation and the intellectual and other resources necessary for mastering the learning task at hand, then the outcome of his learning effort depends heavily upon his strategy or method of attack. In general, the goal is not only to master the task but to do so with a minimal expenditure of time and energy. Since specific study skills are thoroughly covered in elementary texts, we shall simply outline some of the basic procedures for fostering effective learning, particularly as they apply to a school situation.

Using the best facilities and resources. Although some aspects of the task environment are beyond the learner's control, others are of his own choosing. Usually a first step toward making efficient use of learning time and effort is to choose a good place to study —a spot that is well-ventilated, well-lighted, and as free as possible from distraction. Of course, there are wide individual differences in the conditions which students find most conducive to efficient study; the important thing is to structure the situation so that the desired study behavior is most likely to occur and to eliminate stimuli that will make incompatible behavior likely.

Familiarity with available resources also facilitates the effectiveness of learning effort. Most college students could save a great deal of time and avoid much misguided effort if they had a better knowledge of library facilities and a greater skill in using them. Learning efficiency is sometimes impaired, too, by the failure to utilize opportunities for questions and discussion with teachers and other experts.

Establishing a study routine. Scheduling a place and time to study, and sticking with this study pattern until it becomes habitual, is of great importance to efficient learning. Usually the student who works out a good schedule and sticks to it makes more efficient use of his time and hence actually has more free time than the less well-organized student.

When a schedule seems impossible to maintain, it should be re-evaluated. For the student activist or the student who is working to pay his own way, a lighter course schedule may be in order.

Building background and motivation. At the elementary and high-school level, the teacher's task is often viewed as involving a sequence of three steps: (1) building background and motivation, (2) guiding the learning experience, and (3) extending and enriching what has been learned. At the college level these become increasingly the responsibility of the student.

A main reason why informal, out-of-school learning usually comes so easily is that it ties in with our immediate interests and thus is highly motivated. With academic learning, such interest and motivation can be created deliberately if we build a back-

BEYOND PARKINSON'S LAW

"Parkinson's Law" states that a work operation will expand to take up whatever space or facilities are available, regardless of the actual requirements of the job to be done. This general principle has been found to apply also to studying.

In a laboratory experiment, some of the subjects were "by accident" allowed too much time to perform a group of tasks, while others were allowed the minimum time essential. Later, when both groups were presented with a similar task and allowed to work at their own pace, those who had initially been allowed excess time required more time than the others to complete the task. Not only does a piece of work expand to fill the time available, but having once expanded, it continues to require more time (Aronson & Gerard, 1966).

---

ground for the new material and try to relate it to our existing interests and to other things we are studying.

Organizing learning strategy. Assuming adequate background and motivation, the focus moves to planning and organizing the learning experience. This involves actively trying to gain an overall view of the learning task, organize the task in terms of the key elements involved, and distinguish relevant from irrelevant details. Once the task has been clearly delineated, the student then is in a position to formulate the most appropriate study program for ensuring its mastery. As already indicated, different strategies are appropriate for different kinds of tasks.

An integral part of guiding the learning experience is preparing for examinations. Usually the knowledge that one will have to apply what he has learned in practical situations or be tested on it by a formal examination acts as a stimulus to effective learning and recall. The time to begin preparing for an examination, of course, is when the learning task is begun. Distributed study, periodic review, and overlearning all encourage long-range retention and give the learner real confidence in what he knows. Last-minute cramming may get a student through a particular examination, but his understanding will be so poor and his rate of forgetting so high that what he has learned will be of little use to him thereafter. Furthermore, lectures and discussion periods are often little more than a waste of time for the student who puts off all his reading until the last few days before the exam.

Adequate preparation is obviously the first defense against examination jitters, but sometimes test situations elicit anxiety on the part of even the most able students. This is to be expected, for an important examination represents a potential danger to long-range goals, to feelings of self-worth, to the relationship with one's parents or spouse, and so on. It is the student who accepts a certain amount of anxiety as natural, while resolving to function well in spite of it, whose performance shows little impairment under the stress of the test situation. In fact, up to a certain level, anxiety may even improve performance.

Extending and enriching the learning experience. Extending the new learning through study beyond the assignment and through explicitly tying it in with other subject areas —and real life situations, where possible —can contribute both to its meaningfulness and to one's interest and motivation. Often discussing new ideas with others and questioning unclear or doubtful points can help to put the material into perspective and make it easier to understand and remember.

Important here also is promoting positive transfer. Although psychologists generally assume that all of a person's experiences affect his later behavior in one way or another, very little is actually known about how previous learning affects the ease with which we can understand and master other related tasks later. The available evidence seems to indicate that some transfer will occur if there are identical elements in the two learning situations or if they can be understood in terms of the same general principles. Transfer of ideational learning is never automatic, however, but depends upon the learner's ability to perceive the points of similarity between the old and the new. There is always a danger, too, of seeing more similarity than actually exists, in which case previous learning may actually interfere with learning something new.

Feedback

In Chapter 7 we saw how man continuously modifies his adjustive responses on the basis of feedback—the return information he receives concerning the progress or outcome of his behavior. With respect to the learning process, feedback not only tells the learner whether he is proceeding satisfactorily but also serves as reward or punishment.

Knowledge of results. Many studies have shown that adequate feedback facilitates both motor and ideational learning. When the learner must work in the dark, with little or no information about how much he has accomplished or whether he is learning the right things, motivation, self-confidence, and learning efficiency all suffer. Also, he is very likely to learn errors which he will later have to unlearn. For these reasons, frequent short tests are often more useful than occasional long ones. One of the great advantages of teaching machines and computer-assisted learning is that immediate feedback is provided concerning the correctness of the student's responses.

Sometimes the learner is so ego-involved with test results that it is difficult for him to perceive feedback accurately or to put the information to good use. If he receives a poorer grade than he expected, for example, he may become defensive and concentrate on trying to prove that the test was unfair or the scoring invalid rather than on trying to understand where he went wrong and why. Even good test papers should be studied for the information they provide about the desired direction of learning.

In everyday life situations, the variables are so complex that it often becomes very difficult to relate feedback information accurately to the learning situation. Thus a divorced person may be confident that he has learned enough from the failure of his first marriage to ensure his ability to establish a successful marital relationship: he will not again make the mistake, for example, of living near his inlaws or of letting his wife work. But he may never see the *real* causes of the failure—perhaps a lack of common purposes or values—and thus may later discover, much to his bewilderment, that his second marriage is no more successful than his first. Many individuals continue making the same mistakes due to their inability to evaluate and use feedback information. Both in school and in our everyday lives, we often need expert guidance if we are to perceive feedback information accurately and apply it in correcting our failures.

Reward and punishment. Feedback reinforces learning when the return information is a source of satisfaction. Such rewards as good grades, praise, increased understanding, and progress toward specific goals all tend to reinforce what has been learned and to motivate further learning.

Negative or divergent feedback, on the other hand, has the effect of punishment, but its results may vary. Poor grades, for example, spur some students to increased effort while making others discouraged and apathetic or else so defensive that they cannot look at their failure objectively as a learning experience. The effect of divergent feedback upon the learning process depends upon the learner's goals, his attitudes toward learning, the standards of performance he sets for himself, and his general feelings of adequacy or inadequacy. Thus we see again the key role of the individual's self-structure in shaping the entire course of learning. In the next section we shall have occasion to note its equally important influence on problem solving and decision making.

SOLVING PROBLEMS AND MAKING DECISIONS

Life presents a never ending succession of problems to be solved and decisions to be made. In fact, as we saw in Chapter 7, the entire adjustive process is essentially one of perceiving and evaluating problems and then selecting the course of action that seems most likely to meet both the demands of the situation and the overall needs of the individual.

Much of our problem solving is habitual and automatic. Once we have found effective ways to handle the routine problems of everyday living, we devote little or no further thought to them. There are many situations, however, which require a fresh and creative approach. In our work, in our relationships with other people, in our role as citizens, we must use our full intellectual capacities to analyze the problems we encounter and work out the best solutions. Indeed, even some of the problems for which we *do* have habitual solutions merit a more thoughtful approach than we give them, for our habitual ways of seeing and doing things can become outmoded with changes in circumstances and in ourselves. As Glucksberg (1966) has pointed out:

"When faced with a problem it would be well to remember that difficulties often stem from habitual ways of doing things. It is often our particular experiences, our particular ways of looking at things, and our ways of thinking that make problems difficult." (p. 26)

This can be readily seen in the case of the mother who still sees her married daughter as her "little girl" and creates no end of problems by treating her accordingly. On a group level, too, we can see how changes in our society and the world situation may require that we make an "agonizing reap-

praisal" of our habitual ways of perceiving national and international problems.

Common Difficulties in Defining and Evaluating Problems

Basic to the effective solution of any new problem is an accurate assessment. It is often our failure to see the dimensions of a problem—or even to recognize that a problem exists—that accounts for our failure to respond effectively. In discussing the methods of science, Albert Einstein and Leopold Infeld (1938, p. 95) wrote:

"The formulation of a problem is often more essential than its solution, which may be merely a matter of mathematical or experimental skill. To raise new questions, new possibilities, to regard old problems from a new angle, requires creative imagination and marks real advance in science."

Much the same principle seems to hold true in everyday life. With our intellectual equipment and the sources of information available to us, we should be able to find reasonably good solutions to most of our problems, but we are often thrown off the track by our inability to see a problem for what it really is. Our failure here may stem from several sources, among which are faulty assumptions and attitudes, a rigid mental set, an ego-defensive orientation, stress and emotion, and a tendency to oversimplify complex problems.

Faulty assumptions and attitudes. If false information is fed into an electronic computer, there is little probability that valid answers will come out. Similarly, our reasoning powers and "common sense" fail to provide us with good solutions to problems when we start out with false premises. If we assume that marital success can be achieved without any real effort on our part, if we permit our desires to obscure the odds against us in a business venture, or if we assume that material possessions will automatically ensure a happy life, we are likely to encounter serious difficulties in dealing with problems in these areas. Any major inaccuracy in a person's frame of reference is a potential source of error in problem solving.

We have previously emphasized our propensity for perceiving and accepting information and ideas which are compatible with our existing assumptions and attitudes and for rejecting or distorting whatever is not. Faulty assumptions and attitudes tend to be self-perpetuating, although the setbacks of failure may, of course, cause us to revise some of them with time.

Oversimplification. In our earlier discussion of the processing of problems (Chapter 7), we noted our tendency to simplify problems to make them more easily understandable.

This is both necessary and desirable, providing we simplify the problem by delineating its key dimensions. Many problems are not as complicated as they first appear once we have gotten down to the essential elements.

Unfortunately, however, in the process of defining a problem, many people oversimplify it by omitting some of its key facets. Thus we have all heard individuals offering easy solutions to problems ranging from improving international relationships to dealing with women. Although their answers may appear persuasive at first glance, they are not valid because they disregard key dimensions that must be considered if an adequate solution is to be found.

TYPES OF OVERSIMPLIFICATION IN THINKING

Much cloudy thinking can be avoided if we can remain alert to the following sources of error, which underlie many of the false premises from which we reason.

1. *Overgeneralization from limited experience.* If a person fails to consider whether his own experience has been typical or whether it has been broad enough to justify *any* broad conclusion, he may make sweeping generalizations which have no support in fact.

2. *Misapplying general rules.* If he fails to translate the abstract and general into the concrete and specific, a person may apply general principles—valid in themselves—to specific situations where they do not apply. Thus the general rule that a person should be honest does not necessarily mean he should tell a girl at a party that her dress is inappropriate.

3. *Mistaking correlation for causation.* When two things go together, people often jump to the conclusion that one has caused the other. Mistaking correlation for causation, we may be overlooking the operation of other factors which are responsible for the relationship.

4. *Failure to recognize multiplicity of causes.* Closely related to mistaking correlation for causation is attributing an event or situation to a single cause. Having seen statistics which show juvenile

delinquency to be much more prevalent in slum areas than in better residential neighborhoods, we may conclude that a good slum clearance program will eliminate delinquency. Such a conclusion overlooks other factors in delinquency, such as lack of parental guidance, undesirable peer-group affiliations, and frustrations resulting from discrimination and lack of opportunity.

5. *Dichotomous (all-or-none) thinking.* In an effort to simplify problems, we often classify individuals or situations according to the extremes of a continuum. Thus a person may be seen as absolutely good or bad, right or wrong, honest or dishonest.

6. *Thinking in terms of stereotypes.* Stereotypes represent another type of oversimplification. A certain attribute of a group or of individual members in a group is abstracted and regarded as the primary characteristic of every member. Such stereotypes usually give us a false picture of the group as a whole and are even more misleading when we apply them to individuals, who may not fit the stereotype at all.

7. *Uncritical acceptance of majority opinion.* Another source of faulty reasoning is the naïve assumption that a viewpoint or concept accepted by other people must be right. Although one cannot dismiss majority opinion offhand, it is not uncommon for the majority of the group to hold views which are later shown to be invalid.

Rigid mental set. Too often, efficiency in problem solving is impaired by the tendency to think there is only one way to look at a problem and only one possible solution for it. Implicit in a flexible mental set is a questioning and critical attitude, which Berrien (1951, p. 45) described in this way:

"It is a way of thinking characterized by a kind of disrespect for the old answers, the established rules, or the accepted principles. These are not held in reverence as the inevitable and final authority, but are accepted as currently useful generalizations which may at any time be sloughed or revised if new observations fail to support the generalizations. Ideally, there is a flexibility in thinking and a breadth of observation unrestricted by preconceived notions of what one ought to experience in any given situation."

A rigid mental set is often the result of cultural biases. We fail to see the real dimensions of many problems because our perspective is limited by the cultural setting in which we live. We learn certain approved ways of perceiving and dealing with problems and are prone to think of these as the only "right" ways; if we are aware of other approaches at all, we consider them inferior or ridiculous. There is an old story of an American who ridiculed his Chinese friend for putting food upon the graves of his loved ones—a foolish custom, he pointed out, since the dead could not eat. Whereupon the Chinese friend replied that what the American said was true but that the custom was no more foolish than the American one of putting flowers on the graves of loved ones—for neither could the dead see or smell.

Often we are unaware of how much our various group affiliations influence the way we analyze and respond to problems. However, we can readily see the differences which may stem from membership in groups such as labor or management, North or South, and ghetto or suburban communities. Sometimes, of course, cultural biases are exaggerated by group pressures to conform to group-approved views.

Established ways of dealing with problems—whether originally worked out by the individual or learned from his associates—tend to be reinforced because they add to feelings of security and predictability. Also it requires less effort to handle problems in the same old ways than it does to re-examine them.

Defensive orientation. In previous chapters we have noted that an individual who feels threatened and insecure tends to be more concerned with protecting his feelings of adequacy than with coping with a problem. In a group discussion of a problem, for example, he may be intent on proving he is right and be unwilling to examine his own viewpoint critically or to look objectively at the facts of the matter. The individual whose behavior is directed primarily toward enhancing his feelings of adequacy and worth or toward protecting an inaccurate self-concept shows considerable resistance to accepting new information or to facing unpleasant problems. His problem-solving ability is also impaired by a tendency to rationalize away his errors—which, in turn, makes it difficult for him to learn from his mistakes.

The handling of problems in which we are ego-involved is often complicated by such a defensive orientation. For example, a parent usually finds it hard to understand or deal effectively with a delinquent child, for his identification with the child and his need for feelings of parental adequacy are likely to prevent him from approaching the problem with any objectivity.

Emotion and stress. We are often exhorted to "put aside" our emotions in order to think clearly and reasonably. Unfortunately, this is easier said than done, for not all of our emotional processes can be consciously controlled. Whether we like it or not, we cannot banish fear or hate or joy or anticipation simply by resolving to do so. And in dealing with many situations, we may not even recognize the fact that we *are* emotionally involved. We may *think* we are being perfectly objective in our approach to a family problem, for example, not realizing that our analysis of the situation is strongly colored by our complicated emotional relationships with parents or other family members.

As we saw in Chapter 6, it is under conditions of severe stress that emotions have the most dramatic effects in distorting cognitive processes—making it difficult for us to think efficiently when we most need to do so. Fear may exaggerate the severity of the problem and generate an attitude of apprehension which paralyzes action; anger may lead to impulsive and ill-considered action; and anxiety may markedly restrict our ability to see problems clearly or to formulate alternative solutions. Indeed, severe stress of any kind narrows our perceptual field and causes our behavior to become rigid and stereotyped.

Preoccupation, worry, and conflict over serious problems can even impair our ability to solve relatively simple, routine problems. We tend to make mistakes that would be unimaginable under ordinary circumstances, and later marvel at how "stupid" we have been, asking ourselves, "How could I *ever* have done that?"

Some Aids in Problem Solving

As the foregoing discussion suggests, competence in problem solving depends first of all upon personal maturity. Each of the formal aids to problem solving is limited in its usefulness if there are personality characteristics which make it difficult for the individual to look at his problems objectively or to admit the possibility of more than one solution. The individual who is relatively free of such handicaps, on the other hand, can improve his effectiveness in solving problems by applying various intellectual "strategies" such as those we shall discuss in the following pages. Used singly or in combination, they are valuable safeguards against the all too common errors imposed upon us by "common sense."

A basic strategy for problem solving. Whatever specific techniques we may rely upon in solving everyday problems, we can often improve our effectiveness by following a strategy that James Mursell (1951) called the W-E-D approach. The name is derived from the three basic steps in problem solving: (1) obtaining a comprehensive picture of the problem as a *whole;* (2) identifying the essential *elements* of the problem and ordering them in terms of their relevance to the overall picture; and (3) gathering and ordering the necessary *details* for completing the picture and putting a plan of action into effect.

Although it may occasionally be preferable to vary the order of these three steps, and in emergencies to abandon them altogether, the W-E-D approach represents a systematic and efficient strategy for evaluating and solving most everyday problems. The following example helps to illustrate the practical application of this approach:

A large business corporation took over a smaller company which was losing money and placed one of its own top executives in charge. His first step was to undertake a careful and comprehensive study of the situation. He scrutinized accounting records, examined organizational charts, interviewed key personnel, and attempted to gain an overall picture of the new company and its potential role as part of the larger corporation. He listened, observed, and took no major action even though he was eager to get on with the needed reorganization. After a few weeks, however, he had spotted faulty pricing procedures and inadequate communication between departments as critical elements in the company's failure. With further study of the details involved in these two sources of trouble, he was soon able to make a few specific recommendations that overcame the problems without undermining the morale and security of the long-time employees.

These principles of problem solving are applicable to problems as diverse as getting married and climbing Mount Everest. When used by either an individual or a group, the

W-E-D approach facilitates an efficient attack on the problem as a whole, acting as a safeguard against the all too common tendency to become bogged down in relatively unimportant details or particular facets of the problem.

Logic and semantics. Over two thousand years ago Aristotle developed a technique called the *syllogism* for testing whether a given conclusion or generalization follows legitimately from the premises on which it is based. Although we tend to think of logic as an artificial exercise for the intellect, actually we use syllogistic reasoning every day, though usually not the full form. The man who says "Women drivers!" to his wife in a derogatory tone is really saying:

All women are poor drivers.
You are a woman.
Therefore you are a poor driver.

Here the conclusion, although "logically" correct, is based upon a false premise, for all women are *not* poor drivers. This illustrates the greatest limitation of syllogistic reasoning: if we begin with a false assumption, we can never depend on our conclusion. Applying the devices of formal logic can help us with our problems, however, by forcing us to state our premises fully, so that we can examine them objectively in order to determine whether they are valid.

Important to the effective use of logic are the techniques of *semantics,* the branch of linguistic science concerned with the relationship between words and the reality they are intended to represent. Words are symbols for objects and ideas; by using words we are able to refer to things which are not physically present. But when the meaning of words becomes distorted or imprecise, our thinking becomes cloudy, and we may be led to accept a distorted picture of reality. Semantic confusion is most readily illustrated in arguments where several people, using the same words, are actually talking about quite different things.

In semantic analysis there are three trouble spots to watch out for particularly. First, symbols often change with time. The word *liberal,* for example, has quite a different meaning today from what it did thirty-five years ago. Second, the same word may have quite different meanings for different individuals, especially if it is one that commonly arouses an emotional response, such as the word *sex.* Finally, words for abstract or general concepts can be misleading when applied to a concrete or specific situation unless their meaning in the particular instance is precisely defined. In different contexts the word *gentleman* may mean any male, an aristocrat, or a man whose inherent gentleness entitles him to be named such. Our ability to manipulate linguistic symbols can either facilitate or interfere with effective thought, depending upon how accurately our symbols represent the reality with which we must ultimately deal.

Help from experts. Reliance upon the advice of a qualified expert in a given field is one of the oldest problem-solving methods known to man; certainly, in a complicated culture such as ours, we would find it impossible to deal with many of our problems if we did not have experts to call upon. We depend upon the specialized skills and training of the doctor, the lawyer, the political economist, the electrician, the architect, and the television repairman to supplement our own areas of knowledge. Indeed, one mark of intellectual competence is the ability to recognize the limitations of one's own experience and know *when* and *where* to turn for additional information and advice.

In seeking the help of experts, the individual need not forfeit responsibility for making his own decisions. He must first of all check his authorities carefully to determine by what right they *are* authorities. Often he must look not just to one expert but to several, to see if there is agreement among them. And he must determine for himself when he has adequate information on which to base a decision. Frequently, the value of an expert may lie in his ability to help the individual comprehend fully the dimensions of his problem and the variety of ways in which it might be dealt with.

Most people tend to be fairly critical in choosing their authorities in such well-defined fields as medicine and law. But the same individual who insists on having the advice of the best lawyer in the city for help with his legal problems may take his personal problems to friends and relatives who are poorly qualified to give advice. In many cases, too, we mistake experience for wisdom. The new mother who consults the experienced mother of six children will not inevitably get sound advice on childrearing; indeed, the advice may be very bad. Another danger is that of accepting information or advice as valid because it comes from someone we like personally, from someone whose prestige is great in another field, or from a large and influential group.

Group problem solving. There is ample experimental evidence to indicate that some kinds of problems can best be solved by people working as a group rather than individually. Anyone who has had the experience of participating in an effective committee has witnessed the sharing of ideas and experiences, noticed how the faulty logic of one member was checked by the thinking of others, recognized how creative thinking was sparked by the interchange of ideas, and finally seen a solution or plan of action developed which successfully embodied ideas from several different persons.

Every experience of working with a group is not necessarily a happy one, however. Against the saying that "Two heads are better than one," we must match another: "Too many cooks spoil the broth." Sometimes group problem solving is time-wasting and inefficient and frustrates the initiative of individual members. The success of many groups in solving problems which might otherwise defy solution should not obscure the fact that some types of problems can best be handled by individuals.

When group strategy is indicated, the following principles should be considered if the group is to function effectively:

1. The individuals participating should be directly concerned with the problem and prepared with enough background information to discuss it intelligently.

2. Participants should be task-oriented rather than ego-oriented—primarily concerned with solving the problem rather than promoting their own ideas or influence.

3. The entire problem should be clearly reviewed before an attempt is made to attack it.

4. The leader or leaders of the group should see that each member is given the opportunity to express his views and that the group has ample time to evaluate various suggestions before arriving at a final conclusion.

5. The group should formulate its conclusion precisely and develop a plan for putting it into operation. If a solution has not been agreed upon, the group should make specific recommendations for a further attack on the problem.

Many of man's problems are solved in a group setting. When proper safeguards are employed against inefficiency and the stifling of individual initiative, group strategy—by pooling the creative and problem-solving resources of many individuals—can often achieve remarkable results.

Some Aids in Decision Making

Careful and systematic analysis of a problem does not automatically indicate the action we should take. Often we must choose between two or more solutions which seem to be about equally good in terms of the risks they involve, the satisfactions they promise, and the amount of time and effort they demand. Sometimes our choice is not even between two good alternatives but between the lesser of two evils. Usually in choosing one line of action we must forego the benefits that might accrue from another. And because we cannot control all relevant variables or anticipate chance factors, we can never be entirely sure that a decision will work out as we think it will.

In spite of the difficulties inherent in making decisions, however, we must continually choose how to act—or else be acted *upon*. Recognizing that occasional failures are inevitable, we can substantially improve our odds for success by following the general principles outlined below.

Avoiding impulsive action. Acting in haste is an excuse we hear offered to explain mistakes ranging from buying inferior merchandise to quitting a job at the first sign of difficulty. Whenever snap judgments are made —especially in areas where the individual has little knowledge and experience—the likelihood of error is great. Sometimes, of course, a poor decision is of relatively little consequence, and we might rather gamble on an easy choice than waste the time and effort required for evaluating alternate possibilities. But if the decision is an important one that will have long-range effects, it is wise to examine it carefully and often to "live with it" for a time before committing oneself to action. The high percentage of failure of impulsive marriages is a matter of record.

Accepting a reasonable level of satisfaction. Perhaps as dangerous as impulsive action on major decisions is the inability to act until an "ideal" solution can be found. The person who always insists upon maximum satisfactions often becomes the victim of vacillation and indecision. Even if a superior solution is ultimately found, it may not justify the tremendous cost in anxiety and strain.

Besides increasing the difficulty and strain of decision making, perfectionism also tends to create dissatisfaction with choices after they have been made. The man who has delayed marriage until he found a girl who seemed ideal in every respect may be upset by minor irritations in his marriage that another person would consider inconsequential.

When it comes to problems that are routine or unimportant from a long-range point of view, perfectionism has even less to recommend it. The person who debates interminably over what to wear, how to spend the evening, what restaurant to go to, or even what car to buy is wasting more time and energy than any of these decisions justifies.

Reducing the negative aspects of choice. Most decisions involve an element of conflict. We are aware that our choices have negative as well as positive aspects, and as a result we both fear and look forward to the action we are about to undertake. The balancing of plus and minus factors is complicated, as we saw in Chapter 6, by the fact that dread increases more sharply than positive feelings as the point of no return gets closer.

The conflict is most severe when there is approximate equality of strength between approach and avoidance tendencies. Thus the individual who is about equally torn between the desire to marry and fear of losing his freedom is likely to experience severe conflict as his wedding date nears. The balance can be tilted in the direction of marriage either by building up the positive aspects of the choice or by reducing the negative ones. Strengthening the approach gradient, however, is usually a less satisfactory way to resolve conflict than is reducing the avoidance gradient. Among the techniques by which an individual can minimize the negative aspects of a choice are the following:

1. He can clarify his picture of the actual dangers involved in his decision, thus eliminating vague anxiety over the unknown.

2. He can build up the competencies that will enable him to cope with the foreseeable trouble spots. For example, adequate vocational preparation increases the probability of success in a challenging job; the development of social competencies will reduce the fear of difficult but desired new relationships.

3. He can put the decision into proper perspective. Many decisions which seem momentous at the time are actually of such small significance in terms of long-range consequences that even if they are wrong choices nothing much is lost. Recognizing

this can reduce the fear involved in committing oneself to one alternative or the other.

Being prepared to back up a decision. Although it is often foolish to maintain an obviously wrong decision, there are many times when decisions are rescinded without being put to a fair test. Usually this follows from the failure to really commit oneself to the choice made. The indecisiveness that may have preceded the decision is carried over after the decision is put into effect.

Many marriages fail because one of the partners withdraws at the first sign of difficulty. But in any human relationship difficulties may arise and new adjustments may be required. A general who commits his forces to a certain battle area may modify his plan of attack according to how circumstances develop, but while there is a reasonable chance for success he will not cut and run.

Maintaining a reserve of resources. Rarely is it advisable to venture everything on any one decision. "'Tis the part of a wise man," said Cervantes, "to keep himself today for tomorrow, and not venture all his eggs in one basket." Conservation of resources is necessary if, in the event of failure, one is to be assured of a second chance.

Second chances sometimes are no more than the opportunity to make a first decision finally work by calling on available reserves. A man who begins his business on a small, experimental basis may not become a millionaire overnight, but neither need he become bankrupt. He is more likely to spot trouble in certain areas of operation and make changes that will put his business on a more solid foundation; or if the first venture fails, he can put other resources into a more successful attempt. Similarly, the young man or woman who does not summarily abandon his education when love beckons, but either postpones marriage or works out an arrangement for combining it with further schooling, is maintaining reserves that considerably reduce his risk of failure. Even the all-out emotional ex-

penditure demanded in a relationship like marriage should be backed up with reserves in the form of developing one's interests and potentialities as an individual.

Developing clear-cut values as guides. Since the solution of most problems permits considerable choice, it is obvious that the person who has a clear sense of identity, well-defined goals, and an adequate system of values will have an easier time making decisions and investing himself wholeheartedly in them than the person who is not sure who he is, where he wants to go, or what is really important to him. The alternative to being guided by one's own values is to rely upon the advice and values of others. The person who follows the latter course often finds himself making decisions which are inconsistent not only with each other but with his concept of himself.

Minimizing the Effects of Faulty Decisions

A certain percentage of decisions must be expected to go wrong because of human limitations and chance factors which cannot be controlled. When failure comes, it is worth trying to analyze why, perhaps with the help of someone who can be more objective than we, so that we will not repeat the same mistake. The tendency to deny that a mistake has been made, or to rationalize mistakes by decrying unfavorable circumstances, or to project blame for them onto other people is a major stumbling block to the development of increased competence in making choices.

Often it is possible to salvage a good deal from a faulty decision. If, after three or four years of premedical training, a young man decides that his choice of a medical career was a mistake, he may still, after careful investigation and reliable vocational counseling, be able to use his education to good advantage in a profession not completely alien to medicine—perhaps as a biologist, a laboratory technician, or a veterinarian. After the failure of a marriage, professional help is often valuable in helping everyone concerned make the best of the changed situation, especially if children are involved. Most of us have far more inner strength than we realize and despite setbacks can usually rally our hopes and resources for a new assault on our goals.

Life can be viewed as a series of problem situations and choice points—some of them of little importance, others of crucial and lasting importance. It is through learning to deal with the simpler problems and choices that we prepare ourselves for the more complex ones. Increasingly, as we go along, the choices open to us at a given time depend on how well we have solved the problems that came before and how wisely we have acted at each preceding choice point.

CREATIVE THINKING

Creative thinking—thinking which produces new methods, new concepts, new understandings, new inventions, new works of art —is at the very root of human progress. The history of civilization is the history of man's creative triumphs, from his discovery of fire to his investigations of outer space.

In a general sense, all problem solving is creative; each problem is unique in certain respects, and each solution requires the integration of ideas into new and meaningful patterns. On another level, creativity may manifest itself in the speculations of the philosopher and the hypotheses of the scientist; on still another, in the works of the painter, the sculptor, the composer, the novelist, and the poet. On the everyday level, there is the creative thinking that changes one's own personality. It can produce insights into some phase of oneself or one's world which one has not seen before—insights which may drastically alter one's assumptions, motives, and ways of behaving. In every case and at every level, creativity brings into existence something that is new.

The Process of Creativity

On the basis of his comprehensive investigations of creativity, MacKinnon (1962) came to the conclusion that true creativeness, whether it takes place in a few moments or over the span of several years, must fulfill at least three conditions:

"It involves a response or an idea that is novel or at the very least statistically infrequent. But novelty or originality of thought or action, while a necessary aspect of creativity, is not sufficient. If a response is to lay claim to being a part of the creative process, it must to some extent be adaptive to, or of, reality. It must serve to solve a problem, fit a situation, or accomplish some recognizable goal. And, thirdly, true creativeness involves a sustaining of the original insight, an evaluation and elaboration of it, a developing of it to the full." (p. 485)

Although not all investigators would agree completely with MacKinnon's view of creativity, it serves as a useful starting point for trying to answer two key questions: What cognitive processes are involved in the creation of something new—whether an object or an idea? Can we delineate the sequence of events in creativity?

Relation of creativity to cognitive processes. Despite the importance of creative thinking and a considerable amount of research, there is little scientific evidence concerning the precise nature of the cognitive processes involved. However, it is apparent that creativity and problem solving are intimately related since both involve finding novel or uncommon responses.

Guilford (1967) has distinguished three kinds of productive thinking: *deductive* thinking, in which an inference or conclusion is deduced logically from information on hand; *inductive* thinking, in which the individual goes beyond the present information, adding new elements that are not inherent in the known facts; and *evaluative* thinking, in which the individual judges the suitability or appropriateness of an idea. All three may be used in creative thinking. Deductive thinking is creative when the individual sees new relationships that he has not noticed before. Most often, however, creativity requires inductive and evaluative thinking. The individual supplies new formulations or new hypotheses and imagines the possible consequences of untried solutions. Then, as he critically evaluates his work, he may make revisions and changes before it is shaped into final, usable form.

Stages in creative thinking. Psychologists have long been intrigued with the sequence of events involved in the birth of a new idea or the solution to a problem. In dealing with new and complex problems, five steps ordinarily seem to occur:

1. *Orientation*—pointing up the problem.

2. *Preparation*—saturation of the mind with all available data.

3. *Incubation*—a rest period for the thinker, in which the problem is not worked on consciously, though presumably it continues to be attacked even during sleep.

4. *Illumination*—the point at which the solution occurs to the thinker.

5. *Verification*—the critical and often empirical evaluation of the solution.

These steps are not always as clear-cut as such a listing implies. In dealing with a complex problem, for example, there may be many partial illuminations, testings, further incubations, and further illuminations and verifications before the solution is complete.

Characteristics of Creative People

Psychologists have devoted considerable attention to the study of creative persons of various ages in an attempt to clarify the relationship between given personality traits and creativity—that is, to identify the intellectual, motivational, attitudinal, and other characteristics which presumably lead to creativity and without which creativity is not likely to occur.

In general, this approach has taken two forms: (1) delineating and comparing the traits shown by people who have been considered highly creative; and (2) studying creativity itself as a general characteristic of self-actualizing people—by implication, as a characteristic of normal human functioning.

Specific personality traits and creativity. Investigators have found numerous traits commonly associated with creativity. In fact, Craig (1966) has formulated a list of 84 traits that correlate with high scores on various psychological tests of creativity.[1] Included here are such traits as ability for inductive and evaluative thinking, self-acceptance, openness to new experience, sensitivity, courage, self-assertiveness, and originality.

Interestingly, intelligence level does not appear to correlate highly with creativity. For example, in a study of creativity and intelligence in children's thinking, Wallach and Kogan (1967) classified their subjects into four categories: (1) high creativity-high intelligence, (2) low creativity-high intelligence, (3) high creativity-low intelligence, and (4) low creativity-low intelligence. Motivation and cognitive style were found to be more important in creativity than intelligence.

Nor does creativity correlate highly with academic achievement (Bentley, 1966). In his study of creative architects MacKinnon (1962) found that they earned about a B average in college, although they were capable of A performance when a course caught their interest. Curiously enough, Roe (1953), after studying a number of leading artists and scientists in several fields, found only one trait that was shared by all: the willingness to work long and hard. Of course, she assumed a basic minimum of intelligence, ability, and other traits essential to their particular area of endeavor.

---

[1] A number of investigators have questioned the use of psychological tests for measuring creativity. They point out that the individual who shows a high level of novel responses and originality on a test may not actually be creative in real life situations. A good summary of the issues and advances made in the study of creativity may be found in MacKinnon (1967).

It has long been popular to think of creative genius as being closely related to personality maladjustment and mental disorder. Indeed, history has recorded many highly creative persons who suffered from serious personality problems. The names of Van Gogh, Wagner, Poe, and others come at once to mind. In fact, according to psychoanalytic theory, creativity is a form of neuroticism, in which instinctual drives have been diverted into creative activities. The consensus of most current investigators, however, is that personality maladjustment is ordinarily a handicap to creativity—that the individual may be creative despite his handicap but not as productive as he would be if he were better adjusted.

Creativity and self-actualization. A broader approach views creativity not as a combination of special traits but as a normal characteristic of the self-actualizing, fully functioning person. As Maslow (1963) has expressed it:

> *"My feeling is that the concept of creativeness and the concept of the healthy, self-actualizing, fully-human person seem to be coming closer and closer together and may perhaps turn out to be the same thing."* (p. 4)

A distinction is often made, however, between what is called *special talent creativeness* and *self-actualizing creativeness.* An example of the former is a special talent for painting or music; it may make itself manifest despite personality handicaps and other difficulties. The latter is a style of living that grows out of wholeness, involvement, honesty, spontaneity, flexibility, curiosity, openness to experience, and other traits attributed to the self-actualizing person. In short, self-actualizing creativeness is a normal consequence of truly healthy human functioning.

Facilitating Creativity

In the main, attempts to facilitate creativeness have followed two paths: (1) trying to improve creative performance directly by encouraging the development of specific traits, such as openness to experience, and (2) trying to encourage creative performance somewhat indirectly by providing a congenial and stimulating climate for the creative person (Jackson & Messick, 1965).

Of course, for any type of high-level creativity, minimum levels of intelligence, competence, and opportunity are essential. Beyond the intellectual and other special abilities and skills required for creativity in a given area, the following factors appear to be of crucial importance in creativity.

Openness to new experience. A number of investigators, including Rogers and Maslow, have emphasized the importance of being open to new experience. Such openness is the exact opposite of defensiveness, in which new experiences that are incompatible with or threatening to the self-structure are prevented from entering consciousness or are permitted entrance only in a distorted form.

Openness to new experience implies a tolerance for conflict and ambiguity, a lack of rigid categories in thinking, a rejection of the notion that one has all the answers. It is, in a sense, a childlike quality, for the young child is a natural explorer and experimenter who embraces every new experience with open arms and an open mind and who constantly "creates" with thoughts, with words, with pencils and paints (Kubie, 1967). It is only as people grow older that they become timid and conservative in reacting to new experiences. By carefully conforming to all the customs and folkways of their society and placing security before curiosity, many adults cut themselves off from new experiences and new concepts—and thereby close the door on creativity.

Human progress has always depended most on those who have refused to be satisfied with habitual ways of thinking and acting, those whose ideas break away from traditional patterns, those whose minds are endlessly receptive and flexible and active. This, of course, does not mean that all people who break with traditional ways of viewing things or who are "dreamers" are creative and productive. However, most high-level creativity does involve new ways of seeing and doing things. What we mean in essence here was well described by Susanne Langer (1951):

"*The limits of thought are not so much set from outside, by the fulness or poverty of experiences that meet the mind, as from within, by the power of conception, the wealth of formulative notions with which the mind meets experiences. Most new discoveries are suddenly-seen things that were always there. A new idea is a light that illuminates presences which simply had no form for us before the light fell on them. We turn the light here, there, and everywhere, and the limits of thought recede before it.*" (p. 8)

Motivation and set. As we noted, Roe has emphasized the importance of motivation among creative thinkers in terms of their willingness to work hard and long. The dedication of great artists and scientists has sometimes caused them to lead lives of hermit-like isolation, sacrificing the comforts and companionships of ordinary existence in a single-minded drive toward a chosen goal. Although in many more cases powerful motivation has simply served to keep the creative thinker from straying off course, without forcing him to discard or damage healthy interpersonal relationships, the time often comes when he must choose between the safety and security of ordinary living and the danger and uncertainty of pioneering. Frequently, the creative way is the lonely, painful way; history offers many examples of men who paid for their creativity by suffering loneliness, misunderstanding, ridicule, poverty, even death.

Besides motivation, a general mental attitude, or set, toward creativity—whether in terms of problem solving or self-expression—would also appear to be important. As one facet of the ability for evaluative thinking, Guilford (1957) has emphasized the ability to recognize that things are wrong or that they can be improved. Without such

awareness, he points out, creative thinking would never get started. Along with this sensitivity to problems goes a questioning attitude, which has been described by Osborn (1953) as follows:

"*The question technique has long been recognized as a way to induce imagination. . . . Imagination has to be guided by stabs such as 'What about . . . ?' and 'What if . . . ?' And always it must be prodded with 'What else?' and again 'What else?' By bombarding our imaginations with such queries we can pile up a quantity of ore in the form of all kinds of ideas—good, bad, and indifferent. Out of that ore, our own judgment, or the judgment of others, can refine gold in the form of good ideas.*" (pp. 228-229)

This mental set seems to be a key factor in creative thinking as it applies to solving the everyday problems that most of us are concerned with. Solutions to problems often seem so obvious—once we find them—that we wonder how we could have missed recognizing them earlier. The answer is simple: most of us make too few attempts to get away from or even question our habitual ways of thinking and acting.

Social stimulation. In discussing creativity, there is a natural tendency to concentrate on the qualities of the great creators and to ignore the importance of the social setting. Yet, as historians and sociologists point out, some periods and some societies have fostered creativity, while others have inhibited it. In Renaissance Italy the time was ripe for a great artistic flowering; in the United States at the beginning of the twentieth century the inventions and innovations of men like Ford and Edison were welcomed eagerly. But in medieval Europe freedom of scientific investigation was restricted, and in modern totalitarian states innovations in art and literature have been suppressed. In our own society we encourage and support creativity that promises physical improvements in our daily living more than creativity that promises esthetic satisfactions. It is of interest to note also that in science, technology, and even business and government we have come to place increasing emphasis on the creative team, often at the expense of the creative individual, who may not be suited to working efficiently in a "team" setting.

We need creative thinkers today as never before. Our complex social problems and the problem of avoiding nuclear extermination can be solved only by new solutions embodying creativity of the highest order.

SUMMARY AND A LOOK AHEAD

In this chapter we have examined some of the key factors in learning effectively, in solving problems and making decisions, and in creativity.

Among the factors important in learning and retention are the individual's previous learning and resources, his motivation, his frame of reference, and his personal maturity and adjustment, as well as characteristics of the task and the task environment. Learning and retention are both aided by using the best facilities and resources available, establishing a study routine, making the material as meaningful as possible, organizing one's learning strategy, extending and enriching the learning, and making good use of feedback.

Common difficulties in problem solving are faulty assumptions and attitudes, oversimplification, rigidity, defensiveness, and emotional involvement; aids to problem solving include logic and semantics, help from experts, the use of group participation, and the W-E-D approach as a basic strategy. Successful decision making usually involves avoiding impulsive action, accepting a reasonable level of satisfaction, reducing the negative aspects, being prepared to back up decisions, maintaining a reserve of resources, and developing clear-cut values as guides.

One formulation sees creativeness as involving an innovation which is to some extent adaptive to reality and in which the original insight is worked out or elaborated. Creative thinking usually involves evaluative thinking as well as inductive and/or deductive thinking and typically includes orientation, preparation, incubation, illumination, and verification. Assuming a basic minimum of intelligence and ability, it may be that the only personality trait creative people share in common is the willingness to work long and hard. It appears that creativity is fostered by openness to new experience, high motivation, a set toward change and improvement, and social encouragement of innovation.

In the chapter that follows, we shall see the close relationship between intellectual and emotional competence.

Key terms used in this chapter include:

task environment (p. 381)
building background and motivation (p. 381)
extending and enriching learning (p. 382)
knowledge of results (in learning) (p. 383)
W-E-D strategy for problem solving (p. 387)
inductive, deductive, and evaluative thinking (p. 392)
orientation, preparation, incubation, illumination, verification (p. 393)

Chapter 14

EMOTIONAL COMPETENCE

Components of Emotional Competence
Dealing with Problem Emotions

One of the dimensions of personal experience is the emotional or *affective* dimension. As we size up a problem and try to cope with it, we feel pleased, uneasy, elated, angry, or perhaps worried about the situation or our role in it. As we undertake a course of action, we may feel enthusiasm or distaste or perhaps dread. Whatever the situation, we tend to have feelings of some kind about what we are seeing and thinking and doing. Thus emotional processes are not isolated phenomena but components of general experience, constantly influencing and influenced by other processes going on at the same time.

Emotional reactions, as we have seen in earlier chapters, involve not only conscious feelings but also physiological changes, some of which, if they become chronic, can lead to tissue damage. We noted this process in the formation of peptic ulcers and other psychosomatic disorders. In the present chapter we shall be concerned primarily with psychological aspects of emotional competence—with some of the ways we can discourage negative emotions, encourage positive ones, and direct the expression of both negative and positive emotions into healthy and constructive channels. The person who achieves emotional competence in these respects is not likely to be troubled by chronic emotional mobilization or by psychosomatic disorders.

Emotional competence is greatly dependent on an accurate frame of reference and on overall maturity. How we perceive a situation—its meaning for us—determines what emotions will be aroused. If we see no threat, we feel no fear—however great or small the real danger. If we see our performance as superior, we feel elated regardless of the realities of the situation. And if we see ourselves as unfairly treated, we feel angry whether or not our perception is accurate. If we see ourselves as inadequate and unlovable, we feel perpetually anxious and discouraged whether we really are inferior and unlovable or only think we are.

We are as consistent and predictable in our emotional responses as in our perceptual habits, thought patterns, and other aspects of adjustive behavior. The events that arouse emotion in us, the emotions they arouse, and the ways we control and express our feelings are an important component of the overall pattern of coping strategies that makes up our life style.

COMPONENTS
OF EMOTIONAL COMPETENCE

In order to understand the components of emotional competence, we need to understand the ways in which we differ in our emotional reactions and the degrees of difference that seem to be within the normal range.

Patterns of Emotional Experience

Although we often assume that other people "feel about the same way we do," there is considerable evidence that such is not the case. We seem to differ greatly in the depth and range of our feelings, in our moods, and in the proportion of our positive and negative feelings.

Intensity of feeling. Some people apparently feel great intensities of emotion; they react to the ups and downs of living with intense joy, intense disappointment, and intense concern. Others, whether from constitutional limitation or defensive learning, are not easily stirred to either enthusiasm or distress but seem to be insulated from any strong feelings. Most of us are somewhere in between.

Emotional competence would seem to require sufficient depth of feeling to allow active, vigorous, healthy participation in living. Although wide differences in emotionality seem to be within the normal range, the extremes at either end are unadaptive. Overreaction to every minor situation squanders the individual's resources, whereas a very shallow reaction usually indicates a defense orientation with accompanying rigidity and lack of normal richness and meaning in emotional experience.

In terms of intensity, emotions may be described as *mild, strong,* or *disintegrative.* Interestingly enough, different intensities of emotion are apparently related to quite different physiological processes.

With *mild* emotion there is increased alertness, a focusing of attention on meaning-producing factors in the situation, and a slight increase in tension, accompanied by feelings of being "pepped up" and of having increased vigor. Even negative emotions, such as fear and anger, may be experienced as pleasant when they occur in mild form and when the individual believes he has control over the situation and can terminate it if he wishes (Berlyne, 1967). This is readily illustrated by the negative emotions we often experience in watching sporting events or television and movie dramas. In fact, if such events are not emotion-arousing, we are likely to find them dull.

Strong emotions present a quite different picture. In strong active emotions there is an emergency mobilization of bodily resources for immediate, more or less violent action, and the stepping up of physiological processes is both more selective and more extensive. Processes related to digestion are suspended and the mouth becomes dry, whereas heartbeat, blood pressure, respiration, and adrenalin production are all increased. The capillaries along the alimentary canal constrict, while those in the brain and the large muscles enlarge for better circulation. Red blood cells from the spleen and sugar from the liver are released into the blood. Even the factor that induces blood clotting in injuries is increased—just in case. In strong depressive emotions like grief, no action is usually called for, and action potentials are restricted accordingly: pulse rate, blood pressure, and respiration are all depressed.

In addition to our mild and strong emotions, both of which may be normal and healthy, we may experience disintegrative emotions. These may be the outgrowth of normal emergency emotions too long continued, or they may be precipitated by overwhelming stress. In such circumstances, as we noted in Chapter 8, even a stable personality may develop a mental disorder.

The intensity of disintegrative emotions is well illustrated by observations of soldiers who had broken down in combat in World War II and were later given sodium pentothal interviews. Under the influence of this drug, which produces effects somewhat similar to hypnosis, the soldier could "relive" his combat experience and discharge some of his overwhelming fear and anxiety (Grinker & Spiegel, 1945b):

"The terror exhibited in the moments of supreme danger, such as at the imminent explosion of shells, the death of a friend before the patient's eyes, the absence of cover under a heavy dive bombing attack is electrifying to watch. The body becomes increasingly tense and rigid; the eyes widen and the

pupils dilate, while the skin becomes covered with fine perspiration. The hands move about convulsively, seeking a weapon, or a friend to share the danger. The breathing becomes incredibly rapid and shallow. The intensity of the emotion sometimes becomes more than they can bear; and frequently at the height of the reaction, there is a collapse and the patient falls back in bed and remains quiet for a few minutes, usually to resume the story at a more neutral point." (p. 80)

Range of feeling. Human beings have the potential for experiencing a tremendous variety of emotions, from the most intense elation to the depths of depression, from the greatest happiness to the greatest sorrow, from deep and enduring love to lasting hatred.

We all tend to experience unpleasant emotions when our strivings are blocked or our values threatened and pleasant ones when we achieve our goals or anticipate doing so or when we receive confirmation of our values. Thus the events that can lead to pleasant and unpleasant emotions are as varied as our strivings and interests. And of course, the more self-involved we are in a situation or activity, the greater its emotion-arousing potential for us.

Despite their great potential, some people seem to experience a rather limited range of emotions—often with a preponderance of negative emotions such as fear and anger or hostility—while others appear to experience a much wider range of emotions and sentiments—often with subtle nuances and fine shades of feeling. Typically, the failure to develop a full repertoire of emotions with appropriate intensity and depth seems to result from personal immaturity, faulty attitudes, or defenses against emotional involvement. Such a failure—as in the case of an individual who lacks a sense of humor or is incapable of love for someone else—may seriously limit the richness and meaningfulness of one's life.

In addition to emotional responses to particular events, we also experience *moods* —feeling states lasting hours or even days. Lorr, Daston, & Smith (1967) have deline-

ated five mood states: vigor-activity, tension-anxiety, anger-hostility, fatigue-inertia, and depression. Such mood states color our perceptions and provide a background for whatever activity is going on. We have probably all had the experience of being in a bad mood and finding that molehills looked like mountains or of being in a good mood and sailing through a situation that normally would upset us.

The wide fluctuations of the manic-depressive are only a more extreme example of the fluctuations in mood that seem to be typical for the human species. For most of us, moods tend to fluctuate through a fairly predictable cycle that is somewhat independent of external events, though the length of the cycle and the difference between crest and trough are individual matters. People often find it interesting to keep a record of their moods every morning for a few weeks or months to see if they can detect a regular pattern; the individual who feels that his mood swings may be beyond the "normal" range should seek professional assistance.

Positive or negative orientation. Both positive and negative emotions are normal, healthy reactions to certain types of situations. We all experience some of both, and the person who feels he should have only positive feelings is making unrealistic demands on himself. Yet a preponderance of negative feelings is unhealthy and maladjustive. Negative feelings indicate that the individual feels thwarted or threatened in some way, and such a perception, as we have already seen, tends to induce defense-oriented behavior. Furthermore, the person who is chronically fearful or resentful is constantly on the lookout for new dangers and thus tends to see only what confirms his worries and fears. Such a person has trouble maintaining satisfying relationships with other people, and in time his chronic emotional mobilization may even have serious effects on his physical health. Thus a preponderance of negative emotions not only prevents present effectiveness but also interferes with the development of greater competence and maturity.

A predominance of positive feelings, on the other hand, is characteristic of the emotionally healthy person. Repeated studies, both clinical and experimental, have shown that love, sympathy, and other positive feelings are conducive to self-esteem, adequacy, and self-actualization. Although our feelings are, of course, somewhat dependent on what life brings us, this is only part of the story; some people manage to have a predominance of positive feelings despite great adversity, whereas others are constantly fearful, angry, and resentful in what looks to us like a favorable situation. It is our attitudes and values that chiefly determine whether an experience will be gratifying or frustrating to us. Except under the most extreme stress, the emotionally competent person can usually manage to keep the balance on the side of the positive emotions.

Patterns of Expression and Control

People vary not only in their patterns of emotional experience but also in their patterns of expression and control. Some are effusive and demonstrative, freely expressing their feelings in words, gestures, and other behavior. Others hide their feelings— sometimes just from other people, sometimes from themselves as well. Sometimes "admirable" emotions are expressed freely, while disapproved ones are concealed or denied. These may be culturally induced patterns, but usually they serve individual needs and purposes too.

Clearly not every emotionally competent person will have exactly the same pattern of expression and control. As with the experience of emotion, "normal" covers a wide range. The following three characteristics, however, are associated with competence in emotional expression and control: (1) a balance of spontaneity and control; (2) a habit of acknowledging one's feelings and channeling them constructively instead of denying or suppressing them; and (3) an avoidance of distorted and disguised expression.

Spontaneity and control. Children are usually quite spontaneous in the expression of their feelings and emotions. Thus a child may shout "I hate you" at someone to express his anger even before he knows what hating someone actually means. Children, too, are initially quite uninhibited in showing affection for others. With time, however, most of us learn to inhibit the expression of certain

---

DIFFERENCES IN EMOTIONAL RESPONSES (PHYSICAL OR PSYCHIC)

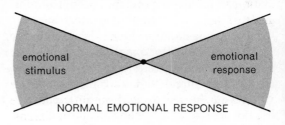

NORMAL EMOTIONAL RESPONSE

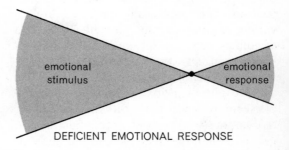

DEFICIENT EMOTIONAL RESPONSE

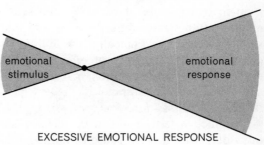

EXCESSIVE EMOTIONAL RESPONSE

Adapted from Menninger, 1945.

In a normal emotional reaction, stimulus and response are proportionate in intensity. An imbalance in either direction—a strong stimulus evoking a negligible response or a negligible stimulus evoking an intense response—indicates some degree of emotional maladjustment.

emotions—such as crying—and to express anger and love only in socially approved ways.

Although some measure of emotional control is necessary, it can be carried too far. Thus an individual may be so inhibited in expressing anger or affection that he seems tense and rigid and lacking in warmth and spontaneity. The person who "plays it cool," avoiding involvements that might arouse strong emotions, misses the sense of emotional involvement in the human enterprise that helps make life exciting and meaningful to those who permit themselves more spontaneity of emotional experience. Although he may avoid the pain of loss or rejection, he also cuts himself off from the warmth, emotional support, and sense of continuity that can come from a deep friendship or love relationship.

With inadequate inner controls, we may overreact emotionally, flying off the handle or bursting into tears in routine situations. With too rigid controls we may be unable to "let ourselves go" or to "be ourselves." Neither extreme is desirable.

Constructive channeling vs. repression. In each society, the child learns what emotions may be expressed and under what conditions. Boys in particular are often admonished not to cry and not to show fear—to act like a "man" and not a "cry baby." The expression of anger is usually discouraged: the child who expresses anger toward parents or siblings may be punished and made to feel guilty and ashamed.

When a child learns that the direct expression of his emotions brings him disapproval and punishment, or when he learns to feel ashamed and guilty for experiencing certain emotions, he may unconsciously resort to repression or emotional insulation as a means of self-protection. Thus he may repress feelings of anger toward his parents and later toward his spouse so that he consciously experiences only love and affection; or he may withdraw and insulate himself from close emotional involvement so that potentially dangerous or uncomfortable emo-

tions will not be aroused. As we have seen, one of the primary tasks of both intensive group experience and psychotherapy is often to reintroduce the individual to his own real feelings.

Direct vs. disguised expression. Emotions that are denied direct expression often find outlets in disguised ways. Hostility, for example, may be expressed through teasing or nagging; anxiety and fear may be expressed through chronic fatigue and somatic complaints. Often the individual is unaware of the causes of such reactions and is quite bewildered by his own behavior. Usually such outlets are not entirely adequate for reducing emotional tensions, or they may reduce the conscious tension but at the price of peptic ulcers or other psychosomatic disorders.

Effectiveness in emotional expression and control, like effectiveness in other forms of behavior, means that both inner needs and outer demands are taken into account. Emotional competence is not achieved once and for all, however. Although we can develop more realistic expectations and greater ability to acknowledge our real feelings, we can expect to have a continuing problem of finding personally satisfying and constructive ways to express negative emotions.

Understanding and Functioning with Emotion

If our emotions are to be adaptive rather than maladaptive influences, we need to understand and accept them and learn to use them instead of fighting them.

Understanding and accepting emotion. The first step in improving our mastery over our emotions is to understand them. Much misery comes from sheer ignorance. Many people worry about mood swings that are actually quite normal, feel a loss of self-esteem over normal sexual urges, or suffer agonies of shame and guilt because of occasional feelings of hostility toward parents or others whom they love—not realizing that such feelings are to be expected. Although an understanding of emotional processes will not automatically solve problems of expression and control, emotional competence starts with a healthy and realistic attitude toward emotion as part of one's equipment for living.

Functioning with emotions instead of fighting them. One important strategy in directing our emotional reactions is learning to function with them, using them instead of trying to fight them. Although some stress situations can be anticipated and made less emotion-arousing by adequate preparation in required skills, other situations will evoke strong emotion no matter how thoroughly we have tried to prepare ourselves. This is fortunate—if we know how to handle it. For example, if the soldier in combat does not experience fear, he will hardly be normal and, lacking the extra energy that fear provides, will probably not fight as well. But if he regards fear as a sign of cowardice and devotes his energy to trying to deny and hide it, he will have less energy for dealing with the actual dangers and will, in addition, be handicapped by continual inner conflict.

In everyday life, too, anger, fear, or anxiety can propel an individual into taking some constructive action—action which he might otherwise not have had the impetus for taking. On the other hand, anger, fear, and anxiety that are not expressed in some kind of action may keep us "churning" inside and may distort our perceptions and undermine our sense of adequacy.

Finding constructive ways to express emotions. When strong emotions are aroused, it is important that they be expressed constructively rather than in disguised or destructive ways. There are many harmless and constructive ways of venting even strong negative emotions once one acknowledges and accepts having them. Strenuous physical activity is a common method; talking the matter out with a trusted friend may help; participating in encounter groups is often of value. Where the situation eliciting the emotion—perhaps an unhappy marriage—is especially difficult

to deal with, professional counseling or psychotherapy may be called for. Just getting our fears, anxieties, and hostilities out into the open where we can see them for what they are often helps to discharge much of the emotional tension and paves the way for more constructive feelings and more constructive ways of dealing with the situation.

Fostering Constructive Emotions

Fortunately, healthy emotional patterns tend to perpetuate themselves just as unhealthy ones do. Thus an important part of emotional competence is fostering constructive patterns of emotional feeling and expression. Often this requires the breaking of negative, self-defeating habits of response and the establishing of new ones.

Keeping a sense of humor. A sense of humor is an important adaptive resource. The person who can remain objective enough to appreciate the incongruities of a situation is less likely to be overwhelmed by it. Laughing at oneself is perhaps as healthy and effective a way of reducing tension and negative feelings as has yet been discovered.

Sometimes, of course, what passes for humor is really an expression of hostility, as when we attempt to feel superior by laughing at the mistakes or misfortunes of others. Even when humor is hostile, however, it may serve to reduce negative emotional feelings. For example, Dworkin and Efran (1967) found that subjects who had been placed in anger-arousing situations appreciated hostile humor more than did non-angered subjects but that both hostile and nonhostile humor significantly reduced feelings of anger and anxiety. Here it is of interest to note that Maslow (1954), in his study of self-actualizing persons, found that his subjects tended to appreciate subtle wit rather than broad humor and that their humor tended to be lacking in hostility.

An ability to use and enjoy humor is both a cause and a result of our attitudes. A defense-oriented person can seldom see anything funny about himself. On the other hand, one who can enjoy a good joke on himself is helped thereby to maintain a task-oriented approach to his problems.

2. *Accentuating positive emotions.* Since it is important to emotional competence and even to good health that positive feelings predominate, we should do what we can to keep the balance on the positive side. Although we obviously cannot decide "Now we shall start having only positive feelings," there is much we can do to encourage healthy emotions. We can choose the activities that seem most likely to yield rich satisfactions both while they are in progress and in their long-term effects. We can concentrate on actualization strivings instead of maintenance ones —on growth instead of on keeping what we have. Rather than nurse a grudge against someone, we can explore ways of building a better relationship with him. Instead of playing a martyr role and wallowing in self-pity,

we can tackle projects that will center our attention outside ourselves. We can make a deliberate effort to be more acutely aware and appreciative of the assets that we usually take for granted.

3. *Striving to achieve a realistic frame of reference.* The key to attitudinal change is not a simple resolve to "think positively" in the sense of denying that problems exist. Rather it focuses on achieving a realistic frame of reference in which our problems and our resources for meeting them are viewed with reasonable accuracy and objectivity. The person who can see his disappointments and frustrations in perspective—without undue optimism or pessimism—is not so likely to get steamed up over a broken date, a bumbling bridge partner, a traffic tie-up, or other irritating but minor events which have little long-range significance. Nor is he likely to react with exaggerated fear and anxiety to more serious stresses.

SOME DETERMINANTS OF EMOTIONAL PATTERNS

CONSTITUTIONAL MAKE-UP	Patterns of reactivity, expression, and control are all influenced by the individual's temperament, mood cycles, activity level, sensitivity, vigor, and other constitutional reaction tendencies.
EARLY TRAINING	Early teaching, models, rewards, and punishments foster certain emotions and discourage others, also induce particular patterns of expression and control. If the child learns to deny and be ashamed of certain emotions, he has unrealistic expectations and is handicapped in learning to cope with such emotions.
FRAME OF REFERENCE	An individual's picture of the world and of himself determines whether he experiences predominantly positive or negative emotions; also determines what events will be seen as significant and hence will arouse emotion.
THE SOCIAL FIELD	Both the arousal of our emotions and the channeling of emotions once aroused depend partly on the expectations and values of the people around us. Their own emotional reactions, especially in a dangerous or unstable situation, may also influence our reactions; for example, hysteria in those around us may make us more emotional, whereas calmness in others may help us to keep our own feelings under control. Different social climates often induce different emotional reactions. For example, a highly competitive climate may induce open aggressiveness; an autocratic climate, aggressiveness which is displaced to a safe target.

If negative feelings predominate and we cannot seem to do anything about them, we may be the victims of unconscious attitudes and defenses which keep us from seeing things in their true perspective. In such cases professional counseling may be necessary to help us examine the real basis for our emotional difficulties and, with this better understanding, achieve a more positive orientation.

Working through emotional "weak spots." The achievement of emotional competence is complicated for most of us by the presence of emotional "weak spots" or "scars." Painful and frightening experiences—particularly those in childhood—are apt to create psychic wounds which never completely heal. As a result, we are left with a particular vulnerability to certain kinds of stress. Learning to recognize and deal with such weak spots is a necessary emotional competency.

Few of us escape at least minor traumas. It is terribly devaluating to a boy, for example, to be beaten up in the schoolyard by the local bully and then taunted for running away. Similarly, when we make a social blunder, forget an important speech, or drop an easy fly ball that brings in the winning run for the other team, we suddenly feel terribly inadequate. Even when we forget such events with the passage of time, the emotional reaction they engendered remains a part of us and is apt to be reactivated in similar situations. Emotional scars are commonly caused, too, by guilt-arousing sexual experiences in childhood, such as participating in forbidden sexual acts or being sexually assaulted by an older person. Often the child is ashamed and afraid to talk about such experiences and may later "refuse" to remember them. But many times they complicate his sexual adjustment as an adult.

Aside from specific traumatic events, the general circumstances of our upbringing may leave emotional scars which time only partially heals. A person who has grown up in grinding poverty may find it difficult as an adult to achieve a real feeling of security even with a high degree of financial and social success. His need for tangible indications of security is insatiable. The deprivation of love during childhood can have even more devastating effects, as we have seen. Many of our emotional difficulties have their roots in faulty relationships with our parents —rejection or overprotection, perfectionism or overindulgence.

In recognizing the sources of emotional weak spots, the idea is not to affix blame— on our parents or elsewhere—or to admit defeat. Rather, by understanding the reasons behind the way we react, and looking to see if we are still reacting to situations that no longer exist, we can hope to make our emotional reactions more appropriate for today's demands.

One common residual effect of a psychic wound is *reaction sensitivity*—the tendency to be acutely sensitive to those elements in a new situation which bear some possible relationship to an earlier painful experience. Thus a person whose home has once burned down may thereafter tend to perceive an unidentified odor as the smell of smoke. An individual who grew up in the midst of marital tension and unhappiness may hesitate to marry because he is more sensitive to the potential risks of marriage than to its potential satisfactions. The person who has been rejected by his parents may see indications of rejection or loss of love in even the best-intentioned behavior of his spouse. The reactivation of such conditioned feelings takes place automatically and therefore is not easily subject to voluntary control.

Unfortunately, early traumatic experiences sometimes create major blocks to growth. Because we fear repetition of pain, we tend to avoid situations in which we fear that the painful feelings might be reactivated. Such avoidance cuts us off from chances to develop adequacy for meeting such situations.

Specific methods by which "weak spots" can be overcome include the following:

1. *Desensitization.* Studies of conditioned aversion reactions with animals have shown that after an animal has been shocked in a particular situation, he will continue to avoid it indefinitely even though the electric current is never turned on again. He gives himself no chance to find out that the situation is now harmless. In like manner, the child who has barely escaped drowning may be so terrified of water that he cannot bring himself to expose himself to situations in which his fear might be overcome and swimming skill developed. Sometimes we go on for years avoiding activities or situations that would no longer hurt us. By exposing ourselves to them we would discover that the anticipated pain did not materialize and our conditioned fear would be extinguished. Especially if we can experience the dreaded situation first in very mild form and in pleasant company or with other sources of reassurance and pleasant emotions close by, it will lose its power to trigger a fear reaction in us. This principle is applied in behavior therapy, as we have seen, but we can also apply it ourselves in trying to overcome avoidance reactions.

2. *Catharsis*. The term *catharsis,* as we have seen, refers to the discharge of emotional tensions. This may be by talking them out or by "reliving" the painful experience which engendered them. In common parlance it means getting things off your chest. Catharsis is particularly helpful in overcoming the embarrassment or shame associated with social failure, and it is invaluable as a means of reducing the tensions associated with anxiety, fear, hostility, and guilt. By verbalizing a trauma, we also get the experience out into the open where we can look at it more objectively and thus begin integrating it into our ego-structure.

Catharsis may take any of various forms. The Eskimos have long used the device of role playing, in which they act out their failures and embarrassing experiences within a group so that everyone can laugh about them together. We have previously noted the use of catharsis in the treatment of mental disorders induced by combat situations; under the influence of a drug such as sodium pentothal the patient almost literally relives his battle experience and thus is able to discharge much of the emotional tension he has built up.

There is a danger in catharsis if one "spills out" to the wrong person—one who might reinforce the fear and anxiety, the guilt and resentment the individual is trying to rid himself of. In severe cases, a professional therapist may best be able to help the individual accept his feelings and integrate a traumatic experience into his ego-structure. In less severe cases, a minister or a doctor or an emotionally mature and discreet friend is able to provide the listening ear and the comments which lead the way to insight.

In therapy it is often difficult to begin working through a problem by catharsis because it brings to consciousness many of the painful feelings the individual has been trying to hide. Sometimes he will terminate therapy when it begins to get uncomfortable. To undertake and carry through with catharsis we must be convinced that this often painful process is worth while.

3. *Insight*. Catharsis often enables us to gain insight into the ways an emotional trauma has been affecting our behavior. When much of the emotion associated with a past experience has been discharged, we are able to see the experience more objectively and may discover that we have been overreacting to it. We may find that we have devalued ourselves unnecessarily, or our aspirations were unrealistic, or that our childish interpretation of an event was inaccurate. We begin to see *why* we feel the way we do— why a small amount of criticism, even if it is constructive, hurts our feelings and makes us feel inferior; why we would rather keep a piece of defective merchandise than face a sales clerk and ask him to take it back; why we are afraid to argue with people even though we are churning with anger over something they have said; why we feel so self-conscious with members of the opposite sex.

4. *Developing new patterns*. It is a mistake to assume that the battle is wholly won either by extinction of faulty reactions through desensitization or by insight into why we feel the way we do. Emotional re-

education is a long laborious process involving the building of new patterns as well as the removal of old ones.

To develop new, more satisfying emotional reactions, the individual needs to put himself into situations where he can experience positive feelings. He can overcome a fear of social gatherings, for example, by participating in such gatherings and having the experience of being accepted. He can learn to reveal his feelings without the fear of disapproval as he discovers that a greater openness of expression makes his interpersonal relationships more rewarding rather than more threatening. Such experiences increase his self-confidence and give him a broadening base for more healthy emotional patterns.

Use of drug therapy for emotional tension. In recent years a great deal of public and scientific attention has been focused on the use of tranquilizers and other drugs in dealing with emotional tensions and maladjustment.

In general, such drugs may be classified as "tranquilizers" and "energizers"; all of them act on the central nervous system. The tranquilizers may be further classified as strong tranquilizers like chlorpromazine, which are used in the treatment of psychoses, and weak or minor tranquilizers like meprobamate, which is perhaps best known under commercial names such as Miltown and Equanil. Weak tranquilizers are used extensively for the relief of anxiety and tension and for help in sleeping. The energizers are used to alleviate feelings of lethargy or depression.

The remarkable success of the tranquilizing drugs in treating mental illness has tended to obscure the fact—at least in the public mind—that they alleviate symptoms rather than causes. Thus many people have turned to minor tranquilizers to reduce the tension and strain of everyday living or to help them get through a particularly difficult period. Some persons have found that minor tranquilizers alleviated their tension and anxiety and made them feel more capable of

dealing with their problems; others have detected no appreciable positive results; still others have suffered undesirable side effects that seemed to outweigh any benefits. There seems to be little substantial objective evidence that the minor tranquilizers are effective; even immediate relief may be short-lived because the individual may adapt to the drug in a few weeks (Rosenhan & London, 1968).

Research efforts continue in an attempt to evaluate the effects and appropriate uses of the minor tranquilizers and to improve them. At the present time, however, it seems that at best they are crutches which are valuable primarily in times of special stress. Used indiscriminately, they may be dangerous because they may produce harmful side effects and/or obscure the need to come to grips with the original source of tension.[1]

DEALING WITH PROBLEM EMOTIONS

The general strategies already outlined for improving emotional competence are, of course, applicable to all the emotions. In addition, however, it will be useful to explore the unique aspects of several of the emotions that most often present problems for us. Although we will discuss them one at a time, it should be emphasized that in our actual experience they rarely occur in isolation. Fear, anxiety, and hostility, for example, commonly go together.

Fear, Anxiety, and Worry

As we have seen, the term *fear* is usually used for a response to a specific danger and *anxiety* for a response to danger or threat which is less clearly perceived. Following this usage, the frightened individual usually "knows what he is afraid of" and what he can

---

[1]Because of possible harmful side effects from minor tranquilizers, several states have passed laws making it illegal to drive an automobile while under the influence of such drugs.

or cannot do about it, whereas the anxious individual "senses danger" but is not clear as to its exact nature or what action to take in dealing with it. Often fear and anxiety go together—fear being elicited by clearly perceived aspects of the dangerous or stressful situation and anxiety by its unpredictable or uncertain implications. For example, a young person approaching marriage may feel fear concerning financial problems and new responsibilities and at the same time feel vaguely anxious and apprehensive about whether he really wants to get married and whether his marriage will be a success.

Worry is a form of fear or anxiety in which the individual is emotionally involved with a troublesome situation but sees no immediate answer and feels helpless and often somewhat hopeless about the outcome. Worries usually focus around unforeseeable future events—about what may happen to the individual or his loved ones, or other matters in which he is self-involved.

Realistic and unrealistic fears and anxieties. Since no life is free of hazard, fear and anxiety are normal and justified experiences. Yet many people consider it a form of weakness or even cowardice to feel fear and anxiety—let alone express them. It is especially difficult for men in our culture to admit their fears and anxieties because of our prevalent stereotype of the male as a strong, confident provider under whose protection his family can feel secure. Recognition of fear and anxiety as normal and permanent parts of the human condition is a first step in dealing effectively with them.

A second step in dealing with these emotions is distinguishing between realistic and unrealistic fear and anxiety. Is the fear elicited by a real danger? Is it proportional to the actual degree of danger, or is it exaggerated? Is it rational or irrational? Is it born of an actual, present stress situation, or does it reflect a pervasive feeling of inadequacy and inferiority? As we saw in Chapter 6, a distinction is often made between *situational* anxiety—anxiety which occurs under particular conditions—and *general* anxiety—in which the individual experiences a chronic, pervasive feeling of anxiety whatever the external circumstances.

Of course, it is not always easy to distinguish between realistic and unrealistic fears and anxieties or to determine whether a given individual is overly prone to fear and anxiety in dealing with the everyday problems of living. However, an awareness of this distinction and an approach to fear and anxiety as reactions to be recognized and understood rather than denied and hidden appear to be important first steps in dealing with these emotions.

As we have seen, fear and anxiety are not always negative in their effects. Fear which leads to caution or protective action is constructive; similarly, a minimal or even moderate level of anxiety may represent a necessary mechanism of arousal in getting us to undertake needed action. Mild anxiety can facilitate learning; and *existential anxiety*—anxiety centering around finding appropriate values and leading a meaningful and fulfilling life—can be a constructive force in our lives. As Levitt (1967) has said:

"Thus anxiety is a Janus-headed creature that can impel man to self-improvement, achievement, and competence, or can distort and impoverish his existence and that of his fellows." (p. 200)

Knowing what to expect and what to do. Since fear and anxiety stem from a feeling of helplessness in the face of danger, the best insurance against them is actual adequacy and competence. Obviously we cannot know ahead of time all the demands we will face, but we can foresee many fairly probable ones and prepare ourselves for them. With specific preparation for marriage, vocation, parenthood, and old age, for example, we are much more likely to maintain a constructive and task-oriented approach in meeting the problems they typically bring. Knowing what to expect and what to do about it can make us feel confident instead of fearful, even in a very demanding situation.

If there are certain types of situations in which we commonly experience fear and

BEING A GOOD WORRIER

Irwin (1968) has suggested the following attitudes and activities to keep worrying from getting out of hand and even use it constructively:

1. Trying to view the problem or anticipated event in perspective. Are we making a mountain out of a molehill? Will it be over, one way or another, in a week or two? Do most of our worries prove groundless?

2. Talking about worries and concerns with someone we trust. This brings the problem out where it can be examined and better defined.

3. Converting worrying into a problem-solving device. If we are determined to worry, we can make it constructive by trying to devise a practical plan for dealing with the "calamity" should it ever occur.

4. Bearing in mind that other people often have similar concerns and worries, and that a certain amount of worrying is both normal and constructive in preparing for future exigencies. Thus the admonition not to worry about worrying.

5. Obtaining psychological assistance when worries seem deep rooted and overly oppressive and are seriously handicapping our everyday personal adjustment.

---

anxiety, we can often take measures to modify our emotional responses—as in working through psychic wounds—or we can learn to carry on despite the fear. As we become accustomed to functioning in fear-producing situations, we may find our fear lessening, although it may not be completely banished.

Taking action in a fear-producing situation may also be of key importance. Fear often tends to a paralysis of action—and paralysis to an intensification of the fear. Action —almost any action—can break this circle and lessen feelings of fear even when it does not lessen the actual danger. The actor usually loses his stage fright once the action begins, as does the athlete once the contest is under way.

Being a good worrier. A certain amount of anxiety and worry is probably an inevitable by-product of modern living. Most of us feel vaguely apprehensive much of the time about possible accidents, failures, setbacks, losses, or other poorly defined future possibilities.

Worrying is a form of fear and anxiety which can be realistic and constructive or unrealistic and destructive. Janis (1968) has referred to the useful "work of worrying" in preparing an individual for coping with future stress. For example, he found that patients who were unworried about impending major surgery were less able to withstand the pain and other stresses of postoperative convalescence, whereas patients who were moderately worried and apprehensive before surgery apparently tended to go through a mental rehearsal of the impending danger and were better prepared for the stressful situation when it materialized.

Chronic anxiety and worry can hamper us in three basic ways. First, as we have noted, anxiety beyond a very minimal level leads to a defensive orientation which makes us less able to face our problems objectively and work effectively toward their solution. Our perception narrows; we become more rigid and less inventive; and we develop a spiraling need to protect ourselves by denial, rationalization, and other defense mechanisms. Second, chronic anxiety keeps us physiologically mobilized for emergency action when no appropriate action is evident; the harmful effects of such anxiety in terms of psychosomatic disorders have been mentioned. Third, chronic worrying deprives us of much of the enjoyment of living. We are continually concerned with the negative and dangerous aspects of living rather than with the positive and enriching ones. Often a chronic worrier will worry about things that never happen and then be taken unawares by the stresses that do occur.

Anger and Hostility

As we have seen, anger may be viewed as a normal response to being interfered with and helps the organism to meet its needs through attack or aggressive action. Rage is anger out of control. Hostility is a more enduring condition of enmity, involving angry feelings and a tendency to inflict harm. Hate (or hatred) is roughly similar to hostility but is a more complex state centering around anger and a wish for harm or misfortune to befall the hated person, group, or object and involving a variety of action tendencies.

Although anger and hostility are normal parts of our adjustive equipment, we differ greatly, both individually and as groups, in the degree and frequency of the hostile feelings we experience. As we have seen, some cultures value and encourage hostility and aggressiveness, whereas others discourage such emotions. In addition, either a repressive social setting or a constantly frustrating one, such as slum residents experience, can be expected to induce much more hostility than one that provides a favorable balance of satisfactions over frustrations. But even in a favorable social setting immature or unrealistic expectations may lead to frequent or chronic hostilities and resentments.

Understanding and expressing anger and hostility. As with other emotions, competence in dealing with anger and hostility begins with an understanding and acceptance of our feelings rather than denial or moral self-condemnation.

We are usually taught early in life that we should love our parents and siblings and later our spouse and children. Yet those close to us inevitably frustrate us at times and hence elicit some measure of anger and hostility. If we believe that we should feel only pure love and affection for such persons, it is often difficult for us to admit and accept hostile feelings and even more difficult to find safe and acceptable ways of expressing them. For expressing anger and hostility toward loved ones bears the risk of alienating

them and eliciting rejection or retaliation and punishment, especially if they, too, believe that anger on our part means rejection and lack of love. Most children learn early that expressions of anger or hostility are likely to lead to punishment and pain for them.

When the individual views his hostile feelings as dangerous and immoral, he may resort to defense mechanisms such as denial or repression as a means of keeping his feelings out of consciousness, or he may turn his hostility inward and engage in severe self-recrimination for having such immoral and unacceptable feelings. Either approach only aggravates the problem. Chronic, unacknowledged hostility can poison the whole relationship and lead to a psychosomatic affliction; intrapunitive handling of the hostility affords some expression but undermines one's feelings of adequacy, worth, and self-esteem.

Unexpressed hostility may build in intensity over time until it blocks out more positive feelings toward the other person. In marital counseling, the individual may spend several sessions expressing his hostile feelings toward his mate before his more positive feelings come to the fore and he can begin to say that she does have some virtues and that he does love her. Thus when feelings of hostility are intense, some channel of expression is considered desirable.

Where it is not feasible to discuss one's hostile feelings with the person involved without damaging the relationship, the individual may find it helpful to discuss his feelings with a trusted friend or counselor. A relatively new approach to the handling of such hostility is the use of encounter groups, as described in Chapter 12.

Constructive vs. destructive hostility. In many situations anger and hostility are normal reactions that may lead to constructive action. Anger and hostility aroused by autocratic and unjust treatment of oneself or others may be used constructively in working for social reforms. On a more personal level, expressing our anger may help another person realize that he is being inconsiderate or selfish and that his behavior is affecting people in unintended ways.

More commonly, however, anger and hostility take destructive forms. We let frustration and hostility interfere with harmonious and satisfying interpersonal relationships or become unduly upset and angered by minor delays, discourtesies, or other irritating situations that are relatively unimportant. Strong anger may lead us to ill-considered and costly action which we may later regret and for which we may receive severe punishment, including imprisonment. On a social level, demagogues often stir up and exploit feelings of bitterness and hatred to gain personal power and lead the society to calamitous action.

Thus it becomes important to distinguish between anger that is appropriate and constructive and anger that is inappropriate and destructive. Although anyone may be aroused to inappropriate anger and hostility when unduly fatigued or under the influence of alcohol, drugs, or special stress, habitual overreacting to minor frustrations or frequent extremes of anger and hostility usually indicate unrealistic expectations or underlying feelings of immaturity and inferiority.

Expecting some hostility from others. As we learn to accept and tolerate hostility in ourselves, we must also learn to accept it in others, even when it is directed against us. Perhaps the most essential aspect of dealing with overt hostility in adulthood is to be prepared for it and to give up the notion of wanting everyone to love and appreciate us at all times. Although there is a certain justice in reacting angrily to the seemingly unjustified anger of another person, this is a form of self-indulgence that seldom pays off. Two people preoccupied with defense against each other or with retaliation for past offenses only feed and perpetuate their feelings of hostility. If we can see another person's anger, especially when it is disguised, as a problem for him rather than as a threat to us, we can often make the response that will lessen his tension and thus make a better relationship possible.

Guilt, Depression, and Grief

Man universally experiences a sense of guilt when he violates ethical or moral principles in which he believes. Guilt is characterized by a feeling of regret, lessened personal worth, and usually some measure of anxiety. And as we have seen, guilt is closely related to depression, with its characteristic discouragement, dejection, and gloomy thoughts. Both guilt and depression are commonly involved in grief stemming from the loss of loved ones.

Although these emotions are part of our adaptive resources, they may take either destructive or constructive forms and often are difficult to deal with.

Normal vs. pathological guilt. The recognition of responsibility for failure to live up to one's ethical and moral values is a necessary concomitant of self-direction. Thus guilt is potentially a normal and useful emotion that can lead to a correction of error and reparation of damage. When guilt is out of all proportion to the magnitude of the "sin" that was committed, however, or when it focuses on self-condemnation and self-devaluation instead of future improvement or redirection of effort, it is pathological.

Normal guilt feelings can usually be dealt with through confession of guilt (to oneself or others), a sincere effort at reparation, and then a willingness to accept forgiveness and look to the future instead of dwelling on the past. This sequence usually leaves one better equipped to avoid the same mistake on subsequent occasions.

In the case of pathological guilt, however, the individual may be convinced that the slate can never really be wiped clean. He feels that he has committed a great and unpardonable sin and suffers pervasive and persistent feelings of unworthiness and self-devaluation. Often he feels dejected and depressed and finds no joy or satisfaction in anything that he does. Usually, too, he suffers from feelings of anxiety and apprehension stemming from his belief that somehow he will be "punished for his sins." Sometimes such an individual resorts to self-defense mechanisms such as projection—thus placing the blame for his misdeeds on others and freeing himself from conscious feelings of guilt and self-devaluation.

Such pathological guilt feelings usually reflect immature, rigid, and unrealistic moral standards that no human being could possibly follow; with such an unrealistic but implacable conscience, the individual is foredoomed to perpetual failure and devaluation. Thus again we see the crucial importance of the individual's assumptions and values in determining the appropriateness of his response patterns.

Guilt and depression. Dejection and discouragement are expected reactions to setbacks and disappointments that keep us from reaching our goals. Where the individual has an unrealistically high level of aspiration, however, he may suffer excessive feelings of dejection and depression over relatively minor setbacks that offer little threat to his long-range goals. Thus a student may be dejected over getting a B grade in a course in which he was aiming and expecting to get an A. Although such reactions subject him to unnecessary misery, they are usually not of key importance and clear up rapidly over time.

Severe depressive reactions, however, are more serious, especially when there is a strong component of guilt and self-devaluation. Such guilt-tinged depression, as we saw in Chapter 8, is often part of a neurotic or psychotic reaction. This seems to be especially true in Christian and Judeo-Christian societies, with their emphasis on personal responsibility (Murphy, Wittkower, & Chance, 1967). Unrealistic aspirations, rigid conscience development, and other conditions that commonly lead to pathological guilt reactions are also commonly involved in pathological depression.

Although it may be useful to examine one's aspirations and values if one is troubled by feelings of guilt and depression, tendencies toward severe and pathological depression usually require professional assistance if they are to be alleviated. Such help is of key importance in view of the suicidal tendencies which often occur in severe depressions.

Bereavement and grief. Grief is a universal reaction to bereavement, found even among animals. It is apparently based on a close identification with the person or thing that has been lost; in a sense, the bereaved feels that a part of himself is gone. This is especially apparent with the death of a close family member, but much the same reaction may occur in public mourning over the death of a well-loved national figure.

Most grief reactions are not severe enough to be incapacitating. Typically there is a depressed mood, sleep disruption, and crying. Usually the individual "works through" the grief reaction; resorting to denial or repression in an attempt to avoid the grief reaction apparently simply prolongs the "grief work" that must be carried out for adjustment to the new situation. The psychological needs of the bereaved person usually center around freedom to express his feelings—not only of sorrow but also of guilt or hostility, if these are involved—and, a little later, emotional support as he tries to build a new life.

Of course, death is not the only source of bereavement and grief. A man's wife may leave him; his son may commit a crime and be sent to prison. The loss of an eye or limb is also a very real source of bereavement. Even the loss of a possession can bring grief if the possession has supplied important emotional supports and gratifications for the individual and, in a general sense, has been viewed as an extension of himself. Our primary concern here, however, is with bereavement and grief stemming from the loss of loved ones.

An individual's reaction to bereavement varies depending upon the meaning of the loss to him and the strength of the ties that have been disrupted. Bereavement may involve a loss of security, friendship, companionship, emotional support, or love—or all of these. Thus it is not surprising that grief may be complicated by feelings of hostility, guilt, and depression—especially when the grief-striken individual has had ambivalent feelings toward the lost loved one. He may engage in self-recrimination for past neglect, for having felt hostility, or for other thoughts and acts of omission or commission for which he now feels guilty. Guilt and depression are almost inevitable, when the individual has actually been involved in some way in the event that caused the death of the loved one—as in an automobile accident in which he was the driver.

Since it is now too late to make reparation for his alleged or actual misdeeds, guilt, self-recrimination, and depression may be severe. Here the process of grief work may be much more complicated and may take a much longer time, and there is a real possibility of suicide. Professional assistance during the most intense period of grief and depression is to be encouraged. In severe cases, where an individual might otherwise be overwhelmed by the intensity of his feelings, tranquilizers or other medication may help him over the crisis until he is able to work through his feelings in a normal way. Except in unusual circumstances, however, the use of drugs only postpones the grief work and makes the individual's readjustment more difficult.

Love As a Problem Emotion

Despite its central importance in human affairs, love, as a psychological phenomenon, has received very little scientific study. In fact, many psychology books do not even have the term *love* in the index, and where the term is used, it is ordinarily in connection with sex and marriage rather than in terms of its more general place in human relationships. Yet it would probably be agreed that an ability to give and receive love is one of the most important of all emotional competencies, for all the evidence points to the necessity of loving and being loved for normal human development and functioning.

Why human beings have such a great need and desire for love has been the subject of considerable speculation. Fromm (1956) believes that love develops from man's awareness of his separateness and his need to overcome the anxiety this separateness brings by achieving union with someone or something. But he stresses the point that the only healthy union is one in which the integrity of the individual is not threatened. We can achieve a feeling of union through dependence on another individual or through conformity to the group, but in so doing, we surrender our own individuality; likewise, we can achieve union through dominating others, but here the others suffer. Only through love, Fromm feels, can the needed sense of union be achieved without loss of individuality and integrity on either side. May (1968) has also emphasized the theme of aloneness as a basis for our need for love in his statement that:

"Every person, as a separate individual, experiences aloneness. And so we strive actively to overcome our aloneness by some form of love." (p. 23)

Whatever its origin, the search for love is an extremely powerful force in human existence.

The meaning and forms of love. Many people have tried to define love. Prescott (1957) has described valid love in terms of the following components:

"**1.** *Love involves* more or less *empathy* with the loved one. A person who loves actually enters into the feelings of and shares intimately the experiences of the loved one and the effects of these experiences upon the loved one.

"**2.** One who loves is deeply *concerned for the welfare,* happiness, and development *of the beloved.* This concern is so deep as to become one of the major organizing values in the personality or self-structure of the loving person. . . .

"**3.** One who loves finds *pleasure in making his resources available* to the loved one, to be used by the other to enhance his welfare, happiness, and development. Strength, time, money, thought, indeed all resources are proffered happily to the loved one for his use. A loving person is not merely concerned about the beloved's welfare and development, he does something about it.

"4. Of course the loving person seeks a maximum of participation in the activities that contribute to the welfare, happiness, and development of the beloved. But he also *accepts fully the uniqueness and individuality of the beloved and . . . accords [him] full freedom to experience, to act, and to become what he desires to become.* A loving person has a nonpossessive respect for the selfhood of the loved one." (p. 358)

There are also, of course, somewhat unique components in the love we feel for a parent, a child, a friend, and a mate. Fromm (1956) delineates five somewhat different love relationships, as described below.

1. *Brotherly love.* Perhaps the most basic kind of love is that for all of humanity. Fromm describes it as "the sense of responsibility, care, respect, knowledge of any other human being, the wish to further his life." (p. 47) Unlike the love of man and woman or mother and child, brotherly love is in no way exclusive. It is the orientation to all human relationships which finds ex-

pression in the Biblical injunction to "love thy neighbor as thyself."

2. *Motherly (parental) love.* Here Fromm emphasizes the parent's unconditional affirmation of his child's life and needs. Parental love involves care and responsibility for the child's well-being and growth, together with a willing acceptance of the fact that the child's life is his own. The parent assumes responsibility for a life entrusted to his care and finds his happiness in seeing that life fulfilled. True motherly love is nonpossessive.

3. *Erotic love.* Fromm describes erotic love as "the craving for a complete fusion, for union with one other person. It is by its very nature exclusive and not universal. . . ." (pp. 52-53) Typically, of course, erotic love finds its culmination in the framework of marriage.

4. *Self-love.* Since love implies concern, respect, and responsibility, self-love is considered a necessity if the individual is to be capable of loving others. Self-deprecation and self-rejection interfere with all healthy love relationships.

5. *Love of God.* In discussing religious

UNHEALTHY LOVE RELATIONSHIPS

Distinguishing between healthy and unhealthy love is not always easy. Assuming outsiders are not being hurt by a relationship, the only yardstick we have for evaluating its healthiness is the extent to which it contributes to the happiness, well-being, and personal growth of both participants. By this criterion, the following types of love relationship would appear to be unhealthy:

1. *Conditional love*—in which the individual gives love only if the other conforms to his needs and dictates while he remains insensitive to the needs of the other.

2. *Possessive love*—in which the person views the loved object as a possession and treats him in a proprietary and exploitative way rather than as an autonomous, self-actualizing person.

3. *Overly romanticized love*—with expectations

of constant excitement and continuous signs of adoration from the loved one.

4. *False or deceitful love*—in which one partner professes deep and enduring love but uses the relationship to deliberately exploit the other.

5. *Two-against-the-world love*—in which the partners view themselves as two persons standing against a hostile world, indicating a defensive and self-centered orientation.

6. *Insecure and devaluating love*—in which one partner feels insecure and anxious and often jealous and in which his self-concept is devaluated rather than built up.

7. *Mutually destructive love*—in which the partners undermine and tear each other down and in which the relationship appears to be characterized more by hate than by love.

CONFLICTING ASSUMPTIONS ABOUT ROMANTIC LOVE

On the basis of intuition, personal experience, and uncontrolled observation, it has been claimed:

1. That romantic love inevitably leads to disillusionment and is the principal cause of our high divorce rate—and also that romantic love mitigates the stresses of monogamous marriage, preventing its disintegration as a social institution.

2. That romantic love is blind and irrational—and also that romantic love involves a sharpening of perception so that the other person is seen realistically but loved for himself anyway.

3. That adequate sexual relationships stem from and can be found only in the context of romantic love—and also that adequate sexual relationships often pave the way for the later development of love.

4. That finding the right person is the most important ingredient in romantic love—and also that one's capacity to give and receive love is the most important determinant.

5. That each successive love relationship is a unique and distinctive experience—and also that one loves as he has loved before so that there is a continuity in his love relationships and he will keep making the same mistakes.

6. That true romantic love leads to harmony and bliss—and also that "the path of true love never does run smooth," that the intensity of feeling in romantic love will inevitably lead to conflict and anxiety.

7. That it is possible in romantic love to lower one's defenses and let one's faults be freely seen by the partner—and also that one must be lovable to be loved and hence must always keep his best foot forward in appearance and behavior.

8. That romantic love can be felt for only one love object at a time—and also that the individual may be romantically in love with more than one person simultaneously.

---

love, Fromm (p. 83) again emphasizes man's "need to overcome separateness and to achieve union"—in this case, union with ultimate reality. This point is elaborated further in Chapter 16 in connection with the quest for values.

Thus love may take several different forms and may have several different meanings. Central to all the forms of love, however, appears to be an attitude of care, concern, and responsibility for the loved one, and a desire to promote his growth, well-being, and concerns. Nor does an individual usually show only one form of love; more commonly, the ability for any of the particular forms of love is part of a broader orientation involving the valuing of other human beings and an eagerness to form warm bonds with other people. As Fromm has put it (1956):

"If a person loves only one other person and is indifferent to the rest of his fellow men, his love is not love but symbiotic attachment, or an enlarged egotism." (p. 46)

In the remainder of this section, we shall be concerned primarily with healthy love relationships in marriage.

Romantic love vs. infatuation. Although economic factors rather than love have often been emphasized in marriage, romantic love has played an important role in most cultures (Kurland, 1953). In our contemporary society, we are constantly exposed to portrayals of idealized romantic love in movies, television, plays, novels, and popular songs. As in the case of other forms of love, however, we know very little about romantic love in real life: speculation about it by various alleged authorities casts little light on the subject.

Some of the many conflicting assumptions which have been held about romantic love are summarized in the chart. Interestingly, virtually the only scientific evidence we have regarding any of these assumptions concerns the last two pairs. In his study of self-actualizing people Maslow (1954) found that these individuals were able to drop their defenses in their love relationships and be wholly themselves without fear or pretense:

"One of the deepest satisfactions coming from the healthy love relationship reported by my subjects is that such a relationship permits the greatest spontaneity, the greatest naturalness, the greatest dropping of defenses and protection against threat. In such a relationship it is not necessary to be guarded, to conceal, to try to impress, to feel tense, to watch one's words or actions, to suppress or repress. My people report that they can be themselves without feeling that there are demands or expectations upon them; they can feel psychologically (as well as physically) naked and still feel loved and wanted and secure." (pp. 239-240)

Whether this finding would hold for less self-actualizing people in less healthy love relationships is a moot point.

In an early study of 500 American college girls, Ellis (1948) reported that 58 per cent admitted simultaneous infatuations and 25 per cent reported being in love simultaneously with two or more men. The findings of Packard (1968) with respect to the sexual patterns of college men and women suggest that the earlier findings of Ellis may be valid for today's generation as well.

Romantic love is characterized by strong feelings of attraction toward and affection for the loved person, a desire to be with him (or her), a concern for his well-being, a willingness to make more of oneself for him, and a desire to contribute to his happiness and personal growth. Usually it also includes a desire for affection from and sexual intimacy with the loved person. Such love may endure and deepen over the years or it may wither away. In some instances there appears to be a shift from romantic love to disillusionment and hurt and sometimes even to hostility and hate.

Despite all these points of similarity any given experience of romatic love is a unique, highly personal experience that may be difficult to describe to others. In fact, writers and poets have described the experience of romantic love in quite diverse ways. It seems unlikely that a person who has never experienced romantic love can understand or imagine the quality of the experience involved.

Often the question is raised as to the distinction between romantic love and infatuation. Lacking a clear understanding of either, we can make only a general distinction. Infatuation is usually considered to be an intense romantic relationship of short duration which is a purely emotional reaction and does not take into account the "fit" of the personalities or any other rational considerations. Often infatuation involves a high degree of wishful thinking in which the lover projects a halo over the head of the loved one and sees only what he wants to see instead of what is there. Once his perceptions become more realistic, the romantic aura may suddenly be lost.

Unfortunately, as Kephart (1967) has pointed out, one usually thinks of his current romantic experience as love rather than infatuation; infatuation is usually recognized as such—at least by the person involved—only after it is over.

Although infatuation may not last, it is a powerful force while it holds sway. It provides both rose-colored spectacles and a sense of urgency to its victims, and when it leads to a hasty marriage, the individual may find himself married to someone he scarcely knows, whose weak points come to him as quite a shock.

Many other irrational elements may also make it difficult for a person to tell if he is really in love. For example, even a relatively mature individual may convince himself that he wants to get married because he is in love when actually what he wants is to have someone take care of him, or to ensure his sexual satisfaction, or to protect himself from loneliness. Often, too, the individual has been indoctrinated with the romantic notion that there is only one person in the world who is right for him; in his eagerness to believe he has found that person, it is easy for him to convince himself that he is in love.

Genuine erotic love grows out of shared experiences of many kinds. The climate of a happy marriage is not necessarily one of complete harmony at all times; but it is one in which the bonds of love are deepened by shared problems as well as by happiness, and one in which both partners can continue to grow as individuals. The latter point is particularly important, for a love which feeds on dependency is apt to destroy itself. Erotic love, like brotherly and parental love, nurtures the growth of the loved one as an individual.

The ability to love. Most investigators believe that people vary greatly in their ability to love and to maintain a durable loving interaction with another person. An individual's ability to love, like other emotional competencies, appears to depend upon a number of factors, including his early experiences with his parents, the extent to which he trusts others, his degree of personal maturity and self-acceptance, and his freedom from exaggerated self-defense.

As we have seen, the ability to give and receive love apparently begins in a healthy infant-mother relationship and then expands as we build satisfying relationships with other family members, friends, and eventually a mate and children of our own. Fromm (1956) has distinguished two components which he considers of crucial importance in such early experiences: (1) the early experience of being loved unconditionally by the mother, and (2) the later experience of having to meet certain standards to ensure love. The first experience is considered a passive one in which the infant is loved simply because he exists; while the second experience, usually largely mediated by the father, shows the child that he can work for love and achieve it—that it is potentially within his control. Later these two trends are integrated into a feeling that one is basically lovable and worthy of love but also that he can behave in ways which will increase or destroy the love that other people will feel for him.

Lacking either part of this experience, the child is handicapped later on. If he has a weak and uninterested father and an indulgent mother, for example, he is not likely to be able to love since his orientation is a receptive one in which he expects others to love him regardless of his own behavior. Or, if the mother is cold and unresponsive and the father authoritarian, the child may later lack the ability for either giving or receiving unconditional love—always suspecting that there are strings attached to being loved.

Whether or not we agree with Fromm's formulation, it is of interest as a model for trying to understand the way in which early family patterns may influence our later approaches to love relationships. It seems a safe generalization that a minimally favorable emotional climate in childhood is usually necessary if the individual is to be able to give and receive love in later years. Yet love is a powerful force, and long-held patterns of self-doubt, cynicism, and of defensiveness may be dissipated by the experience of genuinely loving and being loved by another human being.

SUMMARY AND A LOOK AHEAD

We have seen in this chapter how an individual's constitutional make-up, his early training, the social climate in which he lives, and particularly his frame of reference all help to determine the pattern of emotional responses that he develops. Depending on these factors, his emotions may be deep or shallow, specific or general, and preponderantly positive or preponderantly negative. Similarly, his emotional expression may be balanced or uncontrolled, constructively channeled or suppressed, healthful or damaging. An individual's depth and range of feeling, characteristic balance of positive and negative feelings, and patterns of expression and control are a continuing and consistent part of his life style.

But although each of us develops a consistent emotional pattern, we need not remain the same today, tomorrow, and forever. If we find that our emotional patterns are immature and disruptive, we can take steps to improve them—not by fighting our emotions but by understanding and accepting them, learning to function with them and express them constructively, and accentuating those that are positive rather than negative. Overcoming faulty patterns may include catharsis or other forms of desensitization, gaining insight, and developing new, more appropriate patterns. Common "problem emotions" are fear, worry, and anxiety; anger and hostility; guilt, depression, and grief; and love.

In the last two chapters, we have examined the components of intellectual and emotional competence, faulty patterns that sometimes get in our way, and some of the things we can do to improve our intellectual and emotional resources. In the next chapter we shall be examining some of the same factors in relation to social competence.

Key terms used in this chapter include:

the affective dimension (p. 397)
mild, strong, and disintegrative emotions (p. 398)
constructive channeling vs. repression (p. 401)
direct vs. disguised expression (p. 401)
functioning with vs. fighting emotions (p. 402)
fostering constructive emotions (pp. 402-403)
working through emotional "weak spots" (pp. 404-405)
healthy vs. unhealthy love (p. 413)
love vs. infatuation (p. 415)

Chapter 15

SOCIAL COMPETENCE

Foundations of Good Interpersonal Relationships
Improving Social Competence

Man is a social creature, and his success in dealing with others greatly influences the course of his life and the satisfactions he experiences. An individual's success in attracting a desired mate, in establishing a happy marriage, in raising children, in achieving occupational advancement, and in making friends depends heavily upon his skill in dealing with other people. The electronics engineer who antagonizes his subordinates because he has never learned to offer criticism in a courteous and constructive way is handicapped professionally even though he may know a great deal about the intricacies of electronics. Many people become "unpopular," fail in their work, ruin their marriages, bring up maladjusted children, and go through life feeling alone and friendless because they are unable to establish satisfying relationships with others.

The political, social, economic, and technological complexities of the modern world have put a premium on the ability of very disparate peoples to understand and work with each other. Although in this chapter we shall confine our discussion to interpersonal relations, much of what we shall say applies also to relations between groups and nations.

FOUNDATIONS OF GOOD INTERPERSONAL RELATIONSHIPS

In spite of the importance of good human relations, most of the available literature on the subject has been in the form of popular books and articles which typically describe what the authors consider to be good interpersonal relationships and list techniques which anyone presumably can use to build effective relationships with others. Actually, of course, there are no simple techniques which can be applied effectively without a broad appreciation of the principles which appear to underlie interpersonal relations. For example, the technique of praising others, often mentioned in popular writings, may backfire if the praise is insincere or used primarily to make others more amenable to our own wishes. In this sense, popular approaches are often misleading, and many people who adopt them in order to win good will and affection are shocked to learn that they have, instead, reaped a harvest of dislike and hostility.

While acknowledging the dearth of scientific evidence in this area, we shall endeavor in the present chapter to utilize available findings from which general principles concerning good interpersonal relationships can be established. Then, in the context of this broader understanding, we shall note some of the specific ways in which social competence can be improved, assuming one's general values and attitudes are healthy.

Common goals of interpersonal relationships were briefly outlined in the last part of Chapter 9 in our introduction to the nature of interpersonal relationships in group settings. In assessing interpersonal relationships, two criteria appear of key significance: (1) the extent to which the relationship is achieving the goals for which it was established (in a marriage, for example, meeting the partner's needs for love, approval, and relatedness), and (2) the extent to which the relationship is contributing to or interfering with the well-being and personal growth of the persons involved. When the relationship achieves its goals and contributes to well-being and growth, we may think of it as a good or healthy relationship; when it either does not achieve its goals or interferes with well-being and personal growth—or both—we may describe it as a faulty or unhealthy relationship. Social competence, then, is ability to meet these criteria in one's interpersonal relationships.

Recognition of Mutual Purposes, Rights, and Responsibilities

Psychologists have looked with disfavor upon most popular writing about social skills not only because it tends to oversimplify the problem of good interpersonal relations but also because it typically has a "sales" approach. The emphasis in such works is usually on influencing and sometimes even exploiting others without adequate regard for their own purposes, needs, and rights.

Respect for autonomy and rights of others. A first basic principle in good interpersonal relationships is that of respect for the autonomy and rights of the other person. All relationships are *inter*relationships: they involve mutual interactions. As other people

set the atmosphere of our daily life, so we help to set the atmosphere of theirs. Their approval or disapproval affects us; our approval or disapproval, in turn, affects them. People with whom we have close contact are part of our lives, and we are part of theirs—for better or worse.

This recognition of every man's dependence upon his fellow human beings finds expression in the age-old guide to good human relations: Do unto others as you would have them do unto you. The honesty, concern, and respect implied by the golden rule are necessary not only from a moral standpoint but from a practical one. Lying, deceit, and other evidences of a lack of concern for the rights of others almost inevitably destroys any common ground for mutually satisfying give-and-take.

The golden rule implies more, however, than simply refraining from doing harm to others. Perhaps the Biblical injunction, "love thy neighbor as thyself," gives better expression to the concept, suggesting the need for an attitude of positive care and concern for the needs and rights of others. Mere adherence to the "rules" and a pseudointerest in other people rarely hide an essential indifference toward their well-being.

In general, an attitude of positive concern seems to be most readily established in the context of a democratic approach—an approach which recognizes the right of the other person to autonomy and individuality. The other person must be granted "life space." This does not mean that we must accept his beliefs or values but rather that we acknowledge his right to his own convictions while maintaining the same right for ourselves.

I-Thou vs. I-It relationships. Whereas objects constitute a necessary and important part of our world, we merely manipulate, control, and use them for our convenience. Our transactions with them represent what Buber (1958) has called the *I-It* relationships in our lives. Some people, however, regard other individuals in essentially the same way—as objects or dehumanized things to be manipulated and used. But another person is a "thou," a presence, a person, a dignity and integrity to be respected. A meaningful encounter with another human being is an *I-Thou* relation, not an *I-It* relation.

In our fast-moving, utilitarian, time-pressured society, it is all too easy to establish *I-It* relationships with both the people and the things in our world. To do so, however, is to cut ourselves off from the chance for establishing rich, meaningful, and authentic relationships with other human beings.

Commonality of purpose. Each individual tries to meet certain needs through his relationships with others—perhaps for love and affection, social approval, feelings of self-worth, increased adequacy in attaining certain goals, or simply feeling related to others. Where the relationship tends to meet one person's needs but fails to meet the needs of the other person, it becomes difficult to maintain. Thus even the most generous and devoted friend may become tired of a relationship in which, literally or figuratively, he is continually forced to lend money which is never repaid.

For a relationship to meet the needs of both parties, there needs to be a commonality of purpose. The importance of such shared purposes in establishing mutually satisfying relationships and the harmful effect of a lack of such commonality can be illustrated in many ways. In time of war, common purposes unite nations in alliances, but after the war is over, differences in purposes tend to emerge, and conflicts result. In our highly competitive society, the matter of conflicting purposes is readily apparent in business transactions which are profitable to one party but not to the other and in political activities, advertising, and sports. Labor-management disputes often arise over the seemingly incompatible needs and purposes of the two groups. Many common personal and family problems center around conflicting purposes: parents may want their sons and daughters to remain under their domination even after they reach young adulthood;

a girl may want to get married while her boy friend does not; a married couple may find themselves disapproving of each other's priorities.

Cantril (1950) has pointed to the importance of common purposes in loyalties and friendships:

"Loyalties are mutual in so far as our activity in carrying out our purposes helps other people carry out their purposes. We have no loyalty to a person, a group, a symbol, or an inanimate object that does not in some way help us to act effectively. Hence in peacetime people in many democratic countries have less feeling of loyalty to their 'country' than they do during war times, since in times of peace there are not so many clear-cut common purposes to be furthered by action.

"Friendship involves a high degree of mutual aid in carrying out the purposes of each party. Gibran wrote, 'Your friend is your needs answered.' If friendship is to prove enduring, it must provide for mutual development, mutual and independent experiences of . . . value. Friendships of our early childhood, our school days, our army life, or those we make during a vacation or a long steamer voyage so often prove transient because the purposes that brought us together at the time have dissolved with the changing situation. We no longer need each other." (pp. 112-113)

Commonality of purpose appears to be a basic essential for establishing and maintaining deep and lasting interpersonal relationships.

Reciprocal responsibility. Wolman (1965) has suggested that in interpersonal interactions an individual attempts to form one of three kinds of relationships: (1) *receiving relationships,* in which he does most of the receiving and the other most of the giving—normal in the infant-mother relationship but not in most other relationships; (2) *giving relationships,* in which his objective is to give rather than to receive—as illustrated in parenthood or priesthood; and (3) *mutual relationships,* in which the individuals attempt to satisfy each other's needs—as in friendship and marriage. In the present context we are concerned primarily with the latter.

In recognizing that the relationship that we establish with another person is a reciprocal affair and that we both are partly responsible for whatever satisfactions or dissatisfactions we derive from it, it becomes apparent that both parties must contribute to the relationship if it is to prove mutually satisfying. This is particularly true of intimate relationships such as those with parents, mates, and friends.

Often faulty interpersonal relationships result from a marked discrepancy in the amounts of effort or emotional investment contributed by the parties involved. In a marriage, for example, the structuring may be such that one person is indifferent and preoccupied with other concerns while the other puts in 90 per cent of the effort necessary to keep the marriage going. A friendship may develop in such a way that one person must always take the initiative in maintaining it. Where such discrepancies exist, the individual putting in most of the effort usually comes to feel somewhat devaluated, resentful, and hostile, even though he may not express his feelings to the other person.

Although a relationship may undergo crises in which one person may need to put in disproportionate effort to maintain it, some reasonable balance or reciprocity of responsibility appears to be required under normal circumstances if the relationship is to be a durable and mutually satisfying one. In general, mutual need gratification appears to require mutual responsibility and commitment to the relationship. Such reciprocal responsibility and commitment, of course, are fostered by commonality of interests.

A Realistic View of Self and Others

The accuracy of our view of ourselves and others has a great deal to do with the type of interpersonal relationships we are able to establish.

A realistic view of self. Often we have an inaccurate view of our own "stimulus value" of how others see us. We may see ourselves as generous, while others view our alleged generosity as an attempt to be a "big shot" or as a means of getting others indebted to us; we may view ourselves as brilliant and witty conversationalists, while others think we talk incessantly about trivial things; we may view ourselves as highly endowed with leadership qualities, while others view us as bossy and domineering. We may tend to be hostile, overly competitive, pompous, suspicious, demanding, self-centered, or overly dependent on others without realizing what we are doing.

Because we are often unaware of our negative stimulus value to others, we may be quite bewildered by their lack of appreciation of our merits and abilities, by their lack of approval and acceptance, and by the continuous friction we experience in dealing with them. We do not always recognize that the way others react to us is in part a consequence of how we have acted toward them and how they see us.

Each of us can be characterized by a given *interpersonal style* (Ring, Braginsky, & Braginsky, 1966). For example, some individuals are characteristically poised and adept in their interpersonal relations, while others are painfully lacking in adeptness; some are prone to be trusting and warm in their relations, while others are prone to be suspicious and to "play it cool." Although we all are likely to relate to different people in somewhat different ways, it does appear useful to try to be aware of our characteristic interpersonal style and the motives, values, and skills that it represents.

Understanding our motives in seeking a relationship is especially important. Do we seek relationships in which we can dominate? Or do we try to overcome our feelings of social inadequacy by attaching ourselves to people who are skillful in social situations? Obviously, such motives offer little possibility for building sound relationships. But once we acknowledge them, it is often possible to work out new ways of satisfying our

SELF-EVALUATION AND SOCIAL COMPETENCE

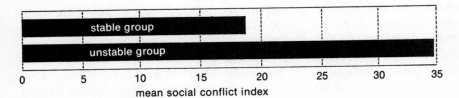

mean social conflict index

Although a person's self-concept cannot be observed directly, a number of studies have demonstrated its far-reaching influence on subjects' perceptions, defenses, and methods of attacking problems. In one such study subjects classified as "stable" or "unstable" (on the Guilford-Martin *Inventory of Factors GAMIN*) were asked to rate themselves on a list of traits in four different ways: as they thought they were, as they hoped they were, as they feared they were, and as they thought others regarded them. The stable group rated themselves more highly than the unstable group did, and, as the above graph shows, had a lower score on the social conflict index—that is, there was less discrepancy between their self-ratings and the way they thought others would rate them. They were also better liked, better adjusted socially, less situation-dominated, and showed less defensive behavior (Brownfain, 1952).

---

own needs and at the same time meeting others' needs.

A clear self-identity is necessary for maintaining coherent inner standards in different social settings—sometimes called *autonomy*. Where the individual lacks autonomy, it is difficult for others to establish a meaningful, consistent, and mutually satisfactory relationship with him.

An accurate perception of others. An accurate view of others is equally important for good relations with them. If we tend to view people as generally egocentric, selfish, and prone to dishonesty, we will establish a different type of relationship with them from what we will establish if we view them as generally honest, kind, and eager to do the right thing.

Of course we make distinctions among individuals we know, but our basic view of human nature leads to characteristic expectations of people in general. Some of us are generally suspicious and wary in our encounters with others and try to prevent them from getting too close to us. Some of us tend to take an opposite approach and are too optimistic and too trusting. Different attitudes toward proposed programs for helping the underprivileged or socially disadvantaged often reflect differences in people's basic views of human nature.

A common source of error in our perceptions of others is the "halo effect": when we know a person to be superior in some important respect, we may tend to put a halo over his head and through a process of generalization overrate his virtuous qualities in other respects. For example, if he is in a high-power position, we may assume that he must have good judgment, a high level of intelligence, and so on. We make similar generalizations from unfavorable judgments: if a person's hair style or speech bothers us, we may assume that he has nothing worth while to say.

Another person is both an *object*—a psychobiological organism whose overt transactions with his environment we can often observe—and a *subject*—another center of conscious experiencing. Thus accurate perception of another person includes perception of both these aspects. Perception of the "inner" aspect is called *empathy*. In a broad sense, empathy involves sufficient understanding of his feelings, attitudes, motives, and general frame of reference to see a situation from his point of view and enter into his feelings about it. Apparently, it involves *apprehending* as well as *comprehending*. In an intimate relationship, for example, empathy means that we are aware of and to some extent share in the desires, hopes, expectations, and worries of the other person and that we know what he hopes to gain from the relationship and what satisfactions he is actually receiving.

Autonomy and empathy appear to be closely related concepts in that uncertainty about either oneself or others is likely to lead to interpersonal difficulties, while a high level of both autonomy and empathy—at least in the context of desirable motives and values —is likely to facilitate good interpersonal relationships.

Adequate Structure and Communication

As the term suggests, "structuring" an interpersonal relationship means giving it shape or form—defining it in terms of limits, responsibilities, and roles. For a relationship to be successful, the individual needs to know what is expected of him and, in turn, to make it clear what he expects of the other person. Where such expectations are not mutually satisfactory, some accommodation must be made if the relationship is to continue without undue misunderstandings and conflicts.

The importance of adequate structuring. In many cases, structuring is inherent in a situation—for example, there is general agreement in our culture about the type of relationship that is appropriate between teacher and student, employer and employee, lieutenant and private, bishop and parish priest. But in most of our more personal relationships—such as those involving husband and wife, parent and child, or friend and friend—the structuring must be determined by the parties involved. Realizing this fact is important for building good interpersonal relationships, since all relationships *do* become structured with time, whether or not the individuals take

any active measures to ensure their development in a particular direction.

To take a simple example, we may examine the behavior of a young couple who are dating. Unless they take active measures to structure the situation in terms of permissible limits of affection, of behavior with others, of mutual effort in maintaining their relationship, of courtesy and honesty in dealing with each other, such limits will eventually become established simply by what actually takes place—whether or not these limits are satisfactory for the individuals involved. Once certain patterns have been established, it becomes increasingly difficult to change the structuring. For example, the girl who has permitted sexual intimacies will find it much more difficult to limit such behavior thereafter than if she had structured the affectional limits differently in the first place.

Unfortunately, structuring is sometimes predetermined by the existence of certain emotional limitations. A person may habitually establish competitive relationships, no matter how inappropriate they may be in some situations, as in marriage. Or he may always be cooperative, so that he is unable to say "no" even when it needs saying. When a person can see in retrospect that he has tried to carry over a type of relationship from one situation, in which it is appropriate, to another, in which it is inappropriate, he can begin to avoid making the same mistake by evaluating new situations in advance, thereby maintaining some control over the structuring.

Many of us are rather naïve in the matter of structuring interpersonal relationships in ways that are appropriate to the situation and person. Often we unwittingly encourage others to be overly familiar or to take advantage of us—and then blame *them* for an unsatisfactory relationship that has been largely of our own making. It is always important to examine in advance the type of relationship that is desirable—whether between employer and employee, executive and secretary, husband and wife, father and daughter, or friend and friend—and to take active measures to establish and maintain the relationship in the form we consider appropriate.

Verbal and nonverbal communication. When lines of communication are open between individuals, each can try to understand the attitudes, point of view, and feelings of the other person. When lines of communication are closed or when communications are misunderstood, there is apt to be conflict. Even in old friendships or established marriages, misunderstandings resulting from inadequate communication can cause serious trouble.

One common communication difficulty stems from our tendency to think of communication solely on cognitive and verbal levels—in terms of ideas and words. Actually, one crucial aspect of communication —and of good interpersonal relationships— is the understanding of *feeling.* The distinction between cognitive and affective elements in communication has been well summarized by Martineau (1957):

"Superficially we think that words are the only form of communication, because we live in such a highly verbal atmosphere. Yet in actuality there is a far greater amount of nonverbal communication going on all the time through the use of other symbols than words. . . . Besides expressing logical thought, our words and our actions are also indicative of the emotions, attitudes, moods, and intention of the speaker. Whenever we speak, we are offering two different kinds of clues. One is manifested by the thought content. The other is at the level where intuition operates, where the speaker conveys his feelings, his intentions, his motives." (pp. 133, 139-140)

There are many situations when we are called upon to answer feelings rather than spoken words; when we fail to perceive these feelings, we may say and do things which fail to support or perhaps unnecessarily hurt and anger the other person. For example, an anxious person asking for information about a problem may actually be more in search of reassurance than facts. Similarly,

we often find it difficult to communicate our *own* feelings adequately. Many of us have learned during early childhood to conceal our fear and anger and even our love; we tend to be embarrassed by emotion or even ashamed of it and to feel we must do or say that which is socially expedient or expected of us.

Child psychologists maintain that children are quite sensitive to the feelings of other people and that they can sense irritation, love, and fear even before they can understand any spoken words. Some adults seem to retain this childhood skill of sensing the feeling behind the words of others and show a great deal of intuition and understanding in dealing with people. Too many of us, however, put our emphasis on the literal meaning of words and tend to take verbal communications at face value.

Differing frames of reference as a source of difficulty. Another common difficulty in communication as well as in structuring situations stems from differences in frames of reference.

If an engaged couple have different views concerning appropriate sexual behavior prior to marriage or even after marriage, the discrepancy is likely to create a problem until some accommodation is worked out which is mutually satisfactory. Similarly, it would be difficult for a Pigmy from the jungles of equatorial Africa to communicate efficiently with a businessman from the United States, since their backgrounds of knowledge and experience are so different. In much the same way, it is often difficult for labor and management to understand each other's point of view, or for a lower-class husband to understand his middle-class wife's reactions; although they seem to be talking about the same problem, they often fail to "communicate." The more divergent the frames of reference of the parties involved, the more likely the message is to be misunderstood. Conversely, commonality of assumptions, values, and motives tends to make people both more able to communicate clearly and more eager to do so.

DIFFICULTIES IN COMMUNICATION

We communicate to other people through all our behavior, not just through spoken or written words. And our actions, even more than our words, are apt to be misunderstood by people whose frame of reference is different from our own. This chart, for example, shows how behavior prompted by one set of assumptions (Norm A) might be interpreted by a person with a different set of assumptions (Norm B).

BEHAVIOR	NORM A	COMMUNI-CATION	NORM B	COMMUNI-CATION
Being "cruel" to animals	Animals are like other forms of material property.	A man who treats animals harshly does not consider them to be very valuable.	Animals are like humans in being sensitive to pain.	A man who is cruel to animals is indifferent to others' pain and probably abuses his own children.
Allowing "junk" to accumulate in front yard	A man's front yard is his castle; it reflects his interests, not his class position.	A man in whose front yard many things accumulate is interested in many things.	A tidy front yard is a mark of respectability.	A man whose front yard is untidy is contemptuous of middle-class virtues.
Collecting rare books	Rare books are matters of good taste as well as a good investment	A man who collects rare books is more interested in enduring satisfactions than in fleeting pleasures.	Rare books are marks of over-refinement.	A man who collects rare books is probably neglecting more practical things.

We can facilitate accurate communication—and hence increase the likelihood of being able to maintain good interpersonal relationships—by remembering that all our actions "say something" to other people and by trying to be aware of what message they are "receiving" from our dress, speech, mannerisms, and other behavior. If this is not the message we are intending to send, and if we care about our true message being received and understood, we may need to code it in ways more familiar to our hearers, even if less comfortable for us.

Chart adapted from Newcomb, 1950.

Factors in Satisfactory Interpersonal Accommodation

As we noted in Chapter 9, interpersonal accommodation is the process by which the partners in a relationship evolve patterns of interaction which permit mutual need satisfaction. Unless they can achieve an adequate accommodation, their relationship is likely to prove unsatisfactory and eventually to disrupt.

Basic processes of accommodation. Accommodation means changing or giving of oneself in response to an adjustive demand. In any continuing interpersonal relationship, both individuals usually need to do some accommodating. As Kelley (1968) has pointed out, this process may involve one-sided compromise and concession or, more often, an exchange of some kind. In fact, through barter, compromise, and concession, there may be a continuing structuring and restructuring of the relationship as the partners attempt to deal with their problems in ways that satisfy them both.

The basic type of interdependence in the relationship helps to determine what pattern of accommodation will emerge. In a relationship in which one person is in authority and the other is a subordinate, there is likely to be a disproportionate giving in on the part of the subordinate, but even in more equalitarian relationships, like a marriage, one partner may have to make most of the compromises if the marriage is to continue. Usually, however, there is some barter and alternation of concessions. One spouse gives in on some occasions, the other at other times. Sometimes one spouse will exact a concession from the other before making one himself. In some instances, a spouse considers it good strategy to make many small concessions and ostentatiously give in on small issues in order to win a concession on one that he considers more important.

Although barter and compromise appear basic means of interpersonal accommodation, other patterns may also be involved. For example, the marriage partner who does not like his in-laws may simply have to learn to accept them as part of the total marriage package; a wife who dislikes her husband's occupation because it keeps him away from home a great deal but realizes that she cannot expect him to make a change accommodates her own attitudes and activities to the realities of the situation.

Accommodation may also involve escape patterns, in which certain problems—such as those centering around sexual relations—are denied and not talked about. Sometimes accommodation is achieved by minimizing one's investment in the relationship and focusing on other life activities, as when the husband is absorbed in his work and the wife devotes her time and thought to the children. Accommodation may also be achieved through mediation, as when the marital partners go to a counselor for assistance in working out their problems.

Conflicting, congruent, and complementary patterns of accommodation. In a study of two-man teams working together in close coordination, Haythorn and Altman (1967) identified three patterns of accommodation:

1. *Competitive or conflicting*—in which both partners could not be satisfied, as when both sought to dominate.

2. *Congruent*—in which the partners had similar needs and purposes, which could be satisfied through their relationship and through joint achievement of the task.

3. *Complementary*—in which the needs of the individuals were different but could be mutually satisfied in the same situation, as when one liked to be dominant and the other dependent.

Although these patterns were identified in men working in isolated settings, such as spacecraft or remote military installations, they also appear applicable to an understanding of patterns of accommodation in marriage and other intimate relationships. And although a competitive or conflicting style of accommodation may appear to predominate, there are likely to be some congruent and complementary elements involved also if the marriage continues.

Haythorn and Altman also found that compatibility and coordination of team members could be strongly affected by personality characteristics. For example, men characterized by egocentric qualities—such as dominance (wanting to control others) and dogmatism (thinking that their opinions and ideas were the only important ones) tended to antagonize their partners and to establish conflictive relationships which impaired team coordination. On the other hand, men with a high need for affiliation appeared to satisfy themselves by satisfying others and tended to establish close and friendly relationships. Similarly, two men with a strong need to achieve would tend to work closely and enthusiastically in the pursuit of their mutual goals.

Interestingly, these investigators did not recommend avoidance of all conflict in space capsules, Antarctic stations, and sea labs; rather, they considered some conflict necessary to enliven an existence of otherwise deadly and crippling monotony and concluded that such conflict could enhance performance. However, they recommended that research be undertaken to ascertain what types and degrees of conflict could be expected to be constructive. This information would be useful also in regard to other close relationships in more usual circumstances.

IMPROVING SOCIAL COMPETENCE

Having examined some of the key factors that determine the nature of interpersonal relationships, we are now ready to consider ways of improving our social competence. As will become apparent, these are essentially applications of the general principles we have already discussed. It should be re-emphasized that social skills are of little use and can be self-defeating unless they are grounded in attitudes of respect and concern for the people with whom we are dealing.

In reviewing ways of improving interpersonal competence, it is also useful to note that three classes of variables influence an interaction between two people: (1) the characteristics of person one, (2) the characteristics of person two, and (3) the characteristics of the setting—physical and social—in which the interaction takes place. Thus the effects of one person's maturity or immaturity, skill or ineptness, always depends partly on the other person involved and on the setting in which they are interacting.

Helping to Meet the Needs of Others

Since people enter interpersonal relationships with certain needs or purposes that they hope to fulfill, the greater the extent to which we help another person to meet these needs, the more likely is his relationship with us to be durable and satisfactory—at least from his standpoint.

When we understand another's need for reassurance, for affection, for feeling important, for being accepted, or for personal growth, we can usually help him satisfy his need without in any way jeopardizing our own needs. Several approaches may be emphasized here.

Helping the other person feel accepted and approved. It is usually pleasant to be around people who obviously like and accept us. Their attitude raises our self-esteem and helps us to feel secure and relaxed with them. On the other hand, people who are hyper-critical of us or who accept us with obvious reservations tend to make us defensive and ill at ease.

Rogers (1961, 1964) has emphasized the crucial importance of "unconditional positive regard" for the other person in healthy interpersonal relationships. This means that we take an attitude of acceptance and respect for the other person as a unique individual. In essence, we respect him for what he is just as we learn to respect ourselves for what we are. Such an attitude enables the other person to feel comfortable in his relationship with us, to lower his defenses, and to express his thoughts and feelings without fear

FACTORS IN INTERPERSONAL ATTRACTIVENESS

In an interesting study, subjects were led to believe: (1) that a person with whom they had interacted either liked or disliked them, and (2) that the person's attitudes on several social issues were either similar or dissimilar to their own attitudes. The subjects' subsequent ratings of the person's attractiveness were then analyzed with reference to these variables.

It was found that if a subject thought the person liked him, he found the person attractive even though they held dissimilar views; on the other hand, if a subject thought the person disliked him, he found the person unattractive even though they held similar views. Interpersonal attractiveness is evidently more affected by evidence that one is liked than by evidence of similarity of attitudes. These findings also indicate that under certain conditions, people can tolerate and even like others who hold contrary opinions and attitudes regarding controversial issues (Aronson & Worchel, 1966).

of being rejected. When such an attitude is mutual, both parties are able to communicate more easily about problems in their relationship and to be more objective in their approach to resolving them.

When we examine our own reactions to various people, we can see more clearly how we have contributed to the success or failure of our relationships with them by making them feel more or less accepted, approved, and adequate. We may tend to be highly competitive in our relationship with others, trying to prove our own adequacy and superiority at the expense of undermining theirs. We may be more quick to judge and criticize than to understand and help. We may express our own views in a dogmatic way that seems to defy contradiction and makes the other person feel that we consider his views of no importance. We may be too proud to admit mistakes or to apologize to others when an apology is indicated. And, of course, racial or other prejudice may lead to attitudes of rejection which tend to elicit defensive behavior from others as well as friction and misunderstanding.

Approving of the other person while disapproving of what he does. Accepting and approving of a *person* does not mean that one accepts and approves of everything he *does* or *says*. In dealing with both children and adults, it is often necessary to make a clear-cut distinction between one's attitude toward the person and one's attitude toward his behavior.

For instance, if a child steals something, it is likely to do much more harm than good to call him a thief and reject him. It is far better to make it clear to the child that he is loved as a person but that his behavior has been wrong and presents a problem that must be worked out. This makes it unnecessary for the child to withdraw or become hostile and defensive in his attitude; it enables him to feel that he is worthy of love and to look at his behavior objectively as something that he himself will benefit from changing in a particular way.

In dealing with adults, too, it is often necessary to make clear that one's disapproval of their attitudes or behavior does not include rejection of them as persons. The adult, even more than the child, is often so ego-involved in his views and behavior that any criticism is interpreted as a threat to his worth. By making it clear that we disapprove of his attitude or behavior but not of him as a person, we are better able to express disagreement and discuss his behavior or attitudes in an objective manner without unnecessarily arousing his defenses.

In this context it is of interest to note Rogers' (1967) findings with respect to the intensive group experience as discussed in Chapter 12. When both positive and negative feelings can be expressed in an atmosphere of trust and mutual acceptance, interpersonal relationships tend to become closer and more positive in nature. As one group member expressed the situation after a workshop, ". . . it would have to do with what I call confirmation—a kind of confirmation of myself, of the uniqueness and universal qualities of men, a confirmation that when we can be human together something positive can emerge." (p. 271)

Expressing praise and appreciation. We can probably all remember how proud we felt as children when our parents praised our efforts and accomplishments; most of us have a continued need for evidence of others' approval and appreciation of us. In adult life our accomplishments are, unfortunately, usually taken for granted unless they are very outstanding. The breadwinner, the homemaker, and the oldster who still tries to do his bit too often have to scratch for acknowledgment of their efforts. As a result, many of us do not receive the praise and appreciation we need for bolstering our self-esteem, sense of adequacy, and need for approval. This is particularly unfortunate because it has repeatedly been shown in experimental studies that praise usually motivates us toward increased effort and tends to bring out warm, positive feelings toward others.

Actually, sincere praise and appreciation should be easy to bestow, for everyone has traits that merit praise, such as generosity, neatness, conscientiousness, a sense of humor, or an ability to cook. Often, too, we can pass on to the individual the compliments others have paid him. Most people find that the quality of the interpersonal relationships improves when they develop a habit of deliberately giving credit where credit is due, verbally and with overt recognition—not just by refusing to detract from another's good points.

It is important, of course, to make a clear-cut distinction between honest praise and insincere flattery designed to exploit the other person. Although some people suffer from such marked inferiority feelings that they grasp at flattery as a drowning man might grasp at a straw, most of us sooner or later recognize insincere flattery for what it is and come to distrust and dislike the person giving it.

Learning how to give criticism. Although there are times when it is necessary to be critical and "tough," it is usually better to temper the hurt of criticism by pointing out the individual's strong points first, thus putting him in a more receptive frame of mind. If an employee must be reprimanded for talking too much on the job, he is more likely to respond in a constructive way if it is first pointed out to him that his contributions to the company are greatly appreciated and that he is considered to be a good worker and valued member of the organization. The wife who must criticize her husband for being untidy around the house will get a much more favorable hearing if she makes it clear that she appreciates his thoughtfulness in other respects. Such an approach avoids making the individual feel that he is being criticized for minor faults while his more important positive contributions are unappreciated.

Criticism may do great harm to a relationship when it is vindictive or spiteful. Even if it is intended to be helpful, criticism never serves a useful purpose when it harks back to old mistakes which are beyond correction and would better be forgotten. Yet as the Overstreets (1956) have pointed out:

"Wherever we turn in today's world, it seems, we find human beings who look guardedly or vengefully at one another across barriers of old mistakes: mistakes that have never been openly acknowledged and that are still, in many cases, being defended; mistakes that, even where an effort has been made to straighten things out, have never been forgiven—much less forgotten." (p. 104)

Usually it is much more helpful to try to understand *how* and *why* a mistake occurred than *who* made it. When a person is repeatedly confronted with an error of the past, any regret he may have felt over the incident will gradually turn into defensiveness and resentment.

Criticisms made publicly also tend to force the person into face-saving and retaliatory behavior. The husband or wife who criticizes his spouse—or his children—in front of friends seldom accomplishes any constructive purpose. Besides showing an insensitivity for the feelings of the person being criticized, public criticism is also embarrassing to the outsiders who happen to be present. Thus it may harm not one relationship but several.

Giving the other person a good reputation to live up to. Most of us attempt to live up to the reputations or roles that other people create for us. This principle is used in the armed forces when the soldier is given a medal for his bravery in action. He now has the reputation of a brave man to live up to, and he becomes a model for others.

In all areas of life, "tags" usually stick to the people who acquire them, in spite of the fact that such labels may not have been too accurate in the first place; somehow or other we tend to become what other people say we are. Unfortunately, this tendency holds true whether the reputation is a good one or a bad one. The child whose mother takes every opportunity to point out his bad behavior and to tell him that he is incorrigible will probably behave accordingly. The husband or wife who receives nothing but nagging criticism may give up trying to be a good mate and increasingly come to warrant the criticisms that have been made. On the other hand, the employee who knows he is regarded as a resourceful, imaginative worker will try hard to live up to this picture.

In deliberately creating a good role for another person, it is necessary, of course, that it be a generally realistic one—one that he can live up to. And continual reinforcement is required until the role becomes an habitual part of that individual's self-perception and behavior. For example, the husband who wants his wife to become a better cook can take the first opportunity that arises to compliment her on her cooking, as when she does a better job than usual or successfully tries a new recipe. If she responds to this encouragement and tries again, he further compliments and encourages her. Chances are, if this continues, she will actually become the fine cook he has made her see herself.

It is unfortunate that we so often try to make changes in the behavior of others by nagging criticism and self-righteous demands which make them so defensive that it is all but impossible for them to attack their problem objectively. It is in helping people become more adequate and secure, rather, that we enable them to grow and improve. A person who constantly feels threatened can hardly approach his shortcomings in a task-oriented way.

Maintaining One's Own Integrity

When social skills are emphasized, we often get the mistaken impression that the goal is simply to avoid friction and to get along with other people at all costs. While it is essential to be sensitive to the needs of others, it is equally essential to maintain one's personal integrity—to have the courage to disagree and take a clear stand when one believes others are wrong. Although tact is an important ingredient in building and maintaining friendships, personal integrity is probably the most essential ingredient of all; for only as an individual is an authentic person and not a "phony," can he relate to others in truthful, valid, and meaningful ways.

Taking a stand when it is indicated. To win the respect of others—and to maintain our own self-respect—we must stand up for what we believe whenever an important issue is at stake, even though our position may elicit antagonism from those who feel we are endangering their purposes. The old saying that one is known for one's enemies as well as one's friends is relevant here. There is a story that when Confucius was asked the question, "If you are a really good person, will everyone like you?" he replied, "No, the good people in the community will like you, but the bad people will dislike you." The hostility we sometimes engender when we stand up for our beliefs need not be devaluating or anxiety-arousing for us if we are prepared for it and if we have faith in our own position. The mature adult does not expect everyone to love and appreciate him, nor does he need universal approval in order to feel adequate as a person.

Everyone distrusts the person who tries to be all things to all men. There is truth in the statement that only one's good friends will tell one the truth even if it hurts. Others may be so intent on maintaining cordial relationships that even in the face of direct questions they will be evasive or even deceitful rather than say anything that might endanger the relationship. Truthfulness with one's friends implies a confidence in *their* integrity as well as one's own—a faith in their ability to look at all the facts objectively and face their problems realistically. As Combs and Snygg (1959, p. 322) have summarized it, such an approach says, in effect, "I am a person of dignity and integrity. I believe you are too. I have no need to attack you nor will I permit you to attack me."

Learning when and how to say "no." For many people, one of the most difficult things in the world is to say "no." We often buy things we don't want, attend social functions that don't interest us, accept responsibilities in social groups we dislike, and otherwise get into difficulties in our personal relationships by our inability to say "no" at the right time. Not infrequently we become angry or resentful because we feel other people are imposing on us or taking advantage of our good nature, but in looking back, we can usually see that we have been partly at fault; if we had said "no" earlier, the entire matter could have been avoided.

Our difficulty in saying "no" apparently stems from our underlying fear of disapproval and hostility from others. We are often so eager to make everyone like us that we become too susceptible to social pressure. Sometimes, too, we find it hard to say "no" because we put ourselves in the other fellow's position and feel sorry for him.

As we become more mature in our social relations, we gradually come to realize that most people respect a firm negative answer more than a grudging consent. Furthermore, we have a right and a need to protect ourselves against excessive demands. The time to take a stand is at the moment when it becomes apparent that we are getting into something in which we don't want to become involved. A courteous but emphatic "no" at the right time—whether in dealing with salesmen or overly aggressive dates—is essential to avoid involvement in situations that may become more difficult to deal with as they progress.

When we have to say "no" to someone, we can often temper our refusal by suggesting some acceptable alternative. In turning down an invitation, a person may make it clear that he would be happy to accept one at a later time. In refusing to take the chairmanship of a fund drive, he may volunteer to help out in some other capacity. The graduate assistant who marks the papers for a college course may tell a student that he doesn't feel justified in raising the student's test grade but offer to refer the problem to the course instructor. Sometimes, of course, there are no reasonable alternatives—for example, some of the many demands on our time and pocketbooks must simply be met with a courteous but unequivocal "no." But in dealing with friends and loved ones, it is usually possible to temper negative responses and thus eliminate or minimize the arousal of hostility.

Being Sensitive to the Requirements of the Situation

Social expectations range from the fundamentals of good manners to highly complex role requirements; many customs and requirements are peculiar to a particular ethnic or religious group, age bracket, sex, or social class. To meet the varied expectations of different people in different situations requires both a knowledge of social customs and an ability to sense what is appropriate.

Sensitivity to the requirements of a situation is basic to social competence. By knowing what is expected of him, the individual is freed of much self-consciousness and fear of doing the wrong thing. And by knowing what to expect of others, he is in a position to understand and give consideration to their feelings.

Respecting social conventions. The argument is often raised that it is more important to be oneself than to worry about good manners. While it is certainly true that strict adherence to the rules of etiquette can never substitute for personal integrity or a genuine concern for others, it is equally true that a disregard for social conventions is more often a sign of self-centeredness than an expression of real integrity and independence. Good manners are merely agreed-upon forms for showing other people that we respect them and do not wish to hurt their feelings. A boy may consider it foolish to open the car door for his perfectly healthy date; but his failure to do so, if the girl expects it, says in effect, "Your feelings are of no concern to me."

While formality and propriety can certainly be overdone, there are few things as unattractive as the sight of the unmannered person—whether a child or an adult—in the act of "being himself" with complete lack of concern for the feelings and needs of others. Somehow many of us are reluctant to see how easily other people can be hurt by remarks that we intend as simply frank and candid. Especially with the current emphasis on being in touch with one's real feelings, there is often a tendency to be so preoccupied with trying to be spontaneous and honest that the expectations and sensibilities of the other person are overlooked.

It is especially important to develop a feeling for what is appropriate in a given situation, whether there are any social rules to cover it or not. On a simple level this can mean knowing what kinds of jokes will be well received in different situations. On a more complex level it may mean knowing how to conduct oneself when involved in an automobile accident. Although some people seem to have an innate sense of the appropriate, their ability is less likely a "gift" than the result of experience and training.

Understanding role requirements. Sensitivity to the requirements of one's social role is also important to good interpersonal relationships; people will inevitably feel uneasy and at odds with the minister who acts like a playboy, the teacher who acts like a juvenile delinquent, or the 60-year-old woman who tries to dress and act like a flirtatious girl of 17. When someone does not conform within reasonable limits to the expectations for his role, other people find his behavior confusing and become uncertain about how to behave in return. A lack of structuring—or highly unconventional structuring—makes everyone feel insecure. For example, an employer who insisted on telling his employees about his marital problems, his worries about the business, and his fears of becoming an alcoholic would be creating almost insurmountable problems in interpersonal relations and in morale. He would not be playing a role to which his employees could comfortably relate—or which would enable them to feel secure in their jobs.

Social competence also requires considerable flexibility in role playing since, as we have previously noted, each of us is called upon to play a variety of roles each day in order to maintain successful relationships in our homes, our occupations, and our various social groupings. The individual who is unable to shift roles as the occasion warrants is likely to make other people uncomfortable or even hostile. This does not mean, of course, that we should be puppets who are manipulated by the strings of social expectation. Success in role playing, like social competence in general, depends upon the individual's having a basic integrity and an understanding of both the value and the limitations of social conventions.

Learning to Communicate More Effectively

We have dealt with communication in Chapter 9 as well as earlier in the present chapter. Here we may simply re-emphasize the importance of good communication—of the accurate expression of thoughts and feelings —in close interpersonal relationships. Inability to communicate effectively about common tasks and problems almost inevitably leads to difficulties in interpersonal relationships.

Being a good sender and receiver. It is all too obvious that communication does not automatically take place whenever two people talk to—or at—each other. Everyone has had the experience of talking to a person who appeared to be thinking only of what *he* was going to say next. Here little real communication was going on. As one exasperated college girl said about her date: "He spent the entire evening talking about himself and ended up thinking he knew all about me." To build and maintain good interpersonal relationships, we must be as skilled at listening to and interpreting what other people say and feel as we are at expressing ourselves.

As a "sender," the individual has to know what he is trying to communicate and how to code the message in such a way that the receiver can interpret it accurately. If the sender is unclear about the message he is trying to convey or if he fails to code the message so that it is meaningful to the person he is communicating with, the message is not likely to be received accurately. The high incidence of failure here is evidenced by our frequent complaints, "I didn't mean that" and "You misunderstood what I was trying to say."

The expectations of both sender and receiver may also distort the communication. If the sender regards the receiver as stupid or biased, his expectation of being misinterpreted may get in the way of a calm, clear presentation of his own thoughts. Or, if he is viewed by the receiver as prone to exaggerating, as suspicious and hostile toward others, or as too weak to take a stand on any issue, his message may be discounted or misinterpreted accordingly, regardless of what he says. In talking with others we need to try to listen to what they are really saying—or trying to say—freeing ourselves as much as possible from preconceptions about what they will probably say or how valuable it will be.

Being sensitive to the feelings of others. As suggested earlier in this chapter, there are many situations in which we are called upon to answer feelings rather than spoken words. The person who is insensitive in this respect often unknowingly does or says things which hurt or anger other people; we characterize him by saying, "Every time he opens his mouth, he puts his foot in it." Although there

---

UNCOORDINATED COMMUNICATION

Below is an example of poor communication between a newly married couple, as reported by the marital counselor from whom they sought help (Rabkin, 1967):

> Wife: Would you like to go to the movies? (asked in an earnest, information-gathering voice)
> Husband: No.
>
> (Ten-minute pause)
>
> Wife: You never take me out! Why did you refuse to take me to the movies?
> Husband: But you never asked me.
> Wife: I never asked! I asked you ten minutes ago. You never listen to me. You don't care about me.
> Husband (to himself): She may be right. I don't remember her asking so I guess I really don't listen to her. Maybe I don't want to hear her.

COMMON SOURCES OF DIFFICULTY IN INTERPERSONAL RELATIONSHIPS

I-IT ORIENTATION

A tendency to regard other people as objects rather than as other feeling, striving beings. Inability to establish I-Thou relationships. Lack of empathy.

EGOCENTRICITY

A concern with one's own interests to the extent of being insensitive to the welfare and rights of others. The egocentric individual is incapable of establishing anything but the most superficial relationships.

MANIPULATION

A tendency, often accompanying egocentricity, to take an exploitative approach in interpersonal relationships, disregarding the needs and purposes of others. Commonly shows itself in the efforts of an "operator" to manipulate people and situations to his own advantage. Often involves deceit.

DECEITFULNESS

A tendency to take advantage of others through deception or duplicity. May involve outright lying, stealing, or fraud or more subtle forms of dishonesty in relationships with other people.

OVERCONFORMITY

An emphasis on getting along with others at the expense of personal integrity, often accompanied by a tendency to be overawed by the authority of those whose good opinion seems important—and, in turn, to be authoritarian and hostile toward those considered inferior.

OVERDEPENDENCY

A tendency to lean excessively upon others for either material aid or emotional support and to rely upon them for making one's decisions. The overdependent person contributes little or nothing to a relationship and usually loses his self-respect as well as the respect of the other person. Occasionally, underlying feelings of dependency are concealed by an exaggerated show of independence (e.g., refusing to become "indebted" to anyone), which is equally destructive of close relationships.

REBELLIOUSNESS

A tendency to rebel against all authority and to become hostile and uncooperative at the slightest suggestion of being "bossed." Sometimes rebelliousness takes the form of flouting all of society's mores and manners in an attempt to prove one's independence.

HOSTILITY

A tendency, usually associated with authority problems, to be antagonistic and suspicious toward other people. When hostility is openly expressed, it creates immediate problems in a relationship. Equally harmful in the long run, however, are such covert expressions of hostility as being gossipy or overly competitive or critical.

INFERIORITY FEELINGS

A basic lack of self-confidence or self-esteem, which may be expressed either in oversensitivity to "threat" or in exaggerated efforts to prove one's own adequacy and worth by such techniques as boasting, showing off, and being hypercritical of other people.

EMOTIONAL INSULATION

An inability to make the necessary emotional investment in a relationship, for fear of being hurt.

PREJUDICE

Reacting to members of other groups on the basis of unfavorable stereotypes. For the holder of the stereotype, false beliefs are perpetuated and corrective experiences prevented; for the victim, the results typically include feelings of rejection, inferiority, hostility, and various defensive and retaliatory patterns.

UNREALISTIC EXPECTATIONS

Expecting a paragon instead of a human being—for example expecting a loved one to be always attentive, patient, thoughtful, and objective. Unrealistic expectations invite frustration and disappointment on both sides.

are no simple rules for improving one's sensitivity to the needs and feelings of others, the following techniques are often very helpful.

1. Let the other person talk, even if it is small talk and seemingly unimportant; the very lack of significant content may give us an opportunity to detect the feeling behind his words. Being alert to his voice, intonation, posture, and facial expression will help us understand what he *wants* to say as well as what he *does* say. In general, a great deal of the lack of social competence stems from talking too much oneself and not listening enough. We may be so preoccupied with our own aspirations, tensions, and problems that we do not even notice that another person is under considerable pressure to discuss a problem with us. We use his every sentence as a springboard for turning the conversation back to ourselves.

2. Ask questions involving the word *feeling* rather than *thinking*. For example, we might ask an employee who is opposed to a new method, "How do you feel about this method?" rather than "Why do you think this method won't work?" If he takes advantage of this opening to express his feelings, what he says may make it apparent that he is opposed to the new method not because he doesn't think it will work but simply because he wasn't consulted about it during the planning stage. Providing him with the opening to discuss his reaction gives him a chance to express his feelings and also suggests that his feelings matter.

3. Mirroring or reflecting the feelings of others, without standing in judgment, is often helpful. This is one method used in psychotherapy, as we have seen: the therapist listens to the individual's statements about his problem and then reflects—by repeating or paraphrasing—the feelings which the individual has expressed, in this way helping him to bring them out into the open where he can examine them for what they are.

Through the use of these techniques, it is often possible to detect the underlying feelings of others and to deal with interpersonal relationships more effectively.

Avoiding Common Sources of Difficulty

There are many sources of difficulty in interpersonal relationships, stemming mainly from violations of the conditions which we have described as being fundamental to good relationships. The actual effects of any one of these faulty approaches in a given case will depend on the personality of the other person or persons involved, and on the context of the relationship, including what other demands, gratifications, and frustrations are present. Some wives are untroubled by deceit or unfaithfulness that others would find intolerable, and behavior that would be a focus of resentment under usual conditions may be overlooked in a situation of unusual stress, as in prison or during wartime. Among the common sources of trouble in interpersonal relationships are those summarized in the chart on page 434.

SUMMARY AND A LOOK AHEAD

Competence in relationships with other people is another basic competence through which we achieve our goals and meet our needs. It cannot be achieved by learning particular skills or techniques but grows out of such conditions as: (1) a genuine respect and concern for others, a sharing of purposes, and an acceptance of reciprocal responsibility; (2) a realistic view of self and others; (3) adequate communication and structuring of the relationship; and (4) willingness and ability to accommodate to the needs of the other person.

Within this general framework, social competence can be improved by special attention to: (1) helping to meet others' needs, including helping them to feel approved and appreciated, making necessary criticisms in a helpful way, and making it clear that we expect reasonable and helpful behavior from them; (2) building I-Thou rather than I-It relationships with other individuals; (3) maintaining our own integrity, including the strength to take a stand and the ability to say "no"; (4) being sensitive to the requirements of the situation; and (5) learning to communicate more effectively, including being open in our communications and listening both to the words and the feelings of others.

The use we make of whatever competencies, resources, and opportunities we have depends on our values—what we think is important and desirable. The foundations on which we make our value assumptions will be the concern of our final chapter.

Key terms used in this chapter include:

I-Thou and I-It relationships (p. 419)
reciprocal responsibility (p. 420)
interpersonal style (p. 421)
autonomy (p. 422)
empathy (p. 422)
structuring of a relationship (p. 423)
verbal and nonverbal communication (pp. 424-425)
interpersonal accommodation (p. 426)
conflicting, congruent, and complementary patterns of accommodation (p. 426)
understanding role requirements (p. 432)

Chapter 16

THE QUEST FOR VALUES

Assumptions About Value
Values and Becoming

In this book we have taken a long and perhaps somewhat arduous journey into the world of man and his behavior. Now as we approach the end of our journey, it is fitting that we come to grips with a problem that has made its presence felt throughout our journey—the quest for values.

We have noted that each individual gradually builds up a unique frame of reference—a set of basic assumptions concerning fact, possibility, and value—which provide him with a coherent picture of himself and his world. We have seen that these basic assumptions may be accurate or inaccurate, conscious or unconscious, and rigidly maintained or tentative and subject to disproof but that whatever their character, they color his perception of each new situation and influence his reactions to it. They constitute the cognitive map by which he tries to pilot his way through the freeways and blind alleys of his existence. And they provide the basis for his answers to the three key questions "Who am I?" "Where am I going?" and "Why?"

In our discussion so far, we have focused on the role of psychology and allied sciences in providing us with information about ourselves and our sociocultural environment—information on which accurate reality and possibility assumptions can be based. Though heavily dependent on our reality and possibility assumptions, our value assumptions go beyond them in taking a position about what is *desirable* or *ought* to be, rather than what is or could be. By their nature, they are not amenable to scientific proof for they are themselves starting points—yardsticks by which we measure the meaning, usefulness, or validity of other ideas or activities.

The quest for values is not an easy one for either the individual or the group; yet on its outcome hinges the personal destiny of the individual as well as the destiny of mankind as a species. In our present discussion, we cannot hope to solve the problem of finding valid values; rather we shall try to clarify the dimensions of the problem and point to some of the directions which a solution may take. As a starting point, we shall examine in more detail what we mean by value assumptions and some of the basic differences in people's value orientations. Then we shall look at the key sources of our values, and some tentative criteria for a sound value system. And finally, in the remainder of the chapter, we shall examine the significance of values for personal "becoming"—for personal change and fulfillment—and for determining what kind of a future man as a species will have.

ASSUMPTIONS ABOUT VALUE

"A value is a conception, explicit or implicit, distinctive of an individual or characteristic of a group, of the desirable which influences the selection from available modes, means, and ends of action." (Kluckhohn, 1954, p. 395)

In selecting goals, in choosing means for reaching them, in resolving conflicts, an individual is influenced at every turn by his conception of the preferable, the appropriate, the important, the good, the desirable—by what he sees as having *value*. The kind of relationship he establishes with his wife and children, the way he transacts business matters, the degree of respect he has for others (and for himself), his political and religious activity, and the patterning of his everyday behavior—all these represent choices from among alternatives according to his hierarchy of values.

Values, of course, are not the only determinants of behavior. Any act reflects a wide range of inner and outer determinants, including the individual's assumptions about reality and possibility, his immediate motivational pattern, and various situational factors. In general, however, it is his key choices that shape the type of life he builds for himself and the kind of person he becomes—and these reflect his basic values.

Value Orientations

There are various ways of viewing or categorizing value orientations. Several broad, comprehensive world views such as those held by communists or Christians, could be delineated. For our immediate purposes, however, the most useful way of categorizing value orientations seems to be: (1) in terms of value types and (2) in terms of conceived and operative values.

Value types. Some years ago Spranger (1928) contended that every person can be regarded as approaching—but rarely fitting perfectly within—one or more of six value types or value directions. In essence, there seem to be six main types of values which appeal to people in varying degrees and around which they build the unity of their lives. These were described by Spranger in terms of pure or "ideal" types of men.[1]

1. *The theoretical.* The primary value of the "ideal" theoretical man is the discovery of *truth*. Since this involves the use of rational, critical, and empirical processes, the theoretical man is an intellectual—often a scientist or philosopher.

2. *The economic.* The "ideal" economic man values what is *useful* and is concerned with the business world or other practical affairs involving the production, marketing, or consumption of goods. Tangible wealth and material possessions are of central interest.

3. *The esthetic.* The "ideal" esthetic man sees his highest value in *form* and *harmony*. He may or may not be a creative artist, but he finds his chief interest in the artistic or esthetic experiences in life. The esthetic man views the economic or theoretical man as unappreciative of and destructive of esthetic values.

4. *The social.* The "ideal" social man places great value on *affiliation* and *love*. The social man values other persons as individuals and tends to be kind and sympathetic. Often he views the theoretical and economic value orientations as cold and inhuman.

5. *The political.* The "ideal" political man places great value on *power*. His activities may not be restricted to the narrow range of politics, but his primary focus in personal relationships is on power, influence, and active competition to maintain and expand his power.

6. *The religious.* The highest value for the "ideal" religious man may be called *unity*. He is mystical and seeks to comprehend and relate himself to the cosmos and to find higher-level value experiences via his religious philosophy.

---

[1] These value types form the basis for a well-known psychological test entitled *A Study of Values*, by Allport, Vernon, and Lindzey (1960).

This classification of value types has been criticized on the grounds that it does not exhaust the possibilities and that it provides an overly favorable view of man. For example, many people appear to have few if any strong values beyond those of hedonism and sensual pleasure. Also the six "ideal" value types appear to represent nonexistent extremes and do not ordinarily exist in such perfect form in real life. Despite such limitations, however, these value orientations have the advantage of being amenable to measurement and help us to understand the general directions that our value orientations may take.

Conceived and operative values. Many people who have studied values systematically distinguish between conceived and operative values. *Conceived* values are conceptions of the ideal. For the most part, these are the values which the culture teaches and the ones most likely to be talked about in any discussion of "morality" or "ethics." But conceived values, even though held with a good deal of intellectual conviction, sometimes have little practical influence on behavior. For example, an individual who thinks he believes in human equality, nonviolence, service to mankind, and complete honesty may not be guided by these values in his actions even when circumstances would make it fairly easy for him to do so. *Operative* values, on the other hand, are the criteria or value assumptions according to which action choices are actually made.

In trying to identify a person's real values, then, we must analyze not only what he says but what he does in situations that involve an element of choice. Sometimes the discrepancy between an individual's conceived and operative values indicates an alarming schism between his "idealized" and "real" self. The businessman who professes to accept the golden rule but violates even the most basic business ethics, the woman who extols selfless mother love but governs her child with refined cruelty, and the politician who praises freedom but denies fellow citizens the right to vote are only very obvi-

ous examples of an all too common phenomenon.

Sometimes a person holds dual standards without realizing it, sometimes knowingly from a conviction that the ends justify the means. Unfortunately, as Emerson said, "The end preëxists in the means," and we tend to become what we do, not what we say we want to be.

It is rarely if ever possible, of course, to bring conceived and operative values into complete harmony. The man who places a high value on nonviolence will usually fight rather than be killed, and the man who values complete honesty may lie to protect a friend. The complexities of human nature and human society make utopia an ideal against which to measure our progress rather than a goal we can realistically hope to achieve. But this does not invalidate conceptions of the ideal or strip them of their practical value. Salvador de Madariaga, a Spanish diplomat and political essayist, made this point well (Smith & Lindeman, 1951):

"Our eyes must be idealistic and our feet realistic. We must walk in the right direction but we must walk step by step. Our tasks are: to define what is desirable; to define what is possible at any time within the scheme of what is desirable; to carry out what is possible in the spirit of what is desirable." (p. 123)

To practice responsible self-direction, an individual must find meaning in his world and must have criteria by which to evaluate alternatives and choose between them. If his values are vague and inconsistent, his behavior will be aimless and confused. Values are necessary, too, for the stability and effectiveness of society, which cannot function unless its members agree on certain standards of responsible behavior and share basic purposes.

We have already commented on the confusion in our values created in our own day by rapid technological and social change. Some people cling rigidly to the values of an earlier time only to find themselves continually at odds with a changing world; others, no more wisely, rebel against *all* traditional values because *some* have proved invalid; still others pay lip service to traditional values but have little faith in them as practical guides. We see many signs of this moral confusion in the rejection by many of our young people of the values and goals of the broader society and in such phenomena as increasing crime, violence, alcoholism, and conflicts between many of the different subgroups in our society.

Sources of Values

One assumption men have been forced to make in the present century is that we are barely on the threshold of understanding the physical, spiritual, mental, and moral forces in our universe. Few people today have the effrontery to claim that they have found the final answers. Where, then, can the individual find reliable values, and how can he determine their validity? How can he arrive at a system of values that is stable and at the same time flexible enough to survive change? The complexity of the problem has been well summarized by Sinnott (1955):

> *"One of man's chief problems is to determine what the basis of a moral code should be, to find out what he* ought *to do. Is the right that which is the word of God given to man in the Ten Commandments? Is it what is revealed to us by conscience and intuition? Is it whatever will increase the sum of human happiness? Is it that which is the most reasonable thing to do? Is it whatever makes for the fullness and perfection of life? Above all, is there any absolute right, anything embedded, so to speak, in the nature of the universe, which should guide our actions? Or are right and wrong simply relative, dependent on time and place and culture pattern, and changing with environment and circumstance? What, in short, is the basis of our moral values? These questions are of vital importance in a day when intellectual power threatens to outrun moral control and thus destroy us." (p. 147)*

In working out his system of values, an individual can turn to four chief sources of understanding: (1) *his culture*—and other cultures with which he has contact; (2) *science;* (3) *religion;* and (4) *life experiences* —his own and those of other people.

Culture. The culture of each social group is based on certain implicit and explicit values, and although each of us has a system of values somewhat different from anyone else's, our values are usually grounded in the core values of our culture. Kluckhohn and Strodtbeck (1961) have suggested that these core values reflect the culture's orientation to five basic and universal human problems:

1. *Orientation toward human nature.* Is human nature basically good, bad, or neutral? Does the individual have intrinsic value or is he only a cog in the social system or only a bundle of atoms in the physical world? Is he essentially good or evil, rational or irrational? As we have seen, beliefs about childrearing and social controls depend on one's orientation to human nature.

2. *Man-nature orientation.* Is man a helpless pawn or does he have some measure of free will? Does the culture take a fatalistic view of the natural world, view it as something to be adapted to, or see it as a resource to be used and conquered. In our own culture, of course, we see our natural environment largely as a challenge to be conquered in the interests of man's comfort and convenience.

3. *Time orientation.* Should man live for the present or for the future? Should old customs and traditions be preserved or should they be replaced by new standards and patterns. Our own culture has often been described as future-oriented and less concerned with maintaining old customs and traditions than with keeping up with the latest ideas and techniques for greater efficiency. There is some evidence, however, that we are becoming more present-oriented, emphasizing and glorifying the "now" for its own sake.

4. *Activity orientation.* What kind of activity is most valued? Making money? Being a good hunter? Service to mankind? Contemplation? Our own society embraces sev-

eral such orientations but appears to be in considerable agreement on the value of "getting going" and "getting things done" with what might be called a *time-pressure* orientation—a compulsion to use time efficiently for useful purposes.

5. *Interpersonal-relationship* orientation. What is the dominant or desired relationship among members of the group? Is it competitive or cooperative, friendly or hostile? Man's relationship to man is strikingly different from one culture to another and often within subgroups in the same society. Our own culture emphasizes both a competitive orientation and one of brotherly love although the latter is not always an operative value.

Against the background of answers generally given to these questions by those in his cultural group, the individual develops his personal system of values. And depending on his conception of what is desirable and good in human life, he selects certain goals over others and patterns his behavior according to standards of what he believes to be right and worth while.

Science. Science has the advantage of providing information that has been checked and rechecked by objective methods. But fact is impersonal and, except as it is interpreted, does not contribute to meaning or provide a guide for action. Even the value of searching for truth—the basic premise of science—cannot be "proved" scientifically. Probably the greatest scientist of our age, Albert Einstein, acknowledged that "the scientific method can teach us nothing beyond how facts are related to, and conditioned by, each other" (1950):

"One can have the clearest knowledge of what is, and yet not be able to deduce from that what should be the goal of our human aspirations. Objective knowledge provides us with powerful instruments for the achievement of certain ends, but the ultimate goal itself and the longing to reach it must come from another source. And it is hardly necessary to argue for the view that our existence and our activity acquire mean-

ing only by the setting up of such a goal and of corresponding values. The knowledge of truth as such is wonderful, but it is so little capable of acting as a guide that it cannot prove even the justification and the value of the aspiration toward that very knowledge of truth. Here we face, therefore, the limits of the purely rational conception of our existence." (pp. 21-22)

Science provides us with dependable information about man and his world, but it helps us make value judgments only as we relate such information to value assumptions we are already making on some other basis. For example, the scientific finding that smoking is bad for our health becomes the basis for a value judgment only if we assume that what is bad for our health is undesirable. Usually, of course, we assume that life is intrinsically of value and that whatever is detrimental to life is undesirable.

Although science has thus helped man greatly in identifying the paths that can take him closer to his goals, the average person often takes a somewhat defensive attitude toward new scientific information when it seems to contradict what he has believed to be true and when it seems to lessen man's stature or significance in the universe. In the same way, Copernicus' discovery in the sixteenth century that the earth moved around the sun, rather than the sun around the earth, met with fierce opposition because it seemed to diminish man's importance and to invalidate his current beliefs.

As modern man learns more about the universe, it is difficult not to see the earth and the human enterprise as an insignificant dot in the vast reaches of the cosmos. But as the astronomer Shapley (1958) has pointed out:

"The new discoveries and developments contribute to the unfolding of a magnificent universe; to be a participant is in itself a glory. With our confreres on distant planets; with our fellow animals and plants of land, air and sea . . . with all these we are associated in an existence and an evolution that inspires respect and deep reverence. We cannot escape humility. And as groping philosophers and scientists we are thankful

for the mysteries that still lie beyond our grasp." (p. 149)

In an age in which every year brings fantastic progress in the physical, biological, and social sciences, we need to develop a positive orientation toward the changing facts of life. New information is not necessarily a threat, even when it requires changes in our present frame of reference. Rather, every increase in knowledge furnishes the potential for a somewhat more adequate view of reality and possibility as well as for a correspondingly more appropriate system of values.

Here it may be emphasized that scientific change need not result in the acceptance of complete cultural relativity. As the anthropologist Clyde Kluckhohn (1954) has pointed out:

"Some values are as much givens in human life as the fact that bodies of certain densities fall under specified conditions. These are founded, in part, upon the fundamental biological similarities of all human beings. They arise also out of the circumstance that human existence is invariably a social existence. No society has ever approved suffering as a good thing in itself. As a means to an end (purification or self-discipline), yes; as punishment—as a means to the ends of society, yes. But for itself—no. No culture fails to put a negative valuation upon killing, indiscriminate lying, and stealing within the in-group.

"Reciprocity is another value essential in all societies. Moreover, the fact that truth and beauty (however differently defined and expressed in detail) are universal, transcendental values is one of the givens of human life—equally with birth and death." (pp. 418-419)

As science discovers more about the "givens" of human life and the various factors that encourage or interfere with the fulfillment of human potentialities, we gain increasingly reliable criteria for making value choices.

Religion. Both science and religion are concerned with truth. But while science remains "ethically neutral" in its pursuit of truth, religion is concerned also with values.

Religion, as we customarily think of it in its institutionalized form, is believed to be built upon the successive revelations of God to man, as recorded in tradition and sacred literature. Typically it involves a formal system of values that can be passed on from generation to generation, as well as a theology and a system of worship and prescriptions for social relationships. Many of the basic values familiar to us in Christianity are found also in other great religions of the world such as Confucianism, Judaism, Mohammedanism, and Buddhism. For example, the mandate "Do unto others as ye would have them do unto you" appears in one form or another in most religions.

Although theologians have used logic, reasoning, and historical arguments to help prove the existence of God and the validity of their beliefs, the "proof" of religious truth must rest finally on faith and judgments of probability. People who have received strength and comfort from their religion may have an unshakable belief in the reality of God, but the correctness of their belief can never, by argument alone, be made convincing to anyone who has not shared a similar experience. In the well-known words of Pascal "The heart has its reasons which reason does not know."

In Western society organized religion has undergone a series of vicissitudes which have tended to undermine faith in many traditional religious beliefs. To some extent this has resulted from what Clark (1958) has called "stimulus-response verbalism" in religious belief. In their search for certainty in a time of change and confusion, many people have embraced formal religion without thinking through its beliefs or values or integrating them into their lives. Thus to many young people, the religious convictions espoused by their elders often seem hypocritical. As someone has put it, "They pray in church on Sunday and they prey on their fellow man the rest of the week." People and nations have inflicted unbelievable suffering on each other in the name of religion. Finally, the frequent concern of the church as an institution with formal trappings, ritual, and ancient dogma rather than with the life problems of crucial significance to people has led many to conclude that *all* religion has lost its relevance and validity.

In part, the advances of modern science have also tended to undermine faith in traditional religious beliefs and values. For example, in discounting various traditional teachings such as the Biblical account of creation, science has cut away many of the artificial props of religion which many people had come to identify with ultimate truth. Perhaps of even greater significance in undermining traditional faith has been the realization that modern science makes it possible not only for man to control his environment but to plan and create his own future. Thus the belief in an all-powerful God who determines each man's destiny has been badly shaken.

Curiously enough, today's young people seem to be searching for what might be called religious or spiritual values as well as for values that are workable in guiding the pragmatic decisions of their everyday life. In essence, they are searching for a coherent value system or philosophy of life which can hold its own against the impact of science and technology on society and provide meaning for the individual's existence and for man's role in the universe.

Life experience. In the life of the group and of the individual, many values originate from experience. Each of us is a valuing organism, experiencing success or failure, satisfaction or dissatisfaction in different situations. We are constantly making judgments about what is good and bad, more desirable and less desirable, more meaningful and less meaningful. And as we make these judgments about our ongoing experiences, we modify our value system accordingly.

We can also draw on the experience of others. Through our libraries and our museums, we can draw upon the experience of men and nations throughout the world since the beginning of human history. We can trace the rise and fall of past oriental and occidental civilizations and examine the causes which led to their downfall. We can observe the effects of dictatorships on human welfare and contrast these governments with more democratic forms of social organization in terms of their long-range contributions to human happiness and social progress. We can observe the effects of greed, selfishness, and ignorance in creating general human misery and leading to warfare. We can note the almost unbelievable cost of man's incessant conflicts in terms of lives, property, and suffering and their futility in solving his basic problems. These and many other lessons can be learned from man's history; although we cannot always scientifically prove such lessons to be accurate, they, too, support certain values and invalidate others.

In guiding our political and social lives, we operate on the basis of hypotheses (somewhat similar to the hypotheses of the scientist) which we continually modify and expand so that they agree more closely with the "facts" of our experience. Tack after tack has been taken through history as men have tried to determine what values they should follow—individually and collectively—to find happiness and to fulfill their destiny as human beings. Usually a society changes slowly, almost grudgingly, by a series of small modifications. At certain critical times in history, however, one human personality, or several, may lead society to accept a new set of values and to put them into action, as our own founding fathers did during the period of the American Revolution. Norman Cousins (1958) has suggested how they were able to work this "magic" of winning acceptance almost overnight for a new system of political values:

"The answer is to be found in the history of ideas. An idea does not have to find its mark in the minds of large numbers of people in order to create an incentive for change. Ideas have a life of their own. They can be nourished and brought to active growth by a small number of sensitive, vital minds which somehow respond to the needs of a total organism, however diffused the parts of that or-

ganism may be. These minds sense both the need for change and the truth of ideas that define the nature of change. When the ideas are articulated and advocated, the popular response is not merely the product of logic reaping its gains but of a dormant awareness coming to life." (p. 16)

Often in the history of ideas new values, once articulated, have been readily accepted because people have *known* them to be right on the basis of their own experience. In the long run, most of the values that actually influence our behavior are validated by the satisfaction we have experienced in pursuing them. Hence experience becomes a key factor in determining what values we follow and what ones we discard.

Criteria of a Sound Value System

Although values are inevitably a somewhat individual matter, worked out by each individual on the basis of what seems most valid to him, any adequate value system must probably meet the general criteria discussed below.

Integration and faith. An adequate value system is both internally consistent and integrated with the individual's total personality. It is something in which he can reasonably have a good deal of faith. An integrated value system also implies a *hierarchy* of values, which enables the individual to choose confidently between things of greater and lesser importance and to be relatively undisturbed by frustrations that interfere only with the attainment of short-range goals.

Values come alive in direct proportion to how much faith the individual has in them. Faith helps close the gap between conceived and operative values and enables the individual to achieve a sense of wholeness in everything he feels and says and does. His behavior reflects an intellectual and emotional surety; there is relatively little conflict between "ought" and "want." This is the kind of faith illustrated in the lives of men whose actions seem in complete harmony with their deepest wishes. Maslow (1954) has described it as one characteristic of the self-actualizing people he studied:

"I have found none of my subjects to be chronically unsure about the difference between right and wrong in his actual living. Whether or not they could verbalize the matter, they rarely showed in their day-to-day living the chaos, the confusion, the inconsistency, or the conflict that are so common in the average person's ethical dealings." (pp. 220-221)

An adequate system of values carries the conviction of truth while remaining fluid enough to allow for correction and expansion. In essence, we need to feel that our reality, possibility, and value assumptions are valid but also to remain alert to information that may prove them false. This is essentially the attitude expressed by Mahatma Gandhi (1948) in his autobiography:

"I am far from claiming any finality or infallibility about my conclusions. One claim I do indeed make and it is this. For me they appear to be absolutely correct, and seem for the time being to be final. For if they were not, I should base no action on them." (p. 5)

Such an attitude enables the individual to take forthright action based on conviction while at the same time maintaining an openness to new or fuller truth.

The kind of faith that encourages self-actualization is quite different from dogmatic faith, which seems to reflect fear and uncertainty more than positive conviction. Dogmatic faith tends to box the individual in and interfere with his spiritual and intellectual growth, whereas dynamic faith pushes him ahead to clearer insights. And as May has pointed out (1957), religion has no monopoly on dogma:

"Dogmatic faith is the kind of faith we cling to when we are scared. It's like building a stockade around yourself. The hope is that if you can protect yourself with these particular beliefs, then you can hide behind them and be safe. You may feel safe, to be sure, temporarily, but you achieve that security

exactly at the cost of the failure to grow. Your life becomes increasingly drab, you have blocked off the human spirit by blocking yourself behind a stockade of dogma. Now in our age this is as prevalent in science as it is in religion. . . . I think most of the dogmatic faith in the 20th Century so far has been faith in progress, faith in mechanical happiness, faith in riches. These have to do not with religion as such, but rather with a crystallizing of dogma of a particular cultural period, and a hiding behind that dogma as though that would then give one security and freedom from anxiety." (p. 185)

In a transitional age such as ours the achievement of reasoned faith is more difficult than in times of greater stability, but it has never been more needed. Some people use the fact of cultural relativity to support the specious argument that *no* value can have any real validity and that the "right" values, therefore, are whichever ones seem most immediately useful. Other people seek security in the face of uncertainty by accepting ready-made the values of their various reference groups—their culture, their socioeconomic class, their church—without thinking them through. Often a further problem is created here when the values of these different groups are inconsistent with each other, so that to live by them the individual must either divide his life into "compartments" or be in constant conflict with himself. Inconsistent faith, dogmatic faith, and lack of faith fail equally to provide the guidelines an individual needs to behave effectively in a changing world and to grow toward self-fulfillment.

ASSUMPTIONS AND THREAT

Depending on one's assumptions of fact, value, and possibility, *(or frame of reference)* the same stimulus situation may be perceived quite differently—and met accordingly with different responses. For example, as shown in the chart below, an impending drought may be regarded as evidence of divine anger, understood on a scientific basis, or not seen as a threat at all. The defense undertaken would depend on the threat as defined by the viewer rather than on the objective stimulus situation. The need for an accurate picture of "reality" is obvious.

STIMULUS SITUATION	THREAT PERCEIVED	DEFENSE UNDERTAKEN
Impending drought	Divine anger	Religious ceremonies
Impending drought	Scientific	Drawing on food resources; irrigation, manipulation of nature
Impending drought	No threat seen	No defense attempted

In general, a culture which places high value on dominance tends to see any threat as an attack and its own defense as a counterattack. When actual danger is great, this value orientation is conducive to objective security, but it is likely to produce high anxiety and perpetual warfare. A group with a submission orientation is more vulnerable to actual danger but, except when a threat materializes, tends to have greater psychological security and peace of mind.

Adapted from Gillin & Nicholson, 1951.

2. *Realism and flexibility.* To behave effectively and find satisfaction, the individual needs values that can stand the test of reality and are relevant to the kinds of problems he must deal with. This means that his value system must provide meaning and practical guidance in a world that is far from being the utopia he might like to create. We need values that give direction and purpose as we go about the real business of living.

A realistic value system implies the need for a certain amount of flexibility. Fundamental values may remain relatively stable, but they must be refined and their compass extended as the individual's understanding broadens. The person whose values today are exactly the same as they were ten years ago has failed to grow in one important dimension. Values must keep pace with changes in the individual himself, in his life situation, and in his physical and sociocultural environment.

3. *Meaning and satisfaction.* A final consideration in judging the adequacy of any value system is the amount of satisfaction that the individual derives from living by it—whether it gives meaning to his life and a sense that he is fulfilling the purposes of his existence. Dorothy Lee, an anthropologist who has made intensive studies of value in other cultures, has emphasized the experience of satisfaction as a universal criterion of value (1959):

> ". . . we experience value when our activity is permeated with satisfaction, when we find meaning in our life, when we feel good, when we act not out of calculating choice and not for extraneous purpose but rather because this is the only way that we, as ourselves, deeply want to act." (p. 165)

VALUES AND BECOMING

Becoming refers to personal change over time. We all are in the process of becoming throughout our lives, for every experience of life leaves some change in us. We like to expect that such continuing change is in posi-

tive directions and that we are becoming more proficient, more capable, and more attractive. But sometimes change is in a negative direction, as in the case of the individual who becomes a chronic alcoholic or the individual who becomes cynical and embittered, feeling that his life has been wasted.

Continuing Personal Growth

In evaluating the course or totality of his life up to the present, a person may experience a sense of fulfillment, of unfulfillment, or even of despair. When asked to tell the story of their lives, Bühler (1968) noted that persons over 50 years of age usually ended with a summarizing statement such as: "All in all it was a good life," or "There were so many disappointments," or "It all came to nothing." (p. 185)

Admittedly, bringing off a life is neither simple nor easy, and it involves far more than simply our values. Opportunities, chance factors, personal resources, and many other conditions all enter in. It is largely through our choices and our actions, however, that we shape the kind of person we will become as well as the kind of personal world that we will make for ourselves to live in.

In our earlier discussion, we have seen that personal growth essentially involves a spiraling sequence of differentiation and integration—of ever increasing knowledge and competencies and their assimilation into more complex levels of personality integration. We also traced several directions in which development toward maturity occurs during the years from infancy to adulthood, such as from dependence toward independence and interdependence, from amorality to morality, from incompetence to competence, and from self-centeredness to concern for others too.

Within this general framework, there appear to be specific directions of personal change or growth throughout an individual's lifetime which are generally considered of positive value by psychologists. Most of these valued directions of personal change appear to fall into one or more of the following categories:

1. *Increased autonomy*—changes in the direction of increased self-reliance, self-regard, and self-direction. Implicit here is emancipation from undue social influence and maintenance motivation, with increased ability to make decisions and to take responsibility for and face the consequence of one's decisions.

2. *More adequate frame of reference*—changes in the direction of increased and more accurate information about oneself and one's world. Such changes lead to more refined and <u>accurate reality, possibility, and value assumptions,</u> to increased understanding and meaning, and to greater capability in problem solving and decision making.

3. *More adequate self-identity*—growth toward a well-differentiated sense of oneself as a worthy and capable person, originator of one's own actions. Important, too, is an accurate assessment of one's abilities and weaknesses, with a realistic level of aspiration and reasonable harmony between self-concept and self-ideal.

4. *Improved competencies*—changes in the direction of increased intellectual, emotional, and social competence. Such improvements lead to greater capability in coping with problems of living as well as in carrying out one's life plans; typically they also lead to improved depth and richness of one's relations with his social environment.

5. *Resolution of conflicts*—dismantling of unnecessary self-defenses and resolving of disabling conflicts, resulting in greater openness to experience, greater inner harmony, increased stress tolerance, and greater general flexibility.

All these changes are in the direction of actualizing one's potentials. They tend to lead to creative self-expression, to more positive attitudes toward the self and others, to warm and loving relationships, and to a greater sense of relatedness to the human

"ALIENATION" OF COLLEGE STUDENTS

Recent years have seen an increase in the number of talented, articulate, imaginative young people who have rejected many of the operative values of the mainstream of American society and have no wish to participate in it. This is a serious loss for the society and, though giving these individuals a high degree of "freedom," cuts them off from many kinds of personal growth.

In an intensive three-year study of twelve male college students, selected because of their extreme degree of alienation as assessed by questionnaires, Keniston (1967) found that most of the subjects came from a similar family background:

MOTHERS	Characteristically described as magnetic, emotional, attractive women toward whom the sons were extremely, often excessively, close. At the same time, however, the mothers were described as confining, possessive, nagging, and intrusive.
FATHERS	Little information volunteered about the fathers. When pressed, the subjects described them as disappointed, frustrated, outwardly cold men. The sons assumed that their fathers had been idealistic, imaginative, and enthusiastic as young men but had lost these qualities through disappointments in life.
APPARENT RESULTS	The investigator concluded that the subjects, determined not to let life break them as they thought it had broken their fathers, were rejecting both their fathers and the society they saw as responsible.

Such a background is, of course, only one possible cause of alienation. As we have seen, our contemporary society provides pervasive sources for such a reaction.

enterprise. Admittedly, however, they offer only general guidelines, and an individual must translate them into specific and meaningful terms in relation to his own life situation.

Two aspects of continuing personal growth are important enough to warrant special consideration: learning to trust one's own process of valuing, and becoming an authentic person.

Trusting our own process of valuing. As we have seen, we derive some of our values from external sources—such as science, religion, our culture, and the experience of others—and some from our own direct experiences of value. Ideally, we are selective in what we accept from external sources—enriching our insights by adding those of other people, weighing the value experiences of others for relevance to us, and choosing from all the possibilities the particular values which have validity for *us*.

When our own experiences of value contradict the value judgments of our culture or the prescriptions of science or religion, we must decide which we trust most—our experience or that of others. Rogers (1964) has found that many of those who seek therapy have, knowingly or not, chosen to follow external value judgments, ignoring or denying their own perceptions of value, with the following typical results:

1. Most of the individual's values are learned (introjected) from other individuals or groups significant to him, but he regards them as his own.

2. The locus of evaluation lies outside himself—he is essentially directed by a "program" which he has received uncritically from others.

3. Often there is a wide discrepancy between the evidence supplied by his own experience and his introjected value system.

4. Since these value assumptions have been accepted uncritically, they tend to be held in a rigid fashion and not to be readily subject to critical evaluation and change.

5. Many of his accepted value assumptions are unsound and even contradictory.

For example, he may calmly discuss the possibility of dropping a hydrogen bomb on an enemy country but feel deep sympathy when he sees the suffering of one small child.

6. The individual feels insecure and easily threatened, for he does not trust his own valuing process to resolve discrepancies and formulate a coherent, meaningful value system. So he clings to his contradictory and confusing values because he sees no reliable alternative.

The ultimate price of depending on the value judgments of others is that the individual loses contact with his own inner processes of evaluation and potential wisdom. This loss of contact appears to be a fundamental aspect of the alienation and estrangement of modern man from himself.

Thus it is of critical importance that the individual's chief locus of valuing be his own inner experience. In fact, it is in viewing man as capable of his own value judgments that we credit him with some measure of free will and self-determination. For it is his ability to weigh the desirability of two courses of action and see one as more desirable than another that makes it possible for him to make a choice. Many choices are not between black and white, but between close shades of gray, which often makes them difficult. But if our choices were made automatically we would lack real freedom, since we would in essence be "preprogramed" and would merely be acting out our destiny. As Kelley (1967) has pointed out:

"Volition is high if you consciously concern yourself with which action to choose and give the choice much consideration, and if you experience uncertainty, conflict, and the potentiality of alternative responses." (p. 218)

There is no guarantee that man will always choose the good or desirable over the bad or undesirable. But the mature person, who is open to his own experiencing, is free to capitalize both on the ability he shares with other animals to utilize feedback in adapting his behavior to meet his needs and also on his uniquely human capacities for self-awareness, critical reflection, and anticipation of future events and consequences. It would appear that when the individual's locus of valuing is internal rather than dependent on what others say is valuable, and when he fully understands the consequences of the alternatives, he can usually be relied upon to choose value directions which are conducive to his self-fulfillment.

As we have seen, making judgments on the basis of one's own valuing does not necessarily entail the rejection of existing social values. As Morris (1966) has pointed out: *"Revolt, rebellion, apostasy are not in themselves the mark of the existential man. Even the man who consents to convention can be the existential man if he is aware of the act of consenting and hence of the necessity that he take personal responsibility for living his life in a conventional way." (p. 48)*

What he does is then done intentionally, out of a conviction that this is the thing to do, regardless of whether or not it happens to follow conventional expectations.

Becoming an authentic person. Closely related to the directions of personal growth enumerated above and to the need to trust one's own process of valuing is the concept of "becoming an authentic person." As Morris (1966) has put it:

"And who is authentic? The individual whose example is perhaps beyond the reach of most of us: the individual who is free and who knows it, who knows that every deed and word is a choice and hence an act of value creation, and, finally and perhaps decisively, who knows that he is the author of his own life and must be held personally responsible for the values on behalf of which he has chosen to live it, and that these values can never be justified by referring to something or somebody outside himself." (p. 48)

As Snyder (1967) says, the authentic person is "being a truth." He is one who has integrity, who has thought through his values and lives by them.

Although the basic theme underlying authenticity is the commitment to be true to oneself—both in terms of being what one is and in terms of shaping oneself through one's own choices and actions—a second and equally important basic theme is concern for and commitment to others. In both the humanistic and the existential models of man, commitment to others follows almost automatically from commitment to oneself. For there is considered to be a basic unity to mankind, and the task of learning to live constructively automatically leads to involvement, obligation, and commitment to one's fellow man. As Rogers (1964) has put it: *"I believe that when the human being is inwardly free to choose whatever he deeply values, he tends to value those objects, experiences, and goals which make for his own survival, growth, and development, and for the survival and development of others." (p. 166)*

VALUES AND THE INDIVIDUAL

Implicit in our discussion of the role of values in personal change or becoming are the following assumptions about human individuals:

1. Individual human beings have some measure of freedom for self-direction.

2. Freedom requires choices, and these choices are ultimately based on the individual's value system—his assumptions about what is valuable, desirable, preferable, and important.

3. The greater the individual's faith in his values, the greater the effort and persistence with which he will pursue them.

4. An individual may hold sound or unsound values or may be unable to find values in which he can place his faith.

5. Each individual is ultimately responsible for his value choices and the actions based on them.

These same assumptions appear applicable to groups as they become aware of and reflect on their value orientations and alternative choices.

In essence, the individual can be authentic and lead a fulfilling life only if his values and choices are both individually and socially constructive.

In this context it is interesting to note the finding of Glasser (1967) that persons in psychotherapy who attempt to clarify and formulate more adequate values and to take greater responsibility for living their lives according to these values show changes in the direction of deeper satisfaction, fewer disruptive conflicts, more profound emotions, more harmonious interpersonal relations, greater meaning in their own lives, and greater concern for the well-being of others. Maslow (1965) has concluded that the authentic person becomes a little less a member of his local groups and a little more a member of his species. He is concerned not only with himself, his family, and his community but with all mankind.

The Greek oracle said "Know thyself"; Emerson said "Trust thyself"; and the Danish philosopher Kierkegaard said "Choose oneself." These appear to be the challenges for the truly authentic person. He must know who he is and what he can realistically hope to become; he must have confidence in himself as an experiencer and judger and in his ability to direct his own life; and he must choose to be himself and to take the responsibility for what he does and what he becomes.

Building a Favorable Life World

Positive becoming is not entirely a matter of change and growth in oneself. Of crucial importance, too, is the type of world one constructs for oneself to live in.

In choosing an occupation, in choosing a mate, in choosing whether to have children and how to bring them up, in choosing his home and its furnishings, in choosing how to spend his money, the individual builds a world for himself which may help him to meet his needs and grow or may present him with one unnecessary problem after another.

Snyder (1967) has dramatically summarized the matter:

"Gradually you build up a life world which, for you, is your destiny in this world. It is the arena where you play out the struggle of life versus death for you. The rest of your life space becomes background. This life world becomes the foreground and pioneer settlement of your life." (p. 19)

The structure of this life world will usually have common elements for most people, for most of us in the course of our lives build friendships, undertake specific occupations, get married, and raise families. Its quality, however, will depend in large measure on our individual value choices. For example, whether we marry, whom we marry, the type of relationships we attempt to build in marriage and other social interactions, and the ways we cope with life stresses all reflect our value choices.

Of particular importance here are our value choices in relation to material things and other people—whether we value and pursue material possessions for their own sake or largely as resources for fuller living, and whether we regard and treat other people as objects or as other valuing, experiencing agents like ourselves.

In our discussion of social competence, we compared I-It and I-Thou relationships, noting that if we view people as objects to be controlled and manipulated rather than as unique persons, we deny ourselves the possibility of establishing meaningful and authentic relationships with them. In a bureaucratic, mass society, which often seems to dehumanize and depersonalize our contacts with each other, it would seem especially important to be sure we are building a life world in which meaningful relationships with people are possible. For although we differ in the value we place upon affiliation with others, it would appear that personal growth and fulfillment, for most of us, is heavily dependent on the quality of the interpersonal relationships in our life world.

In any event, the structure and quality of the life world that we construct for ourselves will be of crucial significance in determining the frustrations and stresses we will face as well as the extent to which we will meet our needs and have opportunities for continuing personal growth.

VALUES AND
THE FUTURE OF MAN

"In a sense earth is a spaceship and we human beings are its astronauts. Our ship has an efficient life-support system which produces our food, purifies our air and processes our wastes. Our main trouble is that the size of the ship remains constant and the capacity of its processing units increases but very slowly while the population of astronauts increases with frightening rapidity. And not only does the population increase but the per capita volume of waste increases as well. We are poisoning ourselves often to the point of death. We must add to this the unhappy fact that the astronauts of this ship fight with each other and kill each other using weapons which steadily become more powerful and effective." (Brown, 1967, p. 15)

As we noted in Chapter 11, the astronauts on our spaceship in the last third of the twentieth century are faced with three herculean tasks: (1) to complete our unfinished business of eliminating poverty and discrimination and provide equal opportunity for all; (2) to cope with problems which have become acute in the course of our technological advances, such as air pollution, the population explosion, and national rivalries among those who possess thermonuclear, biological, and chemical methods of warfare, and (3) to plan for the future—to "invent" a good future for human society which will not only ensure our survival as a species but provide us with a world conducive to personal fulfillment and social progress.

It is the latter problem and its value implications with which we shall conclude our journey into the realm of man and his behavior.

Inventing a "Good" Future
for Man

We are confronted today with the problem of survival, but even more important is the problem of *how* we shall survive—the quality of the life that we will be able to preserve. Saving a man for a future world of *unsanity* is hardly sufficient. But a "good" future will not come automatically.

In recent years, a growing number of scientists and professionals have become directly involved in delineating various possible futures for mankind. For example, General Electric has set up Tempo (Technical Management Planning Organization) where a sizable number of physical scientists, sociologists, economists, engineers, and other scientists devote full time to contemplating the future. Similar enterprises are financed by the Air Force, the Ford Foundation, and other agencies. These "futurists" point to the fact that throughout history, those organisms which have been unable to adapt to the demands of a changing environment have perished. They view with confidence and in considerable detail the potentialities of modern man to escape this fate—partly through adapting to the new environment and partly through our increasing ability to control the changes in it and in ourselves.

Although vitally interested in the possible "shape of things to come," the futurists are thus even more directly concerned with planning and controlling change. This, in turn, means delineating the alternatives available to modern man in terms of possible worlds we might build and possible types of people that might be developed. Man is no longer limited by the "givens" in himself and his surroundings but is increasingly capable of controlling and directing his own destiny by planning and creating the conditions he believes will be most advantageous for him.

Implicit here is the problem of matching man and his environment in such a way as to foster optimal development and adjustment. Computers have proved of great help in enabling us to rehearse the entire range of imaginable options by simulating different possible sequences of change and reactions to it. Ultimately, however, only man can make the value judgments on which plans for his future will be based. For while the computer can relieve man of much routine work and even handle many routine managerial judgments and decisions requiring a repeated analysis of information in terms of a regular set of rules, it still cannot replace man in making the value judgments of which goals are worth while and how much effort they are worth. For better or for worse, man cannot escape from the choices that will determine his destiny. The only question is whether these choices will be made by default or with imagination and use of all the evidence now potentially at his disposal.

Many behavioral scientists—and others —are seriously worried about the possibility that some elite minority may someday plan and exercise control over the rest of us, utilizing behavioral scientists primarily as tools in achieving their goals. We have warnings in such frightening "utopias" as Huxley's *Brave New World,* Skinner's *Walden Two,* and Orwell's *1984.* To safeguard ourselves against such a contingency, scientists are becoming increasingly concerned not only with the possible futures which science and technology are making possible but also with the value orientations on which a choice among these futures may be based.

A Tentative Value Orientation

Modern science and technology are steadily increasing man's power not only to shape his future environment but also to control his own development and behavior.[1] And most scientists consider it inevitable that such controls will be used in shaping the man of the future. This has given rise to a number of anxiety-arousing questions:

What type of controls will be used?
Who will exercise these controls?
What values will they be based on?

Collier (1968) has suggested a basic value with which most scientists and nonscientists alike would probably agree. He defines this value as "the recognition and constructive concern for whatever capacity the individual has (for both self and others) for self-regulation and self-determination." (p. 5) This value orientation involves basic respect for the individual as always a partially self-determining system, with some potentiality for freedom and real choice.

The same basic ethic has been stated in other ways by many prominent Americans. For example, John Dewey (1930) wrote:

---

[1]Many biological scientists think that by the turn of this century, man will be able to change the information contained in the DNA; if so, it will be possible for man to control his own biological make-up and direct his own evolution.

VALUES AND HUMAN SOCIETY

The following assumptions appear to be compatible with and extensions of the basic value orientation discussed in the chapter in relation to the planning of a "good" future for mankind.

1. The survival of man is desirable.
2. The life of each individual has intrinsic worth and is to be respected.
3. Social progress is both possible and desirable.
4. The pursuit of "truth," as exemplified in modern science, can be useful for achieving social progress.
5. Democracy, with its respect for the individual

and its congenial atmosphere for the pursuit of truth, provides the setting most conducive to individual and group fulfillment.

6. Most of the values promulgated by Christianity and other great religions are not only compatible with a democratic society but a necessary basis for it.
7. Each individual and group has the responsibility for preserving and extending the progress made by preceding generations.
8. Man has some role or potential destiny in the universe; we are challenged to find out what it is and use our resources and abilities accordingly.

"Democracy has many meanings, but if it has a moral meaning, it is found in resolving that the supreme test of all political institutions and industrial arrangements shall be the contribution they make to the all-round growth of every member of society." (p. 221)

John W. Gardner, former Secretary of Health, Education, and Welfare, stated it this way (1965):

"What we are suggesting is that every institution in our society should contribute to the fulfillment of the individual. Every institution, must, of course, have its own purposes and preoccupations, but over and above everything else it does, it should be prepared to answer this question posed by society: 'What is the institution doing to foster the development of the individuals within it.'" (p. 814)

The research and writings of Maslow, Rogers, Fromm, and other humanistic psychologists, as we have seen, have all emphasized this general value orientation. The chart on page 452 summarizes the value assumptions that appear to be compatible with and extensions of this basic value orientation.

As man embarks upon the great adventure of shaping his own future, let us hope that he will find new solutions that will change what needs to be changed while preserving essential values that are still valid. For it has taken man many thousands of years to achieve the imperfect level of freedom and opportunity for self-determination that we have reached; if these crucial achievements and other time-tested values are carelessly discarded, the change can bring us more loss than gain, and it may take long effort and suffering just to regain our present position. The warning that "the price of freedom is eternal vigilance" is not one to be dismissed lightly in our age of turmoil and rapid change.

Even if he proceeds slowly in modifying his genetic nature, man will inevitably be transformed as he creates a new and changing environment for himself. The man of the future may well be as different from us as we are from Neanderthal man. In any event, man can, if he will, create a future society which will provide him with a richer life and greater opportunities for self-direction and self-actualization than he has ever known. It would seem a tragedy indeed if by some act of thermonuclear folly he were to commit mass suicide just as his exciting and challenging adventure is getting under way.

In accepting the Nobel Prize for Literature in 1950, William Faulkner made this prophetic statement, which seems equally relevant today and a fitting conclusion for our discussion:

"I decline to accept the end of man. It is easy enough to say that man is immortal simply because he will endure: that when the last ding-dong of doom has clanged and faded from the last worthless rock hanging tideless in the last red and dying evening, that even then there will still be one more sound: that of his puny inexhaustible voice, still talking. I refuse to accept this. I believe that man will not merely endure: he will prevail. He is immortal, not because he alone among creatures has an inexhaustible voice, but because he has a soul, a spirit capable of compassion and sacrifice and endurance." (1961, p. 4)

Readings

EXPLORATIONS IN PERSONALITY AND BEHAVIOR THEORY

In the physical sciences, the student may have to enter graduate school before coming to grips with unresolved issues and future horizons in his field. In psychology, by contrast, the student may find himself glimpsing frontiers of the discipline in his very first course. For though we have amassed a great deal of basic knowledge, questions about learning, motivation, and other topics soon take us from the known to the unknown—to the frontiers of research and thinking.

The following readings have been selected to extend and enrich the basic material that we have covered in this text. The broad range of topics covered by these articles is indicative of the breadth of thinking and research going on in psychology today. An attempt has also been made to provide enough variety that each reader will find something of special interest and be motivated to do more extensive reading in that particular area.

The three readings which accompany Part One of the text are perhaps the most difficult in terms of conceptual and theoretical content of all the readings. The first—Theory of Integrative Levels—deals with the thorny problem of reductionism—of whether we can explain the events on one level, such as the psychological, by exclusive recourse to concepts from lower levels such as the physical or biological. The second—A Dynamic Regulatory Theory of Consciousness—deals with the equally thorny problem of the significance of consciousness and self-awareness in man's development and behavior. The third—Hierarchy in the Brain: Implications for Learning and Critical Periods—deals with the controversial area of critical periods and attempts to show the basis for both critical periods and different kinds of learning in the hierarchical development and organization of the nervous system.

James K. Feibleman

THEORY OF INTEGRATIVE LEVELS

From the study of the relations between the fields investigated by physics, chemistry, biology, psychology and anthropology, some knowledge of a structure is gradually emerging.

The theory of the integrative levels has been growing in recent decades. Men like Bertalanffy (Bertalanffy and Woodger, 1933), Needham, Novikoff (1945) and others have concerned themselves with it. Much remains to be done. Bertalanffy (1950) has envisaged a sort of superscience which shall have as its subject-matter the relations between the sciences. The philosophy of science may yet be the source for the development of an empirical field itself consisting of the integrative levels, a sort of meta-empirical field, with its own entities and processes and laws.

From the *British Journal for the Philosophy of Science,* Vol. 5, 1954, pages 59-66. Reprinted by permission of Cambridge University Press, New York.

SOME LAWS OF THE LEVELS

In this and the following section are set forth some of the uniformities which are found among the integrative levels. A few only are given; others surely exist and can be added as they are discovered.

1. *Each level organises the level or levels below it plus one emergent quality.* Thus the integrative levels are cumulative upward. This proposition implies that everything has at least the physical properties and has led to the position of supreme importance of the physical world in science and philosophy. Chemical elements have mass, density and dimensions, and so do biological organisms; it is possible to weigh aluminum or to measure the height of a horse. But that everything has at least physical properties does not mean that anything except physical objects has only physical properties. Ionic exchange takes

place at the chemical level, and organisms are self-directive; for instance, when hard water is passed through a zeolite, the calcium ions are replaced by sodium ions; and the tissue of horses when slightly injured will heal by itself.

2. *Complexity of the levels increases upward.* This law is a corollary of the first. For if the levels are cumulative upward, each must be more complex than the one before it. The structure of the atom is an organisation of electrons, protons and neutrons. The structure of the molecule is an organisation of atoms. The structure of the cell is an organisation of molecules, and so on. Thus the entire structure of the integrative levels rests on the physical as on a foundation and rises above it in a series of increasing complexity based on complications of the lowest. We have seen this in the structures themselves, but it is not so evident in the emergent qualities. At the higher levels the emergence of qualities marks the degree of complexity of the conditions which prevail at that level. It would be theoretically possible to assign numbers to the levels to indicate their degree of complexity by counting emergent qualities, though this has not yet been done. As yet we are not sure of the qualities. It is the qualities, then, which lend to the integrative levels their relative autonomy. For every quality is as much a quality as any other, and none which is the product of higher grades of complexity is any more qualitative than those which exist at the lower grades of relative simplicity. Qualities at higher levels are somewhat more elusive yet none the less real, none the less qualities *qua* qualities.

3. *In any organisation the higher level depends upon the lower.* That is to say, in an object which extends over more than one level, which it must if it exists at any level above the physical, then the higher level depends for its continuance upon the lower. A culture will not last if its cities are destroyed; a chemical compound will not continue if its bonds are broken; yet both cultures and chemical compounds will leave behind them physical elements; rubble in the case of the cities, and single elements in the case of the compound. The physical properties are more enduring than the constructions raised over them. Destroy the physical properties in any object and the entire object goes, but the reverse is not true. A man run over by a street-grading machine is no longer a man, no longer even an organism but merely a collection of decaying cells; eventually to be reduced to still lower levels, to carbon compounds.

4. *In any organisation, the lower level is directed by the higher.* That is to say, in an object

which extends over more than one level the higher level furnishes the direction of the lower. An army may travel on its stomach but it is its brain that tells it where to travel. Institutions may have physical perquisites, such as buildings and tools, but they take social aims. Just as the mechanism of an organisation is furnished by its lower levels, so its purpose is the product of its higher levels. Purpose in science has been in bad repute for some centuries, and has been replaced by mechanism, chiefly because of its theological reading. Science quite properly avoids all transcendental notions, being committed to what it can learn from the combination of logic with fact, and so has read all teleology as outside its province. But purpose, conceived as vectors built into organisations and discoverable there, has a legitimate function in science. It would be difficult indeed to understand the somatic organism without the aim of adaptation presupposed. One might even add that nobody can understand the mechanism of any organisation without some implicit preliminary assumption of an hypothesis with regard to its purpose. It would be quite possible in perfect innocence to take an automobile apart. But it would not be possible to put it back together without knowing what it was intended to do.

5. *For an organisation at any given level, its mechanism lies at the level below and its purpose at the level above.* This law states that for the analysis of any organisation three levels are required: its own, the one below and the one above. To analyse a mechanism we drop down one level. This is obvious when we consider that analysis moves from the whole to its parts. For we should not expect the parts to be on the same level of analysis as the whole of which they are the parts.

Similarly, to find the purpose of any organisation we would move up one level, for then we are considering the organisation as itself a part of some higher and more complex organisation. We could perhaps study the kidney and its functions without reference to its constituent tissues and without reference to the somatic organism in which it plays a certain role or roles, but we would not get very far without the introduction into our considerations of both adjacent levels.

6. *A disturbance introduced into an organisation at any one level reverberates at all the levels it covers.* It is now well known in psychiatry that mental events can occasion physical difficulties and *vice-versa*. Anxiety may give rise to diarrhoea, or conversely traumasthenia may occur when nervous exhaustion follows physical in-

jury. Disease may occasion loss of weight as well as depression. We are assuming here, of course, the levels as they occur in highly integrated organisations. In less integrated organisations the reverberation would be neither as extensive nor as severe.

7. *The time required for a change in organisation shortens as we ascend the levels.* The evolution of stars requires a longer time than the evolution of biological species, and the evolution of biological species requires a longer time than change in human cultures. Atoms and molecules have been around longer than cells, cells longer than the more complex organisms and these longer than human cultures. The chemical elements are reputed to be something over 3 billion years old, the cultures merely several thousand. The life-span of the genus, horse, has been calculated at about 5½ million years, while 20 million years is the estimated duration of the species of Triassic ammonites (Zeuner, 1950). Evidently the more complex the organisation the more unstable, so that advances are not achieved without a price and advanced positions are not easily held. Hence duration is a function of the integrative levels.

8. *The higher the level, the smaller its population of instances.* The organisation at each level upward is a complication of the organisations of lower levels. Therefore, as we should expect, there are fewer molecules than atoms, fewer cells than molecules, fewer organisms than cells and fewer cultures than organisms. There are more electrons in the universe than anything else, but cultures are rare: Toynbee professes to find no more than twenty-one instances of the species. From the point of view of population the integrative levels form a pyramid.

9. *It is impossible to reduce the higher level to the lower.* Each level has its own characteristic structure and emergent quality. Hence, to reduce a higher to a lower level means to lose the quality and the structure of the higher level. A living organism is not merely a collection of tissues and cells and organs, although it contains these. In the organisations which exist at each of the integrative levels no whole is merely the sum of its parts but each contains the higher organisation of the whole itself. The attempt to reduce the higher to the lower level comes about as a result of the familiarity with analysis in scientific method. Science is seeking primarily the mechanism of the organisations into which it inquires, and this, as we have noted, requires dropping down one level: parts do lie at a level below the whole. However,

this seems to have led some investigators to suppose that the parts are what is real about the whole. The truth seems to be that the whole and its parts are equally real; and indeed the question of which is parts and which is whole becomes merely a question of the level chosen for analysis, for there is some level at which every organisation is a part of some whole and another level at which it is a whole to its parts.

To suppose that the higher level can be reduced to the lower is to commit the fallacy of reduction. The failure to understand this fallacy has led to errors in interpreting scientific method, on the fond assumption that since the wholes are found at the level of common sense and the analytical parts are revealed only in laboratory procedures, the former must be illusive appearances while the latter are the realities. But the table is not merely a collection of whirling electrons, it is also a table, a real culture object as well as a real piece of wood.

10. *An organisation at any level is a distortion of the level below.* Higher organisations disturb the smoothed out distribution of lower organisations. Matter, it has been argued, consists in crinkles in space-time. And organisms have been thought of as distortions in the crystallographical field.

11. *Events at any given level affect organisations at other levels.* This is the same phenomenon as the one discussed in Law 6 above, only this time seen from the outside instead of the inside. The failure of the corn crop is supposed to have destroyed the Mayan culture of Yucatan and Northern Guatemala. Wars at the culture level, on the other hand, may cause the death of many organisms and of many more cells.

12. *Whatever is affected as an organisation has some effect as an organisation.* Examples of characteristic behaviour are: cause-and-effect at the physical level, combination-rearrangement at the chemical level, sensitivity-reactivity at the biological level, stimulus-response at the psychological level and contact-adaptation (as this takes place between cultures) at the cultural level. Every organisation at whatever level it exists has some sensitivity manifested as irritability, and makes its responses in kind.

RULES OF EXPLANATION

1. *The reference of any organisation must be at the lowest level which will provide sufficient explanation.* We are forbidden to call in higher

levels for phenomena which are entirely explicable at the lower. Patients who give allergic reactions to eggs need not be treated for neurosis even though their symptoms may have indicated either. We are obliged by the principle of economy to account for as much as possible by explanations which are as simple as possible, and this means going no higher in the integrative levels than our material requires us to do. Stars do not have souls, but on the other hand men are not merely carbon compounds. If you can entirely account for a compound at the chemical level there is no need to go to the biological for an explanation.

2. *The reference of any organisation must be to the highest level which its explanation requires.* This rule is the converse of the previous one. We must not go any higher in the integrative levels than necessary to provide sufficient explanation, but we must go as high as is necessary. Complex phenomena probably call for higher types of explanation. The lowest levels are complex enough to make explanation a difficult affair, but oversimplification does not explain: it explains away. An organisation, in short, cannot be explained without bringing into the explanation elements which belong to its highest level.

3. *An organisation belongs to its highest level.* This is a very important rule of explanation. All organisations except the physical belong to more than one level but each must be considered as belonging in some peculiar way to its highest level. Chairs like men are not mere physical objects, though they are that too; they are culture objects. Human beings are not mere reactive mechanisms; they are also responsible members of society. An atom is not merely a collection of electrons and protons; it is also an atom.

4. *Every organisation must be explained finally on its own level.* A broken leg cannot be accounted for on social or psychological grounds nor on physical grounds either for that matter. We need to know the tensile strength of the Fibula or Tibia, in this case the physical properties of biological material.

5. *No organisation can be explained entirely in terms of a lower or higher level.* This is obviously a corollary of the last principle. Mechanism and vitalism in biology are attempts to explain organisms in terms of lower and higher levels respectively.

Rex M. Collier

A DYNAMIC REGULATORY THEORY OF CONSCIOUSNESS

The concept of consciousness has been associated with more traumatic history than probably any other concept in psychology. No concept has generated more philosophy from the academically respectable to the misleading mystical verbiage of the quack, and probably no concept has been capable of stimulating, both directly and indi-

From Rex M. Collier, "Selected Implications from a Dynamic Regulatory Theory of Consciousness, *"American Psychologist,* April 1964, 265-269. Copyright 1964 by the American Psychological Association, and reproduced by permission of author and publisher.

rectly, more interprofessional strife. Why, then, should anyone who values his peace of mind and professional standing wish to open this Fibber McGee closet, stuffed as it is with a conglomerate of conceptual hazards? My only answer is that there seems to me no more challenging need in psychology than to restore to our science a valid and usable concept of consciousness, and I have now become involved beyond the point of no return.

More than mere semantics the concept of consciousness will not die either from behavioristic beheading or from relegation to roles of impotence by disregard and belittling kinds of redefinition. Psychology finally has no valid choice except that of dealing with a holistic organism from which no function is excised in the interests of scientific respectability. Even the dichotomy of subjective-objective no longer gives refuge in a right-wing pole, for this convenient dualism must be replaced by a conceptualized continuum of degree of tangibility. With such a continuum new application is made of Leeper's (1951) point that the task of psychological research is to create tangibility where it has not previously existed. Mere mention of the names of Fechner, Ebbinghaus, Binet, and Thurstone will suggest that a history of psychology could be written in terms of the conquests that have made the so-called subjective more tangible and, therefore, more objective and palpable. The day is passing when the concept of consciousness can be swept under a rug of so-called subjectivity with the feeling that a mess has been cleaned up and now the psychological enterprise is ready for respectable visitors from physics and chemistry.

The charge that consciousness had to be disregarded or dropped in the interests of scientific objectivity is and has been based on misinterpretation of history. The concept, as contributed to psychology by structuralism, was static and behaviorally ineffective. In spite of the interactionism of many functionalists, the concept of consciousness was still a world largely separated from behavior. Under such circumstances, the vigorous development of interests in behavior left no choice but to disregard the concept. Consciousness was relegated to a role of unimportance not because of its subjectivity but because it seemed to play an ineffective role in behavior. If it can be shown, on the other hand, that consciousness represents the highest levels of integration, operates as a regulatory field for behavior, and has phylogenetically always been intimately related to action, then psychology has no choice except to create the methodology necessary to make the so-called subjective more tangible.

Several assumptions are necessary in a conceptualization of a functional, effective, regulatory consciousness. The *first* is that consciousness is a product of living protoplasm. *Second,* the principle of continuity in the evolution of the animal series leads to the assumption that human beings have no monopoly on the basic general characteristics of consciousness. The Cartesian type of solipsism, which implies that only human beings are conscious, is hence untenable even if

you must insist that it is currently untestable. *Third,* the living organism may be conceptualized as an open system of energy with many subsystems in the total pattern. *Fourth*, the organization of subsystems tends to be hierarchical with some at functional dominance and others with roles of relative subordination. Earlier papers (Collier, 1955, 1956, 1957, 1963) have shown that consciousness, as it is usually talked about, tends to emerge at the levels of highest dominance or highest metabolic rate. Since such levels are physiologically regulatory, the assumption has been made that consciousness functions as a regulatory subsystem or field. Reference is made here primarily to the attentional function of consciousness. But a more comprehensive concept is both possible and necessary.

In the time remaining, I should like, with brevity, to do the following: *(a)* sketch a functional, three-level, phylogenetically oriented theory of consciousness; *(b)* point out an implied resolution of dualism; *(c)* suggest a revised perspective for Freudian conscious-unconscious dichotomy; *(d)* indicate a different basic approach to methodology; and *(e)* point to a derivable basic value in human relationships.

A FUNCTIONAL THREE-LEVEL THEORY

Suggested, but never developed, are the proposals of Hall (1904), Baldwin (1895), Ribot (1897), and Ruckmick (1936) that consciousness may have had its phylogenetic origins in the affective potentialities of the living organism. More recently Reymert (1950) has said that "Scholars have always been aware of this intangible and intricate 'something,' which we may call feeling, as a very essential and perhaps the most dominating aspect of mental life [p. xix]." But reorientation is necessary, for the history of studies on affectivity, largely in the structuralistic context, has little relevance to behavior.

Functional three-level theory gives Level I phylogenetic priority with its origins in the cell itself. The cell, rated recently as complex enough to require half the total time for biological evolution for its own creation, may be conceived as the focal point for the convergence of three crucial interdependent and probably redundant functions, namely, *(a)* the dissemination on some molecular basis of generalized communicative influence that maintains integration and self-regulation, *(b)* the capacity for simple, generalized contact-chemical-sense-feeling, *(c)* the quality or characteristics of being alive. To solve the problems presented by one of these facets is probably to solve the problems of the other two. Attention is directed to one of these functions.

The simple, generalized contact-chemical-sense-feeling is seen as the phylogenetic basis for all later developments of consciousness. Note a few characteristics of human feeling that can be congruent with such continuity. *(a)* Feelings are generalized. Feelings of fatigue, euphoria, illness, boredom, impotence, energetic readiness are generalized and have no known specialized sense modalities for their propagation. *(b)* Feelings are convincing. For producing conviction, a strong feeling is better than logical argument. *(c)* Feelings are productive of action. Phylogenetically oldest, the chemical sense-feeling always seems to require action. Smells entice or repel and thus invite approach or avoidance. Tastes, in turn, produce acceptance or rejection. The stronger the taste or smell, the more action determining the feeling becomes—one must *do* something about it. The olfactory lobes of aquatic vertebrates tend to be the dominant and regulatory centers. While in human beings other neural centers have become more dominant, the affectivity intimate to chemical sensitivity is clearly an action-determining factor. The basic function of affectivity at all stages of phylogenetic development is the production, regulation, and integration of action.

If this approach is accepted, then the major portion of the literature on affectivity needs reorientation in terms of the new context and its action implications. The door seems open to a whole range of studies which have for some time been somewhat less than respectable. One begins to wonder also how in the history of man's development action and consciousness ever became as systematically separated as they have been.

Functional Level II appears phylogenetically when sense modalities become differentiated and diversified so that informational intake requires central consolidation and unification. This level may be called *situational consciousness*. All the potency for action and action regulation from the affective background of Level I is retained and further augmented by the new sensory and neural equipment. The orientation of the animal, however, is to the immediate in space and time. Neither past nor future is of importance, nor even what lies beyond the range of current sensory intake. The term *situation* is used to represent the fact that the organism can now react to a complex of physical stimuli or informational cues from a variety of sources and give coherence and unity to these stimuli.

Functional Level III is the evolved capacity to become aware of the fact that one is aware or conscious and will be called *reflective consciousness*. To be able to reflect upon or to review the aspects of one's own experience is assumed to be a basic biological achievement in enabling a primate form to become a human being. However, for reflective consciousness to become an asset, a twin capacity had also to evolve, namely, the ability to delay action, under the press of stimulation, while reviewing the alternatives to action. Rosenzweig (1944) has pointed out, "If a response occurs immediately on the reception of the stimulus there is no possibility either for the accumulation of concrete content necessary to abstract thinking or for gratification delay of a providential kind [p. 386]." Reflective consciousness, with ability to delay action, enables man to criticize his own behavior with both constructive and destructive effects; with these capabilities he has invented symbols to facilitate his communication and make his own problem solving more systematic; the development of both civilizations and the uniquely human self are products of Functional Level III.

RESOLUTION OF DUALISM

The foregoing statement of a functional three-level theory of consciousness is brief and in suggestive form only. But special implications may be selected as illustrative. The age old issue of dualism now fades to only an historic role. If consciousness is intimately associated with action at Functional Levels I and II, Level III should be no exception; and a closer look shows that such traditional conceptual separation grows out of a fundamental misconception of consciousness peculiar to reflective consciousness itself. Note that while animals may successfully delay only briefly and then resume relevant action, the human being can manage such delays indefinitely. These twin capacities, to delay action while reviewing either alternatives to action or an elaboration of symbolic representations of action, have resulted in the assumption that action and thought have no necessary relationship. The next step is obvious and easily taken, namely, that the world of thought and the world of action or body or matter are two separate and independent sets of existence. The two supposedly contrasting kinds of existence have been thought of as running parallel or interacting on some mysterious basis, but thinkers have for hundreds of years insisted that basically we deal here with two separate orders of phenomena.

The present theory leads necessarily to the conclusion that the thinkers' assumption is based on misconception and illusion. Thought, cognitive activity, logical processing, and the like are products essentially of Functional Level III and still have action implications even though, at times, apparently divorced from action. Simply because symbolic representations of action may arise at Level III, run their course, and terminate without discharging into obvious action-type responses need not be taken to mean separate orders between thought and physiological process. Closer scrutiny of the processes of Level III will reveal the fact of their action relevance and thus the preservation of the principle of continuity.

The theory at this point seems, at first, to rob man of many cherished beliefs, and frighteningly to complicate the task of psychological research. In my view, the theory gives man intimate kinship to all life, invites him to a more responsible role in relationship to that life and the natural world, dignifies his existence in terms of his phylogenetic and personal achievement, and finally offers to enrich with greater validity the science by which we attempt to understand the nature of man and his behavior.

THE CONSCIOUS-UNCONSCIOUS DICHOTOMY

Freudian dogma, exercising a profound effect on personality theory, has finally come to be accepted by many largely as Freud left it. However, Freudian approaches are at many points unacceptable to the present theory, and much revision of personality theory is eventually to be required. The conscious-unconscious dichotomy has been basic in the Freudian image of man which has included also the characteristics of an impotent consciousness, irrationality of unconscious motivation, dominance of sexual drives, the invalidity of independent attempts at self-understanding, and the individual as a collection of partially independent mechanisms.

The conscious-unconscious dichotomy can now be replaced by a model of the figure-ground relationship which preserves the continuity and integrity within the individual and is consistent with the physiological principle of relative domi-

nance of functional subsystems. In the simple organism, for example the amoeba, the segment stimulated not only increases its rate of metabolism above that of the rest of the organism but that segment becomes temporarily dominant and regulatory; the rest of the organism becomes supportive to the dominant area. This primitive pattern is seen as the simple beginnings of what is finally called attending or attention. As Functional Level II is evolved, the informational intake is so potentially great that this relative dominance pattern, which is basic to organic integrity, is the only way of maintaining situational unity. Thus when some processes are accelerated and become dominant, those relegated to a subordinate role become supportive to the dominant function. As animals increased their range of motility, it became necessary to maintain greater consistencies of internal or organic environments. Thus, a division of organismic labor developed, freeing the animal not only to increased range of movement but also for more continuous, discriminative, coping types of behavior. With development of an autonomic system the supportive background became enlarged and more consistent.

To identify the so-called unconscious with the background which is supportive for processes in clear attention is to accomplish at least the following: (a) Phylogenetic continuity is maintained; (b) continuity between attentional consciousness as figure and the traditional unconscious as background is provided; (c) antagonism between conscious and unconscious is no longer assumed except in special cases not necessarily typical; (d) a basis is suggested for making the unconscious largely a product of the affective-conative predisposition of the organism contributed chiefly by Functional Level I; (e) with the mystery removed from the concept of unconscious, operational definition and relevant experiment become increasingly possible.

A REVISED APPROACH TO METHODOLOGY

A comprehensive theory of consciousness seems necessarily to lead to a theory of the organism. Furthermore, to focus on a basic concept of the organism leads, in turn, to a change in the role of methodology. For psychology, methodology borrowed from the contexts of physics and chemistry has occupied more often the role of end than of means. In the role of end, this borrowed methodology has dictated the nature of the basic concept of the organism with the model of the automaton becoming easily and necessarily adopted. With this model dominating his "apperceptive mass" the psychologist assumes that there is philosophic validity to the dichotomy of freedom and determinism, with resulting necessity to choose the latter in order to be methodologically orthodox. Consider the case of a different approach. The evolutionary developments of consciousness seem to be associated with increasing degrees of independence of the protoplasmic energy system from the surrounding environmental energy systems. Thus, it becomes a short step to posit as a basic model of the organism a semiautonomous open energy system. Under these circumstances the dichotomy of freedom and determinism become poles of a continuum described as degrees of freedom. The midrange of the continuum is seen, then, as realistic and experimentally practical while the terminal regions are unrealistic or fictitious. With a basic concept of subject matter initiating the approach, methodology is assigned its appropriate role as means, and as such it may contribute to but not dictate the nature of the subject matter. Furthermore, methodology will focus more frequently on the probabilistic; predictions will become contingency predictions; and experimenters will more frequently study the self-directing or self-originating responses of organisms.

A BASIC VALUE

A connotation of the automaton model is that the organism waits to react until stimulation produces a reaction. A corollary is that for the automaton, manipulation by external management is part of the accepted order in human relationships. This approach fits conveniently, even though at times undesirably, into many of our methods of adver-

tising, producing, merchandising, and personnel policies in the business world. Since Sputnik I, education has tended more frequently to see the student as a receptacle—a kind of automaton—into which to pour information and as a device to be manipulated toward preconceived ends which are not necessarily shared by the student. Teaching machines fit nicely into this context. Totalitarian propagandas are always more easily spawned from the automaton model as a core concept.

But what happens when the automaton model is replaced by the semiautonomous open system of energy? It becomes immediately important to recognize, as far as possible, the capacity which the organism has for self-regulation, self-direction, or self-management. To disregard the degree to which such potentialities are present is to disrespect and even to do violence to the basic nature of the organism itself. This kind of disrespect easily leads to resentment, anger, alienation, and, when practiced as part of a political policy, can lead to social revolutions. Thus, from this revised basic concept one may derive a basic value. This value is respect defined as *recognition and degree of constructive concern which one has for the self-determining and self-actualizing capacities of other living organisms.*

Love, which has been represented by some as basic, now becomes accepted primarily in the context of basic respect. Love can be predatory, destructive, and crippling to growth potentialities. Love, to be constructive, must be qualified and enriched by the concept of respect as just defined. Thus, respect, so defined and derived from the basic concept of the organism, is seen as having potentialities as a basic value in human relationships and probably also between human beings and the rest of the animal world. Respect so defined will prompt the experimenter not only to be aware of his rights and freedoms but also of his responsibilities and will become a cornerstone in his system of ethical values.

Gordon Bronson

HIERARCHY IN THE BRAIN: IMPLICATIONS FOR LEARNING AND CRITICAL PERIODS

The evolutionary history of man is reflected in the emergence of adaptive mechanisms of increasing complexity in the course of early development. This paper focuses on two of these ontogenetic sequences which seem of particular importance for understanding adult behavior: "critical-period" phenomena, and the development of learning capacities. . . . Many data suggest that learning capacities of increasing complexity emerge with a chronology paralleling the development of these critical periods. An attempt is made to clarify and interrelate these two ontogenetic sequences . . . .

The use of neurological evidence to clarify the meaning of behavioral data requires a conceptual model which focuses on aspects of nervous system functioning pertinent to the issues at hand. The first part of this paper presents such a neurological model. It emphasizes the hierarchical nature of central nervous system (CNS) organization in postulating a series of three "levels" within the nervous system. More complex ("higher") levels are seen as a product of the evolution of successively more differentiating neural networks which in part supersede, and in part build upon, the less complex adaptive mechanisms mediated by the phylogenetically older levels. Ontogenetically, the emergence of new behavioral capacities is seen as a function of the sequential maturation of networks within the different levels.

The second part of the paper considers the different characteristics of learning phenomena mediated by networks at the three CNS levels. Differences in learning capacities are discussed in terms of varying degrees of perceptual and motor differentiation and, more significantly, in terms of the kinds of events which serve as adequate "reinforcement" for learning mediated by neural systems of the different levels. This leads to the proposal of a rough developmental chronology of

From "The Hierarchical Organization of the Central Nervous System: Implications for Learning Processes and Critical Periods in Early Development," from *Behavioral Science*, 1965, Vol. 10, pages 7-25. Reprinted by permission of author and publisher.

learning from classical conditioning, through instrumental learning, to latent learning phenomena, a sequence which parallels the maturation through early infancy of neural networks of increasing cognitive and motivational differentiation. The adult organism, it is assumed, may acquire information under any of these paradigms, depending upon the circumstances of acquisition.

The final part of the paper attempts to interpret evidence from studies of critical-period phenomena in light of the postulated theory of the emergence of learning capacities. Three major critical periods in early development are suggested, each defined by a shifting saliency of different environmental events, and each related to the emergence of more complex learning capacities. Neurologically, each critical period is seen as beginning with the maturation of neural systems of a given CNS level and terminating through several possible mechanisms, including functional inhibition imposed by subsequent maturation of higher-level networks. . . .

HIERARCHICAL MODEL OF CNS FUNCTIONING

The conceptual model. Figure 1 represents the basic characteristics of the model. A gross dichotomy is made between neural tissue which consists of networks of short axon neurons with multiple interconnections (stippled areas of Figure 1) and the systems of long axon neurons which interconnect these areas (broken lines). These latter systems are found both within levels (horizontal broken lines) and between levels of the CNS (vertical broken lines); they constitute an innate programming system channeling the flow of excitation patterns among the areas of short axon networks. Peripheral afferents and efferents (solid lines) connect with the CNS at the several levels so that increasingly refined sensory and motor discriminations can be made directly by the successively

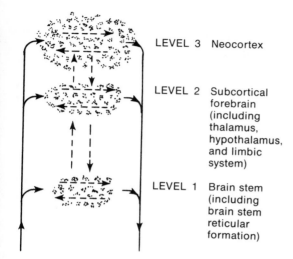

LEVEL 3 Neocortex

LEVEL 2 Subcortical
forebrain
(including
thalamus,
hypothalamus,
and limbic
system)

LEVEL 1 Brain stem
(including
brain stem
reticular
formation)

Figure 1.   Basic characteristics of a hierarchical
model of CNS functioning

more differentiating networks. The networks for vertical integration between levels enable the more primitive systems to exercise an upward control for the general programming of patterns of cerebral activation, while higher levels projecting downward effect a more highly differentiated over-all functioning through tonic inhibition plus a more selective phasic excitation and inhibition of lower-level systems. . . . Finally, note that the increasing diversity of stippled areas within successive levels of Figure 1 represents the increasingly differentiated character of higher-level CNS networks.[1] This evolutionary refinement brings an increasing development of specialized functions among the short axon networks of the higher levels.

Input into all levels is both from peripheral afferents and from connections from other areas in the CNS; activity in levels 1 and 2 is also strongly affected by changes in the internal chemical environment. Information resulting from the interplay of these factors at level l, projected upward to primary sensory and motor areas within the neocortex, affects the general (tonic) level of sensory alertness and motor responsiveness. Similarly, networks within level 2 integrate input from various sources and project output to level 3, modulating the more varied (phasic) activation patterns in "association" areas of the neocortex to effect a more focal alertness to particular stimulus patterns (see Samuels, 1959). Since the networks within levels 1 and 2 include areas particularly responsive to internal biochemical changes, the more discriminative neocortical processes are

partially affected by, and therefore adaptive to, the physiological condition of the organism.

Functions mediated by the various levels. Turning to a more specific consideration of structures incorporated within each of the three levels of Figure l, it is possible to specify further the functional capacities of the various levels. While the generalizations to follow at times require some qualification, the exceptions are not crucial to the main arguments of the paper.

Level 1 networks. The phylogenetic primacy of brain-stem networks of level 1 is reflected in the gross motor functions mediated at this level. The brain-stem reticular system and the various motor nuclei of this level constitute a system for co-ordinating gross body movement . . . . Present also are more discrete stimulus-response systems such as the sucking reflex, rooting reflex, pupillary reflex, etc. (Jung & Hassler, 1960). Brain-stem response patterns are representative of the total behavior repertoire of simple vertebrates; in man they either provide the background pattern for support of the more differentiated motor responses controlled from higher neural systems (Jung & Hassler, 1960), or in the case of more discrete reflexes they may disappear shortly after birth under inhibition from neocortical networks (McGraw, 1943).

Berlyne (1960) has surveyed the extensive data defining an "orientation reaction" mediated by networks of this level. It consists of a complex of responses including: orienting of receptor organs (e.g., turning of head, eyes, and ears); a general skeletal response (arrest of ongoing actions, increase of muscle tonus); autonomic system reactions preparatory for action; changes in receptor organs (e.g., pupil dilation); and an EEG arousal reaction. Its adaptive function in providing a poised alertness to external stimuli is clearly evident. . . . Sharpless and Jasper (1956), working with cats, have demonstrated that brain-stem preparations respond to changes in mode or intensity of stimuli but not to variations of pattern within modes, showing that direct sensory mediation at this level is possible, but that sensory discrimination is severely limited. Berlyne presents data from Russian investigators indicating that the acquired "signal value" of a complex stimulus can influence its saliency in producing an orienting response in humans, a mechanism which

---

[1]Since the neocortex is anatomically continuous, the model at this point reflects the functional rather than the gross structural properties of the neocortex.

must involve the downward control of level 1 processes by perceptual systems of the neocortical level. . . .

Berlyne further describes a "defensive reaction" which apparently can also be mediated by the brain-stem level. It consists of a constellation of responses, largely overlapping with the orienting responses but including "freezing," "blinking," "gasps," and some variations in the reaction pattern within the autonomic system. He notes very intense stimuli, and pain, as being capable of producing this defensive reaction. In addition, the many studies of the conditioning of complex stimuli, using some form of pain as the unconditioned stimulus, demonstrate that the defensive reaction, like the orienting reaction, can follow from neocortically mediated perceptual patterns, as well as from direct level 1 sensory input.

Turning to processes of vertical integration with higher levels of the CNS, the reticular network of level 1 appears as a neocortical activating system. Diffusely projecting afferents to the neocortex affect the general level of neocortical activation, a mechanism influencing over-all sensory and motor responsiveness. In addition to mediating diurnal variations in sensory alertness and motor activity, this level 1 mechanism appears capable of overriding the more focal activation of limited cortical areas controlled by the thalamic reticular system, which is a level 2 mechanism underlying focused-attention phenomena (see Lindsley, 1960, and below). This capacity appears to be a protective device for superseding level 2 mechanisms for focused attention, thereby producing a condition of over-all alertness in situations of potential danger. This alerting response is a component of both the orientation and defensive reactions discussed above.

The reticular system is known to be responsive to the level of nutrients in the blood, to various sex hormones, and to adrenalin. Decreases in the first and increases in the latter two factors heighten reticular activity (Dell, 1958). With regard to peripheral input, the reticular system receives direct afferents from all sensory modalities, but pain and proprioceptor inputs are known to be particularly salient (Samuels, 1959), and it is known also to be richly endowed with afferents from sexual organs (Guyton, 1961). . . . Downward control of reticular activity . . . can effect a more discriminative reticular functioning through the selective excitation and inhibition of reticular networks by neocortical centers, following the recognition of significant objects.

It seems probable, as Berlyne (1960) has suggested, that continued level 1 activation of the higher CNS levels can produce two different orientations in the intact mammal, depending on the intensity of the reticular system excitation. Moderate excitation, initially producing the transient orientation reaction, leads to exploratory investigation until terminated by familiarity with the stimulus object (habituation). This approach orientation, occurring under moderate degrees of level 1 excitation, presumably allows for the subsequent narrowing of attention to specific sensory modes as level 2 attention mechanisms resume control of neocortical activation patterns following the waning of the initial generalized alerting response. More intense reticular activation would produce an initial defensive reaction, followed by innate or acquired fear reactions, and terminated either by escape from the arousing stimuli, or by habituation to a level inducing exploration rather than fear (Berlyne, 1960; Welker, 1961). Response sequences in infant monkeys presented with novel stimuli (Harlow & Zimmermann, 1959) illustrate this latter phenomenon very clearly: the initial fear reaction of clinging to the (surrogate) mother decreases with visual examination, and is gradually replaced by approach and close investigation. . . .

Level 2 networks. . . . For purposes of analysis the networks of level 2 can be classified as providing: (1) more refined sensory discrimination and motor coordination; (2) specific motivational and/or emotional orientations supporting ongoing purposive behavior sequences; and (3) mechanisms for the control of attention. It is the latter two aspects of level 2 systems which are of the greatest interest here. . . .

The motivational networks within level 2, which act to initiate and support diverse purposive orientations to the environment, are responsive (1) to changes in the internal chemical environment and probably (2) to direct input from pain and sexual afferents, and (3) are influenced also by complex auditory and visual perceptions mediated by way of neocortical systems. . . . The complex networks of the limbic system which interconnect areas responsive to the internal environment (i.e., the hypothalamus) and to direct pain and sexual afferents (parts of the thalamus) with pathways from the neocortex (probably via the paleocortex), would appear to be central in the integration of diverse types of motivationally significant stimuli. . . . In addition to motivational functions, the limbic system is central to the mediation of emotional behavior. Fear or rage reactions are the most frequent emotions reported in animal studies;

however, when verbal report is possible human subjects indicate pleasant as well as unpleasant mood changes following diverse limbic system lesions, giving support to the contention of Olds and Olds (1961) that stimulation in numerous limbic loci are "pleasurable" to animals. . . .

The attention-mediating function of level 2 systems in mammals involves the vertical feedback networks between nuclei of the thalamic reticular system and various areas of the neocortex. In contrast with the global alerting capacity of brain-stem activation of the neocortex, the more rapidly fluctuating and more focal alerting mechanisms of the thalamic reticular system allow for the focus of attention to specific sensory modes, and probably to particular input patterns within modes. These diffusely projecting thalamic nuclei activate primarily parietal, occipital, and temporal areas adjacent to the various primary sensory-reception areas. As these cortical areas serve gnostic functions, the control which the neocortex exerts over the thalamic reticular system enables the neocortex to control partially its own excitation level for the selective attention to significant aspects of the contemporary input. . . .

Level 3 networks. For present purposes only a limited discussion of the contributions of level 3 systems is necessary. The highly developed perceptual, cognitive, and motor capacities of the neocortex need no review, and the role of these perceptual and motor capacities in initiating and supporting exploratory or fear reactions has been noted in discussing level 1 networks. Welker (1961) notes that exploratory behavior is more prominent in species with fewer inborn responses to specific stimulus patterns, and also that the dominant sensory mode for exploratory investigation relates to the relative degree of development of various sensory areas of the neocortex in the different species; these facts illuminate the major role of neocortical systems in the instigation and orientation of exploratory behavior. Studies by Krechevsky (1937), showing a decrease in the variability in maze behavior proportional to the amount of neocortical damage in rats, as well as the "lethargic" behavior found in totally decorticate cats (Bard & Rioch, 1937) and monkeys (Travis & Woolsey, 1956), also demonstrate the importance of neocortical processes in supporting an exploratory orientation in mammals. . . .

The hierarchical organization of adaptive mechanisms. One of the consequences of the evolutionary development of the nervous system is what appears as a repetition of the various adaptive mech-

anisms, with refinements, at successive levels of the CNS. The increasingly differentiating sensory and motor mechanisms found at successively newer levels of the CNS is a well-known example; others of equal importance seem less noted and therefore call for further discussion. The interest of this hierarchical organization lies both in the sequential appearance of successively more refined adaptive mechanisms in early human development, and in the later complex interactions among systems of different levels serving analogous functions but with different degrees of complexity. . . .

For the moment consider what may be loosely called a "motivational" hierarchy. . . . Neural tissue sensitive to changes in the internal environment is found both in the reticular system of level 1 and in the hypothalamus within level 2. While both levels are sensitive to the same range of biochemical factors, present evidence indicates that the hypothalamus is more differentiated (1) in having discrete nuclei specifically responsive to particular biochemical changes, and (2) in producing behavior sequences oriented towards various specific goals following the activation of localized hypothalamic areas. Stellar (1960) reviews evidence showing that electrical or chemical stimulation of discrete hypothalamic areas selectively influences eating, drinking, or sexual activities; stimulation of the reticular system apparently affects only the general level of sensory alertness and motor activity (see Samuels, 1959). It seems reasonable, therefore, to speak of a hierarchy of motivational systems: continued excitation of level 1 systems, in the absence of specific hypothalamic activity, produces flexible exploratory behavior oriented toward perceptual novelty; the additional activation of level 2 motivational systems brings a channeling of behavior towards specific goals. This is illustrated in Bruner, Matter, and Papanek (1955), who find less "trial-and-error" behavior in the maze as hunger drive is increased in rats, as well as less incidental learning of nonessential cues. (See Welker [1961] for a review of other pertinent studies.) Some types of stimuli seem to activate motivational systems at both levels, i.e., internal biochemical changes can produce both the "exploratory" components of appetitive behavior (from level 1 activation) and the perceptual sensitivities to particular goal-related objects (associated with level 2 excitation). Other stimuli seem to activate primarily level 1 motivational systems, as when perceptual novelty brings the heightened alertness basic to exploratory behavior. Perception of goal-relevant objects (e.g., food, sex partner) will activate level 2 motivational systems when internal biochemical factors are sufficiently close to "threshold" values. (It is tempting to complete this motivational hierarchy by suggesting that in man neocortical networks have assumed motivational functions beyond the purely perceptual roles mentioned above. It seems likely that cognitive processes relatively independent of the immediate perceptual environment can maintain an alert purposive orientation through the continuous activation of level 1 networks. The Gestalt studies of perseverance towards the completion of interrupted tasks and the desire for cognitive closure, as well as Allport's [1937] early concept of "functional autonomy," and Miller, Galanter, and Pribram's [1960] recent emphasis on the major importance of acquired "images" and "plans" in guiding purposive behavior, all call attention to the characteristically human capacity for maintaining, or returning to, a complex program of flexible goal-oriented behavior which is independent of immediate environmental stimulation, and remote from any recognized physiological need. Current theories of "derived motives" [psychoanalysis] or "secondary drives" [learning theories] perhaps place too exclusive an emphasis on phylogenetically older motivational systems which are activated by biochemical changes and maintained primarily by subcortical systems. . . .)

One final pair of hierarchical systems needs brief discussion here: the development of the transient orientation and defensive reactions into the more enduring exploratory or fear orientations in circumstances where neocortically mediated perception maintains reticular system activity. Since reticular system activity is responsive only to changes in the mode or the intensity of the direct level 1 sensory input, and habituation is fairly rapid, the orientation reaction will be of relatively brief duration in any reasonably stable environment. With the addition of downward activation from perceptual systems of the neocortex, the pattern variability present in the normal environment becomes an adequate stimulus for maintaining a degree of level 1 system activation sufficient for an alert interest in the environment. In conditions of moderate perceptual novelty, this interest outward is manifest in exploratory behavior. The development of aversive response patterns, from the brief defensive reaction mediated directly at level 1 by intense stimulation or pain, to the more enduring fear orientation in response to complex stimulus patterns of extreme novelty, is more complicated. In the many species

showing innate fearfulness in response to perceptual novelty, this reaction develops somewhat later than the capacity for complex pattern discrimination—a chronology often described as allowing time for the development of primary attachments (see section on critical periods, below). Fearfulness in response to novelty, therefore, either requires more extensive visual experience than does object recognition, or is dependent upon still further maturation within the CNS. Analyzing Riesen's (1958) data on the subsequent development of chimpanzees reared from birth to seven months in diffuse (unpatterned) light, it appears that in these animals the fear of strange objects appeared at about the same time as, or even before, clear evidence of visual recognition. This would indicate that maturational processes, which would normally occur subsequent to neocortically mediated object recognition, initiate the fear of strangeness. The maturation may be within any of the several areas within the limbic system known to be involved in fear behavior (see Brady, 1960; Gloor, 1960), but no direct data are available on maturational rates within these networks. If this is the case, the development in infancy from the brief defensive reaction to the more complex and enduring fear orientation is dependent on maturational processes within both level 2 and level 3.

The emergence of the more refined mechanisms within each of these adaptive hierarchies can be observed in early human development. Studies of the maturation of the human CNS (Conel, 1939, 1941) indicate that for about the first month after birth neocortical systems are essentially nonfunctional. The behavior repertoire during this first month is limited to functions noted above as capable of level 1 mediation . . . .

Analyses of the early development of "emotional" capacities limit the neonate to a "quiet-excitement" continuum (see Jersild, 1946), a behavioral range which can be mediated by changes in level 1 reticular activity. In the present terminology, this earliest "emotional" range corresponds to the undifferentiated "motivational" system of the brain stem organism. Furthermore, the range of stimuli influencing this infant motivational system (internal biochemical changes, sudden intense stimuli, and internal or external pain) is identical to the input sensitivities of level 1 networks. Since the nonspecific nature of this primitive motivational state produces no behavioral cue as to the nature of the arousing stimuli (see Jersild, 1946), when not guided by additional information (i.e., hours since last feeding, etc), the parent must adopt a trial-and-error approach to reducing the excitatory stimulus.

Conel's (1947) histological studies show rapid neocortical maturation beginning in the second and third months. . . . Perceptual and motor capacities now reflect neocortical mediation: the appearance of smiling in response to visual stimuli in the second month (Ambrose, 1960) is evidence of the achievement of pattern discrimination and recognition; in the motor area McGraw (1943) documents the inhibition of reflexive responses as voluntary neocortical control brings greater flexibility to motor patterns. Various authors observing early "emotional" development (see Jersild, 1946) give various terms to the emerging patterns, but all agree that the undifferentiated continuum of the newborn expands to a growing spectrum of emotional states beginning at about the second month. Assuming that emotional expression relates to the gratification or frustration of various motivational orientations, this expanding repertoire must reflect an increased motivational differentiation, as well as increased cognitive capabilities. While no neurological evidence on maturation rates within level 2 is available, studies referred to earlier show that level 2 networks are basic to the mediation of emotional and motivational processes. It seems reasonable that networks at this level, maturing along with neocortical systems, underlie this increasingly differentiated range of affective and motivational orientations. . . .

As neocortical perceptual systems mature the complex of brief orienting responses present at birth . . . is extended to include reactions to neocortically mediated perceptions, producing a more enduring and more flexible exploratory interest in the environment. Piaget (1952) and Bühler (1930) mark the second month as the beginning of active visual interest in the environment, with the first overt exploratory behavior appearing around three months (Piaget, 1952). This development is reflected also in Kleitman and Engelmann's (1953) studies of infants' sleep patterns. . . . A similar development of increasingly complex aversive reactions can be seen in the early months of infant development. The initial defensive reaction to intense stimuli or pain is extended by neocortical mediation (and probably also by maturation of level 2 networks) to include more complex fear reactions to patterned stimuli. These developments bring the capacity for acquiring fears of specific objects in the environment, as well as an innate fear of perceptual strangeness. In all of these adaptive hierarchies—sensory-

motor, motivational, attentive, and aversive —more refined mechanisms effect a more discriminating and more flexible functioning as higher-level systems add to the complexity of existing systems. Less emphasized in the above analysis are instances where phylogenetically newer systems supersede, rather than build upon and extend, the more primitive mechanisms. The inhibitory function of the neocortex in replacing the reflexive adaptations of the neonate with voluntary motor control is a well-documented example of this (McGraw, 1943; Terzuolo & Adey, 1960).

. . . Three mechanisms are hypothesized to account for the increasingly complex behavior patterns accompanying the development of the forebrain.

1. Networks of higher levels are increasingly discriminative: capacities for sensory discrimination increase at successive levels; reactions to internal biochemical changes become more differentiated; and motor control is more complex at higher levels.

2. Capacity for complex behavior is also increased as downward control from newer systems extends and refines the responsiveness of lower-level networks through the selective excitation and inhibition of functional systems within the lower levels. Examples of this process of "encephalization" are found in the neocortical activation of motivational networks at level 2 in response to learned visual and auditory patterns, and on the motor side, in the sequences of selective excitation and inhibition of reflexive motor systems within the brain-stem to give postural support for complex voluntary activity.

3. Upward projection from integrative processes at lower levels modulates the activation levels of various neocortical systems, utilizing information from the integrative activities within lower levels for the general programming of complex level 3 capacities. Examples of this upward control are brain-stem modulation of over-all neocortical activation, affecting the general level of alertness in response to gross characteristics of the internal and external environment, and the more specific modulation of attention and motivational orientations by subcortical forebrain networks capable of more limited activation of discrete systems within the neocortex.

The latter two processes of vertical integration will emerge as positive feedback networks in those instances where mutual facilitation occurs between two systems at different levels, i.e., systems activated by internal stimuli at level 2 will sensitize perceptual networks of the neocortex (level 3) toward relevant stimuli; such percepts will in turn further activate the level 2 motivational network.

(It is interesting to note that the integrative processes of successive levels of the CNS appear to contribute increasingly complex qualities of consciousness. Brain-stem activation mediates general alertness and probably also constitutes a basis for experiences of heightened tension and diffuse anxiety; motivational networks of level 2 appear to contribute more specific affective states which can be distinguished by quality as well as intensity; neocortical systems add awareness of pattern, giving ideational content to conscious experience. . . .

HIERARCHY OF LEARNING PROCESSES

The conceptual model of the CNS presented above assumes that integrative processes occur within areas of multiply-interconnected short axon neurons (stippled areas of Figure 1). These processes consist of interactions among various inhibitory and excitatory inputs coming from other parts of the nervous system, from peripheral afferents, and/or from changes in the internal chemical environment. The nature of input to which an area is responsive, and the qualities of innate structure within the area, in part determine the particular characteristics of the integrative processes occurring in the various areas. In addition, it seems a reasonable assumption that the integrative activities themselves produce internal structural changes which also affect the subsequent activation patterns within most, if not all, of these areas. Those changes in subsequent activation patterns which are relatively enduring underlie behavioral phenomena which would be included in a broad definition of learning.

A corollary to the hypothesis that the structural changes underlying learning can be found within integrative networks of all levels is the probability that differences in the complexity of the integrative processes of different levels are associated with behavioral evidence defining different kinds of learning. Within the broad conception of learning presented above are included habituation, classical conditioning, instrumental learning (including "trial-and-error" learning and operant conditioning), and latent learning phenomena. Habituation, while it is recognized as ubiquitous through all levels of CNS and ap-

pears at times to be more than a transient effect (see Berlyne, 1960; Hernandez-Peon & Brust-Carmona, 1961; Sharpless & Jasper, 1956), will be considered mainly in contrast to the remaining three learning processes. . . .

Two characteristics are proposed as distinguishing the quality of learning phenomena occurring through mediation by different levels of the nervous system. Most evident is the degree of sensory and motor differentiation involved: the increased capacities of the higher levels for perceptual differentiation and integration, and for complex motor control, allow for increasingly complex learning phenomena. (Differences in discriminative capacities when input is mediated by different levels of the CNS have been nicely demonstrated by Sharpless and Jasper [1956] in a study of habituation in the cat: level 1 networks habituated to a given sound will respond only to changes in intensity; level 2 networks are capable of alerting the organism when the frequency is changed, and neocortical systems are required to respond to pattern variations. . . .

The second factor distinguishing learning phenomena mediated by networks of various levels is both more interesting and more difficult to specify clearly. It has to do with the nature of the neural excitation which is adequate for the inducement of the enduring structural changes underlying learning. The assumption that some form of central "excitation" is necessary as a reinforcement in learning phenomena distinguishes the three traditional learning paradigms from habituation: repeated input that is not followed by such reinforcement produces only habituation to the afferent pattern.

(That some form of central excitation, rather than "drive reduction," provides the major basis for reinforcement is increasingly evident. Morgan [1957] reviews evidence distinguishing the excitatory effects of consummatory activity from the [often confounded] reduction of physiological needs as the effective reinforcement for learning. Work by Gastaut [1958] on the changing EEG patterns during learning points to the "reinforcing" role of excitatory activation for the reticular system in classical conditioning procedures. Recent studies analyzing the reinforcing effects of direct electrical stimulation in various areas of the hypothalamus and limbic system [see Olds & Olds, 1961] give strong evidence that it is excitation of level 2 networks which provides reinforcement for instrumental learning in birds and lower mammals; electrodes implanted within the brainstem or neocortical levels generally lack this reinforcing capacity. . . . From an adaptive perspective, it seems reasonable that it is those sensory or motor events which prove significant to the organism, i.e., which lead to changes in excitation levels, which are remembered, while events not followed by such reinforcement will produce only habituation.

It is in the analysis of the various kinds of "significant events" which are capable of providing such excitatory reinforcement that the second basis for a hierarchical ordering of learning capacities emerges.[2] The simplest of the traditional learning paradigms, demonstrated in newborn (i.e., "precorticate") humans (Pratt, 1946) and in decorticate mammals (Morgan, 1951), is classical conditioning. A basic requirement for such learning is an unconditioned stimulus capable of exciting level 1 networks, thereby "reinforcing" the conditioned stimulus. The unconditioned stimulus may be a stimulus innately associated with a reflexive network, or a sudden intense stimulus, or pain—all stimuli noted above as directly activating level 1 systems. In the conditioning of intact adult mammals, a more complex stimulus of acquired significance may provide excitatory reinforcement by the downward activation of level 1 systems from neocortical networks. This latter instance, where classical conditioning procedures involve neocortical mediation, can apparently result in learning localized primarily within neocortical systems or mainly within lower-level networks, a complication which will be discussed further below. For the present, it is sufficient to establish that level 1 excitation is adequate for classical conditioning, and that certain types of reinforcement can be directly mediated at this level.

In instrumental learning procedures, the "significance" of preceding events is established by reinforcement through "reward," or by the absence of painful "punishment." Instrumental avoidance learning (learning of a response which prevents administration of "punishment") may seem at first to present some difficulties for the present excitatory theory of reinforcement. There appear to be two possible explanations for the evident reinforcing capacities of a lack of (excitatory) punishment. It could be encompassed by Berlyne's "arousal jag" discussed above: the first stage in avoidance learning, learning that a given stimulus signals impending pain, fits a classical conditioning model, with pain as the excitatory reinforcement; in a second stage, when the anticipated pain does not occur if a specified response is made, there would be a reinforcing decrease in excitation level. Solomon and Brush (1956) present such an analysis, describing reinforcement in this second stage as "anxiety reduction."

As an alternate explanation, note that following the initial stage, which fits the more simple excitatory model, the second step, learning to make the correct avoidance response, could be encompassed within the model for latent learning.

As will be discussed below, the reinforcement in latent learning comes from perceptual novelty, which in this instance is an absence of the anticipated shock when the correct response is made. Since it is to be argued that latent learning phenomena, with "novelty" as reinforcement, requires neocortical perceptual mediation in mammals, it is relevant that learning of instrumental avoidance problems of even moderate complexity seems impossible in decorticated mammals (Hamuy, 1961). More simple avoidance problems, such as the conditioning of a decorticate cat to flex the to-be-shocked leg in response to a buzzer as conditioned stimulus (Hernandez-Peon & Brust-Carmona, 1961), fit into the model of classical conditioning.

In other types of instrumental learning, the "rewards" used as reinforcement are stimuli productive of consummatory activity (e.g., eating, copulation, etc.), and their salience is a rough function of the amount of activity produced and of the degree of physiological need (see Brogden, 1951). . . . No reference can be found to instrumental learning in the absence of level 2 networks, and damage to various areas of the neocortex does not preclude such learning when complex pattern discriminations are not required (Morgan, 1951). It seems probable, therefore, that in instrumental learning the reinforcing effects of consummatory activities are the result of ex-

[2]Note that in the following analysis, which relates different types of learning to excitatory reinforcement mediated by integrative networks of the different levels, the ultimate locus of structural change is not assumed to be always only within the level providing the excitatory reinforcement. The networks for the spread of excitation (vertical broken lines, Figure 1) allow for transmission of excitatory reinforcement to other levels. The particular types of learning associated with structural changes within the different levels cannot be fully specified: that habituation can occur at all levels seems well established (Sharpless & Jasper, 1956). Morgan (1951) reviews evidence indicating that conditioned learning can occur within either neocortical or subcortical networks; the possible loci of structural changes underlying more complex types of learning remain unclear (see Morgan, 1951; Orbach & Fantz, 1958; and Benjamin, 1959).

citation of level 2 networks.

There remain learning processes where the excitatory reinforcement is less evident, i.e., in latent learning phenomena, including sensory preconditioning and the sensori-sensory learning described by Hebb (1949) as basic to early perceptual development in mammals. Learning in these situations, traditionally defined as occurring without reinforcement, is demonstrated in conditions of general alertness and in the absence of any consummatory activity (see review by Thistlethwaite, 1951). This third type of learning seems to reflect the capacity of an alert neocortex to be adequately excited by variation in the immediate perceptual input. The earlier discussion described the role of perceptual novelty in instigating and maintaining exploratory behavior, an orientation providing the basis for latent learning. Since the neocortex was shown to be basic to an exploratory orientation in mammals, and as there is no evidence for latent learning in mammals deprived of neocortical networks, it seems reasonable to assume that perceptual variation, mediated by level 3 systems, provides the adequate excitatory reinforcement for this third class of learning phenomena. (Butler's [1954] evidence that monkeys will learn to open a window when "rewarded" by a view of an adjoining room illustrates the reinforcing effect of perceptual novelty. Welker [1961] reviews other evidence supporting this view of the role of perceptual novelty in latent learning.) In humans it seems reasonable to extend the concept of perceptual novelty to encompass also conceptual novelty as an adequate reinforcement in those learning processes involving only cognitive activity.

Learning situations which allow for effective mediation of input by networks at more than one level introduce a further complexity. It has been long noted that in the classical conditioning of intact mammals the conditioned response may differ from the unconditioned response, both in being incomplete and in containing additional elements that indicate expectancy of the forthcoming unconditioned stimulus. This "anticipatory" component of the conditioned response is a general characteristic of animals with a functional neocortex, and has been reported by Hernandez-Peon and Brust-Carmona (1961) to be seen also in the decorticate cat. While the experimenter may be focused upon the reinforcing effects of the unconditioned stimulus upon the to-be-conditioned stimulus, the subject, human or otherwise, is also attending to, and learning from, other aspects of the experimental procedure.

Maier and Schneirla (1942) analyze this additional component as instrumental learning, and Razran (1955) considers it to be "discriminational and relational" learning. Both of these analyses point out that more complex learning processes, reinforced by consummatory activities (Maier & Schneirla), or perceptual novelty (Razran), may in many experimental procedures occur concurrently with classical conditioning. An analogous situation appears in examples of "incidental learning" occurring in instrumental learning experiments. In such experiments, the subject is motivated towards, and reinforced by, one type of "goal" but shows some evidence of the learning of incidental (i.e., goal-irrelevant) information in the process (see, for example, Bruner, Matter, & Papanek, 1955). Instrumental learning and latent learning phenomena appear to occur concurrently in these latter experimental procedures. In brief, it appears that learning of different types, in response to aspects of the environment which are providing different types of reinforcement, may occur concurrently. This degree of complexity, probably ubiquitous in mammalian learning, would be expected from the hypothesis that mediational processes underlying learning can occur within integrative networks at various levels of the CNS.

The variations in time factors observed in the different learning processes also suggest a hierarchical ordering. Classical conditioning, involving level 1 excitation for reinforcement, requires for effective learning that excitation from the unconditioned stimulus temporally overlap the conditioned stimulus. Instrumental learning, involving level 2 excitatory reinforcement, allows for greater delay between the perceptual or motor events to be learned and the subsequent reinforcing activity. The perceptual organization or reorganization of the environment, reinforced by the excitatory effects of perceptual novelty mediated by level 3 systems, can under ideal circumstances be a relatively continuous process as neocortical mechanisms maintain the focus of attention to salient perceptual sequences for relatively long blocks of time.

As with the sensory-motor, motivational, attentional, and aversive hierarchies discussed earlier, the successively more refined learning phenomena also emerge during the postnatal maturation of the central nervous system. Learning in the human neonate seems limited to classical conditioning reinforced by excitatory activation mediated directly by level 1 networks (see Munn, 1946). During the next two or three months, maturation of networks of the higher levels brings evidence of instrumental and latent learning capacities. Ambrose (1960) concludes that instrumental conditioning provides the basis for the development of social smiling during the second and third months, and Brackbill (1958) has demonstrated differential changes in the strength of the smiling response in 4-month-old infants, depending on whether Brackbill responded to the smile by picking up, cuddling, and cooing at the infant, or by simply remaining a passive observer. Piaget (1952) records the intentional repetition of arm movements in one of his children at about three months after the infant accidentally struck a rattle hung above his crib, which in the present terminology appears to be an early example of latent learning. The general perceptual organization of the sensory world, described by Hebb (1949) as basic to later learning, probably also begins the second and third months, when Piaget (1952) and Bühler (1930) note the beginnings of a general visual interest in the environment. Much of this early organization of the sensory environment must be independent of consummatory reinforcement and must, therefore, be classed as early instances of latent learning.

CRITICAL-PERIOD PHENOMENA

The data from critical-period studies can be described in terms of (1) the nature of the stimuli to which the organism is particularly sensitive during a critical period, (2) the nature of the behavior patterns which are later affected, and (3) the developmental stage within which variations in the significant stimuli have their maximal effects on later behavior. Using all of these characteristics as criteria for ordering the data from the numerous studies, three separate critical periods can be defined: (1) a critical period affecting the later "emotionality" of the animal, with the sensitive period occurring directly after birth, and with the amount of general (unpatterned) stimulation as the significant variable; (2) a critical period affecting primary attachments, occurring at a somewhat later age and dependent on maturation of capacities for pattern discrimination; (3) a critical period when the "richness" of the perceptual and behavioral environment influences later learning abilities, a phenomenon also dependent on the development of pattern discrimination, and probably upon the functioning of complex motor capacities as well, and whose upper age limit remains only vaguely defined.

Note that the defining variables (the significant stimuli, the behavioral effects, and the critical age range) of each critical period correspond closely with the perceptual capacity, the behavioral influence, and the maturational chronology of one of the three levels of the conceptual model. This correspondence suggests that critical-period phenomena are products of the quality of activation patterns occurring in integrative networks of the different levels at the periods when the networks first become responsive to afferent excitation. Each critical period, therefore, begins as the networks involved mature to a level of functional significance. The upper limit may be set by at least two possible developmental factors.

First, the sensitivity of the neural network may decrease, ending the period when rapid structural changes, or more enduring excitatory reverberations, follow from afferent excitation. (This limiting development could be, in part, a product of the excitation itself, as well as of innate growth patterns. For reviews of the accelerating effect of stimulation on development, see Levine [1962] for behavioral data, and Riesen [1961] for neurological evidence.) There is only rather indirect evidence in support of this first possible explanation: Roberts (1960) finds that the inhibitory synaptic transmitter substance GABA, necessary for effective functioning of the innately inhibitory neurons within a neural network, is less present in the immature nervous system, which should make for more extensive and enduring activation patterns in the early stages of CNS development. (See also Riesen [1958] for arguments favoring an early period of "plasticity" of the CNS.)

The second type of developmental factor which might act to terminate some critical stages, is the maturation of neural systems which inhibit or prevent the activation of networks involved in the critical learning. This could be either a general inhibition, such as is found in the tonic effects of neocortical networks upon brain-stem activation, and which might be the terminating factor in the earliest critical stage, or a more specific interference, such as suggestions that the development of innate fear responses terminates imprinting (see Hinde, 1962). The limited evidence available for distinguishing between these possible terminating mechanisms will be presented as each critical stage is considered in more detail.

The effects of unpatterned stimuli (disturbing the animal by shaking the cage, handling, tactile stimuli, electric shock, cooling, etc.; the specific characteristics of the adequate stimuli remain unclear) have so far been established in only a few species: rats, mice, and possibly dogs and cats (see Levine, 1962). The critical period for these effects appears limited to the earliest postnatal stage, before neocortical auditory and visual mechanisms mature. This should limit the phenomenon to those animals born with relatively immature nervous systems, a class including rats, mice, cats, dogs, and the larger primates. The stimuli so far found effective are those which were noted above as capable of directly affecting level 1 networks, a finding not surprising, since this critical period occurs at a developmental stage when higher-level perceptual capacities are, on behavioral evidence, essentially nonfunctional. Nearly all of these studies are on rats or mice, and the later behavioral effects of early stimulation have been clearly established only in these species. Behavioral measures include the rate of avoidance learning and measures of aggressiveness towards other mice, which Levine (1962) interprets to be functions of the strength of a general fear reaction to noxious and/or novel situations in the first type of measure, and of variations in a tendency to "freeze" in the second. Other behavioral measures show variations in autonomic activity in frightening situations, i.e., in open-field tests the amount of urination and defecation is affected by the degree of early stimulation. In the earlier analysis of the defensive reaction, it was noted that all of these kinds of behaviors are associated with an intense activation of level 1 networks. From the rather limited evidence available, it would, therefore, appear that the reactivity of these level 1 networks in later life is in part determined by the extent to which they are activated during very early development. This hypothesis includes this earliest critical-period phenomenon within the broad conception of learning defined above, but limits it to a developmental stage when level 1 networks are either possessed of greater sensitivity, or are characterized by a lack of inhibitory regulation from neocortical systems. . . . [I]t appears to be the more general type of activation, noted to be associated with the complex of defensive responses, which leads to the later behavioral effects.

One of the most striking aspects of critical-period phenomena is the delayed appearance of the behavioral effects of earlier experience. From the present perspective, this appears as a consequence of the hierarchical organization of adaptive mechanisms: later-maturing networks, mediating more complex behaviors, are affected by the degree of activation of level 1 systems. Early experience which affects the reactivity of these networks would, therefore, influence more complex behaviors at later stages. In brief, earlier experiences affecting the reactivity of level 1 networks determine the degree of emotionality of the organism, while later experiences, following maturation of higher-level systems, determine the objects of emotional significance.

The critical period determining primary affectional attachments in mammals appears with the development of neocortically mediated perceptual capacities and is dependent upon the visual and auditory discriminations of this level (Scott, 1962). There is evidence, however, that the neocortex is not primarily involved in the mediation of reinforcement for this type of learning. While the parameters influencing the development of early attachments in mammals are only minimally explored, it appears that the animal becomes attached to that object towards which certain types of responses are directed during the sensitive period. The nature of these responses will vary with species—for example, clinging to soft objects seems basic to attachment formation in monkeys (Harlow and Zimmermann, 1959), a response which is outside the repertoire of puppy behavior, although puppies readily form attachments (Scott, 1962). Chicks become attached to followed objects (Hess, 1959), while human infants show the beginnings of attachment at an age before following is possible. In his consideration of the possible responses providing the basis for forming attachments in humans, Bowlby (1958) points out the innate species-common characteristics of the significant acts. This suggests that the formation of early attachments is a type of instrumental learning: objects perceived while making consummatory responses are remembered and subsequently sought after when the appropriate motivation is aroused. While this analysis must be recognized as highly tentative, it suggests that neural networks within level 2 are primarily responsible for reinforcement of experiences producing early attachment. . . .

It is interesting that evidence reviewed by Scott (1962) and experiments by Moltz (1960) indicate that experimental procedures which would have the effect of a general excitation of level 1 systems—food deprivation, electric shock, painful stimuli, etc.—are effective in producing more rapid attachment learning. This facilitory effect of level 1 excitation has been observed in instrumental learning at later ages also, where electric shock administered in association with the to-be-learned stimuli may increase the rate of learning (see Brogden, 1951). These phenomena could be instances of level 1 excitation projecting upward to supplement reinforcement from level 2 excitation.

Mechanisms terminating this second critical period are far from clear. Many authors note the development of fearfulness in response to novelty as an orientation precluding the development of new affectional ties, but there is evidence indicating other mechanisms also may be involved (see reviews by Hinde, 1962; Scott, 1962). It was suggested earlier that those neural mechanisms associated with fearful behavior that are found within the limbic system may set a maturationally imposed upper limit, but lack of direct evidence on maturational sequences within subcortical forebrain networks prevents further analysis. As with the earlier critical period, the eventual consequences of experience within this stage depend on the influences of subsequent maturation and later learning. For example, the maturation of neural systems releasing sex hormones initiates sexual activities which are in part oriented by early attachments, and in the learning area, the complex vicissitudes of primary affectional bonds in response to later interpersonal experiences appears as a major theme in psychoanalytic theory.

The third type of critical-period phenomena involves the effect of opportunity for complex perceptual and motor experience at an early age upon various learning abilities in later life. Bingham and Griffiths (1952), Forgays and Forgays (1952), and Hymovitch (1952) have shown that rats reared for various periods in cages filled with a diversity of objects inviting perceptual and motor exploration were better maze learners as adults. The latter study is particularly relevant since it included control conditions indicating that improved learning is not an expression of the development of specific motor abilities or of a particular motivational orientation, and that an "enriched" environment provided to adult rats does not counter the effects of early impoverishment. Evidence for similar effects in cats, dogs, and monkeys is available in studies which involve early sensory deprivation rather than enrichment. Melzack and Scott (1957) reared puppies in isolation from weaning to eight months in conditions allowing only minimal perceptual and motor experience (and which incidentally also must have inhibited the development of the affectional bonds which normally would occur in this period). Even after two years experience in a normal environment, these animals showed severe deficits in the visual control of motor behavior in avoiding painful stimuli. From the authors' description of the obtuse behavior of these animals in learning to avoid painful stimuli, the deficiency seemed to be in the perceptual organization of the sensory environment, which contrasts with the hyperemotionality which interfered with avoidance learning in rats as a result of minimal stimulation in the earliest critical period. Riesen (1961) reviews studies of cats reared in total darkness for nine months, or with only diffuse (unpatterned) illumination for five months, which when moved to normal environments failed in some cases to develop normal visual abilities. An apparently irreversible deficit in somesthetic perceptual ability in a chimpanzee reared with cardboard tubes on forearms and legs was shown by Neissen, Chow, and Semmes (1951). Many of the above studies were inspired by Hebb's (1949) analysis of the role of early experience in the perceptual organization of sensory input. That the perceptual deficit following early sensory deprivation was to some degree irreversible often seems to be a secondary finding, and the studies vary in the degree to which this was carefully observed or conclusively demonstrated. There seems adequate evidence, however, to conclude that previous perceptual and motor experience is not only necessary for maximal performance in problems requiring perceptual discrimination and motor skills, but that such experience is more salient in its later effects if acquired when the neocortical systems mediating these capacities first mature. Evidence for setting any precise upper limit to this critical stage is lacking, but since it seems improbable that it is terminated by inhibitory effects due to the subsequent maturation of other functional systems, the waning of the period of maximum sensitivity is probably a very gradual process. . . . This final critical period, therefore, seems to differ from the other two in that (1) the critical period is probably less sharply delineated, (2) effects of deprivation are probably relatively more reversible, and (3) the later effects appear in behavioral areas directly similar to those in which the critical experiences occur. . . .

The readings especially relevant to Part Two cover more familiar territory than the first three and need little introduction. The first article—On Coping and Defending—extends our own discussion of task-oriented and defense-oriented behavior. The second—Computer Simulation of Change of Personal Beliefs—illustrates some of the exciting research in which computers are used in an attempt to understand human thinking—in this case, the development and changes of human beliefs. The third article—The Marihuana Problem—provides the reader with a good delineation of the key dimensions of this contemporary social problem.

Jerome S. Bruner

ON COPING AND DEFENDING

We psychologists have developed a curious posture. It can best be summed up by the apologetic note we strike when we speak of normality. Indeed, my colleagues more often than not insert a quote in their tone of voice or inscribe inverted commas in the air when referring to "normal" controls or to "normal" states, and at a scientific meeting I recently attended a member of the audience addressed a question to the speaker about his "so-called normal group." Yet this wariness about normality is not all a posture. It is in part a compassionate recognition of man's vulnerability to trouble, an awareness that being sick and being well are matters of subtle balance. But a vice is often fashioned from an excess of virtue, and so our attitude about the feather line between health and illness may lead us to overlook some of the important differences between them.

I should like to consider one of the differences between psychological health and illness—the distinction between coping and defending. And I should like to limit the matter further by concentrating upon the reflection these cast on a human being's intellectual life. Coping respects the requirements of problems we encounter while still respecting our integrity. Defending is a strategy whose objective is avoiding or escaping from problems for which we believe there is no solution that does not violate our integrity of functioning. Integrity of functioning is some required level of self-consistency or style, a need to solve problems in a manner consistent with our most valued life enterprises. Given the human condition, neither coping nor defending is found often in pure form. The imperiousness of our drives and the demands of powerful, nonrational, and indocile unconscious mechanisms force some measure of defense. And, save in the deteriorated psychotic, it is rare for defense to cut a person off entirely from the requirements of daily living. Even the most extreme schizophrenic can usually cope with severe emergency—indeed, shock therapy may depend for what effectiveness it has upon the arousal of such coping.

Yet, notwithstanding that there is always a mixture of coping and defending in dealing with life as we find it, I would urge that we distinguish sharply between the two processes. Let me recount what has led me to this conclusion. It begins with a serious error of oversimplification in the design of a research project in which several of my colleagues and I were engaged. Our interest was in studying learning effectiveness. We took it as axiomatic that the object of any particular piece of learning was not only to master the task before one, but to master it in such a way that one would

Reprinted by permission of the publishers from Jerome S. Bruner, *Toward a Theory of Instruction.* Cambridge, Mass.: The Belknap Press of Harvard University Press, Copyright, 1966, by the President and Fellows of Harvard College.

be saved from subsequent learning of identical or like tasks. This seemed to us self-evident and still seems so, for unless learning were rendered generic the organism would be constantly locked in trial and error that would leave him in perpetual danger, and this does not seem to be how organisms act. The question we were asking was, how do organisms benefit from past experience so that future experience can be handled with minimum pain and effort? This constitutes learning effectiveness, of which the problem of transfer is one part. The design of our project was quite conventional. We would study a group of normal children (in quotes, of course) and compare their approach to learning with that of a group of children referred to a guidance clinic for "learning blocks"—children of normal or superior intelligence, without other evident behavior disorders, who were unable to learn in school. Preliminary observation of such children had led us too simply to the conclusion that it was not so much that they had grave difficulties in learning as that they seemingly learned in such a way that there was little or no transfer to new situations, in consequence of which they were constantly having to learn *de novo*. There is a little truth to this observation, but it is quite trivial. It was our hope to design a set of testing and observational procedures that would indicate quantitatively the manner in which the group who were effective differed from the other group who were not.

Fortunately for us, we began our inquiry with a clinical and therapeutic study of some half-dozen children referred to the Judge Baker Guidance Center for "learning blocks." The children were in therapy, and were also tutored in their schoolwork by us with the dual aim of helping them and discovering at close range how they went about learning. The parents of the children were also seeing psychiatric social workers regularly. Withal, we had an opportunity for quite close observation. It became apparent after some months of work that the learning activities of our disturbed children had certain distinctive features that had very little directly to do with the nature of effectiveness—save in the sense that the processes we observed interfered with effectiveness. In a word, their efforts to defend themselves from the activity of learning and from its consequences made it extremely difficult for them to get to the activity of "school learning" itself. Their schoolwork created certain psychological problems that were much more compelling than school problems and that drastically altered their approach to conventional school learning. They could not,

in short, cope with the demands of schoolwork unless and until they were able to defend themselves against the panic of impulse and anxiety that the demands of schoolwork set off in them. Here, then, was a classic antinomy. It was not that they were unable to learn in the conventional sense of that word—for in fact there was much learned canniness in their defensiveness against learning, and later there was often much talent in the way in which they approached school problems when the clamor of defense requirements had been in part quieted.

One will say, "But the difference between these children and the children who do well in school is not in *how* they are learning but in *what* they are learning—the one group geometry and the other, say, how to handle hostility toward their teacher." But this again appears not to be the case. The very texture of the learning in the two instances appears different. Consider the matter more systematically.

Recall first our earlier description of the learning process as it develops in children. At its beginnings, it is shot through with action. It is not surprising that children often hold the belief that thinking something and doing it are somehow equivalent. We shall return to this point later. A second feature of early acquisition of knowledge is that ideas are not isolated from their motivational or emotional context. Thus we find children as old as eleven who block at naming any similarity between one object they happen to like and another they are frightened of—say, a cat and a dog—though they are quite capable of grouping together water and milk as things that you drink. The example is an emotionally trivial one, and later we shall encounter more meaningful instances. When early learning is hemmed around with conflict, as it so often is by virtue of being made a road to parental approval and love or a weapon in the arsenal of sibling rivalry, with the consequence that it becomes highly charged or libidinized, the affective links that relate concepts and ideas often are powerful and relatively intractable, in the sense that they persist in fantasy and can be found to intrude in the child's thinking in later school settings.

At the unverbalized level, then, the child approaches the task of school learning, with its highly rationalistic and formal patterns, with a legacy of unconscious logic in which action, affect, and conceptualization are webbed together. Feeling and action and thought can substitute for each other, and there is an equation governed by what in grammar is called synecdoche: feelings can stand for things, actions for things, things for feelings, parts for wholes. It is as evident as it is both fortunate and unfortunate that these early cognitive structures remain in being into adult life—evident in the sense that the structures appear in dream and in free association and, in a disciplined form, in the products of the artist; fortunate in the sense that without such structures there would neither be poets and painters nor an audience for them; unfortunate in the sense that when this mode of functioning is compulsively a feature of a person's life, he is not able to adjust to the requirements of any but a specially arranged environment.

There are several other features of early learning that are less distinctive but nonetheless important. One of them is the inability of the young child to delay gratification once he has completed a task or to set goals that place that gratification in the far future. These shortcomings have very real consequences. One is that learning is in short pieces, with very little by way of a comprehensive, large-scale structure. That is to say, the more logical and hierarchical structures are lacking—genus-species, cause-effect, rule-example. But though the child may not link many events together in this more logical fashion, he relates them through the associations they share in action and affect. These early, more turbulent forms of learning are extrinsically motivated—being controlled and shaped by gratifications outside of learning itself. Many of the affects and gratifications that give structure to earliest experience are products of taboo and prohibition encountered in socialization. And so too the ideational connections learned under their sway. They become the "dangerous thoughts" of childhood. Such charged cognitive structures may form the core of what later become the *preemptive metaphors* of defensive cognitive activity—a matter that will occupy us shortly. Intrinsic learning that provides its own reward, less subject to such vicissitudes, represents, in contrast, what might be considered the beginnings of a "conflict-free sphere of the ego," characterized by the curiosity and competence-seeking discussed in the essay "The Will to Learn."

Let me suggest now that effective cognitive learning in school depends upon a denaturing process, if I may use such a fanciful and abrasive expression. It involves at least three things. There must first develop a system of cognitive organization that detaches concepts from the modes of action that they evoke. A hole is to dig, but it is also a hole. Secondly, it requires the development of a capacity to detach concepts from their affec-

tive contexts. A hole is not just a reminder of a hidden orifice. Finally, it demands a capacity to delay gratification so that the outcomes of acts can be treated as information rather than as simply punishing or rewarding.

The denaturing process of which I speak probably depends upon the presence of several conditions in the early history of the child. Let me abbreviate them to *stimulation, play, identification,* and some degree of *freedom from drive and anxiety.* With respect to stimulation, what is crucial is that the child have an opportunity to grow beyond enactive representation with its action-bound immediacy and beyond iconic representation with its strong susceptibility to affective linkage . . . . Varied stimulation with relative freedom from stress is about the only way we know of promoting such growth.

With respect to play and playfulness, it is first of all an attitude in which the child learns that the outcomes of various activities are not as extreme as he either hoped or feared—it involves learning to place limits on the anticipated consequences of activity. We have been struck by the difference in parents in respect to their encouragement of playfulness in their children—the children whose learning blocks we have studied and normal schoolchildren. In some instances, among normal children, we are told of "breast play" in which the very consequential act of nursing at the breast is altered into an occasion for playing—nipple in and out in a kind of loving tease. And throughout growth, it is as in the famous remark of Niels Bohr to one of his graduate students who complained of the seeming unseriousness, the amount of horseplay and joking, around Bohr's laboratory: "But there are some things so important that one can only joke about them." In time, the attitude of play is converted into what may best be called a game attitude in which the child gets the sense not only that consequences are limited but that the limitation comes by virtue of a set of rules that govern a procedure, whether it be checkers or arithmetic or baseball. It was a standard line of nineteenth-century evolutionary thinking that the function of play was to permit the organism to try out his repertory of response in preparation for the later, serious business of surviving against the pressures of his habitat. It can be argued equally well that, for human beings at least, play serves the function of reducing the pressures of impulse and incentive and making it possible thereby for intrinsic learning to begin; for if ever there is self-reward in process it is in the sphere of "doing things for merriment," particularly things that might otherwise be too serious in Niels Bohr's sense.

As for identification, recall that willingness to learn, particularly in middle-class families, and particularly among boys, is a prime way of expressing identification with family ideals. One way in which learning becomes highly charged with conflict is through conflict with a family competence model who stands for, and gives rewards for, learning. There are many ways in which identification conflicts arise, but the consequence of most of them is that the child ends up with a rejected competence ideal and no adequate pattern to guide his growth. Whether, in the case of a boy, he is the victim of a father who systematically and sarcastically attacks his son's efforts at mastery, or of one who, as a staff therapist put it, "tip-toes his way through life," the result is that the child fails to develop the sense that he can prevail by his own efforts.

Finally, the matter of freedom from excessive drive. There is good evidence that too strong an incentive for learning narrows the learning and renders it less generic, in the sense of its being less transferable. Where learning is dominated by strong extrinsic rewards and punishments, it becomes specific to the requirements of the particular learning task. It is almost a universal observation of parents that there comes a time of pressure in almost any child's school career when the child blocks, becomes "functionally stupid." A constant pressure of this kind not only produces the narrowing and the transitory block, but may have the effect of keeping active some of the primitive processes of early learning described before—or even leading a child to regress to these more primitive processes to such an extent that action, affect, and thought are fused in a preemptive metaphor, a matter to which we now turn.

What is a preemptive metaphor and what conditions seem to favor its dominance? It represents a principle of cognitive organization that is complexive rather than conceptual. The organization centers upon an affective concept like "things that can hurt me," within which any potentially disruptive or hurtful thing can then be included. For the acceptance criterion of such a concept is the loose rule of synecdoche by which parts can stand for wholes. Let me illustrate by reference to two examples from our case records. In one instance we are dealing with a fourteen-year-old with a severe learning block, a boy with an estimated IQ of 125 whose failing grades are far below what one would expect from one of such intelligence. And indeed, on rare occasions he will show his colors by a sharp improvement in his work, but it is then followed by regression. The mother is the dominant figure in the family, and when she and her husband were high school students before marriage, she helped him through his studies. The boy's sister, the "learner" in the family, is now in the same position with respect to this boy. For the boy, learning is to a degree an act of feminization, in part an act of rejection and hostility toward the father. On the rare occasions when he has shown improvement in his school studies, he has gone out of his way to injure himself by exposing himself to danger—by climbing on roofs, by taking foolish chances skiing, and so forth. The injuries are a retribution for the aggressive act of learning—an act he sees directed against his father.

Angus Strong, to use his clinical name, shows a preoccupation with injury and bodily harm. The range of objects and events that can cause harm, as he acts out his fantasies, is very great and comprises many aspects of his schoolwork. He dislikes fractions, for example, and cannot work readily with them, for he sees them as "cut-up numbers." The elementary operation of cancelation in algebra symbolizes for him the act of "killing off numbers and letters on each side of the equal sign." Asked to extrapolate from three ascending points on a graph, he draws a line through and slightly beyond the points and then has it descend in a sharp drop: "It can get up that far, and then it's sure to explode and fall again." Or he says, "Watch out for that pencil; it has a sharp point," and then later, "That piece of wood is dangerous because you can sharpen its end and it can hurt you."

What Angus appears to be doing is scanning his environment for anything that can be related to his central retribution-and-injury theme. Once he finds it, he then incorporates it into a kind of fantasy about how to avoid hurt or how to bring the harm under his own control rather than being caught out by it. The organization of the concept "what-will-hurt-me" has a seemingly chaotic quality, but only seemingly so. One soon realizes that it is based on a limitless metaphor whose function is to guarantee that Angus will not "miss anything that might hurt me or lead me to hurt those toward whom I feel hostile." It is this type of almost cancerous growth of a preempting metaphor that is the basis of the kind of learning that supports defense and makes coping virtually impossible. For so long as organization is dominated by so exigent an internal requirement—not missing anything dangerous lest one be overwhelmed by it—it is difficult to gain the detachment necessary to treat new materials and tasks in their own terms, free of the compellingly preemptive context to which they have been assigned.

Let me contrast this sample of Angus's behavior with the reactions of a group of twelve-year-old children in seventh-grade arithmetic class—children whom we had observed systematically for three years. Asked what they had liked best in arithmetic up to that year, the majority's response was "fractions." As one child put it, "There are so many things you can do with fractions." So while Angus was locked in the metaphoric significance of fractions as being "cut-up," his agemates were gaining a sense of mastery and manipulation based on such delightful insights as the equivalence of $1/2$, $2/4$, $3/6$, and $n/2n$. But it is not simply this, either, for there are striking differences in how the normal, coping children were going about fractions—their willingness to recognize the generality of the series just mentioned and their practice with such generalities.

There seem to be at least two ways in which preemptive metaphors operate in the blocked child. One is best described as "assimilation." Once an object or event is identified as related to the defensive preemptive metaphor, it is assimilated to the fantasies and "acting out" that are also related to the metaphor. The new object or event is then reacted to in old, established neurotic ways. A second way in which the preemptive metaphor operates is by denial. Once an event is "matched" to the preemptive metaphor, it is then avoided, pushed out of mind, "overignored." Let me illustrate the latter pattern by reference to the case of Dick Kleinman, one of our young patients, in treatment from age twelve to fifteen.

Dick's family was dominated during his early years by a father who relieved his sense of inadequacy by depreciating and punishing Dick for failure to live up to standards far in excess of what could reasonably be expected of the boy—neatness in eating, reasoning ability, and so on. The father suffered a chronic heart condition, but Dick was not told about it because his parents were afraid the information might get back to the father's employer. All Dick knew was that he was not to make noise when his father was about, not to disturb him, and, above all, not to make him angry. Dick was born after the other children in the family were grown. He was an "accident," and his mother rather resented him while getting real gratification from his dependence upon her, a dependence she cultivated. There were episodes during Dick's early childhood of sudden separation from the mother—she went off to the hospital, and another time he was sent off to relatives when she underwent orthopedic surgery. Two considerably older sisters, each of whom had served Dick in the role of mother, departed for marriage during his early childhood. His work in school was indifferent from the start and his teachers complained of inattention. By the time he reached eleven, it was apparent that he was falling further and further behind. He made few friends and was usually in a subdued and depressive mood. As he approached twelve, he began therapy. Shortly afterwards his father died of a heart attack, Dick having no forewarning.

For Dick, inquiry or active curiosity, in contrast to passive acceptance, had led to punishment or to scorn as aggressive and noisy. His attempts at "figuring things out" had been often enough and sarcastically dismissed by his father. The depreciating attitude of the father was reinforced by the mother, who treated Dick as incompetent to do schoolwork. She said to me when we first met after I had become Dick's tutor, "Do you think you can *really* do anything with him?" In his family, Dick had models neither of playfulness nor of competence, and nobody who could help him develop a free and flexible attitude to learning. Indeed, the family attitude toward knowing things was even flawed by a curious "pushing aside" of the unpalatable as unmentionable. This creation of a sphere of unmentionable and unthinkable things—father's illness, mother's health problems, the marriage of a cousin to a Chinese, and so on—took with Dick. He seemed a most uncurious boy.

His approach to learning seemed to lack any aim at mastery. He sought instead to register what was told him or what was read, and made little effort to organize or go beyond. Some examples will give the flavor. His biology class was given the topic of photosynthesis; a tutorial session was scheduled that afternoon. I asked Dick what photosynthesis was. His account was garbled; its one virtue was that he had obviously committed to rote memory the principal words and phrases the teacher had used in describing the process. I asked him whether he felt he understood it, and he replied tentatively in the affirmative. I then said to him that I would tell him my version of it and we'd see whether they matched, and proceeded to set forth an even more garbled account, again using Dick's key phrases. When I was done, he nodded and said that was how he understood it, too, and he then tried to go on to the next topic. The remainder of the hour was given over to giving him a simple picture of photosynthesis that he could really understand, and doing it in a way that would assure him that the effort to understand would not be greeted by scorn or sarcasm. He reacted in a manner that was to become typical—elaborating and going back over the material he had now dared to understand, very much depending upon the tutor's support as he dared try out his mastery. A session on "sentence craft," as it is called, provides a second example. Poorly constructed sentences were to be rewritten so that they would be less ambiguous and more compact. Dick's efforts were of little avail: his rearranged sentences were no better and often even more opaque than those in the exercise book. Again, the same procedure, giving him simple examples so that he would not panic. In time, he got the idea; he would read the original aloud and then his revision, to hear whether the second "made more sense" than the first. A lucky image emerged during the course of all this. When he succeeded for the first time on a simply garbled sentence, I made as if to turn a switch on his forehead, "You see, it is like turning a switch in your head, then you do it the way you just did." He responded with laughing agreement. Some days later he said, "But how will I know I have a sentence right when I do them at home?" I suggested he phone me each morning during the coming week just before leaving for school, and said that I would listen to but not correct his work. For a week he was my guaranteed alarm clock. By the day before our next weekly tutorial, we went through our telephone ritual almost as a joke. He had mastered the task with lots to spare.

In Dick's case, as I have indicated, it was the activity of learning and mental inquiry that had been captured by a preemptive metaphor, the activity of thinking about unknowns and new eventualities. Such activity had led either to dangerous consequences or to punishment. The metaphoric structure that guided his defensive activity included learning, questioning, curiosity, inquisitiveness. Learning tested his mother's right to dominate, renewed his hostile fears of his father, spelled the possibility of failure and loss. The solution was to keep it suppressed, under wraps. What his tutor did was to make it easy for him to discover that learning was neither very dangerous nor likely to evoke punitive and sarcastic response. Unlike Angus, Dick did not assimilate dangerous activity into a fantasy context. Rather, his pattern was one of avoidance and denial—finding techniques of rote learning that would, in effect, keep the dangerous activity from entering the structure of his thinking.

Both the assimilative and the avoidant activities overdefend in a costly way. Each requires a constant scanning of the environment for whatever might be relevant to the core conflict that is the source of trouble. The result is a highly distracting preoccupation: children with this kind of difficulty miss out on a good deal of what is going on because they have such an absorbing investment in scanning the world for danger. It is not surprising, then, that teachers often report that these children are inattentive or that they never participate in class discussions. Our children in treatment often missed what the next day's assignment was—either literally or in the sense of not grasping its purpose—and it has occurred to us that perhaps the time of maximal upset and defense comes just as they are getting into new material and unknown situations, as at the moment of a new assignment.

But there is one other factor operating in the distraction of these children. It has in considerable measure to do with the nature of the conflict that underlies their difficulties. Consider now the origin of learning blocks.

The child with a learning block is the classic case of the double bind—he is damned if he succeeds and damned if he fails. If he fails in his schoolwork, he suffers at school and at home; if he succeeds, he suffers at home and alone. Let me give some typical examples. One child has a younger sister who is mongoloid, a fact the family have had great difficulty admitting to themselves. Their attention is focused on the uncertain progress of younger sister, and great pressure is placed on the twelve-year-old boy to take care of himself and be on his own. In his view, succeeding at school (and his IQ is adequate for that) means less attention from his parents. Indeed, his mother said to the social worker, "If Tony gets along well in school, then that means we don't have to worry about him. We have plenty to worry about already." So success means the loss of a cherished dependency relationship. If, on the other hand, he gets failing grades in school, he is treated harshly at home for his failure, but in any case he gets some of the family's attention. Both success and failure are, then, fraught with difficulties. In the case of another boy, learning is an instrument for controlling and striking back at his parents, though the child is unaware of it, and there is naturally a good deal of anxiety attached to school performance. When he is faced with the idea of growing up, he stands to lose even this much control over his parents. Or, in the case of Dick, the dangers of learning are balanced by praise at home, but also by a sense of his mother's demand that he continue to be her baby. Avoidance of learning satisfies defensive demands, but it too leads to trouble. Finally, with Angus, his failure at school is almost a precondition for peace in the family situation, a condition for his self-identification as a man, where men are assumed to be the ones not good at school and women help them. It is not surprising that learning becomes so consequential for these children that a playful attitude and perspective cannot develop normally.

Yet what must seem patent—and particularly so to those who have children of school age—is that, in some measure, the double bind is the plight of every child growing up in our society. Perhaps there are two or three things that make the difference in the children who become the victims of it. The first is sheer intensity. So tight is the bind in these children that a drastic defensive expedient finally emerges. I am inclined to believe that the second major factor is the absence of an adequate competence figure for the child to identify with. All our cases were boys, and most cases referred to clinics are. The ineffective fathers and the ones who express an impotent rage provide no workable model for mastery, as Barbara Kimball showed a decade ago. And so, too, the overpowering, rejecting fathers who demand so much that only opposition remains as an alternative. Identification seems to provide the modeling or patterning that leads the child toward coping rather than defending. But neither the intensity of the double bind nor the unavailability of a competence model for identification appears sufficient explanation. All of the children we have seen show a tell-tale lack of awareness of what they are doing—whether the pattern is one of assimilation or of avoidance. The learning block is not an instance of rebellion and overt refusal to study or attend to lessons. The children observed fail in their work even when they try—and in some cases (as with Dick) trying was the worst prescription. Whatever "the unconscious" means, these children were operating by its direction. In effect, it amounts, I suppose, to a set of cognitive operations that prevail in the absence of conscious controls. The preemptive quality of the defensive metaphor seems to be the hallmark of such unawareness. To be sure, much ordinary thinking is metaphoric, and surely Wittgenstein has taught us in our generation not to use strict rules of categorization as criteria for judging daily thinking. But it is the absence of the conscious or "logical" check that permits a defensive metaphor to grow by a cancerous metastasis. In the absence of such

checks, it is virtually impossible to "denature" or "delibidinize" learning. In severe cases, defense becomes so habitual that it is almost impossible to make quick therapeutic progress in substituting coping for defending where school learning is concerned.

Consider now the nature of therapy. To what extent does therapeutic progress reflect the kind of processes I have been describing? Let me say at the outset that I lay no claim to wide clinical experience with children. Yet I must at least put down the observations we have made and let those with more experience judge their pertinence to the general problems of therapy with children. It has seemed to us in the first place that therapy with our group of children required considerably more than an intrapsychic working through of unconscious material. Working through, yes, particularly if some insight was to be achieved and the constraints of awareness assisted in containing the defensive activity we have described as the preemptive metaphor. But the tutorial was also a crucial factor in helping the child learn to cope. It mattered first in enabling the child to establish a learning situation free of the double bind. Take the eleven-year-old boy who at one of his first sessions said to the tutor that he was afraid to make an error in reading because his teacher yelled at him. The tutor asked whether his teacher yelled very loud, and, upon being assured that she did, volunteered that he could yell louder than the teacher, and urged his patient to make a mistake and see. The boy did, and his tutor in mock voice yelled as loud as he could. The boy jumped. Tutor to patient: "Can she yell louder than that?" Patient: "Yes, lots." Tutor: "Make another error and I'll try to get louder still." The game went on three or four rounds, and the tutor then suggested that the patient try yelling when he, the tutor, made an error. (The tutor was Dr. Michael Maccoby.) After a few sessions, a playful relation had been built up about mistakes in reading, and the beginnings of transference were at hand. Soon the child was able to take satisfaction in the skills in which he was achieving mastery.

The episodes of "sentence craft" and Dick's reaction to them are similarly relevant. Supporting a dependency relationship up to a point—that point being where Dick had to do the actual work of sentence revision himself and judge whether his own performance was correct, the tutor providing the emotional support—had the effect of getting Dick across the line into intrinsic learning. There were comparable episodes in his algebra, where the idea of unknowns to be solved troubled him. Once that was turned into something of a game we played between us, his grasp of the ways of algebra grew on its own. Biology was the next area, and again tutorial therapy ran from initial emotional support to self-propulsion. To be sure, progress was being made at the same time in dealing both with Dick's family situation and with his own intrapsychic conflicts. Yet what was most observable was the manner in which, once tension was reduced, either by means of conventional therapy or the implicit therapy of a supporting tutorial relationship, the child himself would begin to take over and get a sense of reward from such competence as he had managed to establish. If the supporting relationship remained intact, the competence would be extended and the kind of coping necessary to a task would begin in earnest. The tutor as identification figure became increasingly important in all this, for the tutor provided a new model of coping by showing that problems are both soluble and not dangerous—or, when not soluble, at least not the source of either disaster or punishment.

In the end, then, we too were impressed by the sharpness of the difference between coping and defending. When the child could meet the requirements of the tasks set him, the spreading pattern of defense would fade. There was little in common between the two approaches.

What may we conclude about coping and defending?

What seems clearest to me is that there is a deep discontinuity between the two not only in their objectives but also in the nature of the processes involved. Defense, dominated by the need for locating whatever may be disruptive, overshoots its reasonable goal by including in its range anything that can be construed as dangerous. Unconstrained by conscious processes, defense operates by the use of the unlimited and preemptive metaphor—literally a kind of guilt by association that, under extreme stress, finally implicates so much of the patient's world as being potentially dangerous that he is truly crippled. This is the mode of the unconscious, so called. It

seems highly unlikely that, on its own, "the unconscious" could be much of a creative source of thinking. Rather more likely, it is only when the metaphoric processes come under conscious control in some degree that they can serve a useful function in coping with problems—what in recent years has been called "regression in the service of the ego."

What seems to be required for a proper growth of respect for the requirements of problem solving is a "defusing" of intellectual activity from the demands of immediate action, affect, and drive. We have suggested that such a defusing depends upon a child's having the conditions necessary for playfulness to develop, upon his having an adequate competence model available, and upon the experience of intrinsic reward from increased competence that can start a career of "learning for its own sake." These produce coping.

There is a form of pedagogical romanticism that urges an arousal of unconscious, creative impulses in the child as an aid to learning. One would do well to be cautious about such doctrine. As Lawrence Kubie and others have remarked, unconscious impulses unconstrained by awareness and by the sense of play can be quite the contrary of creative. It is too often taken for granted that the processes that lead to effective cognitive functioning are mere extensions of unconscious dream work and association. I do not believe this to be the case, and a close reading of Freud certainly indicates that he did not believe so. The "primary process" of infantile thinking was surely not for Freud the basis of later, more world-oriented "secondary process."

In a word, then, coping and defending are not, in my opinion, processes of the same kind that differ merely in degree. They differ in kind. What poses the eternal challenge to the teacher is the knowledge that the metaphoric processes can, when put under the constraints of conscious problem solving, serve the interests of healthy functioning. Without those constraints, they result in the crippling decline that comes from a specialization on defense.

Kenneth M. Colby

COMPUTER SIMULATION OF CHANGE
OF PERSONAL BELIEFS

Psychotherapies, whether individual or group, consist of a communicative exchange of semantic information between persons in an attempt to alleviate those personal and interpersonal misunderstandings which are involved in mental suffering. I shall discuss some work in computer science which is intended to contribute to the psychotherapies by increasing our understanding of change in certain thought processes.

MODELS

. . . When we link two systems in a metaphor we are inclined to say "A is a B." We mean in an implied comparison that A, the primary system, is like B, a secondary system, in at least some respects. To say human minds are like computers is only to claim that they are to be taken as alike in those ways which we wish to emphasize. We hope to increase our understanding of minds, something we do not know much about, by comparing them with computers, something which, if we do not know much about, we can readily know much more about because of their properties of tangibility, traceability, and manageability.

This root metaphor connecting mental processes with computer processes should be understood as involving not static entities, but comparable flows of information processing. An inert or idling computer is just hardware. But a computer run, combining hardware and program into a single active system, represents the correct analogy to human thinking. A computer run harmonizes power, energy, and information. It stands as an analog model with its symbolic representations being processed in a physical medium (computer) known to be different from the physical medium (brain) in which thought takes place. . . .

From "Computer Simulation of Change in Personal Belief Systems," from *Behavioral Science*, 1967, Vol. 12. Reprinted by permission of author and publisher.

Some theorists feel that models and theories are the same. If so, one should just say "theory" instead of "model." The useful distinctions are as follows: A theory, particularly in the behavioral sciences, is stated in the form of natural language sentences. The sentences are strings of symbols which describe the properties of a theory. A model, in this instance a running computer program, consists of strings of symbols which do not just state, but *exemplify*, a structure of the system that a theory talks about. . . . When we describe a model we are back to natural language sentences again and this often leads to a confusing of models and theories. These crucial points have been made best by Kaplan (1964).

COMPUTER PROGRAMS
AS MODELS OF THOUGHT

. . . The mind-computer metaphor suggests that mind is like a program running in a computer and that the central nervous system in humans provides the physical medium analogous to computer hardware. The "ghost-in-the-machine," so troublesome to mind-brain theorists such as Ryle, is simply a running program. The mind-brain impasse has awaited a suitable root metaphor with which one could do something in substantive and satisfactory detail.

In attempting to account for the introspectional reports of persons, programs are complex enough to satisfy our notions regarding the complexity of thought and they generate symbols at the proper level of concrete detail to match the output of persons. At the end of a run not only can the output stream be examined, but one can retrace in full the step-by-step operations which generated this sequence. Programs are speculative instruments, strategic simplifications or "undercomplexifications," whose remote consequences can be tested by running them through.

Models must be built for real situations too complex to manage directly or for technological situations which cannot be experimented with during their operation. One should not experiment with a bridge while building it or with a human heart while operating on it. The psychotherapies represent applied technologies which are difficult to experiment with because of the large number of uncontrolled and nonindependent variables. However, models of the processes believed to be involved can be constructed and tinkered with in order to develop the if-then generalizations and law-like statements typically yielded by controlled experimentation. Initial states can be repeated or varied and alternative inputs can be tried to estimate the relative contributions of internal state variables and external input to final output.

THE PERSONAL CALCULI OF BELIEF SYSTEMS

. . . In this essay I shall summarize some work from our laboratory and describe the directions of our current efforts. Details of the actual programs can be found in Colby and Gilbert (1964), and Colby and Enea (1967).

We define a belief as a basic molecular unit of symbol processing. It is a proposition accepted as credible by the system. A belief is represented in the program by a string of words in an internal English-like language, for example, "I like Al." The string is a semantic kernel sentence which can be extracted from a natural language sentence. A semantic kernel in the internal language is that which remains invariant under combination in natural language.

The atoms of a belief molecule consist of concepts about interpersonal relations organized as directed graphs; that is, nodes connected by pointers which indicate interrelation between concepts. Concepts are linked to form beliefs which state propositions, judgments, or attitudes about persons, including the self, and relations between persons.

In addition to this semantic component, a belief has three assigned weights: a credence, a fixed charge, and a current charge. Credence represents personal subjective probability or credibility, the degree to which a belief is held as true. Charge represents the degree of import or interest a belief has in the system. The fixed charge is a more stable weight changing very slowly over time, while current charge fluctuates more readily according to the immediate fates of a belief. The

status of a belief in the program is the product of its credence and its current charge.

A belief may or may not be supported by reasons which consist of other beliefs. Beliefs gain their position of becoming reasons by being warranted by a more general belief termed an implication. For example, a reason for "I criticize father" is "because father rejects me," which is warranted by the implication serving as a substitution rule, "A parent rejects a child implies a child criticizes a parent." These implications also have credences and charges and they are supported by beliefs which instance them.

The program is written in BALGOL and runs on an IBM 7090 connected via a direct-data device to a Digital Equipment Corporation PDP-1. Both the 7090 and PDP-1 connect to an IBM 1301 desk file which permits use of an extremely large data base during on-line experimentations using teletypes and display scopes of the Stanford THOR time-sharing system. The program first forms a pool of relevant beliefs around a nucleus which is the highest charged belief in the system at that moment. Then, successively, the highest charged belief in the pool becomes the regnant and it is matched against the others in the pool in a search for conflict. Two beliefs are considered to be in conflict when they involve the same or similar agents and objects and when action verbs are antonymically related, such as "I hate mother" and "a child ought to love a mother." If no conflict occurs the regnant is expressed as an output belief, along with the values of monitors which keep track of how well the system is functioning at the moment. A belief relevant to the output belief is then selected to take its place in the pool. If high-level conflict occurs, various transformations of the semantic component of the regnant are attempted until one is found which creates a belief not in conflict with other beliefs in the pool, and which hence can be expressed. The transformations change the agents, actions, objects, or combinations of these by computing suitable substitutes from the directed graph of a conceptual dictionary. The resultant belief construction is a distortion of the original regnant. It is such distortions which represent pathological beliefs in a personal belief system. The categories healthy or pathological are not properties of an individual belief but of a belief relative to a belief system.

Given such a personal calculus with its conflicts and self-adjustment processes, the question arises how it can change itself or be helped to change by external corrective input from another source of information to a healthier, more optimal state of consonance. Ideally, such a change would involve a reduction of a severe and wrenching conflict between beliefs which in turn would lead to a reduction of those misbeliefs and misconceptions generated by transforms attempting to cope with conflict. In persons the theoretical problem is how do we change our minds?

TO CHANGE A MIND

. . . There is plenty of evidence that our minds, as indicated by our beliefs, change during a lifetime. A belief which once had great import—"Santa Claus is coming!"—no longer does. A belief once held with a personal probability close to unity— "frogs cause warts"—now brings only a smile. Also it is evident that other persons change our beliefs. Key experiences with other persons change individual beliefs and even entire belief structures. In this sense we can write on one another's programs during that single irreversible pass through the world called life. We remake and revise our own programs continuously, mainly in quite small steps except for key experiences and mostly within character, that is within certain boundaries.

Patients in psychotherapy report that they have changed their perspectives and their ways of looking at old facts about themselves and others. While psychotherapists have some fair, but incomplete theories about origins of mental suffering, they have only the crudest notions about mental change. As a practitioner, a psychotherapist is a decision maker using heuristic rules of thumb which tell him what to say and what not to say in certain contexts. He needs a variable or set of variables he can influence to change and he is interested in facilitating or accelerating mental change which occurs "naturally" in human minds. From clinical experience he knows that the rate at which corrective inputs can be generated and communicated by a therapist and the rate at which they can be accepted by a defensive, ontogenetically battered system, must be measured in calendar rather than clock units, given our present state of knowledge.

A belief system combines external input with stored information in accordance with current values of state variables and parameters of a personal calculus. Input information from another person must first attain some interest and second, it must be evaluated as credible to some degree

before it can be accepted into the system as one of its elements. Belief systems in adults are notoriously conservative. Paradoxically, they are also gullible. Given a trusted source of information, almost anything it reports is accepted as having credibility unless there is counterevidence against it. . . .

Through self-observation one can observe moments called reflective when we engage in an internal dialogue designed to change a belief or belief structure. We bring into play a personal logic in attempting to dislodge or renounce a belief. A belief can be changed by changing its semantic content, its degree of credibility, or its degree of import.

We are currently trying to simulate these processes by an on-line dialogue with the program which first attempts to lessen the credence of a belief by weighing evidence for and against it. This is achieved by consulting all the relevant beliefs in the system to weigh evidence for the contrast of a belief. If more evidence is found for the contrast than the original, the original belief's credence is lessened. This in turn may affect the credence of a belief for which it can serve as a supporting reason. If the main belief serves as a reason in some other belief's reason structure, and so on, the result is a series of small but far reaching chain reactions in the degree to which some beliefs are now accepted as true. Preliminary results indicate that input designed to weaken the reasons for a belief is more effective in changing the program than trying to weigh evidence for and against the belief directly.

In this program, since severe conflict leads to belief distortions and conflict is a function of both credence and current charge, we are also trying to posit mechanisms for reducing the charge on beliefs. It is not clear to us yet how these parameters interact or should interact, but over time credences should probably change more rapidly than charges.

CORROBORATION

Added to the number of difficulties in writing and running these programs is the problem of validating or corroborating the model. As yet we have no satisfactory way of testing models of belief systems for their correspondence with empirical observations on persons being simulated. Since the program simulates an individual belief system, one would like some means of comparing it with output from the individual person involved.

We are developing an on-line method for testing the model by enlisting the research cooperation of a person whose belief system is being simulated (Colby and Enea, 1967). This program tries to build up a cognitive model of a person much in the way a psychiatrist constructs and refines his thought-model of a patient. A person sits at a teletype and participates in a continuous written dialogue in natural language regarding his close interpersonal relations. Each of the natural language input sentences undergoes a pattern recognition analysis in an attempt to find semantic kernels which then become representations of this person's beliefs inside the machine. As information comes in, additions are made to a graph representing beliefs. When some beliefs have been accumulated the program then asks the person whether or not it is correctly representing certain of his beliefs. He is free to confirm, reject or express ambivalence. As in psychotherapeutic practice negation is much more ambiguous than assent, and the program must decide whether to revise its representations of the person's beliefs or whether the semantic area is so conflictive as to give rise to denials.

Having the cooperation of a person in real time and maintaining a continuous and repeated on-line dialogue, we are trying to build up and progressively improve a model of that person's belief system. This type of man-machine communication gives the model a continuous interaction at close range with the system it is representing and gives it a chance to be improved through new information obtained by immediate feed-backs from a person. . . .

THE MODIFICATION OF MAN

Much of what I shall now say is more philosophic than psychiatric or scientific, but this is a good time to look at our presuppositions and suppositions about changing people's minds. We assume that as part of cultural evolution man wants to change himself in some sense of improving his efforts towards a goal. We also suppose as part of this assumption of perfectability that he wishes to liberate himself from beliefs judged to be too heavily weighted or inappropriate to contexts of a changing social and physical environment.

The stored past of a belief system may overinfluence it in attempting to deal with new information from new situations. Clinical examples of this provide a large portion of a psychiatrist's

work. Cultural values of increasing freedom and increasing individual autonomy direct us to find ways of changing our minds about certain personal beliefs, especially the misbeliefs and misinformation acquired from repeated childhood experience with parents and other key persons who lived in a world quite different from our current one.

Physical reality is now easier for many, but painful aspects of social reality remain worthy of being denied and distorted by transformations of their symbolic representations. Granted that some illusions are necessary for everyone, a large number of social misunderstandings could be reduced if people's minds could be changed about their misperceptions and misbeliefs. But change can be seen as threat as well as opportunity because major change challenges fundamental beliefs about the nature of man. If a mind-computer metaphor is taken seriously enough that people work at it, one of the threats is how man is to be looked at in his relations with machines. Metaphor now becomes not only the hub of it but the rub of it.

Opponents of the metaphor claim that if men are viewed as being like machines then men will be treated, like machines, as something less than human. The comparison is seen as inviting dehumanization. It has obviously been useful to view some behavior or persons as machine-like, for example, comparing the heart to a pump. The better question is what *kind* of human activities can be compared to what *kind* of machine. Classical mechanists compared men to clockworks or engines, real or idealized. Now that a lever as a model of physical description has given way to an electromagnetic field, a computer would seem a more appropriate secondary system for the modern mechanist to involve in a man-machine metaphor.

But it is routinely supposed that we are very clear about what a machine is, perhaps because we can see it, point to it, and touch it. We act as if we were confident about the nature of machines and their implications and now all we must do is be to clarify our concepts about the nature of man. Yet if we take a computer as a primary system, it is very unclear what is a suitable secondary system with which it can be compared. As new machines are invented the meaning of the term "machine" changes radically.

To Descartes a machine was a system of ropes and pulleys. To my grandfather a machine was what we went for a ride in on Sunday afternoon. To me a jet airplane is a machine. A computer is a kind of machine which does not look like these and does not do the same kind of work. For a programmer a computer is simply a device for processing symbols which in turn stand for his concepts about some subset of the world. His most direct concerns are not with hardware, but with programming languages and how best to represent his ideas in them. Ultimately, when the program runs these ideas will be represented in the medium of hardware, and naturally someone must worry about keeping the hardware fit. For the *programmer's* practical purposes, a computer as a primary system can be compared to a language as a secondary system. This metaphor then asserts that a computer is a language in that it provides a system of symbols and operating rules which we may relate to our concepts. If man, as part of his cultural evolution, decides he should change his mind—and he seems to have done so—then the problem is whether he can do so aided by a machine such as a computer. Can the study of man-computer communication improve knowledge of man-man communication and its misunderstandings?

By itself a computer does nothing. It is a conceptual and technical aid to a person's thinking and knowing. If it can be used to further our understanding and treatment of mental suffering there can be no question of its value. It it can be used as a psychotherapeutic instrument for thousands of patients in understaffed hospitals, we have no choice but to use it because the healing professions are unable to supply sufficient manpower to meet this great social need. If a computer can teach children better than teachers can because each child is thereby enabled to learn at his own rate, then its use is quite consonant with our values of respecting individual dignity and promoting the growth of autonomy. To me it is dehumanizing to put a child in a class with 40 other children and one teacher. It is dehumanizing to herd thousands of patients into mental hospitals where they will never see a doctor. If a computer can teach and if a computer can provide therapeutic conversation, then there can be no hesitation in exploring these potentials. It may give us a chance to rehumanize people now being dehumanized by our educational and psychiatric systems.

William H. McGlothlin and Louis J. West

THE MARIHUANA PROBLEM: AN OVERVIEW

. . . A reappraisal of the social policies controlling marihuana is clearly needed, but unfortunately there is very little recent research to provide a basis for rational decisions. Virtually all the studies done in this country were conducted some 25 to 30 years ago. The dearth of recent research and absence of long-term studies is a situation largely brought about by giving the same governmental agency control of both enforcement and research.

In assessing the current state of knowledge pertaining to the use of marihuana, probably the

Reprinted from the *American Journal of Psychiatry*, volume 125, pages 370-378, 1968. Copyright 1968, The American Psychiatric Association. Reprinted by permission of author and publisher.

most important fact to keep in mind is that the range in amount used is extremely wide. Since marihuana use has been traditionally defined in legal rather than in health terms, there is a tendency to consider all users as a single group. In fact, there are no physiologically addictive qualities, and the occasional users have always far outnumbered those using it in a habitual manner.

The older studies in this country found that regular users consumed around 6 to 10 cigarettes per day (Charen & Perelman, 1946; Mayor's Committee on Marihuana, 1944); however, a much larger number used it on an irregular basis (Bromberg, 1934). Studies done in Eastern countries, especially India and North Africa, have concentrated on users of a highly potent hashish. Heavy users consume 2 to 6 grams of hashish per day which is equivalent to smoking at least 20 to 60 marihuana cigarettes (Chopra & Chopra, 1939; Soueif, 1967). Moderate use of the less potent cannabis preparations in the East is not considered to be a health problem; and, in fact, bhang (the Indian equivalent of marihuana) is not even considered to fall within the definition of cannabis by Indian authorities and so is excluded from U.N. treaty control (Commission on Narcotic Drugs, 1965).

The recent increase in marihuana use in the U.S. is primarily among middle- and upper-class youth, the large majority of whom do not average more than two or three cigarettes a week. Some members of the hippie subculture and certain other individuals use marihuana in amounts comparable to that found in the older studies (6 to 10 cigarettes per day).

With this as preface, we propose to provide a brief overview of what is known about the effects of marihuana use, followed by some preliminary data from a current study.

CLASSIFICATION

In small amounts marihuana acts as a mild euphoriant and sedative somewhat like alcohol, although in comparable doses it is probably more disruptive of thought processes. In larger doses marihuana effects more closely resemble those of the hallucinogens than any other group of drugs. Most of the phenomena experienced with LSD, such as depersonalization, marked visual and temporal distortion, and hallucinations have been observed with sufficiently large amounts of marihuana and especially with hashish. The effects, however, are generally much milder and easier to control than those of LSD. Isbell and associates recently demonstrated a similar dose effect with tetrahydrocannabinol (THC), an active constituent of marihuana (Isbell, Gorodetzsky, Jasinski, Claussen, Spulak, & Korte, 1967).

On the other hand, there are considerable differences in users' descriptions of marihuana and LSD effects; also, marihuana acts as a sedative and tends to produce sleep, whereas the strong hallucinogens cause long periods of wakefulness. In addition marihuana produces virtually no tolerance, whereas very rapid tolerance accompanies use of LSD-like drugs. Isbell found no cross tolerance to THC in subjects tolerant to

LSD, indicating that the two drugs probably act by different mechanisms.

DEPENDENCE

Mild irritability frequently follows withdrawal from heavy use of marihuana, but there are virtually no other symptoms of physical dependence. Psychological dependence may develop in the sense that the individual prefers the mood state resulting from marihuana use to the undrugged state. The fact that 65 percent of the hashish users in a recent Egyptian survey indicated they would like to get rid of the habit indicates appreciable psychological dependence (Soueif, 1967).

Of course, many forms of socially acceptable behavior (e.g., smoking tobacco, watching TV) may produce a form of psychic dependence. The harmfulness of such behavior should be based on the consequences of the activity rather than its existence.

PHYSICAL AND MENTAL EFFECTS

No long-term physical effects of marihuana use have been demonstrated in this country, although more current studies are needed before this can be resolved with any degree of certainty. Eastern studies of chronic users, who consume several times the amounts generally used in this country, report a variety of cannabis-induced physical ailments. Conjunctivitis is the most frequent, followed by chronic bronchitis and various digestive ailments (Chopra & Chopra, 1939). Sleep difficulties frequently occur, as is the case with opiate users in this country (Chopra & Chopra, 1939; Soueif, 1967). It is interesting to note that from 25 to 70 percent of regular hashish users in two Eastern surveys reported some impairment in physical health due to the use of the drug (Chopra & Chopra, 1939; Soueif, 1967).

There have been several cases of marihuana-induced temporary psychosis reported in this country (Bromberg, 1934; Mayor's Committee on Marihuana, 1944). Panic reactions are not uncommon among inexperienced users, and such reactions occasionally develop into a psychotic episode. These very rarely last more than a day or so, and they do not usually require hospitalization. The danger of a prolonged psychosis from marihuana is very small compared to that for LSD.

On the other hand, in India and other Eastern countries, cannabis has long been regarded as an important cause of psychosis. One study reported that 25 percent of some 2,300 men admitted to psychiatric hospitals were diagnosed as having cannabis psychoses; of the total male admissions 70 percent of the patients admitted to smoking cannabis, and one-third were regular users (Benabud, 1957). Other investigators have argued that the 3 to 1 ratio of male to female hospitalized psychotics is a result of cannabis use being almost entirely restricted to males.

These studies are definitely not in agreement with the findings in this country, and many Western authorities question the adequacy of both the diagnoses made and the methodology of the studies themselves. Although part of the difference may be due to the fact that much larger amounts of the drug are used in the East, it is doubtful that this could reasonably account for the wide discrepancy in the findings.

While there is little concern about marihuana-induced psychosis in this country, there is considerable interest in the possibility of personality changes resulting from marihuana use, particularly in the development of what has been called an "amotivational" syndrome. The older studies of regular users in this country typically described them as tending to be passive and nonproductive. Eastern studies characterize heavy users in a similar manner. However, there has generally been no attempt to distinguish between pre-existing personality traits and the effect of the drug used.

While systematic studies of the recent wave of young marihuana users are not yet available, clinical observations indicate that regular marihuana use may contribute to the development of more passive, inward-turning, amotivational personality characteristics. For numerous middle-class students, the subtly progressive change from conforming, achievement-oriented behavior to a state of relaxed and careless drifting has followed their use of significant amounts of marihuana.

It is difficult to parcel out social factors, as well as the occasional use of LSD, but it appears that regular use of marihuana may very well contribute to some characteristic personality changes, especially among highly impressionable young persons. Such changes include apathy, loss of effectiveness, and diminished capacity or willingness to carry out complex long-term plans, endure frustration, concentrate for long periods, follow routines, or successfully master new material.

Verbal facility is often impaired, both in speaking and writing.

Such individuals exhibit greater introversion, become totally involved with the present at the expense of future goals, and demonstrate a strong tendency toward regressive, child-like magical thinking. They report a greater subjective creativity but less objective productivity; and, while seeming to suffer less from vicissitudes and frustrations of life, at the same time they seem to be subtly withdrawing from the challenge of it.

MARIHUANA AND CRIME

Enforcement agencies have long attempted to justify existing punitive marihuana laws by contending that marihuana use is criminogenic. No acceptable evidence has ever been offered to support these claims, and virtually every serious investigator who has attempted to examine the question has found no relationship between marihuana and major crime. Indeed, many feel that the characteristic passive reaction to marihuana use tends to inhibit rather than cause crime, whereas alcohol consumption is more likely to release aggressive behavior.

One recent study of drug use among juveniles reported that those who were most delinquent preferred alcohol, whereas the "pot-heads" tended to be nonaggressive and stayed away from trouble (Blumer, Sutter, Ahmed, & Smith, 1967). Moreover, a shift from alcohol to marihuana use tended to be correlated with a change toward less delinquent behavior in other respects. There apparently is some validity to the claim that professional criminals sometimes use marihuana as a means of fortifying themselves in their criminal operations; however, other drugs such as alcohol, amphetamines, and barbiturates are equally popular for this purpose.

RELATION OF MARIHUANA
TO OTHER DRUG USE

A possible indirect hazard of marihuana smoking has been much debated. According to the stepping-stone theory, the use of marihuana will lead to the use of heroin in the search for greater thrills. Proponents cite the fact that most heroin users have previously used marihuana. Opponents deny that this indicates causality and cite the fact that while heroin use has remained at virtually the same level during the last few years, marihuana use has experienced a rapid rise.

Although present-day marihuana use has not been shown to predispose to heroin use, it does play a role in initiation to other potent drugs, particularly LSD. To the extent that marihuana contributes to a general disregard for the realistic consequences of behavior in young persons, its use increases the probability of the abuse of other more dangerous drugs. Thus, members of the hippie subculture frequently use methamphetamine and a host of other drugs. There is also some experimentation with heroin.

Finally, to the extent that hashish is available, its use is causally related to marihuana use. Many if not most marihuana users would welcome the opportunity to try hashish, and, if it were available, many would probably continue to use it in preference to the low-potency marihuana. Of course, the use of hashish does not necessarily lead to excess any more than does a preference for distilled liquor over beer or wine. However, the history of mind-altering drugs invariably shows that excessive indulgence increases sharply as more potent preparations of a given drug become available.

MARIHUANA USE AMONG A SELECTED GROUP OF ADULTS

Table 1 presents some characteristics of users and nonusers of marihuana among a sample of 189 persons randomly drawn from a population of 750 who received LSD from a physician in either an experimental or psychotherapy setting during the period 1955-61. The marihuana data are incidental to an ongoing follow-up interview study of LSD effects; however, these results are of interest in two respects. First, they provide information on the use of marihuana among an older group of largely professional persons. Second, the observations of this group concerning the effects of marihuana are based on more experience and are considered to be more objective than assessments made by the less reality-oriented younger groups of marihuana users.

Forty-two percent of this group of 189 have had some experience with marihuana, although only 17 percent have used it ten or more times. One-half of the latter group were introduced to marihuana prior to 1954. About one-third of those who had not tried marihuana indicated

that they might do so in the future, and a slightly higher proportion stated that they might try it if it were legal. The large majority of those who had used marihuana favored its legalization, and about one-half of those who had not tried it indicated a similar preference. . . .

Inquiry was made concerning the effect of marihuana on driving competence. Of the 32 respondents [who had used marihuana ten or more times], eight stated that they never drove under the influence of marihuana. Twenty of the remaining 24 felt that their driving competence was impaired. The reasons given were: perceptual distortion, speed distortion, slower reaction time, less alert, disoriented, poor judgment, and less careful.

Fourteen of the 32 indicated that they sometimes worked under the influence of marihuana; five stated that the effect on work was positive, four, that it was negative, and five, neutral or mixed. Fifteen of the 32 indicated that they sometimes used marihuana to enhance creative endeavors such as art, writing, music, singing, and design. Those who felt it aided in writing generally indicated that the ideas occurred to them while under the influence of marihuana, but the actual writing was done in an undrugged state.

A frequently reported advantage of marihuana over alcohol is the absence of hangover effects. Twelve of the 32 respondents reported that they sometimes experienced undesirable aftereffects the day following the use of marihuana; however, nine of the 12 indicated that such effects occurred only when large amounts were used or when it was smoked just prior to retiring. The most frequently reported symptom was lethargy, followed by inability to concentrate, irritability, and headaches.

Twenty-five of the 32 felt marihuana had resulted in no long-term effects; six reported positive long-term effects (increased insight, tolerance, spontaneity, and sexual freedom); one respondent regarded the long-term effects as mixed. It is interesting to compare these results with those of heavy hashish users in India and Egypt, where up to 70 percent report some harmful effects.

Nine of the 32 respondents were not currently using marihuana. Three said they stopped because they did not particularly like the effect, two stopped due to legal concerns, and four, due to other reasons. Of the 23 currently using marihuana, 18 indicated that they planned to continue at the same level of use and five stated they planned to decrease the frequency of use.

TABLE 1

CHARACTERISTICS OF USERS AND NONUSERS OF MARIHUANA AMONG A SAMPLE OF PERSONS RECEIVING LSD UNDER MEDICAL CONDITIONS, 1955-61

	MARIHUANA USE		
CHARACTERISTIC	NONE (N = 110)	LESS THAN TEN TIMES (N = 47)	TEN OR MORE TIMES (N = 32)
Percent of total group	58	25	17
Mean age (years)	46	40	39
Percent male	63	72	66
Education: B.A. degree or higher (percent)	56	64	44
Income: $10,000 or more (percent)	68	66	58
Used LSD under nonmedical conditions (percent)	7	19	64
Median year of initial marihuana use	—	1962	1954
Used marihuana prior to LSD (percent)	—	30	69
Use of marihuana in future:			
No (percent)	65	40	12
Yes (percent)	7	30	72
Possibly (percent)	28	30	16
Use of marihuana in future if legalized:			
No (percent)	54	32	9
Yes (percent)	15	36	84
Possibly (percent)	30	32	6
Favor removal of legal penalties against:			
Possession (percent)	54	81	97
Both possession and sale to persons over 21 (percent)	40	74	84

Four of the 32 had been arrested in connection with their marihuana use—two cases were dismissed and two received probation. Twenty of the 32 had used LSD under nonmedical conditions and 17 had used other strong hallucinogens such as peyote, mescaline, and psilocybin. Six had some experience with heroin—one had been addicted.

SOCIAL POLICY

Social policy with respect to marihuana and other psychoactive drugs has many important dimensions other than those already mentioned. The most basic issue is whether or not the prohibition of behavior whose direct effects are limited to the individual is within the function of the state. Those who feel it is not argue that the state has no more right to intervene with respect to the use

of harmful drugs than it does with regard to harmful overeating.

Those who take the contrary position argue that the harms are not limited to the individual but burden society in a variety of ways; hence the state is entitled to prohibit its use in the public interest. It is certainly clear that the very existence of government entails individual restraints. Whether or not individual freedoms should be curbed with respect to drug use depends on the extent of the threat to society and whether or not the sanctions against it are effective.

An objective assessment of the threat or benefit to society resulting from the nonmedical use of a drug should consider: physiological effects resulting from occasional or chronic use; tendency to produce physiological or psychological dependence as a function of period of use; release of antisocial behavior; effect on motor activity, especially driving safety; and tendency to produce long-lasting personality changes. Other relevant considerations are: cost; ability to control and measure potency; convenience of mode of intake, oral vs. intravenous, for example; capacity for self-titration to control effect; protection against overdose; availability of an antidote; specific effects attainable without unpredictable side effects; predictable length of action; hangover or other short-term properties which may spill over to affect work or other activities; ability to return to normalcy on demand; and ability to detect the drug, as for monitoring drivers, etc.

One of the most neglected questions in evaluating drug effects concerns the individual benefits which motivate the user. Drug use in many instances may well be an attempt to alleviate symptoms of psychiatric illness through self-medication. In some cases, marihuana use might postpone or prevent more serious manifestations of an illness. Especially for recreational drugs, such as alcohol and marihuana, an objective assessment of user motivation should consider: effectiveness in producing pleasure, relaxation, and aesthetic appreciation; enhancement of appetite and other senses; enhancement of interpersonal rapport, warmth, and emotionality; utility of variety or newness of perception and thinking; and enhancement of enjoyment of vacations, weekends, or other periods devoted to recreation, rest, and pleasure.

Other effects of nonmedical drug use may have more far-reaching ramifications for society in general. Does the drug use provide an emotional escape-valve similar to institutionalized festivities employed by other cultures? What is its effect on personality, life style, aggressiveness, competitiveness, etc.? Does it affect military effectiveness through increased passivity? Would its adoption by large numbers affect the direction of society? For example, the use of peyote changed the direction of the American Indian culture by creating a pan-Indian movement—the hippies would advocate a similar cure for the ills of the present society.

In considering the effectiveness of legal sanctions against the use of a drug, three related questions must be considered at the outset: 1) How many persons would abuse the drug if legal controls were removed or not adopted? 2) Do the laws deter use, or perhaps encourage it, as has been suggested with relation to rebellious youth? 3) Is the drug abuser a sick person who, if one drug is prohibited, will find another drug or some equally destructive behavior as a substitute? More specifically, each of these questions must be examined in the context of criminal sanctions

against both the user and the distributor as opposed to sanctions against sale only.

Clearly, if the law protects against a non-existing harm, society is better off without the law. The recent elimination of all laws pertaining to written pornography in Denmark, for example, apparently resulted in no ill effects. The incidence of marihuana use as opposed to LSD use supports the position that legal penalties are by no means the overriding determiner of drug usage. The number of persons who have used marihuana is several times that for LSD and is increasing in spite of severe penalties. LSD usage is apparently declining because of concern over the hazards rather than because of any deterrent effect of the relatively moderate laws.

The argument that the drug abuser would simply find another means of escape or self-destructive behavior if the drug were not available is probably only partially correct. It is clear that persons are more vulnerable to the abuse of drugs at certain times in their lives, such as during adolescence or other highly stressful periods. If a potential drug-of-abuse is unavailable at these times, an undesirable chain of events may well be avoided. Also, it is known that alcoholism results from sociogenic as well as psychogenic causes, and marihuana abuse can undoubtedly follow a similar pattern.

Concerning the kind of drug-control laws which should be enacted and enforced, there is general agreement that the government has not only the right but also the obligation to enforce certain practices with regard to the distribution of drugs. Disagreement exists as to the point at which the advantages of restricting availability are outweighed by the harm resulting from the illicit supplying of the demand for the drug, such as occurred during the prohibition of alcohol.

Regulation, as opposed to prohibition, permits the orderly control of potency and the conditions of sale, such as age of purchaser, hours of sale, and licensing. It also permits taxation and eliminates the support of organized crime as well as the criminogenic aspects of forcing the user to deal with illegal sources. On the other hand, prohibition of sale clearly indicates social disapproval, whereas open sale does not.

Arguments for criminal sanctions against the drug user primarily stress: 1) their deterrent effect and 2) the aid such laws give to enforcement agencies in apprehending sources of supply. Major arguments against such laws stress that enforcement inevitably encourages the violation of constitutional guarantees of privacy, as well as various other practices, such as informers posing as students, hippies, or other potential drug users, which are ethically questionable though technically legal.

The social control of drug use is most difficult to handle via legal means when the drug in question permits both use and abuse: e.g., alcohol and marihuana. The problem of penalizing the majority because of the abuse by the minority was specifically dealt with by the Supreme Court at the time of the Volstead Act. The Court ruled that the state had the right to deny access to alcohol to those who would not abuse it in order to remove the temptation from those who would abuse it.

On a few occasions, exceptions have actually been carved out of the law to permit use of a drug otherwise prohibited: e.g., sacramental use of wine and religious use of peyote by the Indians. More frequently, society has informally disregarded the enforcement of the law for various groups, conditions, or in certain districts of the city. For example, during the '40s, police frequently overlooked the use of marihuana by jazz musicians because they were otherwise productive and did not cause trouble. Another means of allowing use but controlling abuse is through compulsory treatment.

CONCLUSION

What is especially needed is a concerted effort to produce congruence among the various drug policies and laws. What we have at present is an assortment of approaches which are not only lacking in consistency but often operate in clearly opposite directions. Much of the incongruity is based on unrecognized attitudes and fears which must be made conscious and explicit before a congruent policy can emerge. One means of forcing some of the most glaring inconsistencies into perspective is to treat alcohol abuse and drug abuse as a single problem, an approach suggested by the World Health Organization (1967).

A rational approach to reducing the harm caused to society by excessive drug use must include examination of the contributions of the massive advertising programs for alcohol and tobacco and weigh this against the economic and other costs of intervening in our free enterprise system. If public drunkenness is the manifestation of an illness to be treated rather than punished, is dependency on other drugs not also an illness?

We should critically examine the legal reasoning which concludes that being an addict is not a crime, but possessing the substance necessary to be an addict is a felony deserving a five- or ten-year sentence. The methods of controlling narcotics supply should be weighed against the expense to the victims burglarized, the increased number of prostitutes, and the large profits to organized crime, all of which accompany illegal drug traffic. The deterring effect of the current marihuana laws should be evaluated against the resulting alienation, disrespect for the law, and secondary deviance involving a sizeable portion of an entire generation.

Finally, in a somewhat speculative vein, part of the lack of congruence among drug policies in this country may be due to the fact that economic and technological factors are changing at a faster rate than are cultural attitudes and values. The drug laws in this country have always been an attempt to legislate morality, although they have been justified in terms of preventing antisocial acts. These laws and attitudes evolved at a time when the Protestant ethic and the competitive, achievement-oriented value system were very much in dominance. The freely chosen, passive withdrawal to a life of drug-induced fantasy was an extremely threatening concept.

Now we are told we are verging on an economy of abundance rather than scarcity; an age of automation will eliminate half or more of the labor force necessary for the production of goods. The concept of work will have to be redefined to include nonproductive pursuits which are now considered hobbies; a guaranteed annual income program will likely be in effect within five or ten years. The children of today's middle class have never experienced a depression or any appreciable difficulty in satisfying their material needs. They do not share the materialistic value system to the same extent as their parents because they have little fear of material deprivation.

There also appears to be an increasing acceptance of pleasure in its own right rather than as something that needs to be earned as a reward for hard work.

In conclusion, whether or not the age of abundance arrives, social policy, with some minor reversals, will probably move in the direction of permitting greater individual freedom with respect to drug use. Society will promote the concept of allowing adults the privilege of informed decision. The crucial problem which will remain is that of protecting those who are too young to make an informed decision.

The readings for Part Three cover three topics relating to the individual in his group setting. The first article—Society as a Complex Adaptive System—is a difficult but provocative article which extends our discussion of Systems Theory to the organization, functioning, and adapting of groups. The second article—Anonymity, Dissent, and Individual Integrity—deals with problems which are of deep concern to many young Americans as well as to many older ones. The third article—Sensitivity Training in Industry—shows one application of the method of intensive group experience for fostering personal growth and helps the reader to understand the nature of such experience.

Walter Buckley

SOCIETY AS A COMPLEX ADAPTIVE SYSTEM

We have argued at some length in another place that the mechanical equilibrium model and the organismic homeostasis models of society that have underlain most modern sociological theory have outlived their usefulness. A more viable model, one much more faithful to the *kind* of system that society is more and more recognized to be, is in process of developing out of, or is in keeping with, the modern systems perspective (which we use loosely here to refer to general systems research, cybernetics, information and communication theory, and related fields). Society, or the sociocultural system, is not, then, principally an equilibrium system or a homeostatic system, but what we shall simply refer to as a complex adaptive system.

To summarize the argument in overly simplified form: Equilibrial systems are relatively *closed* and *entropic*. In going to equilibrium they typically *lose structure* and have a *minimum of free energy;* they are affected only by external "disturbances" and have *no internal or endogenous sources of change;* their component elements are *relatively simple* and *linked directly via energy exchange*

Reprinted from Walter Buckley, editor, *Modern Systems Research for the Behavioral Scientist* (Chicago: Aldine Publishing Company, 1968); copyright © 1968 by Walter Buckley. Reprinted by permission of author and publisher.

(rather than information interchange); and since they are relatively closed they have no feedback or other systematic self-regulating or adaptive capabilities. The homeostatic system (for example, the organism, apart from higher cortical functioning) is open and negentropic, maintaining a moderate energy level within controlled limits. But for our purposes here, the system's main characteristic is its functioning to *maintain the given structure of the system* within pre-established limits. It involves feedback loops with its environment, and possibly information as well as pure energy interchanges, but these are geared principally to *self-regulation* (structure maintenance) rather than adaptation (*change* of system structure). The complex adaptive systems (species, psychological and sociocultural systems) are also open and negentropic. But they are open *"internally" as well as externally* in that the interchanges among their components may result in *significant changes in the nature of the components themselves* with important consequences for the system as a whole. And the energy level that may be mobilized by the system is subject to relatively wide fluctuation. Internal as well as external interchanges are mediated characteristically by *information flows* (via chemical, cortical, or cultural encoding and decoding), although pure energy interchange occurs also. True feedback control loops make possible not only self-regulation, but self-direction or at least adaptation to a changing environment, such that the system may *change or elaborate its structure* as a condition of survival or viability.

We argue, then, that the sociocultural system is fundamentally of the latter type, and requires for analysis a theoretical model or perspective built on the kinds of characteristics mentioned. . . . It is further argued that a number of recent sociological and social psychological theories and theoretical orientations articulate well with this modern systems perspective, and we outline some of these to suggest in addition that modern systems research is not as remote from the social scientists' interests and endeavors as many appear to believe.

COMPLEX ADAPTIVE SYSTEMS:
A PARADIGM

A feature of current general systems research is the gradual development of a general paradigm of the basic mechanisms underlying the evolution of complex adaptive systems. The terminology of this paradigm derives particularly from information theory and cybernetics. We shall review these concepts briefly. The *environment,* however else it may be characterized, can be seen at bottom as a set or ensemble of more or less distinguishable elements, states, or events, whether the discriminations are made in terms of spatial or temporal relations, or properties. Such distinguishable differences in an ensemble may be most generally referred to as *"variety."* The relatively stable "causal," spatial and/or temporal relations between these distinguishable elements or events may be generally referred to as *"constraint."* If the elements are so "loosely" related that there is equal probability of any element or state being associated with any other, we speak of "chaos" or complete randomness, and hence, lack of "constraint." But our more typical natural environment is characterized by a relatively high degree of constraint, without which the development and elaboration of adaptive systems (as well as "science") would not have been possible. When the internal organization of an adaptive system acquires features that permit it to discriminate, act upon, and respond to aspects of the environmental variety and its constraints, we might generally say that the system has *"mapped"* parts of the environmental variety and constraints into its organization as structure and/or "information." Thus, a subset of the ensemble of constrained variety in the environment is coded and transmitted in some way via various channels to result in a change in the structure of the receiving system which is isomorphic in certain respects to the original variety. The system thus becomes selectively matched to its environment both physiologically and psychologically. It should be added that two or more adaptive systems, as well as an adaptive system and its natural environment, may be said to be selectively interrelated by a mapping process in the same terms. This becomes especially important for the evolution of social systems.

In these terms, then, the paradigm underlying the evolution of more and more complex adaptive systems begins with the fact of a potentially changing environment characterized by variety with constraints, and an existing adaptive system or organization whose persistence and elaboration to higher levels depends upon a successful mapping of some of the environmental variety and constraints into its own organization on at least a semi-permanent basis. This means that our adaptive system—whether on the biological, psychological, or sociocultural level— must manifest (1) some degree of *"plasticity"* and *"irritability"* vis-à-vis its environment such that it carries on a constant interchange with environmental events, acting on and reacting to it; (2) some source or mechanism for *variety,* to act as a potential pool of adaptive variability to meet the problem of mapping new or more detailed variety and constraints in a changeable environment; (3) a set of *selective* criteria or mechanisms against which the "variety pool" may be sifted into those variations in the organization or system that more closely map the environment and those that do not; and (4) an arrangement for *preserving and/or propagating* these "successful" mappings.

It should be noted, as suggested above, that this is a *relational* perspective, and the question of "substance" is quite secondary here. . . . Also, as suggested, this formulation corresponds closely with the current conception of "information" viewed as the process of selection—from an ensemble of variety—of a subset which, to have "meaning," must match another subset taken from a similar ensemble. Communication is the process by which this constrained variety is transmitted in one form or another between such ensembles, and involves coding and decoding such that the original variety and its constraints remains relatively invariant at the receiving end. If the source of the "communication" is the causally constrained variety of the natural environment, and the destination is the biological adaptive system, we refer to the Darwinian process of natural selection whereby the information encoded in the chromosomal material (for example the DNA) reflects or is a mapping of the environmental variety, and makes possible a continuous and more or less successful adaptation of the former system to the latter. If the adaptive system in question is a (relatively high-level) psychological or cortical system, we refer to "learning," whereby the significant environmental variety is transmitted via sensory and perceptual channels and decodings to the cortical centers where, by selective criteria (for example, "reward" and "punishment") related to physiological and/or other "needs" or "drives," relevant parts of it are encoded and preserved as "experience" for varying periods of time and may promote adaptation. Or, on the level of the symbol-based sociocultural adaptive system, where the more or less patterned actions of persons and groups are as crucial a part of the environment of other persons and groups as the nonsocial environment, the gestural variety and its more or less normatively defined constraints is encoded, transmitted, and decoded at the receiving end by way of the various familiar channels with varying degrees of fidelity. Over time, and again by a selective process—now much more complex, tentative, and less easily specified —there is a selective elaboration and more or less temporary preservation of some of this complex social as well as non-social constrained variety in the form of "culture," "social organization," and "personality structure."

On the basis of such a continuum of evolving, elaborating levels of adaptive system (and we have only pointed to three points along this continuum), we could add to and refine our typology of systems. Thus, we note that as adaptive systems develop from the lower biological levels through the higher psychological and sociocultural levels we can distinguish: (1) the *varying time span* required for exemplars of the adaptive system to map or encode within themselves changes in the variety and constraints of the environment; phylogenetic time scales for organic systems and for tropistic or instinctual neural systems; ontogenetic time scales for higher psychological or cortical systems; and, in the sociocultural case, the time span may be very short—days—or very long, but complicated by the fact that the relevant environment includes both intra- and inter-societal variety and constraints as well as natural environment variety (the latter becoming progressively less determinant); (2) the greatly *varying degrees*

of fidelity of mapping of the environment into the adaptive system, from the lower unicellular organisms with a very simple repertoire of actions on and reactions to the environment, through the complex of instinctual and learned repertoire, to the ever-proliferating more refined and veridical accumulations of a sociocultural system; (3) the progressively greater separation and independence of the more refined "stored information" from purely biological processes as genetic information is gradually augmented by cortically imprinted information, and finally by entirely extrasomatic cultural depositories. The implications of these shifts, and others that could be included, are obviously far-reaching.

One point that will require more discussion may be briefly mentioned here. This is the *relative* discontinuity we note in the transition from the non-human adaptive system to the sociocultural system. . . . As we progress from lower to higher biological adaptive systems we note, as a general rule, the gradually increasing role of other biological units of the same as well as different species making up part of the significant environment. The variety and constraints represented by the behavior of these units must be mapped along with that of the physical environment. With the transition represented by the higher primate social organization through to full-blown human, symbolically mediated, sociocultural adaptive systems, the mapping of the variety and constraints characterizing the subtle behaviors, gestures and intentions of the individuals and groups making up the effective social organization become increasingly central, and eventually equal if not overshadow the requirements for mapping the physical environment.

It was these newly demanding requirements of coordination, anticipation, expectation and the like within a more and more complex *social* environment of interacting and interdependent others—where genetic mappings were absent or inadequate—that prompted the fairly rapid elaboration of relatively new system features. These included, of course: the ever-greater conventionalizing of gestures into true symbols; the resulting development of a "self," self-awareness, or self-consciousness out of the symbolically mediated, continuous mirroring and mapping of each unit's behaviors and gesturings in those of ever-present others (a process well described by Dewey, Mead, Cooley, and others); and the resulting ability to deal in the present with future as well as past mappings and hence to manifest goal-seeking, evaluating, self-other relating, norm-referring behavior. In cybernetic terminology, this higher level sociocultural system became possible through the development of higher order feedbacks such that the component individual subsystems became able to map, store, and selectively act toward, not only the external variety and constraints of the social and non-social environment, but also their own internal states. To speak of self-consciousness, internalization, expectations, choice, certainty and uncertainty, and the like, is to elaborate this basic point. This transition, then, gave rise to the newest adaptive system level we refer to as sociocultural. . . . This higher level adaptive organization thus manifests features that warrant its scientific study in terms as distinct from a purely biological system as the analytical terms of the latter are from physical systems.

THE SOCIOCULTURAL ADAPTIVE SYSTEM

From the perspective sketched above, the following principles underlying the sociocultural adaptive system can be derived:

1. The principle of the "irritability of protoplasm" carries through to all the higher level adaptive systems. "Tension" in the broad sense —in which stress and strain are manifestations under conditions of felt blockage—is ever-present in one form or another throughout the sociocultural system—now as diffuse, socially unstructured strivings, frustrations, enthusiasms, aggressions, neurotic or psychotic or normative deviation; sometimes as clustered and minimally structured crowd or quasi-group processes, normatively supportive as well as destructive; and now as socioculturally structured creativity and production, conflict and competition, or upheaval and destruction. As Thelen and colleagues (1956) put it:

1. Man is always trying to live beyond his means. Life is a sequence of reactions to stress: Man is continually meeting situations with which he cannot quite cope.

2. In stress situations, energy is mobilized and a state of tension is produced.

3. The state of tensions tends to be disturbing, and Man seeks to reduce the tension.

4. He has direct impulses to take action. . . .

2. Only closed systems running down to their most probable states, that is, losing organization and available energy, can be profitably treated in equilibrium terms. Outside this context the concept of equilibrium would seem quite inappropriate and only deceptively helpful. On the other side, only open, tensionful, adaptive systems can elaborate and proliferate organization. Cannon (1939) coined the term "homeostasis" for biological systems to avoid the connotations of equilibrium, and to bring out the dynamic, processual, potential-maintaining properties of *basically unstable* physiological systems. In dealing with the sociocultural system, however, we need yet a new concept to express not only the *structure-maintaining* feature, but also the *structure-elaborating and changing* feature of the inherently unstable system. The notion of "steady state," now often used, approaches the meaning we seek if it is understood that the "state" that tends to remain "steady" is *not to be identified with the particular structure* of the system. That is, as we shall argue in a moment, in order to maintain a steady state the system may change its particular structure. For this reason, the term "morphogenesis" is more descriptive. . . .

Thus, the complex, adaptive system as a continuing entity is not to be confused with the structure which that system may manifest at any time. Making this distinction allows us to state a fundamental principle of open, adaptive systems: *Persistence or continuity of an adaptive system may require, as a necessary condition, change in its structure,* the degree of change being a complex function of the internal state of the system, the state of its relevant environment, and the nature of the interchange between the two. Thus, animal species develop and persist or are continuously transformed (or become extinct) in terms of a change (or failure of change) of structure—sometimes extremely slow, sometimes very rapid. The higher individual organism capable of learning by experience maintains itself as a viable system vis-à-vis its environment by a change of structure—in this case the neural structure of the cortex. It is through this principle that we can say that the "higher" organism represents a "higher" level of adaptive system capable, ontogenetically, of *mapping the environment more rapidly and extensively* and with *greater refinement and fidelity,* as compared to the tropistic or instinct-based adaptive system which can change its structure only phylogenetically. The highest level adaptive system—the sociocultural—is capable of an even more rapid and refined mapping of the environment (including the social and non-social environment, as well as at least some aspects of its own internal state) since sociocultural structures are partially independent of both ontogenetic and phylogenetic structures, and the mappings of many individuals are selectively pooled and stored extrasomatically and made available to the system units as they enter and develop within the system.

Such a perspective suggests that, instead of saying, as some do, that a prime requisite for persistence of a social system is "pattern maintenance," we can say, after Sommerhof (1968) and Ashby (1968), that persistence of an adaptive system requires as a necessary condition the maintenance of the system's "essential variables" within certain limits. Such essential variables and their limits may perhaps be specified in terms of what some have referred to as the "functional prerequisites" of any social system (for example, a minimal level of organismal sustenance, of reproduction, of patterned interactive relations, etc.). But the maintenance of the system's essential variables, we are emphasizing, may hinge on (as history and ethnography clearly show) *pattern reorganization or change. . . .*

To avoid the many difficulties of a one-sided perspective it would seem essential to keep before us as a basic principle that the persistence and/or development of the complex sociocultural system depends upon structuring, destructuring, and restructuring—processes occurring at widely varying rates and degrees as a function of the external social and non-social environment. Jules Henry (1959), among others, has made this point:

. . . the lack of specificity of man's genetic mechanisms has placed him in the situation of constantly having to revise his social structures because of their frequent failure to guide interpersonal relations without tensions felt as burdensome even in the society in which they originate . . . thus man has been presented with a unique evolutionary task: because his mechanisms for determining inter-personal relations lack specificity, he must attempt to maximize social adaptation through constant conscious and unconscious revision and experimentation, searching constantly for social structures, patterns of inter-personal relations, that will be more adaptive, as he feels them. Man's evolutionary path is thus set for him by his constant tendency to alter his modes of social adaptation. (pp. 21-22) . . .

4. The cybernetic perspective of control or self-regulation of adaptive systems emphasizes the crucial role of "deviation," seen in both negative and positive aspects. On the negative side, certain kinds of deviations of aspects of the system from its given structural state may be seen as "mismatch" or "negative feedback" signals *interpreted by certain organizing centers* as a failure of the system's operating processes or structures relative to a goal state sought, permitting—under

certain conditions of adaptive structuring—a change of those operating processes or structures toward goal-optimization. (Thus, one facet of the "political" process of sociocultural systems may be interpreted in this light, with the more "democratic" type of social organization providing the more extended and accurate assessment of the mismatch between goal-attainment on the one hand, and current policy and existing social structuring on the other.)

On the positive side, the cybernetic perspective brings out the absolute necessity of deviation—or, more generally, "variety"—in providing a pool of potential new transformations of process or structure that the adaptive systems might adopt in responding to goal-mismatch. On the lower, biological levels we recognize here the principle of genetic variety and the role of gene pools in the process of adaptive response to organismic mismatch with a changed environment. (And in regard to the other major facet of the "political" process, the more democratic type of social organization makes available a broader range of variety, or "deviation," from which to select new orientations.)

Thus, the concept of requisite deviation needs to be proffered as a high-level principle that can lead us to theorize: A requisite of sociocultural systems is the development and maintenance of a significant level of non-pathological deviance manifest as a pool of alternate ideas and behaviors with respect to the traditional, institutionalized ideologies and role behaviors. Rigidification of any given institutional structure must eventually lead to disruption or dissolution of the society by way of internal upheaval or ineffectiveness against external challenge. . . .

Attempts to analyze a society from such a perspective make possible a more balanced analysis of such processes as socialization, education, mass communication, and economic and political conflict and debate. We are then encouraged to build squarely into our theory and research designs the full sociological significance of such informally well-recognized conceptions as socialization for "self-reliance" and relative "autonomy," education for "creativity," ideational flexibility and the "open mind," communications presenting the "full spectrum" of viewpoints, etc., instead of smuggling them in unsystematically as if they were only residual considerations or ill-concealed value judgments.

5. Given the necessary presence of variety or deviance in an adaptive system, the general systems model then poses the problem of the *selection* and more or less permanent *preservation* or systemic structuring of some of this variety. On the biological level, we have the process of "natural selection" of some of the genetic variety existing within the interfertile species and subspecies gene pool, and the preservation for various lengths of time of this variety through the reproductive process. On the level of higher order psychological adaptive systems, we have trial-and-error selection, by way of the so-called "law of effect," from the variety of environmental events and the potential behavioral repertoire to form learned and remembered experience and motor skills more or less permanently preserved by way of cortical structuring. As symbolic mapping or decoding and encoding of the environment and one's self becomes possible, the selection criteria lean less heavily on direct and simple physiological reward and more heavily on "meanings" or "significance" as manifested in existing self-group structural relations. In the process, selection from the full range of available variety becomes more and more refined and often more restricted, and emerges as one or another kind of "personality" system or "group character" structure. On the sociocultural level, social selection and relative stabilization or institutionalization of normatively interpreted role relations and value patterns occurs through the variety of processes usually studied under the headings of conflict, competition, accommodation, and such; power, authority and compliance; and "collective behavior," from mob behavior through opinion formation processes and social movements to organized war. More strictly "rational" processes are of course involved, but often seem to play a relatively minor role as far as larger total outcomes are concerned.

It is clearly in the area of "social selection" that we meet the knottiest problems. For the sociocultural system, as for the biological adaptive system, analysis must focus on both the potentialities of the system's structure at a given time, and the environmental changes that might occur and put particular demands on whatever structure has evolved. In both areas the complexities are compounded for the sociocultural system. In developing a typology of systems and their internal linkages we have noted that, as we proceed from the mechanical or physical through the biological, psychic and sociocultural, the system becomes "looser," the interrelations among parts more tenuous, less rigid, and especially less directly tied to physical events as energy relations and transformations are overshadowed by symbolic relations and information transfers. Feedback loops between operating sociocultural structures and the surrounding reality are often long and tortuous, so much so that knowledge of results or goal-mismatch, when forthcoming at all, may easily be interpreted in non-veridical ways (as the history of magic, superstition, and ideologies from primitive to present amply indicate). The higher adaptive systems have not been attained without paying their price, as the widespread existence of illusion and delusions on the personality and cultural levels attest. On the biological level, the component parts have relatively few degrees of freedom, and changes in the environment are relatively directly and inexorably reacted to by selective structural changes in the species.

Sociocultural systems are capable of persisting within a wide range of degrees of freedom of the components, and are often able to "muddle through" environmental changes that are not too demanding. But of course this is part of the genius of this level of adaptive system: it is capable of temporary shifts in structure to meet exigencies. The matter is greatly complicated for the social scientist, however, by this system's outstanding ability to act on and partially control the environment of which a major determining part is made up of other equally loose-knit, more or less flexible, illusion-ridden, sociocultural adaptive systems. Thus, although the minimal integration required for a viable system does set limits on the kinds of structures that can persist, these limits seem relatively broad compared to a biological system. And given the relatively greater degrees of freedom of internal structuring (structural alternatives, as some call them) and the *potentially* great speed with which restructuring may occur under certain conditions, it becomes difficult to predict the reactions of such a system to environmental changes or internal elaboration. . . .

Although the problem is difficult, something can be said about more ultimate adaptive criteria against which sociocultural structures can be assessed. Consideration of the grand trends of evolution provides clues to very general criteria. These trends point in the direction of: (1) greater and greater flexibility of structure, as error-controlled mechanisms (cybernetic processes of control) replace more rigid, traditionalistic means of meeting problems and seeking goals; (2) ever more refined, accurate, and systematic mapping, decoding and encoding of the external environment and the system's own internal milieu (via science), along with greater independence from the physical environment; (3) and thereby a greater elaboration of self-regulating substructures in order—not merely to restore a given equilibrium or homeostatic level—but to purposefully re-structure the system without tearing up the lawn in the process.

With these and perhaps other general criteria, we might then drop to lower levels of generality by asking what restrictions these place on a socio-cultural adaptive system if it is to remain optimally viable in these terms. It is possible that this might provide a value-free basis for discussing the important roles, for example, of a vigorous and independent science in all fields; the broad and deep dissemination of its codified findings; the absence of significant or long-lasting subcultural cleavages, power centers and vested interests, whether on a class or ethnic basis, to break or hinder the flow of information or feedback concerning the internal states of the system: and the promotion of a large "variety pool" by maintaining a certain number of degrees of freedom in the relations of the component parts—for example, providing a number of real choices of behaviors and goals. Thus we can at least entertain the feasibility of developing an objective rationale for the socio-cultural "democracy" we shy from discussing in value terms.

6. Further discussion of the intricacies of the problem of *sociocultural selection processes* leading to more or less stable system *structures* may best be incorporated into the frame of discussion of the problem of *"structure versus process."* This is another of those perennial issues of the social (and other) sciences, which the modern systems perspective may illuminate.

Our argument may be outlined as follows:

—Much of modern sociology has analyzed society in terms of largely structural concepts: institutions, culture, norms, roles, groups, etc. These are often reified, and make for a rather static, overly deterministic, and elliptical view of societal workings.

—But for the sociocultural system, "structure" is only a relative stability of underlying, ongoing micro-processes. Only when we focus on these can we begin to get at the selection process whereby certain interactive relationships become relatively and temporarily stabilized into social and cultural structures.

—The unit of dynamic analysis thus becomes the systemic *matrix* of interacting, goal-seeking, deciding individuals and subgroups—whether this matrix is part of a formal organization or only a loose collectivity. Seen in this light, society becomes a continuous morphogenic process,

through which we may come to understand in a unified conceptual manner the development of structures, their maintenance, and their change. And it is important to recognize that out of this matrix is generated, not only *social* structure, but also *personality* structure, and *meaning* structure. All, of course, are intimately interrelated in the morphogenic process, and are only analytically separable.

STRUCTURE, PROCESS, AND DECISION THEORY

Though the problem calls for a lengthy methodological discussion, we shall here simply recall the viewpoint that sees the sociocultural system in comparative perspective against lower-level mechanical, organic and other types of systems. As we proceed upward along such a typology we noted that the ties linking components become less and less rigid and concrete, less direct, simple and stable within themselves. Translation of energy along unchanging and physically continuous links gives way in importance to transmission of information via internally varying, discontinuous components with many more degrees of freedom. Thus for mechanical systems, and parts of organic systems, the "structure" has a representation that is concrete and directly observable—such that when the system ceases to operate much of the structure remains directly observable for a time. For the sociocultural system, "structure" becomes a theoretical construct whose referent is only indirectly observable (or only inferable) by way of series of events along a time dimension; when the system ceases to operate, the links maintaining the sociocultural structure are no longer observable. "Process," then, points to the actions and interactions of the components of an ongoing system, in which varying degrees of structuring arise, persist, dissolve, or change. (Thus "process" should not be made synonymous simply with "change," as it tended to be for many earlier sociologists.) . . .

We can take only brief note of a few of the more recent arguments for the process viewpoint. The anthropologists, for example, have become acutely concerned in the last few years with this issue. G. P. Murdock (1955) seems to be echoing Small when he says, "All in all, the static view of social structure which seeks explanations exclusively within the existing framework of a social system on the highly dubious assumption of cultural stability and nearly perfect functional integration seems clearly to be giving way, in this country at least, to a dynamic orientation which focuses attention on the processes by which such systems come into being and succeed one another over time." (p. 366) . . . "Social structure as Fortes once put it, must be 'visualized' as 'a sum of processes in time.' As I would phrase it, social structure is implicitly an event-structure. . . ." (Nadel, 1958, p. 128) . . .

Among sociologists, a perennial critic of the overly-structural conception of the group is Herbert Blumer. Blumer (1953) has argued that it is from the process of ongoing interaction itself that group life gets its main features, which cannot be adequately analyzed in terms of fixed attitudes, "culture," or social structure—nor can it be conceptualized in terms of mechanical structure, the functioning of an organism, or a system seeking equilibrium, ". . . in view of the formative and explorative character of interaction as the participants *judge* each other and *guide* their own acts by that judgment."

The human being is not swept along as a neutral and indifferent unit by the operation of a system. As an organism capable of self-interaction he forges his actions out of a process of definition involving choice, appraisal, *and* decision. . . . *Cultural norms, status positions and role relationships are only* frameworks *inside of which that process* [*of formative transaction*] *goes on. (pp. 199-201. Emphasis added) . . .*

It can be argued, then, that a refocusing is occurring via "decision theory," whether elaborated in terms of "role-strain" theory; theories of cognitive dissonance, congruence, balance, or concept formation; exchange, bargaining, or conflict theories, or the mathematical theory of games. The basic problem is the same: How do interacting personalities and groups define, assess, interpret, "verstehen," and act on the situation? Or, from the broader perspective of our earlier discussion, how do the processes of "social selection" operate in the "struggle" for sociocultural structure? Instead of asking how structure affects, determines, channels actions and interactions, we ask how structure is created, maintained and recreated.

Thus we move down from structure to social interrelations and from social relations to social actions and interaction processes—to a matrix of "dynamic assessments" and intercommunication of meanings, to evaluating, emoting, deciding and choosing. To avoid anthropomorphism and gain the advantages of a broader and more rigorously

specified conceptual system, we arrive at the language of modern systems theory.

Basic ingredients of the decision-making focus include, then: (1) a *process* approach; (2) a conception of *tension* as inherent in the process; and (3) a renewed concern with the role and workings of man's enlarged cortex seen as a complex adaptive subsystem operating within an *interaction matrix* characterized by *uncertainty, conflict,* and other dissociative (as well as associative) processes *underlying the structuring and restructuring of the larger psycho-social system.*

Process Focus

The process focus points to information-processing individuals and groups linked by different types of communication nets to form varying types of interaction matrices that may be characterized by "competition," "cooperation," "conflict," and the like. Newer analytical tools being explored to handle such processes include treatment of the interaction matrix over time as a succession of states described in terms of transition probabilities, Markoff chains, or stochastic processes in general. The Dewey-Mead "transactions" are now discussed in terms of information and codings and decodings, with the essential "reflexivity" of behavior now treated in terms of negative and positive feedback loops linking via the communication process the intrapersonal, interpersonal and intergroup subsystems and making possible varying degrees of matching and mismatching of Mead's "self and others," the elaboration of Boulding's "Image," and the execution of Miller's "Plans." And herein we find the great significance for sociology of many of the conceptual tools (though not, at least as yet, the mathematics) of information and communication theory, cybernetics, or general systems research, along with the rapidly developing techniques of *relational* mathematics such as the several branches of set theory—topology, group theory, graphy theory, symbolic logic, etc.

Conception of Tension

Tension is seen as an inherent and essential feature of complex adaptive systems; it provides the "go" of the system, the "force" behind the elaboration and maintenance of structure. There is no "law of social inertia" operating here, nor can we count on "automatic" reequilibrating forces counteracting system "disturbances" or "deviance," for, whereas we do find deviance-reducing negative feedback loops in operation we *also* find deviance-maintaining and deviance-amplifying *positive* feedback processes often referred to as the vicious circle or spiral, or "escalation." It is not at all certain whether the resultant will maintain, change, or destroy the given system or its particular structure. The concepts of "stress" or "strain" we take to refer only to the greater mobilization of normal tension under conditions of more than usual blockage. And instead of a system's seeking to manage *tension*, it would seem more apt to speak of a system's seeking to manage *situations* interpreted as responsible for the production of greater than normal tension.

The "role strain" theory of William J. Goode is an illustrative attack on assumptions of the widely current structural approach, using a process and tension emphasis and contributing to the decision-theory approach. Goode (1960) analyzes social structure or institutions into role relations, and role relations into role transactions. "Role relations are seen as a sequence of 'role bargains' and as a continuing process of selection among alternative role behaviors, in which each individual seeks to reduce his role strain." (p. 483) Contrary to the current stability view, which sees social system continuity as based primarily on normative consensus and normative integration, Goode thus sees "dissensus, nonconformity, and conflicts among norms and roles as the usual state of affairs. . . . The individual cannot satisfy fully all demands, and must move through a continuous sequence of role decision and bargains . . . in which he seeks to reduce his role strain, his felt difficulty in carrying out his obligations." (p. 495) . . .

It should be noted, however, that Goode accepts unnecessarily a vestige of the equilibrium or stability model when he states, "The total role structure functions so as to reduce role strain." (p. 487) He is thus led to reiterate a proposition that—when matched against our knowledge of the empirical world—is patently false. Or, more precisely, not false, but a half-truth: it recognizes deviance-reducing negative feedback processes, but not deviance-amplifying positive feedback processes. . . .

Study of Cognitive Processes

A more concerted study of cognitive processes, especially under conditions of *uncertainty* and *conflict,* goes hand in hand, of course, with a focus on decision-making and role transactions. Despite the evolutionary implications of man's enlarged cortex, much social (and psychological) theory seems predicated on the assumption that men are decorticated. Cognitive processes, as they are coming to be viewed today, are not to be simply equated with the traditional, ill-defined, concept of the "rational." That the data-processing system—whether socio-psychological or electro-mechanical—is seen as inherently "rational" tells us little about its outputs in concrete cases. Depending on the adequacy and accuracy of the effectively available information, the total internal organization or "Image," the character of the "Plans" or program, and the nature of the significant environment, the output of either "machine" may be sense or nonsense, symbolic logic or psychologic, goal-attainment or oscillation. . . .

We are reminded here of Robert R. Sears' (1951) complaint that "psychologists think monadically. That is, they choose the behavior of one person as their scientific subject matter. For them, the universe is composed of individuals . . . the universal laws sought by the psychologist almost always relate to a single body." (pp. 478-479) Arguing for the desirability of combining individual and social behavior into a common framework, Sears noted that, "Whether the group's behavior is dealt with as antecedent and the individual's as consequent, or vice versa, the two kinds of event are so commonly mixed in causal relationships that it is impractical to conceptualize them separately." (p. 478)

Fortunately, however, there are recent statements that rally to the side of the sociological interactionist theorists, whose perspective continues to be ignored or little understood by so many personality theorists who are nevertheless gradually rediscovering and duplicating its basic principles. A good beginning to a truly interpersonal approach to personality theory and the problem of stability and change in behavior is the statement of Paul F. Secord and Carl W. Backman (1961), which remarkably parallels Goode's theory of stability and change in social systems discussed earlier. Pointing to the assumptions of several personality theorists that when stability of behavior occurs it is solely a function of stability in personality structure, and that this latter structure has, inherently, a strong resistance to change except when special change-inducing forces occur, Secord and Backman see as consequences the same kinds of theoretical inadequacies we found for the stability view of social systems:

The first is that continuity in individual behavior is not a problem to be solved; it is simply a natural outcome of the formation of stable structure. The second is that either behavioral change is not given systematic attention, or change is explained independently of stability. Whereas behavioral stability is explained by constancy of structure, change tends to be explained by environmental forces and fortuitous circumstances. (p. 22)

Their own theoretical view abandons these assumptions and "places the locus of stability and change in the interaction process rather than in intrapersonal structures." Recognizing the traditional two classes of behavioral determinants, the cultural-normative and the intrapersonal, their conceptualization

attempts to identify a third class of determinants, which have their locus neither in the individual nor the culture, but in the interaction process itself. In a general sense this third class may be characterized as the tendencies of the individual and the persons with whom he interacts to shape the interaction process according to certain requirements, i.e., they strive to produce certain patterned relations. As will be seen, the principles governing this activity are truly interpersonal; they require as much attention to the behavior of the other as they do to the behavior of the individual, and it cannot be said that one or the other is the sole locus of cause. (p. 22)

They go on to analyze the "interpersonal matrix" into three components: an aspect of the self-concept of a person, his interpretation of those elements of his behavior related to that aspect, and his perception of related aspects of the other with whom he is interacting. "An interpersonal matrix is a recurring functional relation between these three components."

In these terms, Secord and Backman attempt to specify the conditions and forces leading to or threatening congruency or incongruency, and hence stability or change, in the matrix. Thus, four types of incongruency, and two general classes of resolution of incongruency, are discussed. One of these latter classes

results in restoration of the original matrix, leaving self and behavior unchanged (although cognitive distortions may occur), and the other leads to a new matrix in which self or behavior are changed. (p. 26)

In sum, contrary to previous approaches, theirs emphasizes that "the individual strives to maintain interpersonal relations characterized by congruent matrices, rather than to maintain a self, habits, or traits."

Maintenance of intrapersonal structure occurs only when such maintenance is consistent with an ongoing interaction process which is in a state of congruency. That most individuals do maintain intrapersonal structure is a function of the fact that the behavior of others toward the individuals in question is normally overwhelmingly consistent with such maintenance. (p. 28)

And this conception also, as most approaches do not (or do inadequately), predicts or accounts for the fact that, should the interpersonal environment cease to be stable and familiar, undergoing great change such that others behave uniformly toward the individual in new ways, the individual "would rapidly modify his own behavior and internal structure to produce a new set of congruent matrices. As a result, he would be a radically changed person." (p. 28)

As we have said, the Secord and Backman theory and Goode's role-strain theory may be seen as closely complementary views. The former argues that *personality* structure is generated in, and continues to have its seat in, the social interactive matrix; the latter argues that *social* structure is generated in, and continues to have its seat in, the social interactive matrix. . . .

FURTHER EXAMPLES

Ralph Turner (1962) has addressed himself to the elaboration of this perspective in that conceptual area fundamental to the analysis of institutions—roles and role-taking. The many valid criticisms of the more static and overdetermining conception of roles is due, he believes, to the dominance of the Linton view of role and the use of an oversimplified model of role functioning. Viewing role-playing and role-taking, however, as a process (as implied in Meadian theory), Turner shows that there is more to it than just "an extension of normative or cultural deterministic theory" and that a process view of role adds novel elements to the notion of social interaction.

The morphogenic nature of role behavior is emphasized at the start in the concept of *"role-making."* Instead of postulating the initial existence of distinct, identifiable roles, Turner posits "a tendency to create and modify conceptions of self- and other-roles" as the interactive orienting process. Since actors behave *as if* there were roles, although the latter actually exist only in varying degrees of definitiveness and consistency, the actors attempt to define them and make them explicit—thereby in effect creating and modifying them as they proceed. The key to role-taking, then, is the morphogenic propensity "to shape the phenomenal world into roles"; formal organizational regulation restricting this process is not to be taken as the prototype, but rather as a "distorted instance" of the wider class of role-taking phenomena. To the extent that the bureaucratic setting blocks the role-making process, organization is maximal, "variety" or alternatives of action minimal, actors are cogs in a rigid machine, and the morphogenic process underlying the viability of complex adaptive systems is frustrated.

Role interaction is a tentative process of reciprocal responding of self and other, challenging or reinforcing one's conception of the role of the other, and consequently stabilizing or modifying one's own role as a product of this essentially feedback-testing transaction. The conventional view of role emphasizing a prescribed complementarity of expectations thus gives way to a view of role-taking as a process of "devising a performance on the basis of an imputed other-role," with an important part being played by cognitive processes of inference testing. In a manner consistent with models of the basic interaction process suggested by Goode and by Secord and Backman, Turner views as a central feature of role-taking "the process of discovering and creating 'consistent' wholes out of behavior," of "devising a pattern" that will both cope effectively with various types of relevant others and meet some recognizable criteria of consistency. . . .

An example is provided by the study by Gross *et al.* (1958) of the school superintendent role. It is found that incumbency in this role (1) actually involved a great deal of choice behavior in selecting among the alternative interpretations and behaviors deemed possible and appropriate, and that (2) consistency and coherence of an incumbent's behavior could be seen only in terms of the total role as an accommodation with correlative other-roles of school board member, teacher, and parent, with which the superintendent was required to interact simultaneously. As Gross puts it, a "system model" as against a "position-centric" model involves an important addition by including the interrelations among the counter positions. "A position can be completely described only by describing the total system of positions and relationships of which it is a part. In other words, in a system of interdependent parts, a change in any relationship will have an effect on all other relationships, and the positions can be described only by the relationships." (p. 53) . . .

In sum, "institutions" may provide a normative framework prescribing roles to be played and thus assuring the required division of labor and minimizing the costs of general exploratory role-setting behavior, but the actual role transactions that occur generate a more or less coherent and stable working compromise between ideal set prescriptions and a flexible role-making process, between the structured demands of others and the requirements of one's own purposes and sentiments. This conception of role relations as "fully interactive," rather than merely conforming, contributes to the recent trends "to subordinate normative to functional processes in accounting for societal integration" (Turner, 1962, p. 38) by emphasizing the complex adaptive interdependence of actors and actions in what we see as an essentially morphogenic process—as against a merely equilibrial or homeostatic process. . . . Rejecting an overly structural view, it is assumed that social order is not simply normatively specified and automatically maintained but is something that must be "worked at," continually reconstituted. . . . On the basis of such considerations, Strauss and colleagues (1963) develop their conception of organizational order as a "negotiated order."

The hospital, like any organization, can be visualized as a hierarchy of status and power, of rules, roles and organizational goals. But it is also a locale for an ongoing complex of transactions among differentiated types of actors: professionals such as psychiatrists, residents, nurses and nursing students, psychologists, occupational therapists and social workers; and non-professionals such as various levels of staff, the patients themselves, and their families. The individuals involved are at various stages in their careers, have their own particular goals, sentiments, reference groups, and ideologies, command various degrees of prestige, esteem and power, and invest the hospital situation with differential significance.

The rules supposed to govern the actions of the professionals were found to be far from extensive, clearly stated, or binding; hardly anyone knew all the extant rules or the applicable situations and sanctions. Some rules previously administered would fall into disuse, receive administrative reiteration, or be created anew in a crisis situation. As in any organization, rules were selectively evoked, broken, and/or ignored to suit the defined needs of personnel. Upper administrative levels especially avoided periodic attempts to have the rules codified and formalized, for fear of restricting the innovation and improvisation believed necessary to the care of patients. Also, the multiplicity of professional ideologies, theories and purposes would never tolerate such rigidification.

In sum, the area of action covered by clearly defined rules was very small, constituting a few general "house rules" based on long-standing shared understanding. The basis of organizational order was the generalized mandate, the single ambiguous goal, of returning patients to the outside world in better condition. Beyond this, the rules ordering actions to this end were the subject of continual negotiations—being argued, stretched, ignored, or lowered as the occasion seemed to demand. . . .

The model presents a picture of the hospital —and perhaps most other institutionalized spheres of social life—as a transactional milieu where numerous agreements are "continually being established, renewed, reviewed, revoked, revised." . . . The daily negotiations periodically call for a reappraisal and reconstitution of the organizational order into a "new order, not the reestablishment of an old, as reinstituting of a previous equilibrium." . . .

Mulford Q. Sibley

ANONYMITY, DISSENT, AND INDIVIDUAL INTEGRITY

The sixties of the twentieth century have been characterized by a restlessness which has but few exact parallels in the experience of the United States. First came the wave of sit-ins during the civil rights movement and, following that, the increasing self-confidence of black men as exemplified in demonstrations, boycotts, and civil disobedience. Then appeared a series of student revolts, which are still very much with us. After 1965, with escalation of military hostilities in Vietnam, came greatly expanded antiwar dissent. Since 1967, these three currents have often tended to coalesce and their techniques to exhibit fundamental dissatisfaction with orthodox processes of social change.

To be sure, these tendencies are still exemplified in only a minority of the American people. But that minority has been growing and includes some of the most significant segments of the population—writers, students, teachers, and even

From Mulford Q. Sibley, "Anonymity, Dissent, and Individual Integrity in America," from *The Annals* of The American Academy of Political and Social Science, Vol. 378, July 1968. Reprinted by permission of the author and the publisher.

politicians. Moreover, the active minority probably speak for many more than themselves.

All this has taken place in an era of economic prosperity without parallel in American history and in a decade which followed the epoch of compulsive conformity which we associate with McCarthyism.

It is small wonder that many are asking about the background of this disquietude. Some are puzzled and distraught by radical criticism of any kind. Many who uncritically accept economic interpretations of politics cannot understand why a people who "never had it so good" should, seemingly overnight, desert ordinary political methods and even reject such values as those which exalt material prosperity. Yet others see rebellion as a harbinger of bad fortune or of decline. This is particularly true as they view the struggles in the colleges. Why, they ask, do we have such stubborn and rebellious young people? Most of the critics, to be sure, do not recognize that this query has been raised in virtually every generation since at least the time of Hesiod. But it is still a question which deserves some kind of answer; and to respond to it against the background of American culture may involve us in unique as well as universal explanations.

Aside from the question of the background and context of events is the issue of justification, if any. When all aberrations are excluded, how, if at all, can we vindicate morally this age of revolt? Does it represent an advance in moral consciousness over previous generations, or a retreat?

Finally, the moralist will wish to ask whether some of the methods of dissenters can be defended. He must examine the means used by the protestors, suggest criteria for judging the legitimacy of the means, and relate the question of methods to issues of both individual integrity and social change.

UNREST: BACKGROUND, PRECEDENTS AND EXPLANATIONS

The background for the unrest of our day can be discerned in the general tradition of American dissent; in the tendency for industrial society and its imperatives to produce feelings of anonymity, against which the individual revolts; and in the fact that the very economic abundance in which Americans take so much pride establishes a material condition for the development of psychological disquietude and moral concern.

The American tradition, some tend to forget, while sometimes exhibiting phases of compulsive conformity and repression, is often the story of rebellion and dissent. If protestors against conscription in our day burn their draft cards, those who helped make the American Revolution burned revenue stamps and threw tea in the ocean. The United States was born in acts of civil disobedience and through dissent generally.

And the history of dissent need only be chronicled to remind us that twentieth-century protest carries on a deeply embedded pattern of conduct. Something like what the British call the Nonconformist Conscience is very much part and parcel of American life. There have been dissenters in religion, the result being a sectarianism which is the wonder of the world. In the nineteenth century, the quest for utopian communities often assumed expressions which outraged conventional morality, the Oneida Community, for example, exalting both communism of sexual love and communism of material goods.

Dissent and conscience with respect to slavery took a diversity of forms, including deliberate flouting of the law, notably in connection with the rescue of fugitive slaves.

Nor have minorities been loath to protest the wars of the past. A militia company threw down its arms at the border when ordered to invade Canada during the War of 1812—on the ground that the Constitution did not authorize use of the militia for invasion of another country. During the Mexican War, many of the ablest men were outspoken in their condemnation of President Polk, the young Abraham Lincoln denouncing the war from his seat in Congress. The Civil War had its Copperheads and its anticonscription riots. Anti-imperialists bitterly denounced the Spanish American War and the war against the Filipinos, calling attention to the atrocities committed by American troops. In World War I, many served jail terms for refusing to support the war, including the great Socialist leader Eugene V. Debs.

The rebellions of our day, then, have ample precedents, back to the very beginning of the American experience.

Much of the contemporary dissent, however, is rooted particularly in certain conditions which industrialism tends to impose on the culture. Extreme division of labor isolates the worker from the final product of his work and often leads to a feeling of meaninglessness. Whatever the material benefits of the machine, moreover, it tends to demand of the worker adjustments in his manner of life which he is often loath to give or which outrage his sense of dignity. Thus, the ways in which the laborer schedules his time must be fitted into the needs of the machine, regardless of personal convenience. The worker's routine must become, as we say, "like clock-work." The rhythm of his life is literally attached to the ticking of the clock. Minutely subdivided labor, too, must be co-ordinated, and co-ordination implies bureaucracy in the industrial process. Not only is the worker forced to bow to the machine, he is also compelled to fit into the routinized directives of a bureaucratic hierarchy.

Nor are these tendencies confined to the industrial process as such. Subdivision of labor affects the professions, education, and indeed, the whole fabric of life. The tendency of industrialism is to separate men from one another psychologically and to substitute impersonal for personal relations. When one pays one's bill, one must not bend the IBM card, for the machine needs unbent cards—the person must adjust his habits to the needs of the machine, since the machine cannot adjust to him. Education tends to become like a factory, with graduates as "products" at the end of the conveyor belt. During the Berkeley student revolt, some students carried cards which ironically said: "Human being. Please do not bend or mutilate." Once, when my grades were late (as they usually are), the Dean's secretary called and asked when they would be submitted. I told her I did not know, since it all depended on how rapidly I read my papers. But she continued to press me. Finally, I said, "perhaps by Tuesday." To this, she responded, very solemnly, "I certainly hope they will be in by then. The machines are waiting."

Personality is a mysterious whole which transcends its parts and reaches into eternity. But the demands of industrialism, and of the bureaucratic structures which it requires, are suspicious of personality. Personality cannot be "rationalized." Hence it must be undermined to fit the machine. The cult of numbers is the result. Each of us is reduced to a series of numbers. Mere names cannot satisfy the machine and the bureaucratic co-ordinators of industrialized society. Thus, each of us becomes one number for Social Security: another for car registration; a third for mailing purposes; a fourth for the needs of the credit card machine; a fifth, if one is a student, for registration in the university; yet another when one is finally "processed"—a ubiquitous word in our day—for burial. Numberhood is the reverse of personality and namehood, and it symbolizes one facet of that anonymity which scholars find so characteristic of complex society.

Confronted by the anonymity, alienation, and sheer complexity characteristic of advanced industrialism, it is not surprising that many human beings revolt in a variety of ways. Some, like the hippies, may simply seek to withdraw, in the hope of restoring personality. The early history of the labor movement was a protest against many of the more obvious imperatives of the machine—the "tyranny of the clock"; the arbitrary boss; the sheer violence through which the system sought to discipline workers. Rebellion is often against impersonal bureaucracy, whatever its guise. Thus, men rebel against the military bureaucracy which processes men (or rather numbers) for the slaughter of war; or against educational bureaucracies, for whom students sometimes become mere statistics useful in gaining appropriations to expand the bureaucracies.

The passive acceptance of the centrality and primacy of technological and economic values produces slums against which men, sorely wounded in their sense of personal worth, sharply react. When these men are also black in color, the alienation and the revolt are compounded.

The human being needs organization and technology, to be sure; but both tend to become ends in themselves, to be idols which men, for a time, worship. When this tendency is pushed beyond a certain point, however, human personality can accept it no longer: there is a rejection of idolatry and an effort to overcome alienation.

Finally, and somewhat ironically, the very affluence produced by industrialism provides material conditions which may lead to psychological disquietude and, in some circumstances, greater social and moral awareness. The person, no longer quite as disturbed about the next meal as before, may become conscious of social inequity and, through introspection, worried about conflicting values and passions within himself. As St. Augustine seems to suggest in *The City of God,* once we are assured of a certain measure of material comfort, spiritual disquietude often sets in, which can be stilled only when the soul finds an integrating point or purpose which will dominate its life and in which it can find ultimate fulfillment. Given a certain economic well-being, men may have time and inclination to reflect on the larger purposes of life, including issues of right and wrong. In our day, moreover, mass communications—themselves the product of at least relative affluence—make us instantly aware of the disquietudes and revolts of others, which may profoundly affect our own conduct.

That threats of revolution and sharp fissions in society arise in communities which have begun to be well-off economically—relative to the past and to others—and not in communities which exist at the very lowest points in the economic scale is a proposition now widely accepted by scholars. The phenomenon of relative deprivation arises when men have a moment to envision what might be, but has not yet been achieved. The French Revolution occurred in a society whose material well-being was higher than that of many other nations. The disquietude of modern American blacks has arisen at a time when average economic well-being of American Negroes is considerably higher than it was a generation ago, and much higher—despite discrimination by whites—than that of most persons in the world.

Thus, current unrest must be seen against the background of a tradition of dissent in the United States, as a reaction to the kinds of alienation and anonymity erupting in a highly complex technological society, and as arising under economic conditions which provide the context for reflection, criticism of merely materialist values, and increased awareness. This is, of course, no exhaustive analysis of our current discontents, but it indicates a few of the factors which must be understood if we are to comprehend what might otherwise seem erratic and inexplicable.

THE JUSTIFICATION FOR DISSENT

To sketch the background and context of modern dissent is not to justify it, any more than a biographical, sociological, and psychological explanation of a murderer justifies his act. Dissenters have been motivated by many considerations, including the power of unrealized ideals embedded in the culture. But to know this is not necessarily to give dissenting acts moral support. One must ask not merely whether and how dissenters justify their position but also whether a given dissenting position itself can legitimately be defended.

Let us maintain at the outset that regardless of the merits of a particular protest, it is desirable that the protest be given expression in some form. From the viewpoint of society, this is true if for no other reason than that feelings and convictions which remain purely private tend to fester within the person only to be released publicly later on in more irrational forms. Beliefs which cannot be expressed, even radically, go underground and emerge eventually in the form of violence and physical destruction. This is true whatever the nature of the beliefs, and the community is thus the loser.

But apart from the loss to society, a dissenting opinion which does not find expression—even, sometimes, to the extent of civil disobedience—may do irretrievable harm to personality; for personality is a fragile thing and its integrity—or wholeness—tends to be eroded when vigorous expression is denied. If we place a high value on personality, then, we must allow it a wide measure for maneuver and dissent. For his own part, the dissenter is attacking himself and undermining the basis for his own personal existence if he cannot reflect his feelings and discontents publicly, even if he does so at the expense of some inconvenience to others. From this point of view, dissent is justified, whatever its substance and even if it does not attain large-scale social objectives.

But the larger question still remains. Can we justify morally the substance of widely heralded recent dissent? Not always, perhaps, for the objectives of the dissenters have varied quite widely. But if we use the civil rights movement, the student revolt, and antiwar activity as examples, the dissent is amply justified, in its ends, on moral grounds.

There is little point in belaboring at length the moral claims of civil rights advocates. Unfortunately, the history of American society has been one of treating black men essentially as things, not as persons. While the Civil War gave the appearance of liberating the slave, it left a heritage of bitterness and irrationality which made true liberation more difficult; and the moralist will see in the outcome of the war a lesson for liberation movements in our day—to seek liberation through mass violence is like demanding hot ice. Long ago, Gunnar Myrdal—in *An American Dilemma* —called our attention to the gulf between professions of equality, so much a part of the American tradition, and the actual way in which black men have been viewed by both Southern and Northern white men. If white America is now confronted by a serious crisis in this respect, it is because for three hundred years we have sown the wind of racism and are now reaping the whirlwind of a sometimes irrational revolt. To change the Biblical figure, our fathers ate sour grapes and their children's and great-grandchildren's teeth have been set on edge. In the black man's many acts of rebellion, one sees a basic protest against being viewed as an anonymous thing. Our age is much more aware of all this than earlier generations of Americans, which found even men like Jefferson and Lincoln ambivalent in their attitudes to Negroes. In this sense, there has been genuine moral progress.

At the same time, we should beware of what might be called the immorality of racism in reverse. In the noble struggle to emancipate black men, it is very easy to allow our sense of corporate guilt to drive us into betraying other ideals. Thus, at the "New Politics" conference at Chicago, during the late summer of 1967, the overwhelming majority of whites consented to give the tiny black bloc a weight equal to that of the much more numerous whites in the decisions of the convention: the principle of individual equality, regardless of race, was surrendered. Moral progress is not to be achieved through separatism based on skin color but rather by means of attitudes which are color-blind. Racism has been so disastrous in the past that it would be a pity if we were to revive it now.

The degree to which we can justify many of the student rebellions depends, of course, on what we think the objectives of education should be and on how we believe it should be organized. As we have suggested earlier, higher education in the United States, in part, reflects certain general tendencies in the culture—the inertia of an often inflexible organization and the technological revolution, with its factorylike imperatives, its stimulation of anonymity, and the tendency for technology to become an end rather than a mere means. Just as the citizen finds himself reduced to a series of numbers, so the student, particularly in a large graduate-study-oriented institution (a multiversity, to use Clark Kerr's expression), sees himself as a zero or a statistic—a kind of faceless consumer of education, being prepared to fit into the technological scheme of things. The anonymity of the general society is reflected in education, and education, in turn, tends to perpetuate the anonymity. I have it from a Ph.D. at a famous university that during the course of his graduate studies, he saw his adviser only a very few times. The adviser gave his dissertation only a cursory reading. When the student was ready to seek a teaching position, he asked his adviser for a letter of recommendation. The adviser consented in these words: "You write the letter of recommendation for yourself and I'll sign it." And so the student went out to seek his fortune.

Now, insofar as the student rebellions of our time—those at Berkeley and elsewhere—are protests against such indignities, they must receive our moral approbation. To be sure, we must, no doubt, compromise with the demands of organization, bureaucracy, and the current fads of the academy, but there comes a point beyond which we cannot go and still preserve any sense of human dignity. In the long run, that society which reduces its students to mere numbers is doomed, whatever its technological accomplishments. When students become mere means to the end of aggrandizing an institution or filling slots in an industrial machine, then revolt is not only justified but becomes morally obligatory. Students of our day are, on the whole, much more aware of moral issues than have been most student generations of the twentieth century, and this in itself represents a net gain. Whether it will lead to yet further progress, depends, in part, on how the general society responds.

As for the claims of the antiwar movement, they become more pressing every day. We have erected in the United States, not a welfare state but a warfare state, as Fred Cook in *The Warfare State* and Tristram Coffin in *The Armed Society* have pointed out. The moral and political ideal of democracy has always contradicted the imperatives involved in war and preparation for war. Today, this tension between democracy and the demands of war has reached a breaking point. War demands secrecy, deception, autocracy; democracy, just the reverse. War calls for destruction and for violation of every tenet of morality which we claim to exalt; democracy has as its center respect for personality and support for every moral notion sustaining or related to that respect. . . .

Essentially, the dissenters rightly see war as a deadly threat to the central values of Judaeo-Christian culture. Those values cannot possibly be reconciled with the demands of war. Hence the draft-card burner; the student obstructionist; the aider and abettor of those who violate the conscription laws; the youths who flee to Canada, as from a plague. It is ironic that thousands of Americans whose ancestors fled Europe to escape the degradation of military conscription are now condemning Americans who flee to Canada for similar reasons. The protestors see this irony.

Many of the war dissenters have been emancipated from the myths and shibboleths which affected earlier generations. They no longer believe in the notion of a "righteous" war—it is too much like proposing to go to the moon astride a broomstick. They no longer believe that the United States has been guiltless in causing earlier wars or in the methods it has used. They are familiar with the wiping out of Indian villages; the "water cure" of the Filipino insurrection; the murder of prisoners of war during World War II; and the frightful slaughter of civilians in Vietnam. In their greater sophistication about such matters, war dissenters in our day are in advance of those who took antiwar positions earlier in American history. In this respect, they may indicate that the United States is finally growing up and is discarding some of the self-righteousness which has often characterized American attitudes. Unfortunately, the vast mass of Americans, whether in government or out of it, still remain to be emancipated in this respect.

War protestors, like civil rights and student dissenters, hope not only to change the public mind but also to preserve their own individual integrity. Even if social change is not accomplished, the quest for individual integrity through protest is to be valued as an end in itself.

THE MEANS: SOCIAL CHANGE AND PERSONAL INTEGRITY

Means and ends are interrelated. Granted a considerable legitimacy in the objectives of modern protest, what means can be regarded as justified?

How much conscience lies behind our modern discontents and how much of the disquietude is a kind of compulsive reaction to events? This is not an easy question to answer. We might turn it around and ask: How much genuine conscience lies behind conformity to the status quo or to policies of the government? The answer would probably have to be, "Very little." Most Americans conform to the crowd out of habit or because of fear. The acquiescence is not a matter of inner conviction. This includes most men who enter the Army: they are not there primarily because their consciences tell them that they should enlist but rather because they are pushed by external economic or legal pressures. Similarly, we have to allow for a certain amount of compulsive or habitual action in the dissenters. All nonconformity is not motivated by conscientious conviction. Some of it is conformity to peer-group pressure and some a kind of irrational reaction against social demands.

But granting this, there still remains a substantial degree of genuine conscience reflected in the restlessness of our day, as there was in such earlier movements as that against slavery.

What, then, about conscience concerning means?

It might be suggested at the outset that once a person has adopted criteria which he holds to be right and, through reasoning, intuition, and evaluation of facts, reaches the conclusion that he ought to act in a certain way—once his decision is an act of genuine conscience, in other words—then he is morally obliged to act in accordance with his decision, even though the community may reject his conclusions. There can be no higher authority than conscience, in this sense of the term—not the State and not the opinions of other men. For if the individual does not regard his own deepest convictions as obligatory, he surrenders his soul. Thus, if he should reach the conclusion that his highest obligation is to assassinate the President, then he ought to begin making preparations to do so. One must follow one's conscience wherever it may lead, even, as St. Thomas Aquinas would put it, a conscience which to others may appear objectively wrong. Thus, throwing blood on draft-board records, burning draft cards, or even burning houses, may conceivably be expressions of genuine conscience. This is not to say, of course, that the law and the community may not also act out of conscience in opposing persons of integrity: at this point, we seemingly reach an impasse, the final moral judgment of which must be left to God.

This having been made clear, however, each of us still has an obligation to examine the criteria which ought to be taken into consideration before he actually reaches his conclusions. The would-be dissenter, it seems, should give the benefit of the doubt to existing law (or custom), on the ground that it may be a deposit of collective wisdom that should be broken, as in civil disobedience, only when a strong case can be made. This does not mean that law should never be deliberately broken —as it has been on occasion in the civil rights, student, and antiwar movements—but only that we have an obligation to obey it, unless we can adduce powerful considerations to the contrary.

A second criterion ought to be whether the proposed act does violence to human personalities. In general, protest movements seek to vindicate the claim of the human being to dignity. To shoot an individual in the name of protecting the universal assertion of human dignity is, on its face, a seeming contradiction between means and ends. It is like the American general saying, as he did, that we must destroy a certain Vietnamese village in order to save it. Mass violence, whether by governments or by private individuals ought to be particularly suspect, since war and the violence of so-called revolution are indiscriminate and tend to be uncontrollable. This principle would condemn both the war in Vietnam and so-called street riots—whatever their purported ends.

The principle of openness might be regarded as a third criterion. Before the decision is reached as to what kind of action one should take, the proposed action should be subjected to the scrutiny of outsiders for their criticism. This will constitute a check on our own mere subjectivity. The decision ultimately must be one's own, but it ought not to be reached rashly. This is a desideratum applicable equally to individuals and to nations. If proposed foreign policies of a nation, for example, were first to be submitted to the critical scrutiny of other nations, they would in all likelihood be more intelligent and responsible, and what is called the "arrogance of power" would not become central.

Within self-imposed limitations of this kind, then, actions could take place; and whether or not a particular policy or action should be adopted at a given time and in a given situation would depend on the circumstances of the moment and the peculiar consequences (judged in terms of the primacy of the common good) which one might expect from a suggested line of action on whether the action involved election politics, demonstrations, boycotts, or ultimately, civil disobedience.

A genuine conscience will, of course, take into consideration possible results, but will also understand the difficulty of forecasting them: after reason and judgment of facts have gone as far as possible there is still an ultimate leap beyond (but not contrary to) reason which every conscience must envision.

It is within some such framework that we should view the legitimacy of means used in the controversies of our time, whether the actors are objectors to the status quo or members of the "Establishment."

By these standards, it would seem the dissenters of our day do not come off badly. The movement led by Martin Luther King, for example, has contributed enormously not only to developing consciousness about civil rights but also to our knowledge of the relation between ends and means. The past generation has been made acutely conscious of the fact that the means shape our ends—a central theme in the writings of men like John Dewey, Mohandas Gandhi, and Aldous Huxley—and the civil rights movement has constituted a gigantic testing of the proposition.

The methods of the civil rights struggle have been emulated in many student revolts and in the antiwar struggle. Nonviolent demonstrations and nonviolent resistance constitute imaginative developments not only in the technique of social change but also, probably, in suggesting a new approach to national defense. They help us see that man is not foredoomed to accept either the status quo of a covert or overt violence, on the one hand, or the disastrous road of violent revolution, on the other. There is an alternative way, that of nonviolent direct action, which preserves personal integrity and at the same time contributes to radical social change. They also suggest that the issue of national defense is not one of passive acquiescence to invasion versus an uncertain and violent counterattack—there is the third method of nonviolent resistance which was used with so much success by the Norwegians and Danes against the Nazis in World War II. With unilateral disarmament and organized nonviolent resistance, the United States could be far more effectively "defended" than it is today (as the late military historian Walter Millis once admitted in a conversation with me).

With respect to this vexing issue of means, the civil rights movement, the students, and the protestors against the war in Vietnam have all made significant contributions. It is these contributions of method—symbolized, for example, in such challenges as that of Dr. Benjamin Spock and his codefendants, in the Montgomery bus strike early in the civil rights struggle, and in the several Berkeley student revolts—which are among the most significant in recent American dissent. Theory and practice have gone hand in hand, as they should.

Activities of this kind have pointed the way to an overcoming of anonymity and an overcoming equally of social inertia; and they reflect in considerable measure an effort to vindicate personal integrity against the forces which tend to undermine it. They exemplify what existentialists like Jean-Paul Sartre and Albert Camus (particularly in *The Rebel*) think of as the role of the rebel—to sustain personality in an often impersonal world and tear down the barriers which are always barring the road to genuine community.

John Poppy

SENSITIVITY TRAINING IN INDUSTRY

They left their offices reluctantly, glancing back at equations half-solved, arguments suspended. Production lines at Space Park kept flowing with insectlike intensity behind them as, one by one, 36 men hurried from scattered buildings into spatters of chilly rain. Habit nagged: Tuesday afternoon is a time for *work*. But they drove their cars away from familiar desks, away from work, out of Redondo Beach, through Los Angeles, 100 miles north of Ojai, where two highways branched into a single country road that poured them into the hush of a grand resort hotel. Closet doors closed on suits and ties. At 3:30, the 36 gathered in a meeting room surrounded by tennis courts and a lime-colored golf course rippling off toward blue mountains. They drank coffee and looked at each other in the damp sunlight, feeling strangely naked in sport shirts and slacks, deflecting talk away from themselves to neuters like the rain, moonshots and absent bosses while they waited politely for the experience to start.

They knew it was intended to change them. In three days, they were supposed to be less scared of each other, more honest, less alone. How would it happen? None could be sure. "What's going to be done to me?" one wrote in his notebook. "Will it be painful, tense . . . or boring?" He slashed a black line, then wrote, "What am I afraid of?"

The men were scientists, engineers, managers, some with Ph.D's. All worked for TRW Systems Group, a California aerospace contractor that has sprouted from 6,000 employees to 16,500 in the last five years. It will go on growing. Half the people at TRW Systems have been there two years or less. They work under pressure, designing and building interplanetary probes, nuclear-detection and communication satellites (including Intelsat III, assigned to relay color TV from this year's Mexico City Olympics), moon-rocket engines and other spaceware too secret to mention

in annual reports of the parent company, TRW Inc. of Cleveland. . . .

The company, even more than most, runs on intricate teamwork. A "system" comprises all the different parts—switches, circuits, valves, sensors—making a thing operate. That includes people. A TRW engineer is no hermit inventor cooped up behind barbed wire. He moves among other specialists, many of them plugged into his daily job. He reports to a project manager, collaborates with scientists, needs support from administrators, feeds work to production-line assemblers and has to make his task—designing an antenna, say—mesh with everyone else's.

Watching the interdependencies wriggle across TRW Systems, its then-president Ruben F. Mettler decided in 1961 that it could grow most successfully if its own human system, the process of co-workers getting along together, were somehow re-engineered. Mettler felt that he could not afford to let creative people act defensive, sly and touchy with each other. What if the antenna engineer hit a snag in his calculations but refused to confess the trouble for fear that it would damage his reputation and chances for promotion? What if he spent a lot of energy defending a mistake once it came to light? What if he felt resentment toward a colleague who offered help? Obviously, the man would suffer. So would the company.

But the competitive culture of most organizations teaches just that sort of behavior. Human hang-ups not only make people miserable; they contaminate the work. Mettler and his personnel managers, sure that they were sitting on a rich pool of untapped creativity, started a program of "Career Development." Their ambition was to reform the basic workings of a culture as big as a town—the internal society of TRW Systems. They weren't just dabbling. Mettler was promoted last February to assistant president of the parent company.

One tool they have used since 1963 is sensitivity training, designed to increase an individual's awareness of the feelings inside himself and of the impact he has on others. The 36 men in the meeting room at Ojai were there to be sensitized to themselves and to each other, like more than 600 key employees before them, in what TRW calls a Leadership Development Laboratory.

Few of them knew each other before volunteering for the lab, but many knew alumni of previous sessions, and all had read about sensitivity training. Reduced to words, it sounded like an ordeal, this business of knocking off facades, opening yourself up, dropping your defenses against other people, groping for cleaner ways to live with them. It's going to be a big waste of time, some thought. But the word was out in the company: Try it. So they would try it.

Pinning on name tags—first name only, no indication of rank or job—they heard some ground rules. "While you're here, try to be absolutely honest," said one of the five "trainers" from the TRW personnel department on hand to help if needed. "Level with each other. Let the people in your group share what you *feel* from the gut. Second, stay in the here and now. Don't be distracted by the past or future; focus on what's happening right here at this moment. Third, no physical violence." A roomful of tough competitors, trained to think rationally about solving problems, listened impassively.

They split into three groups, each with its own meeting room where a dozen men and two trainers would spend from eight to twelve hours a day together. These stretches of concentrated exposure to one another are the heart of the lab. Called T-groups or, on the West Coast, encounter groups, they start with no "givens." Deprived of ready-made handles on each other, the participants have to build a social system, from scratch, inside the room. The subject matter of the group is itself and each of its members.

In Group One, the eyes all turned to Dr. George Lehner, "outside" consultant for this lab. Lehner, a seal-sleek, soft-spoken UCLA psychology professor, is one of nine consultants on human behavior retained year-round by TRW Systems. He was a resource for the group, not a controller, he said, but just to get things started, how about sitting in a circle? "Now, pick someone across from you. How do you react to him? How do you feel about being here?"

Bert, a balding production foreman who kept a suit jacket buttoned over his sport shirt, looked around quickly to see if anyone else was ready, then announced: "I think we can all get a lot out of this. I hope to learn some new methods for being an understanding manager and motivating workers. . . ."

"Methods? You mean like tricks?" The question came from Matt, Irish and aggressive. His voice was sharp. He squinted at Lehner. "That bothers me. He sounds so cold-blooded. . . ."

"Don't tell *me,* Matt," Lehner said. "Say it to Bert."

Matt did. Bert shrugged. Someone filled the silence with another remark. Around the circle went comments carefully phrased as feelings without revealing much feeling, until David, younger than most of the group, said, "You all came up with something so fast, I feel as if everyone is obeying an *order* to talk. Do we have to be so obedient? I don't feel ready yet. I'll wait."

Matt's sideways look down at him was friendly, fatherly, scornful. "Waiting never filled any buckets where I came from," he said. David retreated into silence as the group talked on.

The men found chairs or pillows on the floor. An hour passed. They eased away from addressing Lehner, the authority figure, and started talking straight at each other: ". . . Alec, I just don't feel you're *here.* You're hiding from us. Can't you come out from behind that grin and tell me what you feel about me?"

Alec, leaning back in elaborate comfort on a couch, said dryly and precisely, "I don't know you yet. I really don't have any feeling about you."

"My God, you make me feel *invisible,* Alec. I'll tell you, I'm a human being here in this room with you, and I am hurt that you won't give me a response. Now, do you feel anything? Anger? Annoyance? Remorse? What?"

"No. . . . I just don't feel those things. When they bring me a bunch of proposals six inches thick to print up on Friday night and I have to spend the weekend at the shop, I don't get mad, either. What good would it do?"

"It might make them think twice before they did it again."

"No. . . ."

"Oh, come on!" The new voice was furious. Chris—short, muscular, darkly intense—stuck out his jaw and glared around the room. "We aren't accomplishing a thing. We're supposed to stay in the here and now, and you guys chat about life at Space Park. We're supposed to be making this group function and learning about the process, but frankly, I'd rather be back where I have work to do. You people are wasting my time."

Startled, the group shifted focus. A babble of voices washed over Chris as, to their own surprise, members of the group defended it against the critic: "You're hostile, Chris. . . . Why don't you contribute instead of just bitching, Chris? . . ."

"Ah, some feelings, huh?" Chris challenged

them. "You really squirm when I put the finger on you, don't you?"

Matt bored in with a wide-eyed stare into Chris's eyes: "Yes, I find you just as unpleasant to deal with here as back at Space Park. You come on so strong that I give you a fast answer to get you out of my office—not always the best answer, either, just the fastest."

Chris paused, "Why didn't you tell me that two years ago?"

Lehner intervened, gently: "Why put the burden on him, Chris?"

"Listen, I get impatient with people when they don't react as fast as they should," Chris said. "I know I offend some of them, but there's a lot of pressure. I don't have time to wet-nurse everyone."

"But that probably makes you *less* efficient." David sweated with the effort of making himself face Chris, two feet away. "You muddy up people's reactions when you make them resent you. I'm mad right now, for instance, so I'm probably not functioning too well."

"That's your problem, not mine," Chris said. He smiled, not being brutal, not indifferent; he just felt that David and Matt and the others should be tough enough to fend for themselves.

The light outside faded. Flecks of rain streaked through the glow of garden lamps as the men headed for supper in a reserved section of the hotel dining room. To three tablemates, Chris gracefully revealed that he had manipulated the group: "Thanks for the feedback. I wanted to see if I was getting back to the sort of behavior that bothered me six years ago. It seems I am, so I'll change." He said it as if all he had to do was push a few buttons.

A general session before the evening's encounter groups brought all 36 men together to hear the chief trainer talk theory. "What makes a helping relationship between people?" he asked. Citing Carl Rogers, the psychologist who is an elder statesman of encounter groups, he chalked a list of "helping things" on a blackboard. "TRUST: congruence (saying what you feel) inspires people to trust you. EXPRESSIVENESS: be able to reveal what you feel. CARING: enough to *listen* to others. SEPARATENESS: let others be themselves, not what you want them to be. EMPATHY: put yourself inside another's skin, understand without judging."

By 8:30, Group One was back in its room, resuming the struggle to open up Alec. He slipped every punch, dodged every probe, and finally they turned away from him. Already they were follow-

ing an instinct to zero in on whichever member felt ready to "jump in the barrel." First Bruce, blond and unhappy, talked about his life: ". . . Everything I touch turns into garbage, but I'm the only one who can see it. TRW thinks I'm doing fine, but I feel like a farm kid masquerading around you big-city boys. . . ."

Matt steadied him: "I've got hayseeds in my hair too. I was on my own at 13. Had to fight for everything I ever got. . . . I guess I never had any close friends because I've never wanted to owe anybody anything. I'm damn good at my job, and I know I made it myself. . . ."

Chris stayed silent as the group slipped out of the here and now with Matt and Bruce, then back in. "You don't have to apologize for being tough, Matt," one member said. "I admire you for what you've done with your life." Matt looked up from the floor, pleased and touched. Some of his defiance slid off as the evening ended at 11.

The next morning's general session began at 8:30 with Lehner saying. "I imagine the level of technical skills in this room is fantastically high. But relating to one another takes a set of skills too. All those words on the blackboard last night were *feeling* words, involving the gut rather than the technical training of the cortex. Why develop such skills? Well, we don't complain about fulfilling the systems of a machine—a car, for instance. We make sure we have air in the tires, oil in the engine, water in the radiator, gas in the tank . . . but how much do we do about fulfilling the needs of this ambulatory system, the human being? I'd feel very uncomfortable if I had to drive my car with all the gauges taped over. Shouldn't we feel uncomfortable if we can't read our own gauges?

"Many of us get tremendous kicks from taking a set of data, manipulating it and solving a problem. Yet without satisfaction on the feeling level, technical productivity is useless to us. We already know one of you who has advanced steadily in the company, performs his job so well that he is praised by his superiors, but feels inside like a failure. This man can't enjoy any of his triumphs. . . ."

Group One carefully avoided looking around at Bruce. Protecting their man from the curiosity of the other groups, they drew subtly closer; he could trust them with his revelations.

For the rest of the day, Group One methodically worked on itself. Lehner occasionally cut in: ". . . Try for a win-win situation. If a man brings you a set of plans and you want to modify them, don't just throw them down and overlay your own ideas. That would be win-lose—you win at the other man's expense. Stay with him. *Listen to him*. Try to make yourself understood without smothering him. You can still change the plans and you both win. You are both satisfied at the feeling level." Or ". . . What if you are literally preoccupied, so full of angers and thoughts [*squeak-squeak, a felt-tipped pen drew arrows rushing around inside a circle*] that you leave no room for inputs? Your responses are likely to be irrelevant. If you are full of hidden rage and somebody says, 'Want some help on that wiring diagram?' you might blow up at him. . . ."

Needling, sparring, joking, accepting rough remarks that would have caused a fight two days before, the group began to feel the strength of a new intimacy, pressuring first one member, then another, into the center of the ring.

Sighing in the dark late that night, roommates from other groups sounded envious of Group One: ". . . I'm not sure why we're here, what all this sitting around shooting the breeze in my group is supposed to do for me," said David's roommate from behind the glow of a last cigarette, "but it sounds as if you guys are going great."

"Going smoothly" would have been more accurate. Group One still had its defenses up. Its members had talked about work problems, attacked each other heartily—but on a level that for all its look of freedom, remained tightly cerebral. Everybody was still under control.

The next morning, without warning, it broke. Full of breakfast, bored by a dull general session, Group One was still settling into its room when Paul, a Texas salesman, started trading conversation with David. "You know some writers," Paul said. "What's your idea of a good communicator?"

"Oh, I don't know," David mused. "Underneath everything like technique, I guess if you're going to make a difference—a positive one—in the world, you have to be a good person. . . ."

"So how would you define that?"

"It's more than just a nice guy. I mean a *good* man, someone who *cares*. . . ." Startled by the intensity he felt, David caught a winging, panicky question in the corner of his mind's eye: "Is this my time?" Pressure he could not control swelled behind his ribs. He no longer cared if he broke the rules of here and now. Clasping his hands, elbows on knees, he leaned toward Paul and focused his voice. The group instinct picked up a signal from somewhere inside him. Chatter stopped. They waited.

"I want to be a good man," he said, choosing words slowly. "That means changing the world,

making it a less wasteful place. I can't just rattle through my job, take the money, go home and tune out. . . ." Pause. Words began to spill faster. "You know why what we're doing in this room is important? Think of all the stopped-up energy we can release in here once we quit using up our strength straining against each other, or hiding inside. Once we learn to run free with it, there's no limit to what we might do. . . . And why can't it happen out there?"

He yanked his right hand free and swept it toward the world outside the plate-glass window. Not a head turned away from him to follow the gesture.

"I've had some glimpses . . . people who were wide open, moving together . . . it's like being in a really good kind of love. But most of the time, watching what people do to themselves breaks your heart. . . . It breaks your heart."

The stillness in the room was absolute. His voice sank almost to a whisper, but rose in pitch as his throat began to swell inside. The group saw tears in his eyes. Standing detached from himself for a curious, cool moment, David thought, "Don't blink. The tears will spill, and they'll all see. Don't talk any more. They'll hear you cry." Unblinking, he talked.

"Sometimes you'd think everybody is crazy. . . ." He stared at the light of the window: ". . . flinging incredible amounts of energy around, everywhere you look . . . wasted. We do such violence to each other. We're fighting wars . . . race, we're fighting each other, scaring children at school, scaring them at home. . . . Nobody could do any of it if they weren't so locked up inside themselves, out of touch with the people they hurt. God, I hate all that violence. . . ." He almost stopped, but the pressure to make the group understand was too great.

"I almost killed the person I love the most, last year, because I got sealed up inside. My wife and I are one person, closer than I know how to tell you. But it still happened. . . . We were at a music festival up the coast. We'd taken our seven-year-old along, and . . . I don't know, various little things happened that bothered me, and I built up a bad mood. . . . Sunday afternoon, I wanted more than anything for us to hear Ali Akbar Khan play the sarod. Well, we had to give up our seat in front and sit outside the door, listening to a loudspeaker. . . . My wife went off several times during the music to look for our boy. . . . I just got madder and madder until I said something bitter to her. I don't even remember what it was, but she told me I was a genius at causing pain. We walked out on the grass. I said she was stupid to get mad at *me*. . . . She told me to leave her alone, and . . . and . . . she said it in a way that froze me, as if she meant to cut me off from her. That had never happened before. I was terrified. I didn't know what to do. . . . So I guess I started trying to hurt her."

David tried to dry his eyes with a handkerchief.

"I grabbed her arm as hard as I could, dug in my fingers so they would bruise her through her parka . . . pushed her down a dirt path away from the music. She was crying. Everything in me was focused on my fingers crushing her arm. We got to the end of the path, and she kept saying, 'Let me go, let me go.' . . ."

Swimming in the memory, he bowed his head and let the tears fall on his knees as he spoke to his unseen group.

"I started saying, 'Listen, damn it, listen, don't try to run away,' and I grabbed her by the shoulders. I can remember her eyes, so wide, staring. . . . I started shaking her, but my right hand slipped as I pushed her back and forth, and smashed in her throat."

He smacked his Adam's apple hard.

"She said the strangest thing. 'Wait a minute,' she said. . . . 'Wait a minute,' like in a theater when you want to go back over a line. Then she couldn't breathe, couldn't talk, and I thought I had broken her windpipe. I thought she was going to die. . . . Everything inside me broke. I held her in my arms and cried and said, 'I'm sorry, I'm sorry, I love you. . . .' How could I kill her? What happened to me? . . .

"She got back a little breath after a few minutes. I was so thankful she was all right. But you see what I mean about waste? Hurting? . . ."

Chris had been staring at the rug. He looked up, showing tears of his own, and reached out a hand. "David . . . David," he said, "I want you to know I really feel for you. I'm with you. I didn't know what guts it took for you to show me anger the first night. . . ." David nodded, unable to speak.

Matt said softly, "We're all with you, David." Lehner, Paul, Bruce, others murmured assent. Some stared out the window. Others studied their hands.

Silence. David sat passive, clean and open, unarmored, feeling closer to the group than he had before, not because he knew them but because they knew him. He floated free, ready to respond to the lighest touch. They would not hurt him. Contemplative, tender feelings were loose in the room for the first time. The men in the group tried, haltingly, to express their new feelings.

Before it had a chance to flower, the mood was pinched off. "What's the *matter* with you people?" Chris's face darkened in rage. Too angry to hear the unspoken messages, or perhaps even the spoken ones, he jerked upright in his chair and raked the room with a hot glare. "Here's a man *bleeding* in front of you, and you don't even *try* to help him. You just *sit* there. It makes me sick!"

No, it's all right, David felt himself about to plead, I heard them, we need more time, please don't cut it off now. But he was slow, knocked off-balance by the force of the attack. In confusion, the group wheeled to defend itself. Tenderness boiled off into anger.

"You didn't even know what was happening here," Matt spat at Chris. "The trouble with you, buddy, is that you want to make us do things your way or not at all. Well, you just wrecked something."

Even Lehner stepped out of neutrality: "You took them off the hook, Chris, Anger is a cop-out —it's so much easier to show them what they were struggling with."

Lunchtime. The men scattered, some for golf, most to see *Wild Strawberries,* Ingmar Bergman's film on the horrors of insensitivity. When Group One reassembled at 4:30 for a marathon session that would run until 1 o'clock the next morning, Chris declared that "for my own good and the good of the group," he was leaving. No, he would not discuss his decision. He stalked out into the twilight. Appalled by this amputation, the group worked on, distracted.

Chris went to his room and started to write— 12 pages of tightly scribbled notes to himself: points for them, points for him, questions, answers, analysis. Three hours later, he summed up, read over his conclusion and returned to the group, without comment but with a softer, more supple, more attentive way about him. He had changed.

Chris's new manner enriched the group. Pulling gently instead of attacking, the men surrounded one of their hitherto silent members, Carl, a middle-aged personnel expert who never once removed his white baseball cap or his bland smile. He hadn't talked much because he didn't need their help, Carl said. He was perfectly happy, and besides, he had 50 graduate credits in psychology, "so what can you teach me?" Dodging languidly, Carl answered almost every question with, "Oh, I guess you could say so." Did he want to come to this lab? Would he rather not be there? Did he like his job? Were there things he did not want to reveal? After hours with no breakthrough, Matt laughed in exasperation that he had assumed there were two or three Carls behind that smiling mask, "but I have to take it back. I count at least eight."

"You may be right," murmured Carl. The group went to bed.

Next morning, Friday, was the last of the lab. They would leave after lunch. Carl announced, "I stayed awake last night thinking, and I have to tell you that I've been . . . lying." There were no shouts of "Aha!," no triumphant grins; instead, the group leaned in around their friend and listened intently. Carl felt he was one of the top ten men in his field in the United States, but TRW didn't give him the recognition he deserved. He was becoming reluctant to offer ideas because his bosses hadn't seemed to care for his earlier ones. He was wretched. He had never admitted this to anyone before, he said, but when he saw the group genuinely trying to help and not just snoop, he decided to share the problem.

Time to break up. The men in Group One found they did not want to leave each other. They found they could admit, without embarrassment, feelings of warmth and intimacy that most had not even suspected three days before. "I feel as if we've known each other all our lives," Matt said. "We have to keep this spirit. I get kind of scared when I think we might go back to Space Park and lose it. . . . I don't know exactly what it is, but I want to keep working at developing this new skill of mine."

They all stood up. Beaming, they moved into a circle and joined hands. No one stayed out. All around, the links were firm. . . .

Approaches will vary from group to group, depending on the needs and resources of the people involved. To bear real fruit, they will have to go beyond a quick dip into encounter. Systemwide changes have to be explored, with the knowledge that something that works in one situation may flop in another.

TWR Systems managers did not lift a canned program out of someone else's book; their organic approach is rooted in the realities of their special business. The men from Group One at Ojai got back together for a five-hour follow-on two weeks after returning to the company. It felt like a class reunion, complete with joyful smiles and fervent handshakes. Carl, the man who didn't need help, surprised his friends by looking around the table and announcing, "Fellows, I have a problem I'd like to present to you." Delighted, they listened.

Carl had collected more data than TRW ever had before on wage problems in a big, important group of employees. The morning after this meeting, he was scheduled to make a presentation so a high-level committee could decide what, if anything, to do. The problem: He knew each member of the committee had a different theory. What should he say to weave all the views into a consensus?

"What recommendations are you going to make?" Matt asked.

"Oh . . ." Carl said, doubtfully, "I don't really have any."

"You mean you're just going to dump all your research in front of them and let them sort it out?" David asked.

"Know how I'd feel if you did that in a committee of mine, Carl? I'd be confused, and I'd probably resent it." Chris spoke fast but softly, with the care he had shown in the last day of the lab. "Make a recommendation. Be positive. They'll thank you for solving their dilemma for them. You told us you're one of the top ten in the country, and I believe you. Make the committee believe it too."

Carl pondered. The group sat silent, alert.

"Well. . . ." Carl started slowly. Then his words tumbled out in a rush: "What I really think is that this is a problem we've neglected for a dangerously long time, and we should spend $1.5 million to raise pay for people we can't afford to lose but who are going to go to other companies if we don't give them a raise."

"Wow! SAY THAT!" The whole group lighted up, exploding toward Carl in a burst of ardor. To a roomful of veteran technicians and managers, informed by experience, Carl's proposal felt right.

"Yeah," Carl breathed. He glowed. With a huge smile, he said, "Yeah. . . . Of course. Thanks." He sat back, unable to stop grinning, feeling his new strength.

From the exhilarated babble of voices emerged Chris's, jubilant: "*This* is what TRW hopes will come out of a lab, I bet—more than just *that*." He gestured across the hallway to where two other groups were watching film strips and making lists of management practices to live by. "*This*." He meant the open flow of feeling that allowed the careful judgment of skilled men to emerge spontaneously, immediately, unselfishly for Carl's use.

The next morning, Carl acted. He made his firm recommendation, and the committee bought it on the spot.

The two readings which accompany Part Four of the text take us further into the complex world of meaning and value. The first—Realms of Meaning—is an article delineating the kinds of meaning important to human beings and analyzing the difficulties that may block the pathway to meaning and fulfillment in living. The final reading—The World of Science and the World of Value—looks toward certain changes in our values and priorities which the author considers essential if man is to survive in this time of trouble and change.

Philip H. Phenix

REALMS OF MEANING

Human beings are essentially creatures who have the power to experience *meanings*. Distinctively human existence consists in a pattern of meanings. Furthermore, *general education is the process of engendering essential meanings*.

Unfortunately, the pathway to the fulfillment of meaning is never smooth. The human situation is such that mankind is always threatened by forces that destroy meaning. Values, purposes, and understandings are fragile achievements and give way all too readily to attitudes of futility, frustration, and doubt. Meaning is thus lost in an abyss of meaninglessness.

The perennial threat to meaning is intensified under the conditions of modern industrial civilization. Four contributing factors deserve special emphasis. The first is the spirit of criticism and skepticism. This spirit is part of the scientific heritage, but it has also tended to bring the validity of all meanings into question. The second factor is the pervasive depersonalization and fragmentation of life caused by the extreme specialization of a complex, interdependent society. The third factor is the sheer mass of cultural products, especially knowledge, which modern man is required to assimilate. The fourth factor is the rapid rate of change in the conditions of life, re-

sulting in a pervasive feeling of impermanence and insecurity.

Since the object of general education is to lead to the fulfillment of human life through the enlargement and deepening of meaning, the modern curriculum should be designed with particular attention to these sources of meaninglessness in contemporary life. That is to say, the curriculum should be planned so as to counteract destructive skepticism, depersonalization and fragmentation, overabundance, and transience.

. . . Meaningful experience is of many kinds; there is no single quality that may be designated as the one essence of meaning. Accordingly, we should speak not of meaning as such, but of meanings, or of the *realms of meaning*. Hence, a philosophy of the curriculum requires a mapping of the realms of meaning, one in which the various possibilities of significant experience are charted and the various domains of meaning are distinguished and correlated.

Six fundamental patterns of meaning emerge from the analysis of the possible distinctive modes of human understanding. These six patterns may be designated respectively as *symbolics, empirics, esthetics, synnoetics, ethics,* and *synoptics*.

Each realm of meaning and each of its constituent subrealms may be described by reference to its typical methods, leading ideas, and characteristic structures. These features may be exhibited both in their uniqueness for each realm or subrealm and in their relationships and continuities with the other types of meaning. Leaving the details to be elaborated in subsequent chapters, the six realms can be broadly characterized as follows:

The first realm, *symbolics,* comprises ordinary language, mathematics, and various types of nondiscursive symbolic forms, such as gestures, rituals, rhythmic patterns, and the like. These meanings are contained in arbitrary symbolic structures, with socially accepted rules of formation and transformation, created as instruments for the expression and communication of any meaning whatsoever. These symbolic systems in one respect constitute the most fundamental of all the realms of meaning in that they must be employed to express the meanings in each of the other realms.

The second realm, *empirics,* includes the sciences of the physical world, of living things, and of man. These sciences provide factual descriptions, generalizations, and theoretical formulations and explanations which are based upon observation and experimentation in the world of matter, life, mind, and society. They express meanings as probable empirical truths framed in accordance with certain rules of evidence and verification and making use of specified systems of analytic abstraction.

The third realm, *esthetics,* contains the various arts, such as music, the visual arts, the arts of movement, and literature. Meanings in this realm are concerned with the contemplative perception of particular significant things as unique objectifications of ideated subjectivities.

The fourth realm, *synnoetics,* embraces what Michael Polanyi calls "personal knowledge" and Martin Buber the "I-Thou" relation. The novel term "synnoetics," which was devised because no existing concept appeared adequate to the type of understanding intended, derives from the Greek *synnoesis,* meaning "meditative thought," and this in turn is compounded of *syn,* meaning "with" or "together," and *noesis,* meaning "cognition." Thus synnoetics signifies "relational insight" or "direct awareness." It is analogous in the sphere of knowing to sympathy in the sphere of feeling. This personal or relational knowledge is concrete, direct, and existential. It may apply to other persons, to oneself, or even to things.

The fifth realm, *ethics,* includes moral meanings that express obligation rather than fact, perceptual form, or awareness of relation. In contrast to the sciences, which are concerned with abstract cognitive understanding, to the arts, which ex-

press idealized esthetic perceptions, and to personal knowledge, which reflects intersubjective understanding, morality has to do with personal conduct that is based on free, responsible, deliberate decision.

The sixth realm, *synoptics,* refers to meanings that are comprehensively integrative. It includes history, religion, and philosophy. These disciplines combine empirical, esthetic, and synnoetic meanings into coherent wholes. Historical interpretation comprises an artful re-creation of the past, in obedience to factual evidence, for the purpose of revealing what man by his deliberate choices has made of himself within the context of his given circumstances. Religion is concerned with ultimate meanings, that is, with meanings from any realm whatsoever, considered from the standpoint of such boundary concepts as the Whole, the Comprehensive, and the Transcendent. Philosophy provides analytic clarification, evaluation, and synthetic coordination of all the other realms through a reflective conceptual interpretation of all possible kinds of meaning in their distinctiveness and in their interrelationships.

The symbolics, which have been placed at one end of the spectrum of meanings, encompass the entire range of meanings because they are the necessary means of expressing all meanings whatever. Similarly, the synoptics, which have been placed at the other end of the spectrum, also gather up the entire range of meanings by virtue of their integrative character. Between these two realms of symbolics and synoptics lie the realms of empirics, esthetics, synnoetics, and ethics as four essentially distinct (though interdependent) dimensions of meaning or modes of significant human relatedness to the world and to existence.

The six realms thus charted provide the foundations for all the meanings that enter into human experience. They are the foundations in the sense that they are the pure and archetypal kinds of meaning that determine the quality of every humanly significant experience. From this viewpoint, any particular meaning can be analyzed as an expression of one of the fundamental meanings or as a combination of two or more of them. In practice, meanings seldom appear in pure and simple form; they are almost always compounded of several of the elemental types.

HUMAN NATURE

. . . It is evident at once that there are many different classes of investigators interested in the exploration of human nature and that no one type of expert has a monopoly on knowledge about man. Each kind of investigator sees man from a particular perspective. Each is well equipped to elucidate certain aspects or dimensions of what human beings are.

Physicists and chemists usually do not study man as such. They usually assume that he is part of the general matter-energy system of nature and that a person as a material structure conforms to the same physicochemical laws as rocks, plants, animals, and all other existing things. However, some physical scientists hold that the phenomena of mind, which are not found in developed form except in man, need to be considered even within natural science in order to explain the observed nonrandom organization of energy in the natural world.

Biologists consider man as one species of animal, the most highly developed of all forms of living things within the evolutionary sequence. They draw attention especially to the extraordinary adaptive powers of Homo sapiens that result from the extensive elaboration of his nervous system.

Psychologists divide into two principal groups in their view of human nature. One group, oriented toward the biologists, concentrates on the physiological, chemical, and neurological structures and functions required to explain human behavior. The other group approaches the study of man from the standpoint of his inwardly perceived mental states, using such concepts as consciousness, intention, purpose, value, choice, and the like. Both kinds of psychologists see man as an organism with mind. They differ in the ways in which they interpret the meaning of mind and the data they use to explicate it.

Sociologists and social psychologists see man as a social animal, and they describe and try to explain the many patterns of social organization and transformation that human beings exhibit.

Economists describe man as a producer and consumer of material goods and services, with wants that always outrun resources, and hence, with the need to invent social mechanisms for the allocation of the limited resources.

Political scientists see man as a seeker after power or influence, and they describe the many ways, such as force, reason, propaganda, threats and promises, and economic and social pressures, in which people influence and are influenced by one another.

Anthropologists describe the many types of human beings, with regard to both physical characteristics and cultural patterns. They study the varieties of languages, customs, beliefs, rituals, laws, and forms of social organizations that man has developed. They see human beings as having certain basic biological and social needs which are satisfied in a great many different ways, according to the circumstances of environment and historical development.

Linguists view man in his distinctive capacity for speech. They describe the many different ways human beings have invented to communicate with one another, and they analyze the formal patterns that characterize the languages of mankind.

Geographers study man in relation to his earth habitat. They show how human behavior is conditioned by such factors as climate, food supply, ease of transportation, distribution of natural resources, and population.

For the most part, the natural and social scientists are concerned with describing the distinctive behavior of classes or kinds of human beings, rather than of individual persons. They are also not generally concerned with the inner or subjective life of man except as a means of explaining observed behavior. Other groups of experts on human nature are interested in understanding man more directly from the inside, as it were.

Artists see man as a being with a rich and variegated life of feeling, and they attempt to objectify the most significant kinds of human feelings through various types of works of art, including musical compositions, paintings, sculptures, buildings, dances, poems, plays, and novels. Artists also regard man as a creative agent, and they exemplify the range and power of human creativity through their own works.

Biographers set forth the unique individuality of the person, showing how, through the interplay of many factors, a singular life develops toward its particular consummation.

Moralists portray man as a moral agent, with a consciousness of right and wrong. They see him as free and responsible, fashioning his own destiny through a continuing series of moral decisions. They describe the great moral visions of mankind, by the light of which the way of each person is illuminated and judged.

Historians see man as a being living in time, with memory of the past, anticipation of the future, and the freedom of a creative present in which both past and future meet. They try to understand the real meaning of past events by imaginatively reconstructing the conscious life of the persons who brought these events to pass.

Theologians regard man as dependent for his being upon God and as having a spiritual nature rendering him capable of entering into relationship with the divine. They believe that human beings possess the power of infinite self-transcendence, living in nature but also able by virtue of imagination to look upon natural existence from a transcendent standpoint.

Thus, men of knowledge investigate human nature using a variety of methods and from a great many different perspectives. The natural scientists, by and large, are interested in types of observable human behavior, and they refer to the inner life of man chiefly to render the outer phenomena intelligible. The humanistic scholars, on the other hand, are more immediately concerned with the inner life, and they consider the outer conditions of existence mainly as the background and context for understanding the particular forms of subjectivity. Yet all the different groups of investigators are concerned with the same human reality. What, then, is man?

It is the special task of the philosophers to attempt a comprehensive interpretation of human nature, incorporating and coordinating the work of inquirers from other scholarly specialties with the results of their own reflection. A comprehensive view, first of all, must allow for the many-sidedness of man. Man is everything the various special inquiries show him to be: He is a complex energy-system; an intelligent adaptive organism with highly developed neurophysiological mechanisms and the power to perceive, think, and purpose; an organized social animal with demands for goods and power that need intelligent allocation; a maker of culture and a user of language; a being who lives in a natural and social environment with which he must cope; a creature of feeling and a creator of interesting forms to objectify them; a unique self; a doer and judge of good and evil; a dweller in time, who remembers, anticipates, and celebrates deeds done; a creature of God partaking of the divine nature through the power of boundless self-transcendence.

. . . Is there any unifying idea of human nature of which the experts' testimonies are partial aspects? A classic philosophical answer is that man is a rational animal, that his unique property is the ability to reason, that his distinctive quality is in the life of mind. . . .

This philosophical answer suffers from the limitation that such ideas as rationality, reason, and mind tend to be too narrowly construed as referring to the processes of logical thinking. The life of feeling, conscience, imagination, and other processes that are not rational in the strict sense are excluded by such a construction, and the idea of man as a rational animal in the traditional sense is accordingly rejected for being too one-sided.

This difficulty can be avoided by using a unifying concept that expresses the broader connotations of the idea of reason. The concept proposed is *meaning*. . . .

The proposed philosophic answer to the question about the nature of man, then, is that humans are beings that discover, create, and express meanings. . . .

The import of this fundamental concept may be made clearer by explaining four dimensions of meaning.

The first dimension is that of *experience*. A meaning is an experience, in the sense that it pertains to human consciousness. It refers to the inner life, or the life of mind. This inner life has the peculiar quality of *reflectiveness,* or self-awareness. Automatic reaction to environmental stimuli is not the characteristic human mode of response. The unique human response is one in which the person is aware of his responding. He acts consciously rather than mechanically. As the psychologists say, thought is a "mediating process" intervening between stimulus and response. Reflective mediation is the basis of meaning.

As a reflective experience, meaning presupposes a basic principle of duality, or of self-transcendence. In self-consciousness a person both is himself and yet, so to speak, stands outside himself. He is at one and the same time both subject and object, knower and known, agent and patient, observer and observed. This duality is what enables a person to *know* anything at all. One knows something if he is at one and the same time distinct from and identified with what he knows. All perception of relationships is based on this duality. A relationship is identity-in-difference: two things are united in the one act of consciousness in order that their nonidentity may also be recognized.

All the varieties of human meaning exemplify this self-transcendence. It is the secret of man's unique adaptability. Because of it he can make judgments of truth and falsity, of beauty and ugliness, of right and wrong, of holiness and profanity; he can predict and control events, use tools, create interesting objects, make laws, organize socially, know the past, and project purposes. In short, this inherently dual quality of experience is the source of all that is characteristically human.

Since meanings are experiences in the inner

life, the humanistic scholars give a more intuitively acceptable picture of essential human nature than do the scientific interpreters, for whom the inner life is inference rather than testimony and direct objectification. However, both are valuable and mutually corrective sources of knowledge about man. Direct readings of the inner life need to be checked against inferences from observable behavior, and the outward manifestations need to be humanized and individualized by recognition of the inner sources from which they spring. No matter which method of study is adopted, the objective is the same, namely, to understand the inner life that is the center and substance of human existence and from which all distinctively human actions spring.

The second dimension of meaning is *rule, logic,* or *principle.* The many types of meaning are distinguished from one another by some difference in characteristic form. Each type of meaning has its own rule and makes it one kind of meaning and not another. Each is defined by a particular logic or structural principle. Meaning is not an undifferentiated experience of awareness. Conciousness is differentiated into a variegated array of logical types.

Intention meanings follow a different rule from memory meanings. Social meanings have a different logic from artistic meanings. Moral meanings are based on a different formation principle from language meanings. Similarly, each item in the long, or perhaps even interminable, list of evidences of human mentality has its particular defining characteristics.

The third dimension of meaning is *selective elaboration.* Theoretically there is no limit to the varieties of meaning. Different principles of meaning formation can be devised ad infinitum. New combinations and nuances of rule can be imagined without limit. Not all of these possible kinds are humanly important. From the endless variety selection occurs. The types that are significant in actual human life are the ones that have an inherent power of growth and lead to the elaboration of the enduring traditions of civilization. These are the kinds of meaning that have proven fruitful in the development of the cultural heritage. . . .

These selected types of meaning that have been elaborated into the traditions of civilization can be identified by means of the classes of specialists who serve as the guardians, refiners, and critics of the cultural heritage. These specialists consist of the scientists, scholars, savants, or "wise men" who are recognized as the authoritative interpreters of the human inheritance. Each

of these men of knowledge belongs to a community that is for the most part invisible, comprised of persons bound together by common responsibility for a particular kind of meaning. Each such community has its characteristic discipline or rule by which the common responsibility is discharged. This discipline expresses the particular logic of the meaning in question. . . .

The fourth dimension of meaning is *expression.* Meanings that have civilizing power are communicable. They are not private property. The communication of meanings takes place through symbols. Symbols are objects that stand for meanings. The possibility of symbolization is dependent on the unique human power of self-transcendence, for the dual quality of reflective awareness is required to understand a symbol. The essence of a symbol is that it is both identified with its referent and distinguished from it. For example, the word symbol "tree" is not a tree, and yet by the power of thought the symbol stands for a tree. Symbolization also presupposes self-transcendence in the awareness of a common world, for the symbols are taken as having the same or similar connotation to oneself as to others into whose being one imaginatively projects oneself.

The symbolic expressions of meaning are of particular concern to the communities of scholars representing the various types of meaning. Each kind of meaning has its distinctive expressions, the symbolic forms of each corresponding to the peculiar rule or logic of the type. The symbols of the disciplines are essential to scholars for analyzing, criticizing, and elaborating their domains of meaning.

Summarizing, these are the four dimensions of meaning: the experience of reflective self-consciousness, the logical principles by which this experience is patterned, the selective elaboration of these patterns into productive traditions represented by scholarly disciplines, and the expression of these patterns by means of appropriate symbolic forms. These dimensions all pertain to the idea of meaning and help to explicate it. . . .

MEANINGLESSNESS AND MODERN MAN

The meanings that constitute the proper content of human experience do not appear automatically by a process of natural growth and development. The singular quality of human life is a product of deliberate nurture. It is not a gift of nature; it is a creation of culture. This is another way of saying that meaningful human life is necessarily social. It is only through the educative power of human community that genuine persons are brought into being. . . .

A great deal of attention is devoted by contemporary writers to the loss of meaning. The Viennese psychotherapist Viktor Frankl holds that the secret of all worthwhile human existence is found in meaning and that the basic cause of human deterioration is loss of meaning. He has devised a system of treatment called "logotherapy," the aim of which is to restore meaning to those who have lost hope and faith in the value of life. In this way he seeks to renew the courage to struggle for right and to endure whatever suffering is entailed by the accidents of fortune and the malice and ignorance of men.

Paul Tillich (1952) also sees meaninglessness as an important fact of modern life. In *The Courage to Be* he describes the human condition as one of inescapable anxiety. He finds three principal sources of anxiety. The first, ontological anxiety, arises from the fact of human finitude. Man is anxious because he knows he must die, and all the particular fears besetting him participate in the final horror of annihilation that they symbolize and foreshadow. The second is the anxiety resulting from guilt. Man is anxious because he knows himself to be a transgressor. Consciously or unconsciously, he is aware of having violated the moral law. Do what he will, says Tillich, one can never wholly eradicate the uneasy conscience. The third anxiety is that in which man sees himself threatened by meaninglessness. He is beset with doubts no arguments can dispel, and he asks questions to which he can find no answers and which only lead to deeper perplexities and paradoxes.

Tillich believes that while anxieties are inherent in human existence, they are intensified in periods of transformation when one era of human history is giving place to another. Moreover, the dominant character of the anxiety differs from era to era. Thus, Tillich finds that the end of the classical period in Western civilization was dominated by ontological anxiety—the fear of death—as evidenced, for example, in the Mystery religions and in Christianity by the preoccupation with immortality and resurrection. The end of the medieval period was characterized by moral anxiety, as evidenced by the concern for forgiveness and atonement in the penitential system of the Church and in the spiritual agonies of the great

Reformers. The modern period, which now appears to be ending and giving way to a new "postmodern" epoch, is a time dominated by the anxiety of meaninglessness, revealed in a pervasive skepticism, relativism, aimlessness, and feeling of futility.

All three kinds of anxiety are, however, interfused in every age, including the present. Death is feared because it nullifies the meaning of life and ultimately renders every hope illusory and all striving useless. Guilt also robs existence of meaning because under its burden one cannot accept himself, and the springs of action are poisoned by a bad conscience.

This theme of meaninglessness in contemporary life has been consistently sounded in recent decades by the Existentialists. They believe that the old certainties and securities are gone, and they bid mankind give up the vain hope of progress fostered by the technical successes of science. They point to the ever-mounting social, political, and economic crises as eloquent witness to the impotence of reason in matters of genuine human significance. They see no complete cure for anxiety, no prospect for finally ending human suffering, no reasonable hope for universal safety and peace. Man's life is absurd, they say, since his natural longings and expectations are forever doomed to remain unsatisfied. According to many Existentialists, there is no answer to this human predicament. Through the power of courage, one can only go on affirming one's own being in spite of dread and nausea, creating one's own values out of nothing, and proceeding step by step through the enveloping darkness by acts of defiant and desperate decision.

. . . It can be shown that each of the kinds of meaning earlier discussed is threatened by a corresponding kind of meaninglessness. In every realm of meaning there is also a realm of meaninglessness. If any progress in restoring meaning is to be made, it is necessary to distinguish these different domains. Contrary to the Existentialists, it will be our theme that durable meanings can be found and that the obstacles to meaning can be overcome when the realms of possible meaning and the conditions for their realization are well enough understood. But now let us consider briefly some of the threats to fulfillment in each of the realms of meaning in turn.

Meaning is threatened in the domain of language by the fact of ambiguity. Rarely does language convey to the hearer the meanings the speaker intends. Sincere, serious, and well-informed people are all too often unable to reach common understanding. Even professionals skilled in discourse and devoted to the Socratic ideal seem to make little progress toward secure wisdom by their discussions. In this age of propaganda it has become apparent how easily language can be used as an instrument of power rather than as a channel for truth. Battered by a barrage of words creating incompatible responses, modern man has become cynical about language itself. Flooded by a ceaseless outpouring of symbols through the mass media of communication, language has tended to become a debased currency with little relation to real values and ineffective in the creation of genuine community.

In mathematics and science, strongholds of rational demonstration and experimental proof, modern developments have also brought once secure meanings into question. The axioms of mathematics are no longer regarded as self-evident truths but as arbitrary bases for defining postulate systems, an endless variety of which can be invented. The clockwork simplicity and order of the Newtonian world have been replaced by a universe without absolute space and time, but only relations between space-time events. Statistical probabilities have replaced certainties, and even the principle of causal determination has been radically questioned. Critical scrutiny of scientific knowledge has made untenable the view that science discloses the world as it actually is and has substituted for this naïve realism a variety of operational, instrumental, and constructionist views that recognize the place of arbitrary human activity and purposes in the making of science. Science is thus no longer considered the source of complete and demonstrable truth, but as a system of convenient hypotheses, valid only within specified limits and continually subject to reconstruction in the light of new experience.

In the realm of esthetics the crisis in meaning is evident on every hand. Traditional standards have been widely discredited and many artists have declared their independence of all the conventions of the past. The result, as Richard Weaver and others have argued, is a disintegration of art caused by the destruction of a settled and accepted world for the artist to portray. To most people not belonging to the novelty-hungry and iconoclastic avant-garde, much modern art discloses only the morbidity, confusion, inanity, or plain incompetence of the artist, whether in drama, literature, music, painting, architecture, or dance. Art has become increasingly alienated from the common life, and many artists have reacted against popular hostility and misunderstanding, withdrawing into tight, self-justifying cliques. Inherent in all this confusion and separation is the widespread suspicion that art may not express anything but the private feelings of the artist and that works of art have no universal, permanent, or objective meaning.

In wide areas of modern life the meaning of personal relatedness has disappeared from view. People feel isolated and estranged from nature, from themselves, from one another, and from the ultimate sources of their being. The depersonalization and collectivization of life is far advanced. The plundering of natural resources, the destruction of living things, and the manipulation of human beings are widely practiced. Love has been displaced by lust, loyalty by expedient self-interest, devotion by avarice, responsibility by the unbridled pursuit of power, and reverence by self-sufficient autonomy. Mutual respect and trust have given way to warfare between nations and classes, personal animosity, and suspicion and cynicism regarding the possibilities of building stable and harmonious personal relationships.

Moral meanings also fare badly in the modern world. Pragmatists convincingly wage war on moral absolutes. Positivists deny any cognitive significance to moral assertions, regarding them as expressions of feeling and as disguised commands or means of persuasion. Anthropologists demonstrate the variety of moral codes in the cultures of mankind and usually disapprove of making value judgments about different ways of life. No one appears able to demonstrate the validity of any particular moral injunction so as to convince anyone not already committed to it. Allegedly universal principles seem to reveal more exceptions than rules, and moral obligations are seen as only particular personal expedients within unique specific situations. In short, contemporary life is pervaded by doubts about the basis for moral commitment, and by skepticism as to the possibility of reliable meaning in the ethical realm.

Finally, synoptic meanings are nowadays under sustained attack. Historians, acknowledging the inevitable bias of their interpretations and the limited evidence at their disposal, no longer claim to know what really happened in the past. Despite the revival of grand speculations about the total plan of history by Arnold Toynbee and other neo-Augustinian philosophers of history, the dominant mood is that of Crane Brinton, who heralds the age of "multanimity" and the demise of unanimity, and that of Herbert Muller, for whom the lesson of history is that in the final analysis there is no final analysis. Despite a recent resurgence in popular appeal, religion no longer inspires the serene faith of earlier times. Friedrich Nietzsche proclaimed that God is dead, and millions the world over believe he spoke truly. Doubt is potent even (or perhaps especially) among theologians, for whom belief wins out in the end only by a desperate "leap of faith" into an apparent abyss of meaninglessness. Philosophers, too, generally eschew large speculations about the meaning of life and the nature of reality. Metaphysics is largely out of favor, having been displaced by the more modest and manageable concerns of logic and theory of knowledge, because to many it no longer seems profitable to attempt a comprehensive synoptic interpretation of human experience.

Thus, in all the major domains of meaning modern man is threatened with meaninglessness. . . . Change is the only certainty, and transience pervades everything. These upheavals are a constant source of anxiety and insecurity. They diminish the value ascribed to anything that now exists, in view of the probability that it will soon be superseded. The meanings that enrich human life are found in abiding patterns persisting through time and change. It is the constant and the permanent that help to overcome the anxiety of meaninglessness. It is for this reason that the transience of modern life presents such a threat to meaning.

THE SEARCH FOR MEANING

The attacks on meaning described in the last chapter have not been without countervailing influences. Recent decades have also witnessed a sustained and many-sided search for meaning, the results of which are providing the basis for a renewal of modern man and for an educational program in which human possibilities can be amply fulfilled. . . .

In 1923 C. K. Ogden and I. A. Richards published *The Meaning of Meaning,* a work that has since become a classic in the field of the interpretation of language. These scholars demonstrated the widespread confusion regarding the meaning of "meaning," and they sought by systematic analysis to discard meaningless conceptions and to make proper distinctions among valid modes of interpretation. They discussed and evaluated sixteen major definitions of meaning, and formulated a new theory of signs in which the functions of language were reduced to two, namely,

the referential and the emotive. By such a distinction the authors hoped to strike a decisive blow at superstition, obscurantism, and "word magic," and to provide a comprehensive, contextual, and functional basis for the whole range of language meanings. While it is doubtful whether this division of language functions into the two types—of referential and emotive meanings—does justice to the full range of meanings, there is no doubt about Ogden and Richards' contribution to a revival of concern for meaning and the stimulus they provided in this and later works to the serious study of the varieties of symbolic forms.

The most widely publicized recent movement in the field of language meaning is semantics. Alfred Korzybski's (1948) *Science and Sanity* became the bible of the General Semanticists, who promised solutions to the most vexing problems of mankind through a scientific reconstruction of linguistic meanings. Charles Morris (1938) in his *Foundations of the Theory of Signs* developed "semiotics," which was subdivided into the fields of "semantics," "pragmatics," and "syntactics." Popularizers of semantics, including Stuart Chase and S. I. Hayakawa, brought to the attention of the general public some knowledge of the pitfalls of language and of the methods available for the improvement of verbal communication.

Another group of investigators for whom the problems of meaning are fundamental are the analytic philosophers. These philosophers owe their inspiration to such thinkers as G. E. Moore, Bertrand Russell, and Ludwig Wittgenstein, and their movement currently dominates professional philosophy in England and America. Unlike Existentialists, who are concerned with the "meaning of life" and the problems of selfhood and decision, analytic philosophers undertake the detailed critical scrutiny of various modes of human discourse. In their earlier years the analysts were most interested in the pure constructive languages of logic, mathematics, and natural science. More recently, they have become preoccupied with the problems of ordinary language and have tried to show how most of the traditional philosophical puzzles have been created by philosophers themselves in using concepts without reference to their generally accepted meanings-in-use.

Perhaps the greatest contribution of the analytic philosophers is their personal witness to the importance of meaning and their faith in the possibility of making meanings clear. Furthermore, they have shown that meanings are of different logical orders, which cannot all be subsumed under one type. By this demonstration they have countered the positivistic position limiting all meanings to those of logic, mathematics, and science, and have reaffirmed the possibility of many distinct modes of thought, each valid in its own sphere and justified by its specific human uses.

This recent philosophic emphasis on distinct logical orders of meaning and on the clarification of human understanding by the analysis of the actual uses of symbols is basic to the philosophy of curriculum set forth in these pages. While the method of treatment used herein is not predominantly that of the language analysts, the present work presupposes a similar commitment to the exposition of meanings-in-use and parallel conclusions as to the multiple patterns of human signification.

Ernst Cassirer, using methods quite different from those of the language analysts, has also established the principle of distinct logical orders of meaning. In his great *Philosophy of Symbolic Forms* and his briefer *Essay on Man* Cassirer (1953, 1955, 1957; 1944) shows that the characteristic mark of human activity is the creation and transformation of symbols. The whole world of human meanings, he says, is expressed in the several kinds of symbolic forms contained in such diverse fields as myth, ritual, language, art, history, mathematics, and science. Each of the types of symbolic forms has its unique and legitimate human functions. For example, ritual communicates orders of experience not expressed in speech, and the arts present meanings different in kind from those of the sciences and inexpressible in the categories of empirical description. Each symbolic form has its appropriate field of application, and, though it has relationships with other systems, is not wholly reducible to any other form.

The search for symbolic meaning inherent in semantics and linguistic analysis and comprehensively outlined by Cassirer is paralleled by the inquiries into meaning in each of the other realms of human understanding. Thanks to the labors of philosophers, historians of science, and scientists reflecting on their own enterprise, both the nature of science and its limitations are becoming increasingly clear. Investigators as diverse as James Bryant Conant, Alfred North Whitehead, Bertrand Russell, Percy Bridgman, Rudolph Carnap, Stephen Toulmin, and Ernest Nagel, to name but a few, have critically examined the methods and assumptions of science, showing with precision what scientific knowledge is and what it is not. They have demonstrated the validity and the scope of scientific methods and have de-fined the terms in which empirical descriptions and theoretical explanations are to be interpreted.

In esthetics, too, new exponents of meaning have appeared. Against the criticisms of modern art by those who hold that the classical motifs are the only meaningful ones, and more particularly, that visual art should be representational and music should be limited to the traditional melodies and harmonies, critics like Clive Bell, Roger Fry, Igor Stravinsky, and Roger Sessions have made a strong case for a more generous conception of artistic import. Under the banner of "significant form," those who defend modern art against the charge of meaninglessness have pointed to the wider possibilities of esthetic expression provided by the new artistic forms.

Susanne Langer (1948), taking her lead from Ernst Cassirer, whose general theme she popularized in her book, *Philosophy in a New Key,* makes a particularly cogent case for the distinctively esthetic mode of understanding. She denies that a work of art is only an expression of the artist's personal feelings and argues that artistic import has its characteristic logical forms. She insists that significance is not limited to the literal meanings of factual statements, but extends also to the art symbols objectifying the patterns of feeling found in man's inner life.

In the literary arts the renewed concern for meaning is manifest in the New Criticism in the work of men such as Edmund Wilson, William Empson, W. K. Wimsatt, Jr., John Crowe Ransom, and Ronald S. Crane. In this movement the earlier dependence of literary interpretation on psychology, philology, history, and sociology has been overcome and a fresh recognition of the uniquely literary modes of understanding has been achieved.

Turning next to the synnoetic realm, substantial progress is being made in the articulation and interpretation of personal meanings. Psychoanalysis, though grounded in the identification of unconscious and irrational factors, is primarily aimed at bringing these subterranean forces under the scrutiny and control of reason. What appear as meaningless dreams and fantasies and as inexplicable actions are shown by analysis to be symbols of unconscious meanings. These hidden meanings often reflect disturbances in relationships with other persons and in evaluations of the self. Improvement of relations with others and self may then follow the recognition of unacceptable emotional patterns and understanding of their causes.

Many different systems are employed for the

revelation and clarification of these personal meanings. Sigmund Freud and his followers emphasize infant sexuality and the Oedipus complex. C. G. Jung and his school analyze the interplay of inferiority and superiority feelings. Therapists in the line of Alfred Adler find important clues to behavior in the problems of infantile dependence and the struggle for power. The approach used by Harry Stack Sullivan and his colleagues is to analyze patterns of interpersonal relations, particularly with the "significant persons" in association with whom early self-appraisals are formed. In contrast to the early analysts who regarded the period of infancy as all-important in the development of emotional life, many present-day therapists place as much or more emphasis upon experiences beyond infancy. They concern themselves directly with present behavior patterns instead of tracing everything back to the first few months or years of life.

Others, besides psychotherapists, have joined in the search for meaning in selfhood and in human relationships. The concept of personal meaning is especially important to the Existentialists. As Paul Tillich points out, preoccupation with meaninglessness is itself evidence of a passionate concern for meaning. Rejecting the idea of the subconscious from depth psychology, Jean Paul Sartre proposes a scheme of "existential psychoanalysis," which consists of a thoroughgoing introspective analysis of the content of consciousness aimed at eliminating the self-deceptions by which one tries to avoid responsibility for his own authentic existence. Karl Jaspers, more concerned than Sartre with relationships beyond the self, finds the "way to wisdom" in the will to unlimited communication, and protests against the depersonalized mass culture that has lost faith in "Transcendence," the source of all true selfhood. Martin Buber discovers the source of truly human meaning in the "I-Thou" relation, which he contrasts with the impersonal, manipulative, objectifying "I-It" type of relation. In the act of turning from the personal emptiness of the I-It to the loving, community-creating affirmation of I-Thou, Buber believes the secret of a meaningful life may be found.

Contemporary literature provides further vivid evidence of modern man's search for synnoetic meaning. While typologically poetry, the novel, and drama are art forms communicating esthetic meanings, they can also be powerful expressions of concern for selfhood and for community among persons. In various ways such diverse writers as W. H. Auden, T. S. Eliot, William Faulkner, James Joyce, Franz Kafka, André Malraux, Thomas Mann, Eugene O'Neill, J. D. Salinger, and Tennessee Williams portray some of the deepest concerns of human beings—a concern that in its very seriousness reveals a profound faith in the potential meaningfulness of personal existence, even under conditions that seem to deny all meaning and value to life.

In the realm of ethics, subjectivism and skepticism regarding meaning are encountering strong opposition. Anthropologists are more disposed than they once were to recognize the universality of some moral principles, despite the relativity of laws and customs in the cultures of mankind. Social scientists are taking the normative aspects of human behavior more seriously than before and some are even beginning to assert that it is the proper business of the scientist not only to describe what *is* but also to investigate what *ought* to be. Leading jurists like Justice Brandeis have led jurisprudence away from literalistic interpretations of the legal tradition toward a view of law as an expression of standards for the good life in a dynamic society. Such thinkers are making increasingly clear the dependence of a meaningful social order upon moral principles rather than mere custom and tradition, and they emphasize the need for continual reexamination of laws in the light of these principles.

These developments are complemented by certain trends in ethical theory. Philosophers are largely agreed, as David Hume long ago decisively argued, that an "ought" can never be derived from an "is," i.e., that values are of a different logical order from facts. While this insight exposes the futility of trying to establish morality as an empirical science, and thus contradicts certain of the assumptions implicit in the efforts to develop a scientific ethic, it does support the autonomy of morals and prepares the way for the discovery of distinctively moral meanings. G. E. Moore (1959), in his classic *Principia Ethica,* presents a realistic theory of morals, refuting the "naturalistic fallacy" inherent in every attempt (as in egoism, hedonism, utilitarianism, voluntarism, and supernaturalism) to define "good" by reference to any matters of fact (such as interest, pleasure, utility, or the will of man or God). Later philosophic analysts, including R. M. Hare, Stephen Toulmin, and P. H. Nowell-Smith, though generally rejecting Moore's intuitionism, take seriously the principle of the autonomy of the moral realm and continue to make valuable contributions to the clarification and illumination of moral meanings.

The search for meaning in the synoptic disciplines is also yielding encouraging results. In the discipline of history, nineteenth-century scientific historians had been confident that the historian could strictly present the facts about what really happened in the past. In reaction against this reduction of history to empirical science, the subsequent Historicist movement emphasized the personal, irrational, and contingent factors in historical judgments, thus bringing into question the possibility of any reliable historical knowledge. More recently, the possibility of genuine historical understanding has once again been affirmed, on a broader basis than that of the scientific historians. For example, R. G. Collingwood sees history as a reconstruction of past events— what must have happened—on the basis of an imaginative identification with the thought of the persons who decided the events. Herbert Butterfield, too, holds that in a larger sense than the scientific historians thought, the historian can discover what actually happened by an act of sympathetic understanding in which the historian divests himself of his preconceptions and enters into the life of the past on its own terms.

In religion theologians continue the pursuit of ultimate meanings with great vigor. Having successfully weathered the crises of faith caused by the higher criticism of the Bible, the theory of evolution, and the comparative study of religions, religious thinkers are endeavoring to assess the claims of faith in the light of new developments in knowledge and the social order. Protestant thinkers such as Karl Barth, H. Richard Niebuhr, Paul Tillich, and Rudolph Bultmann are reformulating the doctrine of revelation so as to establish an autonomous logic of religious understanding. Roman Catholic thinkers (e.g., Jacques Maritain and Etienne Gilson) offer contemporary versions of Thomistic theology, reaffirming the common

sense meanings of Classical Realism within a dual framework of Natural and Revealed Theology. Interpreters of Jewish thought in all three of the leading traditions—Orthodox, Conservative, and Reform—are working out ways of making Judaism a relevant and meaningful way of life and thought in the modern world. One of the most impressive signs of the contemporary search for meaning is this development of religious thought which is taking place, despite all the forces of secularization, not only in the various branches of Christianity and Judaism, but also in Islam, Buddhism, Hinduism, and many smaller syncretistic and theosophical sects.

In philosophy, mention has already been made of the signal contribution to the recovery and expansion of meaning made in quite different directions by the logical analysts and the Existentialists. Metaphysics is recovering from the crushing blows administered by logical empiricism and pragmatism. Even some analytic philosophers are now saying that metaphysical statements may be something more than nonsense. A few adventurous spirits, most notably Alfred North Whitehead, have dared to attempt new cosmological schemes after the manner of the great system-builders of the past. In these efforts the possibility of attaining a synthesis of meanings through a comprehensive interpretation of experience is once again affirmed.

The aim of the foregoing summary sketch of some twentieth-century movements reflecting modern man's search for meaning has been twofold: first, to show that the forces of skepticism, frustration, and confusion in present-day life have by no means won the day, and second, to suggest some of the kinds of resources available for the construction of a meaningful philosophy of general education. . . .

Ludwig von Bertalanffy

THE WORLD OF SCIENCE AND THE WORLD OF VALUE

Life and history are no idyll; and when we look back, we find precisely the greatest geniuses—from the Preacher in the Bible to Sophocles, Dante, Michelangelo, and even Goethe—filled with dismay about their times and with what modern philosophers would call existential anxiety, deep-rooted doubts about the meaning and goals of life. Nevertheless, we hardly commit an exaggeration when saying that there never was a deeper, more all-pervading gap between the facts—the world which is—and values—the world which ought to be, a more profound insecurity about our directions. The early Christians in the Roman catacombs did not know whether they would see the next day, but they did know that their martyrdom granted the Crown of Life. The Italian Renaissance was politically one of the most atrocious episodes in history, but it sublimated its gore and cruelty into Giotto's frescos at St. Francis's in Assisi and into the Sistine Chapel and the triumphal glory of St. Peter's. The French Revolution slaughtered thousands at the altar of Liberty, but it brought a new idea into the world which will not perish. We, with all our skyscrapers, space vehicles, comfortable homes, economic abundance, our cars and doubled life-span, are not so fortunate. Whether the abyss of atomic annihilation will devour us or whether we manage precariously to dance at its brink, if everything is said, our creed is that of Iago in Verdi's *Otelo—Sento il fango originario in me; e poi? La morte e nulla:* I come from primeval slime, and my destiny is death and nothing.

Let us not believe that spiritual questions are superannuated in an age of technology. There is an old saying that God is with the stronger battalions. Modern inventiveness has gone only so far as to replace infantry battalions with atomic bombs. In the last resort, however, it is always a system of values, of ideas, of ideologies—choose whatever word you like—that is decisive. It

was an idea that founded the United States, even though little bands of settlers were fighting a mighty empire. An idea was victorious in the group of poor subversives called Early Christians because their imperial adversary governed the world but had lost his basic concept of existence. Napoleon's soldiers, hungry and in rags, conquered Italy and Europe with ideas and determination. We have no reason to assume that this law of history has changed. What has lost its historic meaning will not survive. Military hardware, including the most advanced superbombs, will not save us when the will to live, the guiding ideas or values of life, have subsided. This is one of the few safe conclusions from history.

POIGNANT PARADOXES

At the risk of appearing ridiculous, I would say that one excellent means to grasp the spirit of time is reading newspapers and magazines with the eye of the historian (as what he would call primary sources) and of the naturalist who, in a detached way, looks at the strange ways of ants and termites. On one single page, we may observe all the striking contrasts besetting our time. The report of the latest space exploit is sandwiched between the latest murder and Hollywood divorce . . . . We can do worse than contemplating, for a moment, the symbolic meaning of such arrangements. The conquest of space is not only a most brilliant achievement of science and technology; it is the fulfillment of a millennial longing of humanity, first expressed in the myth of Daedalus, and visionarily anticipated by utopianists from Leonardo da Vinci to Cyrano de Bergerac, Goya, and Jules Verne. . . . Eventually and after centuries, [space flight] materializes in its definitive, never-before-believed form—and is submerged by trivia, by appeals to what is lowest in human nature, by the cheap sensations provided by an almost subhuman killer and the ephemeral amours of a doll.

From *Teachers College Record*, 1964, vol. 65, pp. 496-504. Reprinted by permission of author and publisher.

Ours is the affluent society, so we read, and we have the highest standard of living ever achieved. We are bombarded with astronomical figures of Gross National Product—$20 billion for the first trip to the moon, $11 billion for packaging wares to make them appetizing to the buyer. But we also read of $100 billion which would be required but are not available for slum clearing; we read that 57 per cent of people over age 65 live on less than $1,000 in cold-water flats; that 10 per cent of Americans are functional illiterates. And what is perhaps the most remarkable symptom: Economic opulence goes hand in hand with a peak of mental illness, some 50 per cent of hospital beds being occupied by mental patients. It goes hand in hand with a continuous increase in the rate of crime, especially juvenile delinquency. And, the psychotherapists tell us, beside the classical neuroses caused by stress, tensions, and psychological trauma, a new type of mental sickness has developed for which they have even had to coin a new term—existential neurosis, mental illness arising from the meaninglessness of life, the lack of goals and hopes in a mechanized mass society.

SOCIETY AS PATIENT

The psychiatrist is wont to speak of split personality as a classical symptom of mental disease. If anything, our society is a split personality—not simply a fine Dr. Jekyll and hideous Mr. Hyde, but split into an enormity of disorganized and antagonistic parts. This is the reason why analyses of modern society are not mere book titles anymore but have become part of everyday language: from the Decline of the West to Brave New World, 1984, Organization Man, Hidden Persuaders, Waste Makers, Status Seekers, and many others. This literature in itself is a symptom or symbol; nothing comparable has existed in history, except perhaps in the analogous time of the decay of the Roman Empire. Like physicians examining an individual patient, these modern diagnosticians of society observe different symptoms, use different tools and terms, sometimes err or exaggerate their findings. On the whole, however, their analyses are like a battery of laboratory tests, adding up to a consistent picture. It may be expressed in one brief sentence: We have conquered the world, but somewhere on the way, we seem to have lost our soul.

In more realistic terms, this means that we have lost, or lost sight of those guiding lights for the formation of our lives which are called human values. . . .

A THEORY OF VALUE

. . . Values are things or acts which are chosen by and are desirable to an individual or to society within a certain frame of reference. Although it is admittedly tentative, every word matters in this definition. We obviously have to include both objects and acts—material things like dollar bills or Picasso paintings and immaterial qualities like the goodness of a charitable act are obviously values. We further have to introduce the element of choice. Where there is no choice, there is only necessity, not value. In somewhat different terms, whatever is taken for granted neither is nor has a value. For example, to a perfectly healthy person or animal, health is not a value but is simply taken care of by biological functions. Only if we envisage possible danger and can do something about it does health become a value. Prolongation of human life is possible; physical immortality is not. The first is a value, not the second. We have to pay for food, not for breathing air; therefore, the first has value, the second not, even though it is equally indispensable for life. To the Aztecs, because gold was abundantly available, it had no particular value. To the Spaniards, it was eminently desirable, so they liquidated Montezuma and his Indians. A postage stamp is worth a few pennies to the letter writer; it may be worth thousands of dollars to the collector because it is particularly desirable within the framework of philately. Our criteria equally apply to actions. In the course of a day, we perform innumerable actions which have no value involvement at all. Only where there is both choice and preferability do value judgments appear. Nobody cares what way I choose to arrive at my office—at least so long as I do not commit an undesirable act like a traffic violation; but my consistently coming late or early may be evaluated. On the other hand, if I fall into the river and save myself by swimming, this is not considered to be a moral act because it is presupposed that there is no choice between drowning and swimming. If another person falls into the river and I save him, I may get a medal because it is presupposed that I did have a choice and took the socially desirable action. And so forth *in infinitum*.

From this infinite array of preferences and evaluations, mankind, starting in some prehistoric stage and continuing to the present day, singled out some very general and abstract notions which became values *par excellence*. Pleasure, social virtues, goodness, truth, beauty, deity are a few of them. It is the objective of a theory of value to elucidate where they came from, what they mean, from what ultimate concept they can be derived, and what are their consequences for human behavior and society.

One such theory is the naturalistic one. It is a derivative of the philosophical doctrine known as reductionism which, in this particular respect, can be formulated as follows: Human values are derived from and ultimately reduce to biological needs, drives, and principles. Biological values are essentially maintenance of the individual, survival of the group, and evolution of the species. This basic doctrine can and has been formulated in many different ways. For example, it is the classic philosophical doctrine of hedonism, maintaining that pleasure is the ultimate good. It is also Freud's doctrine that behavior is governed by the pleasure principle and the principle of sustaining the homeostatic equilibrium of the organism in answer to changing environmental influences. Generalizing the original physiological meaning of homeostasis, the terms of psychological and sociological homeostasis were introduced; that is, the ultimate goal of behavior is to maintain the psychophysical organism in a biological, psychological, and social equilibrium. Still other terms for the same idea are psychological and social adjustment or adaptation; from here originate the philosophy of conformity and the ideology of so-called progressive education, both proclaiming social adjustment or equilibrium with existing society as the ultimate goal.

MAN IN TWO WORLDS

With leading biologists, I am in fundamental disagreement with this theory—not because of theological or metaphysical prejudices, but because it doesn't fit the facts. Human behavior is not simply directed toward release of tensions; release of tensions, boredom, emptiness, and *taedium vitae* may be psychopathogenic factors. A large part of behavior—play and exploratory activities, creativity, and culture in general—simply doesn't fit in the scheme. Man (and organ-

isms in general) are not stimulus-response machines, as the theory presupposes; immanent activity going along with so-called function pleasure is an important part of behavior. Life and behavior are not simply utilitarian, trying to come to a so-called equilibrium with minimum expense of physical and psychic energy. This is not even true of organic evolution, which often produces fantastic formations, behavior patterns, colors, and what not, far exceeding mere survival and economic principles of adaptation. It is even less true of man, where not by the wildest flight of fancy can the creativity of an artist, musician, or scientist be reduced to psychological and social adjustment, nor can the self-sacrifice of a martyr be reduced to the principle of utility. The whole of human culture—whether Greek tragedy, Renaissance art, or German music—simply has nothing to do with biological values of maintenance, survival, adjustment, or homeostasis. . . .

In fact, the answer to our quest is very simple. Man, as the old saying goes, is a denizen of two worlds. He is a biological organism with the physical equipment, drives, instincts, and limitations of his species. At the same time, he creates, uses, dominates, and is dominated by a higher world which, without theological and philosophical implications and in behavioral terms, can best be defined as the universe or universes of symbols. This is what we call human culture; and values—esthetic, scientific, ethical, religious—are one part of this symbolic universe. This is what man tries to achieve beyond satisfaction of his biological needs and drives; in turn, it governs and controls his behavior.

We have come a rather long way, but I am now prepared to answer the questions which we have left pending: We have spoken of existential neurosis—mental sickness resulting from the meaninglessness and emptiness of life and a lack of desirable goals. Why has life become devoid of meaning and goals at a time of affluence and high standards of living, whereas it apparently had meaning and goals in times incomparably poorer in their economic and technical resources?

The best answer I am able to find is that that complex structure of symbols and values, called human culture, is, besides many other things, an important psychohygienic factor. If man is surely a creature seeking satisfaction of his biological needs—food, shelter, sex, an amount of security for his biological and social existence—he also lives in the higher realm of culture which is defined by the very fact that it transcends biological needs. Tradition, status in society, full realization of potentialities, religion, art, science—these are a few of the needs deriving from man's cultural existence. Starvation at this symbolic level leads to disturbances of the mental organism just as starvation at the biologic level leads to disturbances of the physical organism. This is a well established fact of psychopathology.

The diagnosis of the sick society, then, is quite simply that it provides more or less abundantly for the biological needs but starves the spiritual ones. All the catchwords I have mentioned—from the Uprise of the Masses to Status Seekers to the Organization Man and so forth— are variations of this one theme. In modern mass civilization, tradition, which made the hard life of a peasant in the Alps tolerable and even enjoyable, is replaced by the titillation of ever new sensations, the cruder the better, from oversexed movies to television bloodies to the hope of fatal events in the boxing ring and the dangerous play even with atomic war as distraction from a dull life. Status-seeking is a perfectly normal human ambition—simply a quest for self-realization, having its precursor even in gregarious animals. But as there is no real status in mass civilization which does not recognize the value of the individual, this yearning can only be satisfied by empty and often silly status symbols—the amount of chromium on the annually traded-in car, higher living than the Joneses, and a larger swimming pool. The human faculty of rational decision is replaced by biologistic factors, by conditioning like that of laboratory dogs and rats, and by exploitation of the unconscious— all brought to mastery in advertising, by hidden persuaders, motivation research, and human engineering in general. The system works to the profit of business because it is psychologically easier to be pushed by conditioned reflexes than to act with reason. But the loss of psychological freedom is paid for by a loss of goals worth fighting for and, consequently, by a feeling of emptiness and meaninglessness. The need for a value system of religion or at least a secular ideology remains unfilled. . . .

WHENCE SCIENTISTS?

A few years ago *Life* magazine published an editorial entitled "Can We Produce an Einstein?" observing that the achievements of modern science were made in Europe. The earlier leaders in American science either came from or studied in Europe. De Tocqueville's famous statement was quoted that the spirit of America, though devoted to practical science, "is averse to general ideas; it does not seek theoretical discoveries." . . .

Since Sputnik I was launched, there has been an enormous debate about American education, science, and research. With a gigantic increase in research and development budgets, there has still been—so far as I am able to see —no change in attitude or any reassessment of basic outlook. These past years have shown an increase rather than a decrease of the Russian lead—and by no means in the space race alone. For example, in the fall of 1960, 80 million people in the USSR were treated with oral polio vaccine, whereas in the United States it was only tested on a small scale. According to a recent book, little Ivan in the first grade is taught a vocabulary of 2,000 words, little Johnny 158 words; in the 4th grade, Ivan is prepared for literature, history, and foreign languages, but Johnny still has to babble about Mommie and Daddie.

If we reject as improbable the hypothesis that Americans are genetically stupider than other people, I believe the answer to *Life*'s question is simple: because we don't want to—because American universities and institutions of learning are not the place for the breeding and care of such abnormalities as outstanding scientists.

Mr. Khrushchev, who is by no means a mediocre intelligence, has given this an almost classical expression. You will remember what he said after another Russian Lunik was launched: The Americans, he said, shouldn't be disappointed about Russia's conquest of space; after all, they are terribly good in inventing new tailfins.

This is precisely the point: American science excels in designing tailfins of all sorts—in diligently working out new touches, new details or convolutions of an already given body, be it the body of a car or of a theory. It is singularly ineffective in inventing new vehicles of space or of thought.

Why is it so? The answer lies, I believe, in a degradation of the democratic dogma. It starts at the level of the elementary school when the democratic ideal of equal rights is converted into that of equal intelligence, whence the retardation of little Johnny in comparison with little Ivan. It culminates in universities and scientific production.

While there is a great hue and cry that scientists are needed and wanted, this means the need and want for trainees to work within a given framework or template of structure and organization—great hustle and bustle, lots of machines and dials to watch, aggressive publicity that so many millions are being spent and new buildings erected, headlines about what often has to be disclaimed, and so forth. It does not mean a genuine welcome for creative individuals who, by definition, are non-conformists, try something new, are sometimes awkward in public relations, less interested in quantitative expansion than in being left alone. As a matter of fact, there is a subtle borderline where achievement is penalized. While universities go desperately hunting for junior scientists and can never have enough of them, seniors are left in the lurch because, as the routine phrase goes, "Unfortunately we have no place for a scientist of your reputation, experience, calibre, superior achievements," etc.

LEADERSHIP AND INTELLECT

The concise expression of this is the American prima donna myth. European universities which, after all, had some six or seven centuries of experience, used to select leaders and pioneers, and it was quite common for students to come to a university not to follow a schedule for a degree, but to hear famous Professor X or Y. In the United States a similar personality is apt to be labeled "prima donna"—and this is very bad indeed. This attitude misses only one detail: You just cannot play opera without prima donnas, even if they sometimes have difficult personalities and lack the desirable togetherness; and you cannot promote science without leaders, individuals who do not fill preconstructed moulds but make new ones. . . .

Take, for example, the matter of scientific publications and grants for research. Roughly speaking, the principle for evaluation used to be that a scientist who, by labors over many years had established a certain reputation, is not likely to make a fool of himself. His previous work doesn't guarantee but makes it more or less probable that his present contribution or project has merit. Our system, however, is totally different. Whether the youngest tyro or an experienced old hand is concerned, everything goes through the same big machinery, as in the stockyards of Chicago pigs of all colors and stocks are processed uniformly to make sausages.

What is the outcome of this procedure? Notwithstanding control by supposedly competent committees, our scientific and medical journals are full of superfluous, repetitive, sometimes incompetent and falsified reports. On the other hand, because of this overflood, it often takes years to have important work published—particularly if it is new and therefore causes headaches to the editorial board. And where grants are concerned, the mildest that can be said is, in the words of Professor Gengerelli of the University of California, that "we have a great plethora of $100,000 grants for $50 ideas." . . .

The interference with scientific productivity goes even farther. Professor H. J. Muller has aptly defined freedom as "the condition of being able to choose and to carry out purposes. . . . A person is free to the extent that he has the capacity, the opportunity, and the incentive to give expression to what is in him and to develop his potentialities." I daresay this freedom is strictly limited in American science. To use Riesman's phrase, American science is "other-directed" to a hardly calculable degree—not only applied research with a prescribed practical or commercial goal, but basic science as well, controlled as it is by fashions in science and medicine, grant-giving agencies, financial considerations, and committees of all sorts, all of which often prove much stronger than the "free choice" (in Muller's terms) of the scientist.

THE GROUP MYSTIQUE

. . . not even in Hitler Germany did I see the thought-control and censorship which appear usual at some American institutions. I had never seen before regulations such as—I quote literally—"all publications, presentations, etc., have to be cleared and approved by the research committee"—which, incidentally, was totally incompetent and only a tool of professional intrigue. I could quote examples where this regulation was made to stick and paralyzed the development of important discoveries.

The underlying philosophy of all these and many other phenomena is the mystical belief in the group, team, committee—and, I should add, exploitation of this pseudodemocratic idea for personal purposes. . . . Roughly speaking, team work will be productive and indeed indispensable wherever elaboration of a given project, discovery, or idea is concerned. The group or team will never, however, replace the individual in inaugurating new developments. . . .

While aware that science is but one limited sector or aspect of modern civilization, I am inclined to believe that it is what the statisticians would call a representative sample; observation of other sectors would lead to conclusions that are different in content but consistent and parallel with those derived from science. . . .

TWO VIEWS OF HISTORY

Again using the way of gross oversimplification, forced upon us by the need for brevity, there are, in principle, two well-known ways to look at the history of mankind. The one is the theory of progress, seeing in it a continuous upward movement, principally caused by an increasing control of nature. Starting with the Agricultural Revolution somewhere in the fourth millennium BC, this movement, although interrupted by dark ages, has continually progressed in an exponential curve since the birth of modern science. We have gained nearly complete mastery of physical nature. Biological technology, such as control of disease by medicine and control of food by applied biology, is advancing. We now enter the age of psychological technology, that is, of controlling human behavior. And if we have once gained the necessary insight into the laws of society and sociological technology—that is, when education, government, and politics have become thoroughly scientific—humanity will establish the earthly paradise with the conquest of space and possible colonies on the planets thrown into the bargain.

The other view is different. It is known as the cyclic theory of history, focusing on a sequence of entities called high cultures or civilizations. Instead of continual progress, each of them goes through a life cycle, being born at a certain time and place, growing, flowering, reaching its apex, and eventually decaying. So it was with the cultures of the past—those of Mesopotamia, Egypt, classical antiquity, China, the Aztecs, and so on. Our own period shows unmistakable symptoms of beginning or advanced decay, and if it does not die a natural death, it may even commit atomic suicide.

To the dispassionate scientist, it looks as if the cyclic model of history were the more realistic one. He would renounce his profession if he could not strongly protest that there has been continual and on the whole uninterrupted progress in one particular sphere of cultural activity, science and technology. But if he keeps an open mind and doesn't forget that these are but one sector of culture—that art, poetry, music, religion and even the modest aspects of customs and styles of living are just as well an expression and need of humanity as are scientific techniques, that, in our period, we have produced grand science but no grand music, sculpture, or poetry —then he cannot lightheartedly bypass the arguments of the theorists of cultural cycles and decline.

This does not imply, however, cowardly acceptance of historical inevitability. History does *not* repeat itself. Patently, our civilization is different from previous ones in two all-important respects. The latter were local phenomena, whereas ours encircles the whole planet. And ours is the first consciously to realize its danger and to possess the means to control it.

And here it is where education comes in. If I say "education," I mean it in the classical sense of the word as unfolding human potentialities; I do not mean it in the sense of "human engineering," handling human beings with scientific techniques for ulterior purposes. We have already alluded to the fact that, with the help of modern technique, the human animal can be engineered just as well as inanimate and subhuman nature. The technique is well known and need not be elaborated here—the control of behavior by conditioning, the use of subconscious drives and motives, of the animal instincts in the human being, and so forth. Roughly speaking, the technique was invented by Hitler for political purposes and perfected by Madison Avenue mainly for commercial ends. I believe the main objection is not in moral indignation about degradation of man as a free entity, in the unpleasant details you find in Packard's *Hidden Persuaders,* and elsewhere; but rather in the fact that human and social engineering, although efficient for particular purposes of commercialism and politics and over short periods of time, is self-defeating in the long run. If you want a less highbrow formula, you may also say that you cannot fool all of the people all of the time. The Persuaders work —to the profit of manufacturers of cars, refrigerators, margarine, toilet paper, etc. But, unfortunately, human nature is not completely satisfied with commercials and commodities, so people in a commercialized society are at the same time headed for mental trouble. And a society consisting merely of mechanized or engineered human beings will not survive. Even *Brave New World* needs some marionette players who themselves are above the conditioning and social engineering they impose on the others.

INDIVIDUALS REAPPRAISED

There is no miracle drug or wonder cure; this is about the most certain knowledge modern medicine and psychiatry has taught us. Nevertheless, some of the unpleasant and dangerous aspects of American life and society patently go back to education. It is, of course, not my intention to suggest any practical measures. But it is, I believe, within the competence of the biologist, philosopher, and social critic to recall some principles or maxims upon which practice should be based. The introduction or, rather, reintroduction of a proper scale of values is a bald necessity.

One such aspect is the value of the human individual, together with its opposite, the theory that all individuals have equal capabilities and intelligence. This, obviously, is a parody of the American Constitution; the Founding Fathers certainly did not envisage or aspire to the manufacture of mass-men in a commercialized society. The consequence of that theory, however, is the orientation of education to fit the lowest common denominator, that is, the lowest intelligence level in the group. The results are that Johnny can't read, that he compares so unfavorably with little Ivan, and that college students can't speak or write decent English.

Intimately connected with this is another theory fundamental in American psychology and education. It is environmentalism, the hypothesis that all individuals are born equal in their dispositions, and that only postnatal influences mould their character and mental outfit. The theory has a long history in English philosophy. It goes back to Locke's *tabula rasa* and found its classic expression by Watson, the founder of behaviorism. . . .

Skinner found "surprisingly similar performances" in organisms as diverse as the pigeon, mouse, rat, cat, and monkey. It is characteristic that the Russians, communism notwithstanding, never fell into this trap: The pope of Russian physiology, Pavlov, reported the enormous variability of his experimental dogs in the conditioning procedure; and if genetic differences are recognized in laboratory dogs, it will be hard to deny them in humans. . . .

THE S-R FALLACY

Again connected is still another biological misconception, the so-called stimulus-response scheme. This is the idea that an organism, the human included, only responds to stimuli coming from outside and does so with maximum economy and for maintenance of its homeostatic equilibrium. In other terms, it does nothing if not stimulated or driven by maintenance needs. I have already mentioned that this theory contradicts biological fact, disregarding as it does spontaneous activities, play, and exploratory behavior. . . .

The S-R theory also implies a utilitarian theory of education. Of course, large parts of education are of necessity utilitarian—from the three Rs to the training of the doctor and lawyer—and they should be made even more utilitarian by eliminating, in view of the enormous extent of present knowledge, everything that is not of use for the particular purpose. But the goal of education as a whole is not utilitarian. It is not to produce mere social automata kept in adjustment and submission by conditioning; it is to produce human beings enjoying themselves in a free society. Here, again, current educational philosophy misses the point. We have already heard that, with respect to one aspect, science, it tends to overemphasize utilitarian know-how against know-why stemming from intrinsic interest in the subject matter, and that, in the long run, this apparently practical approach turns out to be not practical at all. This applies even more to the so-called humanities. It is precisely the definition of the cultural values of theoretical science, art, poetry, history, and so forth, that they have no short-range, utilitarian values; they are, as the Germans have it, *Selbsteweck,* goals in themselves. But for exactly this reason, they have a utilitarian value at a higher level. That poor creature called man, beset with the shortcomings of animal physiology aggravated by domestication, making his living in a continual rat race, under a thousand stresses and chased around in a complex society, becomes something more than an overburdened Pavlovian dog only by those seemingly useless but factually so indispensable realms of his more-than-animal being.

And a last precept: Smash the image of organization man. In our discussion of science, we have already seen that the organization man also belongs to those seemingly eminently practical, but in the long run self-frustrating ideals. . . . It may be eminently comfortable for business administrations when group-think, togetherness, affability, and prefabricated junior executives predominate, but it is equally certain that it will lead to stagnation everywhere. . . .

In trying to outline what the world of values is, I have rather fully discussed certain shortcomings in contemporary science. . . . Within the small compass of my presentation, I have tried to point out at least a few nooks and ribs in our educational and social structure where new timbers should replace old ones. The good old ship is still sailing even though it's overcrowded and its internal arrangement uncomfortable at times. Wondrous to see, it even grew wings and is headed for the abysses of space. But the new frontiers it is bound to reach—they are not outside somewhere in interplanetary space; they are so near and yet so far: discovering a new continent of the human soul.

REFERENCES

The following are the complete citations for names and dates appearing in parentheses in the text.

Abelson, R. P., & Carroll, J. D. Computer simulation of individual belief systems. *American Behavioral Scientist,* 1965, **8**(9), 24-30.

Ackerman, N. W. *The psychodynamics of family life.* New York: Basic Books, 1958.

Allen, J. R., & West, L. J. Flight from violence: Hippies and the Green Rebellion. *American Journal of Psychiatry,* 1968, **125**(3), 364-370.

Allport, F. H. A theory of enestruence (event-structure theory): Report of progress. *American Psychologist,* 1967, **22**(1), 1-24.

Allport, G. W. *Personality: A psychological interpretation.* New York: Holt, 1937.

Allport, G. W. The ego in contemporary psychology. *Psychological Review,* 1943, **50**, 451-478.

Allport, G. W. *The Nature of Prejudice.* Boston: Beacon Press, 1954.

Allport, G. W. *Becoming: Basic considerations for a psychology of personality.* New Haven, Conn.: Yale University Press, 1955.

Allport, G. W. *Pattern and growth in personality.* New York: Holt, 1961.

Allport, G. W., & Postman, L. The basic psychology of rumor. *Transactions of the New York Academy of Science,* 1945, **8**(Series 2), 61-81.

Allport, G. W., Vernon, P. E., & Lindzey, G. *A study of values.* (3rd ed.) Boston: Houghton Mifflin, 1960.

Ambrose, J. A. The development of the smiling response in early infancy. In B. M. Foss (Ed.), *Determinants of infant behavior.* London: Methuen & Co., Ltd., 1960.

American Psychological Association. *Ethical standards of psychologists.* Washington, D.C.: APA, 1963.

Apperson, L. B., & McAdoo, W. G., Jr. Parental factors in the childhood of homosexuals. *Journal of Abnormal Psychology,* 1968, **73**(3), 201-206.

Arkoff, A. *Adjustment and mental health.* New York: McGraw-Hill, 1968.

Aronson, E., & Gerard, E. Beyond Parkinson's law: The effect of excess time on subsequent performance. *Journal of Personality and Social Psychology,* 1966, **3**, 336-339.

Aronson, E., & Worchel, P. Similarity versus liking as determinants of interpersonal attractiveness. *Psychosomatic Science,* 1966, **5**(4), 157-158.

Asch, S. E. *Social psychology.* New York: Prentice-Hall, 1952.

Asch, S. E. Opinions and social pressure. *Scientific American,* 1955, **193**(5), 31-35.

Ashby, W. R. Regulation and control. In W. Buckley (Ed.), *Modern systems research for the behavioral scientist.* Chicago: Aldine, 1968. Pp. 296-303.

Astin, A. W., & Nichols, R. C. Life goals and vocational choice. *Journal of Applied Psychology,* 1964, **48**(1), 50-58.

Azrin, N. H., Holz, W. C., & Hake, D. F. Fixed ratio punishment. *Journal of the Experimental Analysis of Behavior,* 1963, **6**, 141-148.

Azrin, N., & Lindsley, O. The reinforcement of cooperation between children. *Journal of Abnormal Psychology,* 1956, **52**, 100-102.

Baker, L. G., Jr. The personal and social adjustment of the never-married woman. *Journal of Marriage & the Family,* 1968, **30**(3), 473-479.

Baldwin, A. L. *Behavior and development in childhood.* N.Y.: Holt, Rinehart and Winston, 1955.

Baldwin, J. M. *Mental development in the child and the race.* New York: Macmillan, 1895.

Bales, R. F. Task roles and social roles in problem-solving groups. In E. E. Maccoby, T. M. Newcomb, & E. L. Hartley (3rd ed.) New York: Holt, Rinehart and Winston, 1958. Pp. 437-447.

Bandura, A., Ross, D., & Ross, S. A. Imitation of film-mediated aggressive models. *Journal of Abnormal and Social Psychology,* 1963, **66**, 3-11. (a)

Bandura, A., Ross, D., & Ross, S. A comparative test of the status envy, social power, and secondary reinforcement theories of identificatory learning. *Journal of Abnormal and Social Psychology,* 1963, **67**, 527-534. (b)

Bandura, A., & Walters, R. H. *Adolescent aggression.* New York: Ronald Press, 1959.

Bandura, A., & Walters, R. H. *Social learning and personality development.* New York: Holt, Rinehart and Winston, 1963.

Banham, K. M. Senescence and the emotions: A genetic theory. *Journal of Genetic Psychology,* 1951, **78**, 175-183.

Bard, P., & Rioch, D. McK. A study of four cats deprived of neocortex and additional portions of the forebrain. *Johns Hopkins Hospital Bulletin,* 1937, **60**, 73-147.

Bateson, G. Minimal requirements for a theory of schizophrenia. *Archives of General Psychiatry,* 1960, **2**, 477-491.

Bateson, G., & Mead, M. *Balinese culture.* New York: Academy of Science, 1942.

Beadle, G. W. The new genetics: The threads of life. *Britannica Book of the Year.* Chicago: Britannica, 1964.

Beardslee, D. C., & O'Dowd, D. D. Students and the occupational world. In N. Sanford (Ed.), *The American College*, New York: Wiley, 1962. Pp. 597-626.

Beck, J. Guarding the unborn. *Today's Health*, 1968, 46(1), 38-41.

Becker, J. Achievement related characteristics of manic-depressives. *Journal of Abnormal and Social Psychology*, 1960, 60, 334-339.

Becker, W. C. Consequences of different kinds of parental discipline. In M. L. Hoffman & L. W. Hoffman (Eds.), *Review of Child Development Research*, Vol. 1. N.Y.: Russell Sage Foundation, 1964. Pp. 169-208.

Bell, E., Jr. The basis of effective military psychiatry. *Diseases of the Nervous System*, 1958, 19, 283-288.

Bell, J. N. Lifeline for would-be suicides. *Today's Health*, 1967, 45(6), 30-33, 10, 11.

Benabud, A. Psycho-pathological aspects of the Cannabis situation in Morocco: Statistical data for 1956. *Bulletin on Narcotics*, 1957, 9, 1-16.

Benedict, R. *Patterns of culture*. Boston: Houghton Mifflin, 1934. (Republished: New York: New American Library, 1953)

Bengelsdorf, I. S. Technology's role is vital to world peace, well-being. *Los Angeles Times*, June 4, 1966.

Benjamin, R. M. Absence of deficits in taste discrimination following cortical lesions as a function of the amount of preoperative practice. *Journal of Comparative and Physiological Psychology*, 1959, 52, 255-258.

Bennett, E. L., Diamond, M. C., Krech, D., & Rosenzweig, M. R. Chemical and anatomical plasticity of the brain. *Science*, 1964, 146, 610-619.

Bennis, W. G., Schein, E. H., Berlew, D. E., & Steele, F. I. *Interpersonal Dynamics: Essays and readings on human interaction*. Homewood, Ill.: The Dorsey Press, 1964.

Benson, P. The common interests myth in marriage. *Social Problems*, 1955, 3, 27-34.

Benson, P. The interests of happily married couples. *Marriage and Family Living*, 1952, 14, 276-280.

Bentley, J. C. Creativity and academic achievement. *Journal of Educational Research*, 1966, 59(6), 269-272.

Berelson, B., & Steiner, G. A. *Human behavior: an inventory of scientific findings*. New York: Harcourt, Brace and World, 1964.

Beres, D., & Obers, S. J. The effects of extreme deprivation in infancy on psychic structure in adolescence: A study in ego development. In R. S. Eissler and others (Eds.), *Psychoanalytic Study of the Child*, Vol. 5. New York: International Univ. Press, 1950.

Berkowitz, L. *Development of motives and values in the child*. New York: Basic Books, 1964.

Berlyne, D. E. *Conflict, arousal and curiosity*. New York: McGraw-Hill, 1960.

Berlyne, D. E. Arousal and reinforcement. In D. Levine (Ed.), *Nebraska symposium on motivation—1967*. Lincoln, Nebr.: Univ. of Nebr. Press, 1967. Pp. 1-110.

Bernard, J. *Remarriage*. New York: Dryden, 1956.

Bernard, J. Marital stability and patterns of status variables. *Journal of Marriage & the Family*, 1966, 28(4), 421-439.

Berrien, F. K. *Comments and cases on human relations*. New York: Harper, 1951.

Berrill, N. J. *Man's emerging mind*. New York: Dodd, Mead, 1955. Copyright 1955 by N. J. Berrill. Quotation published by Dodd, Mead, & Company, Inc., New York, and reprinted with their permission.

Berry, J. R. What makes a gambling addict. *Today's Health*, 1968, 46(10), 20-23.

Bessell, H. The content is the medium: The confidence is the message. *Psychology Today*, 1968, 1(8), 32-35.

Bettelheim, B. Individual and mass behavior in extreme situations. *Journal of Abnormal and Social Psychology*, 1943, 38, 417-452.

Bieber, I., *et al. Homosexuality: A psychoanalytic study of male homosexuals*. New York: Basic Books, 1962.

Bijou, S. W. Ages, stages, and the naturalization of human development. *American Psychologist*, 1968, 23, 419-427.

Bingham, W. E., & Griffiths, W. J., Jr. The effect of different environments during infancy on adult behavior in the rat. *Journal of Comparative and Physiological Psychology*, 1952, 45, 307-312.

Bladeslee, A. L., Nutritional time bomb. *Today's Health*, 1967, 45(6), 7.

Blau, A., Slaff, B., Easton, K., Welkowitz, J., Springarn, J., & Cohen, J. The psychogenic etiology of premature births. *Psychosomatic Medicine*, 1963, 25(3), 201-211.

Blau, P. M. The flow of occupational supply and recruitment. *Amer. Sociol. Review*, 1965, 30, 475-490.

Blood, R. O., Jr. *Marriage*. New York: Free Press, 1962.

Blood, R. O., Jr., & Wolfe, D. M. *Husbands and wives: The dynamics of married living*. New York: Free Press, 1960.

Bloom, B. *Stability and change in human characteristics*. New York: Wiley, 1964.

Bloustein, E. J. Man's work goes from sun to sun but woman's work is never done. *Psychology Today*, 1968, 1(10), 38-41, 66.

Bluestone, H., & McGahee, C. L. Reaction to extreme stress: Impending death by execution. *American Journal of Psychiatry*, 1962, 119, 393-396.

Blumenthal, M. D. Mental health among the divorced: A field study of divorced and never divorced persons. *Archives of General Psychiatry*, 1967, 16(5), 603-608.

Blumer, H. Psychological import of the human group. In M. Sherif & M. O. Wilson (Eds.), *Group relations at the crossroads*. New York: Harper, 1953.

Blumer, H., Sutter, A., Ahmed, S., & Smith, R. *The world of youthful drug use*. ADD Center Project—Final report. Berkeley: Univ. of Calif. Press, 1967.

Boalt, G. *Family and Marriage*. New York: David McKay Co., 1965.

Bogdonoff, M. D., Klein, R. F., Estis, E. H., Shaw, D. M., Jr., & Back, K. W. The modifying effect of conforming behavior upon lipid responses accompanying CNS arousal. *Clinical Research*, 1961, 9, 135.

Bootzin, R. R., & Natsoulas, T. Evidence for perceptual defense uncontaminated by response bias. *Journal of*

Personality and Social Psychology, 1965, **1**, 461-468.

Bolen, D. W., & Boyd, W. H. Gambling and the gambler. *Archives of General Psychiatry,* 1968, **18**(5), 617-630.

Borow, H. Development of occupational motives and roles. In L. W. Hoffman & M. L. Hoffman (Eds.), *Review of Child Development Research.* Vol. 2. New York: Russell Sage Foundation, 1966, Pp. 373-422.

Bowen, M. A family concept of schizophrenia. In D. D. Jackson (Ed.), *The etiology of schizophrenia.* New York: Basic Books, 1960.

Bowlby, J. The nature of the child's tie to his mother. *International Journal of Psychoanalysis,* 1958, **39**, 1-24.

Boyer, E. L., & Michael, W. B. Outcomes of college: Aptitude. *Review of Educational Research,* 1965, **35**(4), 277-291.

Brackbill, Y. Extinction of the smiling response in infants as a function of reinforcement schedule. *Child Development,* 1958, **29**, 115-124.

Bradford, L. P., Gibb, J. R., & Benne, K. D. *T-group theory and laboratory method.* New York: Wiley, 1964.

Brady, J. V. Emotional behavior. In J. Field (Ed.), *Handbook of physiology. Sect. I: neurophysiology.* Vol. III. Washington, D.C.: American Physiological Society, 1960.

Braine, M. D. S., Heimer, C. B., Wortis, H., & Freedman, A. M. Factors associated with impairment of the early development of prematures. *Monographs of the Society for Research in Child Development,* 1966, **31**(4), 1-92.

Brancale, R., Ellis, A., & Doorbar, R. Psychiatric and psychological investigations of convicted sex offenders: A summary report. *American Journal of Psychiatry,* 1952, **109**, 17-21.

Branden, N. *Psychotherapy and the objectivist ethics.* New York: Nathaniel Branden Institute, 1965.

Bridges, K. M. B. Emotional development in early infancy. *Child development,* 1932, **3**, 324-341.

Broderick, C. B., & Fowler, S. E. New patterns of relationships between the sexes among preadolescents. *Marriage and Family Living,* 1961, **23**, 27-30.

Brogden, W. J. Animal studies of learning. In S. S. Stevens (Ed.). *Handbook of experimental psychology.* New York: Wiley, 1951. Pp. 568-612.

Bromberg, W. Marihuana intoxication. *American Journal of Psychiatry,* 1934, **91**, 303-330.

Bronfenbrenner, U. Developmental theory in transition. In *The 62nd yearbook of the National Society for the Study of Education.* Part 1. *Child Psychology.* Chicago: Univ. of Chicago Press, 1963. Pp. 517-542.

Bronson, G. The hierarchical organization of the central nervous system: Implications for learning processes and critical periods in early development. *Behavioral Science,* 1965, **10**(1), 7-25.

Broom, L., & Selznick, P. *Sociology.* (3rd ed.) New York: Harper & Row, 1963.

Brown, H. Where wonder is taking us. Caltech and the world of science. *Los Angeles Times,* December 10, 1967.

Brownfain, J. J. Stability of the self-concept as a dimension of personality. *Journal of Abnormal and Social Psychology,* 1952, **47**, 597-606.

Bruner, J. S. The course of cognitive growth. *American Psychologist,* 1964, **19**, 1-15.

Bruner, J. S., Goodnow, J. J., & Austin, G. A. *A study of thinking.* New York: Wiley, 1956.

Bruner, J. S., Matter, J., & Papanek, M. Breadth of learning as a function of drive level and mechanization. *Psychological Review,* 1955, **62**, 1-10.

Bruner, J. S., Olver, R. R., & Greenfield, P. M. *Studies in cognitive growth.* New York: Wiley, 1966.

Buber, M. *I and thou.* (2nd ed.) Translated by R. G. Smith. New York: Scribner's, 1958.

Buckley, W. Society as a complex adaptive system. In W. Buckley (Ed.), *Modern systems research for the behavioral scientist.* Chicago: Aldine, 1968. Pp. 490-513.

Bühler, C. *The first year of life.* New York: Day, 1930.

Bühler, C. The course of human life as a psychological problem. *Human Development,* 1968, **11**(3), 184-200.

Bullard, D. M., Glaser, H. H., Heagarty, M. C., & Pivchek, E. C. Failure to thrive in the neglected child. *American Journal of Orthopsychiatry,* 1967, **37**, 680-690.

Burchinal, L. G. Characteristics of adolescents from unbroken, broken, and reconstituted families. *Journal of Marriage & the Family,* 1964, **26**(1), 44-51.

Burchinal, L. G., Haller, A. O., & Taves, M. *Career choices of rural youth in a changing society.* Rosemount, Minn.: Bull. 458, Agri. Exper. Sta., Univ. of Minn., 1962.

Bureau of the Census. *Marital status and family status, March 1964 and 1963.* Series P-20, No. 135. April 28, 1965. Washington, D.C.: U.S. Government Printing Office, 1965.

Bureau of the Census. *Marital status and family status.* Series P-20, No. 159. January 27, 1967. Washington, D.C.: U.S. Government Printing Office, 1967.

Bureau of the Census. *Summary of demographic projections.* Series P-25, No. 388. March 14, 1968. Washington, D.C.: U.S. Government Printing Office, 1968.

Burgess, E. W. The family in a changing society. In A. Etzioni & E. Etzioni (Eds.), *Social change: Sources, patterns, and consequences.* New York: Basic Books, 1964. Pp. 195-202.

Burgess. E. W., Locke, H. J., & Thomas, M. M. *The family.* (2nd ed.) New York: American Book, 1963.

Buss, A. H. *The psychology of aggression.* New York: Wiley, 1961.

Buss, A. H. Physical aggression in relation to different frustrations. *Journal of Abnormal and Social Psychology,* 1963, **67**, 1-7.

Busse, E. W. Geriatrics today: An overview. *American Journal of Psychiatry,* 1967, **123**(10), 1226-1233.

Butler, R. A. Incentive conditions which influence visual exploration. *Journal of Experimental Psychology,* 1954, **48**, 19-23.

Calhoun, J. B. Population density and social pathology. *Scientific American,* 1962, **206**(2), 139-150.

Campbell, J. P., & Dunnette, M. D. Effectiveness of T-group experiences in managerial training and development. *Psychological Bulletin,* 1968, **70**(2), 73-104.

Cannon, W. B. *Wisdom of the body.* N.Y.: Norton, 1939.

Cantril, H. *The "why" of man's experience.* New York: Macmillan, 1950.

Cantril, H. *The politics of despair.* New York: Basic Books, 1958.

Carothers, J. C. A study of mental derangement in Africans, and an attempt to explain its peculiarities, more especially in relation to the African attitude of life. *Journal of Mental Science,* 1947, **93**, 548-597.

Carothers, J. C. Culture, psychiatry, and the written word. *Psychiatry,* 1959, **22**, 307-320.

Carter, H., & Plateris, A. *Trends in divorce and family disruption. Health, Education, & Welfare Indicators.* Department of Health, Education, and Welfare, Office of Program Analysis, September 1963.

Cartwright, D., & Zander, A. *Group dynamics.* (3rd ed.) New York: Harper & Row, 1968.

Caspari, E. Genetic endowment and environment in the determination of human behavior: Biological viewpoint. *American Educational Research Journal,* 1968, **5**(1), 43-55.

Cassirer, E. *Essay on man.* New Haven, Conn.: Yale Univ. Press, 1944.

Cassirer, E. *Philosophy of symbolic forms.* New Haven, Conn.: Yale Univ. Press, Vol. I, 1953; Vol. II, 1955, Vol. III, 1957.

Cattell, R. B., & Scheier, I. H. *The meaning and measurement of neuroticism and anxiety.* New York: Ronald Press, 1961.

Catton, W. R., Jr., & Smirich, R. J. A comparison of mathematical models for the effect of residential propinquity on mate selection. *American Sociological Review,* 1964, **29**, 522-529.

Cavan, R. S. *The American family.* (3rd ed.) New York: Crowell, 1963.

Charen, S., & Perelman, L. Personality studies of marihuana addicts. *American Journal of Psychiatry,* 1946, **102**, 674-682.

Chess, S., Thomas, A., & Birch, H. G. *Your child is a person: A psychological approach to parenthood without guilt.* New York: Viking Press, 1965. Copyright © 1965 by Stella Chess, (M.D.), Alexander Thomas (M.D.), and Herbert G. Birch (M.D., Ph.D.). All rights reserved. Chart adapted by permission of The Viking Press, Inc.

Chilman, C. S. Dating, courtship, and engagement behavior of married, compared to single, undergraduates, with an analysis of early-marrying and late-marrying students. *Family Life Coordinator,* 1966, **15**(3), 112-118.

Chomsky, N. Language and the mind. *Psychology Today,* 1968, **1**(9), 48-51.

Chopra, R. N., & Chopra, G. S. The present position of hemp-drug addiction in India. *Indian Journal of Medical Research,* 1939, **31**, 1-119.

Christensen, H. T. Timing of first pregnancy as a factor in divorce: A cross-cultural analysis. *Eugenics Quarterly,* 1963, **10**(3), 119-130.

Clark, K. B. *Dark ghetto: Dilemmas of social power.* New York: Harper and Row, 1965. Excerpt from pp. 63-65 (hardbound) in DARK GHETTO by Kenneth B. Clark. Copyright © 1965 by Kenneth B. Clark. Reprinted by permission of the publishers, Harper & Row and Victor Gollancz Ltd.

Clark, K. B. Explosion in the ghetto. *Psychology Today,* 1967, **1**(5), 30-39, 62-64.

Clark, W. H. *Psychology of religion.* New York: Macmillan, 1958.

Clausen, J. A. Family structure, socialization, and personality. In L. W. Hoffman & M. L. Hoffman (Eds.), *Review of child development research.* Vol. 2. New York: Russell Sage Foundation, 1966. Pp. 1-54.

Close, K. Giving babies a healthy start in life. *Children,* 1965, **12**(5), 179-184.

Cohen, S. The cyclic psychedelics. *American Journal of Psychiatry,* 1968, **125**, 393-394.

Colby, K. M., & Enea, H. Heuristic methods for computer understanding of natural language in context-restricted on-line dialogues. *Mathematical Biosciences: An International Journal,* 1967, **1**, 1-25.

Colby, K. M., & Gilbert, J. P. Programming a computer model of neurosis. *Journal of Mathematical Psychology,* 1964, **1**, 405-417.

Coleman, J. C. *Abnormal Psychology and Modern Life.* (3rd ed.) Chicago: Scott, Foresman, 1964.

Collier, R. M. Outline of a theory of consciousness as a regulatory field: Preliminary statement. *Journal of Psychology,* 1955, **40**, 269-274.

Collier, R. M. Consciousness as a regulatory field: A theory of psychopathology. *Psychological Review,* 1956, **63**, 360-369.

Collier, R. M. Consciousness as a regulatory field: A theory of psychotherapy. *Journal of Abnormal and Social Psychology,* 1957, **55**, 275-282.

Collier, R. M. A holistic-organismic theory of consciousness. *J. indiv. Psychol.,* 1963, **19**, 17-26.

Collier, R. M. Selected implications from a dynamic regulatory theory of consciousness. *American Psychologist,* 1964, **19**(4), 265-269.

Collier, R. M. A biologically derived basic value as an initial context for behavioral science. *Journal of Humanistic Psychology,* 1968, **8**(1), 1-15.

Combs, A. W., & Snygg, D. *Individual behavior.* (Rev. ed.) New York: Harper, 1959.

Coombs, R. H. Value consensus and partner satisfaction among dating couples. *Journal of Marriage & the Family,* 1966, **28**(2), 166-173.

Commission on Narcotic Drugs. *Report of the Twentieth Session, November 29-December 21, 1965,* E/4140, E/CN.7/488, United Nations.

Conel, J. LeR. *The postnatal development of the human cerebral cortex. I. Cortex of the newborn.* Cambridge, Mass.: Harvard Univ. Press, 1939.

Conel, J. LeR. *The postnatal development of the human cerebral cortex. II. Cortex of the one-month infant.* Cambridge, Mass.: Harvard Univ. Press, 1941.

Conel, J. LeR. *The postnatal development of the human cerebral cortex. III. Cortex of the three-month infant.* Cambridge, Mass.: Harvard Univ. Press, 1947.

Cooper, R. M., & Zubek, J. P. Effects of enriched and restricted early environments on the learning ability of bright and dull rats. *Canadian Journal of Psychology,* 1958, **12,** 159-164.

Coopersmith, S. *The antecedents of self-esteem.* San Francisco: Freeman, 1967.

Cousins, N. What the founding fathers believed. *Saturday Review,* 1958, **41**(12), 15-17.

Crago, M., & Tharp, R. G. Psychopathology and marital role disturbance: A test of the Tharp-Otis descriptive hypothesis. *Journal of Consulting & Clinical Psychology,* 1968, **32**(3), 338-341.

Craig, R. H. Trait lists and creativity. *Psychologia,* 1966, **9**(2), 107-110.

Crocker, W. H. Personal communication to author, 1968.

Crompton, J. *Ways of the ant.* Boston: Houghton Mifflin, 1954.

Cuber, J. F., & Harroff, P. B. *The significant Americans: A study of sexual behavior among the affluent.* New York: Appleton-Century-Crofts, 1965.

Culliton, F. J. Inherited diseases: On the way out. *Science News,* 1967, **92,** 184-185.

Dame, N. G., Finck, G., Mayos, R., Reiner, B., & Smith, B. Conflict in marriage following premarital pregnancy. *American Journal of Orthopsychiatry,* 1966, **36,** 468-475.

Davids, A., & DeVault, S. Maternal anxiety during pregnancy and childbirth. *Psychosomatic Medicine,* 1962, **24,** 464-470.

Davids, A., DeVault, S., & Talmadge, M. Anxiety, pregnancy, and childbirth abnormalities. *Journal of Consulting Psychology,* 1961, **25,** 74-77.

Davids, A., Holden, R. H., & Gray, G. B. Maternal anxiety during pregnancy and adequacy of mother and child adjustment eight months following childbirth. *Child Development,* 1963, **34,** 993-1002.

Davis, C. M. Self-selection of diet by newly weaned infants. *American Journal of Diseases of Children,* 1928, **36,** 651-679.

Davis, D. C. Predicting tomorrow's children. *Today's Health,* 1968, **46**(1), 32-37.

Dean, D. G. Emotional maturity and marital adjustment. *Journal of Marriage & the Family,* 1966, **28,** 454-457.

Dell, P. C. Some basic mechanisms of the translation of bodily needs into behavior. In G. E. W. Wolstenholme & C. M. O'Conner (Eds.), *Symposium on the neurological basis of behavior.* Boston: Little, Brown, 1958.

Dement, W. Effects of dream deprivation. *Science,* 1960, **131,** 1705-1707.

Dement, W. Paper presented at meeting of American Academy of Psychoanalysis, New York, Dec. 7-9, 1963.

De Nike, L. D., & Tiber, N. Neurotic behavior. In P. London & D. Rosenhan (Eds.), *Foundations of abnormal psychology.* New York: Holt, Rinehart and Winston, 1968.

Dennis, W. *The Hopi child.* New York: Appleton-Century-Crofts, 1940.

Dennis, W. Spaulding's experiment on the flight of birds repeated with another species. *Journal of Comparative and Physiological Psychology,* 1941, **31,** 337-348.

Dennis, W. Causes of retardation among institutional children: Iran. *Journal of Genetic Psychology,* 1960, **96,** 47-59.

Department of Defense. *The armed forces officer.* Washington, D.C.: U.S. Gov. Printing Office, 1950.

Department of Health, Education, and Welfare. *Children's Bureau. Health of children of school age.* Washington, D.C.: U.S. Gov. Printing Office, 1965.

Department of Labor. More ex-coeds retaining jobs despite marriage and children. *New York Times,* Nov. 21, 1966.

deSola Pool, I., & Kessler, A. The Kaiser, the Tsar, and the computer: Information processing in a crisis. *American Behaviorial Scientist,* 1965, **8**(9), 31-38.

Dewey, J. *Democracy and education.* New York: Macmillan, 1930.

Dinello, F. A. Stages of treatment in the case of a diaper-wearing seventeen-year-old male. *American Journal of Psychiatry,* 1967, **124,** 94-96.

Dobbing, J. Growth of the brain. *Science Journal,* 1967, **3**(5), 81-86.

Douvan, E., & Adelson, J. *The adolescent experience.* New York: Wiley, 1966.

Dreyfus, E. A. The search for intimacy. *Adolescence,* 1967, **2**(5), 25-40.

Duffy, E. *Activation and behavior.* N. Y.: Wiley, 1962.

Duncan, O. D. The trend of occupational mobility in the United States. *American Sociological Review,* 1965, **30,** 491-498.

Durant, W., & Durant, A. *Rousseau and revolution.* New York: Simon & Schuster, 1967.

Duvall, E. M. *Family development.* (2nd ed.) Philadelphia: Lippincott, 1962.

Dworkin, E. S., & Efran, J. S. The angered: Their susceptibility to varieties of humor. *Journal of Personality & Social Psychology,* 1967, **6,** 233-236.

Dyer, W. G. Analyzing marital adjustment using role theory. *Marriage and Family Living,* 1962, **24,** 371-375.

Earl, H. G. 10,000 children battered and starved: Hundreds die. *Today's Health,* 1965, **43**(9), 24-31.

Ehrlich, D. A. Suicides rising. *Science News,* 1967, **92,** 229.

Eiduson, B. T. The two classes of information in psychiatry. *Archives of General Psychiatry,* 1968, **18,** 405-419.

Eiduson, S., & Geller, E. Biochemistry, genetics, and the nature-nurture problem. *American Journal of Psychiatry,* 1962, **119,** 342-350.

Einstein, A. *Out of my later years.* New York: Philosophical Library, 1950.

Einstein, A., & Infeld, L. *The evolution of physics.* New York: Simon & Schuster, 1938.

Eisenberg, L. A developmental approach to adolescence. *Children,* 1965, **12,** 131-135.

Ellis, A. Questionnaire versus interview methods in the study of human love relationships. II. Uncategorized responses. *American Sociological Review*, 1948, **13**, 61-65.

Ellis, A. Rational psychotherapy and individual psychology. *Journal of Individual Psychology*, 1957, **13**, 38-44.

Ellis, A. Rational psychotherapy. *Journal of General Psychology*, 1958, **59**, 35-49.

English, H. B., & English, A. C. *A comprehensive dictionary of psychological and psychoanalytic terms*. New York: Longman's, Green, 1958.

English, O., & Finch, S. M. *Introduction to psychiatry*. New York: Norton, 1954.

Ennis, P. H. Crime, victims, and the police. *Transaction*, 1967, **4**(7), 36-44.

Erickson, Milton H. Experimental demonstrations of the psychopathology of everyday life. *Psychoanalytic Quarterly*, 1939, **8**, 338-353. Reprinted by permission of the author and publisher.

Eriksen, C. W. Psychological defenses and "ego strength" in the recall of completed and incompleted tasks. *Journal of Abnormal and Social Psychology*, 1954, **49**, 45-50.

Eriksen, C. W., & Browne, T. An experimental and theoretical analysis of perceptual defense. *Journal of Abnormal and Social Psychology*, 1956, **52**, 224-230.

Erikson, E. H. *Childhood and society*. (2nd ed.) New York: Norton, 1963.

Erikson, E. H. Eight stages of man. *International Journal of Psychiatry*, 1966, **2**, 281-297.

Eysenck, H. J. (Ed.) *Behaviour therapy and the neuroses*. London: Pergamon Press, 1960.

Eysenck, H. J. New ways in psychotherapy. *Psychology Today*, 1967, **1**(2), 39-47.

Farberow, N. R., & Shneidman, E. S. *The cry for help*. New York: McGraw-Hill, 1961.

Farnsworth, D. L. Motivation for learning: Community responsibility. In E. P. Torrance & R. D. Strom (Eds.), *Mental health and achievement*. New York: Wiley, 1966.

Faulkner, W. *The Faulkner reader*. New York: The Modern Library, 1961.

Federal Bureau of Investigation. *Uniform crime reports, 1967*. Washington, D.C.: U.S. Government Printing Office, U.S. Department of Justice, 1968.

Feibleman, J. K. Theory of integrative levels. *British Journal for the Philosophy of Science*, 1954, **5**, 59-66.

Feldman, H., & Rogoff, M. Medical briefs. *Today's Health*, 1969, **47**(1), 17.

Festinger, L. Cognitive dissonance. *Scientific American*, 1962, **207**, 93-107.

Fisher, S., Boyd, I., Walker, D., & Sheer, D. Parents of schizophrenics, neurotics, and normals. *Archives of General Psychiatry*, 1959; **1**, 149-166.

Flavell, J. H. *The developmental psychology of Jean Piaget*. Princeton, N.J.: Van Nostrand, 1963.

Fleck, S. Family dynamics and origin of schizophrenia. *Psychosomatic Medicine*, 1960, **22**, 333-344.

Fleck, S., Lidz, T., & Cornelison, A. R. Comparison of parent-child relationships of male and female schizophrenic patients. *Archives of General Psychiatry*, 1963, **8**, 1-7.

Forgays, D. G. The importance of experience at specific times in the development of an organism. Paper presented at the meeting of the Eastern Psychological Association, April 1962.

Forgays, D. G., & Forgays, J. The nature of the effect of free-environmental experience in the rat. *Journal of Comparative and Physiological Psychology*, 1952, **45**, 322-328.

Frankl, V. *The doctor and the soul*. New York: Knopf, 1955.

Frankl, V. *Man's search for meaning: An introduction to logotherapy*. Boston: Beacon, 1959, 1962.

Freedman, D. G., King, J. A., & Elliot, O. Critical periods in the social development of dogs. *Science*, 1961, **133**, 1016-1017.

Freedman, M. B. Personality growth in the college years. *College Board Review*, Spring 1965, **56**, 25-32.

French, R. P., Jr., & Raven, B. The bases of social power. In D. Cartwright & A. Zander (Eds.), *Group dynamics*. (3rd ed.) New York: Harper & Row, 1968. Pp. 259-269.

Freud, S. *Civilization and its discontents*. London: Hogarth, 1930. (Republished: Westport, Conn.: Associated Booksellers, 1955.)

Freud, S. *Psycopathology of everyday life*. (2nd ed.) London: Ernest Benn, Ltd., 1954.

Fromm, E. *The sane society*. New York: Rinehart, 1955.

Fromm, E. *The art of loving*. New York: Harper & Row, 1956.

Fromm-Reichmann, F. Loneliness. *Psychiatry*, 1959, **22**, 1-15.

Frumkin, R. M. Communal interests crucial to marital adjustment. *Ohio Journal of Science*, 1954, **54**, 107-110.

Furth, H. G. Piaget's theory of knowledge: The nature of representation and interiorization. *Psychological Review*, 1968, **75**(2), 143-154.

Gagné, R. M. Contributions of learning to human development. *Psych. Rev.*, 1968, **74**(3), 177-191.

Gandhi, M. *The story of my experiments with truth*. Washington, D.C.: Public Affairs Press, 1948.

Gardner, J. W. The secretary of health, education, and welfare. *American Psychologist*, 1965, **20**, 811-814.

Garn, S. M. Body size and its implications. In L. W. Hoffman & M. L. Hoffman (Eds.), *Review of Child Development Research*. Vol. 2. New York: Russell Sage Foundation, 1966, Pp. 529-561.

Gastaut, H. Conditioned reflexes and behavior. In G. E. W. Wolstenholme & C. M. O'Conner (Eds.), *Symposium on the neurological basis of behavior*. Boston: Little, Brown, 1958.

Gesell, A. *The first five years of life: A guide to the study of the preschool child*. New York: Harper, 1940.

Gesell, A., & Amatruda, C. *The embryology of behavior*. New York: Harper, 1945.

Gesell, A., & Ilg, F. L. *The child from five to ten*. New York: Harper, 1946.

Gesell, A., & Thompson, H. Twins *T* and *C* from infancy to adolescence: A biogenetic study of individual differences by the method of co-twin control. *Genetic Psychology Monographs,* 1941, **24**, 2-122.

Gillin, J., & Nicholson, G. The security functions of cultural systems. *Social Forces,* 1951, **30**, 179-184.

Ginzberg, E. *The development of human resources.* New York: McGraw-Hill, 1966.

Ginzberg, E., Ginsberg, S. W., Axelrad, S., & Herma, J. L. *Occupational choice: An approach to a general theory.* New York: Columbia Univ. Press, 1951.

Glasser, W. *Reality therapy: A new approach to psychiatry.* New York: Harper & Row, 1965.

Glasser, W. Reality therapy—a new approach. In O. H. Mowrer (Ed.), *Morality and mental health.* New York: Rand McNally, 1967. Pp. 126-134.

Glickman, S. E., & Schiff, B. B. A biological theory of reinforcement. *Psychol. Rev.,* 1967, **74**(2), 82-109.

Glidewell, J. C., & Swallow, C. S. *The prevalence of maladjustment in elementary schools.* A report prepared for the Joint Commission on the Mental Health of Children. Chicago: Univ. of Chicago Press, 1968.

Glixman, A. F. Recall of completed and incompleted activities under varying degrees of stress. *Journal of Experimental Psychology,* 1949, **39**, 281-295.

Gloor, P. The amygdala. In J. Field (Ed.), *Handbook of physiology. Sect. I: neurophysiology.* Vol. II. Washington, D.C.: Amer. Physiol. Society, 1960.

Glucksberg, S. *Symbolic processes.* Dubuque, Iowa: Wm. C. Brown, 1966.

Goertzel, V., & Goertzel, M. *Cradles of eminence.* Boston: Little, Brown, 1962.

Goldberg, P. Are women prejudiced against women? *Trans-action,* 1968, **5**(5), 28-30.

Goode, W. J. *After divorce.* New York: Free Press, 1956.

Goode, W. J. A theory of role strain. *American Sociological Review,* 1960, **25**, 483.

Goode, W. J. Family disorganization. In R. K. Merton & R. A. Nisbet (Eds.), *Contemporary social problems.* New York: Harcourt, Brace & World, 1961. Pp. 390-458.

Goode, W. J. *The family.* Englewood Cliffs, N.J.: Prentice-Hall, 1964.

Goodenough, F. Expression of the emotions in a blind-deaf child. *Journal of Abnormal and Social Psychology,* 1932, **27**, 328-383.

Gray, P. H. Theory and evidence of imprinting in human infants. *Journal of Psychology,* 1958, **46**, 155-166.

Gray, S., & Klaus, R. A. An experimental preschool program for culturally deprived children. *Child Development,* 1965, **36**, 887-898.

Greenberg, P. Competition in children: An experimental study. *Amer. J. Psychol.,* 1932, **44**, 221-248.

Greenson, R. R. Sexual roles being reversed, says psychiatrist. *Today's Health,* 1967, **45**(4), 85.

Griffith, J. A study of illicit amphetamine drug traffic in Oklahoma City. *American Journal of Psychiatry,* 1966, **123**(5), 560-569.

Grinker, R. R. (Ed.) *Toward a unified theory of human behavior.* New York: Basic Books, 1956.

Grinker, R. R. *The phenomena of depressions.* New York: Harper, 1961.

Grinker, R. R., & Spiegel, J. P. *Men under stress.* Philadelphia: Blakiston, 1945. (a)

Grinker, R. R., & Spiegel, J. P. *War neuroses.* Philadelphia: Blakiston, 1945. (b)

Gross, N., et al. *Explorations in role analysis.* New York: Wiley, 1958.

Guilford, J. P. *The nature of human intelligence.* New York: McGraw-Hill, 1967.

Guilford, J. P. *A revised structure of intellect.* Report of Psychological Laboratory, No. 19. Los Angeles: Univ. of Southern California, 1957.

Guyton, A. C. *Textbook of medical physiology.* Philadelphia: Saunders, 1961.

Hall, C. S., & Lindzey, G. *Theories of personality.* New York: Wiley, 1957.

Hall, E. J., Mouton, J. S., & Blake, R. R. Group problem solving effectiveness under conditions of pooling vs. interaction. *J. soc. Psychol.,* 1963, **59**, 147-157.

Hall, G. S. *Adolescence.* New York: Appleton, 1904.

Hardy, K. R. An appetitional theory of sexual motivation. *Psychological Review,* 1964, **71**, 1-18.

Harlow, H. F. Motivation in monkeys—and men. In F. L. Ruch, *Psychology and life.* (6th ed.) Glenview, Ill.: Scott, Foresman, 1963. Pp. 589-594.

Harlow, H. F., & Harlow, M. Learning to love. *American Scientist,* 1966, **54**, 244-272.

Harlow, H. F., & Harlow, M. The young monkeys. *Psychology Today,* 1967, **1**(5), 40-47.

Harlow, H. F., & Zimmermann, R. R. Affectional responses in the infant monkey. *Science,* 1959, **130**, 421-432.

Harms, E. "Rock-bottom" problems. *Adolescence,* 1967, **2**, 281-284.

Harmsworth, H. C., & Minnis, M. S. Nonstatutory causes of divorce: The lawyer's point of view. *Marriage and Family Living,* 1955, **17**, 316-321.

Hartmann, E. L. The D-state: A review and discussion of studies on the physiologic state concomitant with dreaming. *International Journal of Psychiatry,* 1966, **2**(1), 11-47.

Haskins, C. P. Report of the president, 1966-1967. Washington, D.C.: Carnegie Institute of Washington, 1968.

Havighurst, R. J. *Developmental tasks and education.* New York: Longmans, Green, 1952.

Havighurst, R. J., & Neugarten, B. L. *Society and education.* Boston: Allyn and Bacon, 1962.

Hayakawa, S. I. Communicating with one's children. In R. E. Farson (Ed.), *Science and human affairs.* Palo Alto, California: Science & Behavior Books, 1965.

Haymuy, T. P. The role of the cerebral cortex in the learning of an instrumental conditional response. In A. Fessard, R. W. Gerard, & J. Konorski (Eds.), *Brain mechanisms and learning.* Springfield, Ill.: Thomas, 1961.

Haythorn, W. W., & Altman, I. Together in isolation. *Trans-action,* 1967, **4**(3), 18-22.

Heath, R. G., Krupp, I. M., Byers, L. W., & Liljekvist,

J. I. Schizophrenia as an immunologic disorder III. Effects of antimonkey and antihuman brain antibody on brain function. *Archives of General Psychiatry,* 1967, **16**(1), 24-33.

Heath, R. G., Martens, S., Leach, B. E., Cohen, M., & Angel, C. Behavioral changes in nonpsychotic volunteers following the administration of taraxein, the substance obtained from serum of schizophrenic patients. *American Journal of Psychiatry,* 1958, **114**, 917-920.

Hebb, D. O. *The organization of behavior.* New York: Wiley, 1949.

Heer, D. M. Negro-white marriage in the United States. *New Society,* August 26, 1965, **6**, 7-9.

Heider, G. M. What makes a good parent. *Children,* 1960, **7**(2), 207-212.

Heilbrun, A. B., Jr., Orr, H. K., & Harrell, S. N. Patterns of parental childrearing and subsequent vulnerability to cognitive disturbance. *Journal of Consulting Psychology,* 1966, **30**(1), 51-59.

Heinstein, M. I. Expressed attitudes and feelings of pregnant women and their relation to physical complications of pregnancy. *Merrill-Palmer Quarterly,* 1967, **13**, 217-236.

Helson, H. Some problems in motivation. In D. Levine (Ed.), *Nebraska symposium on motivation.* Lincoln, Nebr.: Univ. of Nebr. Press, 1966. Pp. 137-182.

Hemingway, E. *The short stories of Ernest Hemingway.* New York: Scribner's, 1955.

Henry, J. Culture, personality, and evolution. *American Anthropologist,* 1959, **61**, 221-222.

Henry, J. *Culture against man.* New York: Random House, 1963.

Hernandez-Peon, R., & Brust-Carmona, H. The functional role of subcortical structures in habituation and conditioning. In A. Fessard, R. W. Gerard, & J. Konorski (Eds.), *Brain mechanisms and learning.* Springfield, Ill.: Thomas, 1961.

Heron, W., Doane, B. K., & Scott, T. H. Visual disturbances after prolonged perceptual isolation. *Canadian Journal of Psychology,* 1956, **10**, 13-18.

Herrick, D. J. *The evolution of human nature.* Austin: Univ. of Texas Press, 1956.

Herzberg, F. Motivation, morale, and money. *Psychology Today,* 1968, **1**(10), 42-45.

Hess, E. H. Imprinting. *Science,* 1959, **130**, 133-141.

Hess, R. D., & Shipman, V. C. Early experience and the socialization of cognitive modes in children. *Child Development,* 1965, **36**, 869-886. Published by the University of Chicago Press for The Society for Research in Child Development, Inc., © by The Society. Excerpt reprinted by permission.

Hetherington, E. M., & Frankie, G. Effects of parental dominance, warmth, and conflict on imitation in children. *Journal of Personality and Social Psychology,* 1967, **6**(2), 119-125.

Hinde, R. A. Sensitive periods and the development of behavior. In S. A. Barnett (Ed.), *Lessons from animal behavior for the clinician.* London: National Spastics Society Study Group and Heinemann Medical Books, Ltd., 1962.

Hoffman, M. L. Child rearing practices and moral development: Generalizations from empirical research. *Child Development,* 1963, **34**(2), 295-318.

Holmes, D. S. Dimensions of projection. *Psychological Bulletin,* 1968, **69**, 248-268.

Hooker, E. The homosexual community. In *Proceedings of the XIV international congress of applied psychology.* Vol. II: *Personality research.* Copenhagen: Munksgaard, 1962.

Hoyt, D. P. *The relationship between college grades and adult achievement: A review of the literature.* Iowa City, Iowa: American College Testing Program, 1965.

Huffman, A. V. Sex deviation in a prison community. *Journal of Social Therapy,* 1960, **6**, 170-181.

Hunt, J. McV. *Intelligence and experience.* New York: Ronald Press, 1961.

Hunt, J. McV. How children develop intellectually. *Children,* 1964, **11**(5), 83-91.

Hunt, J. McV. Traditional personality theory in the light of recent evidence. *American Scientist,* 1965, **53**, 80-96.

Hurley, G. *A replication of the Hill and McGinnis studies of characteristics desired in a mate.* Unpublished manuscript, California State Polytechnic College, 1963.

Hurley, J. R. Parental acceptance-rejection and children's intelligence. *Merrill-Palmer Quarterly,* 1965, **11**(1), 19-32.

Hurlock, E. B. *Developmental psychology.* (3rd ed.) New York: McGraw-Hill, 1968.

Huxley, A. *Brave new world.* New York: Harper, 1932. (Republished: New York, Bantam, 1952.)

Huxley, A. Human potentialities. In R. E. Farson (Ed.), *Science and human affairs.* Palo Alto, California: Science & Behavior Books, 1965.

Huxley, J. *Evolution in action.* New York: Harper, 1953, and London: Chatto & Windus Ltd.

Hymovitch, B. The effects of experimental variations on problem solving in the rat. *Journal of Comparative and Physiological Psychology,* 1952, **45**, 313-321.

Ilg, F. L., & Ames, L. B. *Child behavior.* New York: Harper, 1955.

Irwin, T. Attacking alcoholism as a disease. *Today's Health,* 1968, **46**(9), 20-23, 72-74.

Irwin, T. How to be a good worrier. *Today's Health,* 1968, **46**(11), 28-29, 87-88.

Isaacs, W., Thomas, J., & Goldiamond, I. Application of operant conditioning to reinstate verbal behavior in psychotics. *Journal of Speech and Hearing Disorders,* 1960, **25**, 8-12.

Isbell, H., Gorodetzky, C. W., Jasinski, D., Claussen, U., Spulak, F., & Korte, F. Effects of $(-)\triangle^9$-trans-tetrahydrocannabinol in man. *Psychopharmacologia,* 1967, **11**, 184-188.

Jackson, P. W., & Messick, S. The person, the product, and the response: Conceptual problems in the assessment of creativity. *Journal of Personality,* 1965, **33**(3), 309-329.

Jaco, E. G. *The social epidemiology of mental disorders.* New York: Russell Sage Foundation, 1960.

Jacobson, B., & Kales, A. Deep sleep needed for best health. *University of California Bulletin,* 1967, **15**(37), 168.

Jacobson, P. H. *American marriage and divorce.* New York: Rinehart, 1959.

Jahoda, M. *Current concepts of positive mental health.* Joint Commission on Mental Illness and Health. Monograph Series No. 1. New York: Basic Books, 1958.

James, W. *The principles of psychology.* New York: Holt, 1890.

Janis, I. When fear is healthy. *Psychology Today,* 1968, **1**(11), 46-49, 60-61.

Janowitz, M. American democracy and military service. *Trans-action,* 1967, **4**(4), 5-11, 57-59.

Jarvik, M. E. The psychopharmacological revolution. *Psychology Today,* 1967, **1**(1), 51-59.

Jenkins, R. L. Psychiatric syndromes in children and their relation to family background. *American Journal of Orthopsychiatry,* 1966, **36,** 450-457.

Jenkins, R. L. The varieties of children's behavioral problems and family dynamics. *American Journal of Psychiatry,* 1968, **124**(10), 1440-1445.

Jersild, A. T. Emotional development. In L. Carmichael (Ed.), *Manual of child psychology.* New York: Wiley, 1946.

Johnstone, E. Women in economic life: Rights and opportunities. *Annals of the American Academy of Political and Social Science,* 1968, **375,** 102-114.

Joint Commission on the Mental Health of Children. Statement of the American Orthopsychiatric Association on the work of the Joint Commission on the mental health of children. *American Journal of Orthopsychiatry,* 1968, **38,** 402-409.

Jones, A., & McGill, D. The homeostatic character of information drive in humans. *Journal of Experimental Research in Personality,* 1967, **2**(1), 25-31.

Jones, M. C. A laboratory study of fear: The case of Peter. *Pedagogical Seminary,* 1924, **31,** 308-315.

Jones, M. C. Personality correlates and antecedents of drinking patterns in adult males. *Journal of Consulting & Clinical Psychology,* 1968, **32**(1), 2-12.

Jones, M. C., & Mussen, P. H. Self-conceptions, motivation, and interpersonal attitudes of early- and late-maturing girls. *Child Development,* 1958, **29,** 491-501.

Josselyn, I. M. Sources of sexual identity. *Child & Family,* 1967, **6**(2), 38-45.

Jourard, S. M. *Personal adjustment.* (2nd ed.) New York: Macmillan, 1963.

Jouvet, M. The sleeping brain. *Science Journal,* 1967, **3**(5), 105-111.

Jung, R., & Hassler, R. The extrapyramidal motor system. In J. Field (Ed.), *Handbook of physiology. Sect. I: neurophysiology.* Vol. II. Washington, D.C.: American Physiological Society, 1960.

Kadushin, A. Reversibility of trauma: A follow-up study of children adopted when older. *Social Work,* 1967, **12**(4), 22-33.

Kagan, J. Personality development. In P. London (Ed.), *Foundations of abnormal psychology.* New York:

Holt, Rinehart. and Winston, 1968. Pp. 117-173.

Kagan, J., & Moss, H. A. *Birth to maturity: The Fels study of psychological development.* New York: Wiley, 1962.

Kalachek, E. D. Automation and full employment. *Trans-action,* 1967, **4**(4), 24-29.

Kallmann, F. J. *Heredity in health and mental disorder.* New York: Norton, 1953.

Kallmann, F. J. The use of genetics in psychiatry. *Journal of Mental Science,* 1958, **104,** 542-549.

Kaplan, A. *The conduct of inquiry: Methodology for behavioral science.* San Francisco: Chandler, 1964.

Katz, M. K., Waskow, I. E., & Olsson, J. Characterizing the psychological state produced by LSD. *Journal of Abnormal Psychology,* 1968, **7**(3), 1-14.

Kaufman, I., Frank, T., Heims, L., Herrick, J., Reiser, D., & Willer, L. Treatment implications of a new classification of parents of schizophrenic children. *American Journal of Psychiatry,* 1960, **116,** 920-924.

Keller, S. The social world of the urban slum child: Some early findings. *American Journal of Orthopsychiatry,* 1963, **33,** 823-831.

Kelley, H. H. Attribution theory in social psychology. In D. Levine (Ed.), *Nebraska symposium on motivation—1967.* Lincoln, Nebr.: Univ. of Nebr. Press, 1967. Pp. 192-240.

Kelley, H. H. Interpersonal accommodation. *American Psychologist,* 1968, **23,** 399-410.

Kellogg, W. N., & Kellogg, L. A. *The ape and the child.* New York: McGraw-Hill, 1933.

Keniston, K. College students and children in developmental institutions. *Children,* 1967, **14**(1), 2-7.

Kephart, W. M. *The family, society, and the individual.* (2nd ed.) Boston: Houghton Mifflin, 1966.

Kephart, W. M. Some correlates of romantic love. *Journal of Marriage & the Family,* 1967, **29,** 470-474.

Keys, A., Brozek, J., Henschel, A., Mickelsen, O., & Taylor, H. L. *The biology of human starvation.* Minneapolis: Univ. of Minnesota Press, 1950. © Copyright 1950 University of Minnesota. Graph redrawn by permission.

Kiesler, C. A. Conformity and commitment. *Trans-action,* 1967, **4**(7), 32-35.

Kincaid, J. F. *U.S. News & World Report,* April 8, 1968.

Kind, H. The psychogenesis of schizophrenia: A review of the literature. *International Journal of Psychiatry,* 1967, **3**(5), 383-417.

King, J. A. Parameters relevant to determining the effects of early experience on the adult behavior of animals. *Psychological Bulletin,* 1958, **55,** 46-58.

Kinsey, A. C., Pomeroy, W. B., & Martin, C. E. *Sexual behavior in the human male.* Philadelphia: Saunders, 1948.

Kinsey, A. C., Pomeroy, W. B., & Martin, C. E. *Sexual behavior in the human female.* Philadelphia: Saunders, 1953.

Kirkpatrick, C. *The family as process and institution.* (2nd ed.) New York: Ronald Press, 1963.

Kleitman, N., & Engelmann, T. G. Sleep characteristics of infants. *J. appl. Physiol.,* 1953, **6,** 266-282.

Kluckhohn, C. Values and value-orientations in the theory of action. In T. Parsons & E. A. Shils (Eds.), *Toward a general theory of action.* Cambridge, Mass.: Harvard Univ. Press, 1954.

Kluckhohn, F. R., & Strodtbeck, F. L. *Variations in value orientation.* Evanston, Ill.: Row Peterson, 1961.

Knupfer, G., Clark, W., & Room, R. The mental health of the unmarried. *American Journal of Psychiatry,* 1966, 122(8), 841-851.

Knutson, A. L. *The individual, society, and health behavior.* New York: Russell Sage Foundation, 1965.

Kohlberg, L. The development of children's orientations toward a moral order: I. Sequence in the development of moral thought. *Vita Humana,* 1963, **6,** 11-33.

Kohlberg, L. Development of moral character and moral ideology. In M. L. Hoffman & L. W. Hoffman (Eds.), *Review of Child Development Research.* Vol. 1. New York: Russell Sage Foundation, 1964. Pp. 383-432. Chart adapted and reprinted by permission of Russell Sage Foundation.

Komarovsky, M. *Blue-collar marriage.* New York: Random House, 1964.

Korchin, S. J., & Ruff, G. E. Personality characteristics of the Mercury astronauts. In G. H. Grosser, H. Wechsler, & M. Greenblatt (Eds.), *The threat of impending disaster: Contributions to the psychology of stress.* Cambridge, Mass.: M.I.T. Press, 1964. Pp. 197-207.

Korzybski, A. *Science and sanity.* (3rd ed.) Lakeville, Conn.: International Non-Aristotelian Library Publishing Co., 1948.

Krauss, I. Sources of educational aspirations among working-class youth. *American Sociological Review,* 1964, **29,** 867-879.

Krech, D. Basic intelligence offset. *Science News,* 1967, **91,** 549.

Krechevsky, I. Brain mechanisms and variability; I. Variability within a means-end-readiness. *Journal of Comparative Psychology,* 1937, **23,** 121-138.

Kringlen, E. Nurture, not nature in schizophrenia. *Science News,* 1967, **91,** 328.

Kubie, L. S. The utilization of preconscious functions in education. In E. M. Bower & W. G. Hollister (Eds.), *Behavioral science frontiers in education.* New York: Wiley, 1967, Pp. 89-109.

Kurland, M. Romantic love and economic considerations: A cultural comparison. *Journal of Educational Sociology,* October 1953, **27,** 72-79.

Lacey, J. I. Somatic response patterning and stress: Some revisions of activation theory. In M. H. Appley & R. Trumbull (Eds.), *Psychological Stress.* New York: Appleton-Century-Crofts, 1967. Pp. 14-37.

Lachman, S. J. A behavioristic rationale for the development of psychosomatic phenomena. *Journal of Psychology,* 1963, **56,** 239-248.

Laing, R. D. *The politics of experience.* New York: Pantheon, 1967.

Landis, J. T. The trauma of children when parents divorce. *Marriage & Family Living,* 1960, **22**(2), 7-13.

Landis, J. T., Poffenberger, T., & Poffenberger, S. The effects of first pregnancy upon the sexual adjustment of 212 couples. *American Sociological Review,* 1950, **15,** 766-772.

Landis, P. H. *Making the most of marriage.* (3rd ed.) New York: Appleton-Century-Crofts, 1965.

Langdon, G., & Stout, I. W. *These well-adjusted children.* New York: John Day, 1951.

Langer, S. *Philosophy in a new key.* Baltimore: Penguin Books, 1948.

Langer, S. K. *Philosophy in a new key.* (2nd ed.) Cambridge, Mass.: Harvard Univ. Press, 1951.

Langner, T. S., & Michael, S. T. *Life stress and mental health.* Vol. II. *The Midtown Manhattan study.* New York: Free Press, 1963.

Lazarus, R. S. *Psychological stress and the coping process.* New York: McGraw-Hill, 1966.

Lee, D. Culture and the experience of value. In A. H. Maslow (Ed.), *New knowledge in human values.* New York: Harper, 1959.

Leeper, R. Current trends in theories of personality. In M. Jones (Ed.), *Current trends in psychological theory.* Pittsburgh: Univ. Pittsburgh Press, 1951.

Leeper, R. W. Some needed developments in the motivational theory of emotions. In D. Levine (Ed.), *Nebraska symposium on motivation.* Lincoln, Nebr.: Univ. of Nebr. Press, 1965.

Lehman, H. C. Chronological age vs. proficiency in physical skills. *American Journal of Psychology,* 1951, **64,** 161-187.

Lemere, F. The danger of amphetamine dependency. *American Journal of Psychiatry,* 1966, **123,** 569-572.

Lemert, E. M. Paranoia and the dynamics of exclusion. *Sociometry,* 1962, **25**(1), 2-20.

Lemkau, P. V. The influence of handicapping conditions on child development. *Children,* 1961, **8**(2), 43-47.

Leonard, G. B. *Education and ecstasy.* New York: Delacorte Press, 1968.

Levine, S. The effects of infantile experience on adult behavior. In A. J. Bachrach (Ed.), *Experimental foundations of clinical psychology.* New York: Basic Books, 1962.

Levinger, G. Sources of marital dissatisfaction among applicants for divorce. *American Journal of Orthopsychiatry,* 1966, **36,** 803-807.

Levinger, G., & Senn, D. J. Disclosure of feelings in marriage. *Merrill-Palmer Quarterly,* 1967, **13,** 237-249.

Levitt, E. E. *The psychology of anxiety.* Indianapolis, Ind.: Bobbs-Merrill, 1967.

Levy, D. M. *Maternal overprotection.* New York: Columbia Univ. Press, 1943.

Lewin, K., Lippitt, R., & White, R. K. Patterns of aggressive behavior in experimentally created "social climates." *Journal of Social Psychology,* 1939, **10,** 271-299.

Lidz, T., Cornelison, A. R., Terry, D., & Fleck, S. Irrationality as a family tradition. *Archives of Neurology and Psychiatry,* 1958, **79,** 305-316.

Lidz, T., Fleck, S., Alanen, Y. O., & Cornelison, A. R.

Schizophrenic patients and their siblings. *Psychiatry,* 1963, **26**, 1-18.

Lindsley, D. B. Attention, consciousness, sleep, and wakefulness. In J. Field (Ed.), *Handbook of physiology, Sect. I: neurophysiology.* Vol. III. Washington, D.C.: American Physiological Society, 1960.

Linton, R. *The study of man.* New York: Appleton-Century, 1936.

Lipton, E. L., Steinschneider, A., & Richmond, J. B. Psychophysiological disorders in children. In L. W. Hoffman & M. L. Hoffman (Eds.), *Review of Child Development Research.* Vol. 2. New York: Russell Sage Foundation, 1966. Pp. 169-220.

Locke, H. J. *Predicting adjustment in marriage: A comparison of a divorced and a happily married group.* New York: Holt, 1951.

Lorr, M., Daston, P., & Smith, I. R. An analysis of mood states. *Educational & Psychological Measurement,* 1967, **27**(1), 89-96.

Loughary, J. W. Can teachers survive the educational revolution? *Phi Delta Kappan,* 1967, **48**, 204-207.

Lu, Y. C. Contradictory parental expectations in schizophrenia. *Archives of General Psychiatry,* 1962, **6**, 219-234.

Lynn, D. B. Sex differences in masculine and feminine identification. *Psychological Review,* 1959, **66**, 126-135.

MacKinnon, D. W. Assessing creative persons. *Journal of Creative Behavior,* 1967, **1**(3), 291-304.

MacKinnon, D.W. The nature and nurture of creative talent. *American Psychologist,* 1962, **17**(7), 484-495.

Maddi, S. R. The existential neurosis. *Journal of Abnormal Psychology,* 1967, **72**(4), 311-325.

Maher, B. A. Personality, problem-solving and the Einstellung-effect. *Journal of Abnormal and Social Psychology,* 1957, **54**, 70-74.

Maier, N. R. F. *Frustration.* New York: McGraw-Hill, 1949.

Maier, N. R. F., & Schneirla, T. C. Mechanisms in conditioning. *Psychological Review,* 1942, **49**, 117-134.

Malmo, R. B. Activation: A neurophysiological dimension. *Psychological Review,* 1959, **66**, 367-386.

Maltz, M. *Psycho-cybernetics.* Hollywood, Calif.: Wilshire Book Co., 1960.

Marland, S. P., Jr. Ferment in the schools. *Children,* 1965, **12**, 62-68.

Martin, R. A. The inviolate, but invalid, employment predictors. *Personnel Journal,* 1968, **47**(1), 20-22.

Martineau, P. *Motivation in advertising: Motives that make people buy.* New York: McGraw-Hill, 1957.

Maslow, A. H. *Motivation and personality.* New York: Harper, 1954.

Maslow, A. H. Personality problems and personality growth. In C. E. Moustakas (Ed.), *The self.* New York: Harper, 1956.

Maslow, A. H. Self-actualizing people: A study of psychological health. In W. Wolff (Ed.), *Values and personality.* New York: Grune & Stratton, 1950.

Maslow, A. H. The creative attitude. *The Structurist,* 1963, **3**, 4-10.

Masters, W. H., & Johnson, V. E. *Human sexual response.* Boston: Little, Brown, 1966.

Maudry, M., & Nekula, M. Social relations between children of the same age during the first two years of life. *Journal of Genetic Psychology,* 1939, **54**, 193-215.

May, R. The relation between psychotherapy and religion. In J. E. Fairchild (Ed.), *Personal problems and psychological frontiers.* New York: Sheridan House, 1957.

May, R. The daemonic: Love and death. *Psychology Today,* 1968, **1**(9), 16-25.

Mayor's Committee on Marihuana. *The marihuana problem in the city of New York.* Lancaster, Pa.: Jacques Cattell Press, 1944.

McCann, R. Inconsistency. From *Complete Cheerful Cherub* by Rebecca McCann, © 1960 by Crown Publishers, Inc. Used by permission.

McClearn, G. E. Behavioral genetics: An overview. *Merrill-Palmer Quarterly,* 1968, **14**(1), 9-24.

McClelland, D. C. *The achieving society.* Princeton, N.J.: Van Nostrand, 1961.

McClelland, D. C. Toward a theory of motive acquisition. *American Psychologist,* 1965, **20**, 321-333.

McCord, W., & McCord, J. A longitudinal study of the personality of alcoholics. In D. J. Pittman & C. R. Snyder (Eds.), *Society, culture, and drinking patterns.* New York: Wiley, 1962.

McCord, W., McCord, J., & Verdon, P. Familial and behavioral correlates of dependency in male children. *Child Development,* 1962, **33**, 313-326.

McDavid, J. W., & Harari, H. *Social psychology.* New York: Harper & Row, 1968.

McDonald, R. L., Gynther, M., & Christakor, A. Relations between maternal anxiety and obstetric complications. *Psychosomatic Medicine,* 1963, **25**, 357-363.

McGinnis, R. Campus values in mate selection: A repeat study. *Social Forces,* 1958, **36**, 368-373.

McGlothin, W. H., & West, L. J. The marihuana problem: An overview. *American Journal of Psychiatry,* 1968, **125**, 370-378.

McGraw, M. B. *Growth: A study of Johnny and Jimmy.* New York: Appleton-Century, 1935.

McGraw, M. B. *The neuro-muscular maturation of the human infant.* N.Y.: Columbia Univ. Press, 1943.

McGraw, M. B. In L. C. Carmichael (Ed.), *Manual of child psychology.* N.Y.: Wiley, 1946. Pp. 332-369.

Mead, M. *From the south seas: Studies of adolescence and sex in primitive societies.* N.Y.: Morrow, 1939.

Mead, M. *Male and female.* New York: Morrow, 1949.

Mead, M. The concept of culture and the psychosomatic approach. In A. Weider (Ed.), *Contributions toward medical psychology.* Vol. 1. New York: Ronald Press, 1953.

Mechanic, D. *Students under stress.* New York: Free Press, 1962. Excerpts reprinted by permission.

Medow, H., & Zander, A. Aspirations for the group chosen by central and peripheral members. *Journal of Personality and Social Psychology,* 1965, **1**, 224-228.

Melzack, R., & Scott, T. H. The effects of early experience on the response to pain. *Journal of Comparative and Physiological Psychology*, 1957, **50**, 155-161.

Menninger, K. A. *The human mind*. (3rd rev. ed.) New York: Alfred A. Knopf, Inc., 1945. Illustration adapted by permission of the publisher, Alfred A. Knopf, Inc. Copyright 1930, 1937, 1945 by Karl A. Menninger.

Menninger, W. C. *Psychiatry in a troubled world: Yesterday's war and today's challenge*. New York: Macmillan, 1948.

Merrill, F. E. *Courtship and marriage*. New York: Holt-Dryden, 1959.

Michael, D. N. *The next generation: The prospects ahead for the youth of today and tomorrow*. New York: Random House, 1965.

Miller, D. R., & Swanson, G. E. *The changing American parent*. New York: Wiley, 1958.

Miller, G. A. *Psychology: The science of mental life*. New York: Harper & Row, 1962.

Miller, G. A., Galanter, E., & Pribram, K. H. *Plans and the structure of behavior*. New York: Holt, 1960.

Miller, J. G. Information input overload and psychopathology. *American Journal of Psychiatry*, 1960, **116**, 695-704.

Miller, J. G. Living systems: Basic concepts. *Behavioral Science*, 1965, **10**, 193-237. (a)

Miller, J. G. Living systems: Structure and process. *Behavioral Science*, 1965, **10**, 337-379. (b)

Miller, N. E. Liberalization of basic S-R concepts: Extension to conflict behavior, motivation, and social learning. In S. Koch (Ed.), *Psychology: A study of a science*. Vol. 2. New York: McGraw-Hill, 1959.

Miller, N. E., & Dollard, J. *Social learning and imitation*. New Haven, Conn.: Yale Univ. Press, 1941.

Miller, S. M., Rein, M., Roby, P., & Gross, B. Poverty, inequality, and conflict. *Annals of the American Academy of Political and Social Science*, 1967, **2**, 16-52.

Mishler, E. G., & Waxler, N. E. Family interaction process and schizophrenia: A review of current theories. *Merrill-Palmer Quarterly*, 1965, **11**, 269-316.

Moltz, H. Imprinting: Empirical basis and theoretical significance. *Psychological Bulletin*, 1960, **57**, 291-314.

Money, J., Hampson, J. G., & Hampson, J. L. Imprinting and the establishment of gender role. *Archives of Neurology and Psychiatry*, 1957, **77**, 333-336.

Montagu, A. Man the warrior . . . or child of an imperfect society. *Los Angeles Times*, Sunday May 26, 1968. Section G, pp. 1-2.

Montagu, M. F. A. Man—and human nature. *American Journal of Psychiatry*, 1955, **112**, 401-410.

Moore, G. E. *Principia ethica*. New York: Cambridge Univ. Press, 1959.

Mordkoff, A., & Parsons, O. The coronary personality. *International Journal of Psychiatry*, 1968, **5**, 413-426.

Morgan, C. T. The psychophysiology of learning. In S. S. Stevens (Ed.), *Handbook of experimental psychology*. New York: Wiley, 1951. Pp. 758-788.

Morgan, C. T. Physiological mechanisms of motivation.

In M. R. Jones (Ed.), *Nebraska symposium on motivation*. Lincoln, Nebr.: Univ. of Nebr. Press, 1957.

Morris, C. *Foundation of the theory of signs*. Chicago: Univ. of Chicago Press, 1938.

Morris, M. G. Psychological miscarriage: An end to mother love. *Trans-action*, 1966, **3**(2), 8-13.

Morris, V. C. *Existentialism in education*. New York: Harper & Row, 1966.

Morse, N. C., & Weiss, R. S. The function and meaning of work and the job. In S. Nosow & W. H. Form (Eds.), *Man, work and society*. New York: Basic Books, 1962. Pp. 29-35.

Mowrer, O. H. Civilization and its malcontents. *Psychology Today*, 1967, **1**(5), 48-52.

Mudd, E., Mitchell, H., & Taubin, S. *Success in family living*. New York: Association Press, 1965.

Muller, H. J. Cultural evolution as viewed by psychologists. *Daedalus*, 1961, **90**, 572-573.

Munn, N. L. Learning in children. In L. Carmichael (Ed.), *Manual of child psychology*. New York: Wiley, 1946.

Murdock, G. P. Changing emphasis in social structure. *Southwestern Journal of Anthropology*, 1955, **11**, 366.

Murphy, H. B., Wittkower, E. D., & Chance, N. A. Cross-cultural inquiry into the symptomatology of depression: A preliminary report. *International Journal of Psychiatry*, 1967, **3**(1), 6-22.

Murphy, J. M., & Leighton, A. H. *Approaches to cross-cultural psychiatry*. N.Y.: Cornell Univ. Press, 1965.

Murphy, L., & Associates. *Widening world of childhood*. New York: Basic Books, 1962. Excerpt reprinted by permission.

Murray, E. J. Verbal reinforcement in psychotherapy. *Journal of Consulting & Clinical Psychology*, 1968, **32**(3), 237-242.

Mursell, J. L. *Using your mind effectively*. New York: McGraw-Hill, 1951.

Nadel, S. F. *The theory of social structure*. New York: Free Press, 1957.

Nardini, J. E. Survival factors in American prisoners of war of the Japanese. *American Journal of Psychiatry*, 1952, **109**, 241-248.

National Industrial Conference Board. Factors affecting employee morale. *Studies in Personnel Policy*, 1947, **85**.

Navran, L. Communication and adjustment in marriage. *Family Process*, 1967, **6**(2), 173-184.

Neissen, H. W., Chow, K. L., & Semmes, J. Effects of restricted opportunity for tactual, kinesthetic and manipulative experience on the behavior of a chimpanzee. *American Journal of Psychology*, 1951, **64**, 485-507.

Nelson, H. Sleep: It's the kind you get—not how much. *Los Angeles Times*, April 3, 1967, Part II, p. 6.

Nelson, P. D. Similarities and differences among leaders and followers. *Journal of Social Psychology*, 1964, **63**, 161-167.

Nelson, R. C. Knowledge and interests concerning sixteen occupations among elementary and secondary school students. *Educational and Psychological Measurement,* 1963, **23,** 741-754.

Neubeck, G. The decision to marry while in college. *Acta Sociologica,* 1964, **8.**

Newcomb, T. M. *Social Psychology.* New York: Dryden Press, 1950. Chart adapted from SOCIAL PSYCHOLOGY by Theodore M. Newcomb. Copyright 1950 by Holt, Rinehart and Winston, Inc. Chart adapted and reprinted by permission of Holt, Rinehart and Winston, Inc.

Newcomb, T. M. The prediction of interpersonal attraction. *American Psychologist,* 1956, **11,** 575-586.

Newman, M. T. Biological adaptation of man to his environment: Heat, cold, altitude and nutrition. *Annals of the New York Academy of Sciences,* 1961, **91,** 617-631.

Novikoff, A. B. The concept of integrative levels and biology. *Science,* 1945, **101,** 209-215.

Nye, F. I. Child adjustment in broken and unhappy unbroken homes. *Marriage and Family Living,* 1957, **19,** 356.

Ogden, C. K., & Richards, I. A. *The meaning of work.* New York: Harcourt, Brace & World, 1923.

Olds, J., & Olds, M. E. Interference and learning in paleocortical systems. In A. Fessard, R. W. Gerard, & J. Konorski (Eds.), *Brain mechanisms and learning.* Springfield, Ill.: Thomas, 1961.

Olver, R. R., & Hornsby, J. R. On equivalence. In J. S. Bruner, R. R. Olver, & P. M. Greenfield (Eds.), *Studies in cognitive growth.* New York: Wiley, 1966. Pp. 68-85.

Orbach, J., & Fantz, R. L. Differential effects of temporal neocortical resections on over-trained and non-trained visual habits in monkeys. *Journal of Comparative and Physiological Psychology,* 1958, **51,** 126-129.

Osborn, A. F. *Applied imagination: Principles and procedures of creative thinking.* (Rev. ed.) New York: Scribner's, 1957.

Overstreet, H., & Overstreet, B. *The mind goes forth.* New York: Norton, 1956.

Packard, V. *The pyramid climbers.* New York: McGraw-Hill, 1962.

Packard, V. *The sexual wilderness.* New York: David McKay, 1968.

Panos, R. J., & Astin, A. W. Attrition among college students. *American Education Research Journal,* 1968, **5**(1), 57-72.

Pasamanick, B., & Knobloch, H. Brain damage and reproductive causality. *American Journal of Orthopsychiatry,* 1960, **30,** 298-305.

Pasamanick, B., & Knobloch, H. Epidemiologic studies on the complications of pregnancy and the birth process. In G. Caplan (Ed.), *Prevention of mental disorders in children.* New York: Basic Books, 1961. Pp. 74-94.

Pastore, N. The role of arbitrariness in the frustration-aggression hypothesis. *Journal of Abnormal and Social Psychology,* 1952, **47,** 728-731.

Peck, R. F., & Havighurst, R. J. *The psychology of char-*

acter development. New York: Wiley, 1960.

Pepitone, A., & Wilpizeski, C. Some consequences of experimental rejection. *Journal of Abnormal and Social Psychology,* 1960, **60,** 359-364.

Peterson, C. R., & Beach, L. R. Man as an intuitive statistician. *Psychological Bulletin,* 1967, **68**(1), 29-46.

Pettigrew, T. F. Social evaluation theory: Convergences and applications. In D. Levine (Ed.), *Nebraska Symposium on Motivation—1967.* Lincoln, Nebr.: Univ. of Nebr. Press, 1967. Pp. 241-311.

Pfeiffer, J. *The cell.* Life science library. New York: Time-Life Books, 1964.

Phenix, P. H. *Man and his becoming.* New Brunswick, N.J.: Rutgers Univ. Press, 1964.

Phillips, L. *Human adaptation and its failures.* New York: Academic Press, 1968.

Piaget, J. *The language and thought of the child.* London: Routledge & Kegan Paul, 1926. (Republished: New York, Humanities Press, 1959.)

Piaget, J. *The moral judgment of the child.* New York: Harcourt, Brace, 1932. (Republished: Glencoe, Ill., Free Press, 1965.)

Piaget, J. *The origins of intelligence in children.* Paris: Delachaux & Niestle, 1936. (Republished: New York, International Univ. Press, 1952.)

Piaget, J. Development and learning. In R. E. Ripple & V. N. Rockcastle (Eds.), *Piaget rediscovered.* Ithaca, N.Y.: Sch. of Ed., Cornell Univ., 1964.

Pineo, P. C. Disenchantment in the later years of marriage. *Marriage and Family Living,* 1961, **23,** 3-11.

Pollack, J. H. When parents separate. *Today's Health,* 1967, **45**(6), 17-19.

Pollack, J. H. Five frequent mistakes of parents. *Today's Health,* 1968, **46**(5), 14-15, 26-29.

Poppy, J. The generation gap. *Look Magazine,* 1967, **31**(4), 26-32.

Pratt, K. C. The neonate. In L. Carmichael (Ed.), *Manual of child psychology.* New York: Wiley, 1946.

Prescott, D. A. *The child in the educative process.* New York: McGraw-Hill, 1957.

Pressey, S. L., & Pressey, A. D. Genius at 80: And other oldsters. *Gerontologist,* 1967, **7**(3, Pt. I), 183-187.

Price, D. A technique for analyzing the economic value system. *Journal of Marriage & the Family,* 1968, **30**(3), 467-472.

Pringle, M. L. K. *Deprivation and education.* New York: Humanities Press, 1965.

Proshansky, H. M. The development of intergroup attitudes. In L. W. Hoffman & M. L. Hoffman (Eds.), *Review of Child Development Research.* Vol. 2. New York: Russell Sage Foundation, 1966. Pp. 311-372.

Provence, S., & Lipton, R. C. *Infants in institutions.* New York: International Univ. Press, 1963. Quotation reprinted by permission of the publisher.

Prugh, D. G., & Harlow, R. G. "Masked deprivation" in infants and young children. In *Deprivation of maternal care.* Public Health Paper No. 14. Geneva: World Health Organization, 1962. Pp. 9-29.

Rabkin, R. Uncoordinated communication between

marriage partners. *Family Process,* 1967, **6**(1), 10-15.

Rachman, S. Systematic desensitization. *Psychological Bulletin,* 1967, **67**(2), 93-103.

Rainwater, L. Some aspects of lower-class sexual behavior. *Journal of Social Issues,* 1966, **22**(2), 96-108.

Raker, J. W., Wallace, A. F., & Raymer, J. F. *Emergency medical care in disasters: A summary of recorded experiences.* Disaster Study No. 6, National Academy of Sciences, National Research Council, Publication No. 457, Washington, D.C., 1956.

Rapoport, R. V., & Rapoport, R. N. New light on the honeymoon. In G. Handel (Ed.), *The psychosocial interior of the family.* Chicago: Aldine, 1967. Pp. 332-361.

Razran, G. Conditioning and perception. *Psychological Review,* 1955, **62,** 83-95.

Redl, F., & Wattenberg, W. W. *Mental hygiene in teaching.* New York: Harcourt, Brace & World, 1951.

Reiff, R. Mental health manpower and institutional change. *American Psychologist,* 1966, **21,** 540-548.

Reiss, I. L. How & why America's sex standards are changing. *Trans-action,* 1968, **5**(4), 26-32.

Reymert, M. L. Why feelings and emotions? In M. L. Reymert (Ed.), *Feelings and emotions: The Mooseheart Symposium.* New York: McGraw-Hill, 1950.

Rheingold, H. L., Gewirtz, J. L., & Ross, H. W. Social conditioning of vocalizations in the infant. *Journal of Comparative and Physiological Psychology,* 1959, **52,** 68-73.

Ribot, T. *The psychology of the emotions.* New York: Scribner's, 1897.

Rich, L. D. *Happy the land.* Phila.: Lippincott, 1946.

Richards, I. A. The secret of feedforward. *Saturday Review,* 1968, **51**(5), 14-17.

Riesen, A. H. The development of visual perception in men and chimpanzee. *Science,* 1947, **106,** 107-108.

Riesen, A. H. Plasticity of behavior: Psychological series. In H. F. Harlow & C. N. Woolsey (Eds.), *Biological and biochemical bases of behavior.* Madison: Univ. of Wis. Press, 1958.

Riesen, A. H. Stimulation as a requirement for growth and function in behavioral development. In D. W. Fiske & S. R. Maddi (Eds.), *Functions of varied experience.* Homewood, Ill.: Dorsey, 1961.

Ring, K., Braginsky, D., & Braginsky, B. Performance styles in interpersonal relations: A typology. *Psychological Reports,* 1966, **18,** 203-220.

Roberts, E. Biochemical maturation of the central nervous system. In M. A. Brazier (Ed.), *The central nervous system and behavior: Transactions of the third conference.* New York: Josiah Macy Foundation, 1960.

Roe, A. *The making of a scientist.* New York: Dodd, Mead, 1953.

Rogers, C. R. *Client-centered therapy.* Boston: Houghton Mifflin, 1951. Copyright 1951 by Carl R. Rogers.

Rogers, C. R. *Becoming a person.* Austin: Univ. of Texas, 1958.

Rogers, C. R. *On becoming a person: A therapist's view of psychotherapy.* Boston: Houghton Mifflin, 1961.

Rogers, C. R. Toward a modern approach to values: The valuing process in the mature person. *Journal of Abnormal & Social Psychology,* 1964, **68**(2), 160-167.

Rogers, C. R. The process of basic group encounter. In J. F. T. Bugental (Ed.), *Challenges of humanistic psychology.* New York: McGraw-Hill, 1967. Pp. 261-276.

Rohrer, J. H. Interpersonal relations in isolated small groups. In B. E. Flaherty (Ed.), *Psychophysiological aspects of space flight.* New York: Columbia Univ. Press, 1961.

Rosenblatt, P. C. Marital residence and the functions of romantic love. *Ethnology,* 1967, **6**(4), 471-480.

Rosenhan, D., & London, P. Therapy and remediation. In P. London & D. Rosenhan (Eds.), *Foundations of abnormal psychology.* New York: Holt, Rinehart, and Winston, 1968. Pp. 557-598.

Rosenkrantz, P. L., Bee, H., Vogel, S., Broverman, I., & Broverman, D. M. Sex-role stereotypes and self-concepts in college students. *Journal of Consulting & Clinical Psychology,* 1968, **32**(3), 287-295.

Rosenthal, M. J. The syndrome of the inconsistent mother. *American Journal of Orthopsychiatry,* 1962, **32,** 637-644.

Rosenthal, S. H. The involutional depressive syndrome. *American Journal of Psychiatry,* 1968, **124** (Special No. 5), 21-35.

Rosenzweig, S. The recall of finished and unfinished tasks as affected by the purpose with which they were performed. *Psychological Bulletin,* 1933, **30,** 698.

Rossi, A. Equality between the sexes: An immodest proposal. *Daedalus,* 1964, **93**(2), 607-652.

Rosten, R. A. Some personality characteristics of compulsive gamblers. Unpublished doctoral dissertation, Univ. of California at Los Angeles, 1961.

Rosenzweig, S. An outline of frustration theory. In J. McV. Hunt (Ed.), *Personality and the behavior disorders.* Vol. 1. New York: Ronald Press, 1944.

Rozenzweig, M. R. Environmental complexity, cerebral change, and behavior. *American Psychologist,* 1966, **21,** 321-332.

Ruckmick, C. A. *The psychology of feeling and emotion.* New York: McGraw-Hill, 1936.

Ruff, G. E., & Korchin, S. J. Adaptive stress behavior. In M. H. Appley & R. Trumbull (Eds.), *Psychological stress: Issues in research.* New York: Appleton-Century-Crofts, 1967. Pp. 297-310.

Rugh, R. Ionizing radiation of congenital anomalies of the nervous system. *Military Medicine,* 1962, **127,** 883-907.

Samuels, I. Reticular mechanisms and behavior. *Psychological Bulletin,* 1959, **56,** 1-25.

Sander, L. W. Issues in early mother-child interaction. *Journal of the American Academy of Child Psychiatry,* 1962, **1,** 141-166.

Sarason, I. G., & Ganzer, V. J. Concerning the medical model. *American Psychologist,* 1968, **23,** 507-510.

Sarbin, T. H. Ontology recapitulates philology: The mythic nature of anxiety. *American Psychologist,* 1968, **23,** 411-418.

Satir, V. M. *Conjoint family therapy: A guide to theory and technique.* Palo Alto, Calif.: Science & Behavior Books, 1964.

Scanzoni, J. A social system analysis of dissolved and existing marriages. *Journal of Marriage & the Family,* 1968, **30,** 452-461.

Schachter, S. *The psychology of affiliation: Experimental studies of the sources of gregariousness.* Stanford. Calif.: Stanford Univ. Press, 1959.

Schaefer, E. S., & Bayley, N. Consistency of maternal behavior from infancy to preadolescence. *Journal of Abnormal and Social Psychology,* 1960, **61,** 1-6.

Schaeffer, H. R., & Emerson, P. E. The development of social attachments in infancy. *Monographs of the Society for Research in Child Development,* 1964, **29**(3, Whole No. 94), 1-77.

Schein, E. H. Management development as a process of influence. In H. J. Leavitt & L. R. Pondy (Eds.), *Readings in managerial psychology.* Chicago: Univ. of Chicago Press, 1964.

Schein, E. H. The first job dilemma. *Psychology Today,* 1968, **1**(10), 26-37.

Schildkraut, J. Catecholamine hypothesis of affective disorders. *International Journal of Psychiatry,* 1967, **4,** 203-217.

Schlesinger, B. The one-parent family: An overview. Part I. *The family coordinator,* 1966, **15**(4), 133-138.

Schorr, A. L. The family cycle and income development. *Social Security Bulletin,* 1966, **29**(2), 14-25.

Schuham, A. I. The double-bind hypothesis a decade later. *Psychological Bulletin,* 1967, **68,** 409-416.

Schultz, D. P. *Sensory restriction.* New York: Academic Press, 1965.

Science News. April 1, 1967, p. 307. (a)

Science News. August 19, 1967, p. 80. (b)

Science News. August 31, 1968. (a)

Science News. October 5, 1968. (b)

Science News Letter. Hunger regulates lives. 1950, **58,** 21-22.

Scott, J. P. Critical periods in the development of social behavior in puppies. *Psychosomatic Medicine,* 1958, **20**(1), 42-54.

Scott, J. P. Critical periods in behavioral development. *Science,* 1962, **138,** 949-958.

Scott, J. P. The progress of primary socialization in canine and human infants. *Monographs of the Society for Research in Child Development,* 1963, **28**(1), 1-47.

Scott, J. P. The development of social motivation. In D. Levine (Ed.), *Nebraska Symposium on Motivation—1967.* Lincoln, Nebr.: Univ. of Nebr. Press, 1967. Pp. 111-132.

Sears, R. R. A theoretical framework for personality and social behavior. *American Psychologist,* 1951, **6,** 478-479.

Sears, R. R. Relation of early socialization experiences to aggression in middle childhood. *Journal of Abnormal and Social Psychology,* 1961, **63,** 466-492.

Sears, R. R., Maccoby, E. E., & Levin, H. *Patterns of child rearing.* Evanston, Ill.: Row Peterson, 1957.

Secord, P. F., & Backman, C. W. Personality theory and the problem of stability and change in individual behavior: An interpersonal approach. *Psychological Review,* 1961, **68,** 22.

Seeman, Melvin. Antidote for alienation: Learning to belong. *Trans-action,* 1966, **3**(4), 35-39.

Segal, J. Latest on sleep—what research shows. Interview in *U.S. News and World Report,* Aug. 29, 1966, 60-64.

Selye, H. *The stress of life.* New York: McGraw-Hill, 1956.

Shapley, H. *Of stars and men: The human response to an expanding universe.* Boston: Beacon Press, 1958.

Sharpless, S., & Jasper, H. H. Habituation of the arousal reaction. *Brain,* 1956, **79,** 655-680.

Sherif, M., & Sherif, C. W. *An outline of social psychology.* (Rev. ed.) New York: Harper, 1956.

Shibutani, T. The structure of personal identity. In E. E. Sampson (Ed.), *Approaches, contexts, and problems of social psychology.* New York: Prentice-Hall, 1964. Pp. 231-235.

Shope, D. F., & Broderick, C. B. Level of sexual experience and predicted adjustment in marriage. *Journal of Marriage & the Family,* 1967, **29**(3), 424-427.

Short, J. F., Jr. Juvenile delinquency: The sociocultural context. In L. W. Hoffman & M. L. Hoffman (Eds.), *Review of Child Development Research.* Vol. 2. New York: Russell Sage Foundation, 1966. Pp. 423-468.

Shubik, M. Information, rationality, and free choice in a future democratic society. *Daedalus,* 1967, **96,** 771-778.

Siegelman, M. College student personality correlates of early parent-child relationships. *Journal of Consulting Psychology,* 1965, **29,** 558-564.

Simon, H. A. *Models of man: Social and rational.* New York: Wiley, 1957.

Simon, H. A. Motivational and emotional controls of cognition. *Psychological Review,* 1967, **74**(1), 29-39.

Sinclair, L. Museum of man. In W. R. Goldschmidt (Ed.), *Ways of mankind.* Boston: Beacon, 1954.

Singer, D. L. Aggression, arousal, hostile humor, and catharsis. *Journal of Personality and Social Psychology,* Part 2: Monograph Supplement. 1968, **8**(1), 1-14.

Sinnott, E. W. Reaction wood and the regulation of tree form. *American Journal of Botany,* 1952, **39**(1), 69-78.

Sinnott, E. W. *The biology of the spirit.* New York: Viking Press, Inc., 1955. Copyright 1955 by E. W. Sinnott.

Skeels, H. M. Adult status of children with contrasting early life experiences. *Monographs of the Society for Research in Child Development,* 1966, **31**(3, Whole No. 105).

Skinner, B. F. *Science and human behavior.* New York: Macmillan, 1953.

Smith, C. P. *Child development.* Dubuque, Iowa: Wm. C. Brown, 1966.

Smith, M. B. The revolution in mental-health care—a "bold new approach"? *Trans-action,* 1968, **5**(5), 19-23.

Smith, T. V., & Lindeman, E. C. *The democratic way of life.* New York: New American Library, 1951.

Solomon, R. L. Punishment. *American Psychologist,* 1964, **19**, 239-253.

Solomon, R. L., & Brush, E. Experimentally derived conceptions of anxiety and aversion. In M. R. Jones (Ed.), *Nebraska symposium on motivation.* Lincoln, Nebr.: Univ. of Nebr. Press, 1956. Pp. 212-305.

Sommerhof, G. Purpose, adaptation, and "directive correlation." In W. Buckley (Ed.), *Modern systems research for the behavioral scientist.* Chicago: Aldine, 1968. Pp. 281-295.

Soueif, M. I. Hashish consumption in Egypt with special reference to psychosocial aspects. *Bulletin on Narcotics,* 1967, **19**, 1-12.

Spitz, R. *The derailment of dialogue.* Paper presented at the convention of the American Psychiatric Association, St. Louis, May 1963.

Spielberger, C. D., Parker, J. B., & Becker, J. Conformity and achievement in remitted manic-depressive patients. *Journal of Nervous and Mental Disorder,* 1963, **137**(2), 162-172.

Spranger, E. *Lebensforman.* (3rd ed.) Halle: Niemeyer, 1923. (Translated: P. Pigors. *Types of men.* New York: Steckert, 1928.)

Stagner, R. *Psychology of personality.* New York: McGraw-Hill, 1961.

Stellar, E. Drive and motivation. In J. Field (Ed.), *Handbook of physiology. Sect. I: neurophysiology.* Vol. III. Washington, D.C.: Amer. Physiol. Society, 1960.

Stern, R. L. Diary of a war neurosis. *Journal of Nervous and Mental Disease,* 1947, **106**, 583-586. Excerpt reprinted by permission.

Stinson, M. R. The victims of today's society. *University of Southern California Alumni Review,* 1965, **16**(5), 1-3.

Stodolsky, S. S., & Lesser, G. Learning patterns in the disadvantaged. *Harvard Educational Review,* 1967, **37**, 546-593.

Stoller, F. H. The long weekend. *Psychology Today,* 1967, **1**(7), 28-33.

Strauss, A., *et al.* The hospital and its negotiated order. In E. Freidson (Ed.), *The hospital in modern society.* New York: Free Press, 1963.

Stuckert, R. P. Role perception and marital satisfaction: A configurational approach. *Marriage and Family Living,* 1963, **25**, 415-419.

Suedfeld, P. Social Processes. In *Introduction to psychology: A self-selection textbook.* Dubuque, Iowa: Wm. C. Brown, 1966.

Sullivan, M. S. *The interpersonal theory of psychiatry.* New York: Norton, 1953.

Sundberg, N. D., & Tyler, L. E. *Clinical Psychology.* New York: Appleton-Century-Crofts, 1964.

Snyder, R. *On becoming human.* New York: Abingdon Press, 1967.

Szasz, T. S. *The myth of mental illness: Foundations of a theory of personal conduct.* N.Y.: Harper, 1961.

Terzuolo, C. A., & Adey, W. R. Sensorimotor cortical activities. In J. Field (Ed.), *Handbook of physiology. Sect. I: neurophysiology.* Vol. II. Washington, D.C.: American Physiological Society, 1960.

Thelen, H. A. Emotionality and work in groups. In L. D. White (Ed.), *The state of the social sciences.* Chicago: Univ. of Chicago Press, 1956. Pp. 184-186.

Thistlethwaite, D. A critical review of latent learning and related experiments. *Psychological Bulletin,* 1951, **48**, 97-129.

Thompson, W. R. Early environmental influences on behavioral development. *American Journal of Orthopsychiatry,* 1960, **30**, 306-314.

Thumin, F. J. MMPI profiles as a function of chronological age. *Psychological Reports,* 1968, **22**, 479-482.

Tiedeman, D. V., & O'Hara, R. P. *Career development: Choice and adjustment.* New York: College Entrance Examination Board, 1963.

Tiffany, W. J., Jr., & Allerton, W. S. Army psychiatry in the mid-'60's. *American Journal of Psychiatry,* 1967, **123**, 810-819.

Tillich, P. *The courage to be.* New Haven, Conn.: Yale Univ. Press, 1952.

Time. 1959, **73**(1), 62-63.

Time. 1966, **87**(8), 28-29.

Toynbee, A. *A study of history.* Vol. I. New York: Oxford Univ. Press, 1947.

Travis, A. M., & Woolsey, C. N. Motor performances of monkeys after bilateral partial and total cerebral decortications. *Journal of Physical Medicine,* 1956, **35**, 273-310.

Treisman, M. Mind, body, and behavior: Control systems and their disturbances. In P. London & D. Rosenhan (Eds.), *Foundations of abnormal psychology.* New York: Holt, Rinehart and Winston, 1968. Pp. 460-518.

Trost, J. Some data on mate-selection: Homogamy and perceived homogamy. *Journal of Marriage & the Family,* 1967, **29**, 739-755.

Tuddenham, R. D. Jean Piaget and the world of the child. *American Psychologist,* 1966, **21**, 207-217.

Turner, G. H. Psychology—becoming and unbecoming. In F. T. Severin (Ed.), *Humanistic viewpoints in psychology.* N.Y.: McGraw-Hill, 1965. Pp. 306-321.

Turner, R. H. Role-taking: Process versus conformity. In A. M. Rose (Ed.), *Human behavior and social processes: An interactionist approach.* Boston: Houghton Mifflin, 1962. Chapter 2.

Udry, J. R. Complementarity in mate selection: A perceptual approach. *Marriage and Family Living,* 1963, **25**(3), 281-289.

Udry, J. R. *The social context of marriage.* Philadelphia: Lippincott Co., 1966.

Udry, J. R. Personality match and interpersonal perception as predictors of marriage. *Journal of Marriage & the Family,* 1967, **29**, 722-725.

Ullmann, L. P., & Krasner, L. *Case studies in behavior modification.* N.Y.: Holt, Rinehart and Winston, 1965.

Ullmann, L. P., & Krasner, L. *A psychological approach to abnormal behavior.* Englewood Cliffs, N.J.: Prentice-Hall, 1969.

von Bertalanffy, L. An outline of general systems theory. *British Journal for the Philosophy of Science,* 1950, **1**, 134.

von Bertalanffy, L., & Woodger, J. H. *Modern theories of development.* London: Oxford, 1933.

Vygotsky, L. S. *Thought and language.* Ed. and trans. by E. Hanfman & G. Vakar. New York: Wiley, 1962.

Wallach, M. A., & Kogan, N. Creativity and intelligence in children's thinking. *Trans-action,* 1967, **4**(3), 38-43.

Wallach, M. A., Ulrich, D. N., & Grunebaum, M. B. The relationship of family disturbance to cognitive difficulties in a learning-problem child. *Journal of Consulting Psychology,* 1960, **24,** 355-360.

Watson, J. B. *Psychology from the standpoint of a behaviorist.* Philadelphia: Lippincott, 1919.

Watson, J. B., & Rayner, R. Conditioned emotional reactions. *Journal of Experimental Psychology,* 1920, **3,** 1-14.

Watson, J. B. *Behaviorism.* (Rev. ed.) New York: Norton, 1930.

Watson, J. D. *Molecular biology of the gene.* New York: Benjamin, 1965.

Watson, R. *Psychology of the child.* (2nd ed.) New York: Wiley, 1965.

Webster, H., Freedman, M. B., & Heist, P. Personality changes in college students. In N. Sanford (Ed.), *The american college.* N.Y.: Wiley, 1962. Pp. 811-846.

Welker, W. I. An analysis of exploratory and play behavior in animals. In D. W. Fiske & S. R. Maddi (Eds.), *Functions of varied experience.* Homewood, Ill.: Dorsey, 1961.

Wernimont, P. F. Intrinsic and extrinsic factors in job satisfaction. *Journal of Applied Psychology,* 1966, **50**(1), 41-50.

Werts, C. E. Paternal influence on career choice. *Journal of Counseling Psychology,* 1968, **15**(1), 48-52.

Wetzel, J. R., & Holland, S. S. Poverty areas of our major cities. *Monthly Labor Review,* 1966, **89,** 1105-1110.

Weybrew, B. B. Patterns of psychophysiological response to military stress. In M. H. Appley & R. Trumbull (Eds.), *Psychological stress.* New York: Appleton-Century-Crofts, 1967. Pp. 324-354.

White, R. W. Motivation reconsidered: The concept of competence. *Psychological Review,* 1959, **66,** 297-333.

Williamson, R. C. Dating, courtship, and the "ideal mate": Some relevant subcultural variables. *Family Life Coordinator,* 1965, **14**(3), 137-143.

Williamson, R. C. *Marriage and family relations.* New York: Wiley, 1966.

Wilson, G. T., Hannon, A. E., & Evans, W. I. Behavior therapy and the therapist-patient relationship. *Journal of Consulting & Clinical Psychology,* 1968, **32**(2), 103-109.

Wilson, H. V. Development of sponges from dissociated tissue cells. *Bulletin of the Bureau of Fisheries,* 1910, **30,** 1-30.

Wilson, W. Correlates of avowed happiness. *Psychological Bulletin,* 1967, **67,** 294-306.

Winch, R. F. *Mate-selection: A study of complementary needs.* New York: Harper, 1958.

Winch, R. F. *The modern family.* (Rev. ed.) New York: Holt, Rinehart and Winston, 1963.

Winch, R. F. Another look at the theory of complementary needs in mate-selection. *Journal of Marriage & the Family,* 1967, **29**(4), 756-762.

Winchester, J. H. Iceland: A nation hurrying toward tomorrow. *Reader's Digest,* June 1966, **88,** 197-200.

Winder, C. L., & Rau, L. Parental attitudes associated with social deviance in preadolescent boys. *Journal of Abnormal and Social Psychology,* 1962, **64,** 418-424.

Wingo, H. Hell aboard CVA-59. *Life,* 1967, **63**(6), 22.

Winick, C. The beige epoch: Depolarization of sex roles in America. *Annals of the American Academy of Political and Social Science,* March 1968, **376,** 18-24.

Wintrob, R. M. Sexual guilt and culturally sanctioned delusions in Liberia, West Africa. *American Journal of Psychiatry,* 1968, **125**(1), 89-95.

Witmer, H. L. National facts and figures about children without families. *Journal of the American Academy of Child Psychiatry,* 1965, **4,** 249-253.

Wohlwill, J. F. The mystery of the pre-logical child. *Psychology Today,* 1967, **1**(3), 24-34.

Wolfbein, S. L. Labor trends, manpower, and automation. In H. Borow (Ed.), *Man in a world at work.* Boston: Houghton Mifflin, 1964. Pp. 155-173.

Wolman, B. B. Family dynamics and schizophrenia. *Journal of Health and Human Behavior,* 1967, **6**(3), 163-169.

Wolpe, J. *Psychotherapy by reciprocal inhibition.* Stanford, Calif.: Stanford Univ. Press, 1958.

Wolpe, J., & Rachman, S. Psychoanalytic "evidence": A critique based on Freud's case of little Hans. *Journal of Nervous and Mental Diseases,* 1960, **131,** 135-138.

Wooldridge. D. E. *Mechanical man: The physical basis of intelligent life.* New York: McGraw-Hill, 1968.

World Health Organization. *Services for the prevention and treatment of dependence on alcohol and other drugs.* WHO Technical Report Series No. 363, 1967.

Worsley, P. M. Cargo cults. *Scientific American,* 1959, **200**(5), 117-128.

Wylie, R. C. *The self-concept: A critical survey of the pertinent literature.* Lincoln, Nebr.: Univ. of Nebr. Press, 1961.

Yarrow, L. J. Separation from parents during early childhood. In M. L. Hoffman & L. W. Hoffman (Eds.), *Review of Child Development Research.* Vol. l. New York: Russell Sage Foundation, 1964. Pp. 89-136.

Yarrow, L. J. Conceptual perspectives on the early environment. *Journal of the American Academy of Child Psychiatry,* 1965, **4**(3), 168-185.

Yolles, S. F. Unraveling the mystery of schizophrenia. *Today's Health,* 1967, **45**(4), 42, 82-84.

Zeuner, F. E. Time in evolution. In *The Smithsonian Institution Report for 1949.* Washington, D.C.: U.S. Government Printing Office, 1950. Pp. 247 ff.

Ziller, R. C. Four techniques of group decision-making under uncertainty. *Journal of Applied Psychology,* 1957, **41,** 384-388.

ACKNOWLEDGMENTS

Sources for quoted material and for most charts and diagrams are given in the references. All other sources of illustration are acknowledged below. To all, the author and publisher wish to express their appreciation.

35 Adapted by permission of Dr. Edmund W. Sinnott and the *American Journal of Botany* (left); adapted by permission of the U.S. Fish and Wildlife Service (right).

43 Figures redrawn by permission from T. M. Sonnenborn, The new genetics. *International Science and Technology,* 1962, 1(9), 66-72.

54 C. Capa—Magnum (left); Bruce Davidson—Magnum (center); Elliot Erwitt—Magnum (right).

59 Charles Harbutt—Magnum (upper left); Wayne Miller—Magnum (upper right); Henri-Cartier-Dresson—Magnum (center); Sergio Larrain—Magnum (lower left): Hiroshi Hamaya—Magnum (lower right).

74 Inger Abrahamsen McCabe—Rapho-Guillumette (upper left); Wayne Miller—Magnum (lower left); Hella Hammid—Rapho-Guillumette (right).

75 Hella Hammid—Rapho-Guillumette (left); Burke Uzzle—Magnum (center); Wayne Miller—Magnum (right).

76 Marc & Evelyne Bernheim—Rapho-Guillumette (left); Elliot Erwitt—Magnum (right).

77 Charles Harbutt—Magnum (left); John Rees—Black Star (right).

81 Bob Natkin, photographer—Chicago (left); Erich Hartmann—Magnum (right).

89 Eve Arnold—Magnum.

122 Photos courtesy of Dr. Albert Bandura and the American Psychological Association.

149 Photo by Wallace Kirkland, courtesy of *Life,* copyright 1945 Time, Inc.

159 Culver Service (upper left); Historical Pictures Service, Chicago (upper right); Black Star (lower left); reprinted by permission of the photographer, Vitold de Golish (lower right).

161 Ernst Haas—Magnum.

196 Photos courtesy of Hans Selye.

292 From "Opinions and Social Pressure" by Solomon E. Asch. Copyright © 1955 by Scientific American, Inc. All rights reserved.

294 Burt Glinn—Magnum (left); Charles Harbutt—Magnum (right).

295 Elliott Erwitt—Magnum.

309 Historical Pictures Service, Chicago (upper); Brown Brothers, New York (center); Black Star (lower).

324 Rapho-Guillumette.

332 Cornell Capa—Magnum (left); Lee Balterman Photography (center); United Press International, Inc. (right).

333 Dan Budnik—Magnum (left); U.S. Coast Guard Official Photo (center); News & Publication Service, Stanford University (right).

The artwork on pages 35 and 105 is the work of Franz Altschuler.
The drawings on page 43 are the work of John Mayahara.
The diagram on page 149 is the work of Tom Gorman.

NAME INDEX

SUBJECT INDEX